The Unknown American Revolution

THE
UNKNOWN
AMERICAN
REVOLUTION

*The Unruly Birth of Democracy
and the Struggle to Create America*

GARY B. NASH

Jonathan Cape
London

Published by Jonathan Cape 2006

2 4 6 8 10 9 7 5 3 1

Copyright © Gary B. Nash 2005

First published in the United States in 2005 by
Viking Penguin, a member of Penguin Group (USA) Inc.

First published in Great Britain in 2006 by
Jonathan Cape
Random House, 20 Vauxhall Bridge Road,
London SW1V 2SA

Random House Australia (Pty) Limited
20 Alfred Street, Milsons Point, Sydney,
New South Wales 2061, Australia

Random House New Zealand Limited
18 Poland Road, Glenfield,
Auckland 10, New Zealand

Random House South Africa (Pty) Limited
Isle of Houghton, Corner of Boundary Road & Carse O'Gowrie,
Houghton 2198, South Africa

The Random House Group Limited Reg. No. 954009
www.randomhouse.co.uk

A CIP catalogue record for this book is available from the British Library

Designed by Carla Bolte

ISBN 0-2240-6184-4

Printed and bound in Great Britain by
William Clowes Ltd, Beccles, Suffolk

For CYD

Ever my polestar

＊

CONTENTS

LIST OF ILLUSTRATIONS

INTRODUCTION

Salus populi suprema lex ("the welfare of the people is the supreme law")

—Cicero, *The Laws,* Book 3:8

Truth always makes sad havoc with the frost-work of the imagination and sternly demands the homage of the historian's pen.

—Benson Lossing, *Pictorial Field-Book of the American Revolution* (1850)

"WHO SHALL WRITE THE HISTORY OF THE AMERICAN REVOLUTION? Who can write it? Who will ever be able to write it?" Thus wrote John Adams in 1815 to Thomas Jefferson, his old enemy but by this time his septuagenarian friend. "Nobody," Jefferson replied from Monticello, "except merely its external facts . . . The life and soul of history must be forever unknown."[1]

Not so. For more than two centuries historians have written about the American Revolution, striving to capture the "life and soul" of which Jefferson spoke. We now possess a rich and multistranded tapestry of the Revolution, filled with engaging biographies, local narratives, weighty explorations of America's greatest explosion of political thinking, annals of military tactics and strategies, discussions of religious, economic, and diplomatic aspects of what was then called the "glorious cause," and more. Indeed we now have possession of far more than the "external facts."

Yet the great men—the founding fathers—of the revolutionary era dominate the reigning master narrative. Notwithstanding generations of prodigious scholarship, we have not appreciated the lives and labors, the sacrifices and struggles, the glorious messiness, the hopes and fears of diverse groups that fought in the longest and most disruptive war in our history with visions of launching a new age filling their heads. Little is known, for example, of Thomas Peters, an African-born slave who made his personal declaration of independence in early 1776, fought for the freedom of African Americans, led former slaves to Nova Scotia after the war, and completed a pilgrimage for unalienable rights by shepherding them back to Africa to participate in the founding of Sierra Leone. Why are the history books virtually silent on Dragging Canoe, the Cherokee warrior who made the American Revolution into a two-decade life-sapping fight for his people's life, liberty, and pursuit of happiness? We cannot capture the "life and soul" of the Revolution without paying close attention to the wartime experiences and agendas for change that engrossed backcountry farmers, urban craftsmen, deep-blue mariners, female camp followers and food rioters—those ordinary people who did most of the protesting, most of the fighting, most of the dying, and most of the dreaming about how a victorious America might satisfy the yearnings of all its peoples.

In this book the reader will find, I hope, an antidote for historical amnesia. To this day, the public remembers the Revolution mostly in its enshrined, mythic form. This is peculiar in a democratic society because the sacralized story of the founding fathers, the men of marble, mostly concerns the upper-most slice of American revolutionary society. That is what has lodged in our minds, and this is the fable that millions of people in other countries know about the American Revolution.

I ask readers to expand their conception of revolutionary American society and to consider the multiple agendas—the stuff of ideas, dreams, and aspirations—that sprang from its highly diverse and fragmented character. It is not hard today to understand that American people in all their diversity entertain a variety of ideas about what they want their nation to be and what sort of America they want for their children. Much the same was true two centuries ago. But from a distance of more than two centuries we don't think about our nation's birth that way. It is more comforting to think about united colonists rising up as a unified body to get the British lion's paw off the backs of their necks. That is a noble and inspiring David and Goliath story, but it is not what actually happened. It is assuredly not the story of radical democracy's work during the Revolution.

Introduction

This book presents a people's revolution, an upheaval among the most het-
erogeneous people to be found anywhere along the Atlantic littoral in the
eighteenth century. The book's thrust is to complicate the well-established
core narrative by putting before the reader bold figures, ideas, and movements, highlighting the true radicalism of the American Revolution that was
indispensable to the origins, conduct, character, and outcome of the world-
shaking event.

By "radicalism" I mean advocating wholesale change and sharp transformation rooted in a kind of dream life of a better future imagined by those
who felt most dissatisfied with the conditions they experienced as the quarrel
with Great Britain unfolded. For a reformed America they looked toward a
redistribution of political, social, and religious power; the discarding of old
institutions and the creation of new ones; the overthrowing of ingrained pat-
terns of conservative, elitist thought; the leveling of society so that top and
bottom were not widely separated; the end of the nightmare of slavery and
the genocidal intentions of land-crazed frontiersmen; the hope of women of
achieving a public voice. This radicalism directed itself at destabilizing a society where the white male elite prized stability because it upheld their close
grip on political, economic, religious, sexual, and social power. This radicalism, therefore, was usually connected to a multifaceted campaign to democratize society, to recast the social system, to achieve dreams with deep biblical
and historical roots, to put "power in the people," as the first articles of government in Quaker New Jersey expressed it a century before the American
Revolution.

The pages that follow mostly view the American Revolution through the
eyes of those *not* in positions of power and privilege, though the iconic founding fathers are assuredly part of the story. In reality, those in the nether strata
of colonial society and those outside "respectable" society were *most* of the
people of revolutionary America. Without their ideas, dreams, and blood sacrifices, the American Revolution would never have occurred, would never
have followed the course that we can now comprehend, and would never have
reverberated around the world among oppressed people down to the present
day. Disinterring these long-forgotten figures from history's cemetery, along
with their aspirations and demands, along with the events and dramatic moments in which they figured so importantly, is offered as an antidote to the art
of forgetting.

Many of the figures we will encounter were from the middle and lower ranks of American society, and many of them did not have pale complexions. From these ranks, few heroes have emerged to enter the national pantheon. For the most part, they remain anonymous. Partly this is because they faded in and out of the picture, rarely achieving the tenure and status of men such as John Adams and John Hancock of Boston, Robert Morris and Benjamin Franklin of Philadelphia, Alexander Hamilton and John Jay of New York, or Thomas Jefferson, Patrick Henry, and George Washington of Virginia, all of whom remained on the scene from the Revolution's beginning to the very end. But, although they never rose to the top of society, where they could trumpet their own achievements and claim their place in the pages of history, many other men and women counted greatly at the time. "Lived inequalities," writes the Haitian philosopher-historian Michel-Rolph Trouillot, "yield unequal historical power."[2] The shortness of their lives also explains the anonymity of ordinary people. It is safer to conduct a revolution from the legislative chamber than fight for it on the battlefield, healthier to be free than enslaved, and one is more likely to reach old age with money than with crumbs.

Even a casual reading of the reflections of those who occupy our national pantheon shows that these founders were far from reverent in their views of one another, and far from agreed on how to tell the story of the nation's birth. They thought the story would be messy, ambiguous, and complicated because they had experienced the Revolution in just these ways—as a seismic eruption from the hands of an internally divided people, two decades of problems that sometimes seemed insoluble, a gnawing fear that the course of the Revolution was contradicting its bedrock principles, and firsthand knowledge of the shameful behavior that was interlaced with heroic self-sacrifice during the long travail. "The history of our Revolution," fretted John Adams, "will be one continued lie from one end to the other. The essence of the whole will be that Dr. Franklin's electric rod smote the earth and out sprang George Washington." Adams complained endlessly about how Franklin was overrated and underhanded, and it pained him immensely to think that the story would go on "that Franklin electrified [Washington] with his rod, and henceforward these two conducted all the policy negotiations, legislatures, and war." Adams couldn't decide who would be best remembered in history—Franklin or Washington—but he knew for a certainty that both deserved less credit than he. "I never knew but one man who pretended to be wholly free from [vanity]," Adams wrote of Franklin, "and him I know to be in his heart

Shortly after his death in 1799, portraits of Washington ascending to heaven with mothers, children, and one Indian maiden (at lower right) were done, representing the nation's grief. Yale's president addressed students: "O Washington! How I do love thy name! How have I adored and blessed thy God for creating and forming thee, the great ornament of human kind! . . . Thy fame is of sweeter perfume than Arabian spices. Listening angels shall catch the odour, waft it to heaven, and perfume the universe."

the vainest man, and the falsest character I have ever met with in life." Washington wasn't much better. Adams grumbled about "the superstitious veneration that is sometimes paid to General Washington," because "I feel myself his superior." Growing gray, he told his friend Jedidiah Morse, who had applied to Adams "to assist you in writing history, [that] I know not whether I ought to laugh or cry." Retired as the nation's second president, Adams confessed that history would never give him his due. "I read it [history] as I do romance, believing what is probable and rejecting what I must."[3]

The author of the Declaration of Independence also took his lumps, and administered a few, as he and his band of brothers tried to assess the American Revolution after the smoke had cleared and the ink on the peace treaty had dried. Jefferson found Adams impossible: "He hates Franklin, he hates Jay, he hates the French, he hates the English," wrote the Monticello patriarch in 1783. Adams returned the favor. At one point he assured a friend in Philadelphia that Jefferson was not "a true figure" of the Revolution and that drafting the Declaration of Independence was a "theatrical show" in which the man from Monticello had "run away with all the stage effect . . . and all the glory of it." After losing the presidency to Jefferson in 1800, Adams called his rival so "warped by prejudice and so blinded by ignorance as to be unfit for the office he holds." Many of Adams's Congregational minister friends agreed. One predicted that Americans would "rue the day and detest the folly, delusion, and intrigue which raised him to the head of the United States." Other clergymen bombarded their parishioners with descriptions of Jefferson as an adulterous atheist and a toadying lover of the hopelessly corrupt French, whose revolution was as attractive as a plague.[4]

Washington quickly became the avatar of revolutionary achievement because the nation could hardly do without a conquering hero. But privately— and sometimes very publicly—many of his closest associates thought differently. Charles Lee, who became Washington's third-ranking general and had a low opinion of his commander's generalship, sneered at what he called the "infallible divinity" of the commander in chief and called him "a bladder of emptiness and pride." Tom Paine, even after Washington had virtually been sanctified, told the public that had honored him for the crucial essay *Common Sense* that Washington was "treacherous in private friendship . . . and a hypocrite in public life." In an open letter to the retiring president he capped his denunciation: "As to you, Sir . . . , the world will be puzzled to decide whether you are an apostate or an impostor; whether you have abandoned good principles, or whether you ever had any."[5]

Some of the revolutionary leaders were so convinced that the men being eulogized as the war ended had feet of clay that they decided not to tell what they knew about the conduct of the Revolution. Charles Thomson, for example, had a rare opportunity to pass on to history an insider's view. An immigrant from Ulster who had run away from his indenture to a blacksmith at age ten, he rose to become secretary to the Continental Congress, where he sat in the catbird's seat observing the entire wartime proceedings. Many fellow leaders urged him "to write secret memoirs of the American Revolution," as Benjamin Rush remembered. But after writing a thousand-page account packed with "notes of the intrigues and severe altercations or quarrels in the Congress," Thomson buried and later burned his account, along with all his notes and documents. "I could not tell the truth without giving great offense," Thomson told a confidant. "Let the world admire our patriots and heroes." If he published his memoirs, it would "contradict all the histories of the great events of the Revolution." Better that the American people embrace a mythic version of the revolution; ignorance and misrepresentation would serve the nation better because the boasted "talents and virtues" of the founding fathers would "command imitation" and thus "serve the cause of patriotism and of our country."[6]

While those atop the social pyramid couldn't agree on how to parcel out credit for the outcome of the American Revolution, or even to tell the story honestly, a few of them industriously published histories they hoped would serve to instruct the generations to come. In this effort, they were forerunners of a true people's history of the Revolution because they understood how crucial the rank and file of American society were to the outcome. For example, David Ramsay, transplanted from Pennsylvania to South Carolina, where he served as a delegate to the Continental Congress, organized his *The History of the American Revolution* around the key notion that "The great bulk of those, who were the active instruments of carrying on the revolution, were self-made, industrious men. These who by their own exertions, had established or laid a foundation for establishing *personal independence,* were most generally trusted, and most successfully employed in establishing that of their country." Ramsay also appreciated, even if in muted tones, the centrality of black and Native Americans to the Revolution. Publishing his account just a year after the ratification of the Constitution, Ramsay implored the new American generation—in two pages of advice at the end of his book—to "let the hapless African sleep undisturbed on his native shore and give over wishing for the extermination of the ancient proprietors of this land."[7]

Massachusetts clergyman William Gordon, publishing his *History of the Rise, Progress, and Establishment of Independence* in the same year, also wanted young Americans to learn of both the ignoble and heroic aspects of the nation's birth. "I am in search of genuine truth and not a fairy tale," Gordon wrote Washington in requesting private papers that would enable him to present a multifaceted revolution.[8]

Mercy Otis Warren, wife and sister of two important Massachusetts patriots, also hoped that the readers of her *History of the Rise, Progress, and Termination of the American Revolution* (published in 1805) would find moral lessons in her three-volume account; and she harbored no doubts that this obliged her to dwell on the bitter as well as the sweet, the ordinary as well as the great. Giving considerable play to women's importance in the Revolution, she wrote in detail about how ordinary Massachusetts plowmen and leather-apron men rose up in 1774 in "one of the most extraordinary eras in the history of man"—one that "led to that most alarming experiment of leveling of all ranks and destroying all subordination."[9] Indeed, Warren gave *too much* importance to lesser people and not nearly enough to John Adams, husband of her good friend Abigail—or so John told her. Adams was furious at her history. Putting the writing of his autobiography aside, he wrote ten long letters telling her why. Yet Warren's was one of the accounts that, in paying attention to common people, anticipated Ralph Waldo Emerson's plea four decades later in his famous essay entitled "The American Scholar," where he urged those who would truly know their history to understand "the near, the low, the common."

After the last of the revolutionary generation was in their graves, some began to worry that forward-looking Americans, many of them plunging west, were losing all memory of the American Revolution. Philadelphia's John Fanning Watson in 1825 urged the newborn Historical Society of Pennsylvania "to rescue from oblivion the facts of personal prowess, achievements, or sufferings by officers and soldiers of the Revolutionary war" and to record "the recitals of many brave men now going down to the tomb." Watson was passionately interested in the "great" men of the Revolution but also the "many privates 'unknown to fame' peculiarly distinguished by their actions," for example, Zenas Macumber, a private in Washington's bodyguard who had served through the entire war and survived seventeen wounds.[10]

Watson's fellow amateur historian Benson Lossing, orphaned at eleven and apprenticed to a watchmaker at fourteen in Poughkeepsie, New York, walked eight thousand miles in his midthirties to commune "with men of every social and intellectual grade" and sketch every part of the American landscape involved in the Revolutionary War for a hefty two-volume *Picto-*

rial Field-Book of the American Revolution (1850, 1852). While detailing every major battle of the Revolution, Lossing sprinkled his military history with vignettes about ordinary people: the poor shoemaker George Robert Twelves Hewes, who participated in the Boston Tea Party; the hardscrabble North Carolina farmers living in a region barren of printing presses, newspapers, and schools, who assembled to elect representatives from their militia companies who passed the Mecklenburg Resolutions that all but announced independence in May 1775, far ahead of the rest of the country; a frontier woman who beat off an Indian attack; and Pompey, the slave in the Hudson River valley who led General Anthony Wayne and his men "through the narrow defiles, over rough crags, and across deep morasses in single file" to storm the British fortress at Stony Point in July 1779.[11]

Two years before the public saw Lossing's first volume of the *Pictorial Field-Book*, the granddaughter of a revolutionary soldier, Elizabeth Ellet, published *The Women of the American Revolution*, two volumes that sketched the lives of sixty women "who bore their part in the Revolution." In 1850, she followed with *The Domestic History of the American Revolution.* Prominent women had their place—Abigail Adams, Martha Washington, and Mercy Otis Warren, for example. But most vignettes related the "actions and sufferings" of unheralded women such as sixteen-year-old Dicey Langston, who in the dead of night stealthily moved through woods, forded unbridged creeks, and slogged through marshes to deliver news of Loyalist troops on the march to her brother's patriot camp in backcountry South Carolina.[12] Many of the stories passed down from her remain unknown today.

Contemporaneous with these scribes of revolutionary heroes large and small were radical activists not only interested in ordinary people as agents of revolutionary change but worried about the conservative, reverent, tragedy-free core narrative being peddled in schoolbooks and popular histories by a genteel band of white male writers. Among the first to deplore this was a man remembered by virtually no American today. Born of obscure parents in 1822 near Philadelphia, George Lippard in his early twenties flashed across the literary sky like a meteor. A callow, crusading journalist, he took up labor's cause during the latter stages of the severe depression of 1837–1844. Sharpening his skills as a writer for the penny newspaper *Spirit of the Times*, whose motto was "Democratic and Fearless," Lippard turned into a "literary volcano constantly erupting with hot rage against America's ruling class." His *Quaker City, or, the Monks of Monk Hall* became a best seller in 1844. A muckraker before the term was coined, Lippard described Philadelphia as a stomach-turning subversion of American democracy and an insult to the old ideal of the City of Brotherly Love. Philadelphia's venerated leaders, charged Lippard, displayed a "callow indifference to the poor" that was "equaled only by their private venality and licentiousness." The book made him the most widely read author in the nation. His sales far exceeded those of Nathaniel Hawthorne, Herman Melville, Henry David Thoreau, Ralph Waldo Emerson, or Washington Irving; in fact, Lippard's books sold more than those of all the authors of the transcendentalist school put together.[13]

In 1846, Lippard began churning out legends of the American Revolution, and this is where he becomes relevant to the concerns of this book. Writing at a frantic pace, he freshened the public's memory of local battles at Germantown and Brandywine, British victories that paved the way for the enemy occupation of Philadelphia in September 1777. Mixing hair-raising descriptions of the terrors of war with florid portraits of American battlefield heroism, Lippard presented the Revolution as a poor man's war, one that he hoped would provide inspiration for mid-nineteenth century labor reformers whom he admired and promoted. His stories in *Washington and His Generals; or Legends of the American Revolution* (1847) and *Washington and His Men* (1849) gave Washington his due, but it was the common man on the battlefield who was the true hero. "Let me make a frank confession," Lippard told the City Institute in 1852, after millions had read his books. "I have been led astray. I have looked upon effigies and . . . bowed down to uniforms and done reverence to epaulettes. . . . Gilt and paint and spangles have for ages commanded reverence, while men made in the image of God have died in the ditch." Lippard got more particular: "The General who receives all the glory of the battles said to have been fought under his eye, who is worshiped in poetry and history, received in every city which he may enter by hundreds of thousands, who makes the heavens ring with his name; this General then is not *the* hero. No; the hero is the private soldier, who stands upon the battle field; . . . the poor soldier . . . whose skull bleaches in the sands, while the general whose glory the volunteer helped to win is warm and comfortable upon his mimic throne." Lippard cautioned his audience to "worship the hero . . . [and] reverence the heroic; but have a care that you are not swindled by a bastard heroism; be very careful of the sham hero."[14]

Lippard gave polite history a bad name; but the public loved him. He became their cultural arbiter and provided their understanding of the American

George Lippard was a muckraking journalist half a century before Theodore Roosevelt invented the term. Lippard's attempts to revive Tom Paine's reputation had some success in the mid-nineteenth century, but years of effort to erect a monument to Paine in Washington have been recurrently stalled and now failed.

Revolution. In a separate book, *Thomas Paine, Author-Soldier* (1852), Lippard helped restore Paine's reputation, which had gone into deep eclipse after Paine's attack on Christianity in *The Age of Reason*, written in the heat of the French Revolution. *The Age of Reason* left Paine an unattractive figure in polite circles and deeply offended churchgoing people. Yet Lippard's interest in Paine led to new editions of the revolutionary radical's many works, because Lippard rescued him as the unswerving herald of democracy who had more to say to the struggling mid-nineteenth century urban masses than all the revolutionary generals and statesmen. A year after Lippard's death in 1854, at age thirty-two, the Friends of Universal Liberty and Freedom, Emancipation and General Ruction celebrated "St. Thomas" Paine's birthday in Philadelphia.

Lippard's stories about Paine extended his lesson about heroes and heroism. "You may depend upon it," he wrote, "John Smith, the rent payer, is a greater man, a truer hero than Bloodhound the general, or Pumfrog the politician. True," Lippard continued, "when John is dead there is only another grave added to the graves of the forgotten poor, while your general and your politician have piles of white marble over their fleshen skulls. But judging a hero by the rule that he who suffers most, endures most, works most, is the true hero . . . When you read the praises of Great Statesmen, in the papers, don't be fooled from the truth by these sugar-tits of panegyric. These statesmen are not heroes."[15]

Lippard often dissolved the line between fiction and history in his revolutionary tales. Having Paine convert to Christianity on his deathbed or having the traitor Benedict Arnold don his old Continental army uniform and recant in his dying moments were examples of the liberties he took. The story of the muscular Black Sampson of the "Oath-Bound Five," who avenged the British murder of his white mistress by plunging into the Battle of Brandywine against the redcoats with Debbil, his ferocious dog, was pure fiction. So were other tales he told, though the historical events of which these vignettes were a part were accurate. Philadelphia's *Saturday Evening Post* charged that Lippard had "taken the liberty to palter with and corrupt the pages of history." Lippard retreated not an inch. He countered that in the hands of genteel historians, "The thing which generally passes for History is the most impudent, swaggering bully, the most graceless braggart, the most reckless equivocator that ever staggered forth on the great stage of the world." He embellished, he admitted. But a legend from his hand, he explained, was "one of those heartwarm stories, which, quivering in rude, earnest language from the lips of a spectator of a battle, or the survivor of some event of olden time, fill up the cold outlines of history, and clothe the skeleton with flesh and blood, give it eyes and tongue, force it at once to look into our eyes and talk with us!"[16]

Even as Lippard was publishing his first stories about the poor man's American Revolution, radical abolitionists were taking up the same cause. But they were particularly concerned about how the contributions of free black people, and some slaves, were fading away. John Greenleaf Whittier, poet laureate of the abolitionist movement, took up his pen in dismay and anger after hearing July 4 orations in the nation's capital. Writing in 1847 in Washington, D.C.'s *National Era*, an antislavery newspaper, he expostulated on how "the return of the Festival of our National Independence has called our attention to a matter which has been very carefully kept out of sight by orators and toast-drinkers." Why, asked Whittier, does "a whole nation [do] honor to the memories of one class of its defenders, to the total neglect of another class, who had the misfortune to be of darker complexion?" For a half century, Whittier charged, "certain historical facts . . . have been quietly elbowed aside," that are of "the services and sufferings of the colored soldiers of the Revolution." "They have no historian," he continued. "With here and there an exception, they all passed away, and only some faint tradition of their campaigns under Washington and Greene and Lafayette, and of their cruisings under Decatur and Barry, lingers among their descendants."[17]

On the eve of the Civil War, with the nation torn by sectional tension, Frederick Law Olmsted, later the creator of America's urban parks, tried to administer another cure for historical amnesia by reminding his country that history is with the people and that the people who *made* America were not putty in the hands of the great white men: "Men of literary taste . . . are always apt to overlook the working classes, and to confine the records they make of their own times, in a great degree, to the habits and fortunes of their own associates or to those of people of superior rank to themselves," he wrote as he was traveling through the southern states. "The dumb masses have often been so lost in this shadow of egotism, that, in later days, it has been impossible to discern the very real influence their character and condition has had on the fortune and fate of nations."[18]

Periodically, in the modern period, historians have dug deeper into the social strata to show the underside of the American Revolution. But in schools, historical theme parks, popular culture, film, and television, Olmsted's message about the indispensability of masses of ordinary people in all important social movements has barely been mentioned. The more intensely democratic, the more radical and visionary the idea, the more likely it has been excised from the textbook accounts of the American Revolution. The ideals and ideas that motivate those who want to complete the Revolution's radical agenda today are the very ones that have been leached out of the nation's history, replaced in the core narrative by a partially mythic and incomplete version of the Revolution.

The current generation of historians—a diverse group that looks more truly American than any preceding one—has scoured the records and posed new questions to take to the sources. In the last few decades a remarkable flowering of an American history sensitive to gender, race, religion, and class, which is to say a democratized history, is giving us an alternative, long-forgotten American Revolution. "Each generation," the English historian

Christopher Hill told us several decades ago, "rescues a new area from what its predecessors arrogantly and snobbishly dismissed as 'the lunatic fringe.' " But "it is no longer necessary to apologize profusely for taking the common people of the past on their own terms and trying to understand them," Hill advises.[19] This book responds to this advice.

The aim of this book is to capture the revolutionary involvement of *all* the component parts of some three million wildly diverse people living east of the Mississippi River. I could not have attempted such a study without changes in the historical profession over the past few decades—something akin to a tectonic plate shift. Clio, the muse of history, is hardly recognizable today in comparison to her visage of 1960. The emergence of a profession of historians of widely different backgrounds has redistributed historical property, and the American Revolution is now becoming the property of the many rather than the few. Even the best-remembered heroes are now seen with all their ambiguities, contradictions, and flaws. For example, it is no longer unpatriotic to read of Washington and Jefferson's tortured relationship to slavery, always mentioned in past biographies but usually soft-pedaled and marginalized. Now one can choose from a stack of books with enticing titles on the founding fathers and slavery such as Henry Wiencek's *An Imperfect God: George Washington, His Slaves, and the Creation of America*; Lucia C. Stanton's *Free Some Day: The African American Families of Monticello*; or David Waldstreicher's *Runaway America: Benjamin Franklin, Slavery, and the American Revolution*.

When historians fix their gaze downward or write a warts-and-all American history, they often offend people who cherish what they remember as a more coherent, worshipful, and supposedly annealing rendition of the past. In the history wars of the 1990s, many conservative-culture warriors called historians offering new interpretations of the American Revolution—or any other part of American history—"history bandits," "history pirates," or, sneeringly, "revisionists" intent on kidnapping history with no respect for a dignified rendition of the past. Yet the explosion of historical knowledge has invigorated history and increased its popularity. People who discover in accounts of the past figures like themselves—in color or class, religion, sex, or social situation—naturally find history more satisfying than when it is organized around a triumphalist version of the past in which the occupants of the national pantheon, representing a very narrow slice of society, get most of the play. Narratives of glory will always have a market, and some people will always prefer an uncomplicated, single-message history. But empathy with less than oversized figures, as much in history as in literature, has a market as well.

Unsurprisingly, those of the old school do not like to hear the question "whose history?" It is unsettling for them to see the intellectual property of the American Revolution, once firmly in the hands of a smaller and more homogeneous historians' guild, taken out of their safe boxes, put on the table, and redivided. Yet what could be more democratic than to reopen questions about the Revolution's sources, conduct, and results? And what is the lasting value of a "coherent" history if coherence is obtained by eliminating the jagged edges, where much of the vitality of the people is to be found? How can we expect people to think of the American Revolution as their own when they see no trace of their forebears in it? Historian Roger Wilkins writes: "Tales of the republic's founding—mythic national memories used to bind us together—are often told in ways that exclude and diminish all of us" (and thus, it might be added, keep us divided). In propagating this kind of simplified history "we ensure that our future will be rent along the same jagged seams that wound us so grievously today. There is much pain and loss in our national history, which contains powerful echoes of the pain and loss many of us feel in our daily lives."[20]

A history of inclusion has another claim to make. Only a history that gives play to all the constituent parts of society can overcome the defeatist notion that the past was inevitably determined. Historical inevitability is a winner's story, excusing mistakes of the past and relegating the loser's story to a footnote. Is it not fitting in an open and generally optimistic society that we should portray to a wide range of individuals those who did not see themselves as puppets dancing on the strings of the supposed leaders? If the history we are making today is subject to human will, or what historians call human agency, then yesterday's history must have been fluid and unpredictable rather than moving along some predetermined course. If history did not unfold inevitably in the American Revolution, then surely a great many people must have been significant actors in its unfolding. Conscious of a complex past, readers today can embrace the idea that they, too, can contribute to a different future. Honest history can impart a sense of how the lone individual counts, how the possibilities of choice are infinite, how human capacity for both good and evil is ever present, and how dreams of a better society are in the hands of the dispossessed as much as in the possession of the putative brokers of our society's future.

The Unknown American Revolution

1

ROOTS OF RADICALISM

"Can America be happy under a government of her own?" asked Thomas Paine, the thirty-seven-year-old immigrant, just sixteen months after arriving in Philadelphia on November 30, 1774. The answer was succinct. "As happy as she please; she hath a blank sheet to write upon."[1] That notion—of a slate wiped clean of historical encumbrances, of entrenched class hostilities, of religious bigotry, of racial oppression and conflict, of conventions about gender roles, of genocidal urges directed at Native Americans—was heady, exhilarating, and filled with latent dynamite. In a wide range of communities thousands imbibed the idea that the Revolution must take up, as part of its work, the remaking of America. Millennialist preachers, enslaved Africans, frontier mystics, dockside tars, German-speaking privates in Washington's army, mixed- and full-blooded Indians, urban craftsmen, indentured servants, agricultural workers, ascetic Quakers, disgruntled women, born-again men and women calling themselves Christ's poor—all became caught up in the inner dynamics of the Revolution. If we conceive of them as so many grabbers of quill pens, eager to write on the blank sheet, we can see that the American Revolution was not only a war of independence but a many-sided struggle to reinvent America. It was a civil war at home as well as a military struggle for national liberation.

All revolutions are filled with idealistic hopes, millennial yearnings, desires to redress old grievances, dreams of both individual and societal betterment. The moment of rupture from the old regime has historically presented the moment for cleansing, reinvigorating, reforming, and perfecting; so it was with the American Revolution. What experiences and ideas fueled the desire for change, and who would step forward to unfurl banners of reform? Years after the Revolution, John Adams reflected on just such questions. Writing Mercy Otis Warren, his wife's close friend who was writing her own history of the American Revolution, Adams opined that "the principles of the American Revolution may be said to have been as various as the thirteen states that went through it, and in some sense almost as diversified as the individuals who acted in it."[2]

Even before approaching the beginnings of the American Revolution, we must take our cue from Adams's belief in the diversity of the people caught up in it. War has a way of smoothing out prior disputes and healing angry wounds, because facing a powerful enemy obliges people to embrace a common cause. But when war is more than a struggle with arms to seize independence, and when prolonged conflict necessarily involves the creation of new governments to live under, the abrasions of the past are rarely forgotten. Indeed we will see that past injustices, as perceived by important blocs of people, shaped ideas about how the Revolution could usher in, to use the motto of the Continental Congress, *novus ordo seclorum* (a new order of the ages).

In this chapter, we will examine seven episodes of the late colonial period that set the stage for the multifaceted revolution in North America and prefigured the internal struggle for a radically reformed American society. These seven events took place across a sprawling terrain from Maine to Georgia and from tidewater regions along the coast to the deeply forested backcountry. No one involved in any of these episodes had any notion that they were preparing the ground for the American Revolution. Yet the Revolution could not have unfolded, especially in its thrust for reforming American society, without these unknowing rehearsals for revolt and radical reform.

Jailbreaks at Newark

In mid-September 1745, about 150 New Jersey farmers armed with "clubs, axes and crow bars" descended on the jail in Newark, the capital of the royal colony of New Jersey. They demanded that the sheriff release Samuel Baldwin, who had been arrested for cutting down trees on lands claimed by Governor Lewis Morris, a man of great wealth and the owner of scores of slaves. When the sheriff refused, the crowd mobbed him. They tore the jail door off its hinges and set Baldwin free. Triumphantly making their way out of town, they vowed to mobilize again and bring "fighting Indians" with them on the next occasion that one of their own was imprisoned.[3]

Fourteen weeks later, when the sheriff followed orders from the royal governor to arrest three of the farmers involved in the September jailbreak, the defiant yeomen assembled again. Armed with clubs, they freed one of the prisoners as he was being transferred from one jail to another. Trying to uphold royal authority, the sheriff called out thirty militiamen to surround the Newark jail and prevent further breaks. Undaunted, three hundred determined farmers, marching under a pennant, confronted the militia. "Those who are upon my list, follow me," shouted Amos Roberts, a yeoman leader. With that, the farmers overpowered the militiamen, thrashed the sheriff, freed their friends, and marched out of town.[4]

Other similar events followed. In July 1747, two hundred men marched into Perth Amboy in East New Jersey and vowed that if they were challenged "there should not have been a man left alive, or a house standing." Springing open the town jail, they freed one of their imprisoned leaders.

Mob attacks on the royal jails that summer and fall shattered established authority. "Since that time [in September 1745]," bemoaned the New Jersey Board of Proprietors in early 1748, the yeoman farmers "have gone on like a torrent bearing down all before them and trampling upon all law and authority." Reports circulated that the farmers had established their own jail "back in the woods," where they would imprison their enemies "and then see who durst fetch them out." They operated their own tax system, the worried authorities complained, they elected their own militia officers, and they erected their own courts where justice would be dispensed on their own terms. "Royal institutions and the power of the gentry landowners," writes historian Brendan McConville, "stood on the brink of collapse."[5]

What was amiss in "the best poor man's country," as many European visitors called the mid-Atlantic region? At stake was the question of land and under what conditions it would be owned, leased, or occupied. That had been the story of New Jersey almost from its inception in the 1660s. Indeed, it was the story of all the colonies, for a vast majority of immigrants from the very earliest entries into North America had thirsted for land like the weary

3

traveler in the desert seeks water. A century before, the utopian dreamer Roger Williams had deplored the "depraved appetite [for] great portions of land, land in this wilderness, as if men were in as great necessity and danger for want of great portions of land as poor, hungry seamen have after a sick and stormy, a long and starving passage."[6] Coming from Europe, where land was scarce and beyond the grasp of most people, immigrants made the acquisition of cheap land and secure title to it their most treasured goal. Land was the holy grail, and control of it became a cause of incessant conflict—both with native peoples and among the Europeans who coveted it.

Title to land, the source of political and social power, had a long, tangled, and unique history in New Jersey, so knotty that no single notion of legality in the ownership of New Jersey land gained consensus in the century before the American Revolution. The trouble began because the lands of New Jersey were granted almost simultaneously in 1664 by two legal entities, creating a dilemma of overlapping authority that could not be overcome for generations. The fast-growing yeomanry in the eighteenth century believed that they tilled land originally controlled by the Dutch West India Company and then granted to New England Puritans who had migrated to northern New Jersey after English forces seized control of the Dutch New Netherlands in 1664. They solidified their claims by purchasing these lands from Native American chiefs. Small farmers also held that the labor they invested in developing these lands gave them rightful possession, especially in cases of disputed claims. Opposing these small farmer property claims were gentry arguments that all of northern New Jersey had been granted by James, Duke of York (the brother of King Charles II), to two English aristocrats, Sir George Carteret and Lord John Berkeley, who were vested with the power to create government, sell property, and collect quitrents (a feudal leftover whereby the purchaser made annual payments to the former proprietor in perpetuity).

By 1701, Carteret and Berkeley had sold their vast land grants in East New Jersey to Scottish investors, who organized themselves into a board of proprietors. Trying to transform East New Jersey into an estate-based society where they would dominate tenants, subtenants, and servants, they instead created a perfect formula for instability, violence, and contested authority. Running afoul of migrants from New England and New York who had settled lands and built farming communities, the Scottish proprietors found it difficult to control the land tenure system they wanted. Confronted with a disputatious society pitting Scottish patricians dreaming of feudal-style estates against yeomen farmers coveting freeholds, the English imposed royal government in 1701 in an attempt to stabilize New Jersey.

Royal government could erase neither the Scottish proprietors' property claims nor the yeomen's militant antilandlordism. At first, royal government brought a measure of social and political stability to New Jersey. But in the 1740s, a new generation of proprietors, mostly Scottish, reignited battles over property holding by reasserting their legal claims to vast tracts of land in East New Jersey at the expense of the yeomanry. This second generation of Scottish proprietors was something more than a clique of grasping grandees. They prided themselves as subscribers to the Enlightenment, European intellectuals seeking new forms of social organization and political structures to cleanse a corrupt, monarchy-ridden, religiously torn Europe. These Scottish proprietors imagined they could build a peaceful, orderly society in New Jersey where well-educated, landed gentlemen ruled with virtue and honor and schooled the grateful lower orders. Yet their own property interests led them to imagine the impossible—an enlightened republic of huge estates worked by indentured servants and tenant farmers who had no secure possession of the land they tilled.

The result was a revival of the violent disputes over property rights and control of the courts to mediate them that had punctuated the late seventeenth century. Invoking legal rights tracing back to late seventeenth-century land grants to Carteret and Berkeley, the proprietors began evicting yeomen from property that these smallholders regarded as their own. The yeomen saw nothing "enlightened" about this assault on their property rights and the attempts of leading aristocrats, such as Lewis Morris, his son Robert Hunter Morris, the lawyer James Alexander, and members of the powerful Livingston and Delancey families, to impose "the highly exploitative Scottish-style landholding pattern on the countryside." If the landlords thought of themselves as torchbearers of the Enlightenment, the yeomen were equally sure that John Locke, a pillar of enlightened thinking, championed their cause. Borrowing from Locke's *Second Treatise on Government*, they wrote in defense of land riots that "When Property is made uncertain and precarious, this band [of government] is broken."[7]

The battle between patrician proprietors and prickly plebeians erupted in the mid-1740s. Protecting land in which they had invested their labor for many years, yeomen farmers threatened to follow the venerable English lower-class tradition of house pulling—destroying the house of an offender by attaching ropes to the chimneys, roof beams, and joists and, in pulling them down, reducing the whole structure to lumber. Proprietor John Coxe, who claimed vast tracts of land, was threatened in 1747 that if his evictions caused the jailing of any other people "they would go . . . and pull Coxe's house down about his ears."[8]

From the wealthy gentry's point of view, this was treason against the king—an attempt "to throw off his Majesty's authority," in the words of Governor Andrew Hamilton. Arguing that their property claims originated in grants from the king, which they later acquired, the Scottish proprietors charged that the "Multitude of People [were] trading upon the very heels of rebellion, if not actually engaged in it." The yeomen countered that their claims to the property came from their possession and improvement of it through their own labor since purchasing the land from Indian chiefs. The labor theory of value expressed here was an implicit assault on the political and legal authority embodied in monarchical government. Drawing on Lockean ideas, the yeomen's defense of their Newark jailbreaks argued that "It is a received observation that a settled rule of property . . . impartially applied, is the great ligament of government; and when property is made uncertain and precarious, this bond is broken."[9]

Intensifying the disputes were religious and cultural differences between plebeians and patricians. The yeomen were mostly descended from English and Dutch immigrants, though by the 1740s small northern New Jersey communities were thoroughly mixed. Their churches were Congregational, Baptist, Quaker, and Presbyterian. On the other hand, most of the proprietors were Scottish and Anglican, members of the colony's most hierarchical, stiff-necked church. When the Great Awakening of religious enthusiasm broke out in New Jersey in the 1720s, the yeomanry were most affected by the revivalists' message. Apart from spiritual comfort, the Awakening also provided a potent language with which to contest the gentry's position in the property disputes. The gentry-dominated Anglican Church was predictably hostile to the Awakeners and tried to discredit and undermine evangelical preachers as social incendiaries.

As would happen in the American Revolution, religion and politics became thoroughly entwined in the New Jersey land riots of the 1740s. The message of the revivalist preachers, who served small rural communities, was deeply tinctured with antiauthoritarian, antielitist, and antimaterialist messages that resonated powerfully among those whose land titles were endangered by the gentry proprietors. "Go now, ye rich men, weep and howl, for your miseries will come upon you. . . . Your gold and silver is cankered . . . and shall eat your flesh as if it were fire," preached Theodorus Frelinghuysen, the Dutch Reformed evangelist who touched off the first New Jersey revival in the late 1720s. The itinerant English Awakener George Whitefield, spreading the Awakening with sojourns through New Jersey in 1739 and 1741, further deplored aristocratic fashion and criticized the religious lassitude that came, he cautioned, with the accumulation of material wealth. William Tennent and his son Gilbert, next to Whitefield as the most searing voices of evangelical reform, aroused the plainspoken farmers even more. Crisscrossing New Jersey in the 1740s, Gilbert Tennent, a burly, plainspoken man who, according to one contemporary, was "like a Boatswain of a Ship, calling the Sailors to come to Prayers and be damned," attacked the Anglican clergy as unregenerate and encouraged people to forsake their corrupt ministers. Adapting Whitefield's message to the colonial social landscape, the Tennents infused soul-searching, evangelical preaching with a radical egalitarianism that left many former supporters of Whitefield grasping for their pens. Particularly in the interior hill towns of New Jersey, where land titles were in dispute, the revival reached its peak. The antimaterialist message in the Awakeners' attempt to stimulate a rebirth among the populace produced explicit accusations that the proprietary elite was guilty of "Cut-throat covetousness" in bringing suits of eviction against small farmers living on contested lands.[10]

Though New Jersey was unusually roiled, it was far from the only place where yeoman attacks on property and power holders destabilized society in the late colonial period. In the 1750s, New York's Hudson River valley was torn with tenant revolts against the manor lords who controlled tracts of land so vast as to rival European principalities. In North Carolina, as we will see in chapter 3, thousands of backcountry farmers rebelled against eastern enemies who dominated the colony's government. In South Carolina and northeastern New York, and in the region that would become Vermont in 1777, agrarian insurgents rose up against wealthy men who threatened their livelihoods, which depended almost entirely on land security. In each of these cases, common farmers went "out of the bounds of the law," as Remember Baker put it, bringing charges from the wealthy that the rioters and jail breakers were perpetrating "bold and daring attempts to throw off his

Majesty's authority and their dependence on the Crown of Britain."[11] The agrarian radicals had no intention of overthrowing the English king; they were protecting their land in the face of eviction by local aristocrats. Nonetheless, unbeknownst to them, they were building a legal and political case against monarchical and aristocratic authority; in effect, they were rehearsing for revolution.

Christ's Poor

The fiery comet of the Great Awakening raced through Virginia's foothill Hanover County in the 1740s when Patrick Henry was only a boy. At its core, this firestorm of religious enthusiasm was, in the words of religious historian William G. McLoughlin, "a search for new sources of authority, new principles of action, new foundations of hope" among people who came to believe that "the churches as institutions no longer met the spiritual needs of the people." The Awakeners preached that the old sources of authority were too effete to solve the problems of the day, too encrusted with tradition, self-indulgence, hypocrisy, and intellectualism to bring a sense of hope and faith to a generation that was witnessing the transformation of the world of its forebears. "Our people do not so much need to have their heads stored," pronounced Jonathan Edwards, New England's leading evangelist, "as to have their hearts touched."[12]

When the charismatic George Whitefield from England conducted a tour of the American colonies in 1739–40, he set ablaze Virginia's western frontier counties with the new doctrine of spiritual rebirth. Only twenty-five when he reached the colonies in 1739, Whitefield, the son of an English tavern keeper, was a diminutive youth with a magnificent voice. A master of open-air preaching, he tramped much of the English countryside and then turned his attention to the American colonies. His barnstorming trip evoked a mass response of dimensions never before witnessed in America. It was a response that deeply troubled established leaders—both those in church and those in politics—for Whitefield and the American preachers who followed "the Grand Itinerant," as he came to be known, spread the message that God did not operate through the elite corps of learned clergy and their aristocratic allies. Rather, God worked through the inner light given to every man and woman regardless of their station in life, with lack of education or even slave status posing no barrier to achieving grace through the conversion experience. Whitefield challenged traditional sources of authority, called upon people to become the instruments of their own salvation, and implicitly attacked the prevailing upper-class notion that the uneducated masses had no minds of their own. This was not an entirely new message for nearly a century before, among the millenarian religious sects of England's Civil War period, self-educated preachers such as Mary Cary urged that "the time is coming when not only men but women shall prophesy; not only aged men but young men, not only superiors but inferiors; not only those who have university learning but those who have it not, even servants and handmaids."[13]

In Virginia, such ideas ran afoul of the law and afoul of the colony's established Anglican Church. Patrick Henry's uncle, an Anglican minister in Hanover County, found himself called "a stranger to true religion" and an "unconverted graceless man" who preached "damnable doctrine." Parson Patrick Henry counterattacked. "New preachers ... have lately seduced some unwary people in this parish," he charged in 1745, and he would soon spread a pamphlet attack on the Great Awakening, first printed in New England, with a preface that condemned "a set of incendiaries, enemies not only to the Established Church, but also common disturbers of the peace."[14]

Disturbing the peace? What did an Anglican minister such as Patrick Henry mean by this? And why would he label men "incendiaries" who were bringing streams of people to a state of passionate religiosity and an assurance that they had been reborn? The answer lay in both the message and the medium. The message was one of social leveling, for it put all people on one footing insofar as the conversion experience was concerned. Moreover, the message was one that condemned the established clergy as unconverted and deplored their love of velvet garments and other luxurious trappings. "Christ's poor," as those converted by the Awakeners were called, saw themselves as the true children of God and those most likely to achieve the celestial afterlife.

Lay exhorting summed up all that was wrong with the wave of evangelical enthusiasm in the eyes of conservatives. Patrick Henry, like every other Anglican parson in Virginia, had received his license to teach from the bishop of London, head of the Church of England's overseas Anglican ministers. But now people of no training stepped right from "the plough," or straight from the construction site, as in the case of the self-educated bricklayer Samuel Morris, who refused to attend Anglican services and instead set up religious meetings in a small "reading-house" that he built on his own property. Soon

Morris reading-houses were springing up in Virginia's western counties. This ran hard against the ancient belief within the structured Protestant churches that there was no room for laypersons to compete with the qualified ministry in preaching the word of God. Nor was there room for self-initiated gatherings of people, which were cropping up all over Virginia's western counties, to meet in barns, on riverbanks, or in rude reading-houses instead of licensed churches. This was to relocate authority collectively in the mass of common people. The results were predictable in the conservatives' view. The unlicensed revivalists, Patrick Henry reported to the bishop of London in 1745, "screw up the people to the greatest heights of religious phrenzy and then leave them in that wild state, for perhaps ten or twelve months, till another enthusiast comes among them, to repeat the same thing over again."[15]

Worried Anglican clergymen convinced Virginia's governor to restrain "strolling preachers" who conjured up a world without properly constituted authority. Yet when evangelical Presbyterian ministers from the North, such as the academy-trained Samuel Davies, applied for licenses to preach and establish settled churches, Parson Patrick Henry tried to block them, too. For a time Anglican ministers blocked the licenses through their influence with the House of Burgesses, populated by deacons of the parish churches. But they could not block the word preached by Davies and other evangelists. The slender, handsome young Davies, twenty-four years old when he arrived in Virginia in 1747, found swarms of people lacking "spiritual food" and "nauseated" by comfortless, rigid sermons full of textual references and cold, logical proofs thrown at them by Anglican ministers. Moving carefully, Davies eventually did obtain a license to preach and soon established meetinghouses that were packed on Sunday mornings. "Where I go amongst Mr. Davies' people, religion seems to flourish," recounted a visiting Presbyterian minister. "It is like the suburbs of heaven."[16] As a teenager, Patrick Henry attended Davies's sermons and repeated aloud, at the insistence of his mother, the main parts of the sermon as they drove their carriage home. Henry acquired much of his oratorical skills at the feet of Samuel Davies, whose uncommon artistry in awakening the emotions of his auditors rivaled that of George Whitefield. Henry later claimed that Davies was the most important influence on his life and the greatest speaker he ever heard.

Virginia's ruling class had another reason to fear and oppose religious enthusiasm: It held great appeal for the enslaved. This was partly because the participatory, emotional character of Great Awakening worship provided a spiritual experience akin to that practiced among many Africans. Extemporaneous praying, congregational singing, and voluntary testifying provided the kind of succor for slaves that dry disquisitions from the pulpit before passive churchgoers could never bring. Slaves also eagerly embraced evangelical Christianity because it gave them the nearly irresistible idea that conversion to Christianity would make them free, as passages of the Bible suggested. This was reason enough for masters in the tidewater area densely populated by slaves to quarantine their bondmen and bondwomen from evangelicalism. But in the piedmont counties, where slaves were held in smaller numbers, Presbyterianism took hold rapidly. Samuel Davies counted hundreds of slaves coming to his meetinghouses and commented on their particular love of singing psalms. "Whenever they could get an hour's leisure from their masters," he wrote, "they would hurry away to my house . . . to gratify their peculiar taste for Psalmody." Many, he claimed, "Have lodged all night in my kitchen; and, sometimes, when I have awakened about two or three a-clock in the morning, a torrent of sacred harmony poured into my chamber and carried my mind away to Heaven."[17]

Although Samuel Davies had brought legitimacy to evangelical Presbyterianism by obtaining a license to preach in Virginia, it proved to be only a temporary sanction. In the same month he received his license in 1747, Governor William Gooch and his council issued a proclamation demanding that "all itinerant preachers" be restrained.[18] After the Hanover County Court issued a license to preach to the fiery New Englander James Davenport, in 1750, the governor ordered the suppression of all circuit riders who had no settled place or established church. For another two decades, religious dissenters ministered to their flocks while living in a gray zone where they were always in danger of having their licenses removed or denied. Not until Virginia passed a Declaration of Rights in 1776 was religious toleration guaranteed.

Revolutions have always begun with an insurgent minority, and the American Revolution was no exception. Whether for white colonists of the middle and lower social orders or for the enslaved, the Great Awakening provided a "radical model" for revolutionary activists, as historian Patricia Bonomi has expressed it. The Awakeners created a mass movement; they challenged upper-class assumptions about social order and the deference due to established figures; they seceded from churches they regarded as corrupt and built new, regenerated ones in their place, even without license; they forced religious toleration on those arrayed against it and broke apart attempted unions of church and state; they fractured established churches such as those in Virginia and thereby threatened the existing social order. Guardians of the traditional churches preached to their flocks to "obey them that have rule over you." The Awakeners, to the contrary, claimed the freedom "to question and judge all and refuse subjection to every proper judicature." Here was a "pertinent and usable model" for radicals "in the years that lay ahead,"as Bonomi points out.[19]

Even for those untouched by the Awakening but who emerged as Revolutionary leaders, religious revivalism provided blueprints for the way forward in the decades ahead. Patrick Henry's experience is an example. His mother had warmly embraced evangelical Presbyterianism but his father, brother of Parson Patrick Henry, continued to worship at the Anglican parish church. Growing up, Patrick was both ambitious and cautious, and both qualities led him not toward ecstatic religion but toward the more sober and genteel Anglicanism of his father and uncle. Yet he drew from evangelicalism an appreciation of fiery and theatrical presentation and the needs of the humble. As Henry Mayer, Patrick Henry's biographer, puts it, he learned to "amalgamate the evangelical and gentry styles into a powerful political identity" that enabled him to "reach out to ordinary people, speak to them with fire and conviction, meld them into one community of belief, and turn that massed opinion into a new tool of political control."[20]

Little Carpenter's Dilemma

In the 1750s, by the time the invasion of yeoman property rights had died down in New Jersey, cultivators of the soil hundreds of miles to the south were engaged in another violent confrontation that, like the New Jersey example, foretold elements of the American Revolution soon to unfold. The Cherokee people, whose ancient homelands stretched from the interior of Virginia to Georgia, numbered about 12,000 in 1750. For decades they had been indispensable to the security of the English, Scottish, Scots-Irish, and German settlers who thinly populated the up-country region, where they eked out a hardscrabble existence. Tension always arose wherever land-hungry settlers brushed up against Indian settlements. This was the case in all the southern colonies. But for a long time, more bound the settlers together with the native people than divided them. Especially important were trade and military alliances.

By the 1750s, Indian trade was of signal importance to both sides. It connected native peoples of interior North America with an Atlantic basin network that reached all the way back to European suppliers of worsted materials, glass beads, guns, and other trade goods. Faced with Indian enemies and contending with the Spanish and French for control of southeastern North America, the Virginians, Carolinians, and Georgians also regarded military alliances with powerful Native American tribes as indispensable. In this precarious world, alliance with the Cherokees became the cornerstone of southern Indian policy, and the Cherokees knew this. Their leaders of the 1750s keenly remembered how their people played a decisive role in the bloody Yamassee War of 1715, when British settlers, paying dearly for their abuse of small coastal tribes, faced a militant coalition of the exploited. "The last time they were here [in Charleston]," wrote one white leader in 1717, "they insulted us to the last degree and indeed by their demands (with which we were forced to comply) made us their tributaries."[21]

By the 1730s, abuses by English traders working hard bargains with the Cherokees had weakened Cherokee support. In the 1740s, Cherokee allegiance to the English faded even more because South Carolina's government refused to honor a treaty of mutual support when the upper Creeks, a powerful society to the south of the Cherokees, attacked their old Cherokee enemies. In response, the Cherokees fell upon abusive white Carolina traders, demonstrating that they did not regard themselves as English dependents and had strength enough to control their own destiny. Making overtures to the French, their alternate source of trade goods, the Cherokees kept the English off balance. In 1750, South Carolina's governor reminded the legislature that "it is absolutely necessary for us to be in friendship with the Cherokees, for they are reckoned to be about three thousand gunmen, the greatest nation we know of in America except the Choctaws."[22] With the Choctaws allied with the French in the lower Mississippi area, the Cherokees were the indispensable buffer between the English and their French enemies.

But the day of Cherokee-English alliance was coming to a close. Like other powerful interior tribes, such as the Iroquois and the Creeks, the Cherokees struggled with European smallpox and other diseases that decimated their population. They worried about the corrosive effects of alcohol and other European trade goods that tore at the fabric of their ancient society. And they wondered whether they could continue to play off one colonizing European power against another while the population of the English colonies kept growing at an alarming rate—from about 250,000 in 1700 to 1.2 million in 1750. "To preserve the balance between us and the French," wrote New York's Indian secretary, "is the great ruling principle of modern Indian policy."[23] But the Seven Years' War, breaking out in North America in 1754 and ending in 1763, bringing to a climax nearly a century of Anglo-French hostilities over control of North America, greatly altered the equilibrium between Indian and European peoples. Now the Cherokee stood on the edge of a dangerous and potentially catastrophic new era.

The Seven Years' War, voluminously chronicled in American history, can be treated only skimpily here. For present purposes, it is enough to understand its enormous importance to the Cherokee as well as other Indian nations. Indian involvement in the war, the greatest armed conflict in a century and a half of English colonization in North America, foretold the experience of Native Americans in the Revolution that lay just over the horizon.

In the northern sector of the Seven Years' War territory, the decision in 1759 of the powerful Iroquois nations to abandon their long-held position of neutrality in Anglo-French conflicts proved decisive. Joining the Anglo-Americans, the Iroquois helped bring the French to their knees. They were promptly showered with gifts of trade goods for their efforts. But in the South, power politics worked differently for the Cherokees. At the outset of the war, Virginia's governor, Robert Dinwiddie, worked hard in 1754 to gain Cherokee support for the attempt of the Virginia militia, led by the young George Washington, to dislodge the French from the forks of the Monongahela and Ohio Rivers, a strategic location for controlling the Ohio River valley. Cherokee chiefs at first promised the Virginians a thousand warriors, but they reneged when they could not secure more favorable trading terms with the Carolinians. Washington had no Cherokee warriors with him in the summer of 1754, when he suffered greatly in skirmishes with the French. In July 1755, when English general Edward Braddock suffered a disastrous defeat in the depths of the American wilderness near the forks of the Ohio River, he had only eight Native Americans with his army.

Renewed appeals to the Cherokees brought half promises of support against the French. In 1757, about 250 Cherokee warriors fought with the Virginia militia on the western frontier. But they fought as mercenaries, not as allies. When they were not paid according to agreement, they plundered Virginia frontier settlements in order to collect by force what the white government failed to give them. This occurred again in 1758, when some four hundred to six hundred Cherokee warriors led by Attakullakulla (known to the English as Little Carpenter because he was a skilled orator, politician, and diplomat who could fit together his people's ideas and plans of action like a skilled carpenter joins wood) enlisted in General John Forbes's formidable British regiments. But when Forbes offended Attakullakulla, he tried to withdraw from the impending fray. Attakullakulla was furious about being called a deserter. On top of this insult, Virginia frontiersmen began ambushing Cherokees who were returning from battle alongside the English and living off the land as they made their way home. At least thirty Cherokees lost their lives at the hands of their so-called allies, who proved unwilling to distinguish between friendly and hostile Indians. A few such incidents were all that was required to fan into a roaring blaze the anti-English embers that had been kept alive in the westernmost Cherokee towns (called the Overhill Cherokee towns), where pro-French sentiment still remained. Cherokee messengers went out to the Creeks and Chickasaws in the winter of 1758–59. With spring thaws came backcountry skirmishing from Virginia to South Carolina, and a full-scale war with the Cherokee people was soon under way.

As happened repeatedly in the American Revolution, Indian leaders struggled for a way to preserve their land, their supply of weapons and ammunition, and their political autonomy. For the Cherokees, in the midst of a seriously deteriorating situation with their old English allies, all the signs were ominous. While their warriors had moved north to fight with the English against the French, backcountry South Carolina settlers in the Long Canes settlement were invading the hunting grounds of the Cherokees and diminishing their food supply. This added to the feeling among the young warriors that the white backwoodsmen were no longer their friends. South Carolina's governor William Henry Lyttleton contributed to the decaying situation by spurning Attakullakulla's attempts to mend the rift. By cutting off the supply of gunpowder to the Cherokee, the arrogant and inflexible Lyttleton virtually guaranteed war.

At an impasse, the Cherokee laid siege in January 1760 to Fort Prince George, which the English had built in the Cherokee hill country to counter French influence from the west. Here South Carolina held twenty-two Cherokee warriors hostage. The Cherokees were unable to capture the fort, but within weeks they had attacked frontier settlements from southern Virginia to South Carolina, sending white settlers reeling back to within seventy-five miles of the tidewater capitals of Williamsburg, New Bern, and Charleston. Governor William Bull of South Carolina, succeeding Governor Lyttleton, recognized that the Cherokees were more than a match for the bedraggled force of militiamen at his disposal and agreed to a treaty that made concessions to the Cherokees on "terms that perhaps may not be thought suitable, according to the rules of honour observed among Europeans," as he delicately put it.²⁴ But then the arrival of 1,300 crack Highland Scottish troops under Colonel Archibald Montgomery promised a quick victory over the Cherokee. The British forces devastated the lower towns on the eastern side of the Great Smoky Mountains but were bogged down in the rugged terrain in their attempts to overpower the middle towns, deep in the mountains of what is today Tennessee. Ambushed at every turn and short on supplies, the British retreated to Charleston. In August, Fort Loudoun, the main English garrison in Overhill Cherokee territory, surrendered to a Cherokee siege.

British soldiers and Carolinian militiamen renewed the war in the summer of 1761. This time they succeeded in overthrowing the Cherokee. Always striving for peace, Attakullakulla tried to arrange a truce, but younger chiefs and warriors, preaching a nativist revival, blocked his way. Likewise, white settlers and British officers wanted revenge for the previous summer's defeats. With 700 militiamen from Virginia and South Carolina joining 1,800 British regulars and handfuls of Catawba and Chickasaw warriors, a scorched-earth campaign destroyed the Cherokee middle towns along with their crops. Cut off from their supply of French trade goods, the Cherokees submitted to a peace treaty that acknowledged English sovereignty and established the eastern boundary of the Cherokee territory on terms that yielded some of the lower towns' hunting grounds to the English.

Losing their supply of trade goods and unable to organize a pan-Indian offensive, the Cherokees joined the French as losers in the Seven Years' War. They lost half their villages, a large portion of their hunting grounds, and thousands of their people. The Cherokees would find some comfort when the British, in 1762, appointed John Stuart superintendent of Indian affairs in the southern colonies. Stuart had befriended Attakullakulla, and through his respect for the accommodationist chief pledged to deal less treacherously with

The young Thomas Jefferson, a student at the College of William and Mary, remembered for his entire life Outacite's farewell address in Williamsburg just prior to the chief's departure for London in 1762.

the Cherokee. But Attakullakulla knew, as would be the case in the Revolution soon about to begin, that he had been eclipsed by younger, nativist chiefs who were determined to resist Anglo-American corrupt trading practices, intimidation, and territorial invasion. Stuart and Attakullakulla shared the belief that conciliation rather than conflict was in the interest of both whites and Indians. But it was the burden of the coolheaded Stuart to curb venal traders and land-crazed frontiersmen if ever the friendship of the Cherokee could be preserved. Nearly every facet of the Indians' dilemma in the American Revolution—how to maintain trading relations while preserving their land and political independence—had now played itself out in the brief but punishing Cherokee War of 1759–61. In fact, the Indians' American Revolution had already begun.

"The Mobbish Turn" in Boston

The main cause "of the Mobbish turn in this Town, is its Constitution; by which the management of it is devolv'd upon the populace assembled in their town meetings ... [where] the meanest inhabitants ... by their constant attendance there generally are the majority and outvote the gentlemen, merchants, substantial traders and all the better part of the inhabitants; to whom it is irksome to attend." Thus wrote Governor William Shirley of Massachusetts, standing in New England's chief seaport and reflecting on his neighbors who populated the nerve center of colonial Puritanism. Many years later Thomas Jefferson would call the Massachusetts town meetings deplored by Governor Shirley "the wisest invention ever devised by the wit of man for the perfect exercise of self-government." But for William Shirley, writing in 1747, there was entirely too much self-government. Too many "working artificers, seafaring men, and low sorts of people," he complained, accounted for the "mobbish spirit."[25]

Sitting at his desk penning this letter to the Lords of Trade in London, Governor Shirley was no doubt in a bad mood when it came to Boston's town meeting because, just two weeks before, Bostonians had staged the greatest tumult in the city in many years. When Commodore Charles Knowles brought his Royal Navy fleet to Boston for reprovisioning, in preparation for cruising the West Indies, he sent press gangs ashore before dawn to replenish his depleted crews. Impressment had brought angry protests from Bostonians in recent years, just as it had in the mid-seventeenth century English Civil War, when radical Levellers and Fifth Monarchy Men resisted the seizure of their bodies and called pressing men into armed naval service in an attempt to deprive them of freedom and reduce them to a "slavish condition."[26] Facing impressment this time, Boston commoners defied not only an English commodore but their own governor. Shirley called the militia to arms to stop the raging crowd that was stoning the colony's statehouse windows and burning a royal barge it had hauled to the courtyard of the governor's house. But how could the militiamen heed the governor's call when most of them were in fact part of the defiant stone-throwing crowd? Infuriated, Commodore Knowles threatened to bombard Boston from his warships in the harbor. Great bloodshed was averted only after the release of impressed townsmen.

One day before Governor Shirley condemned Boston's town meeting as a crucible of mob politics, a pamphlet signed by "Amicus Patriae" appeared in the streets. In hard-hitting, plain language, *An Address to the Inhabitants of the Province of Massachusetts-Bay in New England* defended the "natural right" of Bostonians to band together for defense against arbitrary presses by officers of the king's Royal Navy. The author, probably the brawny young Samuel Adams, who made his living as a brewer, started with a diatribe against the crude power of royal government, centered in London, but broadened his argument to indict some of Boston's wealthy elite. Pointing to wealthy Bostonians who had defended the royal impressment action and Governor Shirley's condemnation of the people's spirited fight against it, Amicus Patriae charged that "Some of figure and interest among us live at ease upon the produce" of laboring people who were the targets of press gangs. These "Tools to arbitrary Power [and] . . . slaves to their present petty advantages," he recommended, should be "obliged to serve, as a common seaman, for seven years on board the worst ship of war, and under the worst commander the King has in his service."[27]

If Boston's "mobbish" town meetings gave Governor Shirley a headache, he must have experienced a migraine on January 4, 1748, when Sam Adams and a group of townsmen launched the *Independent Advertiser*. The newspaper's pitch to the laboring classes was obvious from the first issue. "Liberty can never subsist without equality," it pronounced, "so when men's riches become immeasurably or surprisingly great, a people who regard their own security ought to make strict enquiry, how they came by them." Every Boston reader knew instantly that this attack on growing inequality and the rise of a new mercantile elite referred to the wrenching economic derangement in the early 1740s. At that time the liquidation of paper money issued to soften a severe recession led to a drastic deflationary policy that had ruined many Bostonians, including Sam Adams's father. "But some will say," continued the *Independent Advertiser*, "is it a crime to be rich? Yes, certainly, at the public expense." Taken verbatim from *Cato's Letters*, the attacks by John Trenchard and Thomas Gordon on the Robert Walpole government in England and the rise of the new capitalist economy there, this was the most explicit formulation ever heard in Boston that the rise of a wealthy elite was connected with the miseries of many in the middle and lower ranks. Several issues later, still defending the impressment uprising, the *Independent Advertiser* linked Boston insurgency to internal economic problems. The people had warrant in taking the law into their own hands because they had watched "their estates crumbling to nothing, their trade stagnate, and fail in every channel, their husbandry and manufactures rendered for want of hands almost impracticable, and insupportable weight of taxes," while "others thriv[ed] at their expense and [rose] to wealth and greatness upon their ruin." Echoing the Levellers of the English Civil War a century before, the newspaper insisted that "All men are by nature on a level; born with an equal share of freedom, and endowed with capacities nearly alike."[28] In its first month of publication, the *Independent Advertiser* had sowed the seeds for radical attacks on amassed wealth that would flourish less than two decades later when the American revolutionary movement began.

Massachusetts rallied from the economic difficulties of the 1740s, but the Seven Years' War, beginning in 1754, took a terrible toll on the male population that had flocked to fight against the French in Canada. When the conduct of the war shifted to the Caribbean, after Anglo-American victories over the French in Montreal, a postwar depression inflicted greater pain. This brought political controversy to Boston in 1760 when Thomas Hutchinson, lieutenant governor of the colony, and his conservative merchant and lawyer followers decided that the time was ripe to renew attempts to dismantle the town meeting system of government that Governor Shirley had excoriated thirteen years before. Known in the popular press as the Junto, Hutchinson's group was composed of wealthy men surrounding the royal governor, who at this time was Francis Bernard. Most of the Junto members belonged to the Anglican Church, and many were related by blood or marriage. They had long bristled at the indignity of attending town meetings where leather-aproned craftsmen outnumbered them. As the gulf between top and bottom grew, they became more convinced that the herd of common people was congenitally turbulent, incapable of understanding economic issues, moved too much by passion and too little by reason, and unfit to exercise political power.

In the 1750s, poverty had stripped a large part of Boston's lower class from the roll of voters, and the town meeting had become a distinctly unplebeian instrument, sending wealthy merchants to the general court and electing many conservative selectmen to run city affairs. But for Hutchinson's Junto this was not enough, especially when the arrival of a new governor, Francis Bernard, drew them into his inner council and gave them new hopes of consolidating their power. First and foremost, such a consolidation depended on abolishing the town meeting, in operation for more than a century. Their plan was to replace it with a "close corporation," modeled on English city government where aldermen and councilmen elected their own replacements and the lord mayor had great power. A "Combination of Twelve Strangers" calling themselves "the New and Grand Corcas [Caucus]," warned the *Boston Gazette* on May 5, 1760, was determined to "overthrow the ancient Constitution of our Town-Meeting, as being popular and mobbish, and to form a Committee to transact the whole affairs of the town for the future."[29]

Almost as if to prepare Bostonians for events that lay over the horizon, the Junto, cried the *Gazette*, would attempt to keep "tradesmen, and those whom in contempt they usually term the low lived people," from voting at the upcoming election of Boston's four representatives to the colonial legislature. If they could not successfully challenge the eligibility of ordinary Bostonians at the polls, the Junto would attempt to buy their votes by threatening them with loss of jobs or indictment for unpaid debts. In answer, a committee of artisans, working with the "old and true caucus" of Boston's populist party, urged Boston's laboring people to stand up to these threats. Craftsmen should "put on their Sabbath cloathes . . . , wash their hands and faces that they may appear neat and cleanly," go to the polls, and rebuff the "strangers" of the new caucus—"strangers" being the term that the fiercely Puritan popular party leaders still used to deprecate those who worshiped at the Anglican Church.[30]

The election of May 13, 1760, brought out a record number of Boston voters choosing representatives to the colony's legislature. The result was indecisive, with each side electing two members. But the hotly contested election led the city down a path that would soon be littered with issues directly connected to the first stages of radical revolutionary activism.

Shortly after the election, Governor Francis Bernard appointed Lieutenant Governor Thomas Hutchinson as chief justice of the Massachusetts Superior Court of Judicature. Hutchinson, whose house had been mobbed twelve years earlier after he promoted fiscal measures hurtful to the city's ordinary families, was now seen as the personification of grasping, self-serving, narrowly concentrated power. In English liberal thought, this was exactly the kind of man who threatened the rights of a free people. Bostonians soon saw for themselves. In February 1761, Hutchinson convened the Superior Court to consider what would come to be known as the "writs of assistance" case, the beginning of a long series of English policy changes that led to the American Revolution. English customs officials in Boston, under strict orders from London to crack down on smuggling by Boston's merchants, asked the Superior Court to issue general search warrants under which customs officials could enter the warehouses of suspected smugglers. Opposing these writs of assistance were sixty-three Boston merchants.

Peering down from the bench, the bewigged Hutchinson faced his bitter enemy, lawyer James Otis, son of a country politician who had gained popularity among Boston's common folk. The legal issue at stake was whether English law authorized such writs and, if so, whether the Massachusetts Superior Court could issue them. If the answer was yes, then customs officials could obtain these warrants to enter any premise in Boston, regardless of whether there was probable cause for suspecting that imported goods were smuggled to evade the duties that stocked the king's coffers.

In a packed courtroom Hutchinson listened with shock to Otis's oration. A country-bred thirty-five-year-old from Martha's Vineyard had the gall to argue that Parliament was invading the fundamental rights of British subjects by passing trade laws requiring duties on imported goods. Such laws had never been contested since the Navigation Acts were first passed a century before. Brushing aside the technicalities of the law and striding onto higher ground, Otis challenged the principles of British constitutionalism that undergirded the writs. The writs were not really the issue, he exhorted in a passionate, arm-waving speech. What was really under consideration was parliamentary law that shackled the American economy. Writing years later, Samuel Adams recounted that "the child independence was then and there born, [for] every man of an immense crowded audience appeared to me to go away as I did, ready to take up arms against writs of assistance."[31]

Moving cautiously, Hutchinson adjourned the court and wrote to London for advice. After receiving orders to proceed, he reconvened the court, rejected Otis's arguments, decreed that writs of assistance were legal, and issued them to customs collectors. However, the issue had already gone beyond legal procedure, spilling over to infect local politics. Otis and other popular party writers filled the *Boston Gazette* with assaults on the Hutchinson group, which replied in kind in the conservative *Boston Evening Post*. The *Gazette* made sure every reader understood that Hutchinson's circle had become entrenched and dangerous: His brother-in-law Andrew Oliver was the provincial secretary; Oliver's brother was on Hutchinson's Superior Court; one of Hutchinson's brothers and another relative were judges on the Suffolk County Inferior Court; his nephew was register of the probate court and Secretary Oliver's deputy. The web extended into every corner of government.

"Is not this amazing ascendancy of one family foundation sufficient on which to erect a tyranny?"wrote the rising young lawyer John Adams.[32]

Otis's campaign against Hutchinson and his circle has usually been interpreted as the product of family rivalry and the mounting tension over trade regulations. Otis, the sulfurous orator—either mad or brilliant, according to one's views—is generally pictured as the man who called the lower orders into action. But Otis did not simply orchestrate the actions of laboring Bostonians; he also reflected their opinions. Laboring-class people were not so much dough to be kneaded by master rhetoricians and political manipulators, and Otis did not need to create a feeling of alienation among their struggling ranks; that feeling was already there. In truth, Otis was serving two masters: Boston merchants who had evaded the trade laws established by Parliament and were battling the writs of assistance; and laboring people who had suffered in Boston for more than a generation. Otis had more to offer the merchants—a spirited resistance to the writs of assistance—than to laboring Bostonians. For the latter he offered no blueprint for economic reform but only verbal attacks on those who disdained humble Bostonians and totted up their profits while the poor suffered. Accordingly, Otis threw himself into attacking Hutchinson's party surrounding the royal governor. If Otis was insane, as his opponents began to charge, it mattered little, for as one worried conservative put it, "Massaniello was mad, nobody doubts it; yet for all of that, he overturned the government of Naples"—a reference to the peasant fishmonger who in 1647 had mobilized the masses in southern Italy against a hated food tax and led his followers to empty the jails, attack the rich, execute hundreds of public enemies, and briefly stand the political order on its head.[33]

Between 1761 and 1764, spokesmen for the popular and prerogative factions engaged in a furious battle of billingsgate that planted seeds soon to be watered. Newspaper essays became extreme with charges of "Racoon," "stinking Skunk," "Pimp," "wild beast," "drunkard," and dozens of other choice titles. But more important than the invective itself was the deep-seated, class-driven animosity that the polemical pieces exposed: suspicion of laboring people and hatred of their leaders on the part of the Hutchinsonians; contempt and anger toward the wealthy, Anglican elite by the common people. The Hutchinsonians particularly deplored Boston's popular caucus, which they tried to expose in the *Evening Post* as a pack of political manipulators leading ordinary people by their noses. Meeting secretly, they claimed, caucus members decided on the town officers who would stand for election and decide on what issues to raise at town meetings. Then, "for form sake," the Hutchinsonians charged, caucus leaders "prepared a number of warm disputes . . . to entertain the lower sort; who are in an ecstasy to find the old Roman Patriots still surviving." Democracy as practiced by the caucus was nothing but a sham.[34]

There was truth in some of this. John Adams described how he met in the sail loft of Tom Dawes, where caucus members "smoke tobacco till you cannot see from one end of the garret to the other . . . drink [flip] I suppose and . . . choose a Moderator who puts questions to the vote regularly; and Selectmen, Assessors, Collectors, Wardens, Fire Wards, and Representatives are regularly chose before they are chosen in the Town." However, ordinary people saw no betrayal of participatory town politics in this mode of operation because they were most interested in what the town officers delivered. Moreover, ordinary Bostonians believed they had a real voice in local government. "The Rage of Patriotism . . . spread so violently . . . thro' town and country," wrote the *Evening Post* in March 1763, "that there is scarce a cobbler or porter but has turn'd mountebank in politicks and erected his stage near the printing-press from whence his oracular decisions have been stamp'd off and delivered to the world as infallible nostrums." If this horrified the conservatives, caucus writers charged, it was because the rich were obsessed with money and "couldn't have the idea of riches without that of poverty. They must see others poor in order to form a notion of their own happiness." In what was once a flourishing town, "a few persons in power" wanted to control politics and promote projects "for keeping the people poor in order to make them humble."[35]

In 1763, the Hutchinson-led circle made another attempt to abolish Boston's town meeting. They failed again. But each attempt inflamed the public in this town of 16,000, where face-to-face encounters were the norm. The *Evening Post*, Hutchinson's mouthpiece, deplored the "personal invective" that the "modern Politician" of the caucus wallowed in by engaging "hireling Scribblers" to turn out "downright scurrility and gross impudence" by the yard. The Hutchinsonians soon printed a mock report of a London criminal, "Hector Wildfire," who was obviously James Otis. The report told Bostonians that Wildfire had been hanged at Tyburn in London and then removed for autopsy. "Upon ripping open [Wildfire's] belly, which was much distended, it was found to be fill'd with wind which rush'd out violently. . . .

There seemed to be a profuse quantity of liquor in the Gall Bladder, and so extremely corrosive that it ate the instruments of operation like aqua fortis [nitric acid]." The doctors found a heart "very small and very hard" as if gnawed away by wasps. The head had a double row of teeth, a forked tongue, a skull of "uncommon thickness," and a brain cavity so small that its contents would not fill a teacup. After dissection, the doctors threw the pieces of the body to "a kennel of hounds," who had since "run mad."[36]

Like so much tinder awaiting a spark, the output of Boston's newspapers had set the scene for a donnybrook. On the eve of the Stamp Act passed by Parliament and signed by George III in March 1765, Boston was no longer one community. The region's principal seaport was socially fragmented, un-sure of itself, and suffering prolonged economic malaise. The prerogative party, led by the governor and Chief Justice Hutchinson, tried to convince a broad electorate that the very men who had accumulated fortunes in an era when most had fared badly were alone qualified to govern in the interest of the whole community. Middle- and lower-class Bostonians had heard these ideas for half a century, but they understood that aristocratic politicians who claimed to work for the commonwealth could not be trusted. Such men em-ployed the catchwords of the traditional system of politics—"public good," "community," "harmony," and "public virtue"—to cloak their own ambi-tions. The popular party leaders also employed these terms, but accepted a participatory form of politics, which they thought was the only form of gov-ernment that would guarantee economic justice and keep Boston faithful to its traditions.

"Cum Multis Aegis" *in Philadelphia*

On October 14, 1764, one year after wealthy Bostonians made their last at-tempt to dismantle the town meeting in 1763, Benjamin Franklin had one of the worst days of his life. Franklin had made his way from his native Boston to Philadelphia, the center of Quaker pacifism and humanitarian reform, forty-one years before at age seventeen, and he had risen to become the city's most celebrated and public-spirited citizen, known around the world for his experiments with electricity. But on Election Day in 1764, he felt anything but celebrated. Indeed, his heart sank as he witnessed an election unlike any held in the eight decades since William Penn founded his "peaceable king-dom." Philadelphians had produced their share of inflammatory political rhetoric as Quakers, Presbyterians, and Anglicans contended for power in the colony where Penn's descendants still held great proprietary clout, especially in appointing provincial officials, controlling vast tracts of land, and filling the seats on the provincial council (the upper house of the legislature). Philadelphia had even been rattled by a brief but bloody election riot in 1742. But October 14, 1764, shook Philadelphia to its roots—and led to involving ordinary people in politics in ways that would deeply affect the chemistry of revolution making.

Trouble had been brewing for months. At the end of the long Seven Years' War, the uprising of Ottawa warriors, led by Chief Pontiac, against British traders and colonial frontiersmen had set Pennsylvania's western frontier ablaze. Convinced that their legislature meeting in Philadelphia would do little to defend them, the frontier farmers descended on the city on February 4, 1764, with clubs and pitchforks. Along the way, they mutilated and slaughtered twenty Christianized and entirely peaceable Conestoga Indians who lived about a hundred miles west of Philadelphia. Found among the ashes near the burned-out Indian cabins was the treaty that the Indians struck with William Penn in 1701. The treaty promised that the two sides—the English and the Indians—"shall forever hereafter be as one head and one heart, and live in true friendship and amity as one people."[37] Calling themselves the "Paxton Boys," the frontiersmen backed off after being met by a hastily organized volunteer association of citizen soldiers rallied by Benjamin Franklin to save the city from fellow colonists.

British troops squelched Pontiac's Rebellion, Franklin's personal army stood off the Paxton Boys, and the Pennsylvania legislature met some of the backcountry settlers' demands by passing a bill to raise one thousand militiamen to guard the frontier. But the air had been dreadfully poisoned, and Quakers and Presbyterians were soon at each other's throats. Quakers (and others) knew that most of the Paxton Boys were Scots-Irish Presbyterians, and this led Quakers to believe that their frontier lawlessness—Franklin called them "white savages" in a hard-hitting pamphlet—prefigured a Presbyterian takeover of the colony. The unjustifiable murder of Christianized Indians now billowed up into verbal civil war. Quaker pamphleteers pictured the Paxton Boys' march on Philadelphia as part of a global conspiracy, "the latest installment in a perpetual Presbyterian holy war against the mild and beneficent government of the Kings of England" that stretched back to the

This earliest depiction of a bustling colonial city shows voters ascending the stairs at the Philadelphia courthouse to cast their ballots in the election of 1764. The Quaker meetinghouse is on the left.

bloody Presbyterian uprisings in Scotland in the mid-seventeenth century. Presbyterian writers responded with charges that the Quakers were "soft" on Indians and had held on to legislative power during the Seven Years' War when pacifist principles kept the hands of frontiersmen tied behind their backs. Philadelphia's presses struck off so many venomous pamphlets that Franklin wrote friends that he had never seen more "violent parties and cruel animosities" before and feared that "civil bloodshed" would soon occur.[38]

In the greatest mistake of his career, Franklin now joined Quakers and enemies of the Penn proprietorship of Pennsylvania in waging a campaign to put the colony under royal government, where its governor would be appointed by England's king instead of by the grandsons of William Penn. The campaign for royal government politicized Philadelphia to an extraordinary degree, and the timing was disastrous for Franklin and the Quakers, since colonial anger had already been aroused by England's attempts after the Seven Years' War to tighten its grip on the administration of the North American colonies. Known as a herald of people's lives, liberty, and property, Franklin put himself in an untenable position by backing the instituting of royal government when up and down the coast people believed England was in fact laying siege to traditional rights of English subjects.

In the fierce battle over instituting royal government, leaders of both political factions reached downward to mobilize the city's ordinary citizens—
craftsmen, laborers, and mariners—in short, the people that most colonial
leaders had feared as a mindless and dangerous element in political life. This
was by no means the first time that a divided elite had appealed to those
below them in order to win elections—in either Pennsylvania or other
colonies. In the 1720s, a perfectly aristocratic Pennsylvania governor, the
Scottish baronet William Keith, in danger of losing hold on his office, appealed to laboring men and assured them that "We all know it is neither the
great, the rich, nor the learned, that compose the body of the people; and that
civil government ought carefully to protect the poor laborious and industrious part of mankind." His equally well-placed opponent, the lawyer David
Lloyd, tried to match this populist appeal by flatly stating that "a mean man,
of small interest, devoted to the faithful discharge of his trust and duty to the
government" was well enough equipped for high office and vastly preferable
to wealthy, self-interested men. Before this election was over, conservatives
such as the merchant prince Isaac Norris trembled that "the people head and
foot run mad. . . . All seems topside turvy. Our public speeches tell the country and the world that neither knowledge nor riches are advantageous in a
country. . . ." A few years later, with spirits still running high amid a deep recession, Governor Keith was playing to the most ordinary voter by "peram-
bulating our city and popping into the dramshops, tiff, and alehouses where
he would find a great number of modern statesmen and some patriots settling
affairs, cursing some, praising others, contriving laws and swearing they will
have them enacted *cum multis aegis* [by the multitude]."[39]

Franklin and his friends did not have to employ new political tactics and
strategies, nor did they have to fashion new ideological arguments aimed at a
more democratic conception of a just society. Franklin had seen all this just
after arriving in Philadelphia in 1723. The scene described above was, in fact,
his first encounter with popular politics. Still a teenager, he had witnessed the
electoral door open to ordinary citizens like himself, who could regard themselves as capable of reaching an informed opinion and entitled even to serve
as a legislator. Now, in the 1764 campaign to end eighty-two years of proprietary government, the Franklin party had only to draw on earlier precedents.
But they carried Franklin and his followers further—with mass meetings
and door-to-door harvesting of signatures on petitions in favor of royal government. "Taverns were engag'd [and] many of the poorer and more depen-

dent kind of labouring people in town were invited thither by night," wrote one alarmed defender of proprietary government. Some were induced to sign petitions by "the eloquence of a punch bowl," others by "the fear of being turn'd out of business." Going "into all the houses in town without distinction," grumbled the nephew of Thomas Penn, the proprietor, they emerged with the names of "a few ship carpenters and some of the lowest sort of people."[40]

But fire demanded fire in return. The Proprietary Party, needing signatures for counterpetitions, knew where to find them—among "the lowest sort of people." In fact, they outstripped Franklin's stalwarts. Setting aside earlier castigations of the Franklinites for prevailing among "those very generally of a low rank, many of whom could neither read nor write," Proprietary leaders made "unwearied endeavours to prejudice the minds of the lower class of people."[41] Every white male found himself being courted by the leaders of the two political factions. Never in Pennsylvania's history did the few need the many so much.

As the battle thickened, pamphleteers reached new pinnacles of abuse and scurrility. In the process they left in shreds the patrician notion, held by most upper-class colonial leaders, that the middling and lower ranks owed deference to those above them who were better educated, more experienced, and wealthier. Franklin found himself reviled by Hugh Williamson, professor of mathematics at the College of Philadelphia (which Franklin had founded) as an intellectual fraud, a corrupt politician, and a lecher who begged and bought honorary degrees in England, stole scientific knowledge, impregnated a "kitchen wench" who produced his illegitimate son William Franklin, and practiced "every zig zag Machination" in politics. Franklin's hatchet man responded by labeling Williamson "A reptile," who, "like a toad, by the pestilential fumes of his virulent slabber" attempted "to blast the fame of a PATRIOT." William Smith, president of the College of Philadelphia (later the University of Pennsylvania), was presented to the public as a "consummate sycophant," an "indefatigable" liar, and an impudent knave with a heart "bloated with *infernal malice*" and a head full of *"flatulent preachments."* Another Franklinite pamphleteer renamed the Presbyterians "Pissbrute-tarians (a bigoted, cruel and revengeful sect)." Another hired gun reached the summit of scatalogical polemics by suggesting that now was the time for William Smith to consummate his alliance with the proprietary pamphleteer David Dove, who "will not only furnish you with that most agreeable of all foods to your taste, but after it has found a passage through your body . . . will greedily devour it, and as soon as it is well digested, he will void it up for a repast to the Proprietary Faction; they will as eagerly swallow it as the other had done before, and, when it has gone through their several concoctions, they will discharge it in your presence, that you may once more regale on it thus refined." One shocked outsider wrote a friend in Philadelphia: "In the name of goodness stop your pamphleteer's mouths and shut up your presses. Such a torrent of low scurrility sure never came from any country as lately from Pennsylvan[i]a."[42]

But the torrent did not stop. "There has not been a week since you left," wrote one Philadelphian to a friend in May 1764, still five months before the election, "but there has been one or more pamphlets published and sold about the streets." Before the campaign ended, more than thirty-five broadsides and pamphlets, not to mention dozens of newspaper fusillades, filled the streets. Hardly anyone in the river town of 15,000 escaped knowledge that the colony's chief justice, who had risen from sugar boiler to wealthy merchant, was called "Old Drip-pan," an adulterer who had slept with his African slaves for twenty years, and was a "tricking Judge and Presbyterian Jew." David Dove, schoolteacher and pamphleteer, stood accused of sodomy, misogamy, miscegenation, concupiscence, and the almost unheard-of flaw of teratology. The president of the College of Philadelphia was held up to public scorn as a man who spread venereal disease among his female slaves.

Religious leaders were also drawn into electioneering, violating the old maxim that ministers should not meddle in politics. According to one rural clergyman, Presbyterian and Anglican ministers in Philadelphia distributed petitions in favor of retaining the proprietorship of the Penn family, "turned their pulpits into Ecclesiastical drums for politics, and told their people to vote according as they directed them at the peril of their damnation." A "Gentleman from Trans[y]lvania," pretending to be an impartial observer, charged that Philadelphia's Anglican leaders had "prostituted their temples . . . as an amphitheatre for the rabble to combat in." The first committees of correspondence in the revolutionary era were organized not in Boston by radical opponents of English policy but by Pennsylvania Presbyterians who, by May 1764, had created a colonywide network in order to fight Franklin's campaign for royal government.

The flood of polemical pamphlets rife with inflamed rhetoric, the involve-

ment of the churches in politics, and the mobilization of social layers previously unsolicited and unwelcome by political leaders all combined to produce
an election where everybody's integrity was questioned, every public figure's
use of power was attacked, and both sides presented themselves as true representatives of "the people." The effects were dramatic: After polls opened at
9 A.M. on October 1, 1764, and remained open through the night, party workers on both sides shepherded in a record number of voters. Included were the
infirm and aged, some carried to the courthouse in litters and chairs. By the
next morning, party leaders were still rounding up stray votes. The polls finally closed at 3 P.M. Franklin and his friend Joseph Galloway lost their seats
in the provincial assembly, defeated by defecting German voters and propertyless laborers. Franklin no longer sounded like a popular leader. The
leather-apron man, proud of his roughened hands, complained bitterly that
his political opponents had herded to the courthouse "the wretched rabble
brought to swear themselves intituled to vote." "They carried (would you
think it!) above 1000 Dutch from me," cried Franklin. A bit of postelection
doggerel caught the spirit of the contest:

> *A Pleasant sight tis to Behold*
> *The beggars hal'd from Hedges*
> *The Deaf, the Blind, the Young, the Old*
> *T'Secure their priveledges*
>
> *They're bundled up Steps, each sort Goes*
> *A Very Pretty Farce Sir*
> *Some without Stockings, some no Shoes*
> *Nor Breeches to their A__e Sir.*[43]

Franklin, the master politician, who had so often in the past swung the
public behind his programs for reform, had badly miscalculated sentiment
among his own leather-apron men. A great many could not be dissuaded from
the view, as it was later put, that "the little finger of the King was heavier than
the loins of the Proprietor." Deeply wounded, Franklin had to suffer what
John Dickinson, an assemblyman opposed to royal government in Pennsylvania, pronounced: that "no man in Pennsylvania is at this time so much
the object of the public dislike."[44] But, while it marked the low point of his

distinguished career, this astounding rebuff only briefly derailed Philadelphia's most popular and celebrated person. However, permanently derailed were prior beliefs about deferential politics, decorous politicking, the marriage of religion and politics, and the illegitimate role of character assassination in electoral politics.

Although the Philadelphia election of October 1764 was an extreme case and was affected by factors unique to the politics of proprietary Pennsylvania, it reflected a trend in political life in other parts of the colonies. Political innovations involving new organizational techniques, a vocabulary of vituperation, the use of violence, attacks on vested authority and high social position, and the mobilizing of men at the bottom of society that earlier had been deplored were transforming political culture in widely diverse locales. Whenever the elite was divided, as was increasingly the case in the late colonial period, well-born politicians reluctantly worked to activate and obtain the support of the lower classes because this was their only political reservoir to tap. Though they were called "the rabble" and told they had no right to participate in politics if they were illiterate or propertyless, common people were acquiring a sense of their importance despite the manipulations of those above them. The full significance of these developments would become apparent only when local conflicts began to intersect with issues of how and whether England could tighten its rule of the American colonies. This convergence occurred with dramatic swiftness in the shocking events that took place in the summer and fall of 1765.

"Fondness for Freedom"

Historical accounts of the popular politics that roiled Boston and Philadelphia in the early 1760s give almost no sense that many of the witnesses to these events were dark-skinned people born in Africa or descended from Africans who had been brought in chains to the American colonies since the early seventeenth century. In fact, all the colonial cities had hundreds of slaves, as many as 2,600 in New York and 1,500 in Philadelphia by 1760. Many were owned by such emerging revolutionary leaders as Boston's John Hancock, New York's Robert Livingston, and Philadelphia's Benjamin Franklin and John Dickinson. Philadelphia's mayor in 1760, William Masters, owned thirty-one slaves. In northern rural areas, they were held in smaller numbers, though in the tobacco-growing areas of the Connecticut River valley, in the Narragansett region of Rhode Island, and in old Dutch farming areas in Queens and Kings counties in New York they made up hefty fractions of the agricultural laborers. In the South, virtually every political leader was a slaveholder, and the greatest of the emerging revolutionary leaders—for example, Virginia's George Washington, Thomas Jefferson, and George Mason; South Carolina's Henry Laurens and William Henry Drayton; and Maryland's Charles Carroll and his son—were holders of slaves numbering in the hundreds. But their higher mortality rates and lower fertility rates meant that they would make up about one of every five inhabitants of the thirteen colonies on the eve of revolution. They were also unevenly spread throughout the colonies. Nearly nine of every ten North American slaves toiled in the tobacco, indigo, and rice fields of the southern colonies, representing about half of the total population. In New England, they were only 15,000 or so in number, not more than one of every twenty inhabitants.

We know little of the private thoughts of some 350,000 slaves who lived in the colonies in 1760. But we do know a great deal about how they behaved, and from that knowledge we can make reasonable inferences about what they thought as they stood silent witnesses to urban political turbulence, agrarian land riots, Indian frontier warfare, and religious revival. Only a few of them were capable of writing and even the few that were literate had circumscribed lives that left them little time to pen letters, essays for newspapers, or autobiographical narratives. But a handful did give accounts of their lives, rendered orally in the African tradition and captured in print by white writers, usually in the last stages of the storyteller's life or after he or she died. The story of one African American life in particular helps us gain a broad understanding of how black experiences in the late colonial period set the stage for what was to be a massive participation in the American Revolution, an important role in its outcome, and a turning point in the history of the African diaspora. This was the story of Broteer, later known as Venture Smith.[45]

Eight-year-old Broteer was the son of a king. His world collapsed in 1736 when Bambara slave raiders captured his village and killed his father. They marched Broteer and other members of his village to Anamaboe, in what is Upper Volta today, on the Gold Coast of West Africa. This is where Broteer first saw a human with light skin. When a slave ship from Rhode Island arrived to pick up human cargo, Broteer's Bambara captors sold him to the ship's steward for "four gallons of rum and a piece of calico [cloth]." The steward named him Venture on account of his "having purchased me with his own private venture," that is, to sell the young boy for a profit as soon as the ship reached the Americas.

After stopping in Barbados, the ship reached its destination in Connecticut. Here a Connecticut farmer purchased Venture, gave him the surname Smith, and set the boy to work at farm and household tasks. A year later, Smith remembered, "I began to have hard tasks imposed on me . . . or be rigorously punished."[46] The African boy was now part of a growing number of slaves—some 7,000 in New England, about 15,000 in the mid-Atlantic colonies, and at least 120,000 in the southern colonies from Maryland to Georgia. Enslaved Africans had only begun to replace white indentured servants from England, Ireland, and Germany in the late seventeenth century; but now, in the second third of the eighteenth century, societies with some slaves were becoming slave-based societies, especially in the South.

Growing tall and strong in his teens, Smith was a restive slave. Particularly galling was his master's son, who "came up to me . . . big with authority" and "would order me to do *this* business and *that* business different from what my master had directed me." Tempers flared. When his master's son flew into a rage and attacked him with a pitchfork, Smith defended himself and pummeled the white boy until he was in tears. Overpowered by four white men soon on the scene, Smith was hanged on a cattle hook for an hour while another servant gathered peach tree branches to tear the skin from his back. Venture was spared after his master's son, dabbing his eyes with his handkerchief, fled the scene and "went home to tell his mother."

By age twenty-two, Venture Smith was a giant by eighteenth-century standards. Over six feet tall and weighing 250 pounds, he acquired a reputation as a prodigious worker with amazing strength. By day he labored as a farmhand and carpenter. By night he worked for himself, catching fish and game to earn money to purchase his way out of slavery. Shortly after marrying Meg, another enslaved African, Smith made his break for freedom in the early 1750s. He stole a boat and provisions from his master's home and, with three white indentured servants, also chafing under servitude, rowed across Long Island Sound from Connecticut to New York, hoping—with scant geographical knowledge—to reach the Mississippi. Smith had taken to his heels like many other resistant slaves; but like most of them the chances of representing himself as a free black, at a time when only a few had that status, were slim.

Freedom lasted only an instant. One of the white servants ran off with the party's scant provisions, leaving the others to fend for themselves. Heartsick and discouraged, Smith returned voluntarily to his master. As was the case so often with runaway slaves, he was put up for sale. Luckily, Smith's new Connecticut master, Thomas Stanton, soon purchased his wife and their baby girl. But then an argument broke out between Meg and Mrs. Stanton. Smith recalled finding them in a violent quarrel of the kind that frequently occurred when slaves tried to negotiate the terms of their enslavement. "Hearing a racket in the house," Venture recalled, he rushed in and "found my mistress in a violent passion with my wife." Meg stood her ground and ignored Venture's plea to apologize "for the sake of peace." Then "my mistress turned the blows which she was repeating on my wife to me," taking down her horsewhip and "glutting her fury with it." Defending himself, Venture "reached out my great black hand . . . received the blows of the whip on it," and then seized the whip and threw it into the fireplace. When his owner returned, "he seemed to take no notice of it, and mentioned not a word of it to me." But a few days later, when Smith was putting a log in the fireplace, he "received a most violent stroke on the crown of my head with a club two feet long and as large around as a chair post." Staggering to his feet, Venture threw his master to the ground and dragged him out of the house.

Venture and his wife had lived in New England long enough—it was now the early 1750s—to know that the law was rigged against them for they were regarded as chattel property, to be used, abused, and sold like horses as the master and mistress saw fit. But they also understood that slavery in New England had not stripped enslaved Africans of all rights, including the right to read, marry, and assemble on rest days or holidays, as was not the case in colonies such as Virginia and South Carolina. So, thinking himself unjustly attacked, Venture fled to a local justice of the peace to plead his case. The justice "advised me to return to my master, and live contented with him till he abused me again, and then complain." Smith agreed to this, and the justice warned Stanton against abusing his slave. But on the way home, Stanton and his brother "dismounted from their horses . . . and fell to beating me with great violence." The muscular Smith overpowered both of them. "I became enraged, turned them both under me, laid one of them across the other, and stamped both with my feet," he later wrote. After the town constable arrived to restrain him, the local blacksmith fitted Smith with ankle and wrist shackles. Unsubdued, Venture showed off his chains and thanked his mistress for "the gold rings." When his master warned he would sell Venture to the West Indies—the common way of threatening mainland slaves with a living hell—Venture replied: "I crossed the waters to come here, and I am willing to cross them to return."

Venture's owner now knew he could never break Smith, who had a will as powerful as his body. "I continued to wear the chain peaceably for two or three days," Smith remembered. "Not anyone said much to me, until one Hempstead Miner of Stonington asked me if I would live with him . . . and that in return he would give me a good chance to gain my freedom. I answered that I would." But Smith's third master soon sold him for a quick profit to a fourth, Colonel Smith of Hartford, for whom Venture toiled for five years, working on his own time to save money coin by coin. But many coins would be needed because Meg gave birth to two sons during that time.

Finally, at age thirty-six, in the year of the mobbish Philadelphia election of 1764, Venture purchased his way out of twenty-eight years of slavery. Now the race began to set his family free. Venture worked feverishly, while white colonists became entangled with what they regarded as the tyrannical edicts of the British government—the attempts, as they often said of the English, to enslave *them*. "In four years," Venture recounted, "I cut several thousand cords of wood . . . I raised watermelons and performed many other singular labors." Described by historians Sidney Kaplan and Emma Nogrady Kaplan as a black Paul Bunyan "who swung his axe to break his chains," Smith "shunned all kind of luxuries" and "bought nothing that I absolutely did not want." Like Benjamin Franklin, his watchwords were industry and frugality; but for Smith the scramble to break slavery's chains made the work all the more urgent. By 1768, he had purchased his sons out of slavery, soon to be followed by his daughter. Another five years passed before he could purchase Meg, just in time to ensure that their fourth child would be born free (at birth a child followed the condition of the mother, not the father). As the American Revolution approached, Smith acquired a farm on Long Island, purchased a house, and began building a small cash reserve. Here was a truly self-made man—called by the Connecticut editor who published Smith's narrative in

1798 "a Franklin and a Washington in a state of nature, or rather in a state of slavery."

Venture Smith was one of about 250,000 slaves brought to the British colonies of North America between 1700 and 1775, a figure that dwarfed the 28,000 seventeenth-century arrivals. In the 1700s, colonial slavery reached its peak, with slaves outnumbering white European immigrants. Only a small fraction duplicated Smith's success in working their way out of bondage, but few among them did not yearn for freedom. Some waited for the day when their bondage would end; others forced the action. They had a long history of such yearning, almost from their first arrival in the Americas. Cotton Mather, Boston's Puritan intellectual giant, had felt compelled to lecture the city's slaves in 1721, warning them against the "fondness for freedom in many of you" and urging them to rest content with what he called their "very easy servitude."[47] In every colony, this "fondness for freedom" manifested itself in the half century before the Revolution. In the meantime, like Venture Smith, slaves had to endure a code of laws, social rules, and attitudes designed to keep bondpeople and all their descendants (since slavery, by law, was inherited) from freedom. Yet many made the terms of their bondage a matter for negotiation in a multitude of abrasive and often violent encounters with masters and mistresses.

It was with these yearnings for liberty and with a background of resistance against their captors that slaves entered the revolutionary era. What enslaved Africans and a few thousand free African Americans also carried into the argument brewing between the American colonists and their imperial masters was knowledge of the outright rebellions against slavery that had punctuated recent decades. In 1712, in New York City, dozens of slaves rose up to overthrow their oppressors. Without the garrison of English soldiers, one observer reported, the "city would have been reduced to ashes, and the greatest part of the inhabitants murdered."[48] In 1739, South Carolina slaves outside of Charleston seized guns, burned and plundered plantations, and headed south to take refuge with the Spanish in northern Florida, who had established a community of free blacks at Fort Mose. Known as the Stono Rebellion, it was the largest in the colonial era. A year later white authorities nipped in the bud a slave plot to capture Annapolis, Maryland.

To the north, perhaps hearing of the slave revolt in South Carolina, a wave of slave arsonists burned barns in New Jersey in 1740. Other slaves closer to Venture Smith struck in New York City, where nearly one-sixth of the population of 12,000 were enslaved. This insurrection terrified the city and led to prolonged trials of those suspected of treachery. After torture produced sixty-seven confessions, white authorities hanged or burned at the stake thirty slaves and four white co-conspirators and transported seventy-two others out of the colony.

In what turned out to be a prelude to the response of enslaved Africans during the American Revolution, the disruptions arising out of the Seven Years' War gave southern slaves new opportunities to test their chains. With the French enemy on their western frontier offering rebelling slaves "liberty and lands to settle upon," southern colonial militia units were of little help to the British. "The thing is impossible," wrote one white leader; "they have scarce whites enough to prevent the defection of their slaves; and if any considerable [militia] party should happen to be defeated when abroad, it could be scarce possible to prevent their total revolt." In 1756, mindful of unrest in the tidewater region, where most slaves toiled, Virginia's slave-owning legislators allocated over half the military appropriations for that year for militia patrols to control restive slaves.[49]

In 1759, another assault on slavery boiled up in Charleston, South Carolina. Here, more slaves saw North America for the first time, on the harbor's Sullivan's Island, than anywhere else in the colonies. More than half the city's 12,000 inhabitants were black, almost all of them enslaved, and in the colony at large three-fifths of the inhabitants were slaves. White authorities got wind of an uprising led by a free mixed-race man named Philip John, who vowed "that he had seen a vision, in which it was reveal'd to him, that in the month of September [1759] the white people shou'd be underground, that the sword shou'd go through the land, and that it shou'd shine with their blood." Just as he was planning an attack on the Cherokee, South Carolina's governor Lyttleton noted that "a spirit of cabal began to show itself" among slaves outside Charleston and that "their scheme was to have seized some arms and ammunition that were in a storehouse . . . and then with what force they could collect to have marched to this town."[50] Philip John was seized, tried quickly, and executed.

How much enslaved Africans such as Venture Smith and his family knew of these revolts cannot be known with certainty since few slaves were literate enough to leave behind any paper trail to tell us of the state of their minds. But news traveled fast in the colonies, as we will see, and it is reasonable to assume that knowledge of slave rebellions, reported in white newspapers, could not be kept from the part of the population that had the greatest stake in them. The historian of the Stono Rebellion, Peter Wood, argues, "it may well be that, during the generations preceding 1776, African Americans thought longer and harder than any other sector of the colonial population about the concept of liberty, both as an abstract ideal and as a tangible reality."[51]

Heralds of Abolition

In the generation preceding the advent of the American Revolution, the lines of communication that spread news of black insurgents also carried reports about a small number of white colonists who found slavery to be a sin and a curse. Going back to ancient times, only a few holy men entertained the notion of a world without masters and slaves. But if the biblical idea that "[God] hath made of one blood all nations of men to dwell on all the face of the earth" [Acts 17:26] was too exalted for most people to live by, it was also one too worthy to be put out of mind. In the colonies, a few men of great religious intensity—and a complete disregard for social pressures—devoted themselves to making sure that people would not forget. In so doing, they became the first messengers of a radical reform movement that would gain momentum during the American Revolution.

Such a man was Benjamin Lay. Born to poor Quakers in England, Lay spent seven years at sea and then a few more in Barbados, where he and his wife witnessed the barbaric conditions of African slavery. Coming to Philadelphia, the hunchbacked, dwarfish Lay was shocked to see fellow Quakers practicing slavery. So began what some called crazed zealotry, but what others admired as an uncompromising display of conscience. Lay was a strict vegetarian, refusing to eat anything provided through the death of an animal. He sometimes lived in a cave on his small farm outside Philadelphia. He and his wife made homespun clothes to avoid materials made by enslaved Africans. He publicly smashed his wife's teacups to discourage the use of slave-produced sugar. Taking his cause to the quiet Quaker meetings, Lay made himself impossible to ignore. On one occasion, he stood outside a meeting with one bare foot buried in deep snow to dramatize how badly slaves were clothed in winter. He also kidnapped a Quaker child to bring home to Friends the grief suffered by African families when their children were

A modern historian has called Benjamin Lay "a Day of Judgment in breeches."* At the time, very few saw Lay as anything more than an eccentric at best, a disturber of the peace, and a misguided peddler of visionary ideas at worst.

snatched by slave traders or separated from their parents by sale at their owners' hands.

In 1737, after Philadelphia Quaker leaders repudiated Lay's first abolitionist tract, *All Slave-keepers, That Keep the Innocent in Bondage, Apostates*, he upped the ante. Bursting into the annual gathering of Quaker leaders, he plunged a sword into a hollowed-out book resembling a Bible that he had filled with a bladder of red pokeberry juice. By splattering Quaker leaders with "blood," he showed them that they committed spiritual and physical

*George S. Brooks, *Friend Anthony Benezet* (Philadelphia: University of Pennsylvania Press, 1937), 78.

violence by trading and holding slaves, whether or not they treated them well and taught them Christian principles. Invading the churches of other denominations, Lay carried his case to the public that slavery was "the mother of all sins" until he died in 1759.[52]

Lay did not convince Quakers or anyone else to give up slave keeping, but he lit a torch and passed it on to two other men almost as ascetic as he. In the 1750s, a new generation of Quaker leaders came to believe that the Society of Friends had become lax and corrupt, and they pointed to slavery as evidence of it. Seeing the outbreak of war on Pennsylvania's frontier in 1755 as God's punishment for waywardness, they resolved to cleanse the society of sin. In this situation, abolitionists John Woolman and Anthony Benezet were able to hitch their campaign to ban slave ownership to the more general reform movement. The mild-mannered Woolman, a New Jersey tailor and shopkeeper, had awakened to the sin of slave keeping in the early 1740s, and in 1746 made his first journey to the southern colonies to spread his fear among fellow Quakers that they were losing their conscience. He returned home full of remorse at having eaten and "lodged free-cost with people who lived in ease on the hard labour of their slaves." The way of life he observed among slave owners "appeared to me as a dark gloominess hanging over the land." Eight years later, he published his *Some Considerations on the Keeping of Negroes* (1754). Reminding Americans that Africans had not forfeited "the natural right of freedom," he warned that God would rise up and punish a people who engaged in such inhumanity as he saw all around him. Identifying with the Africans themselves, the saintly Woolman said: "[L]et us calmly consider their Circumstance; and, the better to do it, make their Case ours."[53]

Born in France of Huguenot parents, Anthony Benezet rejected a mercantile career and began teaching school for poor children in Philadelphia. In 1750, he began holding free classes for black students in his home and found that they were as capable as white students in both their academic work and in "moral and religious advancement." Benjamin Franklin agreed after visiting a school for black children in 1762. "Their apprehension [is] quick, their memory as strong, and their docility in every respect equal to that of the white children," Franklin wrote. Most Philadelphians probably found it odd that Benezet mixed so readily with the city's benighted blacks and adopted something of a "let-Anthony-do-it" approach. His first eulogist, many years later, recounted how Benezet "would often be seen on the wharves surrounded by a group of these people, whose story afterward served as a basis for an argument or a touching appeal in one of the almanacs or papers of the day." And so it was as Benezet published pamphlets on Africa and the history of slavery in order to convince Americans that Africa was not a dark continent of savages entitled only to servitude. The foundation for all his labors—the abolition of slavery, justice for Native Americans and the poor, education, pacifism, and temperance—was his abhorrence of wealth. "The great rock against which our society has dashed," he wrote, is "the love of the world and the deceitfulness of riches, the desire of amassing wealth."[54]

With Woolman serving as his ideological compatriot, Benezet published his *Epistle of Caution and Advice Concerning the Buying and Keeping of Slaves* in 1754. A stirring renunciation of the slave trade and slaveholding as unworthy of liberty-loving Christian colonists, it earned acceptance of the abolitionist position by the Society of Friends Yearly Meeting leaders. Noting that slave ownership had increased rapidly among Quakers, the Yearly Meeting lectured their followers—but really the world at large—that "to live in ease and plenty by the toil of those whom violence and cruelty have put in our power is neither consistent with Christianity nor common justice." This was one of those rare moments in history when an ideological tectonic-plate shift occurred. Occasional outcries against slavery by eccentric Quakers now reached the policy level for an important religious group—the Society of Friends. "Where slave keeping prevails," pronounced the Quakers' Yearly Meeting of Pennsylvania, New Jersey, and Delaware Friends in 1754, "pure religion and sobriety decline, as it evidently tends to harden the heart and render the soul less susceptible of that holy spirit of love, meekness, and charity, which is the peculiar character of a true Christian."[55]

Over the next twenty years, Pennsylvania and New Jersey Quakers moved from condemning the buying and selling of slaves to forswearing slave ownership. This became a key part of their attempt to revitalize and reform the Quaker commitment to inward purity that they knew had eroded since the days of William Penn. Woolman's second trip through Virginia in 1757 made him the key figure in spreading antislavery principles southward, and he pursued his cause further with another pamphlet in 1762. In *Considerations on Keeping Negroes*, Woolman sounded another note that radical reformers would echo widely in the coming years: that slavery not only outraged humanity but corrupted all white people involved in it. Dominating other humans and treating them brutally was a poor education for a people eager to defend their natural rights and compare their virtuousness with what they claimed was the treachery and covetousness of English overlords. "What had always been a fantasy of prophets in the Society of Friends," writes historian William McKee Evans, "now became a plan of practical men and women."[56] By the time that plan took form, the intertwining of freedom and slavery, locked together in a deadly embrace, could no longer be ignored.

2

YEARS OF INSURGENCE

1761–1766

Given the radical viruses that had infected colonial American society in the pre-revolutionary generation, it is not surprising that imperial decisions made in England as the Seven Years' War drew to a close sparked anger and upheaval in North America. A key element in this destabilization was the remarkable center-stage appearance of lower-class and enslaved people, whom colonial leaders had always hoped to keep in the wings, if not offstage altogether. In some sectors of colonial society, radical insurgency arose quite apart from England's attempts to rule its overseas colonies with a stronger hand. In other cases, external and internal stimuli of radical behavior overlapped and interacted. Whether stimulated externally or ignited internally, ferment during the years from 1761 to 1766 changed the dynamics of social and political relations in the colonies and set in motion currents of reformist sentiment with the force of a mountain wind. Critical to this half decade was the colonial response to England's Stamp Act, more the reaction of common colonists than that of their presumed leaders.

The Crowd Finds Its Own Mind

When dawn broke on August 14, 1765, Bostonians tramping to work found an effigy of Andrew Oliver, who was as respectable and well heeled a man as anyone in the city, clad in rags and dangling from a giant elm tree at the crossing of Essex and Orange Streets in the city's South End. This is where a narrow neck of land led from Boston to the farm villages west of the town. Attached to the effigy was the verse: "A goodlier sight who e'er did see? A Stamp-Man hanging on a tree!"[1] Strung up alongside Oliver's effigy was a worn "Jack-Boot with a Head and horns peeping out of the top." The boot was painted green on the bottom—"a Green-ville sole," said the sign. The boot was a clever pun on the unpopular earl of Bute, King George's trusted adviser, and George Grenville, first lord of the Treasury and chancellor of the Exchequer. Colonial Americans regarded these two men as the architects of detested new imperial policies, especially the hated Stamp Act passed by Parliament on March 22, 1765, and scheduled to take effect on November 1. Oliver had been appointed as the distributor of the stamps for Boston and the entire colony of Massachusetts.

Before the day was over, laboring Bostonians, joined by middling townsmen, turned the city upside down. The "Stamp Act crisis," as historians have called it, had begun. In the cascading reactions to the Stamp Act, we can see how discontent over England's tightening of the screws on its American colonies merged with resentment born out of the play of events indigenous to colonial life. A perceptive witness of the mass disorder occurring from one end of the colonies to the other over the Stamp Act would have seen that several revolutions were about to erupt simultaneously.

George Grenville had become the chief minister of England's twenty-five-year-old king, George III, at the end of the Seven Years' War in 1763. Facing a national debt that had billowed from 75 to 145 million pounds during the war and trying to cope with a nation of weary taxpayers, Grenville pushed for new taxes in England's overseas colonies. He especially believed that the American colonists should pay to support the ten thousand British regulars left in North America to police French-speaking Canada and the Appalachian frontier. The smartly uniformed troops would also remind unruly American subjects that they were still beholden to the Crown. Some colonists grumbled when Grenville rammed through Parliament the Revenue Act (or

Sugar Act) of 1764, which reduced the tax on imported French molasses from the West Indies from six to three pence per gallon, but added a number of colonial products to the list of taxable commodities that could be exported only to England. The Revenue Act also required American shippers to post bonds guaranteeing obedience to customs regulations before loading their cargoes. In addition, it strengthened the vice admiralty courts, where violators of the trade acts were to be prosecuted without benefit of juries drawn from the colonial population.

On the heels of the Sugar Act came the Currency Act. It extended to all colonies the 1751 ban on the issuance of paper money by New England colonies, a popular measure that had helped keep the wheels of commerce turning. Like the Sugar Act, the Currency Act was seen as a constriction of colonial trade and a blow to debtors who usually benefited from the inflationary effects of paper money issues. Then came the Stamp Act, which required revenue stamps on every newspaper, pamphlet, almanac, legal document, liquor license, college diploma, pack of playing cards, and pair of dice.

These moves confused colonial leaders. The new machinery for tightening control of the colonies, asking them to share the burdens of the empire that brought them many benefits, emanated from Parliament, which until now had usually allowed the king, his ministers, and the Board of Trade to run overseas affairs. In a world where history taught that power and liberty were perpetually at war, generations of colonists had viewed Parliament as a bastion of English freedom, the bulwark against despotic political rule. Now Parliament, too, began to seem like a violator of colonial rights.

Bostonians knew vaguely about the tricky constitutional question raised by the Stamp Act: whether Parliament had the right to pass a tax simply to raise revenue—an internal tax—when the colonies had no representation in Parliament. American colonists, with rare exceptions, agreed that Parliament was entitled to pass external taxes meant to control the flow of trade. But ordinary Bostonians knew something beyond a quibble: that Lieutenant Governor Thomas Hutchinson had arranged the appointment of his brother-in-law Andrew Oliver to be the distributor of the hated stamps. Common folk also knew that both men were leaders of the prerogative circle gathered around the royal governor, an imperious group that had recently tried to dismantle Boston's town meeting and showed contempt for ordinary people who dared to think of themselves as entitled to a role in political affairs. All of Boston also knew that their provincial legislature had elected three men to gather with delegates from other colonies to meet in New York in October 1765 to hammer out an intercolonial protest to Parliament about the Stamp Act. The crowd, however, had no intention to wait for the Stamp Act Congress to meet.

At midmorning on August 14, Hutchinson ordered Sheriff Stephen Greenleaf to cut down the effigies, and at that moment the question of rightful authority moved from the chambers of constituted authority to the streets. Quickly, a crowd assembled to stop the sheriff. All day, common Bostonians detained farmers bringing produce into town along Orange Street until they had their goods "stamped" under the great elm standing at the neck of land. At the end of working hours, a mass of laboring men began forming for a mock funeral. Their leader was Ebenezer MacIntosh, a poor shoemaker and veteran of the Seven Years' War. MacIntosh had been a fireman in one of the city's fire engine companies and had emerged a few years before as a leader of the South End's Pope's Day Company, an artisans' social group that paraded on November 5 each year to celebrate the demise of Guy Fawkes, who tried to blow up Parliament in 1605 as part of a plot to place the Catholic Stuart "Pretender" on the English throne. With MacIntosh acting as "the principal leader of the mob," as Governor Francis Bernard described the action, the crowd cut down Oliver's effigy as dark came on and carried it through the streets toward the Town House, the center of government where the legislature met. Then the crowd headed for the South End wharves, where Oliver had built a brick office for distributing the detested stamps. In less than thirty minutes they leveled the building. Saving the timbers, they "stamped" them in derision of the Stamp Act, and hauled them to Oliver's luxurious house at the foot of Fort Hill. At nightfall, they added the timbers to a bonfire atop the hill. By the light of the bonfire, they beheaded Oliver's effigy and then destroyed Oliver's stable house and his horse-drawn coach and chaise—prime emblems of upper-class affluence. Later in the evening, when Lieutenant Governor Hutchinson and Sheriff Greenleaf tried to stop the destruction, the crowd drove them off in a hailstorm of stones after someone cried out: "The Governor and the Sheriff! To your arms, my boys."[2] For another four hours, deep into the night, the crowd tore through Oliver's house, breaking windows and a looking glass said to be the largest in the colonies, demolishing the elegant furniture, emptying the contents of the well-stocked wine cellar, and tearing up the gardens. The next day the shocked Oliver asked to be relieved of his commission as stamp distributor.

Twelve days later it was Lieutenant Governor Thomas Hutchinson's turn. After attacking the handsome houses of the deputy register of the vice admiralty court and the comptroller of Customs, a crowd of men in workaday garb descended on Hutchinson's mansion. Catching the lieutenant governor at dinner with his family, the crowd smashed in the doors with axes and sent the Hutchinsons packing. Working with almost military precision, they reduced the furniture to splinters, stripped the walls bare, chopped through inner partitions until the house was a hollow shell, destroyed the formal gardens, drank the wine cellar dry, stole nine hundred pounds sterling in coin (today this would be about $90,000), scattered books and papers in the street, and carried off every movable object of value. Led again by MacIntosh, the crowd worked into the night, spending almost three hours alone "at the cupola before they could get it down" and then finishing off the building as dawn broke. "Gentlemen of the army, who have seen towns sacked by the enemy," wrote one of the first historians of the Revolution, Boston's William Gordon, "declare they have never before saw an instance of such fury."[3]

Nobody tried to stop the crowd. "The Mob was so general," wrote Governor Bernard, "and so supported that all civil power ceased in an instant, and I had not the least authority to oppose or quiet the mob." The next day, tears in his eyes and bereft of his judicial robes, Hutchinson appeared in his courtroom, savagely discredited in the town he believed he had dutifully served for thirty years. He estimated his property loss at £2,218—nearly one-quarter million dollars today and more than five hundred Boston artisans would earn in a single year. But why "such fury"? Hutchinson knew why his townsmen hated the tightening of trade regulations and the imposition of a new tax. But only by considering the wrath he had incurred among ordinary people over many years could he have understood their determination to bring his house level with the street. He never admitted such understanding in his correspondence or private conversations that have survived in the documentary record. But it is clear that the crowd was giving vent to years of resentment at the accumulation of wealth and power by the haughty prerogative faction led by Hutchinson. Behind every swing of the ax and every hurled stone, behind every shattered crystal goblet and splintered mahogany chair, lay the fury of a plain Bostonian who had read or heard the repeated references to impoverished people as "rabble" and to Boston's popular caucus, led by Samuel Adams, as a "herd of fools, tools, and sycophants." The mobbish attackers were those who had suffered economic hardship while others fattened their

purses. Just the year before, they had listened to their popular leaders condemn those "who grind the faces of the poor without remorse, eat the bread
of oppression without fear, and wax fat upon the spoils of the people." They
had heard it said over and over that "luxury and extravagance are . . . destructive of those virtues which are necessary for the preservation of liberty and the
happiness of the people." They had burned inwardly at hearing some of the
wealthy proclaim from their mansions that poverty was the best inducement
for industry and frugality and that "the common people of this town and
country live too well." And they had cheered James Otis when he replied that
"I am of a quite different opinion, I do not think they live half well enough."[4]

The destructive riots of August 14 and 26 demonstrated the fragile, shifting relationship between different elements of Boston's popular party and
provided a foretaste of what would occur in the decade leading up to the Declaration of Independence. Lawyer James Otis commanded the columns of
the *Boston Gazette*, and brewer Samuel Adams directed the caucus. But who
controlled the streets? The Loyal Nine of the Boston Caucus—printer Benjamin Edes, distillers John Avery and Thomas Chase, braziers John Smith
and Stephen Cleverly, painter Thomas Crafts, and several other craftsmen—
did their best to control the rank and file beneath them. But they left the dirty
work of dismantling the houses of the wealthy to the lower artisans, laborers,
and mariners. They preferred violence in limited doses and hoped to rein in
men like MacIntosh. To this end, Boston's selectmen, equivalent to today's
city council, hurriedly expressed their "utter detestation of the extraordinary
and violent proceedings of a number of persons unknown against some of the
inhabitants" and agreed to form a "military watch, till the present unruly
spirit shall subside."[5]

The selectmen's statement was disingenuous, really only an indication that
anxious merchants and middle-class artisans of the caucus were distressed
that the crowd had developed a mind of its own. But they could not afford to
have hundreds of workingmen prosecuted. They knew that the crowds of
August 14 and 26 were several thousand strong, and the crowd leaders were
by no means unknown to them. Not one Bostonian stepped forward to claim
the £300 reward offered by the governor—a huge amount representing an
artisan's wages for four years or more—for information leading to the conviction of the riot leaders. How to gain control of the mob while not losing
support in the protests against England was the question at hand. Everyone
knew that Ebenezer MacIntosh led the swarming crowd, and indeed he was

arrested by Sheriff Greenleaf. But even before the sheriff could confine Mac-Intosh, several well-to-do Bostonians told Greenleaf that unless he immediately discharged the shoemaker street general, they would cancel the citizens' watch. When a few other suspected rioters were indicted and jailed, all were sprung from confinement by an angry crowd within a few days. Hutchinson sighed that "there was no authority which thought it advisable to make any inquiry after them" once they had escaped.[6] The crowd proved it was more than a match for the authorities when its members were apprehended or threatened with prison.

With the speed of a raging smallpox epidemic, word of the Stamp Act mob attacks in Boston reached other towns. Reports of the sacking of Stamp Distributor Oliver's house on August 14 reached Newport, Rhode Island, in a few days, and firebrands there wasted little time in staging their own demonstration of popular power. On August 27, a crowd gathered at dawn to build a gallows near the Town House. Dispersing to go to work, they reassembled for the midmorning break to carry effigies of Augustus Johnston, Rhode Island's stamp distributor, and two hated conservatives, Doctor Thomas Moffat and lawyer Martin Howard, Jr., through the streets. They hoisted the effigies with halters around their necks fifteen feet high, to the satisfaction of a cheering crowd. The effigies had been carefully prepared: Johnston held the Stamp Act in his right hand and across his chest was inscribed THE STAMP MAN. Doctor Moffat's breast was decorated with THAT INFAMOUS, MIS-CREATED, LEERING JACOBITE DOCTOR MURFY. Out of his mouth trailed a strip of paper reading "It is too late Martinius to Retract, for we are all aground." Over his shoulder hung a boot with a devil peeping out. Howard's effigy was tattooed with inscriptions. One read THAT FAWNING, INSIDIOUS, INFAMOUS MISCREANT AND PARACIDE MARTINIUS SCRIBLERIUS; another read CURS'D AMBITION AND YOUR CURSED CLAN HAS RUIN'D ME. The posts of the gallows were decorated with "We have an hereditary indefeasible right to a halter . . ." and "That person who shall efface this publick mark of resentment will be deem'd an enemy to liberty and accordingly meet with proper chastisement."[7]

The effigy burning of Johnston, Howard, and Moffat was led by three Newport merchants—William Ellery, Samuel Vernon, and Robert Crook—and workingmen gladly followed their lead. This cross-class demonstration gained the common objective: Johnston's assurance he would resign his office as stamp distributor. But then the crowd moved beyond the control of the organizing merchants. Newport's workingmen reassembled again at five in the afternoon, built a fire, and turned the effigies and the gallows into ash. This was not enough. The next day they reassembled at dusk and marched on Howard's house, where they worked as efficiently as any employer would have wished. Not to be outdone by Boston's laboring men, they broke all the window glass, reduced the window frames to kindling, smashed all the elegant furnishings, including a collection of oil paintings, hammered down the interior walls, emptied the wine cellar, threw books down a well, tore up the floors, dismantled chimney hearths and chimneys, sawed down two rows of locust trees leading to the entrance, and leveled the fences around the house. The mob then moved on to repeat the performance at Doctor Moffat's house. Finally, at about two o'clock in the morning, they finished their work. Two of the finest houses in a town of about nine hundred homes had been reduced to shells.

As in Boston, a poor man, John Weber, led the rampaging crowd. This offended the town's respectable Sons of Liberty, the local version of a widely organized revolutionary group, which in Newport included the son of a previous deputy governor, wealthy merchants, and provincial officers. They had already achieved their goal, the resignation of the stamp distributor. Weber had arrived in Newport only recently, probably as a ship's mate for he had the respect of mariners and waterfront maritime artisans. When the sheriff arrested Weber and clapped him on a royal vessel in the harbor, the well-to-do Sons of Liberty turned their heads, believing Weber would take the rap for the wholesale violence and "in some measure atone for the part they had acted," according to the humiliated stamp distributor.[8] Newport's workingmen secured Weber's release with threats that they would pull down the houses of some of the Sons of Liberty who had encouraged protests against the Stamp Act even if they did not approve the mansion destruction. The sheriff released Weber, later arrested him again, and released him still another time. Like MacIntosh in Boston, he slipped offstage—or was sent offstage. As in Boston, the respectable Sons of Liberty struggled to regain control, while those beneath them pursued their own more radical agendas.

Historians have argued that the attacks on the homes of Moffat and Howard were a classic case of an intoxicated mob careening out of control. Historian Edmund Morgan has called Weber "a monster" and deemed the property destruction by the crowd he led "disgraceful." Another historian has described the dismantling of the upper-class mansions as the "revelry" and "mischief" of an out-of-control marauding horde.[9] We can accept this assessment of crowd behavior, however, only by adopting the attitude of the eighteenth-century elite: that the lower orders were by nature unreasonable, entirely moved by passion or alcohol-induced hysteria, not by reason, not by calculation, not by conscious choice. To the contrary, Newport's artisans, mariners, and laborers seem to have acted from brooding resentments, from past experiences, and from knowledge of recent events in other cities where laboring men had settled accounts. They knew particularly of the August 14 crowd destruction of Andrew Oliver's property, and they learned in the *Newport Mercury* of the effigy hangings of London weavers, glovemakers, and other workers who surrounded the Royal Palace and Parliament to protest unemployment caused by a sharp decline in American orders. "Some houses," reported the *Mercury*, had been almost levelled with the ground." It was not necessary to destroy all the emblems of wealth and status—the gilded frames and the oil paintings of *Venus Sleeping*, *Cleopatra*, and *The Countess of Coventry* that hung in Doctor Moffat's parlor—in order to get the stamp distributor to resign his office. Motivating Newport's working people were their day-to-day experiences with Howard as a purse-proud attorney and judge who speculated in Newport land and had the hauteur of an English nobleman. Along with Doctor Moffat and several others, he had been detested since 1761 as part of a clique of foreign-born aristocrats, most of whom worshiped at the Anglican Church. It was an open secret in Newport that this club was in cahoots with Governor Francis Bernard of Massachusetts to create an American "nobility appointed by the King for life." Club members may not have been inside Howard's house, but it was common knowledge that he proudly displayed paintings of the duke of Cumberland and the Jacobite Pretender, figures in England who attracted popular fury for their aristocratic and anti-Protestant views.[10] At a time when Newport's economy had suffered at the end of the Seven Years' War, the opulence, haughtiness, and politics of these men stuck like a bone in the throat of ordinary Newporters.

Ten weeks after the demolition of Hutchinson's house, it was time for Boston's laboring people to celebrate Pope's Day again. By this time, the *Boston Gazette* was calling shoemaker MacIntosh "Commander of the South [End]" and was crediting him for effecting a "treaty" with his North End counterpart, whereby a peaceful and united annual Pope's Day parade would replace the traditional bone-breaking brawl. The governor described how "Captain" MacIntosh, or "General" MacIntosh as he was referred to by some, decked out splendidly in a militia uniform of gold and blue, a gilded chest gorget, and a hat laced with gold, led two thousand paraders through the town. Peter Oliver, brother of the humiliated stamp distributor, called the orderly ranks of marchers a mob, but he described something more like a military regiment, which, if the reported numbers are correct, would have consisted of half of the city's adult males. MacIntosh led the city's workingmen past the statehouse, Oliver wrote, where the "general Assembly were sitting, to display his power. If a whisper was heard among his followers, . . . holding up his finger hushed it in a moment; and when he had fully displayed his authority, he marched his men to the first rendezvous and ordered them to retire peaceably to their several homes and was punctually obeyed."[11] No wonder, given the startling emergence of an unnoticed and obscure shoemaker, that the elite began to refer to MacIntosh as "a Massaniello." Like the Neapolitan rebel of 1647, he had come from nowhere to take command of a force so powerful that neither the royal governor nor the chief justice nor the sheriff nor the city's affluent merchants could stop him. With so many Boston workingmen at his command, how far might this man go? Could the resentments and physical strength of the street rioters be harnessed by the better-to-do Sons of Liberty?

Although Oliver had already promised that he would give up his stamp distributor's commission, the Sons of Liberty wanted a public resignation. Cornered, Oliver agreed to that by publishing it in the *Boston Gazette*. But the city's common folk wanted more—not only a printed resignation but public humiliation. In a scene to be repeated many times and in many places once the war for independence began, the lower orders, so often spurned by those above them, demanded ritual self-abnegation. Oliver twisted and turned, offering to resign at the courthouse—the home ground of governmental authority. But the radicals would not hear of it. Trapped, Oliver succumbed to having Ebenezer MacIntosh march him across the town in pelting rain to the Liberty Tree in the South End, home turf of working Bostonians. There, a huge crowd watched Oliver eat humble pie. He sardonically declared that he would "always think myself very happy when it shall be in my power to serve this people."[12] The drenched observers cheered and returned to their places of work.

To the south, in New York City, everyone in a position of upholding English authority knew about the power displayed by ordinary people in Boston and Newport. Four days after the dismantling of Thomas Hutchinson's Boston house, James McEvers, a wealthy merchant, resigned his post as New

Woodcuts such as this one were not up to graphic standards today, but they were effective at the time. Here the people controlled the streets, a worrisome prospect for those accustomed to political rule.

York's stamp distributor, fearing that "my House would have been pillaged, my person abused, and His Majesty's revenue impaired." But that was not enough. When the stamps for several northern colonies arrived by ship on October 24, to be carried by a king's regiment to Fort George in New York Harbor, placards appeared throughout the town warning that "the first man that either distributes or makes use of stamped paper let him take care of his house, person, and effects. We dare. VOX POPULI."[13] That convinced New York's merchants, meeting on October 31 (the day before the Stamp Act was to go into force), to agree that they should not import any English goods until Parliament repealed the Stamp Act. But New York's plebeian element was not yet satisfied. Going beyond the respectable leaders of the Sons of Liberty, the lower orders rampaged through the town for four days. Some two thousand strong, they threatened the homes of suspected sympathizers of British policy, attacked the house of the famously wealthy governor Cadwallader Colden, paraded his effigy around town, and built a monstrous bonfire in the Bowling Green into which the shouting crowd hurled the governor's luxurious two sleighs and horse-drawn coach.

Four days later, after what contemporaries called the "General Terror of

November 1–4," the crowd regathered at Fort George. Placards had announced that "the sons of Neptune," that is, seagoing men, would lead a new demonstration. This was the sign that the middle-class Sons of Liberty had lost control of the city's masses. Surging to the walls of Fort George, the crowd of several thousand insultingly addressed Governor Cadwallader Colden as the "Chief Murderer of their Rights and Privileges,"[14] taunted the guards to fire, hurled bricks, stones, and garbage, paraded an effigy of the governor in his actual coach, which they had seized from his carriage house, and finally convinced the governor to hand over bundles of the hated stamps.

The situation in New York City was fluid, with contending groups vying for the privilege of harassing men appointed to distribute stamps. At the end of November, an angry crowd flushed out men residing in New York who were commissioned to distribute stamps for Nova Scotia, Maryland, and New Hampshire. A month later, a crowd "followed the custom of most places in America," as the *New York Gazette* reported, by surrounding the home of a suspected stamp distributor and "defacing his house, destroying some furniture in it, and drawing his winter carriages thro' the streets in flames."[15] Middling men such as Isaac Sears and Alexander McDougall, captains of privateers in the Seven Years' War, and John Lamb, a trader, led the Sons of Liberty; but whether the Sons of Liberty could control the mariners, lower artisans, and laborers remained in doubt. As in Boston and Newport, they came to fear the awful power of the assembled lower-class artisans and their maritime compatriots.

In other seaboard towns, resistance to the Stamp Act paralleled that of Boston, Newport, and New York, though it didn't always escalate into actions against wealthy citizens associated with inflamed local issues that predated the act. In Portsmouth, New Hampshire, the crowd assembled to stone an effigy of a stamp master held high on a pole in the town square, and this was enough to convince the stamp distributor to resign. Newburyport townsmen down the coast were stagier—suspending an effigy of the stamp distributor from a large elm tree over tar barrels. Igniting the tar, the crowd cut the rope and dropped the effigy into a flaming barrel. Marylanders held mock funerals for the Stamp Act and drove Zachariah Hood, the local stamp distributor, out of the colony after burning down his warehouse in Annapolis, the colony's capital. North Carolinians in Wilmington dragged the stamp distributor through the streets and forced him to resign his commission, while at the same time imprisoning the governor in his own house. In New Bern, they yanked a superior court judge from his bed in the middle of the night and forced him to defy British orders by holding court without stamped legal documents. In Charleston, South Carolina, an angry mob sprinkled with unemployed seamen burned effigies of the stamp distributor and interred a coffin of "American Liberty." Then they ransacked the house of Henry Laurens, the city's mightiest merchant and slave importer, in search of the hated stamps. "The richer folks" were terrified, according to the *South Carolina Gazette*, by a mob "spirit which [they] themselves had conjured up. . . ."[16] Up and down the coast, people who had never before voted or played any public role surged through the streets to participate in boisterous mock executions, defy royal authority, and initiate themselves in the rituals of revolution.

The reaction of Philadelphians to the Stamp Act was more restrained than in other cities. Just as not all colonists were the same, neither were all colonies nor all seaports. In Philadelphia, a key figure was the rags-to-riches artisan-hero Benjamin Franklin.

Just six months before Parliament and the king issued the Stamp Act, the nasty assembly election of October 1764 colored the response of Philadelphians to the hated measure. Having lost his assembly seat, his first political defeat, Franklin had returned to London as the representative of Pennsylvania and three other colonies. But he was unable to convince Lord Grenville to obtain parliamentary repeal of the Stamp Act, and Franklin's enemies in Philadelphia charged that he had actually helped to write it. Even if that was untrue, there was no dispute that Grenville followed Franklin's recommendation in appointing John Hughes, a baker turned merchant, to the stamp distributor's position in Philadelphia. Philadelphians, though hearing from newspapers about the rioting in Boston and Newport, did nothing to disturb Hughes until September 16. On that evening, after learning that George Grenville had resigned as chief minister, a celebrating crowd assembled at the London Coffee House, owned by William Bradford, printer of the *Pennsylvania Journal* and a member of the Philadelphia Sons of Liberty. Toasts to Grenville's ill health turned to cries that the houses of Franklin, Hughes, and others involved in supporting the Stamp Act "should be level'd with the Street." Only the nimble rallying of artisans who still looked on Franklin as their hero saved his house, where Deborah Franklin stood at an upper-floor window with a musket in her hands. The 1764 issue of instituting royal government had deeply divided the working people of the city, and this permitted upper-class leaders to maintain control. Printer Bradford explained "our body of Sons of Liberty in this city is not declared numerous as unfortunate dissensions in provincial politics keep us a rather divided people."[17] Hughes never resigned his post, but after the stamps arrived on October 5, he promised not to execute the Stamp Act.

In December 1765, all colonial seaports reopened for trade—without using the hated stamps. Colonial Americans rejoiced at having successfully resisted English authority, even if Parliament would not formally repeal the Stamp Act until the next year. But the sweet taste of victory among upper-class merchants, planters, and lawyers who had attempted to lead the resistance movement was soured by the knowledge that in many alarming instances the protest campaign had slipped beyond their control. In trying to resist the punitive British imperial policy, colonial leaders had welcomed the *vox populi.* In fact, they could not do without it. But once the genie was out of the bottle, how could it be imprisoned again? It was the vigor of ordinary people in defining and pursuing goals beyond resistance to the Stamp Act that raised the specter, in the minds of those accustomed to political domination, of a radicalized form of politics and a radically altered society.

The "mob" has been feared throughout history by upper-class power holders, and historians have not been immune from this fear. The fear's source is in the assumption that the masses are irrational, stirred into paroxysms of violence by irresponsible rabble-rousers, and indiscriminate in selecting their targets. Once unloosed, the mob is capable of almost anything. Thus, eighteenth-century writers, including many patriot leaders, referred to the common people on the move as "the unthinking multitude," the "hellish crew," the "impassioned dregs of society," and the like. This was the spontaneous, frenzied, and unprogrammatic mob. Others saw a manipulated mob, acting robotlike under orders from above. This was the view of the brother of Boston's humiliated stamp distributor, Peter Oliver, a dedicated royal servant who believed that Andrew Oliver had been attacked and insulted by a crowd that was a "perfect machine, wound up by any hand who might first take the winch."[18]

Peter Oliver was intimately aware of the political inner workings of Boston, a town smaller than today's Delano, California, or Hanover, New Hampshire. But Oliver was trapped in his perceptions of crowd protest by his inveterate disdain of common people and his veneration of English aristocracy and royalty. In contrast to Oliver's view, the Stamp Act crowds of 1765 are better understood as large groups of disaffected citizens, drawn heavily but not entirely from the laboring ranks, who worked in purposeful and co-ordinated ways to protest British policies, had their own ideas about how an equitable society should operate, and in many cases expressed hatred of op-pressive local oligarchs. To be sure, upper-class leaders worked hard to get crowds to do their bidding, and lower-class citizens often looked for leaders above them because deference was not yet dead and educated men in the upper ranks had the money, organizational skills, and literary talents vital to mounting successful protests. Crowd leadership varied from one place to an-other. In Boston, where the Pope's Day tradition and recurrent street demon-strations since the 1730s had taught the laboring classes the basic lessons of organization and protest, the leader of the urban mass was a poor shoemaker with tenuous ties to those above him. In Newport, Rhode Island, three mer-chants first led the crowd and then saw an obscure mariner, just recently ar-rived, momentarily capture the allegiance of disgruntled workingmen. In New York City, where crowd protests had been less common, the Stamp Act demonstrators were led at first by men higher up on the social ladder—ship captains, master craftsmen, and even lawyers—but then escaped their con-trol. In Philadelphia, where local issues divided artisans and shopkeepers, well-to-do lawyers Joseph Galloway and James Allen led the people into the streets.

Despite these differences, the struggle for political control was everywhere highly fluid, and this continued in the years ahead. Thomas Hutchinson be-lieved that a tight chain of command linked Boston's upper, middle, and lower ranks. It began, he thought, with the Merchants Committee, descended to the master craftsmen organized through the Loyal Nine and the Sons of Liberty, and finally tapped the lower craftsmen, laborers, mariners, and servants. Hutchinson was half right, but he was describing mostly how merchants and lawyers *wished* the political system to operate. He overestimated their ability to control the crowd because he underestimated the self-energizing capabili-ties of common people. "The Boston Mob," wrote General Thomas Gage, who commanded the British regiment in Boston, understood the urban dy-namic better. The crowd, he reported to London, "raised first by the instiga-tion of many of the principal inhabitants, [was] allured by plunder, [and] rose shortly after of their own accord." Gage saw the same process unfolding in New York City. "People of property" at first raised the lower class to protest against the Stamp Act, but after five days of tumult the propertied New

Yorkers lost their influence over the crowd and "began to be filled with terrors for their own safety."[19]

Both loyal supporters of English authority and well-established colonial protest leaders underestimated the self-activating capacity of ordinary colonists. By the end of 1765, an extraordinary year in the history of the English colonies, people in the streets had astounded, dismayed, and frightened their social superiors. Resistance to English policies had emboldened people who previously counted for little in the political arena to find a mind of their own. Colonial leaders, warned the perceptive General Gage, "began to be terrified at the spirit they had raised to perceive that popular fury was not to be guided, and each individual feared he might be the next victim to their rapacity."[20]

Restive Slaves

While crowds took to the streets up and down the Atlantic seaboard shouting "liberty and no stamps," it entered the minds of many colonists that the constant talk about liberty—and its opposite, slavery—might become highly contagious, and applied to an issue far more fundamental than a modest tax imposed by England. In every colony, white leaders began to wonder about how restive slaves might react to the rhetoric fueling the disturbances related to the Stamp Act. While seeking freedom from parliamentary taxes, while deploring English tyranny and supposed attempts to "enslave" colonists, the Americans unexpectedly faced a profound contradiction as they scrambled to suppress enslaved Africans with their own urges to be free.

George Mason, Virginia planter-politician and neighbor of Thomas Jefferson, was one of the many Virginia leaders worried over the huge increase in Africans brought across the Atlantic after the end of the Seven Years' War. "Perhaps the primary cause of the destruction of the most flourishing government that ever existed was the introduction of great numbers of slaves," he wrote in 1765 in a bill he introduced in the House of Burgesses, just after the Stamp Act riots surged through the seaboard cities. Mason was soon joined by other Virginians who had been edgy about slave unrest since the beginning of the Seven Years' War. Many white militiamen were fighting on the frontier, and this raised fear that slaves, who represented 40 percent of the population, would capitalize on their absence as slave patrollers to stage a bid for freedom. "The villainy of the Negroes on any emergency of government is what I always feared," Governor Robert Dinwiddie told Charles Carter, a tidewater planter with scores of slaves, in 1755. Pontiac's Rebellion in 1763 further increased fears of black rebellion. One militia officer told Governor Dinwiddie that the Indians raiding on Virginia's frontier "are saving and caressing all the Negroes they take," and this might "be productive of an insurrection . . . attended with the most serious consequences."[21]

The Indian-African alliance never occurred, but nervousness over the possibility spread as the furor over the Stamp Act filled the air with heated talk about American liberty and British tyranny. In 1766, some of George Mason's slaves joined a plot to mount an insurrection. Other slave rebellions, including ones in Loudoun and Fairfax Counties occurred in 1767, and this convinced the House of Burgesses to double the import duty on slaves in order to limit the number of new Africans entering the colony. In the meantime, white authorities hanged seven slaves, and the heads of four "were cut off and fixed on the chimnies of the courthouse," as a Boston newspaper reported.[22]

In Wilmington, North Carolina, a town of only a few hundred houses on the Cape Fear River, town officials clamped down on the activities of slaves and free blacks. Fearful of slave unrest, white authorities passed ordinances prohibiting an assembly of more than three slaves gathered for the purpose of "playing, rioting, cabaling" and set a curfew at 10:00 P.M. In 1767, north of Wilmington in New Hanover County, shivers went down the spines of white families when about twenty slaves, who had seized their masters' arms, ran away in a coordinated break for freedom.[23]

Charleston, South Carolina, the slave importation center of North America, suffered even greater fears of slave conspiracy after white protesters bandied about assaults on *their* freedom. Black Charlestonians heard and read the word "liberty" repeatedly in the waning months of 1765, and saw the slogan "Liberty and no Stamp Act" emblazoned on a placard hanging from the neck of the stamp distributor's effigy, strung up on October 19, 1765. A few days later, the Sons of Liberty, marching on the elegant house of merchant Henry Laurens to seize bundles of stamps they believed had been stored there, shouted "Liberty, Liberty and Stamp'd Paper." When a huge procession celebrated the resignation of Charleston's stamp distributor, they held aloft a British flag that read LIBERTY.[24]

The repeated use of the word "liberty" was not lost on some five thousand slaves in Charleston. In 1765, the city's grand jury was already apprehensive "that slaves in Charles-Town are not under a good regulation, and that they at all times in the night go about streets rioting," undeterred by the city's handful of watchmen. Within weeks, restive slaves were gathering in knots. More ominous, in mid-December the wife of a wealthy merchant overheard two slaves conversing about a colonywide insurrection planned for Christmas Eve. "This place has been in an uproar for twelve days past," wrote one townsman. "Every company in town mount guard day and night, and the severest orders given which has prevented it hitherto."[25]

Put on close guard, white Carolinians got through the Christmas season unscathed. But in mid-January "a peculiar incident, revealing in what dread the citizens lived among the black savages with whom they were surrounding themselves," reported Henry Laurens, "was furnished by some negroes who apparently in thoughtless imitation, began to cry 'Liberty.' " Laurens was surely mistaken that this action was "thoughtless imitation," but he was accurate that "the city was thrown under arms for a week and for 10 or 14 days messengers were sent posting through the province in the most bitterly cold weather in 19 years." Almost simultaneously, 107 slaves fled their plantations outside Charleston and "joined a large number of runaways in Colleton County, which increase[d] to a formidable Body."[26] Concerned about their liberty with regard to stamped paper, South Carolinians were even more concerned about the liberty of Africans. More than seven thousand Africans had stumbled off slave ships in Charleston Harbor in the year 1765—a huge increase from previous years that made the colony more than 60 percent African. Quaking over real and imagined black insurrections, legislators passed a three-year stoppage of slave imports to take effect on January 1, 1766. But the black revolution in South Carolina had already begun.

In Georgia, where slaves knew that flight to Spanish Florida was their best chance of gaining freedom, a group of slaves, including women and children, fled to a swamp near the Savannah River in the midst of the Stamp Act turmoil. White officials unsuccessfully tried to root out the small maroon band by offering bounties to Indians for their capture. The maroon settlement apparently survived because four years later the legislature had to send a militia detachment into the swamp to destroy the runaways' enclave.

The arrival of at least 25,000 enslaved Africans in the southern colonies during the years the British were clamping down on trade policies almost guaranteed an increase in servile unrest. "Saltwater" Africans, as colonists termed the new arrivals, had always taken poorly to their captivity. "If he must be broke," warned a North Carolinian slave owner to those purchasing newly arrived slaves, "either from obstinacy, or, which I am more apt to suppose, from greatness of soul, [it] will require . . . hard discipline. . . . You would really be surprised at their perseverance. . . . They often die before they can be conquered."[27] Heightening this potential for slave rebellion was the contagiousness of white talk about liberty in the context of the Stamp Act regulations. This potent and dangerous mix of influences was recognized by wary white colonists in the South, who knew that any fissure in white society provided opportunities for black insurgency. There could be no organized black freedom movement at this stage, or even a black radical agenda, for it was not possible for slaves spread across a vast terrain to organize and think collectively. But the single-minded desire for freedom was already surfacing, awaiting the right climate for slaves to take action.

Stricken Conscience

One of the contributing factors to slave unrest during the Stamp Act controversy was news leaking to them that some white leaders were attacking slavery. Making this all the more important to slaves was their discovery that well-known and well-placed white leaders coming to their defense were men very different from such ascetic Quakers as Benjamin Lay, Anthony Benezet, and John Woolman. Rather than basing their opposition to slavery on moral and religious grounds, these proto-abolitionists used economic and political arguments to condemn the practice. Given the battle over the rights of English subjects in the American colonies, it is not surprising that this new secularization of abolitionism took place.

In 1748, the French philosopher Baron Charles Montesquieu published an attack on slavery in his *Spirit of the Laws*, which was circulated widely in the colonies. Residing in the slave-trading port of Bordeaux, Montesquieu "put the subject of Negro slavery on the agenda of the European Enlightenment." Adam Smith condemned slavery as an affront to human progress in his *Theory of Moral Sentiments*, published in 1764. The attacks on slavery by both Montesquieu and Smith inspired questioning of the legitimacy and utility of slavery among educated colonists. Both figured in James Otis's assault on slavery in one of the earliest defenses of colonial rights. In *The Rights of the British Colonies Asserted and Proved*, published in the same year as Adam Smith's *Theory of Moral Sentiments*, Otis made the uncompromising assertion that "The colonists are by the law of nature free born, as indeed all men are, white or black. . . . Does it follow that tis right to enslave a man because he is black? Will short curled hair like wool, instead of Christian hair, as tis called by those whose hearts are as hard as the nether millstone, help the argument? Can any logical inference in favour of slavery be drawn from a flat nose, a long or a short face?"[28]

The work of such men as Montesquieu, Smith, and Otis put the abolition of slavery on the radical agenda of American revolutionists. Otis's attack on slavery was particularly trenchant because he initiated what would become a constant theme over the next decade: that the British infringement of colonial natural rights and the abridgement of African liberties by colonial Americans were joined at the hip. The more Americans cried about British oppression, the more sensitive they were concerning a deadlier oppression of their own. Slave trading and slave keeping, charged Otis, "ha[ve] a direct tendency to diminish the idea of the inestimable value of liberty, and makes every dealer in it a tyrant." "It is a clear truth," he continued, "that those who every day barter away other men's liberty will soon care little for their own."[29]

Otis's pamphlet had an almost immediate effect. In 1765, Worcester's town meeting instructed their delegates to the Massachusetts legislature to propose a law prohibiting the importation and purchase of slaves by any Massachusetts citizen. In May 1766, Boston's town meeting instructed their delegates, including Otis, John Hancock, and Samuel Adams, to push the measure. Legal maneuvering blocked the bill for five years (only to have Governor Thomas Hutchinson veto it when it was finally passed by the legislature), but word was out for all to hear that at least one colony was discussing a new policy to overturn a century and a half of slave dealing. Otis's attack on slavery, soon to be bolstered by others, touched off debates over the legality, let alone the moral justification, of slavery at the College of Philadelphia in 1768 and at Harvard College in 1773. Word of these debates could hardly have escaped the ears of northern slaves. Nor could the thoughts of Nathaniel Appleton, one of the mainstays of Boston's Sons of Liberty. Only months after the Boston town meeting had pushed to stop the importing and selling of slaves, another member of the Sons of Liberty, Benjamin Edes, published Appleton's cogent *Considerations on Slavery: In a Letter to a Friend*. The son of a Cambridge Puritan minister, Appleton had graduated from Harvard and became a merchant in Boston, where he witnessed the workings of the slave trade. In *Considerations on Slavery* he tried to tie the successes of liberty-loving colonists in contesting the Stamp Act to the budding cause of abolition. "The years 1765 and 1766 will be ever memorable for the glorious stand which America has made for her liberties; how much glory will it add . . . if at the same time we are establishing Liberty for ourselves and children, we show the same regard to all mankind that came among us?"[30] Appleton veered from attacks on slavery rooted in religion and morality. Adopting a pragmatic approach geared to the sensibilities of people in a trading community, he flayed the abominable practice of slavery because it encouraged the slave to "throw off his burden" through rebellion, thus keeping all communities in a state of fear. He also deplored that slave labor took the jobs of lower-class whites, leaving them unemployed or—in the case of women—driving them to prostitution.

The hard-hitting words of Otis and Appleton soon reverberated down the coast in Newport, Rhode Island. An anonymous writer in the *Newport Mercury*, probably a member of the seaport's Quaker community, scorned the Americans' self-righteous language about enslavement by Parliament—a "distant prospect"—while they enslaved at the very moment "thousands of tens of thousands of their fellow creatures!" If they truly meant to stop enslavement from their mother country, they must halt "that hellish practice of deluding and enslaving another part of the human species, I mean Negroes." Was liberty applicable only to whites? No, it was applicable to all humankind, and Africans were Sons of Liberty too. As historian Bernard Bailyn has phrased it: "The identification between the cause of the colonies and the cause of the Negroes bound in chattel slavery—an identification built into the very language of politics—became inescapable."[31]

Southern slaves may or may not have heard about the antislavery pronouncements of Montesquieu, Adam Smith, James Otis, Nathaniel Appleton, and others; and they may or may not have heard that Massachusetts' legislature was considering the end of the slave trade. But a Virginia pamphlet, published as the Stamp Act crisis reached its height in late 1765, could hardly have remained unknown to them. In the context of the arguments over England's new measures to rule the colonies more effectively, Colonel Richard Bland, a member of the House of Burgesses from Prince George County since 1742, and an unrivaled scholar of English constitutional law in Virginia, had declared that "under an English government all *men* are *born free*." Upon reading this, John Camm, the feisty Anglican professor of divinity at William and Mary College, rushed into print. Did Bland mean "that *Virginia* is not an *English government,* or that Negroes are not under it *born slaves,* or that the said slaves are not men? Whichever of these confident assertions he undertakes to maintain, and one of them he must maintain, he will find insuperable difficulties to oppose him as soon as he is able to cast an eye on the situation of *Virginia,* the map of America, or on the condition and rational conduct of his own domestics."[32] Reverend Camm and Richard Bland had tangled on a number of issues and cordially disliked each other; but no matter, Camm had gone to the heart of a central contradiction in revolutionary rhetoric: How could Africans, who indisputably were human, be excluded from the principle that freedom was the birthright of all mankind?

By the mid-1760s, knowledge of attacks on slavery was common in Virginia and other southern colonies. The idea that African slavery was incompatible with the natural rights that Americans were coming to depend upon in their argument with the mother country was gaining ground. To be sure, most slave owners, and even people who owned no slaves, did not worry themselves unduly about the contradiction between the enslavement of Africans and the natural rights they were claiming in their mounting fight with England. But slaves did. The vast majority of them could not read, but they could listen; and they could, as inheritors of an oral tradition, spread the word. With the development of larger slaveholdings and the growing population density of slaves from Georgia to Maryland, networks of slave communication grew. Along informal grapevines, as soon became painfully obvious to slave owners, any idea promoting release from slavery moved quickly from one colony to another and from the seaboard towns to the interior hill country. John Adams heard from two Georgia delegates to the Continental Congress in 1775 that "the Negroes have a wonderful art of communicating intelligence among themselves; it will run several hundreds of miles in a week or fortnight."[33] No mass black uprising occurred in the early stages of protest against English policy; but sporadic slave demonstrations that focused on the word "liberty," used repeatedly by Stamp Act protesters, set most white Americans on edge. Considering the odds, still very much against black rebels but soon to change to their advantage, these early foretastes of black revolution were impressive enough to strike fear in the hearts of thousands of slave owners.

The Indian Great Awakening

Restiveness was surfacing in another segment of the peoples inhabiting North America east of the Mississippi River: among Native Americans living in a complex world of villages. As noted in chapter 1, an understanding of the Indians' experience of the American Revolution requires a shift in focus, to events that coincided only in part with those familiar to readers of white revolutionary history. Dramatic events in Indian country in the early 1760s, which set the course for several decades, had their own internal logic. Rather than looking west at Indian country through white eyes, we need to face east, as historian Daniel Richter has urged, to understand events through Indian eyes.[34]

For the powerful Indian nations of the interior, the *pays d'en haut,* as the French designated the midcontinent middle ground, the final stages of the Seven Years' War and the Treaty of Paris that formally concluded it in 1763 had chilling implications. First, after the French surrender at Montreal in September 1761, many Indian nations faced the near certainty of losing their French ally and trading partner. The need for an alternate trade partner was absolute. As Wyandot headmen told the English trader George Croghan a few years before, "You . . . know very well that no Indian nation lives now without being supported either by the English or the French, we cannot live as our ancestors did before you came into our country."[35]

Second, looking to the English for the trade goods that had become essential to their lives, interior Indian people found the English conquerors of New France to be cold and stingy trading partners. At the peace treaty in Detroit in 1761, British general Jeffrey Amherst had demanded the return of Anglo-American war captives, many of whom were white women who had married Indian men and borne them children. (Most had been happily adopted into tribal life in the long-held Indian tradition of replacing their war losses.) Equally offensive, British commanders at Fort Pitt, Detroit, and Michilimackinac withheld weapons, ammunition, and gunpowder upon which the Native American hunters relied in producing the deerskins essential to their trade. But even worse, taking advantage of the new British monopoly on Indian trade goods, Amherst ended the annual "presents" that Indian leaders regarded as tokens of respect and as a kind of rent for land occupied by British forts. On top of all this, Amherst raised the price of English trade goods while offering less for deerskins.

For Amherst, the British had won the war and the Native Americans must accommodate to being subjects of the king. Charged with implementing a policy of financial stringency and knowing that the Indians' military aid was no longer needed, he "blustered into Indian affairs," as historian Richard White puts it aptly, "with the moral vision of a shopkeeper and the arrogance of a victorious soldier."[36] For Native Americans, these were severe blows. For generations they had lived with the French, who were generous in giving gifts, tolerant of native ways (indeed readily adopting Indian customs), and rarely insistent on cessions of land, which the French, with their small settler population, had no reason to acquire. The British, in Indian eyes, were insensitive and greedy, more concerned with subordinating native peoples than in treating, trading, and living with them.

Even for the Iroquois, who had abandoned their long-standing neutrality policy to join the British in the latter stages of the Seven Years' War, the situation became difficult. The Seneca, always the most pro-French of the Iroquois Six Nations, had carried a red wampum belt signifying an intention to go to war to the British garrison in Detroit in 1761, two years before the Treaty of Paris was signed. Although the Iroquois tribes in the Ohio country rejected the Seneca proposal to drive the English back across the Appalachian Mountains, they boiled with resentment at General Amherst's policies. For them, Amherst was renouncing the accommodationist stance the British had always held in order to maintain the allegiance, or at least the neutrality, of the Iroquois people.

In this state of uncertainty over how to adapt to the severe policies of the English, Native Americans began listening to the visions of Neolin, a young Delaware Indian who acted more like a prophet than a warrior. Neolin's parentage and upbringing have never emerged in the documentary record, but it is known that he lived in Tuscarawas Town in present-day Ohio on a stream flowing southeastward into the Ohio River. He appeared on the scene preaching through the territory of the Delawares that native peoples must return to the "original state that they were in before the white people found out their country."[37] The alternative, he argued, was slow extinction at the hands of the settlers swarming across the mountains. Neolin preached that he had received a vision conveyed to him in dreams by the Master of Life, who told him that the Indians' salvation lay not in adopting Christianity and European culture but in returning to ancient Indian customs. They must forswear rum, abandon the material objects of the Europeans, and curb population increase through abstinence. Only by regaining sacred power and reviving traditional ways could Indian people escape the desperate trap in which they now found themselves.

Neolin's message had resonance in part because earlier nativist prophecies had circulated in the country of the Delaware people in the 1750s, including those of a female prophet in the Wyoming Valley of western Pennsylvania. By the time of Neolin's vision, the Delawares had already heard that the Master of Life had created Indians separately from Europeans and Africans, and had sent them hard winters and epidemics to warn the original possessors of the land that they must purge themselves of European ways and return to ancient customs. But Neolin's teachings truly captured the minds of many Delawares when he reminded them of how whites were encroaching on their lands, how the deer populations had thinned, and how the heartless new British policy denied Indians the usual gifts and supply of weapons. As Neolin's message took hold, Delaware chiefs who encouraged moderation and patience in their dealings with the British began to lose status in tribal councils.

By the early 1760s, Neolin's message was reaching Indian villages beyond Delaware country, far into tribal lands to the west from the Great Lakes to Illinois and Kentucky country. "Whence comes it that ye permit the Whites upon your lands?" the Master of Life had asked him, preached Neolin. "Can ye not live without them? ... Ye could live as ye did live before knowing them—before those whom ye call your brothers had come upon your lands. ... Drive them out, make war upon them. I do not love them at all; they know me not, and are my enemies, and the enemies of your brothers. Send them back to the lands which I have created for them and let them stay there."[38]

Throughout 1762, Neolin's teachings passed by word of mouth and then on inscribed deerskin parchment from one Indian village to another. One who heard him and converted to his doctrine was an Ottawa leader named Pontiac. In 1763, he made Neolin's response to the bleak situation confronting the interior tribes the underpinning of a plan to drive the English away. "It is important for us, my brothers," Pontiac exhorted, "that we exterminate from our lands this nation which seeks only to destroy us." By spring 1763, Detroit Indians conveyed to a French outpost that "the Delawares told us ... that the English sought to become masters of all and would put us to death. They told us also, Our Brethren, let us die together. Seeing the design of the English is to cut us off, we are dead one way or another."[39]

68

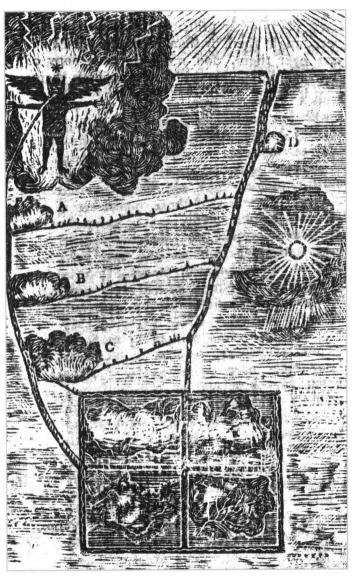

This chart of Neolin's teachings was drawn from memory by a Pennsylvania frontiersman captured during Pontiac's Rebellion. Delaware Indians at the bottom are blocked from following the Master of Life by layers of corruption borrowed from the Europeans.

The Seneca gave British leaders warning of what was coming. "We had been told," the Iroquois complained in 1763 to William Johnson, superintendent of northern Indian affairs for the British government, "that if you should conquer the French, your hands would ever be open to us, and, that as the English were a wealthy and trading people, we should be supplied with goods at a very reasonable rate. . . . But alas we find it quite otherwise; for instead of restoring to us our lands, we see you in possession of them, and building more forts in many parts of our country, notwithstanding the French are dead. This, together with the dearness of goods which are so high that all our hunting cannot supply our wants, gives our warriors and women the greatest uneasiness and makes us apt to believe every bad report we hear of your intentions towards us." General Amherst, comfortably ensconced in New York City, brushed aside reports of impending war, calling them "meer bugbears."[40]

Even before Amherst uttered this monumental misjudgment, the Ottawa chief Pontiac began an assault on Fort Detroit, the strongest of the British garrisons in the Great Lakes region. Launched in May 1763, it was the beginning of a war to cleanse Indian country of the British. The most important pan-Indian alliance in decades quickly took form as some several hundred Ottawa, Potawatomi, and Wyandot warriors laid siege to the fort. By June, warriors of many Indian nations overpowered British outposts as far east as Pittsburgh (where the infamous incident of distributing smallpox-infected blankets to parleying Indians occurred). Only Fort Niagara survived. In one assault, at Michilimackinac, Chippewas "lured the garrison into complacency by playing lacrosse outside the fort for several days and then used a well-placed stray ball as a ruse to storm through the gates."[41] Chippewa women had smuggled hatchets into the fort and were waiting inside. When the Chippewa men poured in, they took up the hatchets and killed sixteen British soldiers while capturing the rest.

The war dragged on through the summer and fall of 1763. Several thousand traders and frontier squatters from Virginia to Pennsylvania fell to Indian ambushes and assaults. One Indian leader insisted "that all the country was theirs—and that they had been cheated out of it" and "would carry on the war 'till they had burnt Philadelphia."[42]

British reinforcements arrived from the east, creating a standoff by late autumn. Pontiac fought sporadically for another two years, while British sol-

diers and American colonists listened apprehensively to rumors that he was
organizing a grand alliance of eighteen Indian nations. But lacking the vital
supplies of powder, shot, and guns, and plagued by a smallpox epidemic that
raced through Indian country, the tribes sued for peace. Without trade goods
available from another European power in North America, they could not
overcome their supply problems.

Londoners first learned about Pontiac's uprising in July 1763. By September, they knew that Amherst's Indian policy had not only failed but had in
fact brought a rain of death down on British garrisons in the North American
interior. Cashiering Amherst was easy—he was replaced by General Thomas
Gage; the difficulty lay in finding a policy to repair the damage with the Indian nations of the *pays d'en haut*. The answer, they hoped, in part was the
Royal Proclamation of 1763, signed by England's young king, George III, on
October 7. Issued as part of an attempt to forge a long-range enlightened Indian policy that would end the incessant border warfare, the proclamation
supported the paramount goal of the Indian nations: protecting their territorial integrity and the political autonomy that came with it. "The several nations or tribes of Indians, with whom we are connected, and who live under
our protection, should not be molested or disturbed in possession of such
parts of our dominions and territories as, not having been ceded to, or purchased by us, are reserved to them." With this unambiguous imperial promise, it followed that "for the present and until our further pleasure be known"
any surveys or land grants beyond the sources of the Appalachian watershed
were forbidden, and all white settlers already beyond the Appalachian divide
were charged to withdraw east of the line.[43]

For Indian peoples, the proclamation was a welcome sign that the hostile
Amherst regime was over. It recognized what William Johnson reported to
London, that "The Six Nations, Western Indians, etc., having never been
conquered, either by the English or French, nor subject to the[ir] laws, consider themselves as a free people." But would the good words on the parchment be observed? And if not, would they be enforced? Time would tell, but
for now Indian leaders were eager to embrace the British shift from military
arrogance to diplomatic protocols grounded in mutual trust. For several
years, William Johnson succeeded in establishing peaceful and profitable relations with the northern Indian nations. One key to this was the restoration
of annual "presents." Listening to Johnson's advice that the best policy was

to "conquer their prejudices by our generosity, [so] they will lay aside their jealousies, and we may rest in security," the English government allocated twenty thousand pounds annually for such presents.[44]

Yet preserving political sovereignty and territorial integrity on paper could not stem the tide of frontier land speculators and farmers. By itself this demographic pressure overcame English efforts to fashion an Indian policy based on respect for land boundaries and political independence. Staggering under an immense debt accumulated in fighting the Seven Years' War, the English government was unwilling to commit resources for maintaining adequate garrisons in the interior to enforce the Proclamation Act. After Pontiac's revolt subsided, the British abandoned most of their interior garrisons and scrapped their plan to coordinate and control the Indian trade and Indian affairs that had been conducted by individual colonies. The line on the map remained, but it was little more than that, simply a thin line on a piece of parchment. Neither colonists nor Indians took it seriously. But for Indian nations of the interior, it seemed at the least that the English king across the Atlantic had repudiated the policies of Amherst and that the new superintendents of Indian affairs—William Johnson in the North and John Stuart in the South—were reasonable men trying to find ways to allow backcountry settlers and native peoples to coexist.

Insurgent Farmers

Budding revolutionary leaders, many of them speculating in lands in the forbidden country west of the Proclamation Line, had to worry about poor backwoods poachers squatting on land they hoped to soon gain title to and control. But they had a more immediate concern: backcountry men and tenant farmers staging minirevolutions in the midst of the Stamp Act turmoil. At stake were liberty, equality, justice, and power. The insurgent farmers, however, were not protesting *British* injustice or tyranny. They were protesting against injustice, inequality, and tyranny exercised by fellow colonists, in some cases the very Sons of Liberty in eastern cities who were acting on behalf of the rights of Englishmen. The dynamics involved in these agrarian revolts prefigured the most radical tactics to be employed by those who would pursue revolutionary reforms: civil disobedience, paramilitary action, defiance of established authority, and insistence that human rights in some cases were superior to property rights. They could not know it at the time, but the small farmers would soon be called upon to support the war against England, and their decisions would be affected by their experiences in the immediate years before the conflict broke out. They would also have in hand, smithied out on the anvil of their pre-revolutionary experience, notions of the kind of society they wanted to create. When it came time to construct new laws to live under and write new state constitutions to govern their lives, their traumatic experiences in the mid-1760s were still fresh in their minds.

In North Carolina and New York, the difficulties of the 1760s, just as in New Jersey during the previous decade, were rooted in land. From the beginning, access to cheap and fertile land had attracted Europeans to North America. Like a great cosmic magnet, land had attracted about 90,000 immigrants from the Rhineland and some 120,000 Scots-Irish into the British colonies in the eighteenth century. Many of them were not disappointed; otherwise, they would not have kept coming. Indeed, the broad ownership of land distinguished farming society from every other agricultural region of the Western world.

Yet a rising population pressed against a limited land supply. Family farms could not be divided and subdivided indefinitely, so by the 1730s farm owners were struggling to provide an inheritance for three or four sons. Decreasing soil fertility compounded the problem of dwindling farm size. When land had been plentiful, farmers planted crops in the same field for three years and then let it lie fallow seven years or more until it regained its strength. But by the eighteenth century, farmers were reducing fallow to only a year or two. Jared Eliot, New England's first agricultural essayist, referred to such intense use of the soil as "our old land which we have worn out." Younger sons drifted to New York, New Jersey, and Pennsylvania; others sought opportunities as artisans in the coastal towns or took to the sea; others migrated to western Massachusetts, New Hampshire, Maine, and Nova Scotia.

Farther south, where sustained population growth along the Atlantic seaboard also spurred heavy migration to the interior, seething discontent emerged by the time the Stamp Act had produced violent seaboard resistance. In three western North Carolina counties, small farmers erupted in 1765. They agreed with some of their superiors that England was unjust, unmindful of American rights, and callously oppressive in passing the Stamp Act. But the backcountry farmers believed that those same charges applied to corrupt and exploitative fellow colonists in their midst who controlled the courts, credit networks, and distribution of land.

73

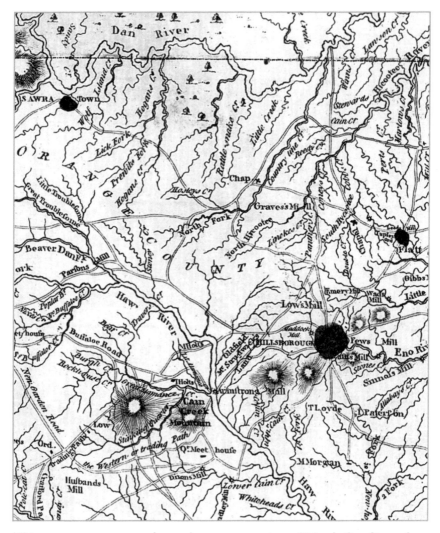

This contemporary map shows the western region of North Carolina where the Regulators rose to defend their rights. The "Buffaloe Road" and "Western or trading Path" show ancient routes traveled by Cherokee and other Indian people. The names given to streams—Wolf, Bear, Buffalo, and Beaver—show how close the farmers lived to nature. Note "Great Troublesome" and "Little Troublesome" rivers at left.

In North Carolina's Granville, Anson, and Mecklenburg counties, hard-scrabble settlers in the Sugar Creek area resisted attempts to eject them after they refused to pay heavy rents to a syndicate of speculators that controlled over one million acres of land. George Sims, a farmer and schoolteacher, distilled the complaints of Granville County farmers in "An Address to the People of Granville County," where he attacked the "damned lawyers who practiced numberless . . . devilish devices to rob you of your livings in a manner diametrically opposite to the policy of our State and the intention of our legislature."[45] A year later, the behavior of extortionate local officials brought Orange County farmers to the boiling point. The farmers hated the county court officials appointed by the governor and a legislature dominated by eastern planter interests. Sheriffs and justices, allied with land speculators and lawyers, seized property when farmers—in a cash-starved economy—could not pay their taxes or debts to local merchants. Seeing their farm tools, animals, and land sold at public auction, often at a fraction of their worth, the farmers petitioned the colony's governor and legislature for lower taxes, paper currency, and lower court fees. When they found no relief, they went outside the law.

Leading them outside the law was a man with unswerving principles, a gift for language, and a family background suggesting anything but a career as a radical reformer. Herman Husband was gentry-born in Cecil County, Maryland. Prosperous, Anglican, and slave-owning, his family could have provided him, as the eldest of twelve children, with a substantial inheritance. But reaching adolescence at just the time when the English evangelist George Whitefield preached in Cecil County, Husband had religious visions and a profound conversion experience that carried him away from the Anglican Church to a New Light Presbyterian Church and finally to the Society of Friends, which he found resembled the apostolic, ancient Christian church that he yearned for. Determined to "take up the Cross" and intensely committed to playing a part on the spiritual battleground he saw around him, Husband, by his early twenties, had enlisted in a Bible-based millennial army to prepare the world for Christ's return.

In the late 1750s, by now married and providing for several children, Husband moved to North Carolina's backcountry. Part of the stream of farmers seeking cheap land, he soon encountered corrupt local officials who controlled property titles. He also found the institution of slavery creeping into what he imagined might be "a new beginning for landless whites to acquire property and build a society based upon small freeholders devoid of a tax supported clergy or slavery."[46] Nonetheless, Husband acquired considerable property in the Granville district. By the time of the Stamp Act crisis, Husband had become the voice of the growing backcountry population of small farmers.

Refusing to pay county and provincial taxes; grating at parish taxes to support the Anglican Church, which they abhorred; forcibly repossessing land taken from them to satisfy debts; and closing the courts to halt judgments against them, the farmers banded together in what they called the Sandy Creek Association. Many of them were Quakers, others Presbyterians, and some Baptists; but all were opposed to the Anglican elite. As their chief spokesman, Husband entered politics for the first time. He preached a doctrine of social justice and the duty of Christians to obtain it. In *An Impartial Relation of the First Rise and Cause of the Recent Differences in Publick Affairs* (1770), Husband asked how the elite could justify the "Conduct of any Government" that had promoted "so many thousands of poor families to bestow their all, and the labour of many years, to improve a piece of waste land, with full expectation of a title," only to refuse the farmers "protection from being robbed of it all by a few roguish individuals, who never bestowed a farthing thereon?" They called themselves Regulators, a term borrowed from England, where it had been used for generations to describe those who reformed "publick grievances and abuses of power."[47]

In challenging and defying men with economic, political, and legal leverage, the Regulators found courage and resilience in the gospel of religious radicalism. Among the people pouring into the backcountry of North Carolina in the middle third of the eighteenth century were Baptists, Quakers, Moravians, and Presbyterians. Like Herman Husband, most of them had been touched by the Great Awakening of the 1740s and 1750s. The Awakeners' message—that if a new wellspring of religious authority was needed, that source was the individual—made a powerful claim on the minds of backcountry farmers. So, too, they came to believe that if they could become the instruments of their own salvation, they might also find ways to neutralize the power of those who trampled on them.

Such ideas spread rapidly through the backcountry of North Carolina in the 1760s. The "New Lights or the Gifted Brethren [who] pretend to inspiration," snorted the crusty Anglican minister Charles Woodmason, "now infest the whole Back Country." Such pretensions of unlicensed and self-educated people were all the more alarming because the "gifted brethren" actually included the gifted sisterhood. Since the founding of the Society of Friends in mid-seventeenth-century England, Quaker women had taken roles denied females in other religious groups. They ran separate women's meetings, played a major role in disciplining wayward Friends, and found their voice as female "Publishers of the Truth," as Quakers called their itinerant early preachers. Now, awakened women in North Carolina's backcountry, particularly among the Separate Baptists, discovered their spiritual gifts and exercised them as exhorters, prophesiers, and leaders of public prayers. Woodmason mocked "a notable She Saint" with supposed "extraordinary illuminations, visions, and communications." Naturally, such subversion of the social order often brought attempts to muzzle such assertive, empowered women. Eunice Williams, who exhorted widely in the 1760s, when charged with taking it "upon herself to exhort and preach Baptist doctrines; was ordered to desist, but not obeying, was (although pregnant at the time), thrown into jail."[48]

The religious radicalism of the Awakened not only dissolved deference to religious and political authority but led to the belief that it was the *duty* of God-fearing people to oppose corrupt governors and their henchmen. Followers of the radical Protestant sects of England's mid-seventeenth-century civil war, the backcountry "enthusiasts," as their detractors called them, used religious commitment as a springboard for political insurgency. Woodmason made the religious-political connection explicit. Speaking in 1767 of the backcountry of both South Carolina and North Carolina, he scorched the Baptist, Presbyterian, "Independent," and Quaker preachers with "Instilling democratical and common wealth principles" into the farmers' minds, "embittering them" against the Anglican Church and "all Episcopal government" and "laying deep their fatal republican notions and principles, especially that they owe no subjection to Great Britain—that they are a free people."[49]

By 1768, the Regulator movement was gathering momentum, almost entirely oblivious to the growing storm between the English government and its American subjects that followed the Stamp Act crisis. Interlocking bread-and-butter issues provided the fuel for the growing conflagration: heavy taxes, assessed regressively, with those best able to pay transferring the burden to those beneath them; the contraction of the supply of paper money; and the corruption of sheriffs who collected taxes and then pocketed much of the funds. Adding to the backcountry farmers' outrage was legislative appropriation of a stupendous £15,000 to build a palace for Governor William Tryon. In the poorest colony in eastern North America, the money was to be raised by the regressive poll tax, where the richest land and slave owners parted with exactly the same amount as the poorest taxpayers. Under attack by small farmers, who overpowered them to repossess livestock and household goods taken as payment for taxes and debts, sheriffs and other local officials convinced the governor to take action to suppress the Regulators. If he did not defang these "traitorous dogs," they would "become sovereign arbiters of right and wrong."[50]

Governor Tryon moved to kennel the "traitorous dogs" by proclaiming "an absolute insurrection of a dangerous tendency . . . in Orange County" and demanding that "riotous and disorderly persons" end "outrages in open violation of the laws of their country." He called out the militia in adjoining counties to restore order, but most militiamen would not respond. After sheriffs arrested Herman Husband and another leader, seven hundred armed Regulators assembled at Hillsborough, west of present-day Durham, and demanded their release. Frightened officers complied. They knew, as the governor did, that "the people are now in every part and corner of the country, meeting, conspiring, and confederating by solemn oath and open violence."[51]

For months, the two sides tried to resolve the issues. At the same time, people in other colonies were embroiled in the Townshend Acts of 1767, which imposed new taxes on the colonists. Governor Tryon threatened the Regulators with charges of treason if they did not admit their "illegal and unwarrantable conduct." But the Regulators refused to comply and repeated their litany of complaints, written by Husband, that boiled down to "the unequal chances the poor and the weak have in contention with the rich and powerful." Through the tense summer of 1768, charges and countercharges flew back and forth. In September, Governor Tryon called out militia units, and word circulated that the governor intended to "try, hang, and condemn all those who bear the title of regulators." That brought a defiant response. The Regulators vowed that, if nothing would "propitiate" the governor "but our blood," they were prepared "to fall like men, and sell our lives at the very dearest rate."[52]

Bloodshed was averted, for the moment, when the governor agreed to accept the Regulators' petition and consider their grievances. "The whole multitude, as with one voice," recounted Husband two years later, "cried out 'agreed.' That is all we want; liberty to make our grievances known."[53] As we will see in chapter 3, the Regulators' grievances went unanswered and the next encounter would not be bloodless. In the meantime, the Regulators, though told to disband and forbidden to use the toxic term by which they called themselves to emphasize their rightful actions, worked to democratize local government and replace corrupt and parasitic officials with farmers like themselves.

Rural insurgency in New York in the mid-1760s was even more intense than in North Carolina. As in the South, militant rhetoric and radical tactics used by small farmers to combat exploitation formed rivulets that fed the mainstream of revolutionary consciousness. The conditions under which land was held in New York caused resentment, then protests, and finally violence and defiance of the law. In this minirevolution, two men who have almost entirely faded from historical memory took leading roles. One was a ship carpenter turned farmer named William Prendergast; the other was Daniel Nimham, grand sachem of the Wappinger tribe. Both were in their midthirties in 1765 when New York erupted with internal disputes.

The Hudson River valley had long been controlled by a few wealthy families with enormous landholdings, which were so large that they rivaled the manors of English nobility. Rensselaerswyck Manor totaled 1 million acres, Philipse Manor 200,000 acres, and Beekman Manor a mere 100,000 acres. By 1710 every acre of some eight hundred square miles of Dutchess County had been patented to a handful of absentee landlords for token amounts of money. Most of these vast tracts were acquired as virtually free gifts from royal governors, and some were obtained by outright fraud. Henry Beekman, for example, had obtained his vast patent in the 1690s from Governor Benjamin Fletcher for £25. The Philipse patent, covering all of southern Dutchess County, was fraudulently obtained because no purchase for it was made from the original owners, the Wappinger Indians.[54]

Manor lords leased land to tenant farmers, who paid annual rents for the right to farm on modest parcels. By the 1760s, about 1,200 tenants farmed on Philipse Manor and nearly as many bowed when their Van Rensselaer landlords rode by. As if living in days of yore, the manor lords tried to exact medieval subservience from tenants, each year obliging them to perform such unpaid services to the manor lord as the corvée—labor to build and maintain the manor roads. More troubling to the farmers, landlords did not allow for eventual land ownership by the tenanted occupants, whom they preferred to think of as peasants. When tenants resisted rent increases or purchased land from Indians, who swore that manor lords had extended the boundaries of their estates by fraud, the landlords began evicting them. Rarely were the tenants favored if a dispute reached the local courts.

The landlords dominated local government, including, most importantly, control of the courts. Dutchess County was virtually the political fiefdom of Henry Beekman, Jr., son of the original patentee to the southern part of the county. Livingstons, Philipses, Van Rensselaers, and Van Cortlandts were likewise local oligarchs and by the mid-eighteenth century had a powerful grip on the colony's legislature. Facing such odds, the grievances of tenants against their landlords had only one realistic channel—going outside the law. Even then, the chances were slim.

Tenant uprisings occurred in both the northern and southern sectors of the Hudson River valley. By the 1750s, the land east of the upper Hudson River was ablaze with disputes. Drifting down from New England, thousands of farmers claimed they had freehold title to land granted by Massachusetts and Connecticut in a zone where the boundaries were murky. The fact that New York and the New England colonies had never fixed the boundary between them created a cornucopia of suits for lawyers, but these were suits that defied easy resolution. An uprising of tenants in 1755 on the Livingston and Van Rensselaer manors, at the beginning of the Seven Years' War, ushered in a quarter century of havoc in the Hudson River region. Not all landlords were imperious and heartless, but those who were learned how intensely they were hated. In 1755, Joseph Paine, a longtime tenant, girdled and felled about 1,200 trees on Livingston Manor and told Robert Livingston's servants dispatched to confront him "that the trees were his and he would go and destroy the timber as he pleased and Robert Livingston [could] kiss his a__s."[55]

This outbreak played out quickly in the face of the superior power held by the "patroons," as contemporaries called them. But this was a lull in what would turn out to be a full-scale storm. The farmers who squatted on land claimed by the Philipses, Livingstons, and Van Rensselaers had the cooperation of Stockbridge and Mahican Indians, who hoped to reclaim the land they believed they had been cheated out of because it had never been purchased from them by the great manor lords of the seventeenth century. Sometimes backed up by the Massachusetts government, which had disputed New York's claims to parts of the upper Hudson River region since the 1730s, Stockbridge and Mahicans made common cause with the antimanorial settlers.

By the time the Stamp Act riots were erupting in the seaboard towns, events leading to what became known as the Great Rebellion of 1766 were under way. The precipitating cause was the determination of Beverly Robinson, a stiff-necked British army officer who had married the daughter of Philip Philipse, to extinguish long-term leases to tenants who had tilled the land for as much as thirty years and replace them with tenants who were given new short-term leases. While the lower Hudson River tenants did not have the support of Massachusetts, which had sparred for years with New York's great landowners in a complex boundary dispute, they had another unusual ally—the Wappinger Indian sachem Daniel Nimham.

Nimham's ancestors were the original owners of a vast territory on the east side of the Hudson River from New York City to north of what is Poughkeepsie today. Over decades of Dutch and English rule, the Wappingers had been devastated by disease and warfare. Once a proud people, they now numbered only a few hundred and had been reduced to an "idle strolling life." Yet they claimed they had never relinquished their ancestral lands to either the English or the Dutch, and certainly not to Adolph Philipse, the original Philipse Highland Patent proprietor. The Wappingers now lived in Stockbridge, Massachusetts, with several other remnants of Indian tribes that had been Christianized over the years. Chief Nimham had taken heart in 1762, when New York's governor, Cadwallader Colden, had promised redress for the unresolved Indian claims in New York. In August 1764, Nimham, working with lawyer Samuel Monrow, issued an announcement that his people were the "Rightful owner" of the vast Philipse Highland Patent, except for five thousand acres, and urged all Philipse tenants to obtain legal conveyances from him, which would specify a token rent. Many tenants gladly accepted this offer, taking out leases from Nimham "for 999 years upon very reasonable terms," such as two peppercorns per year.[56] Nimham urged tenants not to pay rent to Robinson and Philipse while obtaining their conveyances from his tribe.

Predictably, the Philipse manor lords' response was "legal retribution," as Sung Bok Kim, a careful historian of this tangled chapter in the life of New York, describes it.[57] At the end of 1764 the Philipses went to court to obtain ejectment orders against fifteen tenants who had signed Indian leases.

Monrow had arranged with Daniel Nimham that the Wappinger chief would stand trial for all the defendants, a rare case when a colonial court accepted the testimony of a Native American.

Sitting as the high court of chancery, the New York Council heard the case in 1765. To no one's surprise the court was packed with manor lords. Before the bewigged members of the governor's council, the thirty-eight-year-old Nimham testified that Adolph Philipse, the original manor lord, had never purchased title to the 205,000 acres of land he claimed. Furthermore, Philipse's descendants had taken possession of these lands while Wappinger warriors were spilling their blood for New Yorkers and the English king, fighting with British forces in the Seven Years' War. This made no impression on the landlord-jurists, who pronounced Nimham and his legal adviser wrong and indeed guilty of high misdemeanors. They promptly arrested and jailed Monrow in New York City, where he would remain behind bars for two years. Fortified with writs of possession, the jubilant Philipses evicted tenants with Indian leases without compensation for the improvements they had made on their farms. Still determined, Nimham began arranging a voyage to England to present his case before the Crown.

Other manor lords in the lower Hudson River region were beset by tenants and squatters who cared not at all that their exploitative masters were battling British bureaucrats in the heat of the Stamp Act crisis. For example, John Van Cortlandt's tenants in Westchester County had no regard for his leadership as one of New York's Sons of Liberty when they threatened to descend on New York City and pull down his house there. The liberty he was defending in his protests against the Stamp Act made him no less an enemy in his eviction of tenants and squatters.

History is full of situations in which terrible odds cannot deter ordinary people with deep-rooted grievances from taking up arms to fight a battle that in retrospect seems almost suicidal. This, in fact, is how most revolutions have begun. Such a moment now occurred just outside New York City in May 1766, while the metropolis was absorbed in the final stages of the Stamp Act furor. In the face of eviction from their farms and the incarceration of Samuel Monrow, who had provided Daniel Nimham with legal advice, Hudson River tenants and squatters organized to obtain what they thought was simple justice. Banding together, they vowed not to pay the spring rents due on the small farms where they had invested their labor. For landlords, it was a simple matter to go to court and obtain a writ ordering sheriffs to evict delinquent tenants or those who signed Indian leases. But encouraged by the Stamp Act riots in New York City, which gave the farmers, by one account, the notion that "every thing which had the appearance of resisting government might be undertaken with impunity,"[58] the tenants began to offer stiffer resistance to the landlords. They soon formed their own militia bands; elected their own officers; formed popular courts to try enemies they captured; threatened landlords with death; restored evicted tenants by driving off new farmers installed by the manor lords; and broke open jails to rescue friends. In effect, they formed a countergovernment. From the great landlords' point of view, and from the viewpoint of the British government as well, this was treason.

The man whom several thousand Dutchess County tenants urged to take the lead against manorialism was William Prendergast, an Irish immigrant from County Kilkenny. In the early 1750s, he became a tenant farmer on the estate of Frederick Philipse, and here he labored to improve the land. Here was the kind of person who emerged from obscurity in the revolutionary years. In the crucible of exploitation, ideas began to crystallize that Prendergast had probably thought about only fleetingly in the past. In 1755, at age twenty-eight, Prendergast married seventeen-year-old Mehitabel Wing, a Quaker woman who would bear thirteen children before the end of the American Revolution.

Prendergast was respected in Dutchess County and was later described as "always a saving, industrious man." But he was also a man of determination and courage. When the manager of Philipse Manor demanded in 1765 that tenant farmers surrender their long-term leases for new one- to three-year leases, Prendergast stepped forward to lead angry tenants against this attack on their livelihoods. Vowing to "relieve the oppressed," Prendergast led land rioters on a rampage to reclaim the farms on the Philipse and Van Cortlandt Manors from which they had been evicted.[59]

New York's attorney general, John Tabor Kempe, responded by issuing a bench warrant for the arrest of the tenant rioters, and the Westchester County sheriff nabbed three of them and hustled them to jail in New York City, where they would be beyond the reach of Prendergast and other potential jail breakers. But this brought an even greater number of insurgent farmers to a meeting called by Prendergast. Agreeing unanimously that they should march on the city "to do justice and relieve the oppressed"—and perhaps pull down the houses of John Van Cortlandt and Kempe as well—some three hundred armed farmers headed for King's Bridge, which connected Westchester County with Manhattan, on April 29, 1766. Warned that he was defying the authority of the English king, represented in New York by its royal governor, Prendergast retorted that "Mobs had overcome Kings before and why should they not overcome now?"[60]

With Prendergast leading, the men were joined at the bridge by several hundred Westchester farmers. There, Prendergast made a spirited speech in which he anticipated that urban workingmen, who had been so active in the Stamp Act riots in New York, would join them. A man of direct, earthy language, like many farmers, he spoke of how, together, the rural and urban radicals would take any person who "offended us . . . to the first convenient place of mud and water, and there duck them as long as we think proper, from whence we should take them to a white oak tree and there whip them as long as we think proper, and thence take them out of the county and there kick their arses as long as we think fit."[61] The farmers had no difficulty wresting meaning out of these words and cheered their leader.

In a classic case of divided laboring people, a problem that would hobble radical movements for many generations, New York's plebeian ranks failed Prendergast's hopes. Perhaps the artisans, mariners, and laborers he counted on were alarmed by the rumor that the tenant farmers would "set the city on fire in several different places at the same time." Perhaps they were overflowing with excitement over the news, which had arrived just five days before, that Parliament had repealed the Stamp Act. At least as important was the fact that some of the oppressive Hudson River landlords had city mansions and had themselves become active leaders of the Sons of Liberty. Included were the tenants' nemeses John Van Cortlandt and Peter R. Livingston. The "Sons of Liberty [are] great opposers to these rioters," noted Captain John Montresor, the commander of the British regiment quartered in the city. "They are of opinion that no one is entitled to riot but themselves."[62] But most important, the possibility of a rural-urban radical nexus was countered by Governor Henry Moore's order for the city's militia and regular troops to attack the farmers, who were armed mostly with pitchforks, barrel staves, and clubs. Faced down by the governor, and failing to get support of the city's laboring men, Prendergast's legion retreated from the city.

Governor Moore ordered the arrest of Prendergast and other tenant leaders on the spot, but sent a city alderman to arrest them. That the city official gave Prendergast a chance to make his escape suggests the sympathy of many New Yorkers for the small farmer rebels. Within days of the insurgents' retreat Governor Moore issued a proclamation offering a £100 reward "for the taking of Prendergast, Chief of the Country Levellers" and £50 for the capture of each of his two secondary leaders. Prendergast eluded the sheriffs, rejected his wife's pleas to surrender, and vowed to "make daylight show thro'" anyone who attempted to seize him.[63] But in July 1766, a British regiment dispatched to Poughkeepsie finally snared Prendergast. Hauled off to the Dutchess County Courthouse, Prendergast found himself charged with high treason.

On August 6, 1766, a special Court of Oyer and Terminer, filled with landlords, tried him under heavy guard in New York City. Witnesses testified that Prendergast had accepted the leadership role because "it was hard," in his own words, that poor people "were not allowed to have *any property*" and were driven from the land where the sweat of their brows had made the land flourish. "There was no law for poor men," Prendergast testified. In such a skewed legal system, going outside the law was justifiable. Moss Kent, a small farmer (and a witness picked by the great landlords) confirmed that evicted tenants believed they were entitled to defy the law because, though they "had an equitable title," they "could not be defended in a court of law because they were poor and . . . poor men were always oppressed by the rich."[64]

The strong-willed Prendergast had public sentiment on his side, because the Hudson River grandees were hardly popular heroes. A New York newspaper called Prendergast a "sober, honest, and industrious farmer much beloved by his neighbors."[65] But the Irish immigrant had little else going for him. Refusing counsel, he defended himself, with his wife taking the stand to offer extenuating points. In this mismatch, Prendergast lost decisively.

When Robert R. Livingston, chief justice of the court, read out Prendergast's sentence, the entire colony learned how greatly the land war had frightened the rich and powerful. Prendergast "shall be hanged by the neck," intoned Judge Livingston, "and then shall be cut down alive, and his entrails and privy members shall be cut from his body, and shall be burned in his sight, and his head shall be cut off, and his body shall be divided into four parts and shall be disposed of at the King's pleasure."[66] In the colonies, this kind of barbarous punishment was usually reserved for slaves found guilty of murdering their masters or mistresses. As in such slave cases, the point was to terrify miscreants from the bottom of society.

After the court pronounced Prendergast guilty and specified the punishment, his wife rode for seventy miles on horseback to New York to urge the governor to reprieve her husband, but to no avail. Yet if the judges were going to carry out the grisly sentence, they would have to do it themselves. With the execution scheduled for September 26, 1766, the sheriff advertised for assistance in executing Prendergast in the way that was prescribed. Though offering "a good reward" to any takers and promising to disguise them "so as not to be known,"[67] nobody stepped forward. Aware of the widespread sympathy for Prendergast, Governor Henry Moore reprieved him pending the king's approval.

In the northern Hudson River valley, antilandlordism followed a similar course in 1765–66. Robert Noble, a tenant on the Rensselaerswyck Manor, tried again to assert the right to the land that many small farmers had improved. Noble had been a leader in the insurgencies of the 1750s, but this time his followers were more numerous and their determination steelier. The great landed magnates who now became the targets of their tenants' anger were among those same men who protested the Stamp Act and had begun to think about royal tyranny.

The rioters in the upper Hudson River valley attacked those who were loyal to men like Robert Livingston, Jr., but Livingston himself was their main target. In June 1766, they marched on Livingston's manor house, threatening to demolish it and kill him. This led to a bloody confrontation, where a posse organized by Livingston and John Van Rensselaer faced off against Noble's followers. The blood of many men stained the soil, and four did not survive the confrontation.

Trying to cope with this kind of defiance, New York's governor Henry Moore convinced General Thomas Gage, commander in chief of some eight thousand British troops in North America, to dispatch a regiment in the summer of 1766 to break the tenant rebellion. The regiment suffered three casualties in rounding up sixty "miserable, harden'd Wretches" on the Philipse Manor, and their pillaging and burning of the tenants' small houses soon brought about the surrender of about sixty additional insurgents. But on the Livingston Manor, near the Massachusetts border, a British regiment spent two summer months chasing armed tenants who "advance and retire at pleasure," as a British captain put it.[68] The British regulars, about 250 strong, finally routed the rioters, stealing their livestock, carrying off their possessions, and driving several hundred families into the woods for refuge.

Although a royal pardon eventually rescued the hero of the insurgent tenantry, William Prendergast, from the gallows, the bitterness of the Great Rebellion of 1766 endured through subsequent years. Nobody involved in the tenant wars of the 1760s forgot the experience. As we will see in chapter 5, those who fought for the British and those who fought for the Americans carried their local interests, grudges, and unfulfilled yearnings into the Revolution.

3

BUILDING MOMENTUM

1766–1774

IN MARCH 1766, THE FURIOUS AMERICAN REACTION TO THE STAMP
Act convinced Parliament to repeal it. When word reached the colonies in
May, bonfires, bell ringing, drum beating, house illuminations, cannon firing,
and exultant celebrations erupted in nearly every village and town. Some
members of Parliament warned that to retreat before colonial defiance of the
law was akin to coddling wayward children and would ultimately be fatal.
But Parliament bowed to expediency in the Declaratory Act while reminding
the colonists that it still reserved the power to enact laws for the colonies in
"all cases whatsoever."

Although the crisis passed, nothing was solved. Many Americans could
not suppress the notion that a greedy mother country had trampled on her
subjects' rights and would continue to do so. The Stamp Act, one New England clergyman foresaw, "diffused a disgust through the colonies and laid
the basis of an alienation which will never be healed." However, another dif-
fusion had taken place. Scribbled John Adams in his diary: "The people have
become more attentive to their liberties . . . and more determined to defend
them. . . . Our presses have groaned, our pulpits have thundered, our legislatures have resolved, our towns have voted; the crown officers have everywhere trembled, and all their little tools and creatures have been afraid to

speak and ashamed to be seen."[1] The "people" that Adams referred to were not only those accustomed to wielding political power in the colonies but the people at large. Some established leaders, generally cautious in their protests, had been displaced by those lower down on the social ladder. The political consciousness of common citizens rose immensely because they had seen that it was their own mass demonstrations and street violence that had humbled stamp distributors and forced the courts and seaports to operate without the hated, but Parliament-mandated, stamps.

After the repeal of the Stamp Act, ministerial instability in England hampered George III's quest for a coherent, workable American policy. But his ministers tried. In 1767, Parliament approved new laws to enforce customs duties, installing three new vice admiralty courts that did not use juries to try accused colonial smugglers. Still pressed for revenue, Parliament also passed the Townshend duties on paper, lead, painters' colors, and tea imported by the colonists. A final law suspended New York's legislature until it ceased defying the Quartering Act of 1765, which required public funds for support of British troops garrisoned in that colony.

New York knuckled under, but the Townshend duties touched off a new barrage of protests. Massachusetts again led the way. "The Americans have made a discovery," declared Edmund Burke before Parliament in 1767, "that we mean to oppress them; we have made a discovery that they intend to raise a rebellion against us. We know not how to advance; they know not how to retreat." But the British did advance. On October 1, 1768, four regiments of red-coated troops disembarked from their ships and marched into Boston to "dragoon us into passive obedience," as the *Boston Gazette* cried out.[2] Using troops to restore order and compel obedience failed, nor did the Townshend duties accomplish their goal of raising revenue. By 1770, they brought about £21,000 into the royal coffers while at the same time costing British merchants and suppliers about £700,000 because of the colonial nonimportation movement that we will examine later in this chapter.

The game of punch and counterpunch continued through the early years of the 1770s. The final plunge into revolution began when Parliament passed the Tea Act in early 1773. According to this act, the practically bankrupt East India Company was allowed to ship tea directly to North America, eliminating English and American middlemen and reducing import taxes. Americans could now purchase tea cheaper from the company's agents in the colonies, but they were enraged rather than grateful. American merchants had been smuggling Dutch tea into the colonies for several years and now saw a conspiracy to eliminate them as middlemen—tightening a noose around their necks. The movement to stop the tea at the water's edge climaxed when, on December 16, 1773, several hundred Bostonians wearing face paint and Indian headdresses—most of them young apprentices and artisans-in-training—threw £10,000 worth of the East India Company's property to the bottom of the harbor. This cast the die. Thoroughly disgusted with the colonists, Parliament passed the Coercive Acts, stern laws that Bostonians promptly labeled the "Intolerable Acts." The acts closed the port of Boston to all shipping until the colony paid for the destroyed tea and barred local courts from trying British soldiers and officials for acts committed while suppressing civil disturbances. Parliament also prohibited the colony's truculent town meetings, except one each year to elect local officials.

This attempt to strangle Massachusetts into submission (while hoping for acquiescence elsewhere in the colonies) proved popular in England, where sympathy for the American argument about abridged rights had all but evaporated. After a decade of debating constitutional rights and mobilizing sentiment against what many believed was a systematic plot to enslave colonists, who regarded themselves freeborn English citizens, the Americans found their maneuvering room severely narrowed. Again, Massachusetts led the way. Calling for each colony to send delegates to Philadelphia, Massachusetts tried to transform a ten-year debate conducted by separate colonies into a unified American cause. The Continental Congress met for the first time on September 5, 1774, with fifty-five delegates representing all the colonies except Georgia.

After weeks of debate, the congress resisted outright defiance of the Coercive Acts and settled for a restrained Declaration of Rights and Resolves, which defined American grievances and justified resistance to English policies and laws by appealing to the "immutable laws of nature, the principles of the English constitutions, and the several [colonial] charters and compacts" under which they lived. More strenuous was Congress's agreement to form an association throughout the colonies banning all imports and exports between the colonists and the English if they did not rescind the Intolerable Acts by December 1. Boston's cause had now become a national movement. Always dramatic, Patrick Henry was premature in arguing that "All government is dissolved [and] we are in a state of nature." But he was close to the truth in saying, "The distinctions between Virginians, Pennsylvanians, New

Yorkers, and New Englanders are no more. I am not a Virginian but an American."[3] Not all were ready to go that far, but they agreed to meet again in May 1775.

This brief treatment of the road to revolution from 1766 to 1774 takes note only of the highlights of what was a complex and diverse set of dramas played out in a thousand communities from Georgia to Maine. But learning more about the complicated thickening of the argument with Great Britain—a story told in countless histories—would tell us little about the more personal and local matters on the minds of thousands of people in eastern North America. It was not that the imperial argument was irrelevant to these people; but here, the focus is on how the tussle with the mother country sharpened their consciousness about issues of equitable relations in their *own* churches, communities, counties, colonies, and regions. The headline events—chronicled in newspapers, sermons, and pamphlets—engaged particular groups of people in ways that allowed them to carry forward radical ideas as a part of the revolution now brewing.

"The Rising Spirit of the People"

The years between 1766 and 1774 were ones of intense debate and confrontation at every level of society. Thousands of well-meaning people on both sides of the Atlantic were engaged in the yeasty business of defining sound political principles, finding stable constitutional ground upon which to stand, and hammering out ideological positions that made sense within their communities. Only in a time of crisis does such hard thinking usually occur. Complicating matters, the crucial decade after 1765 produced violent economic fluctuations and difficult circumstances for people of all ranks. These difficulties cannot be sensibly separated from the course of politics and political thinking, for all politics takes place within social and economic contexts.

By 1766, most sectors of the colonies had recovered from the depression that followed the end of the Seven Years' War, but nettlesome problems remained. The growing domination of colonial wheels of commerce by English decision makers and English capital was of especial concern. The colonial economy had always been the servant of the metropolitan master; that was what it meant to be a colony, to be "underdeveloped," to be a producer and exporter of foodstuffs and raw products and an importer and consumer of finished goods. But as the colonial economies matured, restrictions on local development began to grate. The Currency Act of 1764, which strictly limited the authority of Pennsylvania and New York to issue paper currency, had a constricting effect because locally issued paper money had provided the circulating medium of local trade. When it was disallowed, internal trade shriveled up, hurting merchants and artisans alike and obliging traders to concoct ingenious schemes for issuing fiat money. The years from 1767 to 1769 were especially difficult in this regard. A number of Boston merchants, including John Hancock's younger brother, closed their doors; and Philadelphians were stunned by the collapse of Baynton, Wharton, and Morgan, one of the city's largest merchant houses that specialized in the Indian trade, with liabilities of £94,000—something akin to the collapse of Enron in 2001.

Even more punishing was the credit crisis of 1772. Touched off by the collapse of a major London banking house, it spread like a summer brushfire. English and Scottish merchants had extended credit liberally to American importers in order to spur the consumption of British goods. American merchants willingly increased their orders and passed their indebtedness on to retailers and consumers as book credit. Accepting credit in order to expand had obvious advantages, but it made borrowers far more vulnerable to cyclical swings in the British credit structure. Responding to a major bankruptcy in 1772, English merchants began to demand payment on colonial debts. When colonial merchants could not meet the demands of their overseas creditors, they declared bankruptcy; or, by calling for retailers to pay off their indebtedness, they forced shopkeepers into bankruptcy. The ripple effect was felt up and down the seaboard colonies. "Daily accounts of heavy failures among the shopkeepers" were reported in Philadelphia in late 1773, and this occurred in other seaport towns as well. The scramble for liquidity hit southern planters and small farmers as well as northern merchants and shopkeepers, for tobacco, rice, and indigo growers had deeply indebted themselves to purchase more slaves and open up more land. When English and Scottish creditors called on them to pay their debts, thousands of southern planters suffered court judgments that took away their "land, Negroes, horses, cows, hogs, and feather beds or old pots or pans," as one Fredericksburg trader explained.[4] The early 1770s thus became a time when punishing economic fluctuations made parliamentary legislation all the more intolerable.

Further down the economic ladder, artisans, farmers, mariners, and unskilled laborers also suffered blows. The sudden contraction of merchants' credit created demands upon artisans to settle accounts. If work had been slow, a laboring man in debt could find himself in court or even in debtor's prison, where his problems quickly compounded because his earning power was then brought to a dead halt. At the very bottom of urban societies, poverty grew alarmingly in the 1760s and 1770s. This did not lead rapidly to the political mobilization of the poor, who had been mostly politically inert before; if some began to stir, the more important effect was on middling men, who viewed the signs of crumbling economic security warily. Urban poverty challenged the governing modes of thought, shook confidence in the internal economic system, and intensified class feeling. "He that gets all he can honestly, and saves all he gets (necessary expenses excepted)," Benjamin Franklin had his Poor Richard say repeatedly, "will certainly become RICH." But city dwellers and many in the small inland towns were learning that this was an illusion. It was hard to ignore the fact that in all the seaboard cities the largest buildings erected after 1765—almshouses, prisons, and cloth factories—were constructed to contain the impoverished, a growing criminal element spawned by poverty, and a noncriminal middle-class group whose only offense against society was its inability to weather the economic storms of the period. This was not the world of their fathers. The main discussion of colonial constitutional rights was thus carried out in urban locales, where nagging poverty at the bottom of society and the crumbling of economic security in the middle gave rise to the most intense concern about the future. This created new tensions in class relations.

Economic difficulties, coupled with the growing crisis with England, produced a growing resentment of wealth, challenges to the elite's conception of the proper conduct of politics, and the gradual hammering-out of artisan and laboring-class interests. This happened especially in the seaport commercial centers, though the smaller inland towns experienced these waves of sentiment as well. As this chapter explains, it was the new vigor of urban laboring people in defining and pursuing their goals that raised the specter, in the minds of many upper-class townsmen, of a radicalized form of politics and a radically changed society. Many of these nabobs later abandoned the resistance movements that they had initially supported and led. They blanched at reading in the newspapers—in this case in New York City—challenges of this sort: "Is it equitable that 99, rather 999, should suffer for the Extravagance or Grandeur of one, especially when it is considered that men frequently owe their wealth to the impoverishment of their neighbours?"

Another New Yorker fumed in 1767 at the rich, who grew mighty by "a pernicious trade at the expence and ruin" of the people at large. "As a Proof of it," he explained, "we have only to look around us to see some rolling triumphantly in their coaches on the profits gotten by a foreign trade . . . [while] the bodies of those who have none crowd our prisons, which of late years have been obliged to be enlarged, whilst the din and noise of prosecutions even tire our Courts of Justice."[5] Such thoughts, gaining ground in the early 1770s, were directed squarely at the upper-class notion that only the idle and profligate could fail in America while only the educated and wealthy were entitled to manage political affairs.

For those in the lower echelons of colonial society, elementary political rights and social justice, rather than the protection of property and constitutional liberties, were the promises of revolution. Many had been deeply infected by evangelical religion, drinking deeply from its egalitarian and communal wells. Their leaders were sometimes drawn from their own ranks, such as shoemakers Ebenezer MacIntosh in Boston and Samuel Simpson in Philadelphia. Sometimes they came from the middle class, such as Philadelphia's doctor Thomas Young, New York ship captains Alexander McDougall and Isaac Sears, and Philadelphia's James Cannon, a teacher. All of these men had risen out of poverty, held egalitarian notions, and still felt a bond with the lowest ranks. Many of them harked back to the Levellers of mid-seventeenth-century England. They found folk heroes in men such as Cornet George Joyce, an obscure tailor in Cromwell's army who leveled a king in 1647 when he captured Charles I, urged his death, and, according to folklore, stood at the executioner's side when the ax fell.

Giving special energy to ordinary men, especially those in the harbor cities, was an idea that had flourished for at least a generation: that laboring men were fully capable of understanding political affairs and not nearly as pliable as their social superiors claimed they were likely to be if given the vote or elected to office. "All candid foreigners who have passed through this country, and conversed freely with all sorts of people here," wrote John Adams, the young country lawyer, "will allow that they have never seen so much knowledge and civility among the common people in any part of the world." Adams attributed this political sophistication to New England's public schools, the high rate of literacy, and freedom of speech and press. He took great pride in this, believing that his Puritan forebears had rescued the mass of people from the kind of bottomless ignorance to be found in absolute monar-

Boston portrait artist Joseph Cole did this oil portrait of Hewes in 1835 and titled it The Centenarian *(which, if not entirely accurate, was close to Hewes's age).*

chies, where the people "were little higher . . . in the scale of intelligence than the camels and asses and elephants." "The education of all ranks of people was made the care and expense of the public," and the wisdom of this had manifested itself in "an hereditary ardor for liberty." Only a politically in-formed citizenry could keep a people free. "The preservation of the means of knowledge among the lowest ranks, is of more importance to the public, than all the property of all the rich men in the country." Still obscure, Adams in-cluded these remarks in an unsigned series of essays published in the *Boston Gazette* in 1765.[6]

To the south of Massachusetts, public schools were uncommon and the lower ranks of urban society did not have so high a rate of literacy as in New

England. But political awareness and the eagerness to jump into political debate was hardly less pronounced. In New York City in the 1750s, a visiting gentleman described "how common it is to see a shoemaker, tailor, or barber haranguing with a great deal of warmth on the public affairs." Askance at this, he complained that the artisans had only "knowledge from the newspapers." But that in itself was a sign of political maturity. The visitor blinked at how a workingman would "condemn a general, governor, or province with as much assurance as if he were of the [king's] privy council."[7]

Philadelphia's ordinary people exhibited the same thirst for political knowledge and the same yen for political debate. "The poorest laborer upon the shore of the Delaware," declared the Anglican clergyman Jacob Duché, "thinks himself entitled to deliver his sentiments in matters of religion or politics with as much freedom as the gentleman or scholar." Benjamin Franklin had played an important role in creating the model of an informed citizen by establishing the Junto, or the Club of the Leather Aprons, for workingmen in 1727. Meeting weekly, tradesmen would debate political and economic issues such as "Does the importation of [indentured] servants increase or advance the wealth of our country?" or "Have you lately observed any encroachment on the just liberties of the people?" By the 1740s, the Junto was both a political club and a reading society, the two being pleated together. Of the first 375 books the Junto members collected—the foundation of North America's first circulating library—more had come from the pen of John Locke than any other author. Here, then, was a model for the self-empowerment and political engagement of ordinary Philadelphians. "Cringing servility," observed Duché, was not in style and "such is the prevailing taste for books of every kind that almost every man is a reader; and by pronouncing sentence upon the various publications that come in his way, puts himself upon a level, in point of knowledge, with their several authors."[8]

In the view of many conservatives, the informed citizen from the lower echelon of society was acting out of place. John Adams was sure that the Boston clique surrounding Thomas Hutchinson wanted to abandon the public schools "for the education of our youth as a needless expence, and imposition upon the rich in favour of the poor." In fact, the Stamp Act, by Adams's reckoning, was purposely "form'd to strip us in a great measure of the means of knowledge, by loading the press, the colleges, and even an almanack and a news-paper, with restraints and duties."[9] Somewhat paranoid on this point,

Adams was nonetheless right that ordinary people eager to protect their liberties would have to contend with more conservative patriots in the decade after 1765. Those accustomed to political clout now had to protect their advantages against those of the lower orders straining to gain them for themselves.

The case of Boston's Ebenezer MacIntosh is instructive. "Captain-General" MacIntosh, who had led a crowd of two thousand with military precision through Boston's streets in November 1765, disappeared from sight as a crowd leader before another year passed. He lost his small leather sealer's office in 1769, and shortly after the Boston Massacre in 1770 was languishing in debtor's prison, where he had plenty of time to ponder why none of Boston's patriotic leaders stepped forward to provide the modest bail required to release him. Sam Adams emerged as the radical leader, assumed the name of "Populus," and wrote that the people should remain quiet and follow the advice of the *Boston Gazette*, the most influential newspaper among laboring people: "NO MOBS—NO CONFUSIONS—NO TUMULTS."[10] Adams came closer than any man in the colonies to becoming a professional politician. Experienced in caucus politicking, a skilled newspaper polemicist, and a man with deep roots among the artisans despite his Harvard degree, he became the patriots' most effective organizer and coordinator.

During the years of nonimportation from 1768 to 1770, Boston's Whig leaders found two men who proved particularly effective in directing street crowds. William Molineux, later celebrated by Nathaniel Hawthorne in "My Kinsman Molineux," was far from a poor shoemaker like MacIntosh. A merchant, he nonetheless worked well with established artisans and petty entrepreneurs, mainstays of the Sons of Liberty. It was Molineux who led nearly every mass action between 1768 and 1771 to harass the Tory publisher of the *Boston Chronicle*, scourge merchants who refused to abide by nonimportation agreements, or tar and feather customs informers. The other street captain and intermediary between resistance leaders and the laboring classes was Thomas Young, the son of immigrant Irish settlers in Ulster County, New York, who acquired medical skills and emerged as a political leader in his early thirties. Young's iconoclastic religious views and hostility toward men of great wealth and power, expressed earlier in his attacks on grasping landlords and speculators in New York, made him an unlikely lieutenant of the merchant patriots of Boston. But, like Molineux, he led crowds to enforce nonimportation, and played a role in halting the violence that genteel patriots feared when he stood in the streets on the night of the Boston Massacre in March 1770, urging the crowd to return to their homes.

In 1770, the repeal of all the Townshend duties except the one on tea drove a wedge deep into the interclass patriot coalition. Merchants wanted to resume importation while artisans did not. The Tea Act of 1773 widened the rift, with merchants attempting to head off a crisis after the Boston Tea Party by subscribing money to pay for the destroyed tea. The Solemn League and Covenant devised by Boston's Committee of Correspondence, another nonimportation agreement meant to bring about a repeal of the Coercive Acts of 1774, was explicitly beamed at the merchants. "This effectual plan," wrote the committee, "has been originated and been thus carried through by the two venerable orders of men styled Mechanicks and Husbandmen, the strength of every community."[11] Boston's merchants lost this tussle in June 1774 when they turned out en masse at a town meeting, where they intended to censure and abolish the Committee of Correspondence. But it was they who were censured.

Boston's patriot leadership successfully regained control of the streets and town-meeting debates through 1774. No independently organized movement of artisans and laboring men emerged. Still, a new political order was taking form. In 1766, the House of Representatives, pushed by the town of Cambridge, had agreed to erect a public gallery—the first time in any colony where ordinary people could come to see their elected representatives debate and vote on particular issues. Passed because resistance leaders need to broaden their support, they turned the House into a "School of Political Learning," as Thomas Young put it. The political community also expanded because Boston was under particular pressure after the British army occupied the city in 1774. By insisting that Boston must fight as a top-to-bottom community against British oppression and discipline traitorous townsmen who acquiesced to British perversions of constitutional rights, Sam Adams and other leaders courted the laboring people, even if they did not have enough property to vote. "The Body of the People," which included everyone, regardless of age, gender, rank, or voting status, became the operative phrase in making nonconsumption boycotts effective. Anyone involved in ferreting out violators, fastening on them the opprobrium of the community, and coercing them to mend their ways could think of himself or herself as a civic actor. The humblest laborers on Boston's wharves, even adolescents and slaves, became part of the political community when they daubed the houses of importers with "Hillsborough paint," a nasty recipe of body wastes, or pummeled zealous royal stalwarts who searched for smuggled goods. In this spirit, when some conservatives challenged the presence of unfranchised mechanics at an important town meeting in 1770, they were shouted down by men who argued that "if they had no property, they had liberty, and their posterity might have property."[12]

In smaller northern towns, the nonimportation movement of 1768 similarly brought into the streets—and into the political arena—masses of men, women, and children who had been quiescent in earlier years. In Newburyport, which had a population of about three thousand, a crowd of ordinary people formed to punish a ship's carpenter suspected of informing a British customs official of a vessel engaged in smuggling. The crowd clapped the culprit in the public stocks, forced him to sit on a sharp stone until he lost consciousness, then pulled him around town in a cart with his hands tied behind his back and a rope around his neck. Bleeding after being pelted with stones and gravel, he was locked in a warehouse, stripped naked, and handcuffed for two days. Another suspected informer got similar treatment—he was stripped of his garments, tarred and feathered, and paraded around town in a cart.[13]

While patriot merchants and lawyers clung precariously to political control in New York City, artisans and mariners gave vent to strong class feelings and often articulated their distrust of their leaders. Laboring men already held many minor offices and, different than in other cities, the status of "freeman" was not tied to property ownership but rather conferred upon payment of a modest fee. But when most of the city's merchants abandoned nonimportation in 1770, shattering a united merchant-artisan front, the mechanics decided to act by themselves. A broadside issued on May 2, 1770, scourged the defecting merchants, who, it was charged, acted only in their own interest and regarded the artisans as "two legged pack horses . . . created solely to contribute to the ease and affluence of a few importers," a "kind of beast of burden, who . . . may be seen in a state but should not be heard."[14] Popular leaders such as Isaac Sears, recognizing that New York's system of *viva voce* balloting, which tied workingmen to their landlords, creditors, and employers so they could watch the workers cast their votes, campaigned in 1770 for the secret balloting used in most other places. Broadside writers argued that this "antidote to corruption" would ensure that "no man of opulence will be able to procure a seat ... by an undue influence upon the fears of the electors." When the campaign failed narrowly in New York's legislature, popular leaders tried again in 1773, after news of the Tea Act reached the city.

Closing the port of Boston in 1774 brought New Yorkers to another fever pitch. Indicative of their growing class consciousness, the artisans now formed a Mechanics Committee, which soon proposed to take over the work of the Sons of Liberty to enforce a new economic boycott. The Merchants Committee responded with its own slate of enforcers. Voters were asked to decide which slate should be endorsed. The young aristocrat Gouverneur Morris reported "a great concourse" of New Yorkers on May 20, 1774: "[O]n my right hand were ranged all the people of property, with some few poor dependents, and on the other all the tradesmen." The tradesmen lost and the merchants crowed that "you may rest assured no non-im[portation], nor non-exportation will be agreed upon. ... The power over our crowd is no longer in the hands of [Isaac] Sears, [John] Lamb, or such unimportant persons." For now, they clung to an uneasy control, though what they were hearing from Philadelphia gave them little satisfaction. Morris vividly expressed their uneasiness: "The mob begin to think and to reason. Poor reptiles! It is with them a vernal morning; they are struggling to cast off their winter's slough, they bask in the sunshine, and ere noon they will bite, depend upon it. The gentry begin to fear this. ... I see, and I see it with fear and trembling, that if the disputes with Great Britain continue, we shall be under the worst of all possible dominions; we shall be under the domination of a riotous mob."[15]

As we have seen, Philadelphia's laboring people had been deeply split over royal government and the Stamp Act. Yet they coalesced so well after 1770 that this was the place where artisans most effectively infiltrated the extralegal committee structure and took steps to redress inequities. For example, "Tom Trudge" complained in 1767 that the poor "sup on a cup of skim milk and have a parcel of half-naked children about our doors," yet laboring men paid their part of the annual road tax supporting the dung carts that cleaned the yards "of the opulent merchants and gentry" but rarely came to the "penurious" alleyways of the poor. With this kind of complaint, the artisans for whom Ben Franklin had stood as a model gathered momentum. They were in the forefront of the nonimportation movement in 1768–70, but then were told by the merchants that they had "no Right to give their sentiments respecting an importation" when the merchants decided, as in New York City, to abandon nonimportation. Refusing to bow to the demand for deference, they promised in June 1770, in a broadside distributed throughout the city by "A Lover of Liberty and A Mechanic's Friend," that importing merchants "will be dealt with by the Mechanics Committee." To call artisans "a Rabble," continued A Lover of Liberty, and to "assert that Mechanics are men of no consequences" was not to be tolerated.[16]

The assembly election in 1770 marked the beginning of a new political party in Philadelphia. Strongly Presbyterian, it combined radical opposition to British policies with a campaign to restructure society internally. Joseph Parker became the first artisan to run for assembly in the eighteenth century, unaffected by "many threats, reflections, sarcasms, and burlesques" hurled at the artisans who deigned to enter the formal arena of politics.[17]

By 1772, artisans were pressing the legislature to end excise taxes on liquor because they fell with greatest weight on "the middling and poorer class of inhabitants." They called for weekly publication of the roll calls and assembly debates on important issues so they could hold their elected representatives to account. They also successfully challenged "the absurd and tyrannical custom of shutting the Assembly doors during debate" and demanded the building of public galleries there. "It is Time the Tradesmen were checked," wrote one alarmed Philadelphian. "They take too much upon them—they ought not to intermeddle in State Affairs—they will become too powerful." Indeed, they grew more powerful with each incident in the struggle with Great Britain. Joseph Reed, a wealthy lawyer, warned at the end of 1773 that "every day [we] perceive it more and more difficult to repress the rising spirit of the people."[18]

The Tea Act of 1773 and the British closing of Boston harbor in 1774 provided a new opportunity for Philadelphia's artisans and small shopkeepers to show their muscle. Some popular leaders, such as merchant Charles Thomson, joined with conservative importers to construct a fusion ticket of candidates to act as a committee of correspondence for coordinating strategies of resistance with other cities. But the artisans called their own meeting, assembled 1,200 strong at the statehouse in June 1774, and forced their way into what they called the "Merchants Committee." Recognizing their growing strength, the artisans put forward a radical ticket in November that excluded every leading conservative from the previous enforcement committee and gave places to craftsmen, shopkeepers, and minor merchants from the city's various religious groups and neighborhoods. A conservative merchant slate went down to defeat. Two months after the first Continental Congress met in

TO THE
Delaware Pilots.

WE took the Pleasure, some Days since, of kindly admonishing you *to do your Duty*; if perchance you should meet with the *(Tea,)* SHIP POLLY, CAPTAIN AYRES; a THREE DECKER which is hourly expected.

We have now to add, that Matters ripen fast here; and that *much is expected from those Lads who meet with the Tea Ship.*----There is some Talk of A HANDSOME REWARD FOR THE PILOT WHO GIVES THE FIRST GOOD ACCOUNT OF HER.----How that may be, we cannot *for certain* determine: But ALL agree, that TAR and FEATHERS will be his Portion, who pilots her into this Harbour. And we will answer for ourselves, that, whoever is committed to us, as an Offender against the Rights of *America*, will experience the utmost Exertion of our Abilities; as

THE COMMITTEE FOR TARRING AND FEATHERING.

P. S. We expect you will furnish yourselves with Copies of the foregoing and following Letter, which are printed for this Purpose, that the Pilot who meets with Captain *Ayres* may favor him with a Sight of them.

Committee of Taring and Feathering.

TO
Capt. AYRES,

Of the SHIP *P O L L Y*, on a Voyage from *London* to *Philadelphia.*

SIR,

WE are informed that you have, imprudently, taken Charge of a Quantity of Tea, which has been sent out by the *India* Company, *under the Auspices of the Ministry*, as a Trial of *American* Virtue and Resolution.

Now, as your Cargo, on your Arrival here, will most assuredly bring you into hot water; and as you are perhaps a Stranger *to these Parts*, we have concluded to advise you of the present Situation of Affairs in *Philadelphia*---that, taking Time by the Forelock, you may stop short in your dangerous Errand----secure your Ship against the Rafts of combustible Matter which may be set on Fire, and turned loose against her; and more than all this, that you may preserve your own Person, from the Pitch and Feathers that are prepared for you.

In the first Place, we must tell you, that the *Pennsylvanians* are, *to a Man*, passionately fond of Freedom; the Birthright of *Americans*; and at all Events are determined to enjoy it.

That they sincerely believe, no Power on the Face of the Earth has a Right to tax them without their Consent.

That in their Opinion, the Tea in your Custody is designed by the Ministry to enforce such a Tax, which they will undoubtedly oppose; and in so doing, give you every possible Obstruction.

We are nominated to a very disagreeable, but necessary Service.---- To our Care are committed all Offenders against the Rights of *America*; and hapless is he, whose evil Destiny has doomed him to suffer at our Hands.

You are sent out on a diabolical Service; and if you are so foolish and obstinate as to compleat your Voyage; by bringing your Ship to Anchor in this Port; you may run such a Gauntlet, as will induce you, in your last Moments, most heartily to curse those who have made you the Dupe of their Avarice and Ambition.

What think you Captain, of a Halter around your Neck----ten Gallons of liquid Tar decanted on your Pate----with the Feathers of a dozen wild Geese laid over that to enliven your Appearance?

Only think seriously of this----and fly to the Place from whence you came----fly without Hesitation----without the Formality of a Protest----and above all, Captain *Ayres* let us advise you to fly, without the wild Geese Feathers.

Philadelphia, Nov. 27, 1773

Your Friends *to serve*

THE COMMITTEE *as before subscribed*

Philadelphia's artisans provided the dockside muscle to stop shiploads of tea from reaching Philadelphia after the Boston Tea Party of early November in 1773. The pungent language from the Committee for Tarring and Feathering bespeaks the artisans' militancy, which frightened many of the merchants: "What think you Captain, of a halter around your neck — ten gallons of liquid tar decanted on your pate — with the feathers of a dozen wild geese laid over that to enliven your appearance?"

Philadelphia in September 1774, artisans were largely in control of the committees that operated outside the law to enforce nonimportation.

Even in Charleston, where the franchise was very limited and the hold of the wealthy merchant-planters rivaled the aristocratic control of politics in France or Italy, artisans groped for some political purchase. They founded the John Wilkes Club—taking as their hero the English radical who had been expelled from his seat in Parliament and with whom Americans identified as a friend of liberty and the freedom of the press—and began to fill places on the nonimportation enforcement committees. By 1774, reported one Charlestonian, "the gentleman and mechanic, those of high and low life, the learned and illiterate" were discussing "American affairs" and claiming a right to shape policy. Even among Anglicans, who were synonymous with wealth and power, it was impossible to tolerate a clergyman after he told his congregation that they most put a stop to a situation where "every silly clown and illiterate mechanic, will take upon him to censure the conduct of his prince or governor. . . ."[19]

Backcountry Crises

By mid-1771, an abatement of the tension over imperial policy in the northern colonies proved to be the lull before the storm. Governor Thomas Hutchinson wrote that "the people about the country have certainly altered their conduct, and in this town, if it were not for two or three Adamses, we should do well enough." But nine hundred miles to the south there was anything but a lull. On the morning of June 19, the sheriff marched six convicted Regulators out of the jail in Hillsborough to a small hill outside the town, where they were led to the newly erected gallows. Governor William Tryon stood alongside his soldiers, who watched over the roughly dressed farmers, many assembled with their wives and children. By the governor's side was the Yale-educated Colonel Edmund Fanning, lawyer, land speculator, and supportive friend of the governor. Also there were most of the eastern merchants and lawyers who controlled the colonial and county offices. Before this assemblage, the six farmers were hanged.

This gloomy day had been ordained over the previous three years. A truce had been arranged after the release of Herman Husband in May 1768, but the governor, advised by Edmund Fanning and other wealthy easterners, stonewalled the Regulators' petitions and moved to reassert his authority.

The farmers' refusal to pay taxes, pending an investigation of reported fraud by highly positioned officials and heightened by outrage over a pretentious palace to be built for the governor, provoked a series of armed standoffs. Farmers charged officials with extortion in the local courts, but they were much more likely to lose as merchants sought writs of ejectment for farmers who could not pay taxes or small debts. "With a deck stacked so heavily against them," writes the most recent historian of the Regulators, "farmers had little success in obtaining justice."[20]

The election of Herman Husband and other Regulators to the provincial legislature by backcountry voters in 1769 heightened the tension. When seated, Regulator representatives proposed extensive reforms: replacement of the regressive poll tax with one obliging "each person to pay in proportion to the profits arising from his estate"; publication of the legislature's debates; replacement of voice voting with secret ballots; new measures to halt the embezzlement of taxes by plundering sheriffs; and a repeal of a recent law passed on behalf of the Anglican Church that disallowed dissenting ministers from performing marriage ceremonies. The petition from several Regulators spoke of how they "labored honestly" for "their own bread and studied to defraud no man, nor live on the spoils of other men's labor nor snatch the bread out of other men's hands." "These demands," historian Marjoleine Kars explains, "were extraordinary. No other such wide-ranging, radical, and concrete vision of agrarian reform has come down to us from the pre-Revolutionary period."[21] But before the legislature considered such measures, the governor disbanded them, furious that they were contemplating a non-importation agreement in response to the Townshend duties.

Exasperated with inattention to their grievances, piedmont farmers packed the Rowan County Courthouse in Hillsborough in September 1770. Brandishing staves, clubs, and whips, they came "to see justice done, and justice they would have." The incensed crowd seized Justice Edmund Fanning, dragged him outside the courthouse, and mauled him. When the presiding judge fled town rather than hold proceedings before the angry Regulators, the farmers unleashed their fury on Fanning, who embodied all the arrogant and exploitative behavior of the piedmont elite. Just as convulsive mobs in Boston and Newport had destroyed the houses of their enemies five years before, the offended farmers broke into Fanning's house, smashed his furnishings, carried his expensive clothes into the streets "by armfuls," and shattered the bell Fanning had donated to the town's Anglican Church, where he worshiped. Then down came Hillsborough's finest house itself. "Debarr'd from justice," as Herman Husband, their spokesman, put it, the plain farmers administered their own rough justice.[22] Two months later, Superior Court judge Richard Henderson's barn, stables, and house went up in flames.

Several months before this house pulling, learning that he would be granted a leave of absence for a year, Governor Tryon convened the legislature on December 3, 1770, to squelch the Regulators. Tryon called for appropriations to support a military expedition against the "seditious mob," which had "torn down justice from her tribunal, and renounced all legislative authority." In signing the Johnston Riot Act, the governor virtually declared war. The act authorized the governor to raise militia units and applied its provisions retroactively to all involved in the September Hillsborough property destruction. Anyone convicted of assembling "unlawfully, tumultuously, and riotously" was liable to capital punishment without benefit of clergy (the one-time reprieve from death customarily allowed). On charges that he was the "principal mover and promoter of the late riots," the legislature expelled Herman Husband from his seat. Husband soon found himself jailed again by Governor Tryon for writing an anonymous letter published in the *North Carolina Gazette*, a charge that Husband denied.[23]

Far from frightening the farmers, the Johnston Riot Act radicalized them further. Recruiting through the winter, the Regulators brought many poor farmers into their ranks. "The spirit of sedition," wrote a Rowan County official to Governor Tryon, "has been propagated with much industry among the lower class of inhabitants here." Spiriting up the farmers was a fulminous pamphlet titled "A Fan for Fanning and a Touchstone for Tryon." The anonymous author provided a minihistory of Orange County, which had been populated "by good industrious labouring men; who knew the value of their property better than to let it go to enrich pettyfogging lawyers, extortionate and griping publicans or tax gatherers and such as delighted in building palaces at the expense of the honest farmer and tradesman."[24]

In May 1771, Tryon readied his military expedition. Recruiting eastern North Carolinians with an enlistment bounty of two pounds (equivalent to a month's wages), Governor Tryon marched his army of 1,100 west with six swivel guns and two cannons, brought in from the British army in New York. In the governor's hands were addresses from the Regulators that "We his Majesty's most loyal subjects [will] take his horse out of the plow tho' at a busy time of the year" to support their governor if he was marching west to suppress "the original offenders in government," by which the farmers meant the sheriffs, lawyers, land speculators, and tax collectors who oppressed them. However, if the governor intended "to force us to submit to that tyranny which has so long been premeditated by some officers of the Province [we will] contend for our just rights." The farmers urged that Tryon stretch "out your hand supported by heavenly justice to heal the deep, the deadly wounds that cause the general groan in our sinking country."[25]

Tryon had no intention of stretching out his hand except in ordering his men to commence firing. Though his numbers were only half of what he wanted (hundreds of men refused to march against the Regulators), his army was formidable and heavily armed. Tryon took prisoners along the line of march and commandeered horses; Regulators, fighting guerrilla-style, stole their horses back and blew up wagons with ammunition. By May 9, 1771, several thousand Regulators had massed together in Rowan County, along the Great Alamance Creek. There they approached Tryon's army. In a last effort to avoid bloodshed, they petitioned Tryon on May 15. Reiterating their many pleas for redress of grievances, they reminded him of their anger that he was "determined not to lend a kind ear to the just complaints of the people." But now, their message continued, "Warlike troops [were] marching with ardour to meet each other. The interest of a whole Province, and the lives of his Majesty's subjects," they pleaded, "are not toys, or matters to be trifled with." Tryon responded that he would send an answer by noon on the next day.[26]

On that day, May 16, Tryon moved his army to within a hundred yards of the Regulators' encampment. He offered no further consideration of their grievances, only a demand to surrender their "outlawed ringleaders" and lay down their arms as the only way to avoid an attack. The Regulators rejected this ultimatum, then shrank back in horror as Tryon ordered the execution of one of their men, who had been captured, within sight of them. Herman Husband and others religiously opposed to war slipped away from the pack. Just before noon, Governor Tryon commanded his artillery to fire on the remaining Regulators. In the melee that followed, about twenty outmatched Regulators crumpled fatally to the ground along with nine militiamen. More than 150 men on both sides suffered wounds. One captured Regulator, a radical Protestant father of newborn twins, was hanged on the battle site, without trial, after refusing to renounce his commitment to the Regulators' cause.[27]

Tryon was not one to practice the art of reconciliation. After the Regulators fled, he sent his troops to destroy the farms of Regulator leaders. His army burned the fields, barns, and farmhouse of James Hunter, a Presbyterian who had been tarred the "General of the Rebels." From there, the army descended on the farm of Herman Husband, leaving "without a Spear of Corn, Grass, or herbage growing and without a House or Fence standing." Burned out, Husband and his family trekked to western Pennsylvania. Traveling in disguise as an itinerant preacher, he took the name "Tuscape Death." On the following days Tryon's army cut through an area populated mostly by Separate Baptists, burning their way from farm to farm. After three weeks of devastating the countryside, Tryon's army returned eastward. The Regulators were broken, but their punishment was not over.[28]

In the final act of this drama, pushing the court in Hillsborough for swift justice and the death penalty, Tryon obtained the conviction of twelve of the fourteen captured Regulators charged with treason. Presiding at the trial was Chief Justice Martin Howard, who had fled Newport, Rhode Island, after the Stamp Act crowd razed his house and confiscated most of his possessions. Shortly before, Howard had issued an arrest warrant so that Governor Tryon could keep Herman Husband from returning to the hill country on a trumped-up charge of libeling royal authority. Now he speeded through the trials on June 15 and 17, 1771, eager to implement the governor's desire to impose the death penalty. The court ordered the hanging of all of those found guilty. At the gallows on the morning of June 19, Tryon commuted the death penalty for six of them. Chief Justice Howard stood beside him as the hangings began.

On the gallows, standing on a barrel with a noose around his neck, Benjamin Merrill, a devout Baptist, quietly announced that he was ready to die "in the cause of his oppressed Countrymen." His last words were a psalm from his Bible. Then James Pugh, Herman Husband's brother-in-law, said that he was prepared to meet his God and told the parable of the sower: When the world came to an end, Jesus explained, the angels would "gather out of his kingdom all things that offend, and them which do iniquity; And shall cast them into a furnace of fire: there shall be wailing and gnashing of teeth." After prophesying that his blood "would be as good seed sown on good ground, which would produce a hundredfold," Pugh spoke of the Regulators' unanswered grievances and began citing a litany of Edmund Fanning's oppressive behavior. Standing next to the gallows, Fanning kicked the barrel out from under Pugh's feet in midsentence.[29]

Governor Tryon rode by horse the next day to New Bern in a hurry to set sail for New York City to accept his new appointment as royal governor of New York. He would soon have to deal with another band of agrarian insurgents, as we will see below. With him went the faithful Edmund Fanning, who would now serve as his personal secretary and—through Tryon's largesse—occupy the role of surveyor general, which put him in a strategic position to amass wealth as a land speculator.

After Tryon's departure, the Regulators fared better. Tryon's successor as royal governor, thirty-four-year-old Josiah Martin, newly arrived from England, was shocked by his tour of the backcountry. The farmers, he wrote home, had been "provoked by insolence and cruel advantages taken ... by mercenary tricking Attorneys, Clerks, and other little Officers who have practiced upon them every sort of rapine and extortion." This drove the oppressed farmers "to acts of desperation and confederated them in violence." In the northern colonies, the radical patriot press was sympathetic to the Regulators' cause because the farmers sought exactly what the Whigs wanted: redress of grievances, the end to abuses of arbitrary government, the restoration of the rights of freeborn Englishmen. Just after the hanging of six Regulators, one writer in the *Boston Gazette* asked whether it was possible "For any man, unless he possess the soul of a Cannibal, to wish success to an administration so corrupt, so absolutely void of humanity, and every Christian virtue as that of North Carolina!!!" Ezra Stiles, minister of the Newport Congregational Church, wrote in his diary: "What shall an injured and oppressed people do, when their petitions, remonstrances, and supplications are unheard and rejected, ... and oppression and tyranny (under the name of Government) continued with rigour and Egyptian austerity!"[30]

The Regulators have not been remembered, and certainly not revered, nearly as much as their persecutors, though at least three-quarters of all men farming in the piedmont counties of Orange, Rowan, and Anson were involved. Many of the eastern men who lined up behind Governor Tryon would become Revolutionary War heroes—Cornelius Harnett, James Iredell, Richard Henderson, Abner Nash, Robert Howe, and others—and it is they who line the pages of North Carolina history books read in the schools. The major tourist attraction in New Bern, then the colony's capital, is Governor Tryon's palace, built on the revenues obtained through the regressive poll tax.

William Tryon could not have been happier leaving North Carolina and its turbulent backcountry farmers behind him, but it was only a matter of a few months after assuming the royal governorship of New York that he encountered a similar conflagration. In early November 1771, nine men marched to the house of Charles Hutchesson in the town of New Perth, at the province's northern frontier, burned the house to the ground, and, in the words of their leader, told the hapless Hutchesson that "they had resolved to offer a burnt sacrifice to the Gods of the World."[31] This was the latest outburst of anger among New Hampshire men who had settled in an area west of the Connecticut River claimed by both New York and New Hampshire. Both provinces had made land grants in what became called the Hampshire Grants, and since 1764 the wrangling over land tenure on this frontier had been almost constant. New York's land speculators had the stronger legal claim after they were upheld by the Crown in 1764. But since New York had granted about two million acres in the region to New York City speculators—and continued to do so in defiance of a royal order to make no further grants—the small farmers of New Hampshire occupied the higher moral ground. The New Englanders refused to acknowledge New York's authority over the land they had cultivated and, when faced with eviction, reacted as did the tenants of the Hudson River valley in the 1760s and the North Carolina Regulators.

By 1769, hundreds of New England farmers were resisting attempts of New York's purported landlords to run survey lines in the region. Also, they protested against paying quitrents to New Yorkers on property they thought they had purchased outright, and soon they were tearing down the houses of those with deeds or leases from New York landlords. By 1770, New York sheriffs found it risky to make the province's writ run west of the Green Mountains. Bringing the matter to a head, New York claimants to disputed land brought nine ejectment suits against New England settlers before the New York Supreme Court in Albany. This brought them face-to-face with a human grizzly bear.

Ethan Allen came from a long line of New England settlers who worked the land. The restlessness of the Allen family seems to have come down to Ethan as part of his genetic inheritance. Whether from genes or some other source, he was a lifelong frontiersman, happiest where the forests were thick, the land plentiful, and the rigors of life challenging. Born in 1737, the eldest of eight children, Allen never had more than a rudimentary education because his father's death, when Ethan was seventeen, made him the head of a large family. In his midtwenties, he met Doctor Thomas Young, then living on the New York side of the New York–Connecticut border, and this helped shape Allen's political ideas.

In his early thirties, hotspur Allen became the leader of the beleaguered New Englanders. He identified with their struggle over titles to land. But, at a deeper level, he also saw this as a conflict between the aristocratic and powerful on one side and the plebeian and seemingly powerless on the other; at stake was the character of the northern frontier. "The plaintiffs appearing in a great state and magnificence . . . together with their junto of land thieves," wrote Allen, "made a brilliant appearance; but the defendants appearing in ordinary fashion, having been greatly fatigued by hard labor wrought on the disputed premises, and their cash much exhausted, made a very disproportionate figure at court."[32] Representing the New York claimants was the New York City lawyer James Duane, who was himself speculating in these lands, and was soon to lay claim to 110 square miles of the Hampshire Grants. The presiding judge, Robert R. Livingston, was also a huge landowner in the disputed territory, as was New York's attorney general, John Tabor Kempe. The decision went for the plaintiffs. The speed with which the court reached its verdict left Allen and his compatriots convinced that "interest, conviction, and grandeur being all on one side easily turned the scale against the honest verdict." Allen later wrote that Attorney General Kempe took him aside in a tavern the night of the court decision and tried to get him to convince his farmer friends to leave the area or recognize that they had new landlords. Said Kempe—at least in Allen's recollection—"We have might on our side, and you know that might often prevails against right." Allen claims he replied, "The gods of the hills are not the gods of the valley," indicating that the New England farmers would not give up their lands without a fight. "We value not New York with all their powers," wrote Thomas Rowley, the bard of the Green Mountains, "for here we'll stay and work. This land is ours."[33]

The victory of the New York landlords was pyrrhic. Almost at once, the New England men resolved to defend their rights to the land they had cultivated, by force if necessary. By late 1770, calling themselves the Green Mountain Boys, they began to form paramilitary units. When William Tryon arrived in New York in June 1771 to assume the governorship, the New Englanders were in a state of rebellion. Tryon might have tried to put out this fire before it spread; but with the Battle of Alamance and the subsequent hangings just a few weeks behind him, he tried less militant measures. First, he declared Allen and other Green Mountain leaders outlaws and offered a reward for their apprehension. Allen's reply mocked the governor: "By Virtue of a late Law in the Province they are Not Allowed to hang any man before they have ketched him." Then Allen read Governor Tryon's warrant aloud to an assembled crowd and said "So your name is Tryon; Try on and be Damned." A few months later, as Allen watched Charles Hutchesson's farmhouse burn to the ground, he told the man, "Go your way now and complain to that damned Scoundrel your Governor. God Damn your Governour, Laws, King, Council, and Assembly."[34]

Such verbal violence was part of the popular culture of rugged backwoodsmen, but, as historian Alan Taylor reminds us, oaths such as these "carried an almost magical power to frighten or harm."[35] Allen was no pacifist like Herman Husband; in fact, he relished bluster and combat and dared the royal governor to take him in. In March 1774, Governor Tryon increased the reward for Allen's capture to one hundred pounds, hoping that this sum—the equivalent of an annual income for an ordinary New Englander—would produce someone willing to betray Allen. Tryon also tried fear. By getting the legislature to pass the New York equivalent of the Johnston Riot Act in North Carolina, he hoped to force the Green Mountain Boys out of their militant stance. The New York Riot Act, which Allen promptly called the "Bloody Act," specified that an assembly of three or more persons with "unlawful intent" would be subjected to the provisions of the law, which included capital punishment for infractions such as destroying fences and outhouses and burning haystacks. With the Continental Congress about to assemble in Philadelphia, Allen defiantly wrote Tryon that "We shall more than three, nay, more than three times three hundred, assemble together if need be to maintain our common cause" and promised that "Printed sentences of death will not kill us.... We will kill and destroy any persons, whomsoever, that shall presume to be accessory, aiding or assisting, in taking any of us."[36]

Historians have called him everything from "comedian-politician" to "frontier bully." But for all his blasphemy, relish of violence, and bullheadedness, Allen ably defended, and certainly inspired, the New England farmers migrating west to the Hampshire Grants. Allen and his brothers were themselves involved in speculating in land in the Onion River region east of Lake

Champlain and not far south of the Canadian border. This reminds us that they were canny opportunists, but that does not alter the fact that they believed deeply in the rights of ordinary farmers who did not aspire to great wealth and toiled under uncertainties of debt, insecure title to their land, and oppressive, exploitative landlords.[37]

If Allen and his Green Mountain Boys had little respect for polite language, what they did admire was John Locke's *Second Treatise of Government*. Like Herman Husband, Allen had only a rudimentary education; also like Husband, he was an autodidact. However, Allen's inspirations came mostly from the radical English political tradition, whereas Husband and many North Carolina Regulators drew deeply from the wells of radical Protestant tradition. It was probably through his deep conversations with Doctor Thomas Young, who was thoroughly familiar with Locke, that Allen imbibed the English philosopher's notions of government. Going back to 1764, relatively powerless farmers on the northern frontier had relied on Locke's principle that legal niceties could not erase the rights of those who improved the land and therefore had a rightful claim to it. Young, whose bone-deep hostility to men of great wealth and power drew him to the New Hampshire wrangle with New York, articulated this for smallholders most cogently in his *Reflections on the Disputes Between New York, New Hampshire, and Col. John Henry Lydius* (1764). Here he had railed against "the great landjobbers" and "monopolizing enemies"—the "accursed aristocracy" of New York— who made it impossible for people of little means, but great potential talent, to raise themselves out of poverty.

Allen took up this line of thought. Drawing from Locke, he appealed to a natural law superior to the common law, as codified by William Blackstone, England's premier jurist, and utilized by the New York "landjobbers." No title to land, argued Allen, especially if disputed (as was certainly the case in the Hampshire Grants area), should outweigh the possession and cultivation of the land, which "is of itself abundantly sufficient to maintain the Right in the Possessor." The New Hampshire farmer's title to the land, Allen argued, was "sealed and confirmed with the sweat and toil of the farmer," a paraphrase of Locke's words: "Whatsoever then he removes out of the State that Nature hath provided, and left it in, he hath mixed his *Labour* with, and joined to it something that is his own, and thereby makes it his *Property*." Locke's treatise also fortified Allen and his Green Mountain Boys in what on its face seems an audacious defiance of royal authority, whether delegated to sheriffs, court judges, or the royal governor himself. Allen probably had in mind Locke's position that "he who attempts to get another man into his absolute power does thereby put himself in a state of war with him; it being understood as a declaration of a design on his life; for I have reason to believe that he who would get me into his power without my consent would use me as he pleased when he got me there, and destroy me too when he had a fancy to it." In such a case, Locke reasoned, it was "Lawful for me ... to kill him if I can."[38]

From these fundamental Lockean propositions on the natural right to property and the right to declare war against any man who tried to hold another man in thrall, Allen proclaimed the right to defy duly constituted government—that is, if such government abused its power. "Laws and Society-compacts, were made to protect and secure the Subjects in their peaceable Possessions and Properties, and not to subvert them," he wrote. "No Person or Community of Persons can be supposed to be under any particular Compact of Law, except it pre-supposeth, that that Law will protect such Person or Community of Persons in his or their Properties." Aiming directly at Governor Tryon and the land-monopolizing elite around him, Allen proposed that "Kings and Governors ... cannot intermeddle" with "the sacred Prerogative of the rightful Owner" of land improved with his sweat and blood. To "resist and depose such Government" was justified. It is "labouring Men that support the World of Mankind," Allen continued, and it is the "Farmers [who] in reality uphold the State." Locke had written, "The *Supreme Power cannot take* from any man any part of his *property* without his own consent ... [and] it is a mistake to think, that the Supreme or *Legislative Power* of any Commonwealth, can do what it will, and dispose of the estates of the subject *arbitrarily,* or take any part of them at pleasure." A Green Mountain backwoodsman, as one historian explains, "had taken John Locke into his own hands, and had appropriated his political theory to meet the needs of a people determined to defend its property."[39]

Though New York's landed aristocracy was victorious in the courts it thoroughly controlled, the court had scant power to enforce the law. Short of royal troops, which by 1773 had their hands full in Boston, Governor Tryon, his legislature, and the moneyed elite with claims to millions of northern frontier acres could not neutralize the five militia groups that the Green Mountain Boys organized. Moreover, the Green Mountain Boys, led by Ethan Allen and his cousin Remember Baker, established courts of their own in defiance of New York law. By trying and punishing those involved in attempting to eject them from the land they had improved, they had, in effect, erected a countergovernment. Baker did not hesitate to say that the Hampshire Grants people "lived out of the bounds of the Law." By 1774, an uneasy truce took hold in the region west of the Green Mountains. All the more to the advantage of the Green Mountain Boys was that they had yoked their cause with that of the colonists' resistance to Parliament and the king. "If the [Hampshire] Grants equaled America, then New York was its Britain," writes Allen's most recent biographer. New York's corrupt and power-hungry government made a compelling parallel to British officialdom, which was portrayed as an avaricious "ministerial tyranny." One Green Mountain townsman in 1774 saw New York's officials in the Hampshire Grants as the local agents of "the British tyrant George the third." The plight of small farmers "diving after redress in a legal way, & finding that the law was only made use of for the emolument of its creatures & the emissaries of the British tyrant" justified resistance—including closing courts or erecting their own—to "the New York cut-throatly, Jacobitish, High Church, Toretical minions of George the third, the pope of Canada and tyrant of Britain."[40] The stage was now set for a final confrontation.

"The Natural Rights of Africans"

The half-million enslaved Africans in the thirteen colonies had no need of stamped paper, drank little tea, cared little about vice admiralty courts where smugglers were now to be tried, and did not concern themselves much about whether New Yorkers should pay for quartering British troops. But they cared passionately about their enslavement, and how they could escape it. This was never far from their minds. They listened carefully to the language employed by white colonists protesting British "tyranny," English attempts to make the colonists "slaves," and Parliament's "horrid oppression." The talk about "natural rights," "immutable laws of nature," and similar phrases fed the slaves' bone-deep conviction that freedom was everyone's birthright. The more such rhetoric became part of public discourse, the more enslaved Africans saw an opportunity to exploit the glaring contradiction that the society and economy of freedom-loving patriots was based on slavery. Moreover, by the late 1760s Africans in America had white sympathizers who were saying as much, helping to lodge the idea of freedom as a birthright in black minds.

White voices that had been but lonely cries in the wilderness before the Stamp Act crisis began to startle the complacency of slave traders and slave owners as the tussle between the mother country and the colonies continued from the passing of the Townshend Acts of 1767 to the Coercive Acts of 1774. Letters and pamphlets appeared mostly in the North but in the South as well. In fact, the first challenges to slavery during these years appeared where slavery was practiced most—in the South—and particularly in Virginia, where almost half of all enslaved Africans in North America toiled.

In the southern colonies, any talk about withdrawing from the slave system was highly subversive, for slavery was the cornerstone of the region's economy. But this is what Arthur Lee, son of an aristocratic, slave-owning Virginia family proposed, though very tentatively. When studying medicine in Edinburgh, the young Lee published an essay defending southern planters, whom Adam Smith had attacked in his *Theory of Moral Sentiments* (1759) with the caustic comment that the enslaved African had "a degree of magnanimity which the soul of his sordid master is scarce capable of conceiving." But Smith's reflections on slaveholding got Lee thinking about how slavery had shaped Chesapeake culture. It must inevitably "deprave the minds of freemen," he concluded, and was "always the deadly enemy to virtue and science." "How long," he asked, "shall we continue a practice which policy rejects, justice condemns, and piety dissuades? Shall Americans persist in a conduct that cannot be justified, or persevere in oppression from which their hearts must recoil?"[41]

Lee's essay was published in London and read by very few Americans. But returning home, he published an "Address on Slavery" in 1767 that was widely read after appearing in the newspaper with the widest circulation in the South—Rind's *Virginia Gazette*. Lee argued that "freedom is unquestionably the birth-right of all mankind, of Africans as well as Europeans," and asserted that slavery "is in violation of justice and religion." He warned that slavery would always be "dangerous to the safety of the community in which it prevails" and that it destroyed the morals of both slaves and masters. The protest to this essay—the only antislavery piece published by a southerner in the pre-revolutionary period—was so great that the publisher of the *Virginia Gazette* refused to publish a sequel essay. Lee at least had the satisfaction of seeing Virginia's legislature increase the import duty on slaves in order to reduce importations from Africa. Slaves who heard of the abolitionist argument must have taken even more satisfaction that a member of one of the colony's most important families had for the first time challenged the system of bondage.[42]

Later that year, writing as "Philanthropos," Lee floated a more drastic scheme. His plan (which hardly qualifies him for the pseudonym he adopted) proposed an end to importing slaves. Then, he proposed, Virginia's government should purchase one-tenth of all slaves each year and subsidize the purchase by selling the slaves to West Indian planters.[43] Virginia free of slaves, not freedom for Virginia slaves, was Lee's objective.

Most Virginia planters and politicians hoped that Lee's inconvenient address on slavery would be quietly forgotten. But a rangy young slave owner, just elected for the first time to the House of Burgesses, stirred further debate on slavery. In 1769, a twenty-eight-year-old, fair-skinned indentured servant named Thomas Howell had fled his master's plantation in Albemarle County and appeared at the door of a young lawyer who he hoped might extricate him from undeserved bondage. Howell explained to Thomas Jefferson that he had been consigned to thirty-one years of labor because his white mother and grandmother had been born out of wedlock and consigned to indentured servitude. Both had been trapped by laws passed in 1705 and 1723 to punish racial mixing. The 1705 law sentenced the offspring of a white woman and a black or mulatto man to thirty-one years of labor, and the 1723 statute held that any child born of such a white woman, even if the father was white, would be held in servitude for thirty-one years if the mother herself was still in servitude. An owner of scores of slaves himself, Jefferson was not so offended by slavery as he was by people who were seemingly white and entirely blameless for their degraded condition being held in bondage. So he took Howell's case to Virginia's highest court with the argument that "Under the law of nature, all men are born free, every one comes into the world with a right to his own person, which includes the liberty of moving and using it at his own will. This is what is called personal liberty, and is given him by the author of nature."[44] Jefferson was unsuccessful, and Howell was returned to his master to fulfill the thirty-one years of labor—a white man held in temporary slavery. The court repelled a challenge that would have opened a small crack in the wall of slavery. Even the slightest allowance was intolerable.

Even before twenty-six-year-old Jefferson lost the Howell case, he drafted a bill that, if passed, would also have opened a somewhat larger crack in the wall of slavery. He proposed that masters, such as Howell's owner, be given the right to free a slave without legislative approval, which at the time was forbidden in Virginia but not in every southern colony. The law did not propose to free a single slave; it would only allow property owners to dispose of their property at their will—a bill, in other words, entirely consonant with the revolutionary credo of the property rights of English citizens. Knowing that a junior burgess would have little chance of succeeding, Jefferson enlisted his cousin Richard Bland, who was twice his age, to introduce the bill. Bland was acknowledged as Virginia's expert on the rights of Englishmen under the common law and had been in the vanguard of constructing arguments against the English policies that were so offensive to the Americans. But Bland's twenty-seven years in the House of Burgesses could not ward off what an embarrassed Jefferson described many years later. Though "one of the oldest, ablest, and most respected members," Bland "was denounced as an enemy of his country and treated with the grossest indecorum."[45] Again the legal wall stood firm.

But slavery was far from unshakable. Slaves themselves helped make the point that slavery was a highly unstable proposition a few months after the House of Burgesses soundly defeated the Jefferson-Bland bill. Forty to fifty slaves at the plantation of Bowler Cocke in Hanover County seized their overseer, whipped him as they had been whipped, "from neck to waistband," and fought desperately from a barn where they had taken refuge against white neighbors assembled to put the rebellion down. Three slaves were killed and five others wounded in the battle; others were sentenced to death. For years, Hanover County people spoke of the uprising as "bloody Christmas."[46]

At Scotchtown, a few miles from the rebellion, Patrick Henry soon had qualms about the men and women he held in slavery. Pulling at his conscience was an unusual planter of the upper James River area. Robert Pleasants, a Quaker with roots in Virginia going back several generations, owned eighty slaves himself and grew rich on the sweat of their brows. Henry had helped Pleasants get pacifist Quakers relief from fines imposed on men refusing to serve in the militia. Then in 1771, Pleasants shocked his Virginia planter friends by announcing that his father and brother had chosen to emancipate all their slaves. Virginia courts blocked this move for many years, but Pleasants continued his efforts in the cause of antislavery. He founded an abolition society in the heart of slave-owning British America and in 1772 sent Anthony Benezet's *Some Historical Account of Guinea*, a cogent attack on slavery and the slave trade, to Patrick Henry, George Washington, Thomas Jefferson, and James Madison.[47]

Unlike the other more revolution-minded Virginia slave masters, Henry responded to Pleasants in one of the longest letters he ever wrote. "It is not a little surprising," he wrote, "that Christianity, whose chief excellence consists in softening the human heart, in cherishing and improving its finer feelings, should encourage a practice so totally repugnant to the first impression of right and wrong." Pleasants must have trembled with emotion at these sensitive words. But there was more. "What adds to the wonder is that this abominable practice has been introduced in the most enlightened ages" and "has brought into general use and guarded by many laws a species of violence and tyranny, which our more rude and barbarous but more honest ancestors detested." How, mused Henry, could "a country [Virginia] above all others fond of liberty" practice such a cancerous evil? "When the Rights of Humanity are defined and understood with precision . . . we find men, professing a religion the most humane, mild, meek, gentle and generous, adopting a principle as repugnant to humanity as it is inconsistent withe the Bible and destructive to liberty."[48]

Henry praised Pleasants effusively for the "noble effort to abolish slavery" and expressed a belief that "a time will come when an opportunity will be offered to abolish this lamentable evil." But pleading that he was "drawn along by the general inconvenience of living without them," Henry pledged that if he could not do without slaves he could "treat the unhappy victims with lenity" and hope for a more opportune time to come when slavery could be abolished. Here, in a nutshell, was the crux of the problem for Virginia's slaveocracy. Having risen in Virginia society through the acquisition of land and slaves, Henry was now reaching a pinnacle of fame by dint of his radical rhetoric on the question of American independence. But what would happen if he followed Pleasants and, as an Anglican worshiper, set an example by putting principle ahead of convenience? "He was a man skilled at political gesture," writes Henry's biographer Henry Mayer, "brave in defiance of convention, but on the question of slavery he would follow the common path of least resistance and, like his contemporaries, only squirm in private agony about what he knew to be a public wrong."[49]

While some southern slave owners squirmed, abolition-minded northerners did their best to create a crisis of conscience in their region of the country.

One of the first places where abolitionist sparks struck was in the heart of New England slavery—Newport, Rhode Island, where by 1770 some 150 slave ships operated and thirty rum distilleries processed the sugar cane raised by armies of enslaved Africans in the West Indies. By early 1768, readers of the *Newport Mercury* were scanning pleas to "put a stop to that hellish practice of . . . enslaving another part of the human species, I mean Negroes." When the Congregational minister Samuel Hopkins took a church there in 1770, he shocked and angered many of his parishioners by "plunging into the abolitionist agitation with great fervor."[50] Hopkins was not a compelling speaker and had almost nothing of the evangelical New Light preacher in him. But he knew what he believed and was not afraid to say it. If his Puritan church members were not ready for his message from the pulpit, he found Newport Quakers eager to work with him to petition the legislature to limit slave importation—always the first step in the abolitionist campaign. Hopkins now began softening up the hearts of slave traders and slave owners with sermons laced with attacks on the sin of slavery and filled with comparisons between British enslavement of white Americans with white enslavement of black Africans. The severity of the first, he preached, was "lighter than a feather" in contrast with the second.

In the Boston area, second only to Newport as a center of New England slave trading and slaveholding, abolitionist ministers—still in the minority—dogged their parishioners and used published versions of their sermons to reach beyond the walls of their own churches. Even more telling, ministers used the traditional Election Day sermons to move the cause along. On May 30, 1770, Samuel Cooke, the uncle of John Hancock, stood before the provincial legislature, which had been ordered by Lieutenant Governor Thomas Hutchinson to meet in Cambridge, across the Charles River from Boston. Sending the legislature across the river was in itself another proof that "a deep laid and desperate plan of imperial despotism has been laid, and partly executed, for the extinction of all civil liberty," in the words of Josiah Quincy, Jr., already a leader in the protests against England. Uttered just eleven weeks after the Boston Massacre of March 5, such words had the intended effect of steeling the legislators' resolve to defend colonial liberty. But the members of the legislature heard more than fusillades against British policy from Cooke. In what one historian has called "the most unusual official election sermon preached since the practice began in 1634," Cooke ended his sermon with penetrating comments on "the cause of our African slaves." "We, the patrons of liberty," admonished Cooke, "have dishonored the Christian name, and degraded human nature, nearly to a level with the beasts that perish." Cooke implored the Massachusetts legislature, where John Adams was sitting after winning his first election, to abolish slavery. "Let not sordid gain, acquired by the merchandize of slaves, and the souls of men harden our hearts against her piteous moans. When God ariseth, and when he visiteth, what shall we answer!"[51] To judge by his later private utterances against slavery, these words had a lasting effect on the rising young lawyer, though Adams never used any of his growing political capital to speak out publicly against chattel bondage.

Partly inspiring men like Cooke who had deep qualms about slavery was the case of a Virginia slave that reached the highest tribunal in England and caused the equivalent of an earthquake in the interpretation of the laws supporting bondage. James Somerset had been purchased in Virginia by a Boston merchant, who took him to London in 1769. Two years later, Somerset escaped but was quickly recaptured. Chained in the hold of a Jamaica-bound ship, Somerset knew his master was selling him into one of the most vicious, death-dealing slave regimes in the Americas. Three London Quaker abolitionists stepped forward to press for Somerset's release, arguing that, while England had put the stamp of approval on many laws sanctioning slavery in the overseas colonies, no law had ever been passed that sanctioned slavery in England itself. The 14,000 slaves in England, counsel argued, were of no great importance to the economy; instead they represented "a nation of enemies in the heart of a state."[52] In June 1772, Lord Mansfield, chief justice of the king's bench, issued his verdict that Somerset must be freed. This was not a general emancipation; it freed only Somerset. But every enslaved African in England was now free to pursue his or her own release from bondage.

Word of Mansfield's decision, reaching the colonies within weeks, was reported in the newspapers from Virginia northward. If the good news inspired white abolitionists, it must have excited slaves even more, though of course the chances of their getting to England were very slim. In September 1773, the *Virginia Gazette* described the flight of a slave couple who imagined they could obtain freedom by reaching England—"a notion now too prevalent among the Negroes, greatly to the vexation and prejudice of their masters."[53] Repeated incidents of this kind occurred as word of the Somerset decision spread. Already, the issue of abolition was of sufficient interest to be the subject of the Harvard College commencement debate in 1773, where two young men, Theodore Parsons and Eliphalet Pearson, addressed whether it was legal to enslave Africans. Within weeks, a Boston printer published the debate.

Support for the budding abolitionist movement in Boston would have benefited greatly from the support of radical leaders such as John Adams, Samuel Adams, James Warren, and John Hancock, who had clipped the wings of artisan street commanders like Ebenezer MacIntosh and regained control of the revolutionary mass movement. But the Adamses and their friends were lukewarm if not opposed to abolitionism, because they saw it as a disruptive side issue that might cripple the intercolonial movement they were trying to build. Warren reported to John Adams, after abolitionists had brought an antislavery bill before the Massachusetts legislature in 1771, that "If passed into an act, it should have a bad effect on the union of the colonies." Boston's trumpet of patriot politics, the *Boston Gazette*, had almost nothing to say on the Somerset case, though it was covered fully elsewhere, even in Virginia. By 1772, concludes historian Patricia Bradley, John Adams "was building an intercolonial movement that avoided direct confrontation on the issue of slavery,"[54] while all around him essayists were decrying calls for American liberty in the land of bondage for one-fifth of the population. Radical when it came to imperial relations, the Adams group was decidedly conservative regarding provincial ones, as would become even more obvious when other issues of colonial reform arose.

Farther south, Benjamin Rush, rising to eminence as one of Philadelphia's best-trained physicians, spoke directly to the contradiction in which colonists who protested odious British acts found themselves. "It would be useless for us to denounce the servitude to which the Parliament of Great Britain wishes to reduce us," he wrote in 1769, "while we continue to keep our fellow creatures in slavery just because their color is different from ours." Four years later, he wrote to Granville Sharp, the English abolitionist, that "Anthony Benezet stood alone a few years ago, in opposing Negro slavery in Philadelphia, and now three-fourths of the province, as well as of the city, cry out against it." No doubt too optimistic, Rush continued that "A spirit of humanity and religion begins to awaken in several of the colonies in favour of the poor Negroes."[55]

If this was naive, it was balanced by Rush's determination. Gently pushed by Anthony Benezet, who understood that it was harder for most white slave owners to ignore a non-Quaker than a Quaker, Rush agreed to take up his quill. In *An Address to the Inhabitants of the British Settlements in America upon*

Slave-Keeping (1773), he called slavery one of those "national crimes" that would "require national punishments" and implored that "Ye advocates for American liberty" renounce "a vice which degrades human nature." A graduate of the College of New Jersey (later Princeton University) and the school of medicine in Edinburgh, Rush commanded far more authority than the eccentric Benjamin Lay or the spartan Anthony Benezet. People could not be moved by words alone, especially when they had a vested interest in slavery. But hearing the argument that "the plant of liberty is of so tender a nature that it cannot thrive long in the neighborhood of slavery" affected at least some. Referring pointedly to the argument now commonly made that the lamp of liberty was going out all over Europe and that the Americans stood guard over this lamp in resisting English encroachments on the natural rights of men, Rush cautioned: "Remember, the eyes of all Europe are fixed upon you, to preserve an asylum for freedom in this country after the last pillars of it are fallen in every other quarter of the globe."[56]

Benezet and Rush were also changing the mind of Benjamin Franklin, one of the colonies' most admired and internationally recognized men. Franklin comes through to us in the history books as the perfect American and the success story nonpareil. Could there be any more inspiring story than that of the twelfth child of a poor Boston candle maker who became an entrepreneur par excellence, an adroit politician and diplomat, a scientist and inventor, an urban reformer, an urbane conversationalist and writer, and author of a best-selling book about how to become wealthy? But we do not know the Franklin who made much money on advertising the sale of slaves and notices of their running away in his *Pennsylvania Gazette*, the man who freed none of his own five slaves even after speaking out against slavery.[57]

Franklin had his first close contact with slavery in Boston, his place of birth, shortly after fleeing an older brother who treated him like a slave when Ben was apprenticed to him. Trading a declining Boston for a rising Philadelphia, Franklin boarded with Widow Read in Market Street, where he was to find his common-law wife Deborah, who was Widow Read's daughter. Having newly purchased the *Pennsylvania Gazette* at age twenty-four, Franklin advertised the "likely Negroe Woman" whom Widow Read wished to sell. This began Franklin's direct involvement with slavery for more than half a century. When Franklin achieved financial independence, he and Deborah bought their first two slaves—Peter and Jemima—probably in the mid-1740s. But Franklin did worry about the issue of slavery. By the 1750s, in his essay on "Observations Concerning the Increase of Mankind," a fascinating set of speculations on population growth in the colonies, Franklin expressed his view, from firsthand experience, that owning slaves was uneconomic because a person denied the benefits of his or her own labor became practiced at the "neglect of business." With slaves living alongside their children in small rented houses, Deborah and Ben worried that, in the presence of slaves, "the white Children become proud, disgusted with labour, and being educated in idleness, are rendered unfit to get a living by industry."[58] Yet the Franklins continued to purchase slaves. When Franklin left for England in 1757, taking his twenty-four-year-old son, William, with him, he took slaves Peter and King to attend to his needs. To help Deborah around the house he purchased Othello, another slave. Franklin made peace with his growing distaste for slavery by rewriting his will, just before his ship left New York, to provide for the release of Jemima and Peter at his death (which never happened, since they predeceased him).

Franklin's personal war over slavery continued over the long years he spent in England, where he lived from 1757 to 1775, but for a brief interlude in Philadelphia in 1764–66. His ideological pendulum swung toward antislavery by 1770 when he took his first public stand in *A Conversation between an Englishman, a Scotchman, and an American, on the Subject of Slavery.* Dubbing a fictional conversation among three worthies, Franklin had the American on the defensive for making "a great clamour upon every little imaginary infringement of what you take to be your liberties," while being "enemies to liberty" in holding tens of thousands of slaves. Franklin's pendulum swung even further toward antislavery in 1772 as Anthony Benezet pressed his case, friends Richard Price and Joseph Priestley began tasking Americans for their deep involvement in slavery, and the Somerset case stirred Londoners. In an unsigned letter to the *London Chronicle* on "The Somerset Case and the Slave Trade," Franklin asked, Is sweetening tea with sugar an "absolute necessity" considering "so much misery produced among our fellow creatures, and such a constant butchery of the human species by this pestilential detestable traffic in the bodies and souls of men?"[59]

Still Franklin freed none of his own slaves. When King ran away from him in England, Franklin found him in the service of a lady who had taught him to read and write and to play the violin and French horn. Franklin consented that King could stay with the lady if she purchased him. When he returned to Philadelphia in 1775, five months after Deborah died, Peter was still at his side. Not needing George, another slave who had served Deborah faithfully during his absence, Franklin passed ownership to his daughter Sally and her husband Richard Bache. The tug-of-war between heart and pocketbook continued as Quakers pushed to end the war in favor of the heart.

Some white slave owners paid heed to the arguments that Rush, Benezet, and Franklin expressed. Even before the Society of Friends made it mandatory for Quakers to free their slaves or allow them to purchase their freedom, Friends in Pennsylvania and New Jersey began to release their human property in sizable numbers. Smaller numbers of Anglicans, Presbyterians, and Swedish and German Lutherans did so as well. Throughout the northern colonies, and even in Maryland, small numbers of conscience-stricken slave owners set their slaves free. However, the armor of economic interest protected the vast majority of slave owners from religious- and natural-rights appeals. Most balked at suffering an economic loss through freeing their slaves, though some severed their connection with an institution that was under moral attack by selling their slaves in the last decade before the Revolution formally began. Old slaves, worn out by years of arduous work, were often more a liability than a source of profit and were likeliest to find themselves the dubious recipients of a master's newfound humanitarianism.

As heartened as they must have been to hear that some masters were ending their slaves' long travail, most able-bodied bondpeople knew that waiting for appeals to conscience to melt the hearts of their masters was a poor gamble. All the time, some saw that it was better to seize the moment. Taking the initiative themselves, they began to pursue three strategies: Make a break for freedom, sue masters individually to redress freedom denied, or petition legislatures to abolish slavery altogether. How many of the half-million slaves pursued one of these strategies can never be known because they left only a slight record behind and because historians have recovered only fragments of documentation explaining slave behavior during this period. But we know enough to be certain that enslaved men and women implemented all three of these strategies well *before* the Declaration of Independence announced that all men are born with certain unalienable rights.

Going to court with charges that their masters robbed them of their liberty took great pluck on the slaves' part, as well as resources to pay a lawyer and court fees. Jenny Slew did so in late 1766 in Salem, just north of Boston. John Adams witnessed the proceedings and wrote in his diary that he had "heard there have been many" such cases.[60] Adams would soon have his chance to further the cause of unalienable rights. In 1769, when William Rotch, a Quaker owner of whaling ships in Nantucket, Massachusetts, became infected by the antislavery efforts of the Society of Friends in Pennsylvania and New Jersey, he encouraged an enslaved whaler named Boston to sue his master for his freedom. A magistrate and jury of the Nantucket Court of Common Pleas awarded Boston his release. When Boston's furious owner vowed to appeal the case, Rotch engaged Adams, who had just heard Samuel Cooke's Election Day sermon railing against slavery, to defend Boston. Adams won the case, his only intervention on a slave matter, and thereafter freedom suits began to grow in number. In 1773, "A True Lover of Liberty" wrote in a small pamphlet published in Boston that "there have been numbers freed in several country towns." This was the case in Newbury, where a slave named Caesar sued his master and was awarded eighteen pounds in damages and costs, along with his freedom, by the local jury.[61] Years later, John Adams remembered, "I never knew a jury by a verdict to determine a negro to be a slave. They always found him free."[62]

Word of successful freedom suits in Massachusetts courts, and knowledge of sermons indicting slavery as an affront to humanity and inconsistent with the protests against England, encouraged enslaved New Englanders to take the next step: a plea for general emancipation. In the first week of 1773, Massachusetts' governor and legislature were served with a petition "of many Slaves, living in the town of Boston, and other towns in the province." It was the first such petition historians know of, though there may have been earlier ones. Apparently, the Massachusetts slaves had taken a page from the patriots' book by organizing themselves so that they could speak as one body, although they came from many towns. Signed by "Felix," the petition sorrowfully related that slaves "who have had every day of their lives embittered with this most intolerable reflection, that let their behaviour be what it will, nor their children to all generations, shall ever be able to do, or to possess and enjoy anything, no not even *life itself,* but in a manner as the *beasts that perish.*" The address continued plaintively: "We have no property! We have no wives! No children! We have no city! No country! But we have a Father in Heaven, and we are determined, as far as his Grace shall enable us, and as far as our degraded contemptuous life will admit, to keep all his Commandments." The petition went on more humbly, expressing that the slaves would not suggest specific legislative remedies to their condition. "The rhetoric of humility," writes historian Linda Kerber, "is a necessary part of the petition as a genre, whether or not humility is felt in fact." But the black petitioners mixed humility with striking self-assertion in a protest statement that almost assumed the character of a broadside to be nailed to tavern doors, lampposts, and other public places. Within weeks, an anonymous friend of the slaves accomplished just this by publishing the petition as a pamphlet with two letters appended—one by "A Lover of True Liberty," the other by "The Sons of Africa."[63]

The petition did not achieve its goal, but it was not a failure. It occasioned a new debate in the legislature on the possibility of abolishing slavery. Three months later, again borrowing from the white protestors' strategy book, four black men published a hard-hitting, less deferential leaflet. The authors indicated that they represented "their Committee" and spoke for "our fellow slaves in this province." They began tauntingly: "We expect great things from men who have made such a noble stand against the designs of their *fellow-men* to enslave them. We cannot but wish and hope Sir, that you will have the same grand object, we mean civil and religious liberty, in view in your next session." The petitioners continued: "The divine spirit of freedom, seems to fire every humane breast on this continent, except such as are bribed to assist in executing the execrable plan"—a reference to the so-called British enslavement of the white colonists.

The petition continued with a remarkable passage that showed how word of the Spanish practice of *coartación*—the legal right of Spanish slaves to buy their way out of slavery—had spread to New England. "Even the Spaniards," the petitioners pointed out, "who have not those sublime ideas of freedom that English men have, are conscious that they have no right to all the services of their fellow-men, we mean the Africans, whom they have purchased with their money; therefore they allow them one day a week to work for themselves, to enable them to earn money to purchase the residue of their time, which they have a right to demand in such portions as they are able to pay for. . . ."[64] The black supplicants implored that they be released from "a State of Slavery." Again, the legislature appointed a committee to consider the petition; but the committee, mindful that the patriot movement included many slave owners, recommended that the petition be tabled. Still another petition, published as a leaflet, reached the legislature in June 1773 and was carried over until January 1774, when it produced no result. Nothing was done to free enslaved Africans, but both houses passed a bill to stop the importation of slaves. Even this half measure failed when Lieutenant Governor Thomas Hutchinson refused to sign it.

Historians have doubted that the signatures on these petitions—Peter Bestes, Sambo Freeman, Felix Holbrook, and Chester Joie—tell us much about the true authorship. Considering that few enslaved blacks were literate, it is thought that white friends of the black petitioners penned the moving appeals. But it is possible that the author was a highly literate black woman, enslaved in Boston and baptized in the Brattle Street Church of Samuel Cooper, who had fifty slave-owning families in his flock. This was Phillis Wheatley, whose eloquence suggests her participation in the petition.

Disappointed in their failure to push legislative action on the issue of slavery, black Massachusetts activists tried again in 1774. The language grew more strenuous. "A great number of Blacks of the Province . . . held in a state of slavery within the bowels of a free and Christian country," read the petition, "have in common with all other men a natural right to our freedoms without being depriv'd of them by our fellow men as we are a freeborn people and have never forfeited this blessing by any compact or agreement whatever." Six weeks later, trying to counter the argument that if freed they would become a public nuisance and a public expense, they asked for a grant of unimproved land for a settlement of their own, where they would withdraw to "quietly sit down under [their] own fig tree" and enjoy "the fruits of [their] labour."[65] Again, there was no legislative result, but the issue was far from squelched, neither in Massachusetts nor elsewhere.

It is too much to claim that a groundswell of abolitionism and slave resistance swept over the colonies as the argument with England wore on and as backcountry insurgencies erupted. More accurately, American protests against English oppression could no longer proceed without raising the slavery issue. As slavery emerged as a major topic of discussion and concern, thousands of enslaved people were brought to a state of anticipation. Most of the northern states, and even Virginia and Maryland, brought slave importation to a halt. Yet after limiting importation for several years, South Carolina resumed the slave traffic with a vengeance in 1773, when about eight thousand slaves staggered ashore in Charleston. This number exceeded that of Africans arriving in the first fifty years of the colony's history.[66] To the north, no more than several hundred slaves received their freedom through voluntary manumission by their masters. So while abolitionist sentiment grew markedly, at least in thought if not in action, so did the number of slaves in the colonies at large. Cracks in the wall of slavery were unmistakably appearing, yet the wall itself was growing higher and thicker.

Indian Hating on the Middle Ground

In the years when the Townshend Acts, the Boston Massacre, and the Boston Tea Party intensified the white colonists' arguments with England, Native Americans saw that the English king had neither the will nor the power to enforce the Proclamation Line of 1763, which promised to protect Indian land and political sovereignty from land-hungry colonists. As a Virginian said in 1773, "not even a second Chinese wall, unless guarded by a million soldiers, could prevent the settlement of lands on Ohio and its dependencies."[67] The truth of this had become evident by the late 1760s. Colonial governors, their hands full with irascible subjects, now had to contend with a bombardment of petitions from important colonial leaders speculating in land west of the Proclamation Line. Bowing to this pressure, royal governors peppered colonial administrators in London with reasons why exceptions should be made to the rule prohibiting white settlement west of the Appalachians. Many of the governors' reports included false assertions that interior tribes had abandoned their claims to various parcels of land west of the mountains. When British government denied such requests to bend the Proclamation Line, governors often turned their heads and permitted land grants, surveys, and private purchases of land from Indian nations such as the Creeks and Cherokees, who did not recognize the right of the English government to demarcate boundaries. When settlers moved onto land still claimed by the Native Americans, governors usually left the backcountry men to fight it out with the Indians.

From an Indian perspective, the sight of colonial governors assisting expansionist-minded speculators and settlers was alarming. On the one hand, they could not do without trade goods and were now bereft of the French lines of supply from Canada. On the other hand, they had to face colonists moving west who were determined to ignore the Proclamation Line. The alternatives for the interior Indian nations were limited. They could seek Indian allies to forge another pan-Indian uprising, as did one faction of the Creeks led by a chief named The Mortar, who had been staunchly anti-English for decades. Or they could try to extend French supply lines from New Orleans while hoping for a renewed French presence on the continent, as did the Choctaws. Or they could bow to the white tidal wave and sell off their land, piece by piece at the best price possible, to private individuals and speculating companies who blithely defied the Proclamation of 1763.

In 1768, England's two Indian superintendents struck treaties with the Cherokee and Iroquois that tore a huge hole in the Proclamation Line and opened the way for a flood of white settlers into the Ohio country. In October 1768, in the Treaty of Hard Labor, Southern Indian Superintendent John Stuart persuaded Cherokee chiefs to cede part of their vast Kentucky hunting grounds west of the Proclamation Line all the way to the Ohio and Kanawha rivers. The Cherokee hoped this would sate the colonists' land hunger and lead to a permanent boundary.[68]

A month later, in what historian Richard White calls "the most tangled agreement reached by Indians and whites in the eighteenth century," some three thousand Iroquois and subsidiary tribesmen agreed with Northern Indian Superintendent William Johnson to the Treaty of Fort Stanwix. By the terms of this treaty, the Iroquois ceded an immense territory south of the Ohio River and west of the Proclamation Line of 1763. This territory constituted the main Kentucky hunting grounds of the Cherokee, Mingo, and Shawnee peoples. White calls it "a cynical compact born in the mutual weakness of its two major parties."[69] Johnson hoped it would bring a permanent peace by satisfying backcountry settlers and eastern land speculators with a chunk of North America about the size of Pennsylvania, Maryland, and Virginia combined. But Johnson could not control the colonists, and in the process he abandoned the Indian people he was sworn to protect. Speaking for the Indian peoples who were supposedly under their protection, the Iroquois chiefs betrayed the Shawnee, Mingo, Delaware, and Cherokee in exchange for the largest supply of trade goods ever issued by the British in a treaty. Rather than damping the white hunger for more land to the west, the Iroquois cession of lands that they neither occupied nor controlled triggered a mania for land watered by the Ohio River and its tributaries.

The betrayed Shawnee, few in number compared to their putative Iroquois masters, worked to mobilize the Miamis, Potawatomis, and other tribes to denounce the terms of the Treaty of Fort Stanwix. But these efforts failed, primarily because Sir William Johnson used his influence to convince these tribes that alliance with the Shawnee would bring Anglo-Iroquois attacks on their villages. Efforts to send a delegation directly to London also failed, as did Shawnee attempts to get Pennsylvania Quakers to intervene on their behalf. Beleaguered, many Shawnee retreated to the west while others kept to their villages hoping for the best.

Nobody could have been happier with the Treaty of Fort Stanwix than the muscular young Daniel Boone. Boone had forsworn his Quaker background as a teenager and had served General James Braddock's army as a teamster in 1755. By 1769, with a growing family and a distinct distaste for farming on the thin soil of the Yadkin River, he left his North Carolina homestead with a brother-in-law, three other companions, and his pack and riding horses to foray west across the Cumberland Gap, the main gateway to the West, to explore the hunting grounds and lush bluegrass meadows of Kentucky. But hunting for land was as important as hunting for deer, elk, bear, and buffalo. Boone's family would not see him for two years. On the first of his "long hunts," Boone reconnoitered the lands that would soon be prized by colonists. Eight months into his trip, Boone and one of his men were confronted by a group of Shawnee on a long hunt of their own. Their Indian leader, Captain Will, warned Boone that the Shawnee scorned the Treaty of Fort Stanwix and intended to defend their Kentucky hunting grounds. "Go home and stay there," cautioned Captain Will. "Don't come here any more, for this is the Indians' hunting ground, and all the animals, skins and furs are ours. And if you are so foolish as to venture here again, you may be sure the wasps and yellow-jackets will sting you severely."[70]

During the two years of Boone's hunt, similarly restless backcountry settlers began filing across the Cumberland Gap and descending into the river valleys feeding the upper Tennessee River. By 1772, Virginia's governor wrote that "finding that grants are not to be obtained, [they] do seat themselves without any formalities wherever they like best." "Wherever they like best" turned out to be beyond the boundaries set by the treaties of 1768. The frontiersmen could not find secure grants because the territory ceded in the Hard Labor and Fort Stanwix agreements was locked up by land company speculators. George Washington, Thomas Jefferson, Patrick Henry, and dozens of other Virginia leaders had engaged in a land rush of amazing proportions. An agent of the Ohio Land Company reported that surveyors were so numerous that "as soon as a man's back is turned another is on his land."[71] Shawnee hunters soon encountered the surveyors' red flags throughout the territory they still regarded as their prized hunting grounds. They knew, as Sir William Johnson explained to the English government in London in November 1772, "that the back[country] inhabitants, particularly those who

In his painting, completed one year after the Mexican-American War, William Ranney has Daniel Boone playing the role of Moses pointing to the Promised Land. It had appeal in an era of national expansion, and few who viewed it noticed the absence of Cherokees or other Indians who were thickly involved in Boone's early forays across the Cumberland Gap. Amidst nature, no violence seemed to beckon.

daily go over the mountains of Virginia, have a hatred for, ill treat, rob and frequently murder the Indians."[72]

Indian Superintendent Johnson now rued his bullying the Shawnee into the Treaty of Fort Stanwix in the hope of creating a permanent peace. The frontiersmen, he judged, were more hunters than farmers, and this made them competitors with Indians for the game upon which the tribal people relied. The "back[country] inhabitants," wrote Johnson in a report to London, "are in general a lawless set of people, as fond of independency as themselves [the Indians], and more regardless of government owing to ignorance, prejudice, democratical principles, and their remote situation." With these words, Johnson had described a different kind of radical in the revolutionary era— men who detested the hand of authority in whatever form it took, longed to make up rules for themselves, prized their "remote situation," and therefore

cared little about stamp taxes, tea duties, search and seizure by customs officials, quartering of British troops, vice admiralty courts, or any of the other
constitutional issues that so troubled seaboard colonists.[73]

These backwoodsmen were also radical in another sense. They had little
use for the French way of cohabitation with the Indians of the *pays d'en haut*.
The Irish-born Indian trader George Croghan, who had lived with the Kickapoos after being captured in 1765, touched on the essence of the French-
Indian relationship by saying that the two peoples had been "bred up together
like children in that country, and the French have always adopted the Indians' customs and manners, treated them civilly, and supplied their wants gen-
erously." General Thomas Gage agreed that the French and the Indians, over
generations in North America, had become "almost one people." The Virginians and Pennsylvanians streaming over the Cumberland Gap were of a
different sort. They had no wish to mingle with the Indians or even have
amiable relations with them. They wanted the Indians' land and the game
that roamed it. In 1767, Gage, Johnson, and Croghan called them "lawless
banditti," people who wished to live under no "landlord or law," "a set of people . . . near as wild as the country they go in, or the people they deal with, and
by far more vicious and wicked."[74]

From this incipient desire for what in the twentieth century would be
called apartheid, came the most radical tendency of all among the backwoodsmen: a hatred of Indians and a desire to drive them west or eliminate
them altogether. If war came, they wanted the colonial militia to the east and
the British army to support them; but "they resented the efforts of the same
military to restrict their actions," as Richard White has said.[75]

Daniel Boone was not one of the Indian haters described by Johnson. But
he was certainly part of those "fond of independency," "regardless of government," and infused with "democratical principles." By 1773, Boone was in the
vanguard of the Kentucky land rush. With his wife and eight children; several families of friends, some with slaves; and horses, poultry, cattle, and hogs,
he set off for Kentucky that October. Without government authorization and
in defiance of boundary lines, Boone's party headed deep into Kentucky. Six
of them, including one of Boone's sons, paid for the intrusion with their lives
after a Shawnee war party attacked. This touched off a cycle of vengeance
that kept the frontiers of North Carolina, Virginia, and Pennsylvania ablaze.

For Cornstalk, main chief of the Shawnee, there was some gratification in
seeing most of the Boone party fall back east of the mountains for the winter

of 1773–74. But with the melting ice the next spring, Virginians and Carolinians touched with Kentucky fever came back in even greater numbers. Numerous among them were surveyors for land companies dominated by the Virginia slaveocracy. But settlers like Boone could ignore the surveyors' lines because the land companies had not received royal consent to bring the Kentucky country under Virginia's authority. Out of this complex situation, the lives of Daniel Boone, Cornstalk, and Virginia's royal governor, the earl of Dunmore, converged in ways that Virginia's founding fathers found to their liking. Though Dunmore deeply offended the Virginian aristocratic tobacco planters by dissolving the obstreperous House of Burgesses in May 1774— after they declared a day of mourning in response to the British closing of the port of Boston—they thanked him profusely, as we will see in the next chapter, for declaring war against the Shawnee and associated tribes in the Ohio country on June 10. If Dunmore was seen as a tyrant in dismissing Virginia's elected representatives, another escalation of the crisis with English rule, he was viewed simultaneously as a protector of land speculators and land-hungry settlers for taking war to the Shawnee, who were trying to protect their homeland in the face of unauthorized white encroachments.

Out of the Shadows

In the late 1760s and early 1770s, while enslaved Africans were stepping out of their subservient and mostly silent roles and interior Indian people were struggling to cope with encroaching frontiersmen, another part of colonial society—white women—were making themselves heard as well. But before addressing this new emergence of women in public life, and their involvement in what historian John Bohstedt calls "the common people's politics," we need to sketch the background of women's place in the late colonial period.[76]

Historians until recently have pictured women of the colonial period as submissive, ladylike, and happy to be so. It is as if they had continued to write in their school copybooks what the young Elnathan Chauncy of Massachusetts penned in the late seventeenth century: The soul, he wrote, "consists of two portions, inferior and superior; the superior is masculine and eternal; the feminine is inferior and mortal." As part of his design, God assigned women special stations in life where they were to be modest, patient, subordinate, and compliant. Regarded by men as weak of mind and large of heart, they existed for and through men, subject first to their fathers, then to their husbands. Taking pride in their domestic life, they stayed out of politics by custom and choice. They did not complain that they were denied the right to vote, hold public office, or serve as jurors in courts of law, because they did not expect to play these public roles. They kept to their place in church as worshipers but not preachers and fulfilled their roles as childbearers and child raisers. The home was their stage; public places belonged to men.

Vibrant new scholarship, propelled by the unprecedented entry of women from diverse backgrounds into the history profession, has been changing our minds about this essentially static depiction of the passive woman. New questions about the lives of women of all classes and colors, their place in the church and community as well as the home, and how their roles were evolving in a changing society have yielded an understanding of women as much less passive than previously imagined and as surprising agents of historical change.

From the earliest waves of immigration, life in frontier North America put a premium on women's hardiness. In colonial courts, wives gained more control over property they brought into marriage than in England and Ireland. They also enjoyed broader rights to act for and with their husbands in business transactions. Large numbers of women worked alongside their husbands in competent and complementary ways. They had limited career choices and restricted rights, but they also shouldered broad responsibilities. In towns and on farms, daily routines of husband and wife overlapped and intersected far more than today. "She is a very civil woman," wrote one visitor to the southern colonies, "and shows nothing of ruggedness or immodesty in her carriage; yet she will carry a gun in the woods and kill deer and turkeys, shoot down wild cattle, catch and tie hogs, knock down beeves with an ax, and perform the most manful exercises as well as most men in those parts."[77] "Deputy husbands" and "yoke mates" were revealing terms used by New Englanders to describe eighteenth-century wives.

Women clearly helped shape the world around them, modeling the behavior of young women, aiding the needy, and subtly affecting menfolk, who held formal authority. They outnumbered men in church life throughout the colonies, wielded influence in seating and unseating ministers, and periodically appeared as visionaries and mystics. In the Great Awakening that swept the colonies in waves from the 1720s to the 1750s, women began to exercise their spiritual gifts, preaching to those gathering in a pasture, a clearing in the woods, or in an urban square. As early as the 1730s, some women put men on notice that they were made of oak, not willow. "We the widows of this city," wrote a group of New York women in 1733, "protest the failure to invite us to court. We are housekeepers, pay our taxes, carry on trade and most of us are she Merchants. . . . We have the vanity to think we can be fully as entertaining and make as brave a defense in case of invasion and perhaps not turn tail as soon as some of the men."[78]

In the late colonial period, women began to involve themselves in political causes, particularly in times of stress or crisis. They could not foresee the American Revolution, but in several instances they paved the way for women to assume a central role in the imperial crisis of the 1760s and 1770s. In New Jersey, for example, Magdalen Valleau became a leader of land rioters in 1740. Daughter of a French Huguenot immigrant, she married another Frenchman, but she became part of the Dutch culture in northern New Jersey, where Dutch farmers were tenanted on the land of the province's English proprietors. Speaking Dutch, Valleau became the central figure in the land riots on the Ramapo Tract in Bergen County. In one mob action, three women and seven men forced a tenant of the Board of Proprietors out of his house and pulled it down. By the end of 1742, the proprietors recognized her as a crowd leader. After 1745, in the riots described in chapter 1, she led some of the largest crowd actions.[79]

Another woman who stepped out of the shadows to take a critical role in the turbulent 1760s was Sarah Osborn. Widowed early, Osborn learned to do for herself. When her second husband's business failed in Newport, Rhode Island, she became the chief support of her family. Like Anthony Benezet of Philadelphia, she became a teacher of poor children and a special friend to black people. As Stamp Act crowds pursued Newport's stamp distributor and hounded the wealthy members of the royalist Junto, Osborn began giving religious instruction in her home. She soon learned that she had uncommon spiritual gifts. By 1767, when Newporters were stewing over the Townshend duties, over five hundred people thronged to her house every evening but Saturday to read the Bible, catechize, sing, and pray. With more than one of every six Newporters of churchgoing age appearing at her door, Osborn separated them into age, gender, and racial cohorts. The largest, proportionately, was black. Among them were Newport Gardner, Quamine, and Bristol Yamma—figures we will encounter later as heralds who preached a return to their African homelands bearing the Christian message. One historian has claimed that the religious revival centered on Osborn was "the only one until the twentieth century initiated, organized, and led by a woman to span the American chasms of sex, race, and age."[80]

With Osborn's house packed "until the house will not contain them," as she wrote to a friend, many Newporters were less than pleased. Seeing a woman with such spiritual power, reminiscent of Anne Hutchinson in Boston 130 years before, Newport men charged she was going "beyond her sphere." Jealousy about her breaking the male monopoly on dispensing God's grace was compounded by fear of her influence with Newport's large black population, which swelled each summer as domestic slaves accompanied South Carolina and West Indian planters and merchants who made Newport their refuge from tropical heat, humidity, and disease. The Christian doctrine, after all, cut two ways: Conservative Christianity prized meekness, humility, and obedience and spoke of deliverance in the afterlife. But radical Christianity stressed the ideals of the brotherhood of man, the story of the Hebrew flight from oppression, and deliverance in this life, not the next. A model of Christian humility herself, Osborn worried herself sleepless in the face of criticism and did everything possible to enlist "the standing ministry" in her revivalist work. She tried to counter charges against her for "keeping a Negro House" and spreading "disturbance or disorder" among slaves by pointing out that some sullen and resistant slaves had been "reform'd" under her tutelage. But men advised her to step away from ministerial work. "Would you advise me to shut up my mouth and doors and creep into obscurity?" she wrote a male friend who quoted Scripture to get her to surrender her charismatic effect. She would not bow down. "I am spirited and gain strength in trying to instruct them," she wrote of her efforts on behalf of slaves. "Man can't determine me. Man's opinion shan't content me."[81] Failing eyes and weary bones overtook her by 1769, and this, not male pressure to disengage, removed her from the scene. But before she put her burden down, Osborn and her church sorority found a replacement to carry on her work of ministering to the poor and enslaved.

The women's choice was Yale-trained Samuel Hopkins, who had studied with Jonathan Edwards, the intellectual giant of New England's Great Awakening. Hopkins had served for twenty-five years as minister at the Congregational Church in Great Barrington, where generations later W. E. B. Du Bois grew up. Hopkins was anything but charismatic and probably lost his church in Great Barrington because of his unpopularity as an uninspired sermonizer. Nonetheless, Osborn and her staunch female allies fixed upon gaining his appointment as the pastor of Newport's First Congregational Church. Hopkins's ideas about a millennial Calvinism rather than his delivery apparently appealed to Osborn and her female cohort. His immediate responsiveness to Newport's large population of slaves suggests that the women also knew of Hopkins's sympathies for enslaved blacks. Whatever the case, the women of the First Congregational Church, according to Ezra Stiles, minister of Newport's Second Congregational Church, were "violently engaged" in the choice of a new minister, and thus "the Sorority of her [Osborn's] Meeting" prevailed.[82]

Osborn had made New England's principal site of slavery and slave trading a center for watchful guidance for black Rhode Islanders. Hopkins now made it the center of New England abolitionism. He later organized and published Osborn's extensive writings, in diaries and letters, and gave her credit for shaping his Sunday sermons. He forged the bond with the black Newporters cultivated by Osborn. In 1773, Hopkins joined Ezra Stiles in sending a circular to hundreds of New England churches advocating a complete ban on the slave trade.[83] Without the support of his congregation's women (who made up two-thirds of the church), Hopkins's antislavery message would almost certainly have doomed him, for sitting in the pews each Sunday were scores of uncomfortable, if not squirming, slave owners and slave traders. By this time, Hopkins was composing sermons that would lead, in 1776, to the publication of one of the most muscular attacks on slavery issued in the revolutionary era.

Deeply engaged in his mission to awaken Americans to the sin of slavery, in 1773 Hopkins purchased seventeen copies of a book of poems that had just arrived in Boston from London. The book bore the imprint of a person who was to become the most famous African woman in America in the eighteenth century. When the author of this slender volume had stumbled off the *Phillis*, a slave ship coming directly from Africa to Boston in 1761, she was only a child of about seven years and was nearly naked. The Boston slave importer told the ship captain it was "the meanest cargo" he had ever seen.[84] A prospering tailor, John Wheatley, and his pious wife, Susanna, purchased the dark-skinned waif and named her Phillis. The Wheatley's teenage daughter, Mary, taught Phillis to read and soon found she was a prodigy. After learning English so well in sixteen months that she could read the most difficult passages of the Bible, Phillis soon showed an uncanny gift for writing. Much of her prose and poetry was inspired by deep religious feelings, but soon she was caught up in the dramatic events in Boston that were bringing revolution closer and closer. She wrote her first poem at age eleven (published in Rhode Island's *Newport Mercury*); three years later, in 1767, she penned her first political verse, a salute to King George III for repealing the Stamp Act, and then lambasted the British customs officer who murdered a teenage member of a crowd that protested British soldiers' occupying Boston in 1768. In "On the Death of Mr. Snider, Murder'd by Richardson," she wrote:

In heaven's eternal court it was decreed
How the first martyr for the cause should bleed
To clear the country of the hated brood
We whet his courage for the common good.[85]

Wheatley had thoroughly absorbed evangelical Christianity from her master and mistress, and she modeled her verses on England's widely admired Alexander Pope. In one of her first poems she wrote that "Twas mercy brought me from my *Pagan* land," and she would later write of Africa as "The land of errors, and *Egyptian* gloom." Over the years, this has brought cruel criticisms of her, summed up almost a century ago by Katherine Lee Bates, who noted that "the rare song-bird of Africa" had been "thoroughly tamed in her Boston Cage."[86] But by 1772, Wheatley inserted a muffled plea for an end to slavery in her odes to American rights and American resistance to British policies. Strategically, Wheatley inserted a stanza on African enslavement in an ode to the earl of Dartmouth, who played a key role in repealing the Townshend Acts of 1767. "Should you, my lord, while you peruse my song / Wonder from whence my love of freedom sprung." Now she made the tie between Whig liberty and black liberty.

I, young in life, by seeming cruel fate
Was snatch'd from Afric's fancied happy seat;
What pangs excruciating must molest,
What sorrows labour in my parent's breast?

Steel'd was that soul and by no misery mov'd
That from a father seiz'd his babe belov'd;
Such, such my case; And can I then but pray
Others may never feel tyrannic sway?

Wheatley was not so passive on the issue of slavery as some critics have said. She was in touch with Obour Tanner, an African woman living in Newport who may have reached New England on the same slave ship that carried Phillis Wheatley across the Atlantic, and who was actively involved in Newport's restive black community. Through Tanner, Wheatley was apparently connected to Newport's abolition-minded Sarah Osborn, and she must have known Samuel Hopkins, who in the spring of 1769 preached at the Brattle Street Church, where Wheatley worshiped and had been baptized. It seems likely that contact with Wheatley became pivotal in Hopkins's growing detestation of slavery, and Hopkins's growing abolitionism affected Wheatley in kind.

That Wheatley's poems were published in 1773 in London is remarkable. Women were not supposed to write publicly in the eighteenth century. Yet it was a young African, still enslaved, who became the first woman in North America to publish anything of a public and political nature. Proud of their prodigy, John and Susanna Wheatley, supported by Boston friends, shipped a sheaf of poems to a London printer and bookseller who obtained the support of the countess of Huntingdon, herself a fervent supporter of evangelical Methodism. Susanna Wheatley had already corresponded with the countess, who for years had been sponsoring evangelical chapels that ministered to the poor and outcast. In Phillis Wheatley, the countess found a religious sister. In the countess, Wheatley found a patroness. Subsidized by the countess, Wheatley's verse appeared under the title *Poems on Various Subjects, Religious and Moral*. Hoping that sea air would clear the clogged lungs of their nineteen-year-old slave, her master and mistress sent Phillis to London to see the volume published. There she was introduced to important reformers and public dignitaries, received a copy of Milton's *Paradise Lost* from the lord mayor of London, and met Benjamin Franklin. Phillis returned to Boston in October 1773 and soon received her freedom from the Wheatleys. She would die at age thirty, just after the American Revolution officially ended with the 1783 Treaty of Paris.

While Sarah Osborn and Phillis Wheatley contributed to one dimension of revolutionary consciousness—the self-fulfillment of spiritual women and their involvement in evangelical ideology aimed at ending slavery—other women became involved in more public ways. Almost of necessity, women became agents of change in the most public of all places—the marketplace where radical economics and politics merged. Pamphleteers by the score,

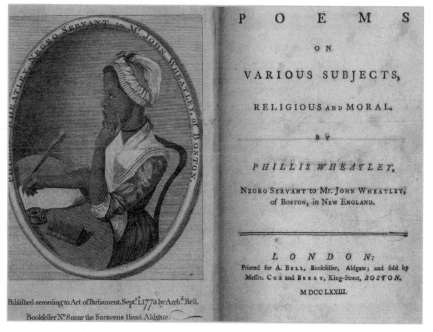

Before the Wheatleys sent their slave's poetry to England, they needed a committee of Boston ministers and political officials to certify that Phillis was truly the author of the poems. In an oral examination, eighteen learned Bostonians quizzed the teenage woman, who many assumed could not have written the poems. On trial was not only Phillis Wheatley but the African people, widely regarded as incapable of such accomplishments.

white men all, appealed to the heads and hearts of anyone who would hear their noble rhetoric about the ancient rights of freeborn Englishmen and the attacks on these rights. But when pleas and prayers and petitions went unanswered, colonists moved to economic sanctions that would squeeze British merchants and manufacturers so hard that they would pressure Parliament to mend its ways. Thus the boycott of imported British goods became the most important weapon in the colonial campaign to alter British policy. And as soon as appeals to the pocketbook became intimately linked with the appeals to constitutional rights in protesting British policies, the involvement of women became essential. Previously functioning primarily within the household, thousands of women for the first time participated in a political process that carried them outside, to the neighborhood and the marketplace. It was here that working-class women, as well as those above them, contributed to the revolutionary movement.

In three waves, the nonimportation movement, married to a nonconsumption movement, drew women who were formally (and often psychologically) proscribed from the political process into the tug-of-war over imperial policy. In 1764, Boston merchants first vowed to halt importation of British goods; the nonimportation movement mounted in intensity after the Townshend Acts of 1767, and reached its peak with the Tea Act of 1773. The strategy of forming nonimportation and nonconsumption agreements depended on mobilizing ordinary men and women. Common people could not write pamphlets or participate in legislative debates, but all of them could change their eating, drinking, and clothing choices and thus become part of a political campaign. They had, in effect, the choice of withdrawing from the Atlantic market in which they had become increasingly involved. As market-goers and arbiters of taste, women became essential. The marketplace, for the most part, was women's terrain. Without the participation of "our wives," wrote Christopher Gadsden, a leading merchant in Charleston, South Carolina, " 'tis impossible to succeed."[87]

Boston, in the vanguard as usual, began speaking of how "the Body of the People" must join the nonconsumption compacts, a specific way of publicly enfranchising those excluded from town meetings because they were female or propertyless. Women as well as men signed the 1767 Boston association pledging not to import dutied commodities. In 1772, Boston's Whigs circulated a Solemn League and Covenant putting into action another boycott. The covenant demanded both women and men of all ranks to sign, leading Peter Oliver, brother of the discredited stamp distributor in Boston, to sneer that it was "highly diverting to see the names and marks to the subscription [paper] of porters and washing women."[88] Of course this made perfect sense, for even washerwomen and delivery boys had to eat and dress themselves. Success depended on coordinating all the shoppers, who made the day-to-day decisions on what to buy and what to shun. Most of them were women. In response to the Tea Act, women by the hundreds gathered in various parts of Boston to sign pledges to drink tea no more. Elsewhere, even in hill towns of the southern interior, it was the same. Women of South Carolina could conceive of their political agency in a new light when a Presbyterian minister told them in the *South Carolina Gazette* that, by shunning imported tea, they would "have it in your power more than all your committees and Congresses,

A Scottish immigrant, Elizabeth Murray became a successful shopkeeper and helped other women set up their own businesses. She may have been among the women who signed the 1774 nonimportation pledge after the call went out that it should "be subscribed by all adult persons of both sexes." Boston merchant Harrison Gray reported that the covenant "went through whole towns with great avidity, every adult of both sexes putting their name on it, saving a few."*

to strike the stroke, and make the hills and plains of America clap their hands."[89]

Women acting on the public scene provided vital support to the resistance movement in another way. Once declared, nonimportation and nonconsumption compacts had to be enforced, because many merchants and shop-

---

*John W. Tyler, *Smugglers and Patriots: Boston Merchants and the Advent of the American Revolution* (Boston, MA: Northeastern University Press, 1986), 210.

keepers, including some women, did not endorse the consumer boycotts. Some were bitter at the restraint of their businesses by what they regarded as "political inquisitors . . . appointed in each town to pry into the conduct of individuals," as one New Yorker complained.[90] Nonetheless, such people had to be admonished, cajoled, scorned, ostracized, condemned, threatened, bullied, and often punished. This was the work of women as well as men. Popular surveillance had to be conducted block by block, street by street, and in this political work women assumed a new public role. The committees of inspection that did the main work of ferreting out boycott violators and tarring and feathering culprits were composed of men. But a much broader public was needed to make the boycotts effective.

In a third way, women proved to be pivotal. To sign a nonconsumption compact was one thing; but what were families to do without the imported textiles upon which colonial Americans had long depended? The answer was obvious: Buy American. In an era before factories, this could mean only one thing: homespun. This shift occurred in every colony, in thousands of homes, but nowhere more than in New England. Boston's town meeting in 1769 proposed to teach large numbers of women and children to spin. Peter Oliver, spitting acid as usual, saw this as "another scheme" concocted by radicals "to keep up the ball of contention." Whether women and children talked politics around their wheels we do not know. But spinning certainly became a patriotic activity and a symbol of defiance against England. From Georgia to Maine, women and children began spinning yarn and weaving cloth. "Was not every fireside indeed a theatre of politics?" John Adams remembered after the war. Towns often vied patriotically in the manufacture of cotton, linen, and woollen cloth, with women staging open-air spinning contests to publicize their commitment. In 1769, for example, about 180 women in little Middletown, Massachusetts, set the standard by weaving 20,522 yards of cloth, about 160 yards each. In the same year, Boston built 400 spinning wheels, and from these wheels came 40,000 skeins of "fine Yarn, to make any kind of Women's wear." Oliver sputtered that "Mr. [James] Otis's black regiment, the dissenting clergy, were also set to work, to preach up manufactures instead of Gospel" until "the women and children . . . set their Spinning wheels a whirling in defiance of Great Britain." Absorbed in this "new species of enthusiasm . . . , the enthusiasm of the spinning wheel," Boston women became part of a "long thread of politicks."[91]

Philadelphia caught the enthusiasm later, where it turned into women's manufacturing outside their homes rather than women's spinning in domestic settings. Drawing on a pool of impoverished women, middling men established a factory where hundreds of women toiled to demonstrate their patriotism while obtaining small wages—and in the process make the nonconsumption compacts work. "In the time of public distress," read a Philadelphia broadside, "you have now, each of you, an opportunity not only to help to sustain your families, but likewise to cast your mite into the treasury of the public good."[92]

It was harder to organize domestic production of cloth in the southern colonies because people were much more scattered across the land. On the other hand, slave owners could command enslaved women to spin and weave. White women also supported nonimportation through domestic production of cloth, simultaneously reducing the indebtedness of their husbands by boycotting English cloth, always a major import item. "With what pleasure must the patriotick eye have sparkled lately to have seen nearly a whole court yard warmly clad in the produce of their wives and daughters," wrote planter-politician Landon Carter. Carter published his account in the *Virginia Gazette* in March 1770, where it would attract attention.[93]

Women's involvement in nonconsumption and nonimportation fed another stream of radical thought: self-purification and a return to a simpler life—or what historian Edmund Morgan has called the revival of "the Puritan ethic" in a revolutionary setting. Radical patriots such as Sam Adams in Boston and Thomas Young and Benjamin Rush in Philadelphia decried the luxury and corruption they saw overtaking commercialized American seaports. Even less radical men such as John Adams saw a "universal spirit of debauchery, dissipation, luxury, effeminacy, and gaming" in Boston. Sam Adams was already imagining that a revolution against England might remake America into a "Christian Sparta," where all would live pretty much on one level and where public virtue would animate every citizen. Ruling the hearth, women again should be the springs of change. Austerity, a key Puritan virtue, began at home. "It is well known," opined the *Newport Mercury*, "that an increase of wealth and affluence paves the way to an increase of luxury, immorality, and profaneness, and here kind providence interposes; and as it were, obliges [the Americans] to forsake the use of one of their delights, to preserve their liberty."[94] Here, the newspaper was talking about tea, the favored drink of the upper echelon of colonial society. Women, the dispensers of tea, must be the agents of reform.

In the same way, women became particularly important in implementing the dictates of the Continental Congress meeting in Philadelphia in 1774, where the delegates put into effect the culminating boycott called the Continental Association. Its eighth article called the tune: "We will, in our several stations, encourage frugality, economy, and industry, and . . . will discountenance and discourage every species of extravagance and dissipation . . . and on the death of any relation or friend, none of us . . . will go into any further mourning-dress, than a black crape or ribbon on the arm or hat for gentlemen, and a black ribbon and necklace for ladies, and we will discontinue the giving of scarves and gloves at funerals." Abigail Adams, daughter of a Congregational minister, was eager to make the sacrifice. Writing to husband John, away at the Continental Congress in Philadelphia, she insisted that "if we expect to inherit the blessings of our fathers, we should return a little more to their primitive simplicity of manners. . . . As for me, I will seek wool and flax and work willingly with my hands."[95]

Allegiance to the Continental Association provided the wealthy a chance to show they were patriotic, too, by putting themselves on a level with those beneath them; but it also obliged "the genteel . . . to renounce aspects of gentility" that they prized because it differentiated them from the hoi polloi. Tea drinking and the equipage it involved was a key part of genteel culture in the late colonial period; now cross-class unity exacted a cost. Forswearing the tea ritual, in effect, accomplished the kind of social leveling that plebeian people wanted, at least symbolically. Affluent and middling colonists could prove their patriotism through conspicuous nonconsumption, but this necessitated a sacrifice of the rank-ordered society they had slowly built over the decades.[96]

Women moved from the parlor and kitchen to the street in one final way—as part of crowd actions that often became disorderly. The crowds protesting the Stamp Act, Townshend Acts, Tea Act, and Coercive Acts were overwhelmingly male; but, as historian Linda Kerber has told us, "women devised their own roles in public ritual." They marched, for example, in public funeral processions for the Boston Massacre victims and the martyred Christopher Seider, the eleven-year-old boy who, just two weeks before the Boston Massacre in 1770, had been shot dead by British soldiers as he participated in a mass protest. In New York City, after Alexander McDougall, a ship captain and radical leader, was jailed for spreading a broadside that slammed the legislature for only wanly resisting the Quartering Act, his wife led a parade in April 1770 of "45 virgins of this city . . . to pay their respects" to their hero. A month later, three of the sixty-seven Bostonians indicted for mobbing Owen Richards, a detested customs officer, on May 18, 1770, were women. Women were also involved in tarring and feathering. Peter Oliver, a thorough patriarch, deplored Boston women engaging in this. "Even the fair sex threw off their delicacy and adopted this new fashion . . . of tar and feathers. . . . When a woman throws aside her modesty, virtue drops a tear." But many women were all too prepared to trade modesty for patriotism, leading them in many cases to urge their husbands, sons, and brothers into the fray. For example, when rumors swept Massachusetts in September 1774 that General Gage's troops had fired on Bostonians, "the women surpassed the men for eagerness and spirit in the defense of liberty by arms," wrote one Worcester County man. The women urged on the men to the point that "they scarcely left half a dozen men in a town unless old and decrepit."[97]

Radical Religion

June 1768 was a beautiful month of ripening wheat and tobacco in the rolling piedmont region of Virginia. But for evangelical Baptist preachers it was a season of violence and persecution. All that spring, their emotional calls to worship were rewarded with ecstatic turnouts. Thousands of people, especially the landless, the poor, and the enslaved, gathered in meadows, on river banks, and in forest clearings. What drew them was a belief in regeneration—of themselves, of their communities, of their society at large. The old Anglican order—hierarchical and dominated by the slave-owning planter aristocracy—had none of the spiritual comfort offered by the Baptists, whose egalitarian religious fellowship brought together worshipers who addressed each other as "brother" and "sister." But the ruling gentry saw this spiritual comfort as unruly and dangerous, a raw display of emotion led by "schismaticks" and defiant zealots. This was precisely what led the sheriff of Spotsylvania County in 1768 to seize four Baptist preachers and jail them for forty days. In neighboring Culpepper County, the sheriff jailed the itinerant Baptist preacher John Ireland, a Scottish immigrant, and allowed a group of galloping horsemen to scatter the crowd that assembled to hear Ireland preach from his cell. The slaves among the worshipers were "stripped and subjected to stripes," Ireland recounted, and he was threatened with "being shut up in total darkness if ever I presumed to preach to the people again." Ignoring the authorities, Ireland continued to preach the Lord's word. Authorities jailed him again and tried to suffocate him with smoke and sulfurous gas. On another occasion, Virginians upholding the old religious order mocked the Baptist credo of immersion by clambering atop a table while Ireland preached "and made their water in my face."[98]

None of this persecution halted the upsurge of religious radicalism. In the decade before the Revolution, Baptist congregations grew from six to sixty. Not far behind them were evangelical Methodists. Speaking for the squirearchy, Virginia's attorney general warned that evangelical preachers were seducing many to "forsake their Church and the cheerful innocent society of their friends and families, and turn sour, gloomy, severe, and censorious. . . . Wives are drawn from their husbands, children from their parents, and slaves from the obedience of their masters." For those drawn to ecstatic religion, the case was just the opposite: The Anglican Church did not represent "the cheerful innocent society of their friends and families" but an authoritarian regime that denied freedom of conscience and compelled everyone to pay taxes to a church that offered them little spiritual comfort.[99]

Edmund Pendleton of Caroline County personified what the Baptists hated about the Anglican Church and its gentry allies. A lawyer, owner of many slaves, longtime member of the House of Burgesses, and avid land speculator, Pendleton was a polished member of Virginia's inner circle of power brokers. Presiding over the Caroline County Court, he meted out especially severe punishment against Baptist preachers. In July 1771, when the minister of the Anglican Church where Pendleton worshiped dragged preacher John Waller into the court, Pendleton watched his parish minister jab the butt end of his riding whip into the preacher's hymnbook and then, when the Baptist began to pray, drive the whip into Waller's mouth. The clerk of the court then dragged Waller from the courthouse, his head beating "against the ground, sometimes up, sometimes down," and delivered him over to the sheriff, who lashed him severely. "In a gore of blood," Waller "went back singing praise to God, mounted the stage and preached with a great deal of liberty."[100]

The Baptist religious revolution of the 1760s was far more subversive than the Presbyterian revivalism of the 1740s and 1750s because it challenged gentry values and their social order more sharply and reached even lower into the social order for its recruits. It was all the more subversive because almost all Baptist preachers were unschooled farmers and artisans—men drawn from

"Christ's poor." They stressed equality in human affairs and insisted that heaven was more populated by the humble poor than the purse-proud rich. It is no wonder that the quest for a personal, emotionally satisfying religion attracted about one-fifth of the white population (and a much larger share of those in the lower levels of Old Dominion society) by the eve of the Revolution. By learning to oppose authority and challenge the values of those accustomed to lead them, ordinary Virginians attracted to the Baptist and Methodist gatherings were continuing the rehearsal for revolution that the Awakeners of the 1730s and 1740s had first initiated.

Like Quakers in England a century before, the Baptists kept careful track of the martyrdom of their laymen preachers, who were stoned, punched, whipped, and jailed for preaching without licenses in the 1750s and 1760s. The man who stepped forward to defend them in the 1760s was Patrick Henry, son of the Anglican minister who two decades before had pilloried the Awakeners. His defense of the itinerant preacher John Weatherford in Chesterfield County made him a hero among Baptists. Honing the rhetorical talents that later would earn him the title of "the Cicero of Virginia," Henry defended Weatherford on charges of disturbing the peace—the usual indictment against evangelical, unlicensed preachers—by pacing before the judge and then, after asking that the indictment be read aloud, expostulating: "Did I hear it distinctly, or was it a mistake of my own? Did I hear an expression, as of a crime, that these men, whom your worships are about to try for misdemeanor, are charged with—with—what? Preaching the Gospel of the Son of God?"[101]

Henry's defense of religious dissenters became the opening wedge of the radicals' demand for complete religious toleration in Virginia. In the history books, the credit for accomplishing this after the Revolution, through passage of the storied Act for Religious Liberty, goes mainly to George Mason, who drafted the act. But it was the Baptists and Methodists who forced the issue and offered their beaten bodies as testimony to religious principles, and it was Patrick Henry who defended them on behalf of what he called "a general toleration of religion."

Elected to the House of Burgesses in 1765, Henry pressed for protection of dissenters' right to practice their religion. Defenders of the Anglican establishment blocked these efforts easily for they enjoyed a large majority in the legislature. But in 1772, the year after the savage assaults on John Waller and other Baptists, a twenty-five-year-old Anglican of liberal views arrived from

England to become a professor of moral philosophy at the College of William and Mary. Asked to deliver a sermon at Bruton Parish Church, where all the members of the House of Burgesses worshiped, Reverend Samuel Henley delivered a thunderclap. "Is *every* state infallible in the doctrines it imposes?" he asked the stunned parishioners. If not, then Virginia's establishment was guilty of legislative bigotry while putting themselves in spiritual danger for imposing religious doctrine on those who refused to recognize it as gospel.[102] To require dissenting preachers of God's word to subscribe to Anglican doctrine as the price of gaining a license was unworthy of men crying out the watchwords of liberty and freedom in their arguments with the English government in London.

Virginia's mightiest planters could not brook the newly arrived twenty-five-year-old who dared lecture them on government and religion. They denied him a rectorship at Bruton Parish Church and dismissed him from the faculty at William and Mary. But Patrick Henry was able to use Henley's indictment to soften up gentry attacks on what the House of Burgesses Committee on Religion chairman called "ill-digested notions of modern refinements" too much "borne on the tide of popularity." Social disorder would accompany an invitation "to every people under the sun to come and inhabit with us," sputtered Robert Carter Nicholas, treasurer of the House of Burgesses. But still, the gentlemen legislators could not ignore Patrick Henry's bill proposing that "all his Majesty's Protestant Subjects dissenting from the Church of England, within this Dominion, shall have and enjoy the full and free Exercise of their Religion, without Molestation or Danger of incurring any Penalty whatsoever."[103] Nicholas tried to load down Henry's measure with enough restrictions on the rights of religious dissenters to weaken the bill. Chief among them was a clause prohibiting religious gatherings in private homes; another forbade offering baptism to slaves without written permission from their masters. The latter measure was particularly sensitive since the gentry, already shaken by the bloody Christmas insurrection of three years before, were convinced that the Baptist egalitarianism and blurring of the color line invited further slave eruptions. In the end, the bill failed to pass, causing the young James Madison to lament the "diabolical Hell conceived principle of persecution" that still "rages."[104]

4

REACHING
THE CLIMAX

1774–1776

FOR GENERATIONS EVERY SCHOOLCHILD HAS LEARNED ABOUT "THE shot heard round the world" on April 19, 1775, at the North Bridge in Concord, Massachusetts, celebrated in Emerson's 1836 verse.

By the rude bridge that arched the flood,
Their flag to April's breeze unfurled,
Here once the embattled farmers stood
And fired the shot heard round the world.

But other shots heard round the world were fired in the same year. In Norfolk, Virginia, on November 14, 1775, John Murray, earl of Dunmore and the colony's royal governor, issued a proclamation that stirred nearly half a million people yearning to become fully American. In Indian country a young bilingual Mohawk took ship to England on a mission that would deeply influence how several hundred thousand Native Americans chose sides in the Revolution. And in Vermont's Green Mountains, Ethan Allen and his backwoodsmen continued volleying in defense of their land before turning their wrath against the British army. By mid-1774 government was coming unhinged throughout the colonies as usually law-abiding people took matters into their own hands. This chapter deals with the two brief years—mid-1774 to mid-1776—during which nearly everyone in eastern North America had to make the most important decisions of their lives.

Abolitionism Under War Clouds

Nobody in England's North American colonies wanted a more radical change than those who abhorred the practice of enslaving and brutalizing fellow human beings. A crescendo of objections to the continuance of slavery, mounting in the two years before the Declaration of Independence, gave hope that an ancient blotch on humaneness and morality might come to an end in a part of the world where people prided themselves on being part of a redeemer society destined to teach the world at large. The abolitionists' pamphlets that rolled off the presses, mostly in the northern cities, were longer, shriller, and more numerous and trenchant than those of the previous decade. The old argument of the Enlightenment *philosophes* that slavery was the central impediment to the march of progress continued. So did the insistence that American patriots be consistent about their proclamations of liberty and unalienable rights. But now, with war imminent, the new militancy of slaves and an astounding royal proclamation made the issue of abolition all the more urgent.

The northern colonies, including Massachusetts, Connecticut, and Rhode Island, banned the slave trade in 1774, as did Virginia and North Carolina. Pennsylvania imposed a duty on imported slaves high enough to dry up the trade. This reconciled the blatant inconsistency between dealing in slaves and appealing to the natural rights of white Americans. Halting the slave trade, however, required no great sacrifice because the slave market, through heavy importations in the early 1770s, was glutted. When the Second Continental Congress formed the Continental Association to ban the importation of British goods as a response to the Intolerable Acts of 1774, it included a ban on the slave trade, which was an extension of the ban that many states (and some towns) had already put in place. Many believed that ending the slave trade was the intermediate step in ending slavery.

Among the many published sermons and pamphlets that reached the public from 1774 to 1776, several were particularly moving. Nathaniel Niles, the Congregational minister in Newburyport, Massachusetts, shook his finger at his parishioners in July 1774: "God gave us liberty, and we have enslaved our fellow-men," he lectured. "Would we enjoy liberty? Then we must grant it to others. For shame, let us either cease to enslave our fellow-men, or else let us cease to complain of those that would enslave us. Let us either wash our hands from blood, or never hope to escape the avenger." Strong as it was, Niles's sermon convinced few, though at least one pew holder freed his slave the next day.[1]

In Philadelphia, where members of the Continental Congress could hardly avoid reading the latest screed rolling off the presses, a recently arrived Londoner, remembered mostly for a sizzling attack on monarchical tyranny, wrote his first Philadelphia essay calling for the total abolition of slavery. Thomas Paine, an unkempt man with fire in his eyes, had just arrived from England with a letter of introduction from Benjamin Franklin and hopes that he could repair his broken career as a minor customs officer. In London, Paine had written an acerbic pamphlet on the wretched pay of customs officers, and this display of literary talent helped him secure a job from Robert Aitken, a Philadelphia printer, to edit the *Pennsylvania Magazine.* Just a few weeks after being carried ashore on a litter, near death from a shipboard fever, Paine looked down on the marketplace from his room above Aitken's store, where slaves were auctioned in front of the London Coffee House. Shocked by the trading in human flesh in what he heard was the City of Brotherly Love, Paine warned Americans that by enslaving multitudes of Africans, they risked retribution from on high. "With what consistency or decency," queried Paine, could American slaveholders "complain so loudly of attempts to enslave them, while they hold so many hundred thousand in slavery?"[2]

By spring 1775, Philadelphians black and white had been exposed to a spate of pamphlets and newspaper articles attacking slavery, and the Society of Friends was on the verge of a dramatic declaration that its members must cleanse themselves of slaveholding or face disownment. Then, just five days before the clash of arms at Concord and Lexington, ten white Philadelphians met at the Rising Sun Tavern to found the Society for the Relief of Free Negroes Unlawfully Held in Bondage. Though not explicitly an abolition society at first, it would flower after the Revolution into the first corporate group in the English-speaking world dedicated to the eradication of slavery. In 1775, it was simply a small group of men, mostly Quaker artisans and small retailers, who had imbibed the humanitarian message of Woolman, Benezet,

The London Coffee House was a favorite gathering place for Philadelphia merchants and a place of sorrow for African Americans, because it was here that slave auctions were customarily held. Memory of this was still acute in 1830 when W. L. Breton sketched the building, which stood at the corner of Front and Market streets. He shows a slave auction in progress to the right, where four African women and a child are being sold.

and others. They assumed the task of redeeming fellow humans who had been snatched into bondage by unscrupulous slave traders.[3]

The first rescue mission of the society was a woman of mixed ancestry—Indian, African, and European—who along with her three children was about to be sold into slavery, even though she claimed she was born free. Led by the Philadelphia merchant Israel Pemberton and the tailor Thomas Harrison, both of whom had been quietly aiding slaves for several years in purchasing their freedom, the society entered a suit on behalf of Dinah Nevill and her children to prevent their being taken from the city by a Virginian who had purchased them from a New Jersey man across the Delaware River from Philadelphia. After four years of wartime delays and disruptions in the legal proceedings, Harrison arranged for the Philadelphia brewer Samuel Moore to purchase Nevill and her children in 1779. Moore then transferred

In this painting by James Peale, mixed-race Dinah Nevill, on bended knee, is about to be freed through the intervention of the Pennsylvania Abolition Society's tireless tailor, Thomas Harrison (in Quaker-style broad-brimmed hat and plain cloth coat). Harrison's wife looks down at Nevill while the gentry-clad Virginian Benjamin Bannerman receives coins for releasing her (and her two children) to the abolition society. This was the first manumission brokered by the first abolition society in the world.

ownership to Harrison, who set them free. The liberation of a single family in the midst of the Revolution required the tenacity and financial resources of committed Quakers in a city that itself was occupied, as we will see, by the British for nine months.

The appeals to conscience and natural rights, as well as the street-level activities of the Society for the Relief of Free Negroes, could hardly have passed unnoticed by Philadelphia's seven hundred slaves, who lived on virtually every street, worked in the taverns and coffeehouses, eavesdropped on their masters' dinner-table conversations, and in some cases, as with those taught in Anthony Benezet's schools, read the newspapers and pamphlets. As tension with England swelled in 1774–75, slaves in the city no doubt heard of slave insurrections and black petitions for freedom in other colonies. They also had opportunities to hear of British plans, in the event of a war that many now thought inevitable, to proclaim freedom for slaves and indentured servants who could reach British forces. The Philadelphia printer William Bradford reported to the young James Madison in January 1775 that a letter from London read aloud in a Philadelphia coffeehouse told of the English plan to declare "all Slaves and Servants free that would take arms against the Americans." "By this," wrote Bradford, "you see such a scheme is thought on and talked of."[4]

The restiveness of Philadelphia's slaves, living in the city where the Continental Congress met during September and October of 1774 and almost continuously after May 1775, could only have increased by the knowledge that some black Philadelphians were being freed by their masters. With appeals to conscience growing more strident amid an increasing preference for free labor, which in uncertain economic times could be hired and discharged at will, some Philadelphia masters began to free their slaves by 1774. Benjamin Rush, a perpetual optimist, believed in 1773 that three-quarters of Philadelphians "cry out against slavery."[5] But while many may have spoken out against slavery, the number who were willing to release their slaves grew only slowly. In 1774, fourteen slaves gained release from bondage or were promised freedom. In 1775, the number rose to twenty-two, and in the following year it climbed to ninety-seven. Most of the manumitters were Quakers, who acted under the new dictates of the Society of Friends. For most others, the armor of economic interest protected them from the ideological arrows aimed at their hearts. The stoppage of slave imports and the unwillingness to enter the colonial slave market were the main factors in the declining slave population of the city. But the step from deciding not to acquire additional slaves, which involved no cost, to a decision to release slaves, which amounted to a divestment of private property, proved to be large.

Most of Philadelphia's large slaveholders who were not Quakers remained resistant to the arguments of the moral reformers and natural-rights pamphleteers that slavery was incompatible with the principles upon which the

Americans based their protests against British policy. Such appeals certainly did not soften the hearts of lawyers Benjamin Chew, James Tilghman, and John Dickinson, all of whom maintained large plantations in Delaware that were worked by numerous slaves; nor could antislavery appeals move artisans such as the baker William Hodge, who owned six slaves; sailmaker John Malcom, who had five; brickmaker John Coats, who also had six; or John Philips, whose thirteen slaves manned the city's largest ropewalk. Even among those in the radical vanguard of the revolutionary movement in Philadelphia, no crisis of conscience developed through 1776. Neither Benjamin Franklin, Benjamin Rush, Charles Willson Peale, William Bradford, James Cannon, nor Christopher Marshall released their slaves, although King, one of Franklin's five slaves, had run away after Franklin took him to England in 1757.

Yet there were those ready to take a radical step and hope that others would follow. The wealthy Quaker merchant Joshua Fisher was such a man. Over many years he had purchased and sold slaves; now, in 1776 at age sixty-nine, he vowed not only to free all the slaves in his possession but to track down all those he had previously owned so he could purchase their freedom, along with the freedom of all their offspring. Fisher spent the last eight years of his life on this rescue mission. Some searches proved futile; others succeeded. Fisher located the son of a slave called Jim (to become James Freeman), paid one hundred pounds for him, and manumitted him in December 1776. He inquired about Sal and her two children, who had served Fisher for ten years before he sold them to his cousin in Delaware. All were now dead, Fisher learned. He had sold Sal in Delaware thirty-one years before and she had died about 1755, but Fisher tracked down her children, all of whom had been born into slavery. He purchased them one by one. Now in their twenties, all of them took the surname Freedom: Glasgow, Paris, Sabina, Moses, and Diana Freedom.

In other parts of the northern colonies, enslaved Africans began a new life as free people on the eve of revolution by ones, twos, and threes, rather than by scores. Freedom came first for slaves in Quaker strongholds such as the rural areas of New Jersey, the coastal towns of Rhode Island, and parts of Delaware. In Massachusetts and Connecticut, slavery withered away mostly through the death of slaves, the decision not to replenish them with further importations or purchases, and the flight of slaves unwilling to wait for the day when their masters' hearts would soften. In most of New York, which had the greatest number of slaves in the northern colonies, manumissions were rare.

Even in the South, talk of abolishing slavery rose to the level of public discussion. In his "Summary View of the Rights of British America," written in the summer of 1774 as a set of complaints against England to be presented by the Virginia delegates to the newly formed Continental Congress, Thomas Jefferson asserted that "the abolition of domestic slavery is the great object of desire in those colonies where it was unhappily introduced in their infant state." This was an extravagant claim, certainly not representing the majority of slaveholders in Virginia or anywhere else. Yet nobody seems to have objected to this statement, soon to be published in Williamsburg as a pamphlet to be discussed by Virginia's first revolutionary convention. Twenty months later, in the spring of 1776, Jefferson's second and third drafts of the Virginia constitution under consideration proposed that "No person hereafter coming into this country shall be held in slavery under any pretext whatever," not only an implicit indictment of the institution of slavery but a formula for setting slavery on the road to extinction.[6] This provision did not survive in the final draft of Virginia's 1776 constitution; but, written at a time when Dunmore's proclamation had thrown into sharp relief the contradiction between the patriots' rhetoric of freedom and the reality of an American slave-based economy, this forthright challenge to slavery made abolition a topic of wide discussion.

"Liberty to Slaves"

Many slaves could not wait for benevolent masters and mistresses to set them free. From northern New England to the Georgia-Florida border, previous strategies to obtain freedom—petitioning legislatures for a general emancipation, bringing individual freedom suits before local courts, and taking flight in the hope of successfully posing as free men and women—now expanded to a fourth highly risky but less complicated option: offering the British their services in exchange for freedom and inducing the British to issue a general proclamation that would provide an opportunity for masses of slaves to burst their shackles.

In Boston, after he had been appointed the military governor of Massachusetts in April 1774, General Thomas Gage was determined to ram the new British policy down the throats of truculent Bostonians. Five months later, he received offers of help in this difficult matter from an unlikely source. Knowing that Governor Gage had dissolved the Massachusetts legislature, thereby foreclosing that avenue of ending slavery, Boston's slaves now offered to take up the sword against their masters. In late September 1774, fourteen months before Virginia's royal governor issued his famous proclamation offering freedom to any slave or indentured servant reaching the British forces, enslaved Bostonians tried to turn rumors of British intentions into concrete policy. "There has been in town a conspiracy of the Negroes," Abigail Adams wrote her husband, now in Philadelphia as a delegate to the First Continental Congress. "At present it is kept pretty private and was discovered by one who endeavored to dissuade them from it; he being threatened with his life, applied . . . for protection." Abigail continued that "They conducted in this way . . . to draw up a petition to the Governor, telling him they would fight for him provided he would arm them and engage to liberate them if he conquered." For white Bostonians, who prided themselves as a different breed from Virginia and Carolina slave masters, this came as a shock. Benjamin Franklin's judgment nearly twenty years before that "every slave may be reckoned a domestic enemy" was being chillingly confirmed.[7]

In reporting the determination of Boston slaves to seize their freedom, Abigail reiterated her hatred of slavery. "I wish most sincerely there was not a slave in the province. It always appeared a most iniquitous scheme to me—fight ourselves for what we are daily robbing and plundering from those who have as good a right to freedom as we have." All over Massachusetts, slaves agreed. In late March 1775, slaves in Bristol and Worcester counties petitioned the local committees of correspondence for assistance "in obtaining their freedom." In mid-April, just before the "shot heard round the world," slaves in Bristol County, Rhode Island, slipped away to join "Col. Gilbert's banditti," a group of thirty-five Loyalists who had obtained arms from a British man-of-war in Newport. Then, in the aftermath of the firefight at Lexington and Concord, Worcester County's convention, sitting outside the law, resolved that "we abhor the enslaving of any of the human race, and particularly of the NEGROES, in this country," and promised to do anything possible "toward the emancipating the NEGROES. . . ."[8]

Not far behind Massachusetts slaves were African Americans in the southern colonies. In November 1774, apparently aware that the English might give them their freedom, a group of Virginia slaves met to choose a leader "who was to conduct them when the English troops should arrive," as the young James Madison revealed to Philadelphia's printer William Bradford. Madison recounted how the slaves "foolishly thought . . . that by revolting to them [the British] they should be rewarded with their freedom." He soon learned that the slaves were not foolish at all but were anticipating what would soon become policy. Madison begged Bradford not to print anything about this plot in the *Pennsylvania Journal* for fear that the news would inspire other uprisings. Two weeks later, the dreaded insurgency surfaced in coastal Georgia when six male and four female slaves murdered their plantation overseer and his wife and then marched to neighboring plantations, where they killed several whites and wounded others. When a patrol captured the rampaging slaves, they were burned alive at the stake, not only to avenge the deaths of white planters but to terrify other slaves with rebellion on their minds.[9]

Word leaking back from England gave southern slaves further reason to believe that their calculations about evolving British policy were not foolish. In early January 1775, the news reached southerners that a member of Parliament had proposed a general emancipation of slaves as a way of "humbling the high aristocratic spirit of Virginia and the southern colonies." The House of Commons did not pass the measure, which would have rocked overseas English slavery to the roots; but in Massachusetts Governor Gage soon expressed interest in such a policy. In a letter to John Stuart, southern superintendent of Indian affairs, Gage noted that if white South Carolinians continued their reckless opposition to British policies, "it may happen that your rice and indigo will be brought to market by negroes instead of white people."[10]

Slaves in tidewater Virginia did their part to shape English policy on the emancipation issue through a rash of uprisings in early 1775. On April 21, only two days after the minutemen riddled Gage's troops, who were sent to capture the colonial arsenals at Lexington and Concord, determined slaves made their move. John Murray, earl of Dunmore, had already moved from the governor's mansion in Williamsburg, Virginia's capital, to the *Fowey*, a British warship anchored in the lower York River. From here he dispatched a detachment to seize barrels of gunpowder in Williamsburg and bring them to the British warships. Edmund Randolph later claimed that the governor's intention was to disarm the Virginians and "weaken the means of opposing an insurrection of the slaves . . . for a protection against whom in part the magazine was at first built." Seeing their chance, a number of slaves in Williamsburg offered to join Dunmore and "take up arms." To cow white patriot Virginians, Dunmore now warned that he "would declare freedom to the slaves and reduce the City of Williamsburg to ashes" if the hastily raised militia units threatened him.[11]

Ten days later, on May 1, 1775, Dunmore made an earthshaking decision in favor of what one white Virginian called "the most diabolical" scheme to "offer freedom to our slaves and turn them against their masters." Writing to the secretary of state in London, Dunmore set out his plan "to arm all my own Negroes and receive all others that will come to me whom I shall declare free." It was a policy, remembered South Carolina's William Drayton, that "was already known" by slaves, who "entertain ideas that the present contest was for obliging us to give them their liberty." Near panic engulfed the South. "The newspapers were full of publications calculated to excite the fears of the people—massacres and instigated insurrections were the words in the mouth of every child," remembered Indian superintendent John Stuart. Stuart himself was part of the potential insurrection. Charlestonians drove him from the city after he was suspected of plotting to draw Creek Indians into the conflict on the British side. Stuart fled to Saint Augustine, Florida, to await the British occupation of South Carolina.[12]

When the Second Continental Congress met in Philadelphia on May 10, 1775, the fight at Concord and Lexington was on everyone's mind. The undeclared war had begun. South Carolina's Henry Laurens pointed out that it was obvious that the government in London had decided "to quell the American troubles by the law of arms and not to quiet them by the laws of reason and justice."[13] Determined not to be gelded by Parliament and George III's ministers, Congress prepared to fight.

But Congress and all the American colonists so disposed had to fight as thirteen united colonies. To this end, one of Congress's first acts was to declare that "these colonies be immediately put into a state of defense." Congress then committed itself to forming a Continental army. The man to lead it, they decided, was the tall, stern-visaged Virginian George Washington, who should "command all the continental forces, raised, or to be raised, for the defence of American liberty." This crucial step on the road to declaring independence is in every textbook on American history. But rarely noted is that the delegates to Congress understood that the preparations for defense were required not only by the clash of arms at Concord and Lexington but by the prospect of a British invasion of the southern colonies in conjunction with a slave insurrection. In South Carolina, one day before Congress decided to form the Continental army, Henry Laurens, president of South Carolina's provincial congress, urged the formation of a state military force to resist the rumored British capture of Charleston linked with an incited slave insurrection. South Carolina's assembly promptly complied. The military association was justified by "the actual commencement of hostilities against this continent—the threats of arbitrary impositions from abroad—and the dread of instigated insurrections at home." Any timidity that white South Carolinians felt about plunging into independence evaporated in an atmosphere of near panic caused by the fear that their slaves, 80,000 of them, who made up about 60 percent of the population, were poised to rise up to seize their freedom.[14]

A few weeks after the Second Continental Congress authorized a Continental army, white Carolinians uncovered the insurrectionary slave plot they had anticipated. The leader was not a slave but a free black man. Jeremiah, a fisherman and boat pilot who knew the shallow waters of Charleston's harbor, hoped to be the agent of deliverance for thousands of slaves. Several months earlier, he had spread the word that "there is a great war coming soon" and that the British would "come to help the poor negroes." After arresting him, white authorities charged Jeremiah with plotting an insurrection and intending to pilot the Royal Navy over the treacherous sandbar that blocked the entrance to Charleston's harbor. On August 18, 1775, white authorities hanged Jeremiah and burned him at the stake, despite the efforts of William Campbell, the newly arrived royal governor, to save his life. Believing that the evidence against Jeremiah was very thin, the governor wrote home that "my blood ran cold when I read what ground they had doomed a fellow creature to death." His efforts to save Jeremiah "raised such a clamor amongst the people, as is incredible," wrote Campbell, "and they openly and loudly declared, if I granted the man a pardon they would hang him at my door."[15]

Executions and burnings at the stake were acts of terror to keep rebellion-minded slaves intimidated. But reducing Jeremiah to ashes or cropping the ears of slaves did not hold back the waves of slave unrest in the summer of 1775. The wave crested in late fall when Virginia's governor, Lord Dunmore, made official what everyone had known he intended for months. On November 7, 1775, aboard the *William*, anchored in Norfolk harbor, he drafted a royal proclamation declaring martial law and labeling as traitors to the king any colonist who refused "to resort to his Majesty's standard." The proclamation included the dreaded words: "I do hereby further declare all indented servants, Negroes, or others (appertaining to Rebels) free, that are able and willing to bear arms, they joining His Majesty's Troops as soon as may be, for the more speedily reducing the Colony to a proper sense of their duty, to His Majesty's crown and dignity."[16]

Lord Dunmore did not publish the proclamation for another week. But the timing and place of the public proclamation were poignant. On November 14, a contingent of British soldiers under Dunmore's command, supplemented by escaped slaves, thrashed a Virginia militia unit at Kemp's Landing, on the Elizabeth River south of Norfolk. Dunmore's force killed several militiamen, captured both militia colonels, and put the rest of the Virginians to flight. One of the colonels, Joseph Hutchings, was captured by two of his own escaped slaves. Flush with this victory, Dunmore issued his proclamation.[17]

Among the first to flee to Dunmore were eight of the twenty-seven slaves who toiled at the stately Williamsburg dwelling of Peyton Randolph, Speaker of Virginia's House of Burgesses and one of Virginia's delegates to the Continental Congress. Hearing almost simultaneously of Randolph's sudden death in Philadelphia and Dunmore's Proclamation, Aggy, Billy, Eve, Sam, Lucy, George, Henry, and Peter slipped away from Randolph's house. Eluding the slave patrols walking Williamsburg's streets, they reached the British forces not far from town. Three weeks after Dunmore issued his proclamation, Lund Washington, manager of his cousin George's Mount Vernon estate, warned the general that among the slaves "there is not a man of them but would leave us, if they could make their escape.... Liberty is sweet."[18]

Within several months, between eight hundred and one thousand slaves had flocked to Dunmore, and many hundreds more were captured while trying. Many of them, perhaps one-third, were women and children. Mustered into what Dunmore named the Ethiopian Regiment, some of the men were uniformed with sashes bearing the inscription LIBERTY TO SLAVES. The slaves of many of Virginia's leading white revolutionary figures now became black revolutionary Virginians themselves. They soon formed the majority of Dunmore's Loyalist troops. Commanding the Ethiopian Regiment was the British officer Thomas Byrd, the son of patriot William Byrd III, one of Virginia's wealthiest land and slave owners.[19]

Dunmore retreated to Norfolk and ventured out on December 9, 1775, with six hundred troops, half of them escaped slaves, to take on the Virginians at Great Bridge on the Elizabeth River. The Ethiopian Regiment fought "with the intrepidity of lions," according to one observer; but the Americans vanquished Dunmore's forces, convincing the governor to withdraw from Norfolk and board his contingent on ships in the harbor.[20] Slaves seeking sanctuary now had to commandeer boats and slip down the rivers emptying into Chesapeake Bay in order to clamber aboard the British ships. Cruising the Chesapeake Bay on Dunmore's ships, they went out in foraging parties to procure provisions for the British.

Escaping slaves augmented Dunmore's Ethiopian Regiment day by day. But an outbreak of smallpox soon reversed these gains. Crowded together on small ships, black men and women who had tasted freedom only briefly contracted the infection rapidly. By June 1776, Dunmore admitted that the killer disease had "carried off an incredible number of our people, especially blacks."[21] Dunmore briefly occupied Gwynn's Island, near the mouth of the Piankatank River, but here, too, smallpox tore through his ranks. By July, he withdrew his disease-riddled forces, sending part of them to Saint Augustine and the Bermudas and others, including three hundred of the strongest and healthiest black soldiers, northward to New York City, then to be sent southward a year later for a land assault through Maryland to Pennsylvania.

The dread of slave insurrection that swept South Carolina and Virginia in 1775–76 also engulfed North Carolina. Especially in the coastal towns of Edenton, New Bern, and Wilmington, patrols searched slave huts for hidden weapons. In the Cape Fear region, where slavery was extensive, white officials nipped a slave insurrection in the bud just before July 8, 1775, when slave leaders, according to the Pitt County Safety Committee chairman, planned "to fall on and destroy the family where they lived, then proceed from house to house (burning as they went) until they arrived in the back country where they were to be received with open arms by a number of persons there appointed and armed by government for their protection, and as a further reward they were to be settled in a free government of their own." "Armed by government" meant that Governor Josiah Martin, who had recently deplored the military force used by his predecessor to crush the Regulators, was the instigator of this slave insurrection. About forty slaves who had fled their plantations were found with arms and arrested. Many were whipped and had their ears severed; one was executed. Governor Martin fled to Fort Johnston, at the mouth of the Cape Fear River, and tried to recruit Loyalists to strengthen the small royal garrison there. Unwilling to keep this serpent in their nest, the Wilmington Committee of Safety, infuriated by the governor's "base encouragement of slaves eloped from their masters, feeding and employing them, and his atrocious and horrid declaration that he would incite them to an insurrection," raised a militia to attack Fort Johnston on July 17, 1775.[22]

Destroying the fort was easy enough, since Governor Martin and his small contingent withdrew without a fight to a Royal Navy ship in the Cape Fear River. When Martin recruited immigrant Scottish Highlanders, especially those who had just arrived in North Carolina and whose land grants depended upon their willingness to uphold the king's authority, the patriot cause became more difficult. But in a pitched battle at Moore's Creek on March 27, 1776, the Americans routed the charging Loyalist Scots and dashed the slaves' hopes for a British victory. However, a powerful British fleet arrived at the mouth of the Cape Fear River in the spring of 1776. This opened the door of opportunity for Cape Fear slaves once again.

One such slave, who has been forgotten in the fog of historical amnesia, was Thomas Peters. Captured in what is now Nigeria in about 1760, he had been brought to New Orleans on a French slave ship. Shortly thereafter, this Egba African of the Yoruba tribe started his own revolution in America, because he had been deprived of what he considered to be his natural rights. He needed neither a written language nor constitutional treatises to convince himself of that. And no amount of harsh treatment persuaded him to accept his lot meekly. This personal rebellion was to span three decades, cover five countries, and entail three more transatlantic voyages.[23]

Peters never adapted well to slavery. He may have been put to work in the sugarcane fields in Louisiana, where heavy labor drained life away from plantation laborers almost as fast as in the Caribbean sugar islands. Whatever his work role, he tried to escape three times from the grasp of bondage. Three times, legend has it, he paid the price of being an unsuccessful black rebel: First he was whipped severely, then branded, and finally fitted with ankle shackles. But his French master could not snuff out his yearning for freedom and seems to have eventually given up on trying to pacify the resistant slave. Sometime after 1760, he sold Peters north. By 1770, Peters was the property of William Campbell, an immigrant Scotsman who had settled in Wilmington, North Carolina, on the Cape Fear River.

In all likelihood, it was in Wilmington that Peters learned his trade as millwright. Three-fifths of the slaves in the Cape Fear region worked in the production of timber products and naval stores—pine planking, turpentine, tar, and pitch. As sawyers, tar burners, stevedores, carters, and carpenters, they were essential to the regional economy's mainstay. The details of Peters's life in Wilmington are obscure because nobody recorded the turning points in the lives of slaves, but he appears to have found a wife and to have begun a family at this time. His wife, Sally, gave birth to a daughter in 1771. Peters may have gained a measure of autonomy because slaves in urban areas were not supervised so strictly as on plantations. Working on the docks, hauling pine trees from the forests outside town to the lumber mills, ferrying boats and rafts along the intricate waterways, and marketing various goods in the town, they achieved a degree of mobility, a knowledge of the terrain, and a taste of freedom.

Like many other slaves in the 1770s, Peters got caught up in the anticipation of what the colonial resistance movement might mean for enslaved Africans. His own master had become a leading member of Wilmington's Sons of Liberty in 1770 and later the Committee of Safety. Peters heard much about the rhetoric of white patriots attempting to secure for themselves and their posterity those natural rights that they called unalienable. In a town of only about 250, it was impossible to keep anything a secret. By summer 1775, Peters was keenly aware of the rumors of British intentions to inspire a slave insurrection that would bring the cheeky white colonists to account. In that month, the town's Committee of Safety ordered all blacks disarmed and declared martial law when they heard that Governor Martin was "collecting men, provisions, warlike stores of every kind, spiriting up the back counties and perhaps the slaves." The visiting Janet Schaw wrote that white Carolinians in the Cape Fear region believed that the Crown had promised "every Negro that would murder his master and family that he should have his master's plantation. . . . The Negroes have got it amongst them and believe it to be true. Tis ten to one they may try the experiment. . . ."[24]

When Dunmore's Proclamation reached the ears of Thomas Peters and other slaves in Wilmington in November 1775, a buzz of excitement must surely have washed over them. But the time for self-liberation was not yet ripe, because hundreds of miles of pine barrens, swamps, and inland waterways separated Wilmington from Norfolk, where Lord Dunmore's British forces were concentrated, and slaves knew that white patrols were on watch throughout the tidewater area from Cape Fear to the Chesapeake Bay. The opportune moment for Peters arrived four months later. On February 9, 1776, white Wilmingtonians evacuated the town as word arrived that the British sloop *Cruizer* was tacking up the Cape Fear River to bombard the town. A month later, four British ships arrived from Boston, including several troop transports under Sir Henry Clinton. For the next two months, the British controlled the river, plundered the countryside, and set off a wave of slave desertions. Seizing the moment, Peters and his family made their escape. Captain George Martin, an officer under Sir Henry Clinton, organized the escaped slaves from the Cape Fear region into the company of Black Pioneers, as Peters testified seven years later at the end of the war. Now, in the spring of 1776, the days of an uncertain freedom began for Peters's family.

Regardless of the horrible death toll at the hands of smallpox, Dunmore's Proclamation reverberated throughout the colonies and became a major factor in convincing white colonists that reconciliation with the mother country was impossible. Dunmore's Proclamation, wrote South Carolina's Edward Rutledge, was more effectual in working "an eternal separation between Great Britain and the Colonies . . . than any other expedient."[25]

Among African Americans, Dunmore remained the "African Hero," as Richard Henry Lee, the fiery Virginia advocate of independence, derisively put it. Indeed, Dunmore did seem like a biblical Moses to slaves. As far north as Philadelphia, where the Second Continental Congress was sitting, news of the "African Hero" galvanized blacks. Encountering a white "gentlewoman" on the street, a black Philadelphian insulted her. When she reprimanded him, he shot back, "Stay you d[amne]d white bitch 'till Lord Dunmore and his black regiment come, and then we will see who is to take the wall." "Hell itself," wrote one Philadelphian, "could not have vomited anything more black than his design of emancipating our slaves. . . . The flame runs like wild fire through the slaves."[26]

Logan's Lament

In late April 1774, as Thomas Jefferson and other members of the House of Burgesses gathered in Williamsburg, Virginia, to establish an intercolony Committee of Correspondence and protest the Intolerable Acts that had closed the port of Boston, a party of armed Virginians led by Daniel Greathouse fell on a canoe filled with nine Shawnee women, children, and a single man as it floated down the Ohio River. They killed all nine, scalped them, and ripped from the womb of one woman a near-term child, which they "stuck on a pole." All of the Shawnee were kin of Tachnedorus, known to the Virginians as John Logan, a half-French, half-Mingo war leader. The pregnant woman was his sister, and the single male in the party was his brother. The white attackers knew Logan well. He was the son of the important Chief Shikellamy and had grown up under the influence of Moravian missionaries. Logan remembered well the murder of many of his Christianized kin at the hands of the Paxton Boys in 1763, and the Virginians remembered that Logan had not retaliated. Logan remained the white colonists' friend and refused to fight against the English in the French and Indian War.[27]

Stricken with grief and anger, Logan gathered a war party and attacked frontier settlements of Virginians along the Monongahela River. He took thirteen white scalps and one prisoner. Thousands of frontier families fled eastward or forted up. These events quickly escalated into a war of Virginians against Shawnee, known as Dunmore's War after the royal governor of Virginia who launched the assault. At the conclusion of this war, to be treated below, Logan sent an Indian messenger to Governor Dunmore with an address that would ricochet down the corridors of history. "I appeal to any white man," began Logan, "to say, if ever he entered Logan's cabin hungry, and he gave him not meat; if ever he came cold and naked, and he clothed him not." Logan recounted his abstention from the Seven Years' War. "Such was my love for the white[s], that my countrymen pointed as they passed, and said 'Logan is the friend of white men.' I had even thought to have lived with you, but for the injuries of one man. Col. Cresap, the last spring, in cold blood, and unprovoked, murdered all the relations of Logan, not sparing even my women and children. There runs not a drop of my blood in the veins of any living creature. This called on me for revenge. I have sought it; I have killed many: I have fully glutted my vengeance." Logan then concluded with reflections on the peace treaty at the end of Dunmore's War in October 1774, by which the Shawnee yielded a vast territory in what became Kentucky. "For my country, I rejoice at the beams of peace. But do not harbour a thought that mine is the joy of fear. Logan never felt fear. He will not turn on his heel to save his life. Who is there to mourn for Logan? Not one."

Logan's address entered the annals of American literature as an example of Indian oratory and pathos. It first became known in January 1775, when Philadelphia's printer, William Bradford, published it in his newspaper after receiving it from James Madison as an example of "Indian Eloquence and Mistaken Valour." A few weeks later, it appeared in the *Virginia Gazette*. But Logan's words attracted a far wider audience when Thomas Jefferson published his *Notes on the State of Virginia* in 1785, where Jefferson included an account of the gruesome attack on the unprovoked Logan family. Here, Jefferson assigned guilt, as did Logan, to Michael Cresap, "a man infamous for the many murders he had committed on those much-injured people." Years later, after his account was challenged in 1797 by Luther Martin, the attorney general of Maryland, an avid abolitionist and Cresap's son-in-law, Jefferson published an *Appendix to the Notes on the State of Virginia* in 1800. He made some corrections to his brief initial account, where he had noted that the attack on Logan's family had been justified at the time by the robbery and murder of "certain land adventurers on the Ohio [River]." Jefferson also changed the place of the attack, and now admitted that the Indian provocation was simple robbery, without murder of any white. However, he failed to mention that he had learned that Cresap had not perpetrated the massacre, though he had taken part in two other attacks at the time that killed other relatives of Logan's. Most tellingly, Jefferson omitted any mention that he had received a letter from his good friend George Rogers Clark, hero of the western campaign against the British during the Revolution, that exculpated Cresap.

Today's leading historian on Jefferson's Indian policy reasons that Jefferson concealed the letter from Clark because Logan's story characterized the butchery of his family as the work of Indian-hating frontier ruffians—Cresap and Greathouse—who greatly dishonored the virtue of revolutionary-era Americans. But the real story that Jefferson did not want to tell was that of the Virginians' systematic plundering of Indian land; the provoking of Indians who dared resist these invasions, justifying their massacre; and the role of Jefferson's friend George Rogers Clark, and Jefferson himself, in looking to these lands as a source of great wealth. "By focusing intensely on a single atrocity perpetrated by a few violent white men," writes Anthony F. C. Wallace, "it distracted attention from a larger set of legal and political issues involving rights to the land west of the Appalachians—issues of which Jefferson was undoubtedly aware."

At heart, the murderous attack on Logan's family was part of an attempt to precipitate a war against the Shawnee, Mingo, Delaware, and other Ohio region Indians in order to seize their lands in Kentucky, western Virginia, western Pennsylvania, and eastern Ohio. John Heckewelder, the Moravian missionary to the Indians whose accounts of this period are the most reliable, described the frontier situation: "The whole country on the Ohio River, had already drawn the attention of many persons from the neighbouring provinces; who generally forming themselves into parties, would rove through the country in search of land either to settle on, or for speculation; and some, careless of watching over their conduct, or destitute of both honour and humanity, would join a rabble (a class of people generally met with on the frontiers) who maintained, that to kill an Indian, was the same as killing a bear or a buffalo." In this way, Heckewelder explained, the land-crazed, Indian-hating frontiersmen "would fire on Indians that came across them by the way; nay, more, would decoy such as lived across the river, to come over, for the purpose of joining them in hilarity; and when these complied, they fell on them and murdered them. Unfortunately, some of the murdered were of the family of Logan, noted man among the Indians."

Jefferson, Patrick Henry, George Mason, George Washington, and most of the other Virginia leaders were not Indian haters, but they were the men coordinating the protests against English policy in the years from 1774 to 1776, while they speculated avidly in Indian lands across the Appalachians. The Proclamation Line of 1763, as modified by the Fort Stanwix treaty of 1768, had denied legal title in most of the Ohio country to Virginia's land speculators; but it did not stop land-hungry settlers from pouring across the line and squatting on unsecured land in the forbidden zone. If the English government lifted the ban, the settlers reasoned, they would gain legal title "on the ground of preoccupancy," as a later legal case put it. Meanwhile, Virginia's land company leaders began to sniff success in their dream of controlling all of Kentucky when Lord Dunmore started fulfilling the promised land bounties to veterans of the Seven Years' War by issuing patents to a few of them. This was enough to revive the hopes of the dormant land companies, which had been dashed by the English government in 1770. George Mason resuscitated the Ohio Company in 1772 and bought up rights to fifty thousand acres. The next year, Jefferson invested in a speculative scheme that he hoped would bring him ten thousand acres. Then, in June 1774, when Parliament passed the Quebec Act, promise turned into pessimism. By declaring all land west of the Ohio River part of British Quebec, "the river that the Virginia gentry had once viewed as a sure route to wealth became a barrier instead."[28]

While the storm over the Intolerable Acts of 1774 occupied most of the colonial leaders elsewhere, Virginian leaders busied themselves with clearing this roadblock. If they could not convince the English government to erase the Proclamation Line of 1763 and if they could not secure title from the Shawnees and Mingos who possessed the region, they would need to take it by force. Near at hand was the pretense the Virginians wanted. They found it in Logan's retaliatory raids on squatting Virginians after white backwoodsmen massacred his family. Logan had been careful not to attack Pennsylvania squatting families but limited himself and his small raiding party to Virginians. Unable to restrain Logan, Shawnee chiefs tried to de-escalate the situation. But John Connolly, Virginia's representative at the Pittsburgh outpost, where the Monongahela, Ohio, and Allegheny rivers converged, declared that Logan's raids amounted to a Shawnee declaration of war. "The Opportunity we have so long wished for, is now before us," declared William Preston, Virginia's Fincastle County militia officer and a land surveyor who was running surveys entirely across the Proclamation Line. In this manufactured war, land, not vengeance, was the cause.[29] Acting unilaterally, the Virginians got the preemptive war they wanted.

Dunmore's War began in June 1774. It was nearing its conclusion in October as the First Continental Congress in Philadelphia prepared to disband after adopting the Continental Association, the pledge to halt imports from and exports to England. Called out by Governor Dunmore, about two thousand Virginia militiamen razed Mingo and Shawnee towns on a branch of the Ohio River. Thwarted in their attempts to avoid the war, the Shawnee sent war belts to the Delawares, Miamis, Wyandots, and Chippewas. Pennsylvania, which was contending with Virginia for the Ohio River lands, stayed out of the war and indeed tried to contain it. With Dunmore himself leading one war party, the Virginians bested the Shawnee at the Battle of Point Pleasant on the Kanawha River on October 10, 1774, where Cornstalk, the fifty-four-year-old Shawnee leader, sued for peace. "The battle," writes historian Richard White, "meant that Kentucky could be settled and that Lord Dunmore and the Virginia elite could now become rich."[30]

Contemplating the loss of their hunting grounds in Kentucky, the Shawnee chiefs must have wondered what the outcome might have been if they had been able to secure Indian allies. It was a question that all Indian nations would face very shortly. From the British point of view, one band of colonists, with their royal governor backing them, had again defied the authority of the Crown. From Boston, General Thomas Gage pronounced the king's disapproval of the Virginians' attack on the Shawnee and ordered them out of the Kentucky zone. But the king might as well have ordered the Virginians out of Virginia.

Overlapping Dunmore's War was a conflict between Georgia backcountry settlers and the Creek Indians who had controlled the southeastern uplands for centuries. But in this case, the royal governor, James Wright, was deeply involved in Indian trade and much opposed to squatting backcountry settlers who, in Virginia, had been the beneficiaries of Governor Dunmore's war on the Shawnee. From 1774 until the end of the Revolution, the Georgia back-country's revolution, as historian Edward Cashin has characterized it, "was from start to finish an Indian war."[31] Backcountry Loyalists were allied with the Creeks; frontier patriots were deep-dyed Indian haters. The Yorkshire immigrant Thomas Brown was typical of the backcountry Loyalists. A large landowner near Augusta, he was mobbed, tarred and feathered, and branded on both feet by patriot "liberty boys." But that did not stop him from enlisting support from some of the Creeks, obtaining British troop support from Florida, and returning to seize Augusta and maintain it as a Loyalist strong-hold for much of the war, finally retreating to form the Loyalist East Florida Rangers.

With Indian lands along the entire southern Appalachian frontier much in play in 1774–76, southerners gained new resolve to resist English authority. The roll call of Virginia revolutionary leaders was also the roll call of Virginia speculators in western land whose rights, they believed, had been oblit-erated by a series of policy decisions, legal judgments, and Parliamentary acts in 1774, including the Quebec Act. The man who was the principal author of Virginia's Declaration of Rights and Virginia's new state constitu-tion, George Mason, "had watched the Proclamation of 1763 destroy first his beloved Ohio Company and then his hopes of obtaining fifty thousand acres of Kentucky land...."[32] The man who would introduce the Declaration of Independence to the Continental Congress in July 1776, Richard Henry Lee, had been appalled by how the 1763 Proclamation Act and the Quebec Act dashed his Mississippi Land Company's hopes to lay hands on 2.5 million acres. The man who would lead the Continental army, George Washing-ton, had thousands of acres of bounty lands that he purchased cheaply from veterans' claims slip from his hands as a result of the English attempt to stop Virginia land speculation. The man who drafted the Declaration of Independence, Thomas Jefferson, had invested in three land companies that would have given him title to 17,000 acres if the ministry in London had not cracked down. And the man whose fiery speeches helped push the colonies to the brink of revolution, Patrick Henry, saw five of his land ventures disappear like smoke. All these disappointments could be undone through a war that would remove the roadblocks—that is, a double war: against England, and against the ancient inhabitants of the fertile region watered by the Ohio River and its tributaries.

The Quebec Act was obnoxious not only to Virginians but to many colonists speculating in lands north of the Ohio River. The act also fiercely offended Protestant New Englanders because it guaranteed Catholic Canadians the right to worship freely. Hence, they folded the Quebec Act into the other Coercive Acts of 1774 and branded them all as "intolerable." But for the Six Iroquois Nations the Quebec Act promised relief from the frantic speculation and squatting in the lands reserved for the Iroquois and other northern tribes. News of the Quebec Act had hardly reached them before the Iroquois had to face the Virginia-Shawnee war, for the Shawnees were their dependents and called on them for support.

The Iroquois council met at Johnson Hall, the mansion of Northern Superintendent of Indian Affairs Sir William Johnson, on July 11, 1774. For years, Johnson had enjoyed great influence with the Iroquois, learning their language, dressing like them on occasion, participating in their war dances, smoking pipes at their councils, and taking the Mohawk name of Warraghiyagey—meaning "man who does much business." Johnson also took as his second common-law wife Degonwadonti, a Mohawk woman known to the English as Molly Brant. In the Mohawk River valley, in today's upstate New York, Johnson was the largest landowner, the most active Indian trader, and the man in whom the king's authority was vested. At the somber July meeting, an ailing Johnson entreated the Iroquois to stay out of the Shawnee-Virginia war and promised that the king would restrain the marauding white frontiersmen. That evening, with the council still in session, Johnson collapsed and died. General Gage in Boston promptly appointed Guy Johnson, William's son-in-law, to succeed him. At a meeting two months later, Iroquois chiefs brought with them "the Great Old Covenant Chain Belt"—a ceremonial wampum belt symbolizing the chain of friendship that the Six Nations had struck with the English seven decades before. Holding the Covenant Chain, the Iroquois pledged "that you may know the bad words of the Shawanese have no effect upon us."[33]

But the full council of the Iroquois Confederacy would have to endorse this decision. At the October 1774 meeting, the brother of William Johnson's Mohawk wife played an important role that would soon make him a central figure in the impending American Revolution. Thayendanegea, called Joseph Brant by the English, was born in an Iroquois village in Ohio country in 1742 and grew up bilingual and bicultural. Schooled at Eleazar Wheelock's Indian school in Lebanon, Connecticut, later to become Dartmouth College, Brant fought as a thirteen-year-old with William Johnson and American colonists against the French at Crown Point in the Seven Years' War. He aided the colonists again by battling the Ottawa leader Pontiac's insurgents, who tried to expel British soldiers and encroaching Americans from the Ohio country in 1763. In 1774, at age thirty-two, Brant was sent by Guy Johnson to the Onondaga Grand Council meeting to take notes and report on the proceedings. In his faithful rendition of the proceedings, Brant established a reputation for reliability and diplomacy.

Attended by some six hundred Iroquois, the Grand Iroquois council endorsed the decision to stay out of the Shawnee-Virginia war. But over the next six months, as tension mounted between the American colonists and England, an even weightier question arose: Would the Iroquois stay out of what they regarded as a family dispute between Mother England and her colonial children; would they maintain their allegiance to the English king by fighting against the Americans; or would they support the American cause against George III? The Concord-Lexington firefight in April 1775 intensified the pressure, especially on the Mohawks, the easternmost of the Iroquois nations and the one most affected by landgrabbing and fraudulent land purchases by white settlers in the newly named Tryon County (to honor New York's new royal governor, who had left the North Carolina Regulators defeated and demoralized).

As the Iroquois pondered their position, the matter became more urgent when several companies of New Englanders and New Hampshire backwoodsmen, completely unauthorized by the Continental Congress, attacked and captured Fort Ticonderoga and Crown Point on Lake Champlain on May 10–11, 1775. Under the joint command of Benedict Arnold and Ethan Allen (who wrestled dangerously for command of this private expeditionary army), the attack at dawn succeeded without a shot being fired. Surrounding the fort, Allen called out to the British officer, who commanded only about forty men: "Come out of there, you damned old rat." When asked in whose name the Americans were fighting, the ever bullheaded Allen replied, "In the name of the Great Jehovah and the Continental Congress."[34] Neither had authorized the attack. But this victory made the Iroquois' problem no less severe. The two forts, lying midway between New York City and Quebec, controlled the trade route from the Atlantic Ocean through the Saint Lawrence River valley to Iroquoia. Now British trade goods, upon which the Iroquois depended, could reach the Iroquois only through American hands. In this bleak situation, most Iroquois leaders stalled for time and continued to waver.

Though embarrassed at first by the attacks of rash New Englanders spoiling for a fight, the Continental Congress was grateful for the scores of cannons, howitzers, and mortars captured at Ticonderoga and Crown Point. This artillery was exactly what the patriots needed to conduct a siege of redcoat-occupied Boston. The vicious battle that now occurred on the Charlestown peninsula across the Charles River from Boston settled the minds of most delegates to the Congress. Here, on Breed's Hill (known in the history books as Bunker Hill), 1,200 New England militiamen, working in the dead of night on June 16, 1775, constructed a fortified entrenchment from which they hoped to dislodge the British troops occupying Boston. At daybreak on June 17, the British reacted swiftly. Two assaults by British infantry fell back before withering patriot fire, but a third succeeded. The Americans sustained more than four hundred casualties; the British lost far more, nearly half of their 2,200 troops. "If we have eight more such victories," one Englishman ruefully remarked, "there will be nobody left to bring the news."[35] It would turn out that this was the bloodiest battle of the eight-year war now in progress. Hearing of this battle, Congress authorized the invasion of Canada, which would proceed from the forts at Ticonderoga and Crown Point that Benedict Arnold and Ethan Allen had bloodlessly captured.

By this time, the Mohawks, most of them attached to Guy Johnson and accompanied by New York colonists who remained loyal to their king, began withdrawing from upper New York to seek refuge to the west. Then in July, Johnson received orders from General Gage to gather as many Iroquois as he could and proceed to Canada, where they would join the forces commanded by General Guy Carleton, governor of the province of Quebec, for action against the invading New Englanders. Another Grand Iroquois council met at the end of July 1775 in Montreal to listen to Governor Carleton's plea for Iroquois support. Joseph Brant participated in a mock feast to devour "a

Bostonian and drink his blood—an ox having been roasted for the purpose, and a pipe of wine given to drink." Along with some 1,700 Indians, Brant listened intently as Guy Carleton promised the Mohawks that if they took up the hatchet "to defend our country," they would recover all their stolen property after the British put the Americans in their place and forced their obedience to royal authority.[36]

Militating against this choice was the cold reality that the bold American capture of the Lake Champlain forts at Crown Point and Ticonderoga had interrupted the Iroquois' supply of trade goods from the English. Most Iroquois wavered, but some five hundred, mostly Mohawks, agreed to take up the war belt against the Americans. Brant now tasted war for the first time in eleven years. He was near the scene of action when the Americans, this time authorized by the Continental Congress, daringly marched to capture Montreal and Quebec in late September 1775. Ethan Allen was again in the midst of the action. Though he thought he had been chiseled out of Vermont granite, Allen lost the confidence of his Green Mountain Boys, who were led into action by the less impulsive and more coolheaded Seth Warner. Reduced to gathering Indians and Canadians, most of them French-speaking, Allen waited for the large American army generaled by Richard Montgomery to arrive. But waiting was not Allen's style. With orders from nobody, he rashly tried to capture Montreal, a city of nearly nine thousand, with his meager force of about 110 men. Finding themselves surrounded and outnumbered, most of Allen's motley band fled the battlefield. With only 38 soldiers still with him, Allen, surrendered his sword to Peter Johnson, the sixteen-year-old mixed-race son of Sir William Johnson. A British officer clapped Allen in irons and put him on the *Gaspée*, from which he would be transferred to a ship carrying him to England to stand trial for treason. In one of the few understatements of his life, Allen wrote, "They were mean-spirited in their treatment of me." Much worse was soon to come.[37]

When Guy Johnson learned that he might now receive the northern superintendentship of the Indians held by his father for many years, he decided to go to London to make his case. With him, to act as secretary and Iroquois confidant, went Joseph Brant, who was deputized by the Mohawks to lay their grievances before the king. On November 11, 1775, the Guy Johnson–Joseph Brant embassy departed from Quebec on the *Adamant* for the long winter trip across the Atlantic. Shackled below decks were Ethan Allen and thirty-three other captured patriots. In his narrative of his watery trip to England in manacles, written years later, Allen never mentions Joseph Brant, though he had much to say about his shipboard captivity: "We were denied fresh water, except a small allowance which was very inadequate to our wants—and in consequence of the stench of the place, each of us was soon followed with a diarrhoe and fever, which occasioned an intolerable thirst." But it is likely that the two men conversed. Guy Johnson's main concern was to secure his commission as northern superintendent of Indian affairs. Brant's concern was to obtain a quid pro quo for the Iroquois. If war continued with the colonists, would Iroquois allegiance to the British be rewarded with redress for the depredations on their shrinking lands? "It is very hard," Brant told Lord George Germain, King George III's colonial secretary and therefore the key figure in managing the strategy to bring the Americans under proper authority, "when we have let the King's subjects have so much of our lands for so little value, they should want to cheat us in this manner of the small spots we have left for our women and children to live on. We are tired out in making complaints and getting no redress." Germain promised what Brant wanted. "As soon as the troubles were over, every grievance and complaint should be redressed" if the Iroquois "fulfilled their engagements with government as they had ever done."[38]

Staying at the Swan with Two Necks for several months, Brant saw all the usual sights in London: the navy yard at Portsmouth, London Tower, Windsor Castle, and the Wimbledon Common, where the king reviewed companies of foot soldiers. Brant spent time with the biographer James Boswell, who gave his impressions of the visiting Mohawk in the *London Magazine*, and he even met George III and the queen. When he boarded ship with Guy Johnson's entourage in June 1776 for the trip back across the Atlantic, Brant was convinced he had accomplished his mission. "We are not afraid Brother," he promised Lord Germain, "or have we the least doubt but our brethren the Six Nations will continue firm to their engagements with the King their father."[39] This, of course, remained to be seen. Turning this expression of good faith into actual reality would become Brant's mission once back in North America.

Recrossing the Atlantic on the *Lord Hyde*, Brant, Guy Johnson, and the others reached British-occupied Staten Island twenty-four days after delegates to the Second Continental Congress agreed to ink their names beneath the Declaration of Independence. Brant now learned of the many events that had occurred during his eight-month absence. The Americans had captured

While he was in London, Joseph Brant sat for this portrait by one of England's eminent portraitists. At least three other American portrait artists, including Gilbert Stuart, took Brant's image, making it all the more remarkable that he is virtually unknown today.

Montreal and Quebec only to have smallpox, a bitter winter, and a reinforced British army that arrived in the spring of 1776 drive them out with horrendous casualties. Throughout New York, as in other colonies, villages, churches, and even families had been torn apart as people were forced to decide on whether to attach themselves to the patriot cause. In hundreds of Iroquois villages, people had debated whether to maintain their neutrality, had puzzled over how they could maintain trade for goods that they could not do without, and wondered if the Americans could possibly win a war against a mighty English navy and army. The British had occupied Newport, Rhode Island, and Charleston, South Carolina. And under Sir William Howe, they were preparing an assault on New York City across the narrows from Staten Island. Brant's wife and children had retreated to her father's village of

Oquaga, far up the Susquehanna River, near where Joseph Brant had been born. Most momentously, the Americans had given up all hope of reconciliation with the British and declared their independence.

A month after Brant's return, more British troops and armaments arrived. Now Howe's vast army of 15,000 began campaigning. Brant apparently took part in several actions to drive the Americans out of New York, which the British accomplished on September 15, 1776. With instructions from Guy Johnson, Brant began a long trek through Iroquoia to convince the Six Nations to support the British in the campaigns that would get under way after the winter season. Slipping out of New York with Gilbert Tice, who had been part of the entourage that journeyed to England and was an appointee to the Indian Department, Brant made his way toward the Susquehanna River region. The Americans were now fighting for their independence. The Iroquois, Brant would argue, must fight to preserve *their* independence.

Plowmen and Leather Aprons

When authorizing the Continental Association in 1774, the First Continental Congress called for the creation of revolutionary committees throughout the colonies to enforce the consumption boycott. In hundreds of communities, voters elected these so-called committees of inspection, installing an estimated seven thousand men. A great many of them now served in a public position for the first time in their lives.[40] In a population of about 400,000 free adult white males, this was one of every fifty-seven citizens. Into these hands fell near control of the colonies' economic life; and hence the committees became centers of political power, or what historian David Ammerman calls "government by committee." As we will see, the committees used this power not only to enforce nonimportation, but to both surmount the remaining obstacles to declaring independence and to bring about democratic reforms at the local and provincial levels. In this interwoven internal and external struggle, people of modest social standing set in motion one of the most radical phases of the Revolution *before* independence was formally declared.

Boston remained the news center of the revolutionary movement in the last two years before the Americans declared independence—the "Metropolis of Sedition," as the sardonic Peter Oliver called it. But it did not remain the center of plebeian mobilization.[41] In areas west and north of the seaport provincial capital, towns that are often thought to have been laggardly in supporting Boston's challenge to British authority began to dismantle local government and defy the Crown. Leading the way were men of no particular eminence; in fact, most of them were distinctly undistinguished. But in the two years before the Declaration of Independence they outpaced Boston's Committee of Correspondence, the city's radical nerve center, and practiced a kind of participatory democracy that we usually associate with twentieth-century politics.

In July 1774, for example, Pittsfield's inhabitants, far from Boston, moved to shut the Berkshire County Court rather than have it operate under the Massachusetts Government Act, which was still making its way through Parliament. Word had reached the colonies that the Government Act would revoke the Charter of 1691, limit Massachusetts towns to one annual meeting, and give the royal governor extensive powers never before conferred upon a colonial governor. The Pittsfield citizens regarded this as "injurious, oppressive, and unconstitutional" and pledged "that the people . . . utterly refuse the least submission" to the act. "The people of this Province," the town meeting decided in August, should "fall into a state of nature until our grievances are fully redressed. . . ."[42] When the Berkshire County judges appointed by Governor Gage appeared in their wigs and robes to open the court, a crowd of 1,500, most of them farmers and artisans, were waiting for them. Surrounding the courthouse, they prevented the judges from entering the building and harried them out of town. The Berkshire County Court would never meet again under British authority.

In other western Massachusetts towns, crowds of club-wielding farmers offered two choices to the wealthy men appointed by Governor Gage to his special thirty-six-man "mandamus" council: resign or abandon their houses and flee to Boston. Mandamus councillors John Murray, Timothy Ruggles, and Timothy Paine of Worcester, the commercial center of western Massachusetts, felt the farmers' wrath on August 27, 1774. A huge crowd from outlying villages obliged them to walk through the assembled masses to the courthouse, read aloud their resignations from the governor's council, and then reread them after taking off their hats. Timothy Paine, who prided himself on his "handsome green coach, trimmed with gilding and lined with satin," was humiliated. The jeering farmers knocked off his wig as he passed through the gauntlet. Paine reported to General Gage that "people's spirits are so raised they seem determined to risque their lives and everything dear to them in the opposition, and prevent any person from executing any commission he may receive under the present administration." It was now impossible for the county court to hold sessions in Worcester. The western towns had taken the lead, jumping ahead of the Boston Committee of Correspondence in defying British authority.

In addition to closing the courts, ordinary citizens in the western towns, soon to be joined by others near the coast, defied the Massachusetts Government Act by conducting their town affairs in time-honored ways. The act allowed them only one town meeting a year, but "the towns through the country are so far from being intimidated," wrote Boston merchant John Andrews, "that a day in the week does not pass without one or more having meetings, in direct contempt of the Act, which they regard as a blank piece of paper and not more." Governor General Gage issued a proclamation declaring such meetings illegal and warned that towns defying king and Parliament would do so "at their utmost peril." But how could Gage visit that peril upon scores of defiant towns spread across the breadth of Massachusetts?

The moment of truth came on August 24, 1774, in Salem, the seaport town of Essex County twenty miles north of Boston. Determined to hold a town meeting to elect delegates to a provincewide convention, Salem's citizens gathered to appoint the men who would help decide how best to respond to the Coercive Acts. Everyone knew this amounted to a double defiance of English authority: meeting illegally and then electing delegates to a legislative body that itself would be illegal. Faced with this affront, General Gage led two companies of the English Fifty-ninth Regiment to Salem to demand that the town meeting disperse. Salem's leaders conferred with Gage, stalling him while the town meeting quickly made their choice of delegates. Never reticent to properly display the king's authority, Gage countered by ordering his soldiers to arrest members of the Salem Committee of Correspondence for calling the meeting "in open contempt of the laws, against the peace, and the late statute [the Massachusetts Government Act]." Some three thousand armed men, gathered from nearby villages, countered back by vowing to rescue them. With eighty British soldiers facing three thousand defiant Americans, Gage backed down.

Ordinary citizens of Massachusetts towns replayed this scenario many times in the hot summer of 1774. They not only overthrew British authority by refusing to allow courts to function under the detested Government Act, but they overthrew some of the mightiest men in Boston's hinterland, men who tried to uphold British rule. Jonathan Judd, a conservative and wealthy Hampshire County officeholder, wrote despairingly in his journal that three to four thousand people in Springfield made it impossible for the county court to sit under the Government Act. "Everybody submitted to our Sovereign Lord the Mob—Now we are reduced to a state of anarchy, have neither law nor any other rule except the law of nature."

By late August, Gage had concentrated his regiments in Boston and turned the city into a refuge for beleaguered Loyalist councillors and other officeholders. "Civil Government is near its end," he wrote to London on August 31, "the Courts of Justice expiring one after another. . . . We will shortly be without either law, or legislative power. . . . Tho the people are not held in high estimation by the troops, yet they are numerous, worked up to a fury, and not a Boston rabble but the freeholders and farmers of the country."[43] Boston had been the fulcrum of revolutionary radicalism for ten years since the Stamp Act crisis, but now it was the farmers' radicalism that pushed Massachusetts to the brink of open war. Their town in a state of siege, Bostonians had their hands full with providing for hundreds of townsmen thrown out of work since the closing of the port. So dire was the situation that Boston's radical leadership, centered in the Committee of Correspondence, could not get a majority vote on the Solemn League and Covenant that would have strictly enforced nonimportation and nonconsumption, though the Continental Congress would soon adopt just such a consumer boycott.

If "civil government" in Boston was "near its end" by late August 1774, that is, civil government functioning under English authority, it was entirely at an end two weeks later in the Berkshire hill country. On September 6, 4,622 militiamen from Worcester County's thirty-seven towns poured into the small town of Worcester to halt the functioning of the county court. Two days later, forming a dense gauntlet on both sides of the main street for a quarter of a mile, they forced the court judges and all other county officials holding office under royal authority to pass through the massed companies. Hats in hand, "in the most ignominious manner," as Peter Oliver wrote of the event, officials recited their "disavowal of holding Courts under the new Acts of Parliament not less than thirty times in their procession." Nearly the entire adult male population of Worcester County had toppled British rule, so far as their own affairs were concerned, and put in its place what amounted to the people's republic of Worcester County. Nonetheless, by 1775, as General

Gage reported home, the people of Massachusetts "are now so spirited up by a rage and enthusiasm as great as ever people were possessed of, and you must proceed in earnest or give the business up."[44]

In New York, a variation of this scenario unfolded. The grip of moderate patriot merchants and lawyers on the politics of protest in New York City began to collapse in 1775 as control of the legislature by the conservative De-Lancey family began to dissolve. The exercise of political power outside formal institutions had grown after 1765, as mass meetings and house-to-house canvassing for support of nonimportation became common. In 1770, for example, opposing factions decided to resolve the importation question by going door to door, conducting what was perhaps the first public-opinion poll in American history. Whether or not individuals were entitled to vote, they were consulted in making a citywide decision of great importance.

By spring 1775, after Concord and Lexington, many believed that war was a certainty. Believing this, many conservative merchants, lawyers, and clergymen abandoned New York for fear that "the leveling spirit of New England should propagate itself into New York." The crusty Anglican clergyman Samuel Seabury spoke for many. If he must be enslaved, he wrote, "let it be by a king at least, and not by a parcel of upstart lawless committee men. If I must be devoured, let me be devoured by the jaws of a lion, and not gnawed to death by rats and vermin." When the time came for a final decision, New York men of this ilk joined the Loyalist cause in numbers unmatched in any other port town, leaving a partial vacuum into which artisan radicals could step.[45]

During the first half of 1776, as radical patriots gathered momentum, New York teemed with cries for social reform. When patriot leaders set about drafting a constitution, the Mechanics Committee demanded that a draft must be put before the people for ratification; moreover, the constitution should include a provision for "an uncontrolled power to alter the constitution in the same manner that it shall have been received."[46] Newspaper essays proposed annual assembly elections, rotation of offices, secret balloting, universal adult-male suffrage, equal legislative apportionment, popular election of local officials, the abolition of slavery, and the end of imprisonment for debt.

In this upsurge of radical political energy, lesser artisans, mariners, and laborers maneuvered for advantage with wealthy moderate leaders such as John Jay, Philip Schuyler, James Duane, and Robert Livingston. Though these upper-class leaders had eagerly sought the support of the lower ranks in their opposition to English policies—in fact, they could not have done much without broad support—they resisted pressure from below on internal issues. In warding off most of the demands of the radicals, New York City's moderate patriots were aided in part by the arrival of Washington's Continental troops in the spring of 1776. For the moment, the exigencies of military preparation trumped internal issues.

Yet what Seabury feared—political rule by "upstart lawless committee men"—was in fact occurring. Historian Edward Countryman likens the situation to the French and Russian revolutions: "Between the end of 1774 and the summer of 1776 [the unsanctioned] committees did in New York what similar bodies would do in Paris between 1789 and 1792 and in Russia in 1917. They created a counter-government on radically different lines from the old one, took power to themselves until the old institutions were hollow shells, and then destroyed in name what they had drained of power in fact." Aptly invoking Leon Trotsky's dictum that "the most indubitable feature of a revolution is the direct interference of the masses in historical events," Countryman shows how the committees of inspection and enforcement—in New York City, Albany, and other parts of New York—were peopled largely by men with little or no previous political status. This was "the most broadly representative government that New Yorkers had ever known," and it performed competently.[47]

During the final year before the Second Continental Congress declared independence, it took all the nimbleness of even radical patriot leaders such as Alexander McDougall, Abraham Lott, and Isaac Sears to control "the sway of the mob," as one New Yorker described the crowd of ordinary New Yorkers controlling the cobblestones.[48] Sometimes sanctioned by McDougall and Sears, sometimes not, the people in the streets by May 1775, after news of Lexington and Concord filled the newspapers, pushed hard for open rebellion and drove key supporters of the British, such as King's College's Thomas Cooper and the Loyalist printer James Rivington, from the city. It was a sign of the crowd's power that they had squelched printed opposition to revolution by the spring of 1776. With little regard for freedom of the press, the crowd first destroyed the printing press of Tory printer James Rivington and then turned their fury on Samuel Loudoun, who announced he would circulate a rebuttal to Paine's *Common Sense*. When Loudoun refused to bow to a people's tribunal, a knot of men from the Mechanics Committee stormed his shop, carried the pamphlets to the city common, and made a bonfire of them.

In this nineteenth-century painting of New Yorkers pulling down the statue of George III that stood on Bowling Green, genteel, fashionably dressed Gothamites watch with approval as workingmen and a few African Americans do the job. Such cross-class unity was part of the nineteenth-century romancing of the Revolution.

The elected New York provincial congress did not lift a finger to redress Loudoun's grievances.

In Philadelphia, the colonies' most united and aggressive artisans outdid their counterparts in New York. Having obtained a third of the places on the committee to enforce nonimportation in the wake of the closing of the port of Boston, they reached for more. In October 1774, after the Second Continental Congress convened at Carpenters' Hall (meeting there in itself was a symbolic victory for artisan radicals, because the impressive building reflected the pride and organizing skill of the city's master carpenters), mechanics put forward a radical ticket for the sixty-six-member Committee of Inspection that sent a conservative merchant slate down to defeat. Both of the tradesmen's main demands—one reflecting external concerns, the other internal—had been fulfilled: that Pennsylvania commit itself unequivocally to an economic boycott and that artisans be fully represented in the committee system that was, in effect, taking over the levers of political action. Seditious utterances in the Philadelphia press were already anticipating Paine's argument in *Common Sense*. All governmental authority, wrote an anonymous contributor in the *Pennsylvania Packet* in November 1774, was derived "from kings or the people," but since "the history of kings is nothing but the history of folly and depravity in human nature," it was the people from whom all authority must flow. After watching the Continental Congress at work, Franklin's old friend Joseph Galloway sputtered that "Nothing has been the production of their two months' labor but the ill-shapen, diminutive brat, INDEPENDENCY."[49]

In the final year before independence, radicalism erupted in the thirty-one companies of the Philadelphia militia that formed after the Concord-Lexington battle in April 1775. Calling themselves Associators and including most of the city's males of fighting age (pacifist Quakers excepted), the militiamen shaped an agenda for radical internal reform while practicing the use of arms. Their goals of curbing individual accumulation of massive wealth, opening up economic and political opportunity, divorcing the right to vote from property ownership, and driving the merchant elite from power became explicit in a flood of polemical literature that now swept the city. "Our great merchants . . . [are] making immense fortunes at the expense of the people," charged a "Tradesman" in April 1775. Sounding the tocsin on economic inequality that English and European republican writers had stressed but genteel American patriots saw fit to ignore, "Tradesman" argued that the merchants "will soon have the whole wealth of the province in their hands, and then the people will be nearly in the condition that the East-India Company reduced the poor natives of Bengal to." Men of this kind must be stopped in "their present prospect of making enormous estates at our expense." Once their "golden harvests" were put to an end, "all ranks and conditions would come in for their just share of the wealth."[50] "Tradesman" doubtless exaggerated in claiming that some Philadelphia merchants made "from 15 to 20,000 pounds per month profit," but the hyperbole was itself a sign of the inequities felt among leather-aproned Philadelphians. The dual themes of independence and greater economic equality were now riveted together.

Who was this "Tradesman," who had such animus against accumulated wealth? It may have been James Cannon, a thirty-six-year-old Scottish immigrant who had served for a decade as a mathematics teacher at the College of Philadelphia. Cannon had played no role in politics in the 1760s and early 1770s but then emerged, as the Revolution drew near, as a radical egalitarian.

The radical Committee of Privates chose him as their secretary in 1775, a position that made him their foremost spokesman. As "Cassandra," he became a pamphleteer in the crucial provincial election of May 1776, where he warned Philadelphians that an "aristocratical junto" was "straining every nerve to frustrate our virtuous endeavours and to make the common and middle class of people their beasts of burden."[51]

But "Tradesman" was probably Thomas Young. Son of poor immigrant Irish settlers in Ulster County, New York, Young had acquired medical skills and played a leading role in the Stamp Act demonstrations in Albany, New York. Moving to Boston in 1766, he continued his engagement in patriotic politics and was among the faux Indians who took part in the Boston Tea Party in 1773. Conservatives such as Thomas Hutchinson gave him a bad name, calling him a "flaming zealot" and one of the "incendiaries of the lower order." In Philadelphia, wealthy merchant Edward Shippen called him a "bawling New England Man . . . of noisy fame." Historians have been content to label Young "an eternal fisher in troubled waters," or a man "drawn to extreme positions." "Part of an international eighteenth-century radical culture," Young never made much money, nor was he interested in doing so. Giving full play to an egalitarian ideology, in fact, shaped his entire life. He called Boston's town meeting "a noble school" where "the meanest citizen . . . may deliver his sentiments and give his suffrage in very important matters." He liked Boston because there, he wrote, "We abound with middling men!" and "many common tradesmen in this town display the wisdom and eloquence of Athenian Senators." Beaten by two British officers and left for dead in 1774, Young and his family fled to Newport, Rhode Island, and then to Philadelphia. Here he found his true milieu: a community of active artisans and a brazen, progressive city to which another international radical, Thomas Paine, was shortly to arrive.[52]

Young quickly established a rapport with Philadelphia radicals and became their clarion voice in the newspapers. In Boston, he had already identified accumulated property as the great danger in a republic of freeborn people. It made its owners "haughty and imperious," "cruel and oppressive," and likely to consider themselves "above the law." If "the upper part of a nation . . . ha[s] the authority of government solely in their hands," Young wrote, the elite "will always be for keeping the low people under." It was time to return to the age of the ancient Saxons, who "considered every man alike as he came out of the hands of his maker." It was the Norman invaders who destroyed "as many of the free customs of the people as [they] possibly could," and grafted upon English people "that infernal system of ruling by a *few dependent favourites,* who would readily agree to divide the spoils of the lower class between the supreme robber and his banditti of feudal lords." In Philadelphia Young saw the telltale signs of a feudal revival, all the more reason for fundamental reform. Working with James Cannon, he pressed for extending the franchise to all taxpayers, many of whom owned no property but paid only a small head tax. And why should not unnaturalized Germans, who were signing up in numbers for militia duty, have the vote? This would counteract "over-grown rich men" who, in Cannon's words, were "too apt to be framing distinctions in society, because they will reap the benefits of such distinctions."[53]

By the fall of 1775, the so-called Philadelphia Associators had become a school of political education, much in the manner of Oliver Cromwell's New Model Army of the 1650s. The Associators, in the words of historian Eric Foner, "quickly developed a collective identity and consciousness, a sense of its own rights and grievances," and "became a center of intense political debate and discussion."[54] Organizing their own Committee of Correspondence, which included men with no previous political experience such as tailor Frederick Hagener and paperhanger Edward Ryves, they pressured Pennsylvania's provincial assembly to take a more assertive stand on independence. They also made three radical demands on the matter of how the burden of fighting for independence should be shared: first, that militiamen be given the right to elect all their officers, rather than only their junior officers, as the assembly had specified in the militia law; second, that the franchise be conferred on all militiamen, regardless of age and economic condition; and third, that the assembly impose a heavy financial penalty, proportionate to the size of his estate, on any man who refused militia service, using this money to support the families of poor militiamen. Journeymen artisans, even apprentices, were making the transition from street activism to organized politics.

Though some upper-class Philadelphians regarded the militia privates as unruly riffraff puffed up with absurd notions of equality, the militiamen saw it differently—they were "composed of tradesmen [artisans] and others, who earn their living by their industry." This was a slap in the faces of those who produced nothing with their hands but grew wealthy manipulating money and speculating in land. By March 1776, the Associators had made gains. The legislature endorsed new rules that any master who refused his apprentice's desire to serve in the militia must pay the same fine imposed on others who refused service. In addition, the fine for non-Associators was raised by about half. In themselves, these were modest accomplishments; but never before had people drawn from the lower ranks moved a legislature in this way.[55]

How did it happen that lower-class activism and group consciousness proceeded furthest in the city where laboring people had been most deeply divided and most politically inactive only eleven years before? Why did the center of radicalism shift south from Boston to Philadelphia? One explanation is the absence of the British army, whose presence in Boston and New York acted as a lightning rod for artisan discontent, especially in times of scarce employment, and promoted interclass unity in the name of confronting a common enemy. With no British troops occupying center stage, Philadelphia's radical reformers focused on internal matters. A second factor was the ability of radical leaders, such as the distiller and small merchant Charles Thomson, itinerant doctor Thomas Young, apothecary Christopher Marshall, hardware retailer Timothy Matlack, and mathematics teacher James Cannon, to capitalize on the city's storied religious diversity. In Boston, patriot leaders used religious homogeneity—they appealed again and again to "the Body of the People"—to curb the formation of class identity. In New York, radical leaders such as Isaac Sears, Alexander McDougall, and John Lamb could never completely overcome Anglican-Presbyterian enmity in trying to build a radical movement. But in Philadelphia, the radicals came from every segment of the religious community and consciously worked to promote interdenominationalism by putting representatives of each ethnic and religious group on the radical committee slates. From the shambles of Galloway and Franklin's old assembly party arose a new popular party. Conservative Quakers and Anglicans labeled it "Presbyterian" because they thought that was a way of discrediting it; but it enjoyed support from laboring men from all congregations except the Society of Friends.

A third development promoting greater internal reform in Philadelphia was the withdrawal of Quakers from politics. Violence in politics and the specter of war with England drove many Quakers into political retirement. In December 1774, the Society of Friends began disowning Quakers serving on the quasi-governmental committees of inspection and enforcement. Filling this partial vacuum of political leadership were reform-minded men from the middle and lower ranks. With Quakers abandoning the political arena, the non-Quaker proprietary elite, which had dominated the executive and judiciary branches of government as well as the municipal government in Philadelphia, found itself under attack. James Allen, archconservative and son of Pennsylvania's supreme court judge, looked out on this unstable scene on the eve of revolution and wrung his hands at the "madness of the multitude" and the train of events that had brought "all dregs to the top."[56]

Breaking the Logjam

The power of artisan and farmer radicalism, vital to gaining momentum toward independence, increased when the down-at-the-heels Thomas Paine arrived in Philadelphia on November 30, 1774. Once recovered from shipboard fever, Paine started writing for the new *Pennsylvania Magazine*. Sharp-featured and dressed in a plain brown coat, he soon became a familiar figure as he tramped the city's cobblestone streets. After the fight at Concord and Lexington, he became a fervid revolutionary. "When the country, into which I had just set my foot, was set on fire about my ears, it was time to stir," he wrote. "It was time for every man to stir."[57]

Paine stirred to be sure. He started writing what would be published as *Common Sense* about November 1, 1775, just after word reached the city that George III had declared the American colonies to be in a state of rebellion. The pamphlet appeared in Philadelphia's bookstalls on January 9, 1776. No author's name was indicated, only the byline, "Written by an Englishman." Composed at breakneck speed, the book Paine later took credit for had "no plan . . . to support it" but "was turned upon the world like an orphan to shift for itself."[58]

Benjamin Rush, who had convinced Paine to write it, claimed correctly that *Common Sense* burst upon the scene "with an effect which has rarely been produced by types and paper in any age or country."[59] Written so it could be understood at the artisans' benches, on the docks, in the taverns, and in the fields and barns, *Common Sense* sold 100,000 copies by the end of the year and thousands after that. If the crack of a rifle at Concord Bridge was the first shot heard round the world in April 1775, Paine's *Common Sense* was the second shot heard round the world in January 1776. In a society where the literacy rate was about half of today's, about fifteen of every one hundred white adults purchased Paine's pamphlet, and it reached many more as it passed around from hand to hand or was read aloud. To reach this best-seller status, a pamphlet today would have to sell about 21 million copies in its first year of publication.

John Adams was not impressed with *Common Sense*, but nearly everyone else was. Adams appreciated Paine's "elegant simplicity," a quality Adams never possessed. But he hated the idea Paine advanced of a "government by one assembly," and confided to Abigail that all of Paine's arguments in favor of independence were stale, already on everyone's lips. Forty-three years later, at age eighty-four, Adams was still fulminating about the pamphlet that changed the world: "What a poor, ignorant, malicious, short-sighted, crapulous mass is Tom Paine's *Common Sense*," he wrote Thomas Jefferson.[60]

The power of Paine's muscular prose lay in its earthiness, its clever turns of phrase, and in its rhetorical strategy. The hard-hitting, pungent language contrasted sharply with the formal, legalistic rhetoric of most protest pamphlets written by lawyers and clergymen. Not everyone could understand the intricate legal arguments of many of the patriot pamphleteers. But every farmer and field laborer could understand what Paine meant when he called William the Conqueror "a French bastard" who made "himself king of England against the consent of the natives," or pilloried George III "The royal brute of Great Britain." Every shoemaker and boatswain's mate could grasp the thought "for as in absolute governments the king is law, so in free countries the law ought to be king." Every dockworker and hired farmhand could understand what Paine meant when he slashed at the arguments of conservatives for reconciliation. How can Americans "love, honor, and faithfully serve the power that hath carried fire and sword into your land? 'Britain is the parent country,' say some. Then the more shame upon her conduct. Even brutes do not devour their young." Every housewife and student understood the logic Paine served up when he proposed that "there is something absurd in supposing a continent to be perpetually governed by an island." And all could shiver at the rendezvous with destiny that Paine proclaimed: "O! ye that love mankind! Ye that dare oppose not only the tyranny but the tyrant, stand forth! Every spot of the old world is overrun with oppression. Freedom hath been hunted round the globe. Asia and Africa have long expelled her. Europe regards her like a stranger, and England hath given her warning to depart. O! receive the fugitive, and prepare in time an asylum for mankind." Such language crashed through the reverence for monarchy that Americans had been taught to honor and removed one of the most potent obstacles to the idea of independence. The man who never got beyond grammar school had created a revolution in rhetoric and struck off one of the most remarkable political pamphlets ever written. Paine was the right man in the right city at the right time.

Though he found *Common Sense* wanting, John Adams was glad enough to see it fuel sentiment for independence, because in early 1776 New Englanders had outpaced many of the colonists in their determination to abandon any further attempts at reconciliation with England. In particular, Pennsylvania's delegates to the Continental Congress were balking. In 1774, Adams had remarked that the idea of independence is "a Hobgoblin of so frightful mien that it would throw a delicate person into fits to look it in the face."[61] In Adams's view, the Pennsylvania delegates were still afraid of the independence hobgoblin. The key to breaking the logjam turned out to be the group that Paine joined shortly after finishing *Common Sense*—a radical knot of intellectuals and artisans that Adams despised.

Bringing Pennsylvania in line with those ready for independence depended on overturning the colony's elected legislature after it dragged its feet on declaring independence in the spring of 1776. The key to unseating the footdraggers was held by Philadelphia's new artisan-filled one-hundred-member Committee of Inspection and Observation, which was charged with enforcing nonimportation. After the committee petitioned the legislature to direct its four delegates in Congress to follow the lead of New England and Virginia in voting for independence, the legislature, controlled by moderates and conservatives still hoping for reconciliation with England, refused. Seeking a new route to revolution, the Committee of Inspection urged greater representation in the legislature for Philadelphia and backcountry counties. The legislature agreed and called the voters to elect seventeen new representatives, four of them from Philadelphia. The Committee of Inspection was sure that once elections were held and new members were added to the legislature, Pennsylvania's representatives in the Continental Congress would break the logjammed vote for independence.

After intense pamphleteering and house-to-house canvassing, Philadelphia moderates won three of the four new assembly seats to the chagrin of the pro-independence radicals. Once again, the Continental Congress was unable to get a clear-cut endorsement for independence from Pennsylvania, soon called the "Keystone State." Exasperated, the independents played their final card. Seizing on John Adams's Continental Congress resolution declaring that "it appears absolutely irreconcilable to reason and good conscience, for the people of the colonies now to take the oaths and affirmations necessary for the support of any government under the crown of Great Britain, and it is necessary that the exercise of every kind of authority under the said crown should be totally suppressed," Paine and his radical friends set about to crush the newly elected Pennsylvania legislature, arguing that it was no longer legitimate because its claim to authority came from the English Crown. Such a government, in the Continental Congress's resolution, must be "totally suppressed." Accordingly, the independents' leaders called the people at large to action. After gathering hundreds of signatures on a petition calling for a mass meeting of Philadelphians on Monday, May 20, the Committee of Inspection, acting without any legal authority, called for "the inhabitants of the City and Liberties to meet . . . in order to take the sense of the people respecting the resolve of Congress."[62]

Attending the meeting on a rainy spring morning, John Adams called it "the very first town meeting I ever saw in Philadelphia." Adams did not cavil that the meeting called out "the inhabitants" and "the people," not just the white male property owners entitled to vote. He would soon attack Paine's "absurd democratical notions," but now he applauded giving power to all the people—of whatever age, status, wealth, or even gender. About four thousand people thronged the brick-walled yard behind the statehouse. They listened to a carefully staged recitation of Congress's resolve to suppress any government derived from the Crown. Then they shouted approval for a resolution declaring that the instructions from Pennsylvania's legislature to its delegates not to vote for independence "have a dangerous tendency to withdraw this province from that happy union with the other colonies."[63] With three cheers and hats flying, this resolution passed without dissent. The follow-up resolution stated that since the legislature no longer derived its authority from the people, it could not legitimately sit in session. Only one man in the immense crowd voted against this, perhaps amazed that an open-air meeting of Philadelphians could legitimately shout out of existence a legislature seated by all enfranchised Pennsylvanians. Having voted to cast the province into a state of nature, the people at large now called for an assembly of county committees to draw up plans for a constitutional convention.

In the next month, the elected legislature surrendered itself to the will of Philadelphia's people. After word arrived that Virginia had passed a resolution on May 27 asking Congress to declare the colonies free and independent

states, the Pennsylvania Assembly caved in on June 8. Abandoning its recon-
ciliationist position, it told its delegates they could vote for independence if
they wished. John Dickinson, one of the four delegates, refused, bitterly condemning Pennsylvanians for marooning him by scuttling his policy of moderation. But Charles Thomson, a moderate himself, beseeched Dickinson to
"do justice to your 'unkind countrymen.' They did not desert you. You left
them. Possibly they were wrong in quickening their march and advancing to
the goal with such rapid speed. They thought they were right, and the only
'fury' they had against you was to choose other leaders to conduct them."[64] To
the bitter end, Dickinson would not comply and refused to sign the Declaration of Independence. On June 14, the assembly adjourned and left the construction of a new state government in the hands of a committee. Four days
later, on June 18, a provincial conference held its first meeting to construct a
constitution for Pennsylvania.

While finally breaking the olive branch approach of Pennsylvania's timo-
rous delegates to the Continental Congress in May and June of 1776, the radical leaders centered in Philadelphia had prepared the soil for thoroughgoing
internal reform. It was a prime example of a revolution within a revolution.
In trying to change the legislature's mind on independence, the radicals also
changed the way the legislature would be constituted. Two breathtaking
propositions, best articulated by Paine, Young, and Cannon, promised to
make Pennsylvania the most advanced democracy in the world: First, all laws
would be passed by a unicameral legislature; second, the franchise and privilege of officeholding would be severed from property ownership. As early as
April 1776, "Eudoxus" argued that the notion of a two-house legislature,
with the upper house protecting the interests of the wealthy, was an anti-
quated and inappropriate model for Pennsylvania, where at "present there
seems to be but one order to people among us, and in consequence there can
be but one common interest." Of course, it was absurd to argue that there was
"one common interest" and only one order of people. But "Eudoxus" was
hoping to point the way toward a society reconstructed along egalitarian
lines. That was his point in warning that "the Barons of America" had not yet
pushed for a legal aristocracy that would replicate feudal Europe but that
"some choice spirits have contracted a prodigious itch for such patents."
"Elector," probably Young, argued that men of high rank wanted to stand
at the top of "the system of Lord and Vassal." To scrap the entire idea of a

bicameral legislature now became the answer to overthrowing those seeking a constitutional system where they could advance their aristocratic pretensions in an upper house that could overween a popularly elected lower house.[65]

To extend the franchise to all white men was the most alarming of the "absurd democratical notions" that sent shivers down the spine of John Adams. But this is what the radical leaders in Philadelphia now proposed as the debate over independence reached its climax. Suffrage at the time was limited to men with property worth fifty pounds—the equivalent today of about ten thousand dollars. Now radicals attacked this venerable tradition. If a man was good enough to sacrifice his blood for independence, as many young men who served as apprentices and servants were prepared to do, then he "should have a voice" in the state's councils. For "Civis," such "ambitious innovators" with notions of an expanded suffrage threatened to plunge Pennsylvania "into a scene of anarchy." Responding, "Elector" charged that "Civis" "thinks liberty the *peculum* of men of *some rank,* who by one means or another . . . can continue themselves and *favorites in power.*" This argument, reeking of distrust of the wealthy by one side and distrust of ordinary people by the other, filled Philadelphia newspapers through the spring of 1776. Toryism—the reluctance to take the plunge for independence—was linked with opposition to reconstructing government on democratic lines; fervor for independence and internal reform were equally linked. "Take heed Tories," wrote a commentator in the *Pennsylvania Evening Post* three weeks before July 4, "you are at your last grasp!"

Several hundred miles south of Pennsylvania, ordinary farmers who lived at a great social distance from Jefferson, Mason, Madison, Washington, and the other planter aristocrats who are generally credited with leading Virginia into the Revolution, were also the driving force for independence. As in other areas, they pushed a second, intertwined agenda—a program to bring greater equality and justice to their local affairs. Historian Woody Holton has argued this point forcefully, that "insurgent Virginia farmers pushed the gentry toward Independence," and, "by creating great disorder, convinced the planter aristocracy that they could suppress disorder only by getting out of the state of nature they had created by establishing a new Virginia government which they could control."[66] Getting that control was far from easy, for it had to be gained in the face of a rising agrarian insurgency.

Virginia's state of nature became obvious in June 1774 when the colony's county courts closed, even before farmers closed them in western Massachusetts. Closing courts served the interests of both large planters and small farmers because both were indebted to British creditors, who could only sue them if the courts were open. It was not necessary to close the courts by force; they closed by default. When Governor Dunmore adjourned the House of Burgesses on May 26, 1774, the provincial government officially ended; with it ended the operation of the county courts. In their stead, the provincial convention that first met in Williamsburg in August 1774, operating without authorization, provided a semblance of colonywide government. It looked a lot like the dissolved House of Burgesses, largely dominated by the "gentleman freeholders." But now it had an immensely weighty task: the creation of an armed force to defend Virginia against British depredations and against rebellious slaves. In attempting to do this, Virginia's leaders found themselves severely challenged from below.

To mobilize a fighting force for Virginia, the convention held to the gentry model of a layered, disciplined society. But it was the wrong model for a society already in a state of flux. The long-simmering tension between the gentry and the far more numerous small farmers bubbled to the surface amidst debate on how to mobilize Virginia's multilayered society. At first, the convention ordered the creation of a regular army of independent volunteer companies composed of "gentleman of the first fortune and character." They were to pay for their own weapons and uniforms, complete with white stockings. Gentlemen all, they would elect their own officers. "While hostilities had yet to break out," writes historian Michael McDonnell, "the units resembled elite gentlemen's clubs, rather than formal military units." Mainly, they were designed to "rouse the attention of the public" but not involve the public at large.[67]

The next spring, almost simultaneous with news of Concord and Lexington, Governor Dunmore snatched the colony's main supply of gunpowder out from under the Virginians with a midnight raid on Williamsburg's public magazine. Men of all classes rushed to join the "Independent Companies of Volunteers." In Jefferson's Albemarle County, a slender band of twelve gentlemen volunteers swelled to seventy-four socially mixed men by June 1775; many more soon joined up. Most of the new volunteers had no white stockings, blue and buff uniforms, or rifles, only tough canvas hunting shirts, Indian boots, and tomahawks or scalping knives. To elect their own officers was much to their liking. And rather than sip sherry, they wanted to fight, particularly to march to Williamsburg to recapture the colony's gunpowder and harass the royal governor. Over one thousand men of all classes assembled at Fredericksburg, one hundred miles from Williamsburg, most of them with their hunting shirts emblazoned with the motto of the fiery, hawk-featured Patrick Henry: "Liberty or Death." Alarmed that they would push Virginia down the road to revolution too quickly and destabilize society in the process, the convention ordered the transformed companies "to desist from carrying their resolutions into execution."[68]

As the swelling independent companies pushed for armed resistance, they began ostracizing Virginians who were reluctant to join them. William Byrd, owner of thousands of acres and hundreds of slaves, lamented that he was "often threatened with visits from the valiant Volunteers of some of the neighbouring counties" and insulted and given "great offence" for refusing to volunteer for military service. Gentrified Virginians now saw the specter of a plundering army and concluded that the "wild irregular sallies" of fortified companies must be checked.

Afraid of losing control, the Third Virginia Convention that met in the summer of 1775 took a bold, ill-advised step: to replace the independent volunteer companies with eight thousand minutemen who would train for brief periods and stand ready, at a moment's notice, to sally forth. But the convention miscalculated and immediately fractured the white unity that Virginia's leaders so much wanted to preserve. Looking for a more disciplined force, it imposed new rules that ended the popular election of officers. The convention also called for longer periods of training, and pay for only the training period or actual military engagement.

Ordinary Virginians balked. Making up the bulk of the minutemen, they opposed not only part-time pay but the convention's edict that officers should be elected by county committees, where the elite held sway. Also galling was the convention's rule that owners of more than three slaves and servants were exempt from militia duty. "It is calculated to exempt the gentlemen and to throw the whole burthen on the poor," admitted George Gilmer, Jefferson's physician. Offended by this blatant class bias, poor and middling men also objected to paying senior officers eleven times as much as ordinary soldiers. The minuteman scheme, according to its most recent historian, "failed miserably." Promoted by the gentry's desire to quash the egalitarian sentiments of ordinary Virginians and end the disorder they associated with plebeian attempts to alter the planter's aristocracy, the minuteman system injured those who were supposed to make up its rank and file. By the fall of 1775, Jefferson's physician and Albemarle County friend warned his neighbors that "we were once all fire, now most of us are become inanimate and indifferent." Who would fight for Virginia and the united colonies—if the colonies agreed to unite—remained an open question.

For the last year before the Declaration of Independence, the burdens that the Virginia elite tried to impose on middling and poor farmers remained contentious. Many plantation owners had tenant farmers on their land who found it "cruel in the land holders to expect their rents when there is no market for the produce of the land," as Washington's Mount Vernon manager told him in December 1775. Since nonexportation compacts were a major cause of the dried-up market for Virginia produce, tenant farmers felt entirely justified in opposing landlords demanding rent. Sensing that the revolution in the offing would mostly benefit the mighty, tenants in Loudoun County refused to pay their rents to landlords at the end of the year. Lund Washington, George Washington's nephew, reported that the rent strikers "are not at all intimidated" by attempts to crush their leaders. Threatened that local courts would put their belongings up for auction, the farmers promised to "punish the first officer that dare distrain for rent." No county officer, in fact, attempted to seize their modest property—tools, house furnishings, farm animals, and rude clothing—and the farmers continued to oppose the class-biased organization of the militia and slave patrols. By spring 1776, the tenant disturbances in Loudoun County spread into neighboring Fairfax County, where "here all the talk is about the tenants," reported Lund Washington.[69]

On the brink of revolution, Virginia was severely divided "between those dictating the terms upon which the colony would fight and those expected to bear the brunt of those terms."[70] Added to this interclass conflict was intraclass division as the gentry itself divided over whether Virginia should support the momentum building in the Continental Congress for the creation of a new nation. In the vanguard of those pushing for independence were ordinary Virginians. They took the lead not only because of disgust with the long argument with England but because they hoped for a new, more equitable and just Virginia government in which they would play a broader role.

This was the rub for the gentry class, however. The latent dynamite in declaring independence in fact affronted many of the Virginia gentry whom our textbooks celebrate for their role in leading the colonies into revolution.

"Hurray for Independence, Sedition, and Confusion," wrote conservative planter Landon Carter sardonically in his diary on May 1, 1776. Yet for other Virginia gentlemen, "sedition and confusion" pushed them all the more vigorously toward independence. "The political usefulness of the mounting agrarian insurgency," writes Woody Holton, became obvious to men like wealthy planter Francis Lightfoot Lee. Without reinstituting stable, gentry-led rule, which was possible only after severing ties with England, Virginia would fall into the anarchy that Landon Carter and others deplored. Lee blamed the tenant disturbances on both "the mismanagement of the gentlemen" and the collapse of provincial government with "no new one substituted in its stead." "Anarchy must be the consequence," Lee wrote Carter, the land- and slave-rich planter who was morbidly afraid of the rising poor. "Do not you see the indispensable necessity of establishing a government? ... How long popular commotions may be suppressed without it, and anarchy be prevented, deserves intense consideration."[71]

Carter's gloomy stance was not unreasonable because he, like all the other planters, had seen the plebeian fever that had spread even among Virginia's voters. In the November 1775 elections for county committees of correspondence, and in the election of April 1776 for delegates for a new convention, the "voice of the people," as Jefferson's doctor expressed it, made itself heard. Carter knew there had been no wholesale rejection of gentlemen planters accustomed to rule but rather a shrinking of their power as middling planters, of no family prominence or vast estates, won seats. The power of "Mr. Common Sense," reported Carter, was plainly demonstrated when many who would not stand for election in April 1776 on the platform of endorsing independence, knowing that small farmers closely linked independence and a more democratically structured Virginia government, lost their seats. Carter Braxton, who came from one of Virginia's finest families, agreed. He knew many who favored independence, he snorted to Carter, because it would give them the opportunity to establish "their darling Democracy." Writing Washington on May 9, 1776, Landon Carter complained that many "inexperienced creatures" who had been elected to the Fourth Convention defined independency as "a form of government that, by being independent of the rich men, every man would then be able to do as he pleased." Owner of hundreds of slaves, Carter grieved that one of the delegates opposed a law providing for militia patrols to thwart slaves from taking up Lord Dunmore's offer of freedom because "a poor man was made to pay for keeping a rich man's slaves in order." Carter relished the fact that he "shamed the fool" for uttering such a thought. The dunce, he said, "slunk away." Yet Carter admitted that the fool "got elected by it," thus confessing that even in a colony where the vote was far more restricted than in northern colonies, "such rascals" were winning elections and contesting the privileges of the rich.[72]

Six days later, on May 15, the adoption by the Continental Congress of John Adams's radical resolution that each colony establish a government standing independent of English authority gave the Virginia gentry pushing for independence the card they needed to win the game with their conservative fellow planters, who feared that independence and the disintegration of Virginia's gentry rule could not be uncoupled. Seizing on Congress's resolution, Francis Lightfoot Lee urged his fellow gentlemen to "make an establishment, as will put a stop to the rising disorders . . . and secure internal quiet for the future." For the next two months, pro-independence Virginia planters "played on their conservative brethren's fear of disorder to try to dissolve their allegiance to Britain." They finally succeeded. For the gentry, the task would now be to stave off "those wild and turbulent republics, which hold out dissensions, civil war, massacres, and bloodshed in perpetual prospect."[73]

The Genie Unbottled

The common understanding of the final breach between the American colonists and the British government in July 1776 centers on the story of the Continental Congress's tortured decision to declare independence, and the consequent imperative to establish a government that would unite thirteen colonies under the Articles of Confederation. But the colonies had already been through a decade of establishing quasi-governments at the local level— North Carolina, New York, and New Hampshire are examples we have explored—to address problems that were home-bred, not imperial. Those who for decades held little formal power had begun seizing the levers of government in order to find solutions to festering internal problems. Some of these reform efforts failed, as with the Regulators at Alamance in 1771. Others succeeded partially, as in the case of the Green Mountain Boys, who stared down New York's elite-controlled provincial government. But regardless of whether they won all they wanted, the process of standing ruling power on its head accustomed ordinary people to think about themselves as agents of history rather than the passive recipients of whatever history had in mind for them.

This heady notion of grasping history by the throat spread through the widely separated and poorly connected parts of the colonial eastern seaboard. Congress had nurtured the idea of popular participation in government by calling for the enforcement of the Continental Association through locally constructed committees in every town and county. But even without this encouragement, plebeian elements of society nearly everywhere displayed a new assertiveness in the public arena. Even in South Carolina, which of all the colonies had the most entrenched political rule by a narrow elite, men accustomed to commanding others rather than listening to them saw their power under attack. "Men of property," wrote Lieutenant Governor William Bull in March 1775, "begin at length to see that the many-headed power of the people, who have hitherto been obediently made use of by their numbers and occasional riots to support the claims set up in America, have discovered their own strength and importance and are not now so easily governed by their former leaders." In Salem, Massachusetts, a town of fishermen and maritime artisans, the mighty merchant William Pynchon complained bitterly that "the threats and insults of the rabble have been insupportable to many." In the process of providing the determination and sheer physical presence in the streets to enforce nonimportation and nonconsumption, the "body of the people" had targeted the wealthy. "People of property," continued Pynchon, "had been so often threatened and insulted that at length several more proposed to leave the town of Salem."[74]

Of course, the wealthy were particularly susceptible to attacks on their persons and property if they were known to oppose the nonimportation association, or continued to advertise their loyalty to the Crown or counseled reconciliation rather than armed resistance in the final months before July 1776. Daniel Coxe, a leading member of New Jersey's council, the political club of the well-heeled that served the Loyalist royal governor (Benjamin Franklin's son), expressed the elite's horror of the popular force that had been unleashed: "What then have men of property not to fear and apprehend, and particularly those who happen and are known to differ in sentiments from the generality? They become a mark at once for popular fury, and those who are esteemed friends to government, devoted for destruction. They are not even allowed to preserve a neutrality, and passiveness becomes a crime. Those who are not for us are against us is the cry, and public necessity calls for and will justify their destruction, both life and property." In Philadelphia, "Candidus" made the connection between Loyalism and upper-class pretensions to aristocratic rule.

Sounding very much like Thomas Young, he wrote that those opposing independence were the "petty tyrants" who could best "carry on their oppressions, vexations, and depredations" by keeping Americans under British rule. "They tell you," wrote Candidus, "they had rather be governed by the mild and wise laws of Great Britain than the decrees of an American mob. . . . If the people by any means obtain an adequate share in the legislature of this country, they know their visions of golden mountains, and millions of acres of tenanted soil, will all vanish, and themselves remain in the despised rank of their honest and contented neighbors."[75]

A common interpretation of the surging popular sentiment is that the elite, having need of the masses, could not put the genie, once released, back in the bottle. Much of this interpretation is based on elite contemporary opinion at the time. For example, New York's Loyalist council, advising Governor Tryon, warned the Continental Congress in June 1775 that "contests for liberty, fostered in their infancy by the virtuous and wise, become sources of power to wicked and designing men; from whence it follows that such controversies as we are now engaged in frequently end in the demolition of those rights and privileges which they were instituted to defend."[76] "Wicked and designing men" were here understood to be the likes of Ethan Allen, and the "rights and privileges" under attack were the rights of wealthy landowners, with questionable land titles, to evict and beleaguer ordinary farmers.

It was not only wealthy colonists committed to Loyalism who quivered at what the struggles in the streets portended. Even the heartiest upper-class proponents of independence felt themselves under attack, knowing that beneath them stood men in great numbers who experienced class oppression firsthand and were learning to express themselves openly. Philadelphia's wealthy James Allen, who had joined the militia to demonstrate his patriotism, despaired in March 1776, "The mobility [is] triumphant. . . . I love the cause of liberty; but . . . the madness of the multitude is but one degree better than submission to the Tea Act." The time was now at hand when men of this kind would have to decide. Weighing heavily on their minds were bitter charges that they were the "great folks," as "A Common Man" writing in a New York paper put it, who "are the only gainers from arbitrary government," men who lie in bed with English officials "to enable them to carry on their wicked and greedy schemes of stripping and oppressing the body of the people."[77]

Waverers faced similar sentiments, and many were driven off the fence to stand with their king for fear of the politically charged, street-savvy people. In New Jersey, struggling to decide which way to turn, lawyer Gouverneur Morris believed that the aristocracy of which he was a part would not survive American independence. In the end, he cast his die with independence, but he spent most of the war years worrying about the power of the people. So did John Adams. Nobody doubted John Adams's stance on independence, and it was common knowledge that the still struggling young lawyer had no mansion, four-wheeled carriage, slaves, or other accoutrements of wealth. Adams had nothing to fear from those who railed against the pyramid of wealth and power, and his reading of the classics told him that republics collapsed at just this stage of evolutionary development. But Adams was temperamentally conservative, had little appetite for a thorough democratization of colonial society, above all prized social stability, and therefore was nervous about the rising masses. In writing to Patrick Henry, a man with deeply democratic sensibilities, Adams could sound liberal: "The dons, the bashaws, the grandees, the patricians, the sachems, the nabobs, call them by what name you please, sigh, and groan, and fret, and sometimes stamp, and foam, and curse, but all in vain," he wrote one month before the Declaration of Independence. "The decree is gone forth, and it cannot be recalled, that a more equal liberty than has prevailed in other parts of the earth, must be established in America." Adams commended this because he knew from firsthand experience that the Hutchinsons, Olivers, and other Bostonians with princely fortunes had scorned and exploited the ordinary citizens who had always been on the razor's edge that separated those with a "decent competency," as it was often called, from poverty. "That exuberance of pride, which has produced an insolent domination in a few, a very few, opulent, monopolizing families," Adams ventured, "will be brought down nearer to the confines of reason and moderation than they have been used to. . . . It will do them good in this world, and in every other." In the same vein, looking south, Adams regretted the "inequality of property" and worried that "the gentry are very rich and the common people very poor." This, he believed, "gives an aristocratical turn to all their proceedings and occasions a strong aversion in their patricians to Common Sense." If they could not swallow Paine's *Common Sense*, Adams concluded, "the spirit of these barons . . . must submit."[78]

Yet Adams, especially in his public pronouncements, had nervous fits about the leveling spirit breaking out in all the colonies. It was one thing to bring the high and mighty down a rung or two, but quite another to allow those on the bottom rungs to spring upward. Like his cousin Sam, he believed that in a republic the distance between rich and poor should not be too great. But if this leveling of income and wealth shaded into indiscipline or challenges to the authority of the well-born and educated, he saw the beast of anarchy beckoning. Writing from Philadelphia to Abigail, who was tending the farm and raising their four children in Braintree, Massachusetts, three hundred miles to the north, Adams complained that "our struggle has loosened the bands of government everywhere. That children and apprentices were disobedient—that schools and colleges were grown turbulent—that Indians slighted their guardians and Negroes grew insolent to their masters."[79] This casting off of deference disturbed Adams. Released from the bottle, could the genie ever be recaptured?

That the genie was not always masculine also troubled Adams. His wife Abigail tasked him on just this issue. Her husband's long absences from home and the strain of running their farm by herself just outside British-occupied Boston, along with the death of her mother in the fall of 1775, all seemed to bring her to a new state of consciousness about what the looming revolution might hold for the women who were playing such an important role in the nonimportation and homespun movements. "In the Code of Laws which I suppose it will be necessary for you to make," she wrote John on March 31, 1776, "I desire you would remember the ladies, and be more generous and favourable to them than your ancestors." In this much quoted passage, Abigail went from desire to demand. "Do not put such unlimited power into the hand of the husbands. Remember all men would be tyrants if they could. If particular care and attention is not paid to the ladies, we are determined to foment a rebellion, and will not hold ourselves bound by any laws in which we have no voice or representation." A few paragraphs earlier Abigail had wondered about just how real the "passion for liberty" was among those who still kept fellow humans enslaved. Now she pushed the point home about men enslaving women. "That your sex are naturally tyrannical is a truth so thoroughly established as to admit of no dispute, but such of you as wish to be happy willingly give up the harsh title of master for the more tender and endearing one of friend. Why then, not put it out of the power of the vicious and lawless to use us with cruelty and indignity with impunity? Men of sense in all ages abhor those customs which treat us only as the vassals of your sex."[80]

In this letter we see clearly how women of Abigail Adams's intellectual mettle nimbly made the connection between civil and domestic government.

The more male leaders railed against England's intentions to "enslave" its colonial "subjects," to rule arbitrarily, to act tyrannically, the more American women began to rethink their own marital situations. The language of protest against England reminded many American women that they too were badly treated "subjects"—the subjects of husbands who often dealt with them cruelly and exercised power over them arbitrarily. Most American women, still bound by the social conventions of the day, were not yet ready to organize in behalf of greater rights. But the protests against England stirred up new thoughts about what seemed arbitrary or despotic in their own society, and many women began to think that what had been endured in the past was no longer acceptable. This paved the way for change. Abigail's reference to the cruelty men used against their wives probably refers to the "rule of thumb" that the law upheld. Deeply imbedded in England's common law, and encoded in Blackstone's *Commentaries on the Laws of England*, the rule of thumb made it permissible for husbands to beat their wives so long as the stick or club did not exceed the thickness of a male thumb. The reference to using women with indignity probably referred to the emotional and psychological domination of wives by husbands. For all his love of Abigail, John's reply to her letter of March 31, 1776, confirmed the point. "As to your extraordinary code of laws," he wrote, "I cannot but laugh." Then referring to the growing insubordination of children, apprentices, Indians, slaves, and college students, he sniffed that "your letter was the first intimation that another tribe more numerous and powerful than all the rest were grown discontented. This is rather too coarse a compliment but you are so saucy, I won't blot it out."[81]

Adams was less than honest in saying that he had no notion of women's discontent. Adams knew very well of James Otis's 1764 *The Rights of the British Colonies Asserted and Proved*, in which his lawyer friend had included in an "Introduction of the Origin of Government" the time bomb of a question: "Are not women born as free as men?" and followed it up with the query that if this was so, then had not "every man and woman . . . a natural and equitable right to be consulted in the choice of a new king or in the formation of a new original compact or government if any new form had been made?" At Yale, seniors had recently debated "Whether women ought to be admitted into the Magistracy and Government of Empires and Republics"—a telling indication that the concept of a political woman was now a matter of public discussion. But rather than open up the topic for further comment, Adams drew a line in the sand. "Depend upon it, we know better than to repeal our masculine systems." He claimed that the laws subordinating women "are little more than theory," and that men "dare not exert our power in its full latitude." Since "we are obliged to go fair and softly" with women, men would not allow themselves to be subjected to "the despotism of the petticoat." Adams was seemingly trying to disarm his wife with humor by saying that it appeared to him that the British ministry, after stirring up "Tories, Landjobbers, Trimmers, Bigots, Canadians, Indians, Negroes, Hanoverians, Hessians, Russians, Irish Roman Catholicks, [and] Scotch Renegadoes, at last . . . have stimulated the [women] to demand new privileges and threaten to rebel." But doubtless he had limited tolerance for change in women's rights and opportunities. When Abigail saw to it that their oldest daughter, Nabby, studied Latin, John did not oppose it but warned that Abigail "must not tell many people of it, for it is scarcely reputable for young ladies to understand Latin and Greek."[82]

Abigail was not amused. She knew that it was not the British ministry that stirred up women and others grating against their subordination. Instead of writing John after receiving his dismissive letter, she unburdened herself to her friend Mercy Otis Warren, the sister of John Otis and wife of James Warren, a Massachusetts legislator. "He is very saucy to me in return for a list of female grievances which I transmitted to him," she wrote Mercy. "I think I will get you to join me in a petition to Congress." Why, she wondered, was her husband so insensitive to what seemed an opportunity to enact a more "generous plan," "some laws in our favor upon just and liberal principles" by which the law would curb "the power of the arbitrary and tyrannic to injure us with impunity?" Under revised law, women could gain court protection against abusive husbands and not lose their property and wages to men once they married. For raising just and liberal principles, she bitterly told Mercy, he scoffed at her and called her saucy. "So I have helped the sex abundantly," she closed, "but I will tell him I have only been making trial of the disinterestedness of his virtue, and when weighed in the balance have found it wanting."[83] Mercy Otis Warren, who had already crossed the boundaries of correct female behavior by writing two patriot plays that pilloried Thomas Hutchinson and other Loyalists, sympathized with Abigail and told other women that the criticism of females who interested themselves in politics should be resisted.

Abigail stewed about John's dismissiveness and waited far longer than was her habit before answering his letter of April 14. "I believe tis near ten days since I wrote you a line," she wrote on May 7. "I have not felt in a humor to entertain you. If I had taken up my pen perhaps some unbecoming invective might have fallen from it." Then she let out the steam building in her on the matter of women's rights. "I can not say that I think you very generous to the ladies, for . . . you insist upon retaining an absolute power over wives." Again, she was using the same catchwords and phrases so familiar from the years of protesting British arrogance and insensitivity—"absolute power," "tyranny," "unlimited power." "You must remember," she continued, "that arbitrary power is like most other things which are very hard, very liable to be broken—and notwithstanding all your wise laws and maxims we have it in our power not only to free ourselves but to subdue our masters, and without violence throw both your natural and legal authority at our feet." In this reference to Lysistrata, who rallied the Grecian women to withhold their sexual favors from husbands who would not listen to their pleas for peace, Abigail played her last card—at least for now. When John received her latest parry on the question of arbitrary and tyrannical men, he chose to withhold further comment. It was not that he put the matter out of mind. Rather he chose to express his dismay and horror to James Sullivan, superior court judge in Massachusetts and member of the legislature, who had offered his view that propertyless adult men should be allowed the vote. "Depend upon it, Sir," Adams wrote Sullivan: "There will be no end of it" if propertyless men were given the vote. "Women will demand a vote." Young lads would be next. "It tends to confound and destroy all distinctions and prostrate all ranks to one common level."[84]

Adams tried to end the argument on a high note by complimenting Abigail as a "Stateswoman" as well as "a Farmeress." But for Abigail, the matter was not closed. Years later she insisted that "I will never consent to have our sex considered in an inferior point of light. Let each planet shine in their own orbit. God and nature designed it so—if man is Lord, woman is Lordess—that is what I contend for."[85] Like a stone cast into a pond, ripples radiated outward from this family argument—a private argument auguring currents of change far beyond the Adams family.

5

THE DUAL REVOLUTION

1776–1778

ON JULY 13, 1776, WHEN SHE RECEIVED A FIRSTHAND ACCOUNT from her husband that the Continental Congress had issued the Declaration of Independence, Abigail Adams had just been inoculated against smallpox, along with the four young Adams children. For days people had been making their way into Boston—at least thirty alone from the small town of Braintree where the Adams family lived—to undergo inoculation. The British had evacuated the city four months before, in March 1776, but they left behind a more insidious enemy that took no prisoners and refused to spare even non-combatants. Smallpox had raced through Boston and the surrounding countryside throughout the previous year. Desperate to ward off the dreaded killer, about five thousand people underwent inoculation in Boston in the summer of 1776.[1]

As she nursed her children and struggled against the harsh regimen involved in the inoculation procedure, Abigail read John's prediction that "the Second Day of July 1776 will be the most memorable Epocha in the history of America. I am apt to believe that it will be celebrated by succeeding generations as the great anniversary festival. It ought to be commemorated as the day of deliverance by solemn acts of devotion to God Almighty. It ought to be solemnized with pomp and parade, with shows, games, sports, guns, bells, bonfires and illuminations from one end of this continent to the other from this time forward forever more." Many did just what Adams recommended—celebrate and solemnize. In one of the most telling celebrations of all, a milling crowd of New York City citizens roped the marble-mounted equestrian statue of George III, toppled it on Bowling Green, and fell upon the leaden monarch. Mutilating the face, cutting off the head, and displaying the royal visage atop a flagpole, they left the rest of the torso on the ground. It would end up in Litchfield, Connecticut, where women and children turned it into about 42,000 musket balls—hunks of "melted majesty," as one wit put it—to be fired at the king's redcoated troops.[2]

When Abigail read the declaration, she was overjoyed. But one deletion from an earlier draft bothered her. "I cannot but feel sorry that some of the most manly sentiments in the declaration are expunged from the printed copy," she wrote John. "Perhaps wise reasons induced it." Apparently, Abigail was referring to the complaint Jefferson drafted about the slave trade, which he asserted was entirely the work of "the *Christian* king of Great Britain." The king, Jefferson charged, "has waged cruel war against human nature itself, violating its most sacred rights of life and liberty in the persons of a distant people, who never offended him, captivating and carrying them into slavery in another hemisphere, or to incur miserable death in their transportation thither." Moreover, the king vetoed every effort of the American colonies to stop "this execrable commerce."[3]

It is no surprise that delegates to the Continental Congress stripped out this language because it was patently false and because Georgia and South Carolina insisted on continuing their importation of Africans, even if the other colonies had prohibited it or made it prohibitively expensive with stiff import duties. John Adams, second only to Jefferson on the drafting committee, liked this antislavery language, but it did not survive the scrutiny of the full Congress, which also rubbed out Jefferson's charge that the king "is exciting those very people [enslaved Africans] to rise in arms among us, and to purchase that liberty of which he has deprived them, by murdering the people upon whom he also obtruded them; thus paying off former crimes committed against the liberties of one people, with crimes which he urges them to commit against the lives of another."[4] In place of this emotional language, Congress inserted a brief phrase in the midst of a charge that the king was rousing "the merciless Indian savages." The king, the revised and adopted declaration charged, "excited domestic insurrections amongst us," an ambiguous turn of phrase that could have referred to the North Carolina Regulators and New York land rioters—white colonists all—as well as slaves answering Lord Dunmore's call. Congress had certainly erased some "manly sentiments" that Abigail Adams wished had remained. This was the most important deletion made to Jefferson's draft.

Why would Jefferson make such preposterous charges against the king? He owned more than one hundred slaves himself, was making no attempt to free them, understood that planters like himself had clamored for slaves for many generations, and had never objected that English kings had "obtruded" Africans upon them. He also knew that American slave traders were as avid to participate in the trade as the British merchants whose interests, Jefferson charged, the king was trying to protect. To suggest that Americans were unwilling partners in the slave trade and were really not complicit in the institution of chattel bondage was, on its face, outrageously dishonest. Roger Wilkins, calling this section of Jefferson's draft a "bloated roar of rage,"[5] suggests that this was "beyond mere hypocrisy." Rather, it was "the product of the irreconcilable tension between earned guilt and the aspiration to honor," resulting in a "gusher of overheated rhetoric, [a] jumble of charges disconnected from reality." Mostly cleansed of the most preposterous charges against George III, the revised declaration was rushed before the congressional delegates on July 2. Though they unanimously affirmed on that day that "these United Colonies are, and of right, ought to be, free and independent states," they took several days more to amend the draft, to be finally endorsed on July 4.

The Declaration of Independence released a torrent of festering emotions and allowed the great task at hand to move forward. For many people in North America, the stirring words of Thomas Paine, in his revision of *Common Sense* published in late February 1776, now rang true: "We have it in our power to begin the world over again. A situation, similar to the present, hath not happened since the days of Noah until now. The birth-day of a new world is at hand."[6] But what would the new world look like? The answers to that were various, depending on one's condition and shaped by one's hopes for the future. People of all stripes began to step forward with different agendas for a born-again America. Necessarily, these agendas would have to be pursued in the midst of an armed conflict of the greatest intensity and duration that the inhabitants of the American colonies had ever known.

Unalienable Rights for Whom?

"We hold this truth to be self-evident, that God created all men equal, and is one of the most prominent features in the Declaration of Independence and in that glorious fabric of collected wisdom, our noble constitution. This idea embraces the Indian and the European, the Savage and the Saint, the Peruvian and the Laplander, the white man and the African." So spoke Philadelphia's prosperous black sailmaker, James Forten, thirty-seven years after the declaration first received printer's ink.[7] Was Forten mistaken that white Americans of the revolutionary generation subscribed to the notion that unalienable rights were universal, not limited just to white European males? Many historians believe that men such as Forten were wrong, that the founders really meant all *white men* are created equal, that only they were entitled to the fabled "unalienable rights." Conventional wisdom has it that white revolutionary leaders believed Africans—even those who were free—were not endowed with fully human attributes and therefore were not considered to be among "all men" claimed in the declaration to have been created equal.[8]

To be sure, many white Americans did not intend to include African Americans and others (such as women) under the canopy guaranteeing unalienable rights and equality as a birthright. But many did. Forten did not misremember the days of his early service in the Revolution; nor did he invent the climate of opinion in his hometown of Philadelphia. Hardly any writer who attacked slavery in the 1760s and 1770s imagined that Africans were not part of the human race. James Otis made this explicit in his *Rights of the British Colonists* in 1764, and a decade later the Massachusetts General Court debated a bill premised on this principle. Abigail Adams expressed the same view in 1774, insisting that black Americans had "as good a right to freedom as we have." In the same year, Tom Paine insisted that "the slave, who is the proper owner of his freedom, has a right to reclaim it."[9] Samuel Hopkins, writing in 1776 from Newport, Rhode Island, the center of New England slave trading, made it his business to keep the matter squarely before the Second Continental Congress. The enslaved Africans, he exhorted, "behold the sons of liberty oppressing and tyrannizing over many thousands of poor blacks who have as good a claim to liberty as themselves, [and] they are shocked with the glaring inconsistence." Hopkins warned that if the leaders of the nation struggling for independence did not erase this "national sin," the American people would never survive God's wrath. Almost simultaneously, the New York legislature stated that slavery was "utterly inconsistent with the avowed principles in which this and other states have carried on their struggle for liberty."[10]

In southern as well as northern colonies important leaders acknowledged the universality of rights proclaimed by the declaration. As early as 1767, Virginia's Arthur Lee stated baldly that "Freedom is unquestionably the birthright of all mankind, of Africans as well as Europeans." Two years later, Jefferson argued before Virginia's highest court, in a case involving a mulatto consigned to thirty years of labor, that "under the law of nature, all men are born free, every one comes into the world with a right to his own person, which includes the liberty of moving and using it at his own will."[11] Nearly all Virginia leaders admitted as much as they began drafting a constitution for the state in 1776. George Mason's draft, in the very first article of the Declaration of Rights, stated "that all men are born equally free and independent, and have certain inherent natural rights, of which they cannot, by any compact, deprive or divest their posterity; among which are, the enjoyment of life and liberty." Objections immediately arose for fear that the first clause would "have the effect of abolishing" slavery or might be "the forerunner of . . . civil convulsion." The language had to be manipulated "[so] as not to involve the necessity of emancipating the slaves."[12]

Edmund Pendleton, a shrewd lawyer and expert wordsmith, rescued the Virginia leaders from the problem of making the essential claim of natural inborn rights while not giving slaves an opening. The accepted revision averred that "All men are by nature equally free and independent," but acquired rights only "when they enter into a state of society." The last clause solved the problem because it could be said that slaves were not in a state of society. Such sophistry would do for the moment, though many Virginians were already on record saying that Africans were part of humanity and therefore as possessed of natural rights as Europeans, Asians, or anyone else. Though Jefferson would use many of the key words in the natural-rights proposition in the preamble of the Declaration of Independence, he knew better than to slip in the weaselly clause about "when they enter into a state of society."

Virginia's crafty circumlocution later proved useful in legal matters, but it did not change the minds of many southern leaders that Africans were born with natural rights, including the essential right to freedom. John Laurens, the son of South Carolina's largest slave trader and one of the colony's largest slave owners, believed the half-million slaves in North America were "unjustly deprived of the rights of mankind."[13] The young Laurens, infected by study in the Enlightenment hub of Geneva, Switzerland, made this statement in 1778. But most white southerners held negative views of Africans' attributes, and some, like Jefferson, speculated that such negative qualities were innate. But even in disparaging descriptions of African moral and intellectual capacities, and even in arguments that abolishing slavery was impractical, the claim was rarely made that Africans—or any other caste or class of people—were born without unalterable rights. The revolutionary generation's problem was not in its conception of universal rights, as expressed in the declaration, but rather its inability to honor them.

British writers, fellow inheritors of the Enlightenment, agreed. "How is it that we hear the loudest *yelps* for liberty among the drivers of Negroes?" inquired England's Samuel Johnson, a former schoolteacher and creator of *A Dictionary of the English Language*, the masterpiece that today still commands such encomiums as "a portrait of the language of the day in all its majesty, beauty, and marvelous confusion." Johnson asked this question in 1775 in the context of his disapproval of American pretensions to independence, a position he spelled out piquantly in his *Taxation No Tyranny*, where he flummoxed American colonists by calling them selfish, ungrateful children—"these lords of themselves, these kings of *Me,* these demigods of independence."[14] John Lind, a British government writer equally eager to unmask American hypocrisy, put it as strongly: "It is their boast that they have taken up arms in support of these their own self-evident truths—that all men are created equal, that all men are endowed with the unalienable rights of life, liberty, and the pursuit of happiness." If so, why were they complaining to the world "of the offer of freedom held out to these wretched beings [by the British], of the offer of reinstating them in that equality which, in this very paper, is declared to be the gift of God to all; in those unalienable rights with which, in this very paper, God is declared to have endowed all mankind?"[15]

If Jefferson's draft of the Declaration of Independence blithely absolved American colonists from complicity in the slave trade, he was equally dishonest in his blanket indictment of Native Americans. The charge that Jefferson buried in the declaration among the long list of grievances against king and Parliament must have astounded Joseph Brant, Attakullakulla, Logan, Daniel Nimham, or any other Indian leader whose stories we have followed.

They would surely have agreed with the charge that the king had blocked "new appropriation of lands," since they knew full well that Parliament had issued the Proclamation Act of 1763 and the Quebec Act of 1774 to create a buffer between the land-hungry colonists and the interior Indian nations. But they must have been deeply offended at the assertion that the king had "endeavored to bring on the inhabitants of our frontiers the merciless Indian savages, whose known rule of warfare is an undistinguished destruction of all ages, sexes, and conditions." These pungent words from Jefferson's hand, "submitted to a candid world" and borrowed exactly from his preamble to the Virginia constitution, were left untouched by drafting committee members Benjamin Franklin, John Adams, Robert R. Livingston of New York, and Roger Sherman of Connecticut, and by the Continental Congress sitting as a committee of the whole.[16] The silence of historians on this disingenuous charge is deafening in the most notable studies of the Declaration of Independence spanning more than eighty years. In Carl Becker's *The Declaration of Independence* (1922), in Garry Wills's *Inventing America* (1978), and in Pauline Maier's *American Scripture* (1997), not a word appears on this vicious caricature of the American Indians, who had been trading partners, military allies, and marital consorts as often as enemies for two centuries.

Jefferson, like most signers of the declaration, knew that this inflammatory charge was duplicitous. The first part of it—that the king had incited Indians against white settlers—had been charged in grievances expressed by several colonies and in Congress's "Declaration on Taking Up Arms" in 1775. But the second part of the loaded sentence—that the known rule of destruction followed by Indian "savages," where no woman, child, or person of any condition was spared, was Jefferson's own formulation. To write this, Jefferson had to bury recent memory. Fourteen years before, finishing up his study at the College of William and Mary, the nineteen-year-old Jefferson had been spellbound by Chief Outacite, one of the Cherokee leaders who passed through Williamsburg on their way to take ship to London, where he hoped to find justice for his people. After spending two days in Virginia's capital, Outacite gave a farewell speech that Jefferson remembered so vividly that he described it in detail, even to the phase of the moon, fifty years later in a letter to John Adams. "I knew much the great Outacite, the warrior and orator of the Cherokees," Jefferson told Adams. "He was always the guest of my father on his journeys to and from Williamsburg. I was in his camp when he made his great farewell oration to his people the evening before his departure for

England." It was a moment burned into Jefferson's psyche, though he buried it while writing the Declaration of Independence. "The moon was in full splendor, and to her he seemed to address himself in his prayers for his own safety on the voyage, and that of his people during his absence, his sounding voice, distinct articulation, animated actions, and the solemn silence of his people at their several fires, filled me with awe and veneration, though I did not understand a word he uttered."[17]

What had happened to this awe and veneration when Jefferson drafted the declaration, sitting in a rented room looking down on bustling Market Street in Philadelphia? Of course, it was no time for Jefferson to be sentimental. In drafting the declaration, he was all too aware that he was writing a propaganda missive, a legal brief to justify American independence. He knew from his own experiences in Virginia's piedmont region that attributing a genocidal urge against "all ages, sexes, and conditions" to Indians more appropriately described the "rule of warfare" practiced by Virginia's white frontiersmen. We can never know how his sleep at night might have been disturbed by his suppression of the recent atrocities against peaceable Native Americans, for example the massacre led by the Paxton Boys in 1763 and the slaughter of Logan's family in 1774. Jefferson knew of these heinous attacks in all their gory details, but in the flush of finding stirring rhetoric to voice the sentiments of an aroused colonial people, Jefferson ignored his deep respect for native people. A few years after penning the Declaration of Independence, he returned to his remembrance of Outacite's stirring oratory and noble composure. In summing up his drama-filled years during the Revolution, he decided that nobody could find in the "whole orations of Demosthenes and Cicero and indeed in all of European oratory" a "single passage superior to the speech of Logan."[18]

Jefferson's reduction of half a million Native Americans east of the Mississippi River to "merciless savages" had propagandistic value, but many who read the toxic words in the declaration at the time knew that most of the troubles with Indian nations began with *white* land hunger, unscrupulous trading, and arrogance. The judgment of Thomas Pownall, the governor of Massachusetts only a few years before, was well known and uncontested: that "the frauds, abuses, and deceits that these poor people have been treated with and suffered under have had no bounds." Nor were Jefferson and other members of the Continental Congress unaware of the much circulated report of 1755 that proposed a plan for biracial comity. Edmond Atkin, the Indian trader of South Carolina who had years of intimate contact with southern Indian nations, wrote that "In their public treaties, no people on earth are more open, explicit, and direct. Nor are they excelled by any in the observance of them. . . . With respect to . . . all ruptures of consequence between the Indians and the white people, and the massacres that ensued . . . the latter were the first aggressors, the Indians being driven thereto under oppressions and abuses, and to vindicate their natural rights."[19]

Many colonists agreed, admiring the Indian traits of morality, generosity, bravery, and the spirit of mutual caring. Indians seemed to embody these Christian virtues almost without effort while colonizing Europeans, attempting to build a society with similar characteristics, were pulled in the opposite direction by the natural abundance around them—toward individualism, disputatiousness, aggrandizement of wealth, and the exploitation of other humans. "As a nation," wrote John Brickell of the Delawares, with whom he lived for more than four years, "they may be considered fit examples for many of us Christians to follow. They certainly follow what they are taught to believe more closely, and I might say more honestly, in general, than we Christians do the divine precepts of our Redeemer."[20]

Whether members of the Continental Congress who pored over Jefferson's draft of the declaration considered the effect the insulting language used to describe Native Americans might have on the Indians themselves is not clear. But as historian Daniel Richter points out, they knew that England, as the war clouds loomed in 1774–75, had neither attempted to make formal military alliances with Native Americans nor encouraged them to descend on the frontier settlements. To be sure, English ministers were *discussing* how to mobilize Indian support if the undeclared war mushroomed into a full-scale fight. So was the Continental Congress. In fact, Congress had already enlisted the support of the Christianized Mahicans, Wappingers, and Housatonic Indians living in Stockbridge, Massachusetts, in 1775. Seventeen Stockbridge warriors fought with the Americans at Breed's Hill in June of that year.[21] A few months later, commissioners of the Continental Congress met at Pittsburgh with the Shawnee, Wyandot, Seneca, and Delaware to secure their pledge of neutrality. Once again, just as Congress was declaring independence, American commissioners at Fort Pitt received a renewed Six Nation pledge of neutrality.

Creating a generic, colonist-hating Indian might be useful in kindling fears of a British-Indian conspiracy, but how could it serve to woo Indians to the American side or even convince them to remain neutral? The American seizure of Sir John Johnson, son of William Johnson (who was beloved by the Mohawks), and the imprisonment of his wife and confiscation of his property gave the Iroquois further reason to distrust the Americans.

The Myth of the Minuteman

"We must all be Soldiers *pro Aris et Focis* [for God and country]," John Adams wrote Samuel Cooper, minister of the storied Brattle Street Church in Boston, on May 30, 1776.[22] Six months later, General Charles Lee, who fought as a British officer in the Seven Years' War and then returned to North America to offer his services to Washington's army, believed that Congress should oblige every free male of fighting age to serve at least one term. Deeply etched in American memory is just what Adams and Lee proposed: that the citizen-soldier, embodied in the minuteman, step forward from all walks of life to carry on the war for independence. The statue of the minuteman created by the nineteenth-century sculptor Daniel French for the centennial celebration of the firefight at Concord Bridge has surfaced repeatedly—on postage stamps, life insurance policies, war bonds, and intercontinental ballistic missiles. The citizen-soldier, emotionally bonded to his home and community, fighting for short terms and then returning to the workbench or plow, provided the backbone of true republican virtue. This was Paul Revere, Ethan Allen, Molly Pitcher, Thomas Paine, and Yankee Doodle Dandy.

But Yankee Doodle Dandy took the field to fight in the "glorious cause" mostly in the first eighteen months of conflict that began at Lexington and Concord, when the *rage militaire* ruled supreme. Within months of the signing of the Declaration of Independence—certainly by the end of 1776—the cross-class character of American fighting forces changed sharply. As military historians Mark Lender and James Kirby Martin have observed, "Each year, as a general rule, fewer and fewer people wanted to have anything to do with Continental service." For six long years of war, climaxing at Yorktown in October 1781, but not culminating for another year, the men who fought under Washington were a far cry from the celebrated minutemen. Especially those who fought in the Continental army had shallow roots in *any* community. They were overwhelmingly from the lower layers of society and were mainly enlisted to bear arms so that the mythic citizen-soldier could avoid

This mid-nineteenth-century painting perpetuated the myth of the citizen-soldier, stirred by a patriotic speech and surrounded by townspeople in a festive mood.

military service and stay at home. This led to tension, dissension, and disillusionment with the Continental Congress among the common enlisted men. Finally, it led to mutiny. The "bedrock facts of the American Revolutionary struggle," writes historian John Shy, "especially after the euphoric first year, are not pretty."[23]

State militias as well as the Continental army would have to fight in the Revolution, and the militia system seemed to promise a truly broad blood sacrifice because a large proportion of men were subject to militia duty in the late colonial period, usually from age sixteen to sixty. Probably a majority of white male adults served at least one short militia term—often just a few months—during the prolonged military contest. But as the Continental Congress, Washington, and all his generals knew, the war could not be won without long-term soldiers marching in a regular army. One of the main problems of the war was how to fill the thirty-eight regular regiments, which at full strength consisted of some eight thousand men (not even half the soldiers the British fielded throughout the war). Upon inspection, most of these soldiers turn out to be those with pinched lives, often fresh from Ireland or Germany, recently released from jail, or downright desperate. In fact, only a small sliver of white American males of fighting age served in the Continental army under Washington and his generals. The people celebrated as citizen-soldiers "got tired of serving, and they got tired of contributing." Louis Duportail, who came from France to become the chief engineer of the Continental army, reported to his government at home in 1777 that "There is a hundred times more enthusiasm for this Revolution in any Paris café than in all the colonies together."[24]

In recent years, historians have combed muster lists, town records, and military pension applications to come up with a composite picture of Washington's Continental army. How men were lured or dragooned into service varied according to the quotas set by the Continental Congress. What the men had in common, regardless of their place of enlistment, was their youth, their poverty, and their tenuous attachment to any particular community. The town of Concord, where the shot heard round the world was fired, is a good example of recruiting New Englanders. After the initial blush of patriotism, Concord found it difficult to induce its citizen-farmers to enlist as part of the town's quota, even though Massachusetts was peerless in glorifying its citizen-warriors for generations of fighting against Indians and the French. So Concord scoured the countryside for free blacks and other footloose men who could be bought up as substitutes for those who had lost their fire for military service. Ezekiel Brown, who apparently heard the first shots at North Bridge from the town's jail, where he languished as a debtor, was typical. "With little or nothing to lose," as he later related, he joined up. Landless and voteless, he had drifted around eastern Massachusetts for several years before the Revolution, a foot soldier in the army of "strolling poor." Half of the sixteen men who signed up from Concord in the first five years of the war were much like Ezekiel Brown, without "any known connection to the town," according to historian Robert Gross.[25]

So it went from town to town. To be sure, at the beginning of the war in 1775 and soon after that, when the British army hovered nearby, towns such as Peterborough, New Hampshire, engaged in a cross-class people's war rather than fighting a poor man's war. When General John Burgoyne invaded New York in 1777, many of the townsmen saw action. But thereafter, few men with land and voting privileges stepped forward to enlist. According to the town's historian of the revolutionary experience, most of the soldiers for the remainder of the war were "an unusually poor, obscure group of men, even by the rustic standards of Peterborough."[26]

Even those who served far more than a few months were not necessarily fired by ideological rage toward English policies and practices. "Long Bill" Scott (so named to distinguish him from his cousin "Short Bill" Scott) was typical of this group. He did not spring to arms out of patriotic fervor after Lexington and Concord; rather, he was a shoemaker who "got my living by my labor." He saw the chance to better himself—"the only motives for my entering into the service," he related after the British captured him at Bunker Hill. "As to the dispute between Great Britain and the colonies," he told his British interrogator, "I knew nothing of it; neither am I capable of judging whether it is right or wrong."[27] Scott was atypical only in that he was a bit better off than most of his townsmen who enlisted for service, for the majority of them served short terms, were poor when they enlisted, came home to remain obscure for the rest of their lives, or became transients looking somewhere else for something better.

In the mid-Atlantic states, as in New England, the yeoman farmer of revolutionary lore, shouldering his weapon and bidding his family goodbye, was mostly a myth. Mostly landless, drawn from unskilled laborers or lower artisans (such as shoemakers), and overwhelmingly drawn into service by bounties provided by those wanting to avoid Continental service, they differed from the dispossessed New Englanders only in one respect: The majority were foreign-born, and most of them had only recently arrived in North America. Fortuitously for middle-state recruiters, about 127,000 immigrants had poured into the colonies between 1760 and 1775. Most hailed from Scotland, Ireland, and England, but about 20,000 came from Germany. The majority of them settled in the mid-Atlantic region. Henry Lee, later to become famous as "Lighthorse Harry" Lee, called the Pennsylvania battalions "the Line of Ireland," but he might just as well have called them "the Line of Germany."[28]

In the southern states the recruiting process was much the same. Maryland's Continental soldiers, who froze at Valley Forge in the winter of 1777–78, were mostly young, poor, landless, voteless, and, in about half the cases, immigrants. Maryland was unusual only in trying to take choice out of the hands of the dispossessed. By legislative decree, any local court could require a person considered a vagrant to serve at least nine months in the

Continental army. Prime candidates for this kind of conscription were the thousands of convicts transported by the British to Maryland and Virginia— some 24,000 from 1746 to 1775—in order to sweep clean the jails of England.[29] Once in the field in American uniforms, they stood a good chance of fighting against men from their own impoverished villages in Ireland, Scotland, and England, where the British rounded up jailbirds who were "chained to ringbolts and fed with bread and water" until they agreed to head into the War of Independence in British uniforms. In Virginia, substantial bounties lured lower-class youths, some as young as fourteen, into the regular army. By the end of 1776, looking for more men, the Virginia government followed Maryland by authorizing the impressment of "rogues and vagabonds"—a vagabond being described as any man neglecting to pay his county and parish taxes or any man with no visible estate. Looking over this army of the dispossessed, Charles Lee called them "riff raff—dirty, mutinous, and disaffected."[30]

Washington's officers had no illusions about the human material they had to shape into fighting units. "Food for Worms . . . , miserable sharp looking caitiffs, hungry lean faced Villains," Anthony Wayne labeled them. Tench Tilghman, Washington's aide-de-camp, called the recruits from New York City "mostly old disbanded Regulars and . . . foreigners." Other officers called them "the sweepings of the York [England] streets," or "a wretched motley Crew." Indeed they were. Many had arrived in North America like one numbed London weaver who landed in Virginia in 1758 in the company of indentured servants: "They all was set in a row, near a hundred men and women and the planters come down [from] the country to buy [them]. . . . I never see such passels of poor wretches in my life," wrote the weaver, "some almost starved by the ill usage in their passage by the captain, for they are used no better than so many negro slaves that are brought in here and sold in the same manner as horses or cows in our market or fair.[31]

Notwithstanding all these unpleasant comments, Continental army officers could not do without such men. Absent such human material, the war would have quickly ended with a British victory. What is more, it was these down-and-outers who were most likely to endure the awful conditions of camp life and battlefield gore. Washington knew this. "Men just dragged from the tender scenes of domestic life; [and] unaccustomed to the din of arms" were almost worthless, he wrote. The fabled minuteman who left his farm to shoulder arms was also difficult to discipline and difficult to restrain from deserting. "Men accustomed to unbounded freedom, and no control," he concluded, "cannot brook the restraint which is indispensably necessary to the good order and government of an army; without which, licentiousness, and every kind of disorder triumphantly reign."[32] It was only the poor, particularly the unmarried and young, who could stand up against England's professional army. The poor man's fight was the only fight that the Americans could wage.

For all his obscurity, the foot soldier was, in fact, one of the main reasons that the Americans were able to sustain a series of disheartening defeats in the first two years of the war and still continue the fight. Washington and his generals relied on the poor unsung youth—the guerrilla fighter whose capacity to survive in horrendous conditions proved crucial. Washington understood what would later become a famous dictum of war, one that also applied in Vietnam two centuries after the American Revolution: The standing army that does not win, loses; the guerrilla army that does not lose, wins. Private Joseph Plumb Martin, an out-of-work farm laborer who joined the Eighth Connecticut Regiment, was the kind of young, penniless soldier who made all the difference. In plainspoken but penetrating prose, inscribed in a diary kept through several enlistments, the seventeen-year-old Martin, born in the tiny farming village of Becket in western Massachusetts, showed what the common soldier faced, endured, and—sometimes—survived. "We had nothing to eat for two or three days previous, except what the trees of the fields and forests afforded us," he wrote in mid-December 1777, as Washington's army marched along a rutted road from Gulph Mills, on the Schuylkill River west of Philadelphia, to the Valley Forge encampment where they would spend the winter. "But we must now have what Congress said," Martin recalled, "a sumptuous Thanksgiving to close the year of high living we had now nearly seen brought to a close." Congress had indeed called for a day of thanksgiving on December 18, a day of wind and freezing rain, to remind Americans that their tattered army still survived. "Our country, ever mindful of its suffering army, opened her sympathizing heart so wide upon this occasion as to give us something to make the world stare. And what do you think it was, reader?" wrote Martin sardonically. "Guess. You cannot guess, be you as much of a Yankee as you will. I will tell you: It gave each and every man *half a gill of rice* and a *tablespoonful* of vinegar!" With four ounces of rice, "this extraordinary superabundant donation," Martin continued, "we were ordered out to attend a meeting and hear a sermon delivered upon the happy occasion. . . . The army was now not only starved but naked. The greatest part were not only shirtless and barefoot but destitute of all other clothing, especially blankets. I procured a small piece of raw cowhide and made myself a pair of moccasins, which kept my feet (while they lasted) from the frozen ground." Though the hard edges of the moccasins "galled my ankles," this was better than going barefoot, "as hundreds of my companions had to, till they might be tracked by their blood upon the rough frozen ground."[33]

Martin recounted the sermon the men were obliged to hear. The minister urged the soldiers to fulfill their obligations honorably. He added that the preacher might also have told the freezing soldiers to be "content with your wages. But that would not do, it would be too apropos; however, he heard it as soon as the service was over, it was shouted from a hundred tongues." But despite the misery and the soldiers' resentment at Congress's pitiful ration for the day of thanksgiving, Martin showed his true colors. "Our prospect was indeed dreary. . . . However, there was no remedy, no alternative but this or dispersion [desertion]; but dispersion, I believe, was not thought of—at least I did not think of it. We had engaged in the defense of our injured country and were willing nay, we were determined, to persevere as long as such hardships were not altogether intolerable."[34]

Martin reenlisted in 1777 for the duration of the war—which made him one of a small stouthearted minority determined to stick it out. Year in, year out, life in the army improved little. Benjamin Rush, appointed physician general of the military hospitals in spring 1777, found "scenes of distress shocking to humanity and disgraceful to a civilized country. . . , sons of our yeomanry . . . shivering with cold upon bare floors without a blanket to cover them, calling for fire, for water, for suitable food, and for medicines—and calling in vain."[35] A year later, when he could not get support for cleaning up the filthy, military field hospitals, often barren of medicine, Rush resigned in disgust.

Though humble in origin and humble in status, the rank-and-file soldiers were anything but humble in their conception of their rights, either as Continental soldiers or state militiamen. Prompt payment of wages, adequate food and clothing, medical attention when wounded, and support for their families in need were the most important issues that aroused them. In April 1776, one of Washington's generals was warned that a mass of disaffected men promised to "go home in a Body" if not given their clothing allotment and pay. The counterthreat of the "severest Punishment" had some effect, but many of the soldiers deserted anyway. Desertion, from that point forward, was the bane of the commander in chief and his generals. More than four of every ten New Jersey troops in 1777 deserted. In New York, about one of every three privates deserted. Even in Washington's handpicked Life Guard, eight soldiers deserted during the war. Nearly desperate to keep troop levels up, Washington considered invading Vermont's Green Mountains, which had become "an asylum to all deserters" from the Continental army; but he gave up on trying to capture deserters, concluding that his soldiers could not be convinced "to imbue their hands in the blood of their Brethren."[36]

For most Continental army soldiers, deserting was disgraceful. Like Private Joseph Plumb Martin, they endured bouts of homesickness, depression, disillusionment, boredom, and stark fear; yet the majority stood in place while contending for their rights. From the beginning of enlistment, the soldier's struggle was for food, clothing, medical attention, effective weapons, brave and just officers, and the pay they were promised. In a later chapter we will follow this quest and consider their many tribulations.

Fighting to Be Free

If any group within America's diversified people came close to answering John Adams's plea that "we must all be soldiers," it was black Americans. No part of revolutionary society responded to the call for arms with anywhere near the enthusiasm of those who were black. Proportionate to their number, African American males—and some females—were more likely to join the fray than white Americans. But, as we will see, Adams should have been careful about what he wished for, because the "spirit of '76" manifested among enslaved and free blacks mainly took the form of fighting *against* the side that proclaimed all men were born free, equal, and endowed with certain unalienable rights.

Those who fought at Lexington and Concord in April 1775 must have noticed the dusky Lemuel Haynes among the contingent of militiamen from Granville, Massachusetts, who rushed to the scene. Born in West Hartford, Connecticut, Haynes was twenty-two at the time. He was the son of a full-blooded African and a young white woman. After his mother gave him up when he was just five months of age, the town's selectmen indentured Haynes out to a farmer and Congregational church deacon in Granville, Massachusetts. There on the frontier he learned to plough, chop wood, and read. "I could vie with almost any of my age," he wrote many years later in telling of his love for books.[37]

Full of martial ardor, Haynes joined the local militia in Granville in 1774. He marched with Captain Lebbeus Ball's militia company to arrive on the scene just a few days after the firefight between the minutemen and the redcoats at Concord and Lexington. Haynes then became part of the siege of Boston and the Battle of Bunker Hill. Fresh from this battle, his unit marched to secure Fort Ticonderoga. He mustered out after several weeks, reenlisted in October 1776, and was sent home with typhus a month later.[38]

Haynes fought with his quill as well as his rifle; but the target of his quill was not the British but his fellow colonial Americans who practiced slavery. Now twenty-three, Haynes stole time in camp to work out "Liberty Further Extended: Or Free Thoughts on the Illegality of Slave-keeping." The only known essay by an African American of the revolutionary era, it drew from Anthony Benezet's *Some Historical Account of Guinea*, a pamphlet published in Philadelphia in 1771 to prod the Americans to cleanse themselves of slave trading and slave keeping. Haynes pointed to how the monster tyranny was "lurking in our own bosom" and argued that "an African . . . has an undeniable right to his Liberty." Quoting the book of Acts in the Old Testament, he wrote that "It hath pleased God to make of one blood all nations of men, for to dwell upon the face of the Earth." "What is precious to one man," Haynes proposed, "is precious to another, and what is irksome, or intolerable to one man, is so to another. . . . Those privileges that are granted to us by the Divine Being," he continued, "no one has the least right to take them from us without our consent."[39]

Haynes never published his essay. Perhaps he could find no publisher for it. But he carried his message with him after laying down his weapon to take up the ministry. For many years, he pastored white congregations in different parts of New England, preaching some five thousand sermons and becoming, in the words of his first biographer, "a sanctified genius." Marrying a white woman, he became the first black minister to white Congregational churches in New England. His life's work, his biographer reasoned in 1837, could "hardly fail to mitigate the unreasonable prejudices against the Africans in our land."[40]

Among enlisted men, Haynes was unusual, indeed nearly unique, for fighting with words as well as bullets. But he was by no means the only free African American who joined the patriot cause in the early years of the war.

Crispus Attucks, half African and half Wampanoag, had already shed blood in the Boston Massacre of 1770. "The first to defy, and the first to die," wrote a Boston poet a century later of the muscular Attucks, who had charged the British soldiers with a stout cordwood stick.[41] At Lexington and Concord, Prince Easterbrooks was one of the first wounded patriots. After this, many more black New Englanders joined up, including one of Venture Smith's sons. Some of them were free but many were slaves, fighting alongside or in place of their masters. White Americans were fighting to protect their liberty; enslaved Americans fought to attain it.

Those who fought as slaves held the hope that their masters would reward them with freedom. Sometimes they were actually promised it. Peter Salem signed up in the village of Framingham with his master's pledge of granting his freedom. Salem served at Lexington and a few weeks later at Bunker Hill, where he killed Major John Pitcairn of the British marines, who led the attack on the patriots' fortifications. Salem later fought at Stony Point, Monmouth, and Saratoga, survived the war, and built a cabin in Leicester, Massachusetts. In another case, Salem Poor fought alongside his master, Lieutenant Thomas Grosvenor, at Bunker Hill. So honorable was Poor's performance that fourteen Massachusetts officers petitioned the Continental Congress to award freedom to this "brave and gallant soldier." Poor went on to fight with Washington's army at White Plains, New York, in 1776, and endured the trying winter of 1777–78 at Valley Forge. He became a small property owner after the war. In still another case, Prince Whipple, the slave of a New Hampshire officer, pulled the stroke oar on a small boat carrying George Washington across the Delaware River in a piercing snow and sleet storm on Christmas night in 1776.

Peter Salem, Salem Poor, and Prince Whipple were the kind of men celebrated by William C. Nell, the first African American historian of the black revolutionary experience. Writing in the 1850s, while he worked to integrate Boston's public schools, Nell hoped to further the abolitionist crusade by pointing to the blood shed by black Americans for the "glorious cause." Nell meant to stimulate racial pride while countering the white Negrophobia that had spread rapidly throughout the North in the early nineteenth century. Rather than reaching for a broad understanding of how those of African descent reacted to the revolutionary tumult, Nell focused on specific black contributions to the struggle for independence. Harriet Beecher Stowe hoped Nell's *The Colored Patriots of the American Revolution* would "redeem the

Born free in Northampton, Massachusetts, Agrippa Hull enlisted in 1777 at age eighteen. He served as an orderly to the Massachusetts general John Paterson and then for the Polish officer Thaddeus Kósciuszko. Washington signed his discharge after Hull had served in the army for six years. He comes down to us in paint because he served a key officer from overseas.

character of the [Negro] race," and abolitionist orator Wendell Phillips similarly wished that Nell's efforts would "stem the tide of prejudice against the colored race."[42]

Intent on showcasing black patriots, Nell waxed eloquent about figures such as James Forten, the fourteen-year-old Philadelphia son of a free black sailmaker. Five years into the war, Forten enlisted on Stephen Decatur's privateer as a powder boy and soon "found himself amid the roar of cannon, the smoke of blood, the dying, and the dead" in a naval duel between Decatur's *Royal Louis* and the British *Lawrence*. When the British captured Decatur's ship after another battle at sea, the young Forten wore the colors of patriotism nobly, refusing the offer of the British captain to transport him to England to

Probably more than one thousand African Americans served in the small American navy, many of them as slaves. White ship captains frequently owned slaves, so the seagoing African American was not at all uncommon. This black sailor very likely served on a privateer that took many enemy prizes, because only his share of the prize money would have allowed him to dress in such finery.

stay with his son, who had befriended the black American lad aboard the British ship. "NO, NO!" exclaimed Forten, according to Nell, who based his account on oral recollections, "I am here a prisoner for the liberties of my country. I never, NEVER, shall prove a traitor to her interests."[43] Noble as it was, this was far from a typical story.

Nell's attempt to show that black Americans partook of the "spirit of '76" was unbalanced, ignoring entirely the large number of African Americans who fought on the British side. This is understandable and likely was intentional. What would Nell, the historian-activist, have done in the 1850s with evidence of the tens of thousands of slaves who sought freedom by fighting against the Americans? Probably he concluded it was best to bury this chapter of history because publicizing the general belief among slaves that life, liberty, and the pursuit of happiness were best pursued with the British would have crippled the abolitionist cause. William Lloyd Garrison felt the same, publishing his *Loyalty and Devotion of Colored Americans in the Revolution and War of 1812* on the eve of the Civil War with the same basic narrative.

For black Americans who wanted to serve on the side of the Americans, the first battle was to acquire the right to fight. At first, free black men such as Cash Africa, from Litchfield, Connecticut, were welcomed into Washington's Continental army. Nearly 150 served at Bunker Hill (along with six Native Americans). But pressure from white southern leaders to purge the army of African Americans led to Washington's general order on November 12, 1775 (just five days, ironically, after Virginia's Governor Dunmore had offered freedom to slaves reaching his encampment), to exclude them all, whether enslaved or free. Within six weeks, Washington partially reversed his general order; with congressional approval, he reopened the Continental army to free blacks, though not to slaves. Cash Africa was back in the army by 1777 and served for the remainder of the war. By one estimate, some five hundred Massachusetts free blacks served in the war, roughly one half of all free black men of military age in the state. A Hessian officer fighting with the British observed in 1777 "that the Negro can take the field instead of his master; and, therefore, no regiment is seen in which there are not Negroes in abundance, and among them there are able-bodied, strong and brave fellows."[44]

By the winter of 1777–78 Washington further amended his policy on black troops. Struggling to regroup his manpower-starved army, he accepted the plea of Brigadier General James Mitchell Varnum to raise a regiment of black soldiers from Rhode Island. The state's legislature quickly endorsed the idea with lofty language: "History affords us frequent precedents of the wisest, the freest, and bravest nations having liberated their slaves and enlisted them as soldiers to fight in defense of their country." But at heart, the motives were less lofty. In deeming the proposal "inspired by stark necessity," historian Lorenzo Greene is surely right.[45] Rhode Island's First and Second Regiments, created at the beginning of the war, were composed mostly of poor white men, with a sprinkling of free blacks. By early 1778, the regiments were close to disintegration, their pay in arrears, uniforms tattered, and ranks thinned by disease, absenteeism, and desertion. One of its colonels described the First Regiment as "scandalous in its appearance in the view of everyone— as a result of their appearance townspeople provoke them with epithets of the Ragged Lousey Naked Regiment."[46] If this was not enough, the term of enlistment for most men was up, and few were ready to reenlist under the three-year terms that had now been made the norm for Continental army service. Moreover, the British occupied much of Rhode Island, leaving the state's economy tottering.

In these dire straits, Rhode Island's considerable slave population—about 3,700—proved to be a godsend. In February 1778, desperate to fill the thinned ranks of its regiments, the state offered freedom to "every able-bodied Negro, Mulatto, or Indian Man slave in this state . . . to serve during the continuance of the present war with Great Britain." Every black enlistee would be "immediately discharged from the service of his master or mistress, and be absolutely free, as if he had never been encumbered with any kind of servitude or slavery."[47] Slaves could not simply walk away from their masters and enlist; this had to be done with the consent of their owners. But many of Rhode Island's slave owners found this proposal too good to turn down. Releasing their slaves relieved them of army duty themselves and promised to fill the state's quota for Washington's army. In addition, they would receive compensation for their lost slave property from the state legislature at the market price. However, many slave owners vehemently opposed the plan, since they would lose their strongest, most valuable slaves.

Roughly one of every four able-bodied male slaves in Rhode Island obtained his master's consent to enlist. The First Regiment (dubbed the Black Regiment many years later), where almost all of them served, became almost entirely black and Indian below the rank of corporal. Leading the regiment was Colonel Christopher Greene, an entrepreneurial Quaker from Warwick who had given up pacifism in 1775 to lead white Rhode Island troops. African and Indian names roll off the muster lists, which can still be viewed today at the Rhode Island Historical Society: Bristol Prime, George Sambo, Quam Cook, Quacko Wanton, Thomas Sachems, Narragansett Perry, Peter Mohawk, Aaron Sucknesh, and dozens more. About two hundred slaves enlisted to fight as free men in the Continental army. Their masters were promised about £120 each, equivalent today to about $2,400.

The newly liberated slaves had to learn the manual of arms in a hurry. Luckily, Christopher Greene, their white commander, was a hardened veteran. He had been captured during the assault on Quebec on New Year's Day in 1776, returned in a prisoner exchange, and dispatched southward in November 1777 to defend Fort Mercer, a Delaware River fort guarding Philadelphia. Now in the summer of 1778, after a few months' training under his command, Greene threw his black recruits into the breach in the Battle of Newport, where a large American army, supported by a French fleet, sought to dislodge the British forces occupying Newport and southern Rhode Island. Assigned to a hot sector, the Black Regiment repulsed three assaults of Hessian mercenaries, inflicting heavy casualties and minimizing patriot losses in what became an American fiasco. From there, Rhode Island's First Regiment moved on to defend a post on the Croton River in New York, where an American Loyalist unit, in a surprise attack, killed Colonel Christopher Greene. The story passed down to William Nell, the Boston historian of *The Colored Patriots*, has it that Greene was "cut down and mortally wounded; but the sabres of the enemy only reached him through the bodies of his faithful guard of blacks, who hovered over him to protect him, and every one of whom was killed."[48]

Sent south a few months later with Stephen Olney as their new white commander, the black Rhode Islanders fought at Yorktown in September 1781. There, they found no black southerners under arms for reasons we will examine in chapter 7. The French officer François Jean Marquis de Chastellux described the First Regiment as three-quarters black and, of all the regiments in Washington's army, "the most neatly dressed, the best under arms, and the most precise in its maneuvers" he had seen.[49] Knowing of its previous exploits, Lafayette and Washington handpicked the Rhode Island regiment to participate in the assault on Redoubts 9 and 10, the strongholds that held the key to victory. Remembering the night of October 14, when he led the Black Regiment forward to storm the moated and heavily fortified redoubts, Colonel Olney recorded how "the column marched in silence ... many no doubt thinking that less than one quarter of a mile would finish the journey of life with them." By the time they mustered out in late 1783, after nearly five years of fighting, only one third of the former slaves survived to taste freedom as civilians.[50]

Though white northerners turned to slaves and impoverished free blacks to help supply their manpower needs, they had to confront the awful reality that the British had already recruited great numbers of the same people. Chapter 4 showed how Dunmore's Proclamation of November 1775 inspired people such as Thomas Peters to make their break for freedom. But by mid-1776, what had been a small stream of escaping slaves now turned into a torrent. Over the next seven years, enslaved Africans mounted the greatest slave rebellion in American history. Wherever the British army moved, slaves bolted from their masters and headed toward British lines to claim freedom. Even when the British forces were small, slaves took their chances. For example, a week before Congress signed the Declaration of Independence, eight slaves belonging to Landon Carter, whose vast Virginia plantation lay along the Rappahannock River in Richmond County, made their break. "Last night after going to bed," he wrote in his diary, "Moses, my son's man, Joe, Billy, Postillion Tom, Mullatto Peter, Tom Panticove, Manuel, and Lancaster Sam ran away, to be sure to Lord Dunmore."[51]

The main theater of war from 1775 to 1778 was in the North, and even in eastern Pennsylvania, where slave masters exercised their rule less harshly than in the South, the flight from slavery was remarkable. Thomas Peters, marching in the Black Guides and Pioneers, was among those who occupied Philadelphia in September 1777. There he watched droves of slaves, many of whom were women and children, fleeing to the British. Surveying the state's losses in 1779, a white legislator lamented, "By the invasion of this state, and the possession the enemy obtain of this city and neighborhood, [a] great part of the slaves hereabout were enticed away by the British army."[52]

In northern New Jersey, a slave named Titus, who renamed himself Colonel Tye, took a leading role. When his Quaker master refused to free his four slaves, as required by the Society of Friends, the twenty-one-year-old Tye fled. He somehow reached the British in Virginia in 1775. Several years later he was back in New Jersey, organizing other escaping slaves and free blacks to fight against the Americans. For five years, he led a local guerrilla band that fought alongside white New Jersey Loyalists to terrorize and kidnap patriot farmers, seize their crops and cattle, and control border posts between the British and Americans. At the bloody Battle of Monmouth near Freehold in June 1778, where 750 African Americans were sprinkled through the fourteen American brigades, Tye captured an American militia captain and quickly earned respect from the British as an effective fighter. In the next year, Tye was part of a Tory brigade that plundered Shrewsbury in northern New Jersey. Hiding out in swamps and inlets, Tye led many raids, incorporating enslaved New Jerseyans bolting for their freedom into his ranks. All over New Jersey, white patriots held him in awe.

Tye died of battle wounds and lockjaw in 1780. The first notice of his death in a local newspaper described him as "justly to be more feared and respected than any of his brethren of a fairer complexion."[53] By this time, as chapter 7 will relate, the war had moved southward, where black rebels at the time also fled to the British in large numbers.

Rioting to Eat

"There has been much rout and noise in the town for several weeks," wrote Abigail Adams to her husband, who was still in Philadelphia in the summer of 1777. "Some stores had been opened by a number of people and the coffee and sugar carried into the market and dealt out by pounds." On July 24, women took the lead in battling a perfectly patriotic Boston merchant, Thomas Boylston. Indeed, two years before, Boylston had been on the British blacklist—a dangerous and vehement patriot. But while wealthy and eminent, Boylston was also "miserly" and "stingy," to use Abigail's terms. Seeing an opportunity for windfall profits by withholding coffee and sugar from the market, thus driving up the price, he now faced a horde of angry Boston women. When he refused to sell his coffee at a reasonable price, "a number of females, some say a hundred, some say more," related Abigail, "assembled with a cart and trucks, marched down to the warehouse, and demanded the keys, which he refused to deliver." When Boylston (who happened to be the first cousin of John Adams's mother) tried to face the women down, "one of them seized him by his neck and tossed him into the cart. Upon his finding no quarter, he delivered the keys, when they tipped up the cart and discharged him, then opened the warehouse, hoisted out the coffee themselves, put it into the trucks and drove off." Abigail doubted, she told John, that the women administered "a spanking" to the purse-proud Boylston, as some said; but she was certain about the fact that "a large concourse of men stood amazed silent spectators of the whole transaction."[54]

Abigail Adams was describing what in Europe was called *taxation populaire*—the people's seizure of basic commodities and their subsequent sale at a fair price. Historians have seen this an example of "the moral economy" at work, the implementation of an age-old principle where no individual economic actor—whether merchant, miller, farmer, or shopkeeper—was entitled to enrich himself at the public's expense, especially in a crisis situation.

On the home front, female militancy revolved around obtaining subsistence commodities. While their husbands and sons fought the British, the women and children had to eat. Almost by definition, the war between the Americans and England dislocated the market economy. The prolonged clash of arms cut off avenues of trade to the West Indies and continental Europe, created shortages as marauding American and British armies requisitioned food and livestock, forced the Americans to rely on paper currency (which soon led to rampant inflation), and offered unusual opportunities for unscrupulous merchants, retailers, and even farmers to manipulate the price of foodstuffs.

Replying to Abigail's account of Thomas Boylston's comeuppance, John Adams made light of the incident, telling his wife that her letter "made me merry with the female frolic with the miser."[55] But it was far from a frolic for women in Boston and countless other towns. Many of them were managing their families, farms, and urban shops in the absence of men. Trying to cope with a disordered economy, women became involved in a majority of these food riots and often were the principal organizers. Striding onto the public stage, they became arbiters of what was fair, what was patriotic, and what was necessary to serve the needs of the whole community. Fighting for ethical marketplace conduct was consonant with supporting "the glorious cause"; conversely, men like Thomas Boylston displayed antipatriotism by contributing to the misery of middle- and lower-class families—those who bore the brunt of battlefield blood sacrifices.

Marketplace riots began almost before the ink was dry on the Declaration of Independence. Just a few days after the Continental Congress had agreed to sever ties with England, merchant Samuel Colton and retailers Jonathan and Hezekiah Hale felt the anger of their neighbors for marking up prices on scarce molasses, sugar, salt, and rum in the close-knit village of Longmeadow, a few miles from Springfield in the Connecticut River valley. Not mincing words, Longmeadow's citizens warned that "every man whose actions are unfriendly to the common cause of our country ought to be convinced of his wrong behavior and made to reform, or treated as an open enemy." The tongue-lashing continued: "We find you guilty of very wrong behavior in selling at extravagant prices, particularly West Indian goods. This conduct . . . is very detrimental to the liberties of America. We therefore your offended brethren demand satisfaction of you . . . by a confession for your past conduct and a thorough reformation for time to come."[56]

Sharply chastised, the Hales recanted, agreeing to sell at prices specified by the assembled crowd. But Samuel Colton resisted. The town's wealthiest man, his roots traced back to Longmeadow's founders in the 1640s. Ship owner, slave owner, head of a large household, and owner of the town's finest dwelling, he was accustomed to the respect that most "river Gods" of the Connecticut River valley enjoyed. But now he had to eat humble pie. Deep into the night, a knot of blackfaced Longmeadow townsmen, wrapped in blankets "like Indians," broke into Colton's store, carried off his cache of sugar, salt, rum, and molasses, and put the liberated goods in the hands of the town clerk. The crowd included the deacon of Longmeadow's Congregational Church and the cousin of Colton's wife. After selling the scarce commodities at a fair price, the town clerk tried to give the proceeds to Colton. When he refused to accept the money, crowd leaders entered his house, plunked the sum down on a table, and left. They had made their point: Those who tried to line their pockets at the expense of ordinary members of the community must answer for their misdeeds and yield to the collective will.

Six months after this incident, in early 1777, the Massachusetts legislature instituted price limits for the sale of rum, beans, cloth, and many other essential items in response to petitions from many towns that all goods "should be sold upon reasonable terms." At the same time, thirty-eight Connecticut River valley towns set uniform prices throughout the area. The legislature later abandoned price controls because they had no way of enforcing them in the face of widespread defiance by both farmers with produce to sell and merchants with money to buy. Still nursing his injured pride, and encouraged by the abandonment of price controls, Samuel Colton struck back. In 1780, he sued the night raiders for their seizure of his goods on that rainy night in July 1777. Colton charged that "there was no color for the people at large interposing and in this violent outrageous manner depriving any man of his property."[57]

The defendants, Deacon Nathaniel Ely among them, protested that they had seized Colton's property because he used it "in such a manner as essentially to injure the whole [community]." They had struck by night, they testified, "to hinder some members of the community from acting contrary to the general welfare just as their humor or malice should direct." Here, in microcosm, was one of the central disputes that divided Americans as they strove to secure their independence. "Colton had preferred his own private profit to the welfare of the community," sums up Barbara Clark Smith, the main historian of this revealing incident. "Private property had its rights, but it still had to yield to the larger good."[58] Adam Smith's core idea of the hidden hand properly regulating all economic transactions to the benefit of the greatest number had been gaining ground for many decades, and it would become the reigning philosophy of the nineteenth century. But for now, in small villages such as Longmeadow, the hidden hand was that of blanket-wrapped, black-faced, upright citizens responding not to abstract propositions but to concrete, everyday dinner table needs.

The villagers in Longmeadow—and in hundreds of other places—were trying to force back a tide that had been sweeping onto the shores of North America for a long time. Colonists had become enmeshed over many decades in the broad Atlantic economy, exporting wheat, tobacco, rice, indigo, timber products, beef, fish, and many other commodities to Europe and the West Indies; balancing their books, they had imported finished goods, sugar, coffee, slaves, indentured servants, rum, molasses, and much more. Increasingly, they participated in credit relations and markets extending far beyond their local economies. But this engagement with a wide, capitalistic Atlantic market was part of an incomplete transition, one that proceeded "unevenly within any one community." The market economy was most enthusiastically embraced by prospering farmers, town retailers, and seaport merchants, and most warily regarded by those in the lower ranks.[59]

Amid wartime dislocations, insistence on equity and crowd action to enforce it bubbled to the surface. After all, the movement toward independence had been fueled by anger over British policies that seemed blatantly unfair to colonists at all levels of society. Withdrawing from the British-controlled Atlantic market was as much a part of proclaiming independence as withdrawing from membership in the British empire. But this immediately boxed the Americans into an uncomfortable and stress-filled place. Cutting themselves off from British imported fabrics, they would have to produce homespun clothing. Depriving themselves of West Indian sugar, they would have to give up their sweet teeth. If tea and coffee were no longer available, they would have to drink cider and milk. Upper-class Americans would have to do without imported luxuries: ornate furniture, four-wheeled carriages, expensive dinnerware, fashionable attire, and the like. "Buy American" must be the watchwords.

Just as important, every economic actor or actress must be part of the common sacrifice that the war required. Reaping windfalls by manipulating the market, putting personal gain ahead of community welfare, and taking advantage of ordinary people in a pinched economy were as repugnant as refusing allegiance to the Revolution. Fair dealing and patriotism became virtually synonymous; inequitable dealing and Loyalism became partners. Among the many things it did, the Revolution fueled a revival of the idea of a moral economy that condemned the untrammeled manipulation of the market. It could hardly have been otherwise. The notion that a free, unregulated market would benefit all, at least eventually, made little sense for those suffering real privation at a time when they were bearing the greatest burdens for the glorious cause.

Food riots and other crowd interventions with respect to the operation of a free market occurred widely in the years from 1776 to 1779, in rural as well as urban areas and in the South as well as the North. Barbara Clark Smith has analyzed more than thirty such food riots. She shows how they were central to ordinary people's understanding of how political and economic affairs were spliced together. In the view of those who held to the idea of a "moral economy," the exchange of goods and the setting of prices were not simply impersonal transactions governed by the laws of supply and demand operating across a vast Atlantic commercial network. Rather, they were intensely personal and local transactions that must work for the greater good of the community. As Boston's minister Jonathan French expressed it in 1777, every economic exchange should be "mutually advantageous."[60]

Boston and the towns in its commercial orbit lay at the center of food rioting. Fourteen times between December 1776 and the fall of 1778, crowds sprang into action to punish those who raised prices inordinately or withheld goods from the market in order to reap windfall profits. Typical was a "concourse of people to the amount of 500," who seized five well-to-do men, forced them into a cart, carried them past the gallows across the Charles River to Roxbury, dumped them in the street, and "told them," as Abigail Adams wrote to her husband, "if they were ever catched in the town again it should be at the expense of their lives." At the head of the "concourse" was "Joyce Junior," a reference to the poor tailor George Joyce who captured King Charles I in 1647 during the seventeenth-century English civil war, became his executioner, and thereafter became a potent symbol for Boston's lower classes. Decked out in a red coat and white wig, a sword at his side,

Joyce rode a horse at the head of the shouting crowd, which was incensed at how, at a public auction in nearby Salem, the five men had "bid up the articles to an enormous price," as Abigail Adams explained, and refused to sell them for paper currency, which, in the general absence of silver, was the main medium of exchange. "There is a general cry against the merchants, against monopolizers etc. who tis said have created a partial scarcity . . . , not only of luxury, but even the necessaries of life," Abigail lamented to John.[61] Though she labeled the five merchants "Tories," Abigail complained that "a spirit of avarice, a contempt of authority [referring to frustrated attempts at price control in Boston], an inordinate love of gain . . . prevails not only in town but every where I look or hear from." By the evening of the carting to Roxbury, handbills signed "Joyce Junior" were nailed up in the streets of Boston warning monopolists to sell at a fair price and for paper money, as the legislature had already specified.

In the spring and summer of 1777, crowds marched to obtain bread, coffee, and other table items at a reasonable price on seven other occasions in Marblehead, Salem, and Boston, Massachusetts. People's extralegal actions were increasingly "expressive of the beliefs and grievances of the cities' lower classes." They included the women's carting of Thomas Boylston recounted earlier. Two months later, in September 1777, a crowd carted monopolizers and price gougers out of Boston. In November, about sixty women and a handful of men seized the sugar of a merchant in nearby Beverley, forced other merchants to surrender *their* sugar, and put a woman shopkeeper in charge of selling all the commandeered sugar at an equitable price. At the same time, about five hundred North End Bostonians commandeered the sugar of merchant Jonathan Amory, who was withholding it from the market to jack up the price.

Controlling prices in the name of the community's need troubled many moderate patriots and infuriated conservative ones. Many states set price limits in 1776 and 1777 on such essentials as bread and meat, but they did so reluctantly. By 1777–78, merchants, retailers, and some farmers began pressuring state governments to repeal price control laws, seeing them "as directly opposite to the idea of liberty," as Boston merchants argued to the legislature. The power of the crowd, as demonstrated in Joyce Junior's humiliation of price gougers, also worried these men. They were all the more unsettled by seeing women, traditionally excluded from public and political action, playing assertive, outdoor roles. By late 1777, legislatures in New Hampshire and

Massachusetts did repeal price control laws, but this did not stop the people from confronting merchants and retailers. In harassing Jonathan Amory, Bostonians obtained the justice they sought, carting his sugar to a neighboring store, added sugar wrested from other merchants, and taking satisfaction in seeing it distributed through the summer of 1778 at a fair price by three Boston officials.

Free-trade advocates, composed especially of merchants and retailers, gradually got their way in dismantling price controls late in the war. Their strongest argument was that "in a free country no man ought to be divested of his property, but by his own consent or the law of the land," as New York merchants insisted. But in the depths of revolution in 1777–78, ordinary people took the law into their own hands in order to feed their families. In this way they upheld the idea of a moral economy that earlier had prevailed. All the more extraordinary, "women cast themselves as competent actors in a political context from which they had largely been excluded." "With or without price control laws on the books, and with or without the support of men," writes Barbara Clark Smith, "women acted."[62]

Radical Loyalism

"What have you to expect from those who have cut down liberty poles and in direct opposition thereto, have erected the King's standards and in an avowed manner drank his health and success and destruction to Congress and conventions?" Thus in March 1777 wrote Maryland's General William Smallwood, who had earned laurels by leading the Maryland Regiment north to fight against the British in the battles of Long Island and White Plains in August and October of 1776. But now, back home, he was in charge of quelling an insurrection of Marylanders on the state's Eastern Shore. From neighboring Dorchester County, wealthy patriot planter Joseph Dashiell bemoaned "those who held out, from a blind and obstinate attachment to the old form of government, and whose wish and inclination was still to fall down and worship the golden image of royalty."[63]

Who were these Maryland worshipers of George III? Called "Tories" by their patriot enemies, the Loyalists are known in the history books mainly as selfish ultraconservatives who preferred English rule to American self-governance. It is true that most Anglican clergymen, who owed their licenses to preach to the Church of England, remained loyal to England. So, too, large numbers of lawyers trained in England and wedded to English common law became Loyalists. Also, thousands of wealthy merchants and planters, with much to lose if an internal revolution succeeded alongside a victory over the British, swore fealty to the king. But these groups made up only a fraction of the Loyalists who numbered hundreds of thousands and made up about one fifth of the American population. Far more numerous among the Loyalists were ordinary farmers, artisans, and others of modest means. Among these plebeian Loyalists were the tenants of the Hudson River valley treated in chapter 3; North Carolina Regulators still bitter over their treatment at the hands of those who were now leading the patriot movement; backcountry farmers in South Carolina who hated the patriot merchants and planters centered in Charleston; and ethnic German farmers and artisans in the middle states who feared control by an Anglo-American majority. In many cases, Loyalists "were the king's friends and others . . . were the patriot's enemies," as historian Ronald Hoffman has put it.[64]

In history, the Loyalists have come down to us as not only faithful subjects of the English king but also those afraid of too much social change. This fits men such as William Franklin, Benjamin Franklin's son, who became the royal governor of New Jersey, or Joseph Galloway, Franklin's old lawyer friend whose social conservatism was bone deep. Both were indeed frightened by what they regarded as liberty-mad men engineering a needless revolution. Yet many of the Loyalists were among the most radical proponents of a transformed American society, people who sought a place in the body politic for ordinary people and an overhauled legal system where those in the lower classes could obtain simple justice. These are the Loyalists that history has forgotten.

The case of Maryland's Somerset and Dorchester counties on the lower Eastern Shore of the Chesapeake is instructive. Most of the insurrectionists of March 1777 described above occupied the lowest rung of Maryland society. "Humanity can scarce forbear to drop a tear on reflecting on the circumstances of many of them," Joseph Dashiell told Maryland's governor. "With a poor wretched hut crowded with children, naked, hungry and miserable without bread or a penny of money to buy any; in short they appear as objects almost too contemptible to excite the public resentment." Yet impoverished and uneducated as they were, these people had their own ideas about an equitable society. In fact, they thought all too much, Dashiell lamented: "[T]hese are the wretches who set up to be the arbiters of government; to knock down independence and restore the authority of the British King in Parliament which by testimony taken by us was the avowed design of some of the[ir] principles. . . . Despicable as those creatures really are, they have their influence within their own peculiar sphere."[65]

A few months before the March 1777 insurrection, the wavering allegiance of county militias became obvious. More eager to redress local grievances than defend "liberty" against English encroachments, the Dorchester County militiamen, defying their officers, confiscated salt from a monopolizing local merchant. The gentry-led Dorchester County Committee of Observation tried to apprehend and punish the rioters, even as the riots spread to other locales. But "many of the men swear they will support what they have done at the hazard of their lives," reported one officer. More ominous, they declared their readiness to use their weapons on behalf of the king. "By their declarations against the present measures of the country, and in favor of the king," wrote the Dorchester planters, "[they] show themselves entirely disaffected to our cause." Worse still, "they have a very formidable number to protect them from Caroline [and] Worcester [counties], and Sussex [County] in Delaware." Some county militia colonels turned to indentured servants to fill the ranks and quell the disturbances. This backfired too. "So general a desertion prevails amongst the servants enlisted into our army," wrote Colonel William Richardson of Caroline County, "that I have ordered my officers to forbear enlisting any more of them, seeing that it was only recruiting men for the enemy, not for us."[66]

A riot in Baltimore County in October 1777 provided further evidence of radical Loyalism. When a sheriff tried to levy fines on those resisting militia duty, hundreds of men rose up in defiance. The Maryland Council of State ordered militia units from other counties to turn out to suppress the insurrection, and this worked in part. But the state never solved its military manpower problem, and Maryland leaders continued to grit their teeth under the many threats. One colonel informed the governor that his men promised "they will shoot several of their field officers."[67]

How do we explain the determination of these Eastern Shore outcasts to thwart American independence and restore the authority of George III and Parliament? General Smallwood's understanding of the matter provides some clues. "What can be expected," he asked, "from the inhabitants of a place which becomes the reception of deserters, escaping prisoners, and most of the disaffected who have been expelled from the neighboring states?"[68] But this stops short of a full explanation, describing the insurgents' social condition but not their mind-set. That can be grasped only by understanding the success of socially conservative patriot planters and lawyers in blocking attempts of equally patriotic Marylanders to obtain taxpayer suffrage and a reformed Maryland government. The Eastern Shore radicals became Loyalists because conservative patriots, with a history of class imperiousness and insensitivity, drove them into the arms of the British. If social justice could not be obtained under the rule of Maryland's elite, perhaps it could be found under England's royal banner. It would be sought in this manner by men of a certain disposition noted by a young visiting Englishman just a few years before: "An idea of equality seems generally to prevail," wrote William Eddis, "and the inferior order of people pay little but external respect to those who occupy superior stations."[69]

General Smallwood's difficulties in suppressing the Eastern Shore insurrection should have given him a clue that the rebels were not just escaped prisoners, faithless militia deserters, and refugees from Virginia and Delaware. The state government had tried to defuse the "alarming and dangerous insurrection in Somerset County," by issuing a proclamation ordering an end to all disorder and offering immunity from punishment if the poor rebels obeyed.[70] When the proclamation produced no results, the patriot planter elite tried more draconian measures: a law prescribing the death penalty for treasonous acts against the state; the confiscation of property belonging to anyone withholding information on such activities; the empowerment of the governor to suspend habeas corpus during an invasion of the state; and the publication of a blacklist of fourteen insurrectionist leaders. Again, this produced no results. In fact, the insurrection spread to Dorchester, Worcester, and Caroline counties. Either Continental troops or Maryland's militia units would have to solve the problem.

But no Continental troops were available in the spring of 1777 as the insurrectionists flouted the law. Washington was more than fully engaged after a series of disastrous defeats in the New York City area—at Long Island, White Plains, and Fort Washington—that decimated his army. The Maryland Council of State next ordered county militia colonels to raise three hundred volunteers to overpower the Loyalist rebels. The pitiable result was another example of the minuteman myth revealed earlier. "Such backwardness prevails generally amongst us," wrote Colonel William Whitely from Caroline County, "that I am almost certain the number (though so very small) can not be got voluntarily; nothing but a draft will accomplish the design." In fact, Whitely was having difficulty bringing out already enlisted men for normal training. "Two thirds of the people remain at home abusing and ridiculing the honest few who think it their duty to attend constantly," he explained. Even his officers "deliver sentiments very prejudicial to our cause."[71] Of the three hundred militiamen requested, only fourteen had been procured by the end of June 1777.

At the heart of the problem was the hauteur and domineering posture of Maryland's planter elite. A prime example of this was the clause in the state constitution giving the governor sole power to appoint militia officers. Forbidden to elect their officers, ordinary men refused to serve. Even in usually placid Queen Anne's County, militia colonel Thomas Wright informed its council of safety that "the people have been induced to believe they ought not to submit to any [officer] appointments but those made by themselves." Wright was probably wrong that ordinary people—poor white farmers, mostly—had to be "induced" to insist on electing their own officers. Throughout the country, enlisted men demanded this right, and in Maryland the sentiment was held all the more passionately after ordinary farmers heard from such haughty officers as Richard Chew that "no poor man was entitled to a vote, and those that would insist upon voting, if he had his way, should be put to death" for "a poor man was not born to freedom but to be a drudge on earth."[72]

Also fueling the resentment of yeomen, tenanted agricultural workers, and indentured servants were waves of Methodist evangelicalism that swept over the Eastern Shore at this very time. Tory insurrections were led by itinerant "scoundrel Methodist preachers," as William Paca, a wealthy tobacco merchant, described them in 1777.[73] Perhaps this was an overheated exaggeration, but Methodist preachers such as Cheney Clow had great influence among the poor farmers, servants, and slaves of the area. Attacking slavery as immoral and ungodly, Clow, Freeborn Garretson, and other Methodist ministers made many converts with their fiery outdoor preaching, where they indicted the proud, domineering Anglican-based gentry. In 1778, Clow led an attack on the Queen Anne's County Courthouse. Two years later, wrote one alarmed Eastern Shore planter, "the spirit of Methodism reigns so much amongst us that few or no men will be raised for the war." As soon as a man converted to Methodism, he "lays down his arms and in that way declares himself an enemy to his country."[74] The Anglican gentry could arrest, beat, harass, imprison, and—in at least one case—try to assassinate the "strolling" Methodist ministers, as they often did, but this only confirmed the view from the bottom of society that in the midst of revolution, the British were their natural allies, not the wealthy and oppressive patriot tobacco gentry.

Loyalist radicals of the Eastern Shore had opportunities to join the king's forces because during late 1776 and most of 1777, the British navy controlled Chesapeake Bay, sending troops ashore to seize American arms, requisition food, and recruit disaffected Marylanders. But most of the Loyalist radicals, many with families, saw no future in serving with the British army or navy, which, in any event, was on the move. When the British fleet sailed up the Chesapeake Bay to land the king's regiments for their overland march to capture Philadelphia in the fall of 1777, the Eastern Shore radicals lost an important ally. Yet they continued to lash out against the patriot gentry. In the spring of 1778, after a fact-finding tour of the Eastern Shore, patriot lawyer Luther Martin reported that armed bands of "the disaffected inhabitants" of Somerset County had seized tobacco- and wheat-filled boats of local planters and brazenly stormed the house of a county militia captain.[75]

The offscourings of Maryland society gained two of their main objectives— a reform of Maryland's regressive tax system and partial relief for the state's debtors—not through the support of the British but through two radical planters. Rezin Hammond and John Hall, both descended from seventeenth-century Maryland settlers, became the tribunes of the poor. Hammond was thirty-one years old in 1776 and one of six sons of a venerable Anne Arundel County planter who left nearly 20,000 acres and hundreds of slaves when he died in the early 1770s. Hammond's share was about 4,000 acres, not on par with the immense holdings of some Maryland planters, but nonetheless enough to put him in the top tenth of planter society. He soon served as a lieutenant colonel in the Anne Arundel County militia, a mark of the respect he commanded from hundreds of residents in his county. His leadership of a radically democratic party in Maryland had deep roots. With his brothers, he had been among the most fervent anti-British Marylanders in the years leading up to revolution. John Hall, an Annapolis lawyer, had also emerged as a popular party leader in the stormy days leading to revolution and became closely associated with Hammond. Both played leading roles in the masses' burning of the *Peggy Stewart*, a British ship carrying tea to Maryland—a popular upsurgence discountenanced by many conservative patriot leaders. Hammond and Hall differed from their fellow wealthy Marylanders in their sensitivity to the hard lives that many indentured servants, tenant farmers, and agricultural workers endured.

Maryland's propertied elite controlled the convention that wrote the state's constitution in 1776, the most conservative of all the state constitutions put in place. Moreover, the first legislature elected under the constitution guaranteed the continued political rule by the state's wealthy. But this did not ward off the reformist sentiment surging up and down Maryland's coast. Meeting in Annapolis in February 1777, the new legislature, controlled by the same men who wrote the constitution, trimmed their sails in the face of a gale. Within a year they "moved to subdue the class antagonisms fomenting internal unrest," as historian Ronald Hoffman explains, "by enacting a radical fiscal program . . . , the price they must pay to save their class and the Revolution."[76]

Rezin Hammond and John Hall pushed the populist radical agenda, and they started by proposing to reform the most egregiously reactionary tax system known on the west side of the Atlantic. Almost all states levied taxes regressively, drawing revenue disproportionately from middle- and lower-class citizens. In Maryland, the wealthiest landholder and slave owner paid exactly the same tax as the poorest agricultural laborer. Those who passed the laws took care of themselves, yet self-interest had its limits. Responding to widespread social unrest and difficulties in raising volunteer militiamen, the legislature pragmatically enacted a graduated property tax based on landholdings in February 1777. Eight months later, the legislature included slaves as taxable property. The immensely wealthy Charles Carroll of Carrollton called this the "price of revolution."[77] On the heels of this reform, Hammond and Hall proposed a more radical plan: to make paper money legal tender. This was a clear concession to the debtor class because, with the Continental paper dollars authorized by Congress already depreciating in value, the bill promised relief for debtors. Those benefiting were not all bottom dwellers; included were planters with extensive ownership of land and slaves and merchants in Annapolis and Baltimore.

Many Maryland grandees bitterly opposed the paper money bill. Charles Carroll, the Annapolis patriarch of the princely Carroll family, exploded that such a law "will surpass in iniquity all the acts of the British Parliament against America," and told his son that he would regard Maryland legislators who voted for the law as "highway men" and "pickpockets." But his son, Charles Carroll of Carrollton, advised his father that "this unhappy civil war" was bound to bring some social leveling. "I have long considered our personal estate, I mean the money part of it," he wrote, "to be in jeopardy. If we can save a third of that and all our land and negroes, I shall think ourselves well off." Well off they indeed remained, and the father slowly learned the art of "yielding to the times."[78] The Eastern Shore tumults, the dissipation of the patriotic military fervor in the lower ranks, the widespread desire of militiamen to elect their own officers, and the willingness of some of the state's poorest people to welcome a return of British authority chastened most of the Maryland legislature. To retain their leadership they would have to bend to the people at large, even if these people lacked the vote or the right to hold office. "The [paper money] law suits the multitudes," Carroll of Carrollton wrote his father. "Individuals must submit to partial losses; no great revolutions can happen in a state without revolutions or mutations of private property." Carroll did not argue with his father's view that the popular will— "popular frenzies and delusions," he called them—was unjust. But the people would bring "violence and greater injustice" down on the heads of those who opposed them. "There is a time when it is wisdom to yield to injustice."[79] For the poor enlisting in the ranks of radical Loyalism their behavior was the opposite of injustice.

The Loyalism of the dispossessed was not confined to Maryland. In New York, one of the Loyalist strongholds, most of those remaining faithful to the king were ordinary people, and many of them lived on the edge of poverty. For example, among the twenty men rounded up as dangerous antirevolutionaries by New York City patriot authorities in June 1776 were five taverners, four leather workers, two smiths, four laborers, a teacher, a constable, and a pensioner.[80]

William Prendergast, saved from the gallows by royal reprieve, was another radical antilandlord leader who had to make a decision about where to place his allegiance once the Revolutionary War began. His eldest son, Matthew, twenty years old in 1776, had no qualms about joining the Loyalist contingent formed by Abraham Cuyler, mayor of Albany. Fighting with a Loyalist unit on Long Island, Matthew Prendergast captured many Connecticut patriots. He was one of thousands of Loyalists who sought refuge in Nova Scotia after the war. The decision was more difficult for his father. Like so many other tenant farmers, he tried to stay out of the Revolution; but this became difficult as marauding American and British armies scourged the Hudson River valley repeatedly in the early years of the war. Three times between 1775 and 1779, local committees of observation and safety demanded

Prendergast's oath of allegiance, but his support for the American cause was passive at best.

On the Livingston Manor of 160,000 acres, however, tenant farmers knew almost reflexively that as soon as landlord Robert R. Livingston threw in his lot with the patriots, they would take the other side. Land was the key. As Livingston wrote his friend John Jay in May 1775, "Many of our tenants here refused to sign the [Continental] association, and resolved to stand by the king as they called it, in hopes that if he succeeded they should have their lands." The rhetoric of freedom and unalienable rights for freeborn Englishmen rang hollow for men who for years had struggled for security on the land they worked. For them, the tyranny of their landlords was far more injurious than the English tyranny bemoaned by the American patriots.

When pressed to join patriot militia units, the Livingston tenants tried to stay neutral, arguing that their leases would expire in the event of their deaths and therefore leave their families bereft. Robert Livingston's mother and father promised new leases to the widows of fallen tenant-soldiers, but most tenants had little confidence in this. One tenant, Jury Wheeler, promised in September 1776 that if he was drafted into a militia unit from the Livingston Manor, he would turn his musket first on the militia captain.[81] By this time, some of the tenants were signing the "King's Book," promising to "Come to the King's people" and join British regulars if they reached Livingston Manor.

The spring thaw of 1777, as historian Staughton Lynd has chronicled, brought a series of tenant uprisings. "Almost everybody in the upper manor . . . appears to have engaged with the enemy," wrote a patriot commissioner charged with rooting out the tenant Loyalists, "first by taking an oath of secrecy, and then an oath of allegiance to the King." Believing that English General John Burgoyne would sweep down the upper Hudson River valley from Montreal, the tenants expected "to have pay from the time of the junction [with the British regulars] and each 200 acres of land."[82]

Though they had their priorities straight, the radical tenant Loyalists' uprising was ill timed. They carried weapons and powder stolen from Livingston's powder mills and lead they had pilfered from nets strung by the patriots across the Hudson River to block British ships; but they could not match the firepower of the well-equipped patriot militia units marching under orders to "fire upon every man fleeing before them." Some tenants died in skirmishing, others were hanged, but most fled to the woods or penitently signed oaths of loyalty to the patriot cause. Retribution would have been more severe except for the fear that gripped the Livingston Manor lords. Robert Livingston, Jr., was so disgusted with his tenants that he wished "that they may be all hanged and their children starved." But he knew he had little influence with them and in fact was afraid "from riding about in his own manor," as an intimate remembered after the war.[83]

For the remainder of the war, the chastened tenants dodged militia service and often recanted their oaths of allegiance to the patriot cause. Those who did join militia units deserted in droves. Radical in economic and social matters because their life situations made "hearth and home" their chief issue, they saw no contradiction in pitting themselves against patriot landlords who professed political liberty as their goal.[84]

For the Regulators of North Carolina, as for the tenant farmers of New York, the Revolution presented difficult choices. Many of the defeated Regulators joined North Carolina Loyalists at the Battle of Moore's Bridge in February 1776, but many melted away when they did not find the large contingent of British regulars they had been told would rendezvous with them. A limited number enlisted for Continental army service, and some turned out for patriot militia duty. But most tried to sit out the war, battle-shy after Alamance and unsure which side offered the best hope for a better future. Both the royal governor, Josiah Martin, and the provincial revolutionary government that evicted him, promised Regulators pardons for any past sedition. Throughout the war, both Loyalists and patriots sought the support of the radical prewar farmers. However, the Regulators found little reason to choose sides, and the constitution that the patriot elite created in 1776, which made only modest reforms to the old colonial regime, gave them meager hope that the "glorious cause" was worth fighting for.

Choosing Sides

For some 200,000 Native Americans composing eighty-five nations east of the Mississippi River, the onset of full-scale war between the American colonists and the British in 1776 greatly complicated goals of political independence and territorial preservation—their guiding principles since the first encounters with intruding Europeans. African Americans who had neither liberty nor land now fought for the former in order to someday gain the latter. But Native Americans, who had both, reached a critical point in struggling to preserve them. Like most African Americans, the majority of Native Americans painfully reached the conclusion that preserving political and territorial integrity could best be achieved by fighting *against* the side that proclaimed the equality of all men and with the side that the Americans accused of trampling their God-given, natural, irreducible rights. The logic of nearly two hundred years of abrasive contact with colonizing Europeans compelled the choice. After all, it was the settler-subjects of the English king who most threatened Indian autonomy, just as it was royal power before the Revolution that had attempted to protect Indian land from colonizer encroachment.

In pursuing their revolutionary goals, Indian societies shared with the Americans the problem of overcoming long traditions of local identity and intertribal friction to forge a confederated resistance movement. Just as the white "tribes" of Connecticut and New York had to put aside local attachments and long-standing disagreements, just as Virginians and North Carolinians had to bury nagging animosities, just as northern and southern colonies had to settle their differences, so did the Iroquois, Shawnee, Cherokee, Delaware, Creek, Miami, and other tribes have to find ways to forge a pan-Indian movement against a background of generations-long intertribal conflict. For the white revolutionaries, as John Adams said, the trick was to make thirteen clocks strike as one. For the red revolutionists, the problem was identical. In both societies, new leaders emerged in the process of wrestling with this central question. Usually they were men whose military abilities or political acumen gained them attention, suggesting that the fate of their people lay in their hands. Our history books rarely record the names of Red Jacket or Cornplanter of the Seneca, Attakullakulla and his son Dragging Canoe of the Cherokee, Alexander McGillvray of the Creek, Cornstalk of the Shawnee, George White Eyes of the Delaware, or Little Turtle of the Miami. But in Indian society they were as much the dominant figures of the revolutionary era as were Washington, George Rogers Clark, Nathanael Greene, Richard Henry Lee, John Paul Jones, Alexander Hamilton, Thomas Jefferson, and other white founding fathers in colonial society.

As Congress's war strategists surveyed the landscape in 1775, they knew from generations of colonial experience that it was essential to keep the many Indian nations neutral. If they did not, the native peoples allied with the British would face off against the Americans along a thousand-mile-long second front to the west. Yet to keep them neutral, the Americans had to deal with the two matters foremost in the minds of native people: land and trade. Maintaining trade was expensive, and the English, with a network of Indianist administrators and traders, were much better prepared than the Americans to supply the Indians' needs. As for land, native people could rarely be convinced that the Americans would protect their lands. It was no mystery to them that the white population explosion of the eighteenth century had translated into a feverish desire to expand into Indian territory west of the Appalachian Mountains. On both key Indian issues the odds heavily favored the British. And on top of their self-interest, Native Americans could consider the only reference to them in the Declaration of Independence—Jefferson's blanket indictment of the "merciless Indian savages" who knew only an indiscriminate desire to kill.

Congress succeeded in its neutrality policy through 1775 and into 1776, but primarily because the British followed the same strategy of keeping native people out of the war. Then two months before signing the Declaration of Independence, congressional delegates authorized Washington "to engage up to 2,000 Indians for war against Canada."[85] The Indian recruits, at the most seven hundred, were mostly from the small Penobscot and Abenaki tribes in Maine. This was nearly Congress's last success in wooing significant numbers of Native Americans to the patriot side. Throughout the course of the war, native warriors enlisted in Washington's Continental army and in state militia companies as individuals and in small groups, but these were usually men from severely weakened and dependent Indian tribes. Where the great reservoir of Indian fighting manpower resided, in Iroquoia, the Ohio country, the Kentucky hunting grounds of the Cherokee, and the interior Creek lands of the Lower South, the appeals made by congressional diplomats fell decidedly on deaf ears. Congress might as well have written off Indian support from these areas, because many of its white members were offending Native Americans by speculating heavily in their ancient homelands or had friends who were doing so. Native people knew all too well that the rebelling Americans rising up to secure their liberty in the East were equally desirous of establishing an empire in the West.

As Iroquois people surveyed the territorial and political landscape, neutrality seemed the best policy. But if the Iroquois stayed out of the war, would the war stay out of Iroquoia? Through the eyes of Mohawk Joseph Brant, this seemed very unlikely. He was ahead of most Iroquois leaders in seeing, as historian Francis Jennings puts it, that "while the colony-states fought for in-dependence from the Crown, the tribes had to fight for independence from the states."[86]

As recounted earlier, Brant had trekked through Iroquoia after his return from London in 1776 to coax leaders of the Six Nations from the position of neutrality, which most of them preferred. Brant recalled many years after the Revolution that "Every man of us thought that by fighting for the King we should ensure to ourselves and children a good inheritance."[87] But this was far from the case in 1776. Trying to convince the Iroquois that their lives, lib-erties, and property depended on American defeat, Brant and British agents had to contend with the efforts of the Continental Congress, which relied on Samuel Kirkland, Presbyterian missionary to the Oneida and Tuscarora, to keep the Iroquois neutral or bring them to the American side. Mary Jemison, the "White Woman of the Genesee," who had been taken captive by the Shawnee as a young girl during the Seven Years' War and given to the Seneca, with whom she lived contentedly for the rest of her life, remembered how the Iroquois met with Americans and pledged their neutrality in late 1775. They were "well pleased that they could live on neutral ground, sur-rounded by the din of war, without being engaged in it."[88] But thereafter, for many months, Iroquois people wavered. Militants, usually young warriors, leaned toward alliance with the English in the hope of regaining lost terri-tory. Conservatives, typically those drawn to Christian doctrine, counseled accommodation with the Americans. Between the two sides stood the "neu-trals," including most older chiefs and most women, who hoped that the fight among the whites would blow over and spare the lives of Indian people.

For more than two years after the battles at Concord and Lexington, the Iroquois neutralists prevailed. But by late 1777, their position became unten-able. Joseph Brant's own military exploits from 1776 through 1778 became an important part of how the Iroquois Six Nations reached their ultimate deci-sions and were drawn into the war on both sides. Emerging as a militant anti-American leader, he became instrumental in a train of events that led to ritually extinguishing the Six Nations council fire in 1777 for the first time in the history of the League of the Iroquois.

In late 1776, Brant began recruiting Mohawk and Oneida warriors, along with some white frontiersmen—most of them immigrants from England, Ireland, and Scotland who had mingled with the Iroquois—in the upper Susquehanna River region. To a casual observer, the Europeans and Indians were hardly distinguishable because the whites dressed and painted themselves as Indians. Supported by British paymasters, they fought together as Brant's Volunteers. Provisioned by other white Loyalist farmers, they harried patriot farmsteads in northern New York. Brant acted without sanction from the Iroquois Confederacy or even from Mohawk chiefs. In this sense, he was as hotheaded as Ethan Allen, who, marching to his own drummer, had gathered a private force of volunteers for the calamitous attack on Montreal.

In July 1777, when Brant and his contingent reached Oswego, on the southeastern shore of Lake Ontario, his position among the Iroquois gained stature. Among a large number of warrior chiefs, Brant spoke passionately in favor of taking up the hatchet against the Americans. Brant's position was strengthened twofold: First, several companies of German mercenaries, British regulars, and the white Loyalist King's Royal Regiment of New York were in attendance; second, the British showered the Iroquois with a shipful of goods ranging from ostrich feathers and small jingling bells to gun barrels and barrels of rum. In this context, the warriors debated at length. Finally, about seven hundred warriors agreed to join a British expedition for an attack on the Americans at Fort Stanwix. Seneca warriors did not want to participate, but were coaxed "to come and see them whip the rebels" while smoking their pipes and staying clear of the action, as Mary Jemison remembered.

Also at the Oswego parley was a man whose life became entwined with Brant's, a war captain who became a folk villain in the years after the American Revolution. John Butler was descended from three generations of Connecticut people on his mother's side. His father had come to North America as a British regimental officer sent to help New Englanders attack French Canada in Queen Anne's War (1702–13). He remained in British service and in the 1750s became closely connected with William Johnson, who was soon to become superintendent of Indian Affairs for the northern colonies. In this way, John Butler was raised as an Indianist. After fighting in the Seven Years' War alongside other colonists, Butler married the daughter of a prominent Dutch family in the Mohawk River valley and became one of the largest landowners in the Mohawk region. He lived only a few miles from Johnson Hall, the manor estate of William Johnson, who had married Joseph Brant's sister. Butler, like Johnson, learned the language of the Iroquois and became an interpreter for the Crown's northern Indian department.[89]

As the Revolution loomed, Butler became an invaluable British go-between with the Iroquois, a man of military experience and a person well respected in the Mohawk River valley. Deeply attached to the Iroquois and a faithful servant of the British Indian Department, Butler recruited ten companies of enlisted men, more than five hundred in all, from the Mohawk River valley and the upper Susquehanna River region in 1777–78. Marching under the banner of George III, Butler's Rangers were a mix of immigrants or sons of immigrants, some German, others Highland Scots, others Irish, and many married to Iroquois women.

In American memory, Butler became the consummate turncoat, rivaled only by Benedict Arnold. An early-twentieth-century historian of the Mohawk River valley called him "not only arrogant, and supercilious in a high degree but barbarous, treacherous, revengeful, ferocious, merciless, brutal, diabolically wicked, and cruel, with the spirit of fiends [committing] cruelties worthy of the dungeons of the Inquisition."[90] D. W. Griffith may well have read this passage before casting Butler in a leading bad-guy role in *America*, the moviemaker's last big-cast spectacle, which brought the American Revolution to the silver screen for the first time. To the modern-day historian, where serious probing of Loyalist sympathies and ideology is no longer akin to writing "treason texts," as was the case three generations ago, Butler emerges differently—a sympathetic Indianist, a frontiersman par excellence, and a man loyal to the Crown like most of his Mohawk River valley neighbors. After the war, Butler led those who served with him, along with other Loyalists whose farms had been confiscated by the victorious Americans, to the Niagara peninsula of Upper Canada. Today, John Butler is honored there as a founding father.

From the Oswego parley, the Iroquois warriors, many of them mixed with Brant's Volunteers, moved down the Mohawk River valley to join British forces in laying siege to Fort Stanwix, the westernmost American post (renamed Fort Schuyler to honor one of Washington's generals). Fighting alongside hundreds of white Loyalists recruited by Colonel John Butler, Brant's Volunteers were conspicuous in ambushing an American militia regiment of eight hundred men and boys hurrying to the relief of Fort Stanwix's defenders. Led by General Nicholas Herkimer, the relief unit was only six miles from the fort when they fell into a trap near Oriskany that led to appalling American and British-Iroquois casualties. Returning to the ambush scene in a ravine a few days later, a British scout described "the most shocking sight I had ever witnessed. The Indians and the white men were mingled with one another, just as they had been left when death first completed his work. Many bodies had also been torn to pieces by wild beasts." Blacksnake, later a Seneca chief, remembered his shock. "There I have seen the most dead bodies all . . . over that I never did see, and never will again. I thought at the time the blood shed [was] a stream running down on the descending ground during the afternoon, and yet some living crying for help."[91] Among the casualties on the British side, the greatest losses were sustained by the Mohawk and Seneca, the latter having thought they were only to be onlookers. When the pro-British Iroquois slipped away to mourn their losses, the British also abandoned the siege and retreated without accomplishing their goal.

The key result of the fierce battle at Oriskany was to convince the Iroquois people that this was going to be a difficult war and that abandoning "modern Indian politics," the old strategy of playing one white power off against another, was going to be very costly. During the following years, writes historian Barbara Graymont, the Iroquois, like the English, "would become a divided people—nation against nation, clan against clan, lodge against lodge."[92]

For the remainder of 1777 and into the spring of 1778, Joseph Brant and his sister Molly, the widow of Sir William Johnson, played a key role in persuading the Seneca and Cayuga, the westernmost tribes of the Six Nations, to support the British. They had to counter the effect that General John Burgoyne's surrender to the Americans at Saratoga in the fall of 1777 had on northern native peoples, who feared that the British would now be vanquished. Molly Brant was especially important in holding most of the Iroquois to the British side. "One word from her goes farther with them," said Daniel Claus, a veteran of Indian affairs in the pay of the British, "than a thousand from any white man without exception who in general must purchase their interest at a high rate."[93] For Joseph Brant, his mission was being fulfilled.

While the pro-British Seneca, Cayuga, Onondaga, and Mohawk conducted their traditional winter hunting to replenish their food supplies, Brant, on foot and by canoe, traveled hundreds of miles in the interior to recruit warriors for the spring and summer campaign of 1778. Also urging the warriors on were three Tory Indian traders: Simon Girty, Matthew Elliott, and Alexander McKee, all of whom dressed Indian-style, with even their noses pierced for nose rings. In early July, mixed white Loyalist–Indian war parties fell on frontier settlements in the Mohawk River valley and then

*Cornplanter, a Seneca chief, was second in command at the Wyoming Valley
campaign. His mother was Seneca and his father white. Nose rings and ear
pendants were typically Seneca, but the uniform is probably fanciful.*

engaged the Americans in a major battle at Forty Fort, situated along the
Susquehanna River in the Wyoming Valley near present-day Wilkes-Barre,
Pennsylvania. The Iroquois outflanked the Americans sallying forth from
the fort, routed them, and killed all but a handful of the hundreds of patriots
at the expense of only a few of their warriors. The remaining Americans
surrendered the fort on the next day. For another week the British and their
Indian allies lay waste to the small settlements of the Wyoming Valley, plundering farms and sending the terrified frontier families into the hills. Among
the attacking Seneca was the husband of Mary Jemison.

Though the Americans were thrashed, they converted the Wyoming Valley assault into one of the great propaganda victories of the war. The fleeing
patriot survivors promptly circulated atrocity stories, turning the battle into

This sensationalist rendition of the so-called Wyoming Valley Massacre, painted in 1858, shows the scalping of one of the hapless Americans. An even more lurid illustration, appearing in Josiah Priest's Stories of Early Settlers in the Wilderness *(1837), showed Joseph Brant with his foot on a corpse and other Mohawks braining prisoners or tearing off scalps with their teeth.*

the Wyoming Valley Massacre. The patriot press reported that the attackers set the American fort on fire and pitched the forty surrendering prisoners into the flames. Newspapers claimed that the Indian Queen Esther, the daughter of Catherine Montour, who had married a well-known Indian trader, personally tomahawked fifteen prisoners pinned to the ground with pitchforks while shrieking a bloodcurdling war song. Joseph Brant, soon to be labeled "monster Brant," was said to be in the thick of the carnage, though he and his volunteers were actually far away on raids in the Mohawk River valley. The Wyoming Valley Massacre soon became the grisly story of Tory and Indian brutality, sadistic enjoyment of human sacrifice, and disregard for civilized rules of warfare. Modern scholarship supports none of this. The surrendering garrison that remained in the fort was given written immunity, and no Indian woman was with the warring Iroquois and Butler's Rangers.

Nonetheless, on the basis of the fabricated atrocity stories, Americans began preparing for a campaign that would be filled with *real* atrocities.

Later that summer, Joseph Brant did join the frontier war. Raiding the Lake Otsego area, he carefully protected women and children as his volunteers burned houses, barns, and haycocks and drove off their enemy's cattle. Americans now targeted his home camp at Oquaga on the upper Susquehanna River, one of the Mohawk staging points for backcountry attacks. In nearby Cherry Valley, patriot patrols fanned out with the cry that they would castrate Brant. In September 1778, with support from the Continental Congress, American rangers burned the now abandoned Indian villages of Oquaga, Unadilla, Tioga, and Queen Esther's Town. Oquaga was especially important. The attacking American officer in charge called it "the finest Indian town I ever saw; on both sides the river, there was about 40 good houses, square logs, shingles and stone chimneys, good floors, glass windows, etc."[94] The next day, the American unit burned two thousand bushels of corn and seized the livestock. Though this caused little loss of life, it stiffened Iroquois determination to resist the invasion of their territory that straddled the New York–Pennsylvania border. Adding to the anger of the Iroquois was an atrocity against Oquaga children. A veteran of the American expedition later recounted that "when they were mowing the corn they found several small children hid there, and he [the veteran] boasted very much, what cruel deaths they put them to, by running them through with bayonets and holding them up to see how they would twist and turn."[95]

In retaliation, Brant's Volunteers and Butler's Rangers attacked a cluster of farming villages in Cherry Valley in November 1778. Indian warriors brutally killed several dozen women and children in their attacks on farmhouses, and the number would have been much larger if Brant had not restrained the Iroquois warriors. The number of noncombatants taken prisoner more than doubled the number killed, and most of them were released unharmed the next day. Among those taken to be used for a prisoner exchange were about twenty black slaves owned by the Cherry Valley farmers.

The attack at Cherry Valley became additional fodder for the patriot press, and in this case the newspapers could accurately point to the Iroquois slaughter of noncombatants. Cherry Valley became the center of a long, bitter correspondence between American general Philip Schuyler and British general Sir Henry Clinton, in which charges of atrocities were traded freely. Two centuries later, historians agree that atrocities occurred on both sides and were about evenly divided between the American and the British-Iroquois warriors. But the correspondence of generals and the conflicting eyewitness accounts that we read today mattered little at the time. Once in the press, stories about Iroquois warriors ripping open the bellies of white women and hanging their quartered body parts from trees, or accounts of babies torn from their mothers' breasts and brained against tree trunks, became established truth. These truths, as Anthony Wallace has written, fueled "a vindictive hatred for and contempt of the Iroquois that would later cost that people and the British dear."[96]

Most of the southern Indian nations, like those in the North, sided with the British, usually after agonizing discussions. The Cherokee case demonstrates the perilous situation the southern Native American peoples confronted. The Cherokee had choked at seeing their lands ceded away by Iroquois delegates in the Treaty of Stanwix in 1768. In the half-dozen years after that, village headmen such as Attakullakulla had tried to maintain peace and trade. The Cherokee position worsened in 1775 when North Carolina's Richard Henderson claimed an astounding 27,000 square miles of prime Cherokee hunting land between the Cumberland and Kentucky rivers. Henderson claimed that Attakullakulla and other Cherokee chiefs had agreed to the cession for £10,000 worth of trade goods at the Sycamore Shoals Treaty in March 1775. The chiefs later swore they had been deceived and that one of the chief's signatures had been forged by Henderson. It is likely, however, that older headmen had agreed to the cession in order to obtain the guns, powder, and shot that the young Cherokee hunters relied on.

From this critical confrontation emerged a young warrior called by a recent Cherokee historian "the greatest military leader ever produced by the Cherokee people."[97] This was Dragging Canoe, the son of Attakullakulla (Little Carpenter to the English). Born about 1740, he gained his name through a boyhood feat that prefigured his military career. Longing to join a Cherokee war party against his father's wishes, he hid in a dugout canoe at a rendezvous portage. His amazed father now told him that if he could carry the canoe over the portage, he could join the warriors. Unable to meet this test of strength, the boy began dragging the canoe by one end. *"Tsi'yugûnsi'ni,"* shouted one warrior ("He is dragging the canoe"). In this rite of passage, the leader of a new generation of Cherokees emerged.

At the Sycamore Shoals conference, again defying his father, Dragging Canoe denounced the land cession and stormed out with a promise to

Henderson that in claiming the Cherokees' prime hunting ground, "you will find its settlement dark and bloody." Seventeen months later, Dragging Canoe told Henry Stuart, British Indian deputy superintendent, that the old chiefs (his father included) "were to blame for making private bargains." They were "too old to hunt and, . . . by their poverty, [they] had been induced to sell their land." Dragging Canoe complained that the Cherokee "were almost surrounded by the white people, that they had but a small spot of ground left for them to stand upon, and that it seemed to be the intention of the white people to destroy them from being a people." Dragging Canoe promised "he had a great many young fellows that would support him and that were determined to have their land." It was the beginning of deep fissures in the Cherokee nation, mirroring those occurring simultaneously among the Iroquois Confederacy.[98] In this case, a generational conflict rent the Cherokee. For young men, who regarded hunting as the essence of manhood, the loss of prime hunting grounds was intolerable, even if ceded by their elders, ironically, to obtain the trade goods necessary for hunting.[99]

In July 1776, the Cherokee fell upon white backcountry settlers who had squatted on their land by dint of the Sycamore Shoals Treaty, refusing the offer of free land in Florida promised by the British if they would vacate the disputed grounds. They were led by Dragging Canoe. Carrying torches and tomahawks to the cabins of frontiersmen, the young Cherokees threw backcountry Virginians and Carolinians into a state of terror. However, the odds were much against the Cherokee, in contrast to the situation of the Iroquois in the North and the Shawnee in the West. Compounding their difficulties, the Cherokee failed to obtain support from the powerful Creek nation to the south and were cut off from British trade sources. The Cherokee warriors soon found themselves short of ammunition and other supplies. With southern militiamen eager to carry out genocidal attacks commanded by Virginia and South Carolina leaders—South Carolina's William Henry Drayton urged that "you cut up every Indian cornfield and burn every Indian town and every Indian taken shall be the slave and property of the taker and that the nation be extirpated and the lands become the property of the public"—the Cherokee were outmatched. In the summer and fall of 1776, four expeditions of southern militiamen, some six thousand strong and not yet engaged in the fight against the British, severely punished the militant Cherokees, burning food and supplies, destroying orchards, razing villages, and selling captured Cherokees as slaves.[100]

This proved to be the training ground for southern militiamen mustered to fight against the British. David Ramsay, the South Carolinian who wrote a history of the Revolution in his home state just after the conflict, observed that "the expedition into the Cherokee settlements diffused military ideas and a spirit of enterprise. . . . It taught them the necessary arts of providing for an army, and gave them experience in the business of war." So thorough was the scorched-earth policy of the patriots that one militiaman believed the Cherokee "were reduced to a state of the most deplorable and wretched, being often obliged to subsist on insects and reptiles of every kind."[101]

Dragging Canoe and most of the warriors took refuge farther south and west along the Chickamauga and Tennessee rivers, regrouping to fight another day. Not all were young. Included was Outacite, the chief who had voyaged to London in 1762 and impressed the young Thomas Jefferson in Williamsburg. Also joining Dragging Canoe's militants were many Scottish and English traders, most of them married to Cherokee women. But most of the older chiefs remained behind, trying to maintain the peace. Sadly, they could do so only by surrendering more land. At the Treaty of Long Island in the summer of 1777, they ceded five million acres, roughly the size of New Jersey. The Chickamauga Cherokee, mostly young and accepting Dragging Canoe as their leader, began calling themselves *Ani-Yun'wiya*, the "Real People." They contemptuously referred to the old beloved chiefs as "Virginians." From Pensacola the British supplied the Chickamauga Cherokee but denied the desperately needed goods to the neutralist Cherokee still living in the smoldering remains of the old Indian villages. The winter of 1776–77 was one of great deprivation for the Cherokee who had not followed Dragging Canoe. The unwillingness of Virginians, Carolinians, and Georgians to assist them wore at their allegiance, leading some to slip away to join Dragging Canoe's Chickamauga faction.

The building of new villages along the Tennessee River, near present-day Chattanooga, brought the Chickamauga Cherokee closer to the powerful Creek nation. Here they regathered, only to be struck by a smallpox epidemic in 1778 that swept southward all the way to the Gulf of Mexico. For several years, the Cherokee stayed on the sidelines as the war began to move farther south in 1779. Dragging Canoe's so-called militant nationalists were not yet done with the Revolutionary War.

If the young Cherokee warriors overestimated their ability to protect their ancient homelands, the miscalculation was based on ignoring the advice of John Stuart, the British head of southern Indian Affairs. Stuart warned Dragging Canoe that the British could provide little military support in 1776 and counseled the breakaway Cherokees to remain neutral until the English were in a position to help them. Dragging Canoe and his followers spurned this advice, instead conducting the war in their own way and on their own terms.

The situation of the Shawnee and Delaware Indians of the Ohio country paralleled that of the Cherokee. As the war unfolded, militant young Shawnee warriors still smarted at the encroachments on the their Kentucky hunting grounds, but older chiefs, whose spokesman was Cornstalk, worked to maintain the peace. Eager to obtain pledges of Shawnee neutrality, Virginia and Continental Congress delegates met with chiefs of the Shawnees, Delawares, and Six Nations at Fort Pitt in September 1775. The treaty signed there endorsed the Fort Stanwix land cessions of 1768, engineered by the Iroquois at the expense of the Shawnee. White delegates promised to stop settler encroachment north of the Ohio River. Cornstalk expressed the hope that "our children now growing up will live in peace."[102]

Militant Shawnee warriors, like those among the Cherokee led by Dragging Canoe, did not abide the neutralism agreed to at Fort Pitt. Striking Virginia's frontier forts along the Ohio River in the fall and winter of 1776–77, they laid the ground for George Rogers Clark's Ohio campaign against the Shawnee, which we will examine in chapter 7. Cornstalk pleaded with Shawnee militants to put down the hatchet, but he also asked the Continental Congress to restrain settlers violating the agreed-upon boundaries. "Our lands are covered by the white people," he entreated, "and we are jealous that you still intend to make larger strides. We never sold you our lands which you now possess on the Ohio between the Great Kanawha and the Cherokee and which you are settling without ever asking our leave or obtaining our consent. . . . Now I stretch my arm to you my wise brethren of the United States met in Council at Philadelphia. I open my hand and pour into your heart the cause of our discontent in hopes that you will . . . send us a favorable answer that we may be convinced of the sincerity of your profession."[103]

Cornstalk's efforts to keep the militant Shawnee off the warpaths were increasingly compromised by Congress's inability—or unwillingness—to restrain the encroaching settlers. But Cornstalk continued to talk peace in Shawnee country through the winter and spring of 1776–77. In the summer of 1777 he sent his sister Nonhelema, called the Grenadier Squaw by the Americans, to warn the Americans that parts of the Shawnee nation were sealing agreements with the British at Fort Detroit. That November, as Joseph Brant led his volunteers on raids in the Mohawk River valley region, Virginian militiamen ended Cornstalk's hopes to keep Ohio country Indians neutral. Coming to Fort Randolph on the Kanawha for another peace council, Cornstalk found himself, his son, and two other Shawnee held as hostages in exchange for the militant Shawnees' good behavior. Confined to a cabin within the fort for a month, Cornstalk and the others must have all but lost hope for the elusive peace. On November 10, 1777, Virginia militiamen stationed at the fort burst into the cabin and slaughtered Cornstalk, his son, and the other two Shawnee. Patrick Henry, Virginia's governor, and the Continental Congress sent messages of regret to the Shawnee, though the perpetrators went unpunished. American hopes for Shawnee neutrality were now shattered. "Indian haters," writes historian Richard White, "killed or alienated the very men who were willing to act as alliance chiefs or mediators for the Americans."[104]

A small number of Cornstalk's followers (his sister included) and the Turtle Clan of the Delaware, led by George White Eyes, moved to Coshocton, on the Muskingum River. There they maintained allegiance to the Americans under the guardianship of Moravian missionaries. But most of the Shawnee and Delaware accepted the British war belt sent from Detroit in the spring of 1778, shifting the odds faced by George Rogers Clark, Daniel Boone, and other American frontier leaders fixated with conquests in Indian country.

For the Catawba of North Carolina, no division occurred between peace advocates and militants because they were a much smaller Indian nation with a much different history than the Cherokee, Shawnee, or Iroquois. Once numbering several thousand, the Catawbas had dwindled to four or five hundred by the eve of the American Revolution. They had already suffered walking the first "trail of tears" in North America. Displaced from most of their homelands, they were confined to a small reservation on the North Carolina–South Carolina border by the 1760s. By the time of the Declaration of Independence, white settlers surrounded them. The Catawba understood that the politics of survival dictated firm support of the American cause. Dependent, desperately poor, and nearly powerless, they had little choice.[105]

Neutrality would have served the Catawbas better; but summoned to

Charleston in July 1775, they heard South Carolina authorities lecture them that "your case and our case is just the same" and that "if you do not mind what we say, you will be sorry for it by and by." From that point on, Catawba men dutifully served the Americans. In a punitive expedition against the Cherokee in July 1776, twenty Catawba scouts accompanied the South Carolina militia.[106] This was the first of several battles where the Catawba joined the Americans, sometimes against the Cherokee, sometimes against British soldiers and American Loyalists.

American patriots were grateful for whatever support they got from the Catawbas, even if the contributions were small. But once the war was over, Catawba blood sacrifices profited them little. The 225 square miles allotted the Catawba in the 1760s shrank to 12 square miles by the end of the war. Even their pinched reservation became fair territory for land speculators and settlers, and the forest game that had been the basis of their sustenance became ever more scarce.

To the north, another Indian tribe, similar to the Catawba with its small population and shrunken territory, cast their lot with the Americans—and with much the same results. Daniel Nimham, whose attempts to recover the land of the Wappinger tribe we examined in chapter 2, had led the remnants of his people to Stockbridge, Massachusetts. There he waited for the New York courts to adjudicate his claims that the Philipse family had defrauded his tribe of 200,000 acres. When the Revolution erupted, fewer than forty able-bodied Wappinger men were capable of mustering, but almost all of them volunteered for service with Washington. They fought in one campaign in 1777 as part of Washington's Continental army, suffered at Valley Forge that winter, and fought again in spring 1778 under General Lafayette at Barren Hill, Pennsylvania, eleven miles west of Philadelphia, where they skirmished with the British forces preparing to evacuate Philadelphia. That August, Chief Nimham's warriors engaged the British again at Kingsbridge in what is today the north Bronx. A cavalry charge by the British Queen's Rangers, under Colonel John Simcoe, overwhelmed the Wappingers, who struggled desperately to drag red-coated cavalry men from their saddles. Urging his warriors to retreat, sixty-year-old Chief Nimham gasped, "I am an aged tree; I will die here." About half his men, including his son, perished in the attack.[107]

The surviving Wappinger men served on through the Revolution under a new chief, the twenty-one-year-old Hendrick Aupaumut. But like the other remnants of Indian tribes that had gathered at Stockbridge, at war's end the Wappingers had been severely reduced. Only about forty men, twice as many widows, and perhaps a hundred children remained. Desperately poor, they applied for pensions and bits of land to live on. When the states of New York, Massachusetts, and Vermont shuffled the Indian petitions around and did nothing, the Stockbridge people accepted the offer of the Oneidas to take them in. In one of the most plaintive documents of the entire war, Stockbridge leaders wrote the Massachusetts government in 1783: "In the late war we have suffered much, our blood has been spilled with yours, and many of our young men have fallen by the side of your warriors, almost all those places where your warriors have left their bones, there our bones are seen also. Now we who remain are become very poor. Now Brothers, we will let you know we have been invited by our Brothers, the Oneidas, to go and live with them. We have accepted their invitation."[108] It was a story of heartbreak and shattered dreams.

6

WRITING ON THE
CLEAN SLATE

1776–1780

BY 1776, COLONISTS WERE PRACTICED AT OVERTHROWING GOVERN-
ment, but not at constructing it. In one colony after another they had closed
courts, driven royal agents to cover, evicted king-appointed governors from
their residences, and, at the urging of the Continental Congress, elected new
men to sit in extralegal provincial legislatures and conventions. But creating new constitutionally sanctioned governments was infinitely more difficult, akin to instantly growing a new, fully formed tree after chopping down
a venerable old oak. And the work of constitution making was all the more
tricky because it had to be accomplished, state by state, in the vortex of a war
for national liberation that was going badly.

Composing his autobiography two years after yielding the presidency to
Thomas Jefferson in 1801, John Adams remembered how he urged the Second Continental Congress on October 18, 1775, "to resolve on a general recommendation to all the states to call conventions and institute regular
governments." This was the beginning of "our desire of revolutionizing all
the governments"—governments that had already formed outside England's
authority, but only as conventions or temporary bodies, after royal governors
had disbanded their legislatures.[1]

Adams was pleased in 1775 that most members of Congress agreed with him about constructing new state governments (at a time when Congress was still deeply divided on declaring independence), but he was mortified at the kind of government most of his friends desired. Pressed to come up with a model plan of government that might serve the states, he began penning "Thoughts on Government." But Adams chose not to suggest the form of government he had in mind on the congressional floor. In fact, he was chary of having Congress take a stand on *any* kind of government. "I dared not make such a motion," he recalled, "because I knew that if such a plan was adopted, it would be if not permanent yet of long duration, and it would be extremely difficult to get rid of it."

Adams would have been thrilled to see state constitutions constructed that conformed to his idea of a wisely structured government. The raw country lawyer of a decade before had now emerged as a diamond-edged intellectual deeply immersed in the science of politics. He had gained great respect in Massachusetts and in the Continental Congress for poring over the works of political theorists all the way back to classical authors, but especially those of the main English political thinkers of the last century: Hobbes, Harrington, Sydney, and Locke. "I had in my head and at my tongue's end as many projects of government as Mr. [Edmund] Burke says the Abbe Sieyes [noted French political philosopher] had in his pigeon holes." However, Adams knew that many others had been reading the same political theorists but had reached different conclusions about what constituted balanced government.

In fact, Adams had to remain mute because, for all the respect he had garnered, he was out of step with most members of Congress. Later he wrote, "I knew that every one of my friends, and all those who were the most zealous for assuming government, had at that time no idea of any other government but a contemptible legislature in one assembly, with committees for executive magistrates and judges." Even his cousin Sam Adams, fellow Massachusetts delegate to the Continental Congress, was enamored of a single-house legislature, as was his friend Thomas Cushing, a wealthy merchant and another of the Massachusetts delegates. For Adams, the idea of a unicameral legislature with a weak executive branch was naive, almost juvenile, and certainly dangerous. "The child was not yet weaned," he sputtered, and "I took care, however, always to bear my testimony against every plan of an unbalanced government."

Thus in 1776 the epochal work of making government began with sharply divided views among the leading statesmen of the revolutionary movement.

On one point, consensus had developed—that the consent of the governed was the only true source of political authority. But that was a vague and elastic notion. From that one powerful idea emerged intense debate, fierce passion, and bitter controversy, in many cases so rancorous that it interfered with the armed struggle for independence. Thirteen states had to create thirteen constitutions, all to be made in the midst of war. More than five years elapsed before all thirteen were in place.

First Attempts

The necessity to create new law began months before July 4, 1776. New Hampshire crafted a constitution six months before the Second Continental Congress declared independence. Then on May 10 and 15, 1776, Congress voted for what amounted to a virtual declaration of independence: that "the exercise of every kind of authority under the said crown should be totally suppressed, and all the powers of government, exerted under the authority of the people" be put into place. Three other states—South Carolina, New Jersey, and Virginia—had their constitutions up and running before July 4. Thereafter, delegates to constitutional conventions in seven other states rushed to construct a framework for self-governance and create fundamental laws to protect the people's basic liberties.

Constitution making absorbed people's interest, energy, and passion as never before. Heightening popular interest in making rather than obeying law was a flood of printed material issuing from printing presses up and down the seaboard. Cascading newspaper dialogues and political pamphlets fanned political debates. It was "a spectacle . . . without parallel on earth," remembered Samuel Miller, a clergyman, many years later. "Even a large portion of that class of the community which is destined to daily labor have free and constant access to public prints, receive regular information of every occurrence [and] attend to the course of political affairs. . . . Never were [political writings] so cheap, so universally diffused, and so easy of access."[2]

The need for a unified story of the nation's birth—a founding mythology that would underpin a national identity—has obscured the fact that Americans were deeply divided when the time came to construct these state constitutions. From a great distance, we imagine that nearly everyone involved in the call to arms would unite in creating new governments. This was hardly the case, because the opportunity to create fundamental law was an invitation to experiment, all the more so since no blueprint of a model state constitution existed, either in North America, Europe, or anywhere else. The prospect was exhilarating, but the gritty work of hammering out a constitution was divisive and exhausting. John Adams enthused over the opportunity: "How few of the human race have ever enjoyed an opportunity of making an election of government, more than of air, soil, or climate, for themselves or their children? When, before the present epocha, had three millions of people full power and a fair opportunity to form and establish the wisest and happiest government that human wisdom can contrive?"[3]

But whose wisdom? That of a few, the many, or *all* the people? Who might participate in the process of drafting a constitution, and how would they acquire that right? Who could look at the draft and decide whether it established "the wisest and happiest government that human wisdom can contrive"? Would the old property restrictions on the right to vote and hold office remain in place? Would there be a governor with veto power over laws passed by the legislature? Would the governor be elected or appointed by the legislature? How would the natural rights of life and liberty be reconciled with slavery, which ensnared one-fifth of the population and promised their offspring only a life of perpetual servitude? These and a host of other questions faced constitution drafters, whoever they were and however they were selected.

That the constitutions varied from state to state is not surprising because no state's history, economy, labor system, religion, and social composition was a replica of another's. Each had experienced its own turmoil and internal disputes, conditioning people to think in various ways about reforming government. Also, the people of each state sent a unique set of constitution writers to the table. Neighboring Maryland and Pennsylvania, for example, had grown into very different societies by 1776. Thirty percent of Maryland's population was enslaved, but only 4 percent of Pennsylvania's. Maryland's established Anglican Church contrasted with Pennsylvania's religious diversity. Quaker pacifist tradition in Pennsylvania had no counterpart in Maryland, and Maryland's mostly Anglican tidewater aristocracy had no parallel in Pennsylvania. Hence, Maryland's constitution writers were predominantly slave-owning planters experienced in holding office and making law; Pennsylvania's constitution drafters were mostly farmers and middling urban artisans or struggling doctors and teachers with scant experience as officeholders, lawmakers, or legal experts. Out of these differences came sharply different constitutions.

They shared some elements but contrasted in crucial ways: Pennsylvania's constitution shifted the center of political gravity downward in the ranks of society, while in Maryland political power remained in the hands of an elite that strictly hedged in popular sentiment.

Not every state thought it necessary to write a constitution *de novo*. Connecticut and Rhode Island amended their English charters simply by deleting all reference to the English Crown. Letting it go at that, they continued to govern themselves as before. By itself, this decision *not* to change was a slap in the face of those who wanted to write afresh on a clean slate. But in all other states, the view prevailed that "we have it in our power to begin the world over again," as Thomas Paine expressed it, and therefore the people needed a fresh beginning with a body of fundamental law to live under as free people. Rather than have their existing legislatures draft a constitution, most states called for a freshly elected convention specifically charged with the task. Many subscribed to the idea expressed by Boston's town meeting that such a body should exist "no longer than the Constitution is forming."[4]

Never before had the people dared to think of themselves as the source of authority for constructing fundamental law. This was radical, breathtaking, and inspiring. "Divine providence is about to grant you a favor," wrote Pennsylvania's provincial congress, "which few people have ever enjoyed before, the privilege of choosing Deputies to form a government under which you are to live." Far to the south, two young Charleston, South Carolina, men watching the procession of those charged with writing that state's constitution reported that the spectacle was "beheld by the people with transports and tears of joy. The people gazed at them with a kind of rapture."[5] In other states, people were similarly awestruck with what they were themselves creating: specially elected groups of constitution writers who understood that, having done their best, they must return home with no further power vested in them. Among the eleven states that wrote new constitutions, nine followed this radical innovation, with only South Carolina and Virginia allowing their sitting legislatures to assume the responsibility of drafting a constitution.

A Militiaman's Constitution

If only an extraordinary, task-specific political body could be entrusted with the creation of fundamental law, who could vote for these special, almost godlike delegates? In this matter, Pennsylvania first strode onto radical ground. In a sharp break from nearly a century of elections in England and its far-flung colonies, Pennsylvania's lawmakers opened up the vote on the belief that all taxpaying men, rather than only property-owning men, were entitled to it. All "associators"—that is, men who had agreed to associate in the militia units as bands of brothers—were permitted to vote if they were at least twenty-one years of age, residents of Pennsylvania for at least one year, and had paid even the smallest tax. This broadening of the suffrage potentially brought about nine of every ten free adult males into the political community. But it had one important qualification: It applied only to those ready to swear allegiance to the independence movement. Deprived of the vote were those unwilling to vow that they would not "by any means, directly or indirectly, oppose the establishment of a free government in this province by the convention now to be chosen, nor the measures adopted by the congress against the tyranny attempted to be established in these colonies by the court of Great Britain." This test of loyalty, along with the widened suffrage, proved crucial in the composition of the convention's delegates.[6] By neatly disenfranchising Tories and "Moderates," those still opposed to an outright declaration of independence, the provincial conference calling the convention paved the road for a lawmaking body that was not representative of Pennsylvania's people in their entirety but of those committed to independence and internal change. Yet a crucial step had been taken—moving from property-owner suffrage to taxpayer suffrage, which included everyone but slaves, indentured servants, and those too poor to pay even a small "head tax."

Twelve days before the election to choose constitutional convention delegates, James Cannon's broadside, addressed to the "Several Battalions of Military Associators in the Province of Pennsylvania," gave a foretaste of what was to come. Reminding the men who were shouldering arms and preparing for battle with the British that the "judiciousness of the choice which you make" will effect "the happiness of millions unborn," Cannon pinpointed the "qualifications which we think most essential to constitute a member of the approaching Convention." A teacher of mathematics at the College of Philadelphia, Cannon urged the soldiers to reject the upper-class view that in order to write a constitution, men needed "great learning, knowledge in our history, law, mathematics, etc., and a perfect acquaintance with the laws, manners, trade, constitution and policy of all nations."[7] Such men were exactly those to be distrusted if the great work to be accomplished must serve "the common interests of mankind." Reminding the militiamen of decades of simmering class hostility, Cannon warned that "Great and over-grown rich men will be improper to be trusted. . . . They will be too apt to be framing distinctions in society, because they will reap the benefits of all such distinctions— gentlemen of the learned professions are generally filled with quirks and quibbles of the schools; and, though we have several worthy men of great learning among us, yet, as they are very apt to indulge their disposition to refinement to a culpable degree, we would think it prudent not to have too great a proportion of such in the Convention."

What should be preferred to deep learning and professional status? "Honesty, common sense, and a plain understanding, when unbiased by sinister motives," counseled Cannon. These qualities "are fully equal to the task." Men like the voters themselves "are the most likely to frame us a good Constitution," he told the militiamen for "we are contending for the liberty which God has made our birthright: All men are entitled to it, and no set of men have a right to anything higher." At all costs, he concluded, do not vote for any delegate "who would be disposed to form any rank above that of Freemen."

Here was an argument that divided the elite from the common in every region and would continue to do so for many generations. William Henry Drayton, a South Carolina grandee, had fumed in 1769 that popular leaders had given credence to "men who were never in a way of study, or to advise on any points but rules how to cut up a beast in the market to the best advantage, to cobble an old shoe in the neatest manner, or to build a necessary house." From the other end of the coast came the rejoinder of the anonymous New Hampshire author of "The People the Best Governors," who pledged that "God . . . made every man equal to his neighbor and has virtually enjoined them to govern themselves by their own laws. . . . The people best know their own wants and necessities and therefore are best able to rule themselves. Tent-makers, cobblers, and common tradesmen composed the legislature at Athens."[8]

The voters listened all too well so far as conservative Pennsylvania leaders and other politicos at the Continental Congress were concerned. For John Adams, who believed the *sine qua non* of a republican government was "a decency, and respect, and veneration introduced for persons in authority," this was social dynamite, in fact a perversion of good republican government. Would Pennsylvania voters, their numbers swelled by men who never before had cast a ballot, choose men of humble status and limited education simply because they seemed to be individuals of "honesty, common sense, and a plain understanding"?

It was just this prospect, that a broad suffrage would make lawmakers out of ordinary men, that made the franchise the key to the democratization of politics. In the radical view, political rights traditionally rooted in property must now be vested in the people. "The Great Secret of Government," wrote one Massachusetts town in the midst of its constitutional debate, "is governing all by all." This was the principle that now emerged in Pennsylvania. Colonies varied only modestly on how much property conferred voting rights on men. English election laws going back to 1429 limited the vote to landowners whose property yielded an annual rent of forty shillings (about one month's wages for an ordinary worker). For more than three centuries this figure "recurs like a mystic number in English and American suffrage laws," writes historian Willi Adams.[9]

Other colonies were far less radical in stipulating who could vote for the constitution-writing delegates. Propertied freemen in Maryland's Anne Arundel County, which contained the colony's capital town of Annapolis, called for the suffrage of all free adult men, but wealthy and politically experienced men such as the grandee Charles Carroll thought this "impudent and destructive of all government." This conservative view prevailed, and thus Maryland followed the old suffrage requirement with some modification. The Committee of Mechanics of New York City argued that if every artisan was not capable of writing a constitution, every citizen could *judge* one, and ought to be consulted in a referendum of a draft constitution. "That share of common sense, which the Almighty has bountifully distributed amongst mankind in general," they reasoned, "is sufficient to quicken every one's feeling, and enable him to judge rightly, what advantages he is likely to enjoy or be deprived of, under any Constitution proposed to him." The craftsmen did not prevail in this case, and neither did their counterparts in most other states. Yet the old maxim that men without property possessed no independent judgment and therefore had no right to vote was under attack. Of all the radical steps taken in the bright light of early revolutionary enthusiasm, this was the most significant: the insistence, in the face of received wisdom dispensed by the upper class, that ordinary men struggling for a foothold on the ladder of property-owning status had just as much right to inclusion in the political community as the wealthiest shipowners, plantation proprietors, money lenders, and slaveholders.[10]

Sitting in the East Room of the Pennsylvania Statehouse with other members of the Continental Congress, Adams must have shaken his head at seeing the delegates filing into the West Room across the hall on July 15, 1776. These were the men just elected for the weightiest political task assigned in Pennsylvania since William Penn had drafted a Frame of Government for his colony in 1681. A month before, Adams had worried that new constitutions would be influenced by a "spirit of leveling, as well as that of innovation." Now, his fears materialized. The delegates numbered ninety-six. Most were farmers, a few were merchants and lawyers, others were artisans, shopkeepers, and schoolteachers. It was not unusual for an ironmonger born in Upper Silesia to be flanked by an Ulster-born farmer and an Alsatian-born shopkeeper as the deliberations went forward. A majority were immigrants or sons of immigrants from Ireland, Scotland, and Germany, and many were in their midtwenties. All but eight represented the rural counties outside Philadelphia. About half had joined up as militiamen, and most of them had been elected officers by the rank and file. Francis Alison, Philadelphia's Presbyterian minister, called them "mostly honest well meaning country men, who are employed; but entirely unacquainted with such high matters [and] hardly equal to the task to form a new plan of government."[11]

It is unlikely that more than a few of the delegates had read John Adams's advice in "Thoughts on Government," the pamphlet the Sage of Braintree had published in Philadelphia three months before. Adams had tried to neutralize Paine's most radical notions in the wildly popular *Common Sense*. But even if they had consulted Adams's "Thoughts on Government," which stressed the need for a balanced government where popular interests would be offset by conservative ones, the assembled delegates had something much different in mind.[12]

As they met in the midst of great apprehension over the British demonstration of military superiority in the summer of 1776, seven men emerged to guide and shape the debates. Four were from Philadelphia: clock maker David Rittenhouse, doctor Thomas Young, mathematics tutor James Cannon, and brewer Timothy Matlack. These were just the kind of men celebrated by Benjamin Franklin, who three decades before had gathered such artisan-citizens in the Junto, where they could improve their minds through collective reading and discuss issues of the day. Lawyers George Ross of Lancaster County and James Smith of York County, and Robert Whitehill, a farmer with legal training from Carlisle, completed the cadre. Franklin him-

In the room where the Continental Congress voted for independence, shown here by English painter Robert Edge Pine and later completed by Edward Savage, John Adams and other delegates deliberated as the Pennsylvania Convention constructed the state's 1776 constitution across the hall.

self sat impassively as president, much of the time asleep (though sometimes he stepped across the hall to sit at sessions of the Continental Congress). Thomas Paine was absent, but his ideas were much in the heads of many delegates.

Working for eight weeks, the constitution drafters considered and then rejected three of the most honored elements of English republican thought. First they scrapped the idea of a two-house legislature with the upper house reflecting men of wealth and the lower house mirroring the common people—a replica of the British government where the House of Lords represented the aristocracy and the House of Commons represented the people at large. The case for unicameralism rested primarily on long historical experience showing that upper houses in the colonies had generally reflected the interests of the wealthy and gave institutional form to a contest of interests that did not, at least in the minds of ordinary people, serve the common good. Other historical experiences fortified the unicameralist argument: that town meetings, the Continental Congress itself, and almost a century of one-house rule in Pennsylvania had proved that dispensing with an upper house could well serve the interests of all.

Second, the drafters abandoned the idea of an independent executive branch with extensive power, especially to veto legislative bills—a governor's power commonly found in British colonies. Instead, the convention provided for an elected weak plural executive branch, composed of a president and council. It was empowered to appoint important officers, including the attorney general and judges, but given no legislative veto power. Its duty was to implement the laws passed by the legislature, not to amend or veto them.

Finally, the constitution drafters scuttled the old franchise that allowed the vote only to free, white, property-owning males, and created the most liberal franchise known in the Western world to that date. Only apprentices and the deeply impoverished, excused from paying any tax, were excluded. This was a flat-out rejection of the hoary idea that only a man with "a stake in society" would use the vote judiciously. After all, was not risking one's life on the battlefield evidence of a stake in society? How then could those risking their lives to protect the property of voting citizens be denied the vote?

Other provisions of the Pennsylvania Constitution erected hedges to prevent concentrated political power. Annual elections by ballot, used in the colonial period, were continued. "Instruct your deputies, when chosen," advised James Cannon, "to reserve an annual return of all power into your hands." Also, the constitution guaranteed that the doors of the legislative house remain open to "all persons who behave decently," so the people from whom government derived its authority could monitor their elected legislators. Also to this end, the legislative debates and votes were to be printed weekly, in English and German, for all to see. Reflecting the fear of corrupt politicians and the determination to hold lawmakers accountable to their constituents, these measures were followed by all other states except South Carolina. Even conservative patriots endorsed these innovations promoting transparency in the decisions reached by the people's representatives.

The Pennsylvania constitution writers provided a final check against corrupt or unresponsive legislators. Having drafted, debated, and passed a law, the legislature must print and distribute it "for consideration of the people." This allowed time for public discussion of each law before the next annual election of representatives. This next legislature would then finally vote on the law passed by its predecessor. Vermont was the only state to follow Pennsylvania on this. For some conservatives, such as William Hooper of North Carolina (to whom John Adams sent his first draft of "Thoughts on Government"), this was an especially offensive constitutional requirement. "The mob," he sputtered, "made a second branch of legislature—laws subjected to their revisal in order to refine them, a washing in ordure by way of purification. Taverns and dram shops are the councils to which the laws of the state are to be referred before they possess a binding influence." "K," writing anonymously in the *Pennsylvania Packet*, agreed that this amounted to a veto power on legislation by "a part of the people, particularly such as frequent public houses where the laws are to be always posted up for consultation."[13]

Three final provisions nailed down the radical democracy desired by the Pennsylvania delegates. First, they imposed term limits that restricted a man from serving more than four one-year legislative terms every seven years—a term limit provision adopted in no other state for the lower house. This rotation of legislative power jibed with the idea that many citizens were capable of performing well in public office. Second, they specified the popular election of a "Council of Censors" once every seven years to review the constitution to ensure that it had "been preserved inviolate in every part; and whether the legislative and executive branches of government have performed their duty as guardians of the people."[14] Only Vermont mimicked this provision for monitoring the constitution's effectiveness. Third, the convention stipulated the reapportionment of the legislative assembly every seven years on the basis of census returns. This commitment to proportional representation was followed by only three states and achieved by the U.S. Congress only in 1962, when the Supreme Court ruled in the "one man–one vote" *Baker v. Carr* case.

In one proposed feature of the constitution, the Pennsylvania draftsmen went beyond the wishes of the full convention. Radical leaders Cannon and Young proposed a clause giving the state the power to limit private ownership of large tracts of land. The rationale was that "an enormous proportion of property vested in a few individuals is dangerous to the rights and destructive of the common happiness of mankind; and therefore every free state hath a right by its laws to discourage the possession of such property." This clause, a so-called agrarian law to redistribute wealth, marked the outermost boundary of radical thought. It was not a homegrown idea but one harking back to England's seventeenth-century civil war era, later to be proposed by James Burgh in his *Political Disquisitions* (1774), a treatise on politics widely read in the colonies. The *Providence Gazette* had published an excerpt of it in December 1775, arguing the need for putting a limit on the accumulation of wealth.[15]

Imbedded in this tenet was the notion that inequality was not the result of different degrees of talent or ambitiousness or the product of impersonal economic forces—the argument of conservatives. Rather, gross inequality resulted from avarice and oppression by those who, for whatever reason, had risen to the top. But the convention did not pass this agrarian law, perhaps because of its vagueness about how the state could limit the accumulation of wealth without actually confiscating private property, and partly because the delegates were unwilling to tamper with the bourgeois inclinations of most Pennsylvanians. Yet in agreeing on a clause abolishing imprisonment for debt, and on another providing for public education supported by taxes on property holdings, the constitution drafters took important steps toward achieving a more equitable society.

The constitution was a victory for small farmers, especially Scots-Irish frontiersmen with small holdings of land; for urban artisans, many of whom could not vote; and for radical intellectual reformers. It was a heavy blow to wealthy merchants, large property owners, and assorted conservatives who wanted to hold on to the old political system, which, they feared, was already slipping from their grasp. It was the culmination of a move toward a democratized polity that had been occurring piecemeal for several generations and had gained momentum as revolutionary leaders saw the necessity to mobilize the bottom as well as the middle of society. Here was the idea that the producing classes were to be valued most in a republic, and that the wealthy nonproducers, who lived by manipulating money and land, were to be valued least.

After completing its work in September 1776, as Washington's army was abandoning New York City and retreating precipitously across New Jersey at the time, the Pennsylvania Convention ordered the distribution of four hundred copies of the constitution for public consideration and debate. This in itself was a further radical innovation—to send back to the people the fruit of their elected delegates so they could endorse or reject it. The process was left vague, however, so the invitation to the public was more of an informal public-opinion poll than a formal ratification. The constitutional convention proclaimed that the document was adopted on September 28, 1776.

For Pennsylvania's militiamen, the constitution was all they hoped for. While the convention delegates were drafting the document, they had been honing their own democratic skills. Under Cannon's tutelage, privates formed their own committee to debate the selection of two brigadier generals for the Pennsylvania militia. Should the Pennsylvania assembly make the choice, as the Continental Congress recommended on June 3? Or should the militia officers make the choice? Or, should the enlisted militiamen be included in the choice of the colony's two most senior military officers? In a decision unimaginable today—perhaps equivalent to the election of the two highest officers for the National Guard of Texas—a meeting of the Committee of Privates and the board of officers decided that each battalion should send two privates and two officers to Lancaster on July 4, 1776, to elect the brigadier generals. Before ever taking the field, the Committee of Privates had won a political victory—"the right of appointing officers to command them," as they put it, and not only junior officers, but all officers up to the brigadier generals. When most of the militiamen returned to Philadelphia in late August 1776 after a six-week enlistment, they became part of the debate on the newly instituted Pennsylvania constitution.

The Frightened Response

The militiamen for whom James Cannon had become spokesman found plenty of reasons to applaud the constitution put before Pennsylvanians in September 1776. For them, it was like a fresh wind blowing down the corridors of established power. But for moderates and conservatives, both inside and outside Pennsylvania, the constitution was more like a gathering storm poised to wreak havoc in the Keystone State. Pennsylvania's constitution departed so radically from conventional political thought that it shocked and dismayed some patriot leaders, including Pennsylvanians Benjamin Rush, John Dickinson, James Wilson, and Robert Morris. A firestorm of criticism took only days to develop after the *Pennsylvania Evening Post* published the draft on September 10. The ensuing public debate in the Philadelphia newspapers continued far beyond the adoption of the constitution. Benjamin Rush called it "our rascally constitution" and "our state dung cart with all its dirty contents" that made the state government as dreaded as "the government of Turkey." Though he had grown up under a unicameral legislature, Rush now complained that "a single legislature is big with tyranny" and that the constitution "substituted a mob government to one of the happiest governments of the world." "Good god!" gasped John Adams after seeing the full constitution. "The people of Pennsylvania in two years will be glad to petition the crown of Britain for reconciliation in order to be delivered from the tyranny of their Constitution."[16]

Many elements of the constitution appalled conservatives and some moderates, but none more than the enlargement of the electorate. "The most flourishing commonwealths that ever existed, Athens and Rome," wrote an anonymous Philadelphian in the *Evening Post*, "were RUINED by allowing this right to people without property." The prospect of taxpayer suffrage deeply troubled John Adams. With Abigail pressing him on the right of women to vote and even conservative friends in Massachusetts advocating that the franchise should be opened to all free men, Adams upheld the traditional view on limiting suffrage to the propertied. His friend and fellow jurist James Sullivan shocked Adams by arguing that "every member of society has a right to give his consent to the laws of the community or he owes no obedience to them." Sullivan explained further that "a very great number of the people of the colony" were disfranchised for lack of an "estate worth 40 shillings per annum"—that is, property that would produce a rent of forty shillings per year. Sullivan called the traditional practice feudal, one based on the false premise that "men [without property] are unable to account for the principles of their own actions." "The poor and the rich," he insisted, "are alike interested in that important part of government called legislation."[17]

Adams responded with a tortured defense of the age-old definition of political competency. Thinking back to his wife's ministrations, he fumed rhetorically, "Whence arises the right of the men to govern women, without their consent?" And "whence the right of the old to bind the young without theirs?" Because women's "delicacy renders them unfit for practice and experience in the great business of life . . . as well as the arduous cares of state," he explained. Adams knew very well that his wife, from her management of the Adams farm, her arduous care in the smallpox inoculation of their children, and her sage comments on the political scene, was far from "unfit for practice and experience in the great business of life." But he pressed on. "Children have not judgment or will of their own," he reasoned, but this was off the point since not even the most utopian reformer suggested that children should vote or hold office. Back on point—the competency of propertyless males to exercise the vote responsibly—Adams argued that "Men in general in every society, who are wholly destitute of property, are also too little acquainted with public affairs to form a right judgment, and too dependent upon other men to have a will of their own." Only three years before, Adams had voiced no objections; indeed he applauded the political savvy of the mass of Bostonians, some five thousand strong, who thronged the public meeting that preceded the Tea Party. This, he noted in his journal, was an "exertion of popular power."Adams saw the Revolution as a "people's war," but he was unwilling to have a people's war produce a people's polity. Adams loved liberty but not equality, and from this position he would not budge through the entire course of the long Revolution.[18]

But in other states people *were* budging. In only two states—Virginia and Delaware—did state constitution writers retain the existing property qualifications (and even in Virginia some, including Thomas Jefferson, favored widening the suffrage). In New York, New Jersey, Maryland, and Georgia, constitution writers lowered the property qualifications substantially, thus broadening the electorate. North Carolina, South Carolina, and New Hampshire followed Pennsylvania's taxpayer suffrage, and Vermont enfranchised all adult males, even those who paid no tax at all. Rhode Island kept its ancient charter but enlarged the franchise to include almost all white men. In Maryland and Massachusetts, taxpayer suffrage came close to taking effect, thwarted only by close votes that favored scaled-down property qualifications.

Pennsylvania conservatives regarded the new unicameral legislature, unfettered by a governor armed with the power to veto its bills, as the second most disturbing and dangerous element of the constitution. Timothy Dwight, to become president of Yale in 1795, sputtered that "a legislature by a single house is of course no other than an organized mob. Its deliberations are necessarily tumultuous, violent and indecent." North Carolina's William Hooper called it "a beast without a head." In his "Thoughts on Government," Adams had listed six reasons for treating a one-house legislature like poison. He predicted that "A people cannot be long free, and never can be happy whose laws are made, executed and interpreted by one assembly." Fear lurked behind all his reasons, rooted especially in the pessimistic view that legislators left to themselves would "make arbitrary laws for their own interest, and adjudge all controversies in their own favor." Adams wrote this before seeing how Pennsylvania's constitution drafters carefully hemmed in the legislators with provisions for open legislative hearings, published arguments and votes, annual elections, turnover in offices, rules against plural office-holding, and review of laws by the electorate before final endorsement or amendment by the next elected assembly. But these safeguards changed Adams's mind not one bit. Both his cousin Samuel Adams and his friend Thomas Cushing favored a unicameral legislature in 1776, but Adams was adamantly opposed.[19]

From the fall of 1776 through the autumn of 1777, Pennsylvania conservatives, led by Robert Morris and John Dickinson, fought to defeat or cripple the 1776 constitution. One tactic was to argue that the next elected assembly should amend or rewrite the constitution. This mustered little support. The next tactic was for conservatives to withdraw from the legislature elected in November 1776 so that the majority supporting the constitution would be unable to obtain quorums for other legislative business. Another ploy was to refuse to serve as justices of the peace, sheriffs, and militia officers, even when popularly elected. Accusations flew in the pages of the Philadelphia press for months. Radicals charged that the conservatives' problem was that they could not "stand to be governed by leather aprons." Conservatives returned fire with charges that the radicals were "coffee-house demagogues," who would bring anarchy to William Penn's peaceable kingdom. The arguments continued in the press, in the streets, and in the taverns well into 1777. Only when the British army drove northward from the Chesapeake Bay region to capture Philadelphia in September 1777 did the anti-Constitutionalists, as opponents of the constitution called themselves, temporarily quit their attempts to scuttle the constitution. The argument was far from over, but with the British army occupying Philadelphia from September 1777 to June 1778, the Constitutionalists held their ground.

Vermont and Maryland

To the north and south of Pennsylvania, Vermont and Maryland devised constitutions that showed how differently delegates imagined the societies they wanted to live in if the Americans succeeded in casting off the British yoke. In early 1777, the New York area known as the Grants, where so much prerevolutionary populist activism had surfaced, finally declared itself independent. Ethan Allen, their swaggering leader, was rotting in a wretched English prison, but the Green Mountain Boys saw the war for independence as the perfect opportunity to realize their separatist dreams. Six conventions of hill town delegates met between April 1775 and January 1777 as British forces threatened to sweep all northern American combatants from the field.

Led by Heman Allen, Ethan's brother, the delegates voted in January 1777 to "be a new and separate state; and for the future conduct themselves as such."[20] New York leaders regarded this as outrageous and illegal, but their governor, George Clinton, could hardly afford to send provincial troops against fellow Americans also involved in the war against England.

Calling themselves the Republic of Vermont (the name was suggested by Philadelphia's Thomas Young), the Grants residents petitioned Congress for admission as an independent state. Strenuous New York opposition convinced Congress to deny admission and admonish the Vermonters in July 1777. But that did not deter Grants residents, most of them small landowners and most of them resolutely democratic. While waiting for Congress to recognize their legitimacy, they set about constructing a constitution. Thomas Young, peripatetic ideologue, spurred them on, arguing that "you have as good a right to choose how you will be governed" as any other state, and urging them to form a government where "the people at large [are] the true proprietors of governmental power." A few years later, back in the country, Ethan Allen wrote that "They were a people between the heavens and the earth, as free as is possible to conceive any people to be; and in this condition they formed government upon the true principles of liberty and natural right."[21]

"Liberty and natural right" indeed captured the essence of the Vermont plan of government. The constitutional convention met in early July 1777 as General John Burgoyne's British forces overwhelmed the Americans at Fort Ticonderoga and rampaged through the towns where many of the delegates lived. Out of this unpromising situation emerged a constitution that in most respects followed the Pennsylvania model: a unicameral legislature; a public review of each law drafted before the next elected assembly amended or ratified it; a governor with no veto power over laws passed by an annually elected legislature; and a Council of Censors meeting once every seven years to monitor the faithful execution of constitutional principles. If the council believed the constitution was functioning improperly, it could call a popularly elected new convention to amend the constitution so that future generations would have "the same privileges of choosing how they would be governed." Whiffs of the limitation on the concentration of wealth proposed in Pennsylvania appeared in the Vermont constitution where the preamble—a "Declaration of Rights"—declared "that private property ought to be subservient to public uses" and that the state had the right of eminent domain and therefore could appropriate private property for public use if the owner was fairly compensated. Vermont was more conservative, however, in allowing multiple office-holding (such as a legislator serving simultaneously as a justice of the peace).

Vermont's constitution went further than Pennsylvania's in several respects: It provided for unrestricted manhood suffrage without even a taxpayer qualification; made all judges elective; gave special protection to debtors; and declared all slaves free, without compensation to their owners, as soon as they reached the ages of twenty-one, if male, and eighteen, if female. To be sure, few slaves resided in Vermont. Yet the state was the first to say constitutionally that slavery was illegal as a violation of "natural, inherent, and unalienable rights." The abolitionist principle received real application when Yale-trained David Avery arrived in Bennington to assume the pulpit of the Congregational church in 1779. There he found that his congregation refused to commune with him because he owned a female slave. Encouraged by Ethan Allen, the woman sued for her freedom. In another instance, a judge in 1784 ruled in favor of a runaway slave whose master produced a bill of sale proving his ownership, only to be admonished that to retain his slave property he would have to provide a bill of sale from "God Almighty."22

With a constitution in hand, Vermonters still had to gain legitimacy for their self-proclaimed state. Here, the old warrior Ethan Allen reentered the stage. After he was released from England in a prisoner exchange, he became Vermont's state attorney in 1778. Using what Thomas Jefferson called "the Vermont logic," that is, the right of people to create their own state, Vermonters set up courts to adjudicate the laws that their elected legislature passed. From his pivotal position as Vermont's prosecutor, Allen helped protect the land grants of Green Mountain farmers. Meanwhile, the New Yorkers still remaining in the Grants region, many of whom had become Loyalists, had to be confronted one last time. The New Yorkers regarded the self-created state of Vermont as the "offspring of anarchy," and they had resolutions from the Continental Congress to back them up. But neither they nor Congress could make the words stick. New York's legislature went so far as to threaten to withdraw from the war against England unless Congress took "speedy and vigorous measures for reducing them [the Vermonters] to an obedience."23 This, too, was a toothless threat.

New York's passage of a conservative constitution in 1777 ended any chance that Vermonters would recognize New York's old colonial claims to the Grants region. In many respects, the New York constitution was the most conservative passed by the states, contrasting sharply with those of Vermont and Pennsylvania. It lacked a bill of rights; installed a powerful executive branch that could disband the elected legislature; created a Council of Revision of appointed supreme court judges and the elected governor with veto power over legislative bills; maintained the hefty colonial property qualification that narrowed the electorate more than in all but a few states; made most officials—from the local level to the highest state offices (except that of governor)—appointive rather than elective; and upheld all land grants issued in the colonial period (which would have invalidated the deeds of most Vermonters). Ira Allen, Ethan's youngest brother, carried the constitutions of New York and Vermont from town to town in the Green Mountain region in 1777, inviting the citizens to compare them carefully. This worked well. Most Vermonters saw in the New York document a blueprint for preserving the power of New York's elite (minus those who remained loyal to Great Britain). By one estimate, only 10 percent of Vermont's adult males would have been able to vote for the Senate and governor.[24] Forty towns in the region endorsed the Vermont constitution while rejecting New York's as perversely undemocratic.

Politically empowered as first-class citizens, men of the Grants region joined the Vermont militia, commanded by Ethan Allen after 1778, in impressive numbers. This was virtually unique among the states. Elsewhere, the war had become a poor man's fight; in Vermont it became every man's fight. Within a society filled with farmers struggling for economic security, radical politics merged with radical militarism. They fought under elected officers and were as willing to fight New Yorkers to uphold Vermont's claim to independence as they were to defend the northern frontier against the British.

Radicalism also tinctured the creation of Vermont courts. Presided over by elected judges with little formal legal training, the courts confiscated the land of Loyalists, put the land up for public auction with preference to veterans, protected the land titles of small farmers, and shunned the legal technicalities employed by trained lawyers in other states that prolonged legal proceedings and made the system of justice expensive to administer. "New York used its courts as instruments of the central state government and the interest that ran it," writes historian Michael Bellisles. But Vermonters, while they "also saw courts as a means of social control," used them especially to protect "the well-being of the immediate community rather than the success of a distant elite."[25] Created from the bottom up by the populace of the Grants region, the courts stood prepared for a final day of reckoning in the long-standing New York–Vermont dispute.

Far to the south of Vermont, other delegates were at work on their own constitutions in the spring and summer of 1776. Among the southern states, the sharpest contest took place in Maryland. Ordinary Marylanders had been gaining voice in the turmoil of revolutionary protests against English policies, and this surging populism quickly infused the debates on creating a state constitution. As in other states, the first question became: Who was entitled to vote for the delegates who would write the fundamental laws under which generations would live? In Maryland, the propertyless *seized* the vote, not waiting for radical leaders to legislate taxpayer suffrage for the purpose of electing constitution-writing delegates, as happened in Pennsylvania and Vermont. After Maryland's provincial convention in August 1776 called for the election of delegates to write a constitution, people in five counties who did not meet the property qualifications thronged the polls, threw out the election judges, and insisted that anyone who bore arms was entitled to vote. In Prince Georges County, "the inhabitants . . . agreed, that every taxable [man] bearing arms . . . had an undoubted right to vote for representatives at this time of public calamity." When the election judges resigned in protest, the people at large elected judges of their own, who then submitted the election results to the constitutional convention. In Frederick County, the Committee of Safety chose new election judges who then ratified the vote of a mass of voters, the majority of whom "had armed in defense of the country." Also, in Kent, Worcester, and Queen Anne's counties, election judges counted the votes of propertyless militiamen.[26]

The suffrage rebels also struck in Anne Arundel County, where the Carroll family had built an immense fortune. After election judges opened the polls, a knot of men "insisted on every man having a vote that bore arms." When the judges closed the polls and ordered James Disney, an election clerk, to read the election regulations that restricted the franchise, infuriated militiamen shouted "pull him down, he shall not read, we will not hear it, and if you do not stop and let every free man vote that carries arms, we will pull the house down from under the judges." The militiamen finally backed down, but one of the men standing for election, Rezin Hammond, "advised the people to lay down their arms if they were denied the privilege of voting, for it was their right and they ought not to be deprived of it."[27]

The entrenched elite from other Maryland counties moved to stem this radical tide. Elected to the constitutional convention under the restricted franchise rules, they quickly ordered new elections in the five insurgent counties where militiamen and other propertyless men had seized the vote. But even after militiamen were turned away from the polls, the propertied voters elected radical leaders John Hall and Rezin Hammond from Anne Arundel County. It was Hammond and Hall who now carried the banner for a liberal, if not radical, constitution.

Months before the constitutional convention met, even before Congress declared independence, Hall, Hammond, and other radical reformers hammered out the equivalent of a Pennsylvania militiamen's constitution. Meeting in June 1776 in Annapolis, where representatives of the Anne Arundel militia battalions met, they had their document ready for publication in the *Maryland Gazette* by July 18, just days after word of the Declaration of Independence reached Maryland. Their draft was not as democratic as those constructed in Pennsylvania and Vermont, but it called for reforms that were radical compared to neighboring Virginia's constitution. A bicameral legislature would be elected annually by the people. This legislature would choose a governor with no legislative veto power and appoint all state judges. The legislature would publish its proceedings and votes annually so that the electorate could judge the responsiveness of their representatives. At the county level, the people would choose all officials, including tax assessors and sheriffs. More radical, the constitution would abolish "the unjust mode of taxation heretofore used," replacing it with taxes paid "in proportion to every person's estate." Also to serve those injured by a disordered economy, the constitution proposed to restrict all debt proceedings in court until "this time of public calamity" had ended.[28]

Armed with this reform constitution, signed by 885 Anne Arundel freemen, Rezin Hammond arrived at the constitutional convention in August 1776. The convention received even more radical proposals from Anne Arundel freeholders. Key provisions allowed the election of militia officers by militiamen themselves. Most radical was broadening the franchise to include all freemen of the state who were at least twenty-one years of age and "well affected to the present glorious cause."[29]

The gulf separating the militiamen's constitution and the gentry's notion of good government led to inflamed rhetoric and bitter disputes. Charles Carroll of Carrollton, the eldest son of the immensely wealthy Charles Carroll of Annapolis, saw no merit in framing a more democratic society and a more equitable economic system. Hammond and Hall's advocacy of the militiamen was class betrayal. They were not honest men promoting a constitution responsive to Anne Arundel citizens, who at this moment were marching north in "flying camps" to serve with Washington and his Continental army. Rather, Hammond and Hall were "evil and designing men." "Should their schemes take place, and it is probable they will, unless vigorously counteracted by all honest men," Carroll wrote to his father, "anarchy will follow as a certain consequence; injustice, rapine and corruption in the seats of justice will prevail, and this province in a short time will be involved in all the horrors of an ungovernable and revengeful democracy, and will be dyed with the blood of its best citizens." To allow broader suffrage, to give an elected legislature more power than the governor, and to provide for debtor relief was the work of "selfish men, who are everywhere striving to throw all power into the hands of the very lowest of people, in order that they may be their masters from the abused confidence which the people have placed in them."[30]

In this view, the propertyless were incapable of voting intelligently, always tethered to their landlords, employers, and creditors, whose bidding they would promptly do as soon as they filled out a ballot. "A Watchman" in Maryland, probably Rezin Hammond, responded that "Every poor man has a life, a personal liberty, and a right to his earnings; and is in danger of being injured by government in a variety of ways" and therefore "should enjoy the right of voting for representatives, to be protectors of their lives, personal liberty, and their little property, which, though small, is yet, upon the whole, a very great object to them." Claiming that the old property qualifications in Maryland stripped the right to vote from half the state's freemen, who paid "a very heavy share in the support of government" through poll taxes that fell disproportionately on the propertyless, "Watchman" insisted that taxpayer suffrage was a natural right and "the ultimate end of all freedom."[31]

For all his dyspeptic exclamations, Carroll of Carrollton need not have feared that Maryland's emerging constitution would overturn the interests of the ruling elite. The composition of the constitutional convention almost guaranteed a conservative outcome. Three-quarters of the Maryland delegates, who had to own at least fifty acres of land to stand for election, claimed more than five hundred acres. Half of them owned more than twenty enslaved Africans, and only a handful had no slaves at all. About four of every five delegates had fortunes of at least one thousand pounds (equivalent to

$200,000 today). Four immensely wealthy planter lawyers became key figures in writing the constitution: Charles Carroll of Carrollton, Samuel Chase, Thomas Johnson, and William Paca. They owned on average 17,500 acres and one hundred slaves each. Rivaled only by New York's constitution writers, the Maryland delegates represented the most entrenched political and economic elite in North America.

"Connected by ties of kinship and interest," as Charles Carroll aptly put it, conservatives fought off the minority of delegates who wanted a democratic constitution. The result was a constitution designed to perpetuate a deeply conservative aristocratic government. This was clear from its key provisions: limited suffrage as under the old colonial qualifications; officeholding restricted as in the past to those owning extensive property; elections for lower-house representatives once in three years for candidates possessing an estate of at least five hundred pounds; voting *viva voce* as in the past, ensuring that the old patronage and clientage system remained in place; an electoral college, elected to seven-year terms by enfranchised Marylanders, consisting of upper-house delegates who must have an estate of at least one thousand pounds; election of a governor, who must have an estate of at least five thousand pounds, by the two legislative houses; and election of county and local sheriffs qualified by possession of an estate worth one thousand pounds or more. Recent research shows that the constitution, as proposed, would have limited those eligible for office in the lower house of the legislature to the top tenth of free white males and those eligible for the upper house to the wealthiest fourteenth.[32]

By the time Maryland's full constitutional convention took up the drafting committee's plan of government in October 1776, the war was going badly for the poorly clothed, armed, and provisioned American army. When radical opposition to the ultraconservative constitution surfaced, Charles Carroll of Carrollton despaired. "We are miserably divided," he wrote his father, "not only colony against colony, but in each colony there begins to appear such a spirit of disunion and discord that I am apprehensive, should we succeed against Great Britain (which I think very improbably under our circumstances), we shall be rent to pieces by civil wars and factions." It might be better, he thought, rather than "hazard civil wars amongst ourselves," to abandon the quest for independence and sue for peace with Great Britain.[33] Carroll's pessimism deepened as the convention delegates deliberated. But in fact conservatives had to make only small concessions to the radicals. They reduced the terms of office for upper-house legislators from seven to five years and lower-house legislators from three years to one year. The convention's radical minority pushed hard for broadening the electorate but lost by narrow votes on proposals to eliminate all property qualifications or reduce them to five pounds Maryland money. Instead, the convention agreed to lower the property qualification to fifty acres of land or property worth thirty pounds Maryland money. This became the threshold for membership in the political community, still denying suffrage to about half the white adult male population.

In one progressive move, the convention restored political and civil liberties to Catholics and disestablished the Church of England. Finally, the delegates signed the constitution without public review. Compared to other state constitutions, perhaps excepting that of neighboring Virginia, where aristocratic planters also controlled the constitutional convention, Maryland had shaped its political future according to the wishes of a minority of wealthy citizens. In the preamble the delegates affirmed that "All government of right originates from the people."[34] But in Maryland's case "the people" were actually only half of the white male citizens.

E Pluribus Unum?

Whether reducing property qualifications for voting, broadening the suffrage to include all taxpayers, or extending the vote even to nontaxpaying white males, state constitution writers were unwilling to open the franchise to women, with one exception. Those in New Jersey, whose legislature met just across the Delaware River from Philadelphia, took this momentous step. In one of the telling oddities of written history, most textbooks and scholarly treatments of the American Revolution ignore this pivotal advance in democracy. Those that do mention it claim, or infer, that New Jersey's constitution writers allowed female suffrage by an oversight in the choice of words governing the right to vote. This was not the case.

New Jersey's constitution writers, as recent scholarship has demonstrated, began debating the vital topic of suffrage as early as January 1776, and they considered numerous petitions insisting on extending the franchise. Though they rejected demands for taxpayer suffrage, they lowered the property ownership bar to fifty pounds of *personal* property, which included a farmer's or artisan's tools, furniture, household goods, or any other form of transportable property. Then, in a remarkable stroke, the Third Provincial Congress, which in January 1776 had usurped the legislature sanctioned under the royal charter, conferred the vote, in gender-neutral language, on "all freeholders, and householders . . . worth fifty pounds clear estate." Many weeks of debate ensued, while John Adams, across the river in Philadelphia, made explicit his opposition to opening the suffrage to women or the propertyless. The Jersey constitution makers were no doubt aware of the argument by "Essex" (who may have been a delegate in the provincial congress) that "widows paying taxes . . . have an equal right to a vote as men of the same property." After much discussion, the constitution drafters abandoned the personal pronoun "he" in the crucial phrasing of the suffrage law. From this point forward, from 1776 to 1807, single women—either unmarried women or widows— "routinely participated in the state's electoral process." Their votes were often solicited by males running for office. No records survive that tell us how many women took advantage of this groundbreaking opportunity, but it is clear that enough did so to keep the matter controversial. In 1790, when the issue was raised again, the all-male legislature wrote a new election law that wiped away any ambiguity about women's entitlement to vote. Referring to voters as "he or she," it solidified a right for which Abigail Adams and others had spoken during the Revolution. For more than a quarter century, until the legislature disenfranchised women by amending the state constitution in 1807, a precedent had been set, crashing through the age-old gender barrier that had kept women from entering the political community.[35]

Historical amnesia about this early pathbreaking case of women's suffrage (not to be followed at the state level until 1869, when Wyoming enfranchised women) is all the more remarkable because the topic was not confined to New Jersey. Important male leaders, as well as women, were ready to take the plunge. For example, Richard Henry Lee, longtime delegate to the Continental Congress, signer of the Declaration of Independence, and friend of Samuel and John Adams, supported women's suffrage. When his sister Hannah Corbin pushed him on the issue, he agreed in March 1778 that "widows having property" deserved the vote. Lee argued further that married women had "as legal a right to vote as any other person" in electing local tax assessors who established the value of taxable property. In taking this position, Lee broke ranks with the vast majority of men of his generation; the same could be said of the beginning of almost every important reform movement in American history, in which a lonely band of individuals first must swim against a strong tide. As historian Marc Kruman writes: "Given the rigid exclusion of women from the public sphere in the preceding decades, any discussion of woman suffrage, for or against, testified to the transformative impact of the American Revolution."[36]

In Massachusetts, Abigail Adams was not ready to go quite so far as Virginia's Richard Henry Lee. She had raised the issue of woman suffrage with her husband even before the Declaration of Independence, and a month after it passed, still groping her way toward such a major reform, she asked John how a republic could produce "heroes, statesmen, and philosophers" without "learned women?"[37] Clearly this was not an explicit call for admitting women into the political community, but it was a step in that direction. If the republic needed educated women to sustain itself, then how long would these females wait before insisting on their right to put their intellectually equipped minds to work in the public sphere?

No evidence exists to show that free African American women entertained such advanced ideas, but most free black males insisted on the right to vote, too. Virginia, South Carolina, and Georgia denied the vote to freedmen, but in the North only Massachusetts constitution drafters attempted to strip away the suffrage of free African Americans. This retrograde step aroused voters in many of the state's numerous towns. When the draft of the first constitution was put before them in 1778, many towns objected to this race-based exclusion. The town of Sutton, for example, protested the suffrage provision as "diametrically repugnant to the grand and fundamental maxim of humane rights; viz. *That law to bound all must be assented to by all.*'" Objecting that "Negroes . . . are excluded even though they are free and men of property," Sutton's townsmen pointed out that disenfranchising African Americans added to "the already accumulated load of guilt lying upon the land in supporting the slave trade when the poor innocent Africans who never hurt or offered an injury or insult to this country have been so unjustly assaulted [and] inhumanely murdered."[38] Obliged to rewrite the constitution, the drafters removed the color bar in Massachusetts.

Betrayal in Massachusetts

Nowhere was the debate over a constitution more protracted than in Massachusetts. Many years ago, John C. Miller, a biographer of Sam Adams, put the matter straight: "After the outbreak of war between the mother country and colonies, Massachusetts failed lamentably to take the lead in framing a new state constitution."[39] In no other state did ideas about the people as the fountain of all political authority ebb away so quickly in the face of a resurgent conservative view that favored strict limits on popular power. This regressive movement in Massachusetts constitution making is all the more intriguing because of the particularly vibrant quality of involvement of ordinary citizens who were repeatedly asked for comment and advice on several drafts of the constitution. Brought to action, the state's town meetings produced an outpouring of down-to-earth political thinking, spawned not out of arguments among political theorists and educated lawyers, clergymen, and leisured men but mostly out of the local political experiences of men who worked with their hands.

Historians are still coming to grips with the peculiar difficulties that Massachusetts had in agreeing on a constitution. At first blush, it seems that many factors favored reaching an early settlement. Leading up to revolution, after reining in radicals such as Ebenezer MacIntosh, popular leaders had fashioned an interclass alliance that set an example for other colonies resisting abhorrent British policies. Also, they had in John Adams a student of political science to whom many other colonial leaders turned for advice in forming state constitutions. Further, by the spring of 1776, the British army had evacuated eastern Massachusetts, never to reoccupy the state and tear up the countryside, as occurred in most other states. Most Loyalists left with the British, removing many of Massachusetts' ultraconservatives, thus sparing the state the civil war between patriots and Loyalists that shredded the social fabric in New York, New Jersey, and most southern states. Yet for all the conditions conducive to constitution making, Massachusetts failed repeatedly in devising a consensus constitution. Why?

Pennsylvania, Maryland, and several other states were already working on their constitutions when the Massachusetts legislature, at the beginning of June 1776, chose a drafting committee. But the legislators were unsure that they were entitled to clothe themselves with this grave responsibility. Nonetheless, they agreed to proceed. Yet nearly four months later, with the war going badly, the legislature had no draft to show. The problem was not the lack of ideas, but a fear among conservative leaders of the radical political innovations put forward by some legislators, especially those representing the hill towns of western Massachusetts. Sitting with the Continental Congress in Philadelphia, Adams sickened at what his friends reported to him. John

Winthrop, distinguished scientist at Harvard and member of the legislative council, sent a distressing account of how thirty to forty men, brandishing large sticks, kept the justices from entering the Bristol County Courthouse in Taunton. Similar uprisings staged by those who opposed courts dispensing justice under commissions running in the name of George III convinced the legislature to suspend most county courts, though there was suspicion that debtors were trying to escape their creditors. For Winthrop, "these commotions" were part of "a spirit of innovation." "It seems as if everything was to be altered," he reported. "Scarce a newspaper but teems with new projects." Among these innovations were county assemblies to make local rules, and the election in each town for committees to probate wills. All of this would place authority closer to the people and reduce the high court fees detested by people of modest means. "Tis like repairing a house that is on fire," Winthrop moaned.[40]

The new mood of ordinary people in Massachusetts, it seemed, could not be ignored, swept away, or even steered in conservative directions. Or could it? Responding to Winthrop's alarmed description of populist schemes, John Adams confided that he was "grieved to hear, as I do from various quarters, of that rage for innovation, which appears in so many wild shapes in our province." Adams's greatest fear was coming to pass: a government of ordinary people. A decade of plebeian involvement in the fracas with England had unnerved him. Adams was keenly aware that to bring the colonies into a state of open rebellion, moderate and conservative patriots had energized ordinary citizens, and in some cases, as chapter 4 relates, ordinary farmers and artisans had themselves taken the lead before beckoned to the fracas from above. In either case, ordinary citizens had become alarmingly unwilling to content themselves with the *status quo antebellum*. Reflecting his pessimistic view of ordinary people in the Bay State, Adams frowned on "ridiculous projects" such as "county assemblies, town registers, and town probates of wills," and sputtered that these projects aimed at putting authority in the hands of locally elected officials "are founded in narrow notions, sordid stinginess and profound ignorance and tend directly to barbarism." Adams would not have dared say this in front of the Boston town meeting, or in the town meeting in Braintree, where Abigail knew every attendee. But he expressed these innermost thoughts privately to Harvard's John Winthrop two weeks before he signed the Declaration of Independence.[41]

For moderates and conservatives in the legislature, the best course was to slow down on writing a constitution in the hope that the fever of the ordinary people would eventually subside. On September 17, the legislature asked the towns whether they wished them to draft a constitution. Bowing to the current understanding that creating fundamental law required special approval of those who would live under it, they promised, if sanctioned to proceed, to publish their handiwork "for the inspection and perusal of the inhabitants."[42]

Responses to this canvass were varied, and the legislature, already deeply divided, took eight months to act on the town meeting responses. This in itself was evidence of the conservatives' hope that democratic sentiment would exhaust itself. It was not to happen. Some towns, such as Concord, advised that the people should elect special delegates to perform this epochal task, drawing a clear line between lawmaking and constitution making. In neighboring Lexington, and in Pittsfield in western Massachusetts, the people wanted guarantees that town meetings across the state would have the opportunity to ratify or reject the constitution rather than simply to "inspect and peruse" it. Other towns, such as Concord and Boston, held that the suffrage must be broadened so that delegates elected for the weighty business now at hand should mirror all of the people asked to commit their lives and property to the Revolution, not just the propertied part. Consistent with the way the city had acted "as a body of the people" in the years of protest against the British, "every individual," insisted Boston's town meeting, "ought to be consulting, acting, and assisting." The towns of Worcester County, always a hotbed of radicalism, assembled in a convention in November 1776 to present a united front. Rankled by the recent redistribution of legislative seats as unfair to western parts of the state, most of the towns opposed the present legislature writing a constitution. Many of them wanted a special election for delegates to an assembly with only one task: to write a constitution that people of the commonwealth would live under for untold generations.[43]

On May 5, 1777, the upper and lower legislative houses finally reached a compromise on the most important points raised by the towns: that in the upcoming general election voters who met the old property requirement would choose delegates specifically empowered to draft a constitution, then to continue as a legislative body; that the draft would be published in Boston newspapers and sent to all towns where all males "free and twenty-one years of age" would be asked to vote up or down on the draft; and that if two-thirds of the voters approved, the constitution would be final. Seemingly, it was an adroit compromise. Conservatives had avoided a specially elected convention chosen by all free white men, the formula already adopted in other states, and in this way could screen out those most likely to represent the state's lower ranks. But they conceded that *all* adult male citizens should participate in rejecting or ratifying the constitution.

Boston's town meeting was not pleased with the compromise. By "a unanimous vote of a full meeting," Bostonians denied that it was proper for a legislative body to form a constitution. They called for an election by "the people at large," not just the propertied, to choose men specially elected to write the august document. Bostonians had zeroed in on precisely the two hedges that conservatives had erected to block a constitution resembling Pennsylvania's or Vermont's. But the election went ahead. Convening on June 15, 1777, the delegates rolled up their sleeves to begin work. They quickly agreed that one man from each county and five chosen at large should sit on a drafting committee. Thirteen came from the the lower house of the legislature and four from the upper house. Boston merchant Thomas Cushing was chosen to chair the committee.

Through the summer and fall of 1777, and into early winter, the committee struggled to agree on a draft. Sometimes deadlock seemed to seize the committee. But one important breakthrough for reformers came early: It was agreed that the franchise should be broadened to include all adult freemen who paid taxes. James Warren, sitting on the drafting committee, reported to John Adams that he wanted to retain the old property requirements but "as it [the constitution] is to have the sanction of the people at large" it was best to concede this point. Conservatives on the drafting committee then dug in their heels, knowing that reform-minded committeemen wanted to bring government closer to the people through a unicameral legislature and a weak executive branch. "The Council are almost to a man against the new constitution," Warren wrote to John Adams "and are forced to come to it with the greatest reluctance." So the committee labored through six months, searching for compromises.[44]

The deliberations of the drafting committee went unrecorded or have not survived; but Boston newspapers were filled with commentaries on the raging arguments, and these accounts help us understand why the deliberations were so protracted. Essayists showered readers with arguments over the constitution, echoing the barrage of viewpoints expressed in Pennsylvania when that state formed its constitution a year earlier. "My idea of government," wrote "Clitus," is that it is easy, simple, and cheap." A unicameral legislature elected by free manhood suffrage and a strict avoidance of an upper house and a powerful governor were the alpha and omega of democratic government. "We debase ourselves in reintroducing the worst parts of British rule. The plain question is, are we fighting and lavishing our blood and treasure to establish the freest and best government on earth, or are we about to set up a formidable court interest?" From the opposite side, "Faithful Friend" contended that "the stuff of power never was, nor never can be, in the nature of things, in the people's hands." Displaying his pessimism, shared by most conservatives and most of the wealthy, "Faithful Friend" lectured that "Man, considered abstractly and individually, is perhaps the most selfish, fierce and cruel animal in the whole creation of God." Give the people power, and "anarchy and confusion" would result. Splitting the difference was the Salem minister William Gordon. "A restricted suffrage is not fit for a free society," he argued, but he feared a unicameral legislature because "ambitious men will have more than a little ground for building up their own particular greatness upon their country's ruin."[45]

Most scholars who have scrutinized the protracted debate over the Massachusetts constitution of 1778 have considered it as an abstract document reflecting various political theories and differing assessments of the capabilities of the ordinary citizen. That was truly the case. But it needs remembering that the debate was conducted in the midst of deteriorating economic conditions in Massachusetts, amid a war that was going disastrously, and, as chapter 7 will explain, in the context of a growing clamor over war profiteering and the desirability of price controls, tension between seaboard towns and interior villages, and sinking hearts that the virtuous people counted on to make the republican ship float were becoming as scarce as hard money.

Amid these uncertainties, the drafting committee veered toward the conservative position. John Adams's return to Massachusetts in late November 1777 possibly convinced some of the committeemen to hold to the conservative line. Whatever the case, the draft was finally ready on December 11. Now the full legislature must approve it before sending it to the people.

The constitution put before the full legislature in December contained the two most important elements the conservatives wanted: a two-house legislature and a powerful executive branch. The governor would have powers greater than in almost any other state: to adjourn, prorogue, or recess the legislature with the advice of the upper chamber; to lay embargoes on any commodities for up to forty days; to appoint (with the upper house) all general, field, and staff officers of the militia; to appoint judges and justices of the peace; and, most important, to have the legislative veto power so much favored by John Adams and most conservatives. Conservatives also squelched the reformers' effort to prohibit multiple officeholding; fought off attempts to allow Catholics and other non-Protestants free exercise of religion and the right to hold office; disenfranchised free blacks and Indians; overrode a provision to end slavery in Massachusetts; and rebuffed efforts to end mandatory taxpayer support for the Congregational Church.

When the legislature met in January 1778, calling itself the convention to distinguish its constitution-writing responsibilities from its legislative tasks, it found itself no less divided than when it had first selected a committee to do the drafting. With Boston's Thomas Cushing and Salem's John Pickering acting as the principal negotiators, three changes were made. Bending to the reformist delegates, who mostly represented western towns, the legislators stripped the governor of his veto power, giving him only one vote with the upper house on laws proposed by the lower house. Also, they increased slightly government representation of western towns. Offsetting these concessions to reformers, conservatives got much of what they wanted: graduated property requirements to vote for candidates and run for office. All free white men could vote for lower-house candidates, but the candidates themselves must have personal estates of two hundred pounds, including real estate worth half of that. Only men with sixty pounds of personal estate (actually more than had been required in the colonial period) could vote for upper-house and gubernatorial candidates. The candidates themselves were to be chosen from the upper ranks of Massachusetts society. Only men with personal estates of four hundred pounds and real estate worth half of that could stand for an upper-house seat. And only the very wealthy could run for governor—those worth one thousand pounds, including real estate of five hundred pounds. One historian characterizes the constitution as a blueprint for "a government dominated by the Whig aristocracy."[46] Even this is too mild. The draft of 1778 was by far the most conservative in the North and in its restricted suffrage and candidate property qualifications were exceeded in the South only by Maryland and South Carolina.

On March 4, 1778, the general court ordered the constitution printed and sent it to the towns with a request that they vote for or against the draft by June 15. Nearly four of every five towns rejected the constitution. Those that voted unanimously against it, or had only a handful of votes in favor, testify to how far the document's drafters had turned their backs on the democratic sentiment that had been indispensable in committing Massachusetts to revolution and supporting the war. In Boston, the center of revolutionary mobilization, 968 citizens gathered at a town meeting and renounced the constitution unanimously. Just outside Boston, Cambridge, Newton, and Brookline registered their opposition with votes of 79–0, 75–5, and 45–0, respectively. On the seacoast north of Boston, the vote was 108–0, 147–0, 109–0, 64–0, and 46–0, respectively, against the constitution in Salem, York, Gloucester, Kittery, and Halifax. To the south of the state's capital, Scituate, Plymouth, Ipswich, and Methuen voted against the constitution by votes of 134–2, 122–8, 190–1, and 80–0. In Concord and Lexington, where the war had first erupted, townsmen were unanimously opposed. Farther west, in the hill country populated mostly by middling farmers and village artisans, opposition to the constitution was also widespread. Among the small towns opposed were South Hadley (58–4), Amherst (53–0), Sturbridge (52–0), West Springfield (52–3), Worcester (49–9), Greenwich (111–0), Sutton (220–0), and Petersham (77–0). Other towns voted narrowly for the constitution, and a few small towns voted unanimously for it. But the weight of public opinion was massively against it.[47]

Certain elements of the document were particularly offensive. The brunt of criticism—in many cases overflowing into indignation—boiled down to what voters saw as an attempt to deny political rights to ordinary men, to shield the state government from popular control, and to concentrate power in the hands of the few. For many townsmen, this smacked of the British assault on liberty. Many townsmen decried the conservatives' disfranchisement of those without sufficient property and the erection of a political color bar. From the small farming community of Lenox, in western Berkshire County, came strong language: The clause limiting the suffrage to those with sixty pounds of property "declares honest poverty a crime for which a large number of the true and faithful subjects of the state, who perhaps have fought and bled in their country's cause, are deprived" of the right to vote. Why, asked another town, should a man "born in Africa, India, or ancient America or even being much sunburnt" be stripped of a vote? William Gordon, Salem's Congregational minister and hardly a radical, predicted that any advocate of the Enlightenment would look askance after seeing that the constitution's drafters "mean their own rights only and not those of mankind."[48]

The abiding worry over concentrated political power led many towns to deplore the rejection of a unicameral legislature while creating a powerful governor—precisely the "balanced government" that John Adams wanted. Little Boothbay, on the eastern frontier of what would become Maine, insisted that the governor and lieutenant governor were "needless in a free state," as was the upper house. All were programmed to be chosen from the wealthy, who would therefore "control the people's representatives" congregated in the lower house. Related to this complaint was fear over the appointive power handed to the upper house and governor. This was a constitution that reminded townsmen of why they had been willing to risk all in treasonous acts against their king. Like many towns, the rural village of Westminster, in Worcester County, expressed its dismay at a constitution that "deprives the people at large of appointing their own rulers and officers and places the power where it may (and no doubt will) be greatly abused"—that is, the power of judicial and militia appointments in the hands of a "selected number of men." "No officer whatsoever," the town maintained, "from the highest to the lowest ought to be put in trust but by the suffrages of the people." The lessons of the 1760s and early 1770s had taught Massachusetts this. "Who has the boldness—without blushing—to say the people are not suitable to put in their own officers?" they asked. "If so, why do we waste our blood and treasure to obtain that which, when obtained, we are not fit to enjoy—if but a selected few only are fit to appoint our rulers?" Other towns scorched the drafting convention for turning a deaf ear on widespread sentiment to prevent plural officeholding, one of the main bugbears of the late colonial system under British rule. By a unanimous vote of 111–0, the townsmen of Greenwich, in Hampshire County, admonished the convention for divesting "the good people of this state of many of the privileges which God and Nature has given them," while giving power "to a few individuals." With one voice, they called for a unicameral legislature and the election by all free males of all offices, including the state's militia general and all judges.[49]

If most towns opposed a constitution designed to minimize the power of the people at large, a small number thought it did not go far enough to ensure the rule of the well born and wealthy. A gathering of towns in Essex County, center of seaboard mercantile interests north of Boston, submitted the most pointed criticism from the conservative point of view. Their spokesman was Theophilus Parsons, a rising young Harvard-educated lawyer whose essay, "The Essex Result," argued that the constitution left propertied men insufficiently protected and open to predation from the unpropertied. Parsons reflected the views of many of the wealthy who believed that a leveling spirit had coursed through Massachusetts during the last decade, a situation exacerbated by the erosion of public virtue—the selflessness and commitment to the public good—that Adams and others had always thought necessary to sustain a republic. Parsons departed from most conservatives in believing that "all the members of the state" were entitled to the vote unless, like women, "they have not sufficient discretion or are so situated as to have no wills of their own." But their representatives, sitting in the lower house, must be strictly checked by the upper chamber, which should be the preserve of "gentlemen of education, fortune, and leisure" who made up the vast majority of those "possessed of wisdom, learning, and firmness and consistency of character." With the governor, these men must have an absolute veto power over laws passed by the lower house. "The holders of property must be in the majority in any question affecting property," he argued. In this line of thought, Parsons and the Essex County elite had John Adams's concurrence, though Adams hoped for the political domination of the wise and virtuous rather than that of the wealthy minority whose status was based on property.[50]

Why did the Massachusetts constitution writers ignore the widespread desire for taxpayer suffrage and offices open to any free adult male citizen? And why did they dismiss the popular concern about concentrated power and the fear that men of great fortune would checkmate the lower house from their upper-house positions? One explanation is the gnawing fear of constitution writers that Massachusetts would fall into the internecine warfare that erupted in Pennsylvania after the adoption of its radical constitution. Another explanation is the absence of popular leaders who in other states—Pennsylvania is a notable example—were able to channel debate and argue forcefully for a broad-based electorate, offices open to talent, and curbs on concentrating political power in the executive branch and the upper house of a bicameral legislature. No such popular leader emerged in Massachusetts during the protracted years of constitution making. Urban radicals who might have served as the people's tribune—Boston's Sam Adams or William Molineux—were in eclipse. From the western towns, where sentiment was strongest for a constitution empowering common people, nobody emerged to promote their cause. In 1778, Northampton's Joseph Hawley, who for years had carried the radical banner, was so ill that he could not serve as a delegate to the convention. Absent such radical leaders, conservative men such as Thomas Cushing, James Warren, and John Pickering, all friends and ideological compatriots of John Adams, became effective floor leaders.

Rebuffed by a large majority of the people who had elected them to write the fundamental law, the constitution drafters of the general court stalled, waiting eight months after receiving a storm of negative votes and arguments before asking the towns in February 1779 whether they wanted to elect delegates to a new constitutional convention. The answer to that was obvious; of course there had to be a constitution. The legal system was in disarray, with courts lacking legitimacy even to function. The economy was on the edge of collapse, with problems of depreciated currency and volatile prices for basic commodities and calls for the confiscation of Loyalists' property creating a reservoir of uncertainty and disgruntlement. Even those favoring a conservative constitution were worried that merchants who had been lukewarm toward the Revolution were plundering the economy. Finally in mid-June 1779 the newly elected general court directed the towns to choose delegates for the sole purpose of writing a constitution, and enfranchised all free adult males for doing so. The convention met in Cambridge on September 1, 1779, to deal with a badly fractured, frustrated, and philosophically broken state.

This was the moment John Adams had been waiting for. Adams had returned to Massachusetts in August 1779 after a year in Paris, where he and his fellow commissioners appointed by Congress had negotiated a treaty of alliance that greatly strengthened the American cause. Chosen to represent Braintree, he was ready to restore virtue to his beloved Massachusetts, which seemed almost hopelessly ensnared in trying to agree on a constitution. He was not only chosen to be among the thirty members on the drafting committee but asked by that committee to serve as a subcommittee of one. He "had the honor to be principal engineer," he later recalled with satisfaction.[51]

The engineer now charged with rescuing Massachusetts from its constitutional morass had changed greatly during four years of war. The people in whom he had such faith in his early years as a lawyer had disappointed him. He could not have agreed more when he read a plaintive *cri de coeur* from Mercy Otis Warren just after returning from France. "The spirit of party" had overtaken Massachusetts, she wrote, and the wealthy would not involve themselves in public affairs or only "worship at the shrine of *Plutus*," while only "a solitary few" of the "old republicans . . . still persevere, their hands untainted by bribes—though poverty stares them in the face—and their hearts unshaken by the levity, the luxury, the caprice or whim, the folly or ingratitude of the times."[52] Adams assuredly considered himself one of the "old republicans," and now he meant to show that a proper constitution would reestablish stability and restore virtue, the indispensable qualities of a true republic. As we will see, his plan did not offend those who worshiped at the shrine of Plutus but those who stared at poverty.

Adams knew that four years of war had frayed the Bay State's social fabric and deranged the economy in ways that had set farmer against merchant and urban consumer and pitted western and eastern Massachusetts communities against each other. To harness these divisions, he proposed what he had plotted out almost four years before in his "Thoughts on Government." The answer was to balance interest groups by giving the generality of people and those of wealth and status each a place in government. The people at large—Adams did not include free but unpropertied men—would elect legislators to the lower house of the legislature. Those of greater amounts of property would elect an upper house. Both houses together would elect a governor, who would have veto power over laws passed by the two-house legislature. The governor would also have great appointive power: to choose judges and justices of the peace, all militia officers, the attorney general, and even lesser state officials such as town sheriffs with the consent of a governor's council elected by the upper house. Adams called this "mixed government." In the main, this was the form of government Massachusetts had lived under since the Charter of 1691 and different only in detail from the failed constitution of 1778. The largest change from that document was to make the franchise more restrictive. Ignoring the outpouring of town criticisms of the narrowly drawn franchise in the draft constitution of 1778, Adams imposed a property requirement for voting for lower-house delegates, hence disenfranchising a large part of the adult males, and increased the amount of property the 1778 constitution required to run for the upper house and governor. Only those owning one thousand pounds of property (about $200,000 today) could run for governor, making the office more restrictive than in any other state besides Maryland and South Carolina.

In the more innovative parts of his draft, Adams made his case for moral rejuvenation. He proposed that the state actively promote Harvard College, the common schools, and both public and private institutions for disseminating knowledge about manufacturing, commerce, the arts and sciences, agriculture, and natural history. Without knowledge, there would be no virtue;

without virtue, a republic could not survive. By the same token, the state should sponsor religion, specifically to ensure that the towns provided support for "the public worship of God, and of the teachers of religion and morals."

When the full convention met in late October 1779 to consider Adams's draft, which the larger drafting committee accepted, Adams and his committee made a few concessions to alarmed democratic reformers. Conservatives beat back the reformers' desire for fixed terms for supreme court justices rather than life terms, but they got the governor's absolute veto power reduced to a veto that could be overturned by a two-thirds majority in both houses of the legislature. Other matters of contention were postponed to a winter session. This was the undoing of the reformers, mostly from western towns, because severe winter weather prevented most of them from reaching Cambridge. Now in command, the conservatives yielded only in allowing militiamen to choose their officers up to the rank of captain, but this simply restored the militia election system that had been in place for the entire war.

On March 2, 1779, the constitutional convention concluded its revisions, ordered the constitution printed and sent to the towns, asked the towns to indicate their approval or disapproval by June 1, and specified that the constitution would take effect if two-thirds of the people voting indicated their consent. Five years into a wearying war, Massachusetts adult males were asked to vote for a constitution that was no closer to the people than the rejected constitution of 1778, in fact one that ignored almost all of the reformers' objections to that document. It was one of the most conservative constitutions created among the states.

Reconvening to count the votes in early June 1780, the convention declared that the requisite two-thirds of the voters had given their approval. Massachusetts citizens were told that after a prolonged struggle, they had a constitution. But it was not a constitution that they had actually approved. Of 290 towns returning votes (only 207 have survived), only 42 accepted it without amendment. According to Stephen E. Patterson, the historian who has examined the returns most closely, nearly half of them rejected the constitution because it strangled the voice of the people at large in favor of a government controlled by the elite. Seventy-eight of these 101 towns were from the three western counties—Hampshire, Worcester, and Berkshire—where only nineteen towns approved the constitution. Eight towns in eastern Bristol County and a smaller number of towns in eastern Massachusetts also demanded democratic changes. As against these 101 dissatisfied towns, 86 endorsed the constitution in the main, and a handful wanted amendments that would have concentrated power even more narrowly. Twenty towns, as analyzed by Patterson, were so mixed in their responses as to defy categorization.[53]

The objections of Northampton were typical of the anger of many towns at the constitution put before them. In the valley town of the Berkshires, where Jonathan Edwards had long ago roused the people to worship in the Great Awakening, the sick revolutionary radical leader Joseph Hawley girded his loins for one last battle. Agreeing to moderate the town meeting convened to ratify or reject Adams's constitution, he penned a scorching critique. After a meeting that lasted until sundown, the townsmen adopted his report on May 22, 1780. The constitution, wrote Hawley, violated "the natural, essential and inalienable right" of every freeman to vote and hold office. Why should the disfranchised agree to be governed by laws in which they had no voice? The constitution would impose taxes on them and obliged them to perform public service; but they were not to vote. "Shall these poor polls," the Northampton report asked, "who have gone for us into the greatest perils, and undergone infinite fatigues in the present war to rescue us from slavery ... some of them leaving at home their poor families, to endure the sufferings of hunger and nakedness, shall they now be treated by us like villains or African slaves? God forbid!" "Shall we who hold property," continued Hawley's report, "be content to see our brethren, who have done their full share in procuring that security ... ; on election days, standing aloof and sneaking into corners and ashamed to show their heads, in the meetings of freemen?"[54]

Historians and political scientists have lauded constitution making in Massachusetts, pointing especially to two elements: a broadly elected constitution-writing convention and the popular ratification of its work. Three other states had already adopted constitutions written by specially elected delegates, so in this regard Massachusetts was not a pioneer. As for popular ratification, where Massachusetts was indeed unique, the process may have been followed, but the results were overturned. Only by manipulating the town votes did the convention decide that the constitution had been endorsed by a two-thirds majority. "The counting of votes," writes Patterson, "was neither mechanically nor honestly conducted, for the committee fixed upon a method of counting that would almost inevitably result in the acceptance of the constitution."[55] The people of the Commonwealth of Massachusetts would now live under a constitution they had rejected.

Most of the convention delegates probably feared that another failure to pass a constitution would fuel the conflict of interest groups that had become endemic. With legal cases piling up for lack of courts sanctioned by a constitution, creditors were especially frantic to restore the legal system. But if the convention was mainly hoping to restore stability, they did so at the price of honesty.

Objections to the constitution were not long in coming. Particularly offensive was the imposition of property qualifications for voting and officeholding. The town of Stoughton, outside Boston, expressed a common view that "taxation and representation are reciprocal and inseparably connected." On this issue, the Revolution began. But why would the constitution annul what was "not only a civil but . . . a natural right"? Belcherstown, at the opposite end of the state in Hampshire County, objected that the constitution denied that "liberty and freedom which we are at this day contending for." Many towns pointed out that the suffrage requirements would take away the vote from those who had elected delegates to the constitutional convention. "How many sensible, honest, and naturally industrious men, by numberless misfortunes, never acquire and possess property of the value of sixty pounds?" asked the townsmen of Mansfield, in eastern Bristol County. The town of Tyringham agreed: "We are very sensible that a very large number of the good inhabitants of this state that pay a very considerable part of the taxes of the same are by the frame of the constitution debarred of the privilege of freemen."[56]

After the constitutional convention declared its document upheld, the restricted Massachusetts electorate made John Hancock their first governor. Within days, he heard how bitter it was for men who had put their lives on the line to find that they were voteless and ineligible to hold office. It was not militiamen, but two militia captains who first protested. Captain Samuel Talbot and Lieutenant Lemuel Gay, both from Stoughton, wrote of how they, like many soldiers under them, had been "by the Constitution disfranchised, for want of property lost by many in their struggle for freedom." These were men who had previously owned property but saw their small farms or artisan's shops dwindle in value as they fought in the war. What was the point of fighting for freedom? they asked. "We can no longer with truth encourage our fellow soldiers, who are so poor as to be thus deprived of their fundamental rights, that they are fighting for their own freedom; and how can an officer possessed of the generous feelings of humanity detach any of them into a service in which they are not interested?"[57] Declining to act "under such a form of government . . . that appears repugnant to the principles of freedom," Captain Talbot and Lieutenant Gay resigned their commissions.

Constitution writing was over for now in Massachusetts. It had produced the lengthiest and most thoughtful discussions about government arising from the people themselves in the nineteen decades since European immigrants had settled in North America. And it had involved common people in making government, not simply living under government. In tiny hamlets with hardly more than a cluster of families as well as in large towns, men confirmed John Adams's judgment years before when he boasted that it was "as rare as a comet or an earthquake" to find a Massachusetts citizen who was not literate and capable of clear thinking.[58] But the constitution they would now live under, heavy with the fingerprints of John Adams, was not the one they wanted.

7

RADICALISM AT FLOODTIDE

1778–1781

THE YEAR 1778 FIGURED CRUCIALLY FOR THE AMERICAN PATRIOTS. The British occupation of Philadelphia through the first half of the year, the collapse of morale in Washington's army, the waning of patriotism on the home front, and the repeated failure of most states to fulfill the request of the Continental Congress for soldiers and supplies presented bleak prospects for winning the war. But Benjamin Franklin's charm and genius in Paris plucked the American cause from near disaster. By engineering a treaty of commerce and amity with the French, announced in March 1778, the Americans soon celebrated the French declaration of war on Great Britain and the arrival of French troops, a formidable French fleet, and great quantities of war matériel. American prospects brightened, at least momentarily.

Yet French intervention did not yet tip the balance. Though the British withdrew from Philadelphia in June 1778, pulling back thousands of troops and naval forces to New York City, the war in the North produced only a stalemate. By the end of 1778, British strategists decided to move the war south in an attempt to cut the southern states off from the northern states. For two more years, the war wore on, sapping American resources, producing abrasive conflicts within the Continental Congress, and convincing a divided Congress to print prodigious amounts of paper money to support the war.

The French alliance kept the American nation in the war but could not enable them to win it. Emblematic of the struggle to create a unified young nation, ratification of the Articles of Confederation under which the Congress acted could not be secured from all the states until March 1, 1781.

During the years from 1778 to 1781, when the fortunes of the quest for independence hung in the balance, revolutionary radicalism reached its apogee. Up and down the seaboard and from tidewater to up-country regions, those bent on transforming their society or changing the prosecution of the war greatly complicated the thrust for independence. In these years, the American Revolution had to be carried forward on multiple fronts. The front familiar in our history books is the one on the battlefield, which mostly moved south by December 1778. Unfamiliar to most of today's public is the chapter of the war involving African Americans, who from 1778 to 1781 rebelled in large numbers. A second largely unremembered front involved Native Americans, who in these same years struggled to stave off an imperialist nation in the making. In addition, a third conflict developed in which fellow patriots fought wrenching battles with one another. Building on earlier hopes for a rejuvenated and reconstructed American society, elements of the independence-minded American people reacted militantly to economic injustice in urban areas, even to the point of outright class warfare under the eyes of the Continental Congress in Philadelphia. In Virginia, class tension ripped apart efforts for the state to defend itself. And in Washington's Continental army, men by the thousands who had pledged their lives to the American cause rose up in mutiny. It is well enough to chronicle the battlefield action—some of which is interwoven with other matters below—but the hidden history of radical America is what this chapter seeks to recapture.

Blood in the Streets

The War of Independence entered a new military phase as the action moved south in late 1778, as we will see below. But at the same time it entered another phase: A meltdown of the fiscal structure undergirding the war effort now brought demands for radical intervention in the imploding economy.

Dislocations of the economy have been endemic to most wartime societies, usually characterized by shortages of essential commodities, inflation, and profiteering. The American Revolution was no different. In the history books, the Continental Congress gets most of the blame, especially for issuing

Scales of Depreciation of Continental Money.

	Of Congress.			Of Pennsylvania, by act of Assembly,	From the merchants' books: For Philadelphia.	For Virginia.
1777.						
January				1 1-2	1 1-4	1 1-4
February	*Value of* 100			1 1-2	1 1-2	1 1-4
March	*Continen. dol-*			2	2	2
April	*lars in specie.*			2 1-2	2	2
May				2 1-2	2 1-2	2
June				2 1-2	2 1-2	2
July	*Dollars.*	*90ths.*	*8ths.*	3	3	3
August				3	3	3
September	100	00	0	3	3	3
October	90	77	3	3	3	3
November	82	73	0	3	3	3
December	74	70	0	4	4	4
1778.						
January	67	85	0	4	4	4
February	61	83	2	5	5	5
March	56	79	6	5	5	5
April	48	74	4	6	6	5
May	42	77	5	5	5	5
June	36	86	1	4	4	5
July	32	79	3	4	4	5
August	27	87	3	5	5	5
September	24	78	5	5	5	5
October	20	84	5	5	5	5
November	17	88	0	6	6	6
December	14	89	2	6	6	6
1779.						
January	12	85	1	8	7 8 9	8
February	10	85	6	10	10	10
March	9	87	1	10 1-2	10 11	10
April	8	89	7	17	12½ 14 16 22	16
May	7	89	5	24	22 24	20
June	6	89	2	20	22 20 18	20
July	6	40	0	19	18 19 20	21
August	5	89	6	20	20	22
September	4	88	5	24	20 28	24
October				30	30	28
November	3	89	6	38 1-2	32 45	36
December	3	30	0	41 1-2	45 38	40

SCALES

Chart of the Depreciation of Continental Money; from Pelatiah Webster, Political Essays on the Nature and Operation of Money, Public Finances, and Other Subjects *(1791).*

SCALES of DEPRECIATION of Continental Money.				
	Of Congrefs.	*Of* Pennfyl-vania, *by act of Affembly,*	*From the merchants' books:* For Philadelphia.	For Virginia.
1780.				
January	3. 40 0	40 1-2	40 45	42
February	2 89 1	47 1-2	45 55	45
March	2 45 0	61 1-2	60 65	50
April	2 45 0	61 1-2	60	60
May	2 45 0	59	60	60
June	2 45 0	61 1-2	60	65
July	2 45 0	64 1-2	60 65	65
Auguft	2 45 0	70	65 75	70
September	2 45 0	72	75	72
October	2 45 0	73	75 80	73
November	2 45 0	74	80 100	74
December	2 45 0	75	100	75
1781.				
January	2 45 0	75	100	75
February	2 45 0	75	100 120	80
March	2 45 0	75	120 135	90
April	2 45 0	75	135 200	100
May.	2 45 0	75	200 500	150

May 31, 1781, Continental money ceafed to pafs as currency, but was afterwards bought and fold as an article of fpeculation, at very uncertain and defultory prices, from 500 to 1000 to 1.

The exchange of State-money of *Pennfylvania,* in *May* 1781, was 2½, 6, 7, 5, and 4, to 1 hard Money.

huge quantities of paper money—Continental dollars—to finance the Revolution. But Congress had few alternatives. It had no authority to levy taxes to pay for the war, and the states taxed far too little to underwrite a long and expensive conflict. While hoping for massive loans from France and Holland, Congress issued what amounted to IOUs—promises to pay in the future what it could not pay at the time. With the economy collapsing—torn by a sharp decline in agricultural and artisanal production—the flood of paper money backed only by hopes for a robust future economy produced galloping inflation. The worth of a Continental dollar in specie (gold or silver) fell from one hundred cents in September 1777 to fifty-six cents in March 1778 and to twenty-five cents in September of that year. Within another six months, by which time the dollar was worth ten cents, the expression of the day became "not worth a continental"; Mercy Otis Warren called the dollars "immense heaps of paper trash." For an ordinary family this translated into devastating price hikes: A gallon of molasses costing 2 shillings in early 1776 cost 20 shillings in early 1778 and 200 hundred shillings at the end of 1779; the price of a bushel of corn rose from 3 shillings in mid-1776 to 100 shillings in April 1779 to 180 shillings in February 1780.[1]

Every state government wrestled with this difficult situation and none harder than Pennsylvania's. We focus on the problem as it developed in Philadelphia, the nation's largest city, because the economic crisis struck with unusual force there, and because it was there that it led to the spilling of blood among patriots just a few blocks from Pennsylvania Statehouse, where an alarmed Continental Congress sat.

Although Congress halted its program of issuing paper money to feed the war machine in the fall of 1779 (by which time the dollar was worth four cents in specie), this came much too late to avert a disastrous confrontation. For Pennsylvania's wartime government the key issue was how far the powers of government should reach in regulating the economy for the public good. Aside from indicting economic criminals who violated laws prohibiting forestalling—the purchasing of flour and witholding it from the market in anticipation of highly advantageous price increases—and monopolizing, regulation boiled down to one thing: price controls. Could Pennsylvania's legislature balance the claims of farmers and merchants who wanted the best price for commodities against the claims of urban consumers, especially those living close to the poverty line, who demanded the necessities of life at an affordable or "just" price?

Though Pennsylvanians had elected the most radical body of lawmakers ever known in the state, the legislature could not agree on instituting price controls, primarily because most of the legislators represented the farmers, who opposed controls limiting the price they could charge for their produce. This left urban people, the main sufferers of an economy careening out of control, bereft of legislative remedies. This vexing issue was not a collision of ideology from above and ideology from below. The Supreme Executive Council of Pennsylvania, as early as January 1779, recognized the genuine privation of "the industrious poor" and attributed their distress to the "heinously criminal" forestalling and monopolizing practices of merchants. Three months later, the legislature tried to stop "the forestalling and regrating of provisions." But neither political body was able to clamp a lid on the rising prices of "bread and other necessaries of life," because they could think of no device for enforcing a price control law.[2]

Even in urban centers the artisan population was divided on governmental intervention in the economy. Lower artisans for the most part advocated strict regulation of prices as a way of reinstituting the "moral economy" at a time when inflation was pushing the cost of life's necessities beyond the reach of ordinary families, many of whom had sacrificed the male head of household to military duty. Many upper artisans, however, cleaved to the ideology of free trade and laissez-faire principles of political economy, which gave merchants and retailers freedom to charge whatever the market would bear. In maintaining this position, they demonstrated the resilience of the bourgeois values of those swept from office in the final days before independence and those bested in the struggle over the Pennsylvania constitution of 1776.

As early as mid-1777, rising prices created distress in the homes of ordinary people, who quickly found a cause of their misery in opportunistic merchant practices. "Every article of life or convenience was raised upon us, eight, ten, or twelve fold at least," Philadelphia militiamen complained in June 1777. They were "at a loss to this day, what course or station of life to adopt to support ourselves and families."[3] An anonymous writer in the *Pennsylvania Packet* raised the tocsin: "To all FORESTALLERS and RAISERS of the price of GOODS and PROVISIONS. Take notice that a storm is brewing again[st] you. Warning the first." By September, as the British moved closer to capturing Philadelphia, militiamen began deserting in large numbers, unable to leave their jobs and families with a military salary that could not keep up with the cost of basic foodstuffs.

The situation worsened throughout 1778, with prices rising relentlessly and the Continental Congress frustrated at its lack of authority to implement a national plan to tax heavily enough to start retiring the mountain of paper money it had issued. "A Fair Dealer" argued that those who practiced "monopoly and extortion" were making "the poor almost clamorous." Writing in a Philadelphia newspaper, "Mobility" used a little history to put profit-maximizing merchants and retailers on warning: "It has been found in Britain and France, that the people have always done themselves justice when the scarcity of bread has arisen from the avarice of forestallers." Reminding Philadelphians that in Europe the distressed had "appropriated stores to their own use" and sometimes "hung up the culprits who have created their distress without judge or jury," "Mobility" continued with a veiled threat: "Hear this and tremble, ye enemies to the freedom and happiness of your country.... We cannot live without bread—hunger will break through stone walls and the resentment excited by it may end in your destruction." These were strong words, but they were only a little stronger than those of the commander in chief. Washington had already deplored the "want of virtue" among merchants and expressed his belief to Congress that "unless extortion, forestalling, and other practices, which have crept in and become exceedingly prevalent and injurious to the common cause, can meet with proper checks, we must inevitably sink under such a load of accumulated oppression."[4]

In January 1779 more storm signals arose. Angry seamen, seeking higher wages as the cost of basic foodstuffs headed skyward, removed the rigging from ships in order to prevent the departure of the merchants' vessels. On January 19, the state's executive council issued a proclamation "threatening the heaviest penalties of the law against those who, by engrossing quantities of flour, had enhanced the price of bread and other necessaries of life."[5] The response of the engrossers was magisterial repudiation of those who criticized their behavior.

By May, the situation grew more critical for the poor while providing Philadelphia's leading grain and flour merchants new opportunities for profit. With prices still rising and wages lagging far behind, laboring people faced an outrageous affront to the community: Knowing that the French fleet was approaching with hard money—gold—to pay for foodstuffs, flour merchants refused to sell for paper currency, the only medium of exchange available to the city's ordinary families. Overnight, bread was not to be bought at any price.

With prices rising at the compound rate of 17 percent a month, tempers flared on the eve of a militia muster. Hurrying through the streets late at night, radical militia organizers tacked up a broadside on city lampposts and tavern doors that urged the restoration of prices prevailing five months before. At dawn, Philadelphians moving through the streets read words that fairly jumped off the broadside: "In the midst of money we are in poverty and exposed to want in a land of plenty. . . . Down with your prices, or down with yourselves. For by the living and eternal God, we will bring every article down to what it was last Christmas, or we will [put] down . . . those who opposed. We have turned out against the enemy and we will not be eaten up by monopolizers and forestallers." When some Philadelphians began tearing down the broadsides, militiamen collared them and roughed them up. They chased one merchant down the street, wrestled him to the ground, put him on a horse, and paraded him bareheaded around the city. Men with clubs went from store to store to "oblige" shopkeepers to lower their prices.[6]

At the end of the workday, a rowdy town meeting, gathered behind the statehouse, shouted approval of Pennsylvania militia general Daniel Roberdeau's passionate speech on behalf of the city's militiamen and poor. He attacked merchants for forming a combination to raise food prices and asserted the community's right to "set limits to evils" created by those "getting rich by sucking the blood" of ordinary people. From the meeting came an ad hoc Committee of Trade composed of middling traders, several ship captains and ship's carpenters, and members of a company of the radical City Artillery. Though they lacked legal authority, they had a long history of customary law behind them. Acting much as the citizens of Longmeadow, Massachusetts, as recounted in chapter 5, the committee set a plan to fix prices, cajole merchants and retailers to comply with them, and distribute bread and flour to the poor. Warning that the "want of flour has in all countries produced the most fatal resentments," the committee told the offending merchants that "discontents, far beyond our power to remedy," would erupt if forestalling continued. Speculators and monopolizers who avoided militia duty, they charged, could easily pay the stiff fines imposed on "non-associators" with the profits they were making. But "the middling and poor will still bear the burden, and either be totally ruined by heavy fines, or risque the starving of their families, whilst themselves are fighting the battles of those who are avariciously intent on amassing wealth by the destruction of the more virtuous part of the community." Congress chimed in, wagging its finger at offending merchants and farmers in a sharply worded report.[7]

But words could not correct the situation. Conservatives tarred the town meeting as a motley crew of "printer's devils, barber's boys, apprentice lads," and militiamen, as one later wrote, who were ignorant enough to think that the "old rags and lampblack" used to print Continental dollars could be converted "into gold."[8] But more ominous than slander was defiance. Reasoning that the Committee of Trade had no legal authority to compel reduction in prices of the commodities stored in their warehouses, merchants refused to sell their goods at controlled prices. This brought the city closer to the precipice.

Word of the Committee of Trade's plan of action brought plaudits from other parts of the country. Citizens of Albany acclaimed Philadelphians for opposing the free-trade merchants "who lately had the name of the greatest extortioners on the continent," and announced that their town and its surrounding region had "followed [Philadelphia's] example." Word arrived from Boston that merchants themselves, warning that the crowd's fury would "burst on the heads of monopolizers, as it did on the odious stampmasters" of the mid-1760s, agreed on their own schedule of price controls.[9]

Through the summer of 1779, advocates of an unrestricted market economy and supporters of a managed moral economy stared and shouted at each other over a widening chasm. The militiamen of the City Artillery, just finishing a tour of duty, marched to the statehouse and then to the College of Philadelphia on June 27 to support the price-fixing committee. A few days later they promised that "We have arms in our hands and know the use of them—and are ready and willing to support your honorable board [the price-fixing committee]—we will no longer be trampled upon." Merchants stonewalled their critics. Many of them had formed the Republican Society in March 1779 with the avowed purpose of overturning the 1776 state constitution; from this same group now came the argument that "freedom of trade, or unrestrained liberty of the subject to hold or dispose of his property as he pleases is absolutely necessary to the prosperity of every community."[10]

Contributing to the anger of Philadelphia's lower and middle orders was their belief that price control resisters were wealthy merchants and lawyers who hated the goals of revolutionary radicals, were plotting to overturn the radical constitution of 1776, and were Tories or Tory sympathizers who had welcomed the British occupation of the city from September 1777 to June 1778. Many of the upper-class Philadelphians had profited from the free-spending soldiers, in some cases married their daughters to British officers, and gaily joined in sumptuous British social events. Everyone knew how sympathy for the enemy surfaced at the Meschianza, the lavish fete staged by British officers to honor their commander, General William Howe, as he left Philadelphia in May 1778, just ahead of the British evacuation. The estate of wealthy Loyalist merchant Joseph Wharton on the southern border of the city provided the scene. British officers came to the Meschianza costumed as medieval knights, with Philadelphia ladies turned out as Turkish maidens. Life-size hand-painted dummy boards of British grenadiers decorated the regal Wharton gardens. A mock-medieval chivalric tournament amused the guests before dinner. Then twenty-four slaves in Turkish outfits served courses almost beyond count. Fireworks and dancing followed, keeping some of the celebrants away from their beds until six the next morning.[11]

The knightly splendor of the Meschianza, at which slaves were displayed conspicuously as symbols of subordination and aristocratic privilege, caused great resentment among ordinary Philadelphians and came to haunt Philadelphia's aristocracy after the British decamped. On July 4, barely two weeks after the British evacuation, a raucous crowd paraded a local prostitute through the streets overdressed in high-fashion headgear similar to that worn by Tory Philadelphia women during the British occupation. Hannah Griffitts, a young Quaker woman, scribbled in her notebook verses deploring the affair: "A shameful scene of dissipation; / The death of sense and reputation; / A deep degeneracy of nature; / A Frolick, for the lash of Satire."

In the context of rising prices and scarce household commodities, the memory of the Meschianza was all too vivid. One newspaper account reported that elderly Philadelphians could not remember "such a frequency of public entertainments and dissipation" while "fellow citizens [were] suffering every hardship . . . destitute of the necessities of life for . . . themselves and their little ones."[12] Aristocratic, purse-proud behavior, reeking of Toryism, did not really leave the city with the British army but remained behind to increase the misery of common Philadelphians.

In July 1779, at a town meeting convened to elect a new and larger price control committee, militiamen wielding clubs shouted down the wealthy merchant John Cadwalader as he rose to oppose price controls. Philadelphians then chose between two slates—one reflecting merchant interests, headed by flour merchant Robert Morris, the other drawn to reflect a cross-section of the community. The people's ticket prevailed by a vote of 2,115–281, showing clearly that the mass of Philadelphians wanted some kind of restriction on the market behavior of merchants. Yet even a few dozen determined merchants and several hundred supporters were able to hobble attempts at price control. By refusing to sell, or directing incoming shipments to land at other ports, Philadelphia's merchants crippled the effort.

Robert Morris, a wealthy merchant who was soon to be treasurer of the Continental Congress in charge of running the finances of the war, became a lightning rod for the surging debate. The argument pivoted on the extent of private property rights in a situation where the free exercise of property ran squarely athwart the public interest. Morris insisted that his freedom included the right to send his ships where and when he wanted, even laden with flour desperately needed in the city; or to withhold incoming cargoes until he decided that the moment was ripe to sell advantageously; or to sell flour to whomever he chose at whatever price he could obtain. Did private property, then, while indisputably individual in most cases, have no social nature that put limits on its use?

Morris and his merchant supporters answered that question with an emphatic "No!" Using Philadelphia's conservative newspaper, they argued that every individual should be able to "taste and enjoy the sweets of that liberty of person and property, which was highly expected under an independent government." For them, that was the promise of the war for independence. "It is a sad omen to find among the first effects of independence," wrote Pelatiah Webster, the merchants' chief essayist, "greater restraints and abridgements of natural liberty, than ever we felt under the government we have lately renounced and shaken off."[13]

The counterargument of the city's price control committee was that there "are offenses against society which are not in all cases offenses against the law." The city's ship carpenters and other artisans took this argument a step further, using the building of Morris's ships as an example. "We hold that though by the acceptance of wages we have not and cannot have any claim in the property of the vessels we built for you," they argued, "we nevertheless have—and the people of the state in general have—a right in the *service* of the vessel because it constituted a considerable part of the advantage they hoped to derive from their labors." Morris and Webster stood their ground: "Take off every restraint and limitation from our commerce. Let trade be as free as air. Let every man make the most of his goods and in his own way; and then he will be satisfied." The shipbuilders fired back: "That the property of the vessel is the immediate right of the owner, and the service of it is the right of the community collectively with the owners, is ... rationally deduced from the purpose for which all mercantile vessels are built."[14]

The argument over whether the good of the community took precedence over the profit margins of its individual members brought Philadelphians face-to-face with conflicting ideas of why they were fighting the Revolution. For the shipbuilders and many other artisans, private property was a social institution because every economic transaction had a social dimension. For the merchants, every man had a "natural liberty" to obtain prices dictated by whatever the market would bear, and this, even if it harmed the community in the short run, would benefit the people as a whole in the long run.

During the summer of 1779 the city's radical leaders faced an ideological crisis. Militiamen had looked to Thomas Young and James Cannon a few years before, but Young had died of a "virulent fever" in 1777 while serving as a surgeon in a military hospital, and Cannon had moved to South Carolina. Now they turned to General Daniel Roberdeau, the popular Quaker doctor James Hutchinson, artist-soldier Charles Willson Peale, brewer Timothy Matlack, Thomas Paine, watchmaker Owen Biddle, and clock maker David Rittenhouse for inspiration and clout. Some of these men had helped construct the radical state constitution three years before and a few of them represented Philadelphia in the legislature elected in October 1778. But faced with merchant recalcitrance on scaling back prices of foodstuffs, the radical leaders' options boiled down to several equally repugnant choices: Either admit that price controls could not work without voluntary merchant compliance, or lead the militia into an extralegal enforcement strategy.

None of the principal radical leaders left clear accounts of the tortured decision making thrust upon them in the summer of 1779. But it is clear that with merchants unwilling to yield and the legislature declining to pass a price control law, the alliance between middle-class radical leaders and their lower-class militia constituency began to unravel. In June, the Committee of Trade hedged its bets by advising the people to "exercise your industry [in] discovering concealed hoards" of foodstuffs—an attempt to needle merchants into a compliance that they had already disavowed—but "to do [put up] with some men whose subtlety is equal to their delinquency and who while they commit the offense, will artfully evade the punishment properly due thereto."[15]

More worrisome to committee members was the vociferousness of the militiamen's rhetoric. A few weeks after Robert Morris defended his free-trade position, a broadside spread around the city in late August urged the price control committee elected earlier that month to press forward. The radicals' broadside of late May had been signed "Come on Cool[l]y." But this time the radicals' broadside was signed "Come on Warmly." We will probably never know the author's name, but we know he was anything but temperate. He called "upon you all, in the name of our bleeding country, to rouse up as a lion out of his den, and make those beasts of prey, to humble and prove by this day's conduct, that any person whatever, though puffed like a toad . . . shall dare to violate the least resolve of our committee, it were better for him, that a millstone was fastened to his neck, and he cast into the depth of the sea, or that he had never been born."[16]

With the gauntlet thrown down by those socially beneath them, the middle-class radical leaders retreated. The Committee of Trade dissolved itself on September 24, 1779, in effect raising a white flag of truce to the merchants. Charles Willson Peale lay low and even Tom Paine retreated from the vanguard position he had occupied since writing *Common Sense*. If radicals such as Peale and Paine lost the fire in their bellies, the militiamen did not. Two days after the Committee of Trade disbanded in late September, militiamen met on the city's common and reconstituted the Committee of Privates. They tried to rebuild the cross-class alliance that had served them well in the past. But Peale, James Hutchinson, and two others they summoned to support them refused to attend. It was a sharp blow to the rank-and-file militiamen, though most of their elected junior officers stood with them. Thus constituted, they moved forward to accomplish in the streets what they could not achieve in the legislative hall.

On October 4, 1779, handbills appeared on Philadelphia's streets exhorting militiamen "to drive from the city all disaffected persons [Tories] and those who supported them." The handbill named offending monopolizing and engrossing merchants, including the prominent Quaker John Drinker, and urged that the chief offenders be "put on the prison ship to be sent to New York," which the British still controlled. Gathering at a tavern on the city's edge, the militiamen mustered and sallied forth to do battle with the principal British-leaning Philadelphians whose free-market behavior was pinching their lives intolerably. If the Committee of Trade or the legislature would not protect the most vulnerable members of the community in the face of "a few overbearing merchants, a swarm of monopolizers and speculators, [and] an infernal gang of Tories," then the poor would protect themselves.[17]

Why did Philadelphia's women not stand forth at this critical juncture as they did in Boston to parade merchant Thomas Boylston around the city in a cart and confiscate the coffee he had engrossed? There is no good answer, though one can speculate that their husbands, brothers, and sons in the militia promised to obtain justice themselves. Indeed, that is what happened. Seizing four detested merchants—John Drinker, Thomas Story, Buckridge Sims, and Matthew Johns—the militiamen paraded them around the city with a drum beating "The Rogue's March." Then they prodded them along toward the large house of James Wilson, a leading conservative lawyer, vigorous opponent of price controls, and defender of two Tories executed a year before. Ritual humiliation was the purpose of this forced march. Cooler heads tried to avert a confrontation; but Wilson, fearing that he was slated for a trip to New York on the prison ship, barricaded his house with armed friends, including Robert Morris. Here they prepared for the militiamen, who were determined, according to one of their leaders, a poor carpenter, "to support the constitution, the laws, and the Committee of Trade."[18]

With bayonets fixed on their muskets, the militiamen marched by Wilson's house with their four human trophies. Then shots rang out, with conflicting accounts of who fired first. In the next ten minutes, militiamen of the artillery company rolled a cannon into position to fire on the house and tried to batter down the doors with iron bars and large hammers. From inside, Wilson's friends fired on the militiamen, and hand-to-hand fighting broke out as some militiamen poured into the house. In what became known as the Fort Wilson Riot, five were killed and fourteen wounded at Third and Walnut streets. "Poor Pennsylvania has become the most miserable spot under the surface of the globe," lamented Benjamin Rush. "Our streets have been stained already with fraternal blood—a sad prelude we fear of the future mischiefs our constitution will bring upon us."[19]

It was not the constitution that caused the Fort Wilson bloodshed, and it was not a riot. Rather, it was an organized, purposeful confrontation, as one militia leader put it, of "the laboring part of the city [that] had become desperate from the high prices of the necessities of life." "They call it a democracy," Rush anguished, "a mobocracy in my opinion would be more proper." Members of the Continental Congress in Philadelphia saw the bloody confrontation more realistically. A Delaware delegate wrote home: "God help us—terrible times. . . . The poor [are] starving here and rise for redress. Many flying the city for fear of vengeance."[20]

Trying to restore order after the bloody confrontation, Pennsylvania's Supreme Executive Council president Joseph Reed called for all attackers to surrender to the sheriff and submit to prosecution. After the sheriff arrested twenty-seven militiamen, continued agitation convinced authorities to release and pardon them, hoping this would heal the wounds. At the same time, the state assembly authorized distribution of flour to Philadelphia's poor with special attention paid to militiamen families. Three weeks after the bloodshed, President Reed issued a broadside warning merchants that without self-restraint, there could be no peace: Do not expect to "live in ease, plenty, and safety, while such a body of your fellow citizens were destitute of all the necessaries of life."[21]

Bitterness over the underlying causes of the incident continued. In the election of November 1, 1779, just four weeks after the Fort Wilson bloodshed, radicals won nearly every seat in the legislature, showing the widespread sympathy for the plight of the poor. But that did not bring price control legislation. Pennsylvania lawmakers continued to look to Congress to solve the problem. In April 1780, radicals plastered the city with a broadside urging militiamen to deliberate the still-rising prices and unequal militia obligations—the old sources of discontent. "We are determined to be free," the broadside announced, and its postscript warned that anyone tearing it down would experience "the just resentment of an injured people." Fearing another Fort Wilson, President Reed issued a proclamation forbidding the militiamen to assemble or speak out publicly and offered a one-thousand-pound reward for the identity of the author or printer. Such an enormous amount, equivalent to an urban worker's income for several years, brought no informant forward, indicating the solidarity of the dispossessed. Congress finally acted in the spring of 1780, drastically devaluing the Continental dollar and issuing new bills, thus initiating fiscal reform.[22]

Philadelphia's radicals voiced their ire one more time in the fall of 1780, turning their wrath on Benedict Arnold and his Philadelphia-born aristocratic wife. The gallant, thirty-eight-year-old Arnold had been the military commander of Philadelphia after the British decamped in June 1778, and had charmed the beautiful nineteen-year-old Peggy Shippen, daughter of one of the city's wealthiest merchants and a distinctly Tory-leaning member of the city's conservatives, into marriage. One year after the Fort Wilson carnage, Arnold's treasonous plot to deliver West Point to the British had been discovered. A day after the news broke, the crowd swung into action. Erecting a life-size papier-mâché effigy of Arnold, they paraded it through the streets in a horse-drawn cart with fifes and drums providing "The Rogue's March." The procession culminated with a bonfire, where the crowd celebrated the unceremonious burning of Arnold's effigy. This was patriotic revelry but also a reminder to the city's aristocratic elite, from which Arnold had drawn his main associates for the lavish parties he hosted in 1778–79, of ordinary Philadelphians' ownership of the streets.[23]

New Choices for African Americans

"Altho our skins are different in color, from those whom we serve, yet reason and revelation join to declare that we are the creatures of that God, who made of one blood, and kindred, all the nations of the earth. . . . We are

Dressed in a red coat for Loyalism, with two faces symbolizing his duplicity, Benedict Arnold is advised by a huge black devil shaking a purse of money at the traitor. One conservative Quaker dismissed the boisterous procession as "a frolick of the lowest sort of people,"* though Charles Willson Peale, the radical leader and creator of this drawing, claimed it was led by mounted "gentlemen, Continental Army officers," as well as "a guard of the City Infantry."

endowed with the same faculties with our masters, and there is nothing that leads us to a belief or suspicion that we are any more obliged to serve them than they us. . . . We can never be convinced that we were made to be slaves. . . . Is it consistent with the present claims of the United States to hold so many thousands of the race of Adam, our common father, in perpetual slavery? Can human nature endure the shocking idea?" These were the words of the enslaved Prime and Prince, on "behalf of themselves and other petitioners" in the towns of Fairfield and Stratford, Connecticut, on May 11, 1779, in a plea to the wartime state legislature. "Can your honors any longer suffer this great evil to prevail under your government? . . . We ask for nothing but what we are fully persuaded is ours to claim."[24]

Eight weeks later, a British squadron, under William Tryon, no longer royal governor of New York but now organizer of New York Loyalists and commander of the British Seventieth Foot, pummeled Connecticut towns along Long Island Sound. New Haven first felt the torch. Then at Fairfield

---

*Gary B. Nash, *First City: Philadelphia and the Forging of Historical Memory* (Philadelphia: University of Pennsylvania Press, 2002), 98–100.

the Connecticut patriots lost ninety-seven homes, sixty-seven barns, forty-eight stores, three churches, two schools, and the town jail to British destroyers. The torching continued at Norwalk. In all three towns, slaves fled to the British, seizing their freedom as the fires burned. Some of the towns' white citizens also joined the British—men and their families who had never been comfortable with the American claim to independence. In some cases, they were unable to drag their slaves with them as they sought refuge with the king's banner. Such was the case of Pomp, slave of Jeremiah Leaming of Norwalk. While the British troops razed Norwalk and his master joined them, Pomp fled. Nine days later, still technically part of Leaming's property forfeited to the state, he petitioned the Connecticut legislature for his freedom.[25]

Prime, Prince, and Pomp were among the thousands of slaves who surveyed the chaotic wartime landscape, calculated the odds, and struck out to gain their freedom as the Revolution entered its fifth year in 1779. By this time, the British had shifted the war south. Stalemated in the North, their strategists hoped to win the dragged-out war by delivering blows in South Carolina and Georgia, where Loyalists were as numerous as patriots, and then drive north to smash Washington's army. For northern slaves, except those who could claim freedom under English protection in the New York City area, where the redcoats still maintained their hold, this was a blow. But just as this escape hatch closed, new ones opened up. Some northern states took steps to abolish slavery, either at a stroke or gradually, and slave masters, without legislative dictate, slowly began to grant freedom to their bondmen and bondwomen.

Pennsylvania again earned its title as the Keystone State, this time as the abolitionist vanguard. The constitutional convention of 1776 had sidestepped the controversial issue, though their Declaration of Rights included the maxim "that all men are born equally free and independent, and that they have natural, inherent, and unalienable rights"—words much referred to thereafter by those pursuing abolition. In May 1778, just before the British withdrew from Philadelphia after occupying the city for eight months, the legislature moved to implement the Declaration of Rights. Legislative moves to abolish slavery began in 1779, when Chester County's radical Committee of Correspondence petitioned the legislature to pass a gradual abolition act. For slaves in northern states, word of attempts in Pennsylvania to abolish slavery came as the biblical balm of Gilead.

It was not the Quakers who took the lead in fashioning a gradual abolition bill but an immigrant Presbyterian. George Bryan had established himself as a small merchant in the 1750s after arriving in Philadelphia from Ireland. By 1770, he was playing a leading role in the radical Scots-Irish Presbyterian bloc that controlled state politics during the Revolution. Becoming acting president of the Supreme Executive Council in 1778, Bryan urged the legislature to consider an abolition act. Absorbed with the price control crisis and other issues, the lawmakers took no action. But Bryan kept the matter alive, reminding the legislature in November 1778 that "no period seems more happy for the attempt than the present as the number [of slaves] has been much reduced by the practices and plunder of our late invaders"—an oblique reference to the flight of hundreds of slaves to the occupying British army. Slavery was "the opprobrium of America," he chided the legislators; it astonished Europeans "to see a people eager for liberty holding Negroes in bondage."[26]

Rather than waiting for the legislature to write a bill, Bryan offered one of his own. He did not propose to liberate those already enslaved, but to promise freedom to those born of slave women. When the legislators took no action, the executive council prodded them again in February 1779, arguing that slavery was "disgraceful to any people, and more especially to those who have been contending in the great cause of liberty themselves." Offering something akin to immortality, the council declared that "honored will that state be in the annals of history, which shall first abolish this violation of the rights of mankind."

Though beset by the inflation and price crisis, the legislature drafted its own law in mid-1779 and ordered it printed for public discussion. There are many claimants for authorship of the bill, with Thomas Paine, Benjamin Franklin, Quaker lawyer William Lewis, and others receiving credit. Bryan's tombstone gives him the honor, though his role was mostly in shepherding the bill through the legislature. The poignant preamble contained language suggesting that Anthony Benezet was involved. In a pointed history lesson, the preamble called attention to the tragic retrogression of human progress in the New World, where "the practice of domestic slavery, so highly detrimental to morality, industry, and the arts, has been, in the instance of the natives of Africa and their descendants, in modern ages revived among Christians." Thus America had been "made the scene of his new invasion of the rights of mankind after the spirit of Christianity had abolished it from the greater part of Europe."

The specifics that followed have been celebrated in the history of antislavery because this was the first time in America, or anywhere else, that an elected political body abolished slavery. But the abolition act of 1780 was not so altruistic as often portrayed. From the beginning, not one legislator proposed freeing a single slave, for this would raise treacherous problems regarding compensation for slave owners at a time of economic derangement. The bill called only for emancipating children born to slave women after the act took effect, and it required these children to serve, in the manner of indentured servants, until age eighteen if they were female and twenty-one if male. The law exempted congressmen and foreign ministers entering Pennsylvania with slaves, but any other person arriving with slaves must release them within six months, though they could be indentured until age twenty-eight if a minor or for seven years if an adult. The bill also banned slave importations and repealed the slave code in effect since 1726, while retaining the former legal prohibition of racially mixed marriages and the old practice of binding out free black people to servitude if they were unable to maintain themselves.

Held up for public discussion, the bill attracted plenty of opposition, particularly from nonslaveholding Germans from Lutheran and Reformed backgrounds, who dominated the agricultural hinterland in a wide arc sweeping west and north of Philadelphia. Equally opposed were slaveholding Scots and Scots-Irish Presbyterians west and south of Philadelphia. In the face of considerable opposition, the legislature took no final action on the bill, carrying it over to the next legislative session of late 1779.

The new legislature, one of the most radical ever elected in eighteenth-century America, took up the bill again, made an important concession to slave owners, and then passed it in revised form. Elected to the legislature from Philadelphia, George Bryan chaired the committee to redraft the bill. Though the language of the preamble spoke of the "sorrow of those who have lived in undeserved bondage," the new bill provided that all children born after the law took effect would serve for twenty-eight years. Compared to the initial draft, this added ten years to the term for girls and seven to that for boys in the prime of their lives. Thus, the first Pennsylvania slave born after the law took effect on January 1, 1780, would not have walked in freedom until 1808. Given the life expectancy of laboring people—one commentator, signing his name as "Phileleutheros," believed that most people "used to hard labor without doors begin to fail soon after thirty"—this provision offered Pennsylvania slave owners what historians Stanley Engerman and

Robert Fogel have called "the opportunity to engage in philanthropy at bargain prices."[27]

While making this concession to slave owners, the revised abolition bill extended a hand to former slaves and those with white spouses. The clause for binding out free African Americans if they could not maintain themselves was dropped and so was the ban on interracial marriage. Placed again before the public, the bill sparked another spirited debate, some arguing that it was a halfway measure that left thousands of slaves with little hope for the future, while others argued against any form of abolition as an intrusion on property rights. Conducted in the same month of the Fort Wilson bloodshed, it is remarkable that the debate occurred at all. Anthony Benezet visited every member of the legislature asking for support of the bill, and George Bryan published a set of anonymous newspaper articles appealing to religion, morality, and patriotism. By a vote of 34–21, the bill passed the third reading on March 1, 1780.

Pennsylvania's gradual abolition act of 1780 has drawn effusive praise as exemplifying the spirit of enlightened reform in the revolutionary era. The first historian of the Pennsylvania Abolition Society (PAS), writing in 1847, called it a law "which for justice, humanity, and philanthropy, has seldom been equaled, and which raised the State of Pennsylvania to a high position amongst the nations of the earth."[28] With historical hindsight, less enthusiasm is warranted. It was, in fact, the most restrictive of the five gradual abolition laws enacted by the northern states between 1780 and 1804, mostly because of the long service—twenty-eight years—required of any child born to a slave after the law took effect. If the law was a death sentence for slavery, it was a sentence with a long grace period for slave owners. In fact, it was designed to avoid an abrupt end to slavery and to accomplish abolition at little cost to those who claimed ownership over other human beings. Legislators had found a way to satisfy those who saw slavery as inconsistent with the principles undergirding the revolutionary struggle while touching nobody's chattel property and depriving them of future human property only on a nearly cost-free basis.

The law drew sharp criticism from thoroughgoing abolitionists. New Jersey Quaker John Cooper was far from satisfied. "If we keep our present slaves in bondage and only enact laws that their posterity shall be free," he wrote in a newspaper circulating in Philadelphia, "we save that part of our tyranny and gain of oppression, which to us, the present generation, is of the most value." Pennsylvanians were telling their slaves that "we will not do justice unto you, but our posterity shall do justice unto your posterity." A few years later, the French reformer Brissot de Warville reached the same conclusion. Why did the legislature not "extend at least the hopes of freedom to those who were slaves at the time of the passing of the . . . act?" he asked. He received the answer that slaves were property "and all property is sacred." Yet what is property "founded on robbery and plunder?" retorted the Frenchman. At the least, the legislators should have limited slavery "to a certain number of years, in order to give at least the cheap consolation of hope," or given the slave the "right of purchasing his freedom."[29]

Yet Pennsylvania had taken an important step that neighboring New Jersey and New York would not take for many years. The stage had been set for further action. The language of the law had condemned slavery, admitting that it deprived African Americans of "common blessings that they were by nature entitled to." Furthermore, it expressed a belief in the unitary nature of humankind—a "universal civilization." "It is not for us to enquire why, in the creation of mankind," the preamble stated, "the inhabitants of the several parts of the world were distinguished by a difference in feature or complexion. It is sufficient to know that all are the work of an Almighty Hand . . . who placed them in their various situations [and] hath extended equally his care and protection to all."[30]

Watered down though it was, the 1780 abolition act continued to draw fire from antiabolitionists. Some slave owners refused to register their slaves, as the law required, and they raged against those slaves who had fled to claim their freedom, as guaranteed in the law, when their masters refused to register them. Opposition to the law became a factor in the political revolt of October 1780 that swept 60 percent of the previous Pennsylvania assemblymen from their seats and replaced them with more conservative representatives. This led to a hard-fought battle to save the partial abolitionist victory in the face of repeal efforts. A full-scale defense of slavery appeared in the *Pennsylvania Journal* early in 1781, arguing that the Bible justified slavery and denying that "all mankind are born alike free." Free black Philadelphians, engaging in one of their first political acts, petitioned the legislature to resist rearguard attacks on the abolition act and penned newspaper appeals. Writing in *Freedom's Journal*, Cato wrote that "to make a law to hang us all would be merciful, when compared to this [proposed] law for many of our masters would treat us with unheard of barbarity, for daring to take advantage (as we have done) of the law made in our favor." Another group of free African Americans in Philadelphia, pointing to the phrase that slaves had "lived in undeserved bondage," declared their confidence that "this honorable house, possessed of such sentiments of humanity and benevolence," would not pass an act to reenslave those who had gained their freedom. In a close vote of 27 to 21, the legislature defeated an attempt to dismantle the first legislative action against slavery in the new nation. Now the law gained unquestioned acceptance in the state.[31]

The most dedicated antislavery advocates held to the belief that a half victory was insufficient because immorality and un-Christian behavior should not be half-corrected. Anthony Benezet carried the banner forward even when others rested, content with the progress already made. He kept peppering the public with appeals to end slavery and the slave trade unequivocally. In June 1782, the *Pennsylvania Evening Post* published his letter to Abbe Raynal, the aristocratic French reformer, calling for an abolition of slavery, along with Raynal's approving reply. Two months later, Benezet's moving plea calling for the end of "the galling chains, the cruel stripes, the dying groan" of slavery lest America lose its soul appeared in the *Pennsylvania Packet*. But by now, most white Pennsylvanians were content to rest on their laurels, and death would soon remove Benezet from the scene.

South of Pennsylvania, some 400,000 slaves looked not to southern legislatures for freedom but to the British army. From New Year's Day in 1779, when the British southern campaign began with the capture of Savannah, Georgia, until the final capitulation at Yorktown in October 1781, African Americans struggled to take advantage of the massive tearing of the social fabric in the South. With British forces, Loyalist Americans, and patriot Americans engaged in the ugliest, bloodiest, and most destructive warfare of the Revolution, opportunity beckoned for slaves as never before in the long history of North American bondage.

British strategists selected Georgia as the base from which the southern states could be severed from the North because it was brimming with Loyalist Americans. If this separation was successful, they believed, American resistance would crumble. By land and sea attack from East Florida, the British required only a month to gain control of Georgia. For 15,000 slaves, this victory had little to offer, for most of them were the property of white Loyalists, whom the British could not afford to violate. Slaves who belonged to white patriots had a better chance at freedom, but a mass exodus of patriots fleeing the British carried most of them out of the state. William Moultrie, an American officer, described "the poor women and children, and negroes of Georgia, many thousands of whom I saw. . . , traveling to they knew not where."[32]

Yet in this chaotic situation, slaves imagined for a brief moment that the desperation of Georgia and South Carolina patriots might work to their advantage. Hope arose out of one of the boldest steps of the entire war taken by Congress—one that had the promise of riveting together the War of Independence with the revolution to reform America. In March 1779 (and again in December), considering the pillaging and plundering British sweeping across the Georgia border into South Carolina, Congress urged the two southernmost states to raise "three thousand able-bodied negroes" to help repulse the British. Congress promised to compensate masters for each released slave. The slaves themselves would receive no enlistment bounty or pay; but if they served "well and faithfully" and survived the war, they would receive their freedom and fifty dollars each. Not for another eighty years would the nation's government again propose the military recruitment of slaves and underwrite their manumission.[33]

Eager to supervise the recruitment was the twenty-five-year-old South Carolinian John Laurens, scion of one of the colony's wealthiest and most politically powerful figures, aide-de-camp to George Washington, and a visionary reformer who hoped that American independence would eventually break the chains of half a million slaves. Laurens knew firsthand that black men would fight bravely, for he saw them in the thick of battle at Newport in August 1778, where the contingent Laurens led fought almost alongside Rhode Island's First Regiment, mostly composed of black men. A few months after this, Laurens had urged a compensated emancipation of slaves who would promise to fight against the British in all-black regiments. This would reward "those who are unjustly deprived of the rights of mankind." New Hampshire's William Whipple, delegate to the Continental Congress, agreed with Laurens that if the plan was now implemented, "it will produce the emancipation of a number of those wretches and lay a foundation for the abolition of slavery in America." Alexander Hamilton and many others in Washington's military family circle endorsed the plan. So did Henry Laurens, John Laurens's father and president of the Continental Congress from November 1777 to December 1778. Both father and son knew that white soldiers, even militiamen, were nearly unrecruitable for action against the British because they were "at home to prevent insurrections among the Negroes and prevent the desertion of them to the enemy," as Daniel Huger, South Carolina delegate to the Continental Congress, reminded everyone.[34]

Washington withheld support of this astonishing idea of enlisting slaves with a promise of freedom, a notion heretofore unthinkable because it conjured up the specter of black men under arms who would become the vanguard of an uncontrollable liberation movement. Thinking of his own slaves, who at the moment he was considering selling, Washington feared that enlisting slaves would "render slavery more irksome to those who remain in it." Writing directly to John Laurens, he continued: "[M]ost of the good and evil things of this life are judged of by comparison; and I fear a comparison in this case will be productive of much discontent of those who are held in servitude."[35]

It is possible that Washington's support of the plan would have convinced South Carolina and Georgia's planter-politicians to accept it, which would have changed the entire character of the American Revolution. This was unlikely because the horror at the prospect of black men under arms was real. Yet Washington's enormous prestige has been noted repeatedly by historians, and it is one of the staples of the "great man" theory of history that such a figure often triggers epic historical turning points. Absent Washington's support, Congress's proposal "was received with great resentment," huffed Christopher Gadsden of South Carolina, "as a very dangerous and impolitic step." South Carolina's council was so indignant that it considered sending a flag of truce to British general Augustine Prevost, when it appeared that the city would be overwhelmed or beaten down with a siege. Under the white flag, South Carolinians would quit the war for independence to preserve their dependence on slavery. Writing her history of the American Revolution after the war, Mercy Otis Warren condemned the Carolinians' surrender offer as "the only instance in America of an offer made so derogatory to the honor of the nation."[36]

Amidst great confusion and wholesale violence, as the British army swept into South Carolina, the soft underbelly of the South, in spring 1779, thousands of slaves fled. Some sought refuge in the woods and swamps; others took to roads knowing not where they might find shelter; others tried to reach British units, hoping that Dunmore's Proclamation, issued hundreds of miles to the north more than three years ago, would cover them. Some carried stolen arms, others fled on stolen horses. Many women with small children were among them. Henry Laurens thought one-third of the 80,000 South Carolina slaves made a break for freedom. Always, their flight was perilous. Patriot militia units often intercepted them and returned them to their masters, if the masters were on the American side. Others biding their time with Loyalist masters found themselves seized by patriot units and claimed as booty. In one case, patriot raiders fell on the lightly protected plantation of the royal lieutenant governor John Graham outside Savannah and carried off 130 slaves along with all of his horses. Transferred from a Loyalist master to a patriot master, many of them fled and ended up as laborers in the British army, where they hauled provisions, cleared roads, and dug latrines. A few who knew the terrain served as scouts, spies, and pilots. In some cases, particularly in the unsuccessful American attempt to recapture Savannah in September and October of 1779, the British gave slaves who had reached their lines their freedom and formed them into companies of armed black volunteers. Some of them faced other armed blacks when several hundred French-speaking freedmen from Saint Domingue arrived with a French fleet to support the American attempt to recapture Savannah. In a further attempt to regain the city in April 1780, American forces engaged with about four hundred former slaves under British arms.[37]

In the siege of Charleston in May 1780, slaves played a role on both sides of the battle. Those captured by the British as they approached the city were equipped with shovels and axes to prepare for the siege. Likewise, inside Charleston, the slaves of American patriots did most of the fortification building, though they proved to be too few in number. John Laurens, trying to defend the city, lamented the thin forces available to him—"far too few for defending works [fortifications] of nearly three miles in circumference ... and many of the Continental troops half naked."[38] Laurens himself fell prisoner to the British, and was released in a prisoner exchange six months later.

In what many historians regard as the most ignominious defeat of the war, the American surrender on May 11, 1780, led the English command to make a decision that shaped the fate of thousands of South Carolina slaves. Attempting to pacify the sprawling South Carolina interior, Sir Henry Clinton moved "to use slaves as weapons against their masters." Even before leaving Philipsburg, New York, to lead the British forces south by sea in mid-1779, Clinton implemented this strategy by issuing a proclamation pledging that all slaves *seized* from American rebels would be sold for the benefit of British combatants but that all slaves *fleeing* the American rebels would be accepted into British military service with "full security to follow within these lines any occupation which he shall think proper."[39] Like Dunmore's Proclamation, the Philipsburg Proclamation was more an announcement of military strategy than a pronouncement of abolitionist principles. Its fourfold purpose was to weaken the southern rebels by bleeding off their main labor source, to bulk up British manpower, to maintain morale among British officers by awarding them captured slaves, and to hold the allegiance of white southern Loyalists by respecting their slave property. It differed from Dunmore's Proclamation in one crucial respect: Slaves seized from American rebels would not be given freedom.

As mentioned above, the British were careful not to offend the Loyalist support they so badly needed. When the fleeing slaves of southern Loyalists reached their lines, British commanders regularly returned them to their owners as soon as they discovered the slaves' identities. In many cases, they sold slaves captured from patriot masters back to the Americans in order to purchase supplies for the army with no qualms of conscience.

Far from demoralizing white patriots in South Carolina, the Philipsburg Proclamation further aroused them. It also plunged the South into what many historians regard as the fiercest, most savage phase of the American Revolution, in which far more deaths occurred through fratricidal combat than through British-American combat. Historian Sylvia Frey calls this the "triagonal war" among white patriots of the Lower South, the British and their loyal followers, and the slaves. With the triumphant British threatening to seize their slaves unless they renounced their allegiance to the American cause, thousands of patriot planters, including many of the former leaders of the American cause, took an oath of fealty to England's king in order to keep their slaves. The idea of independence had its limits.[40]

For slaves, the massive British military presence presented the opportunity of a lifetime. But they did not flee en masse to the British. Many feared reprisals of their kinfolk if they deserted, and the uncertainty about what fate awaited them if they reached British lines must have gnawed at many. Yet large numbers took their chances on the freedom that the Philipsburg Proclamation promised. Some fled alone, some in pairs, some in families and in large groups. Old Ross, a fifty-six-year-old Ibo woman, led two of her daughters, a son-in-law, a son, a granddaughter, and four nonfamily members to the British lines.[41] In another case, sixteen slaves fled the plantation of Andrew Lord, a Charleston slave merchant. Rawlin Lowndes, one of South

Carolina's wealthiest slave owners, lost thirty-four slaves in March 1780, and most of his neighbors in the area also lost many slaves. David George, a former slave who later became a Baptist missionary in Sierra Leone, recalled in his autobiographical account how his master fled his plantation as the British approached, leaving the slaves to fend for themselves. George, his wife, two children, and about fifty other "of my master's people" walked "about twenty miles . . . [to] where the King's forces were." Boston King, another South Carolina slave, who met up with David George in Nova Scotia after the war, remembered how he fled to the British after his master promised a severe beating.[42]

Many slaves who reached the British lines found opportunities to practice the crafts they learned on American plantations. Wheelwrights, carpenters, blacksmiths, wagon builders, sawyers, and butchers served the British in camp and in the field. British officers put black women to work making cartridges for muskets and serving as nurses in field hospitals. Hundreds of other fleeing or captured slaves were assigned to British officers in a ranked system where senior officers had four to six semiservile attendants, noncommissioned officers had at least one attendant, and nearly every soldier had a black carrier who lugged provisions and equipment. A Hessian officer described how even white women accompanying British officers had their black attendants.[43] The wife of David George served as washerwoman for one Loyalist company of troops, while Boston King served one stint as the body servant of a British officer.

Black refugees served the British most importantly as organized foraging parties. When supplies ran low, the king's troops lived off the countryside, and slaves knew the terrain much better than the British. By one report, Cornwallis's army, on its march north through North Carolina in the spring of 1780, sent two thousand black foragers afield to seize anything edible. One British officer may have exaggerated the case in claiming that "Negroes who flock to the conquerors . . . do ten thousand times more mischief than the whole army put together"; but it is doubtless that the thousands who took refuge with the British added significantly to the British war machine.[44]

Near the end of the war, the British took a step they had previously employed sparingly—militarizing the black refugees. Preparing to evacuate Charleston, they formed black military units, usually led by white officers but occasionally with black captains. About seven hundred strong, the Black Dragoons, as they were called, battled white South Carolinians in the last stages of the war in early 1782. Though they inflicted limited damage on the rebel South Carolinians, they raised the possibility that the sight of armed black men would encourage the patriots' slaves to think of themselves in the same way.

In the latter stages of the war, slaves became the victims of a free-for-all among American soldiers turned bounty hunters. Desperate for recruits by 1781, American general Thomas Sumter offered "one grown negro" to every militiaman who would promise to serve for ten months and "three large and one small negro" to officers. Civil authorities followed suit in trying to raise recruits for Washington's Continental army. Attempting to raise a modest 1,300 men in early 1782, South Carolina's legislature promised even the poorest white enlistee a slave between the ages of ten and forty confiscated from Loyalist estates. Used as "wartime money," as historian Benjamin Quarles puts it, slaves found themselves commodified even more than in peacetime.[45]

Such promises of a slave bonus were not easy to keep because many Loyalists had fled with their best slaves, leaving behind only the infirm and aged. So the slave-bonus system limped along with both militia and Continental army quartermasters always in arrears, just as they were in salary payments. Colonel William Hill, for example, dunned the state government for seventy-three large and three and a half small Negroes due his regiment. Colonel Wade Hampton's men were in arrears by ninety-three and three-quarters grown slaves and "three quarters of a small Negro." For a decade after the war, attempts to indemnify men shorted their slave bonus in 1781–82 clogged the courts.[46] South Carolina's patriots and Loyalists fought for lofty principles, but they battled even more for slave property.

We will never know the fate of thousands of slaves who, through several years of fratricidal war in the Lower South, were seized as war booty by one side or the other. How many slaves reached the British lines cannot be determined with precision. Writing from firsthand experience in the war, South Carolina's David Ramsay believed that when the British first invaded the state in the spring of 1779, fleeing slaves "collected in great crowds, near the royal army," which he estimated at three thousand, almost as large as the British army itself.[47] Ramsay's judgment was that by the end of the war some 20,000 (of about 80,000) slaves in South Carolina had reached the British lines. A Pennsylvanian transplanted to South Carolina, Ramsay welcomed this because he hoped it would impel the Carolinians to stop their folly of "accumulating negroes" and turn instead to "encouraging the settlement of poor white people." King George III, he wrote Benjamin Rush in Philadelphia sardonically, "for once in his life is promoting the grand cause of American liberty and republicanism ... by diminishing the number of slaves."[48] The most careful modern historian of black revolutionary experience in the South agrees that slaves striking out for freedom "streamed in like a tidal flood, their sheer numbers overwhelming the [British] army." Whatever the number, it is certain that a great many of them, probably a majority, died, particularly after smallpox broke out in Charleston in November 1779 and raged through the countryside, laying waste to the uninoculated, both black and white.[49]

The hopes of thousands of slaves for a better future by fleeing to the British were shattered by rampant disease that struck the British army recurrently during the southern campaign of 1779–81. Typhus, dysentery, smallpox, and typhoid, familiar camp fevers, killed white and black combatants alike in the makeshift camps. But in dire circumstances, the British also abandoned sick ex-slaves, consigning them to almost certain death. This occurred in 1779 when General Augustine Prevost's army retreated down the Georgia offshore islands. Without medical attention and sufficient rations, hundreds of fever-stricken former slaves were left to die on Otter Island. A year later, the most severe smallpox epidemic in seventeen years swept through South Carolina, cutting down thousands of black refugees in the British camps. When the British thrust pox-infected blacks out of their camps in an effort to prevent the grim disease from spreading, hundreds died and were left unburied in wooded areas. Boston King was one of those sent a mile from Charleston and left to fend for himself.

Some fifteen to twenty thousand slaves in South Carolina responded to the half promise of freedom hinted at in the Philipsburg Proclamation, testimony to the slaves' willingness to gamble on even the *possibility* of emancipation. Certain that they and their children would never see freedom, unlikely odds often seemed better than none. But only a fraction of the many thousands who fled achieved full liberty. When British military strategists decided to hold only Savannah and Charleston and strike north through North Carolina to Virginia in August 1780, some four to five thousand black males and females of all ages trudged behind the baggage train of Lord Cornwallis to meet an uncertain fate. Thousands of others remained, to be evacuated from Savannah and Charleston in July 1782. Most of them sailed away as slaves, thousands of them with their white Loyalist masters and thousands more as the contraband property of British officers. Most landed ashore in East Florida and Jamaica, once again to toil as field laborers. Only a small minority—perhaps a thousand or so—went as free men and women to pursue lives largely hidden to historians to this very day.[50]

For about 230,000 slaves in Virginia (nearly half of all North American slaves), five years had passed since Lord Dunmore had issued his famous freedom proclamation in late 1775, inspiring hundreds of bondpeople to flee to his banner. But when the war unfolded in other regions, not to return to Virginia until 1780, they lost the chance to cash in on Dunmore's offer. British naval forces intermittently conducted spoiling operations along the shores of the Chesapeake Bay from 1777 to 1780, stirring the hopes of slaves for freedom. However, only in small numbers could they escape their masters and commandeer small craft to reach the British vessels.

The prospects for slaves changed radically when British schooners and barges began maneuvering up the rivers flowing into the Chesapeake in November 1780. "Slaves flock[ed] to them from every quarter" as the British swept ashore to burn houses and barns, reported a local planter. This was the opportunity Virginia slaves had been waiting for since 1775. Whereas Governor Dunmore had fled Williamsburg to operate from a royal ship at Norfolk, which made it possible only for slaves in a small geographical area to reach his forces, the rampaging British now operated over a vast part of tidewater Virginia and westward into Virginia's hilly interior. This opened the way for massive slave defections, as became apparent in January 1781 when Benedict Arnold's squadron, with 1,600 men, made it all the way up the James River to Richmond. Coming ashore, they plundered the region and opened the gates for fleeing slaves. James Madison's father wrote him that "families within the sphere of his [Arnold's] action have suffered greatly. Some have lost 40, others 30, and one a considerable part of their slaves." In March 1781, Arnold continued his forays in the James River area, and once again, reported Robert Honyman, a Hanover County physician, slaves "flocked to the enemy from all quarters, even from very remote parts." Many planters lost from thirty to seventy slaves, along with cattle, horses, and sheep.[51]

British raids up the Potomac River in April 1781 brought more new opportunities for Virginia slaves. Robert Carter, one of the largest planters of the area, lost thirty of his unresisting slaves when a British warship landed at his Cole's Point plantation. Sailing to the landing of Washington's Mount Vernon plantation, the British sloop *Savage* carried off fourteen enslaved men and three women. In the face of this onslaught, hundreds of tidewater planters loaded their most valuable possessions in wagons and headed for the piedmont region with slaves in tow, trying to move beyond the reach of the British forces. Jefferson, wartime governor of Virginia, was not spared. In Goochland County, Cornwallis made his headquarters at Jefferson's Elk Hill plantation, and for ten days his troops, accompanied by escaped slave foragers, destroyed barns and rustled cattle, sheep, hogs, and horses. When they left, Black Sall, three of her children, and fifteen more of Jefferson's slaves joined the British. Twelve others fled from his Cumberland County plantation. When Cornwallis dispatched Banastre Tarleton's dragoons to capture Jefferson and members of the Virginia legislature who had retreated to Charlottesville, Jefferson escaped with his family, but four of his Monticello slaves, including Old Jenny, decamped with the British. Richard Henry Lee counted the loss of slaves on other plantations: forty-five from the plantation of his brother William Lee, all of the slaves of Richard Taliaferro and Edward Travis, and all but one slave of John Paradise. Thomas Nelson, Jefferson's successor as governor of Virginia, lost all but eighty to one hundred of his seven hundred slaves, according to Ludwig von Closen, a German officer who served with French troops. "This is the general case of all those who were near the enemy," Lee wrote to his brother in July 1781. Hessian officer Johann Ewald believed "well over four thousand Negroes of both sexes and all ages" were now part of Cornwallis's army.[52]

Virginia's stricken plantation owners liked to think that the British compelled their slaves to abandon them. "Whenever they had an opportunity, the soldiers and inferior officers likewise, enticed and flattered the Negroes and prevailed on vast numbers to go along with them," noted Robert Honyman in his diary. Richard Henry Lee was indignant that "force, fraud, intrigue, theft, have all in turn been employed to delude these unhappy people and to defraud their masters!"[53] But this was usually not the case. It was hardly unknown to enslaved Virginians that the British were motivated by short-range military tactics—bleeding off the labor of the patriots that undergirded their economy and eager to provide themselves with refugee slaves to do the brunt of the drudge work—rather than long-term benevolence. Nor were slaves unaware that life on British ships and in makeshift camps was dangerous and difficult and that lethal diseases often mowed down appalling numbers of people in the army, always on the move.

Yet whenever Cornwallis's army approached, slaves determined to make their move could have fled *from* the British rather than *toward* them. This happened in some cases, as slaves, acting "under the combined weight of prudence, caution fear, and realism," as historian Sylvia Frey puts it, remained with their masters as the British approached.[54] But those who struck for their freedom in the face of unfavorable odds were hardly "deluded," as Richard Henry Lee believed, and most would doubtlessly have laughed at the notion that they were "defrauding" their masters. Almost all slaves in the path of the onrushing British army had the opportunity to make a conscious choice: to flee or not to flee. The majority stayed where they were; but we need to appreciate that a great many of these stay-at-homes were children too young to make any kind of move, pregnant or suckling women with limited chances of surviving a flight to the British, disabled and elderly slaves with limited physical capabilities, and an abundance of others who prized the place where they lived and feared the uncertainty of life with the rarely reliable British. But slaves by the tens of thousands had waited years for the British army to move into sight. Believing that this was their best chance, they demonstrated an unquenchable thirst for freedom by fleeing to the British on the eve of the momentous military climax at Yorktown.

A particularly vivid account, scribbled in the diary of a Hessian officer far away from home, gives insight into how the most intrepid slaves, both women and men, fled to the British lines and exacted their pound of flesh from their tormentors. Officer Johann Ewald described how escaped slaves reaching British camps or going out on foraging expeditions plundered the wardrobes of their masters and mistresses with great relish. They "divided the loot, and clothed themselves piecemeal with it," he wrote. "A completely naked Negro wore a pair of silk breeches, another a finely colored coat, a third a silk vest without sleeves, a fourth an elegant shirt, a fifth a fine churchman's hat, and a sixth a wig. All the rest of the body was bare!" Here was a demonstration of primitive justice. "The one Negress wore a silk skirt, another a lounging robe with a long train, the third a jacket, the fourth a silk-laced bodice, the fifth a silk corset, the seventh, eight, and ninth—all different styles of hats and coiffures." The overall tableau amazed Ewald: "These variegated creatures on thousands of horses" trailing behind the British army's baggage train reminded him of "a wandering Arabian or Tart[a]r horde."[55] For slaves who for years had little but skimpy and worn clothing, here was one of freedom's rewards, momentary to be sure, but nonetheless sweet.

But the gamble for freedom in the heart of the Virginia slave country was almost at an end. Decamping from Richmond and moving down the James River, Cornwallis's army reached Williamsburg on June 25, 1781. After occupying the small town for ten days, the British general moved his army on to Jamestown and then in August to the small tobacco port of Yorktown. Forming several thousand black refugees into shovel brigades, Cornwallis built stout fortifications, where his seven thousand troops prepared to do battle with the French naval force moving into the Chesapeake Bay and the American land forces gathering to lay siege. Meanwhile, even before they reached Yorktown, hundreds of absconding slaves were struck down by a terrifying outbreak of smallpox. "Within these days past, I have marched by 18 or 20 Negroes that lay dead by the wayside, putrifying with the small pox," noted a Connecticut soldier. Others, similarly infected, marched on to Yorktown, where Cornwallis put them to work building redoubts.[56]

The siege that began on September 28, 1781, soon made hunger the biggest problem for Cornwallis, but disease was not far behind. When feed ran out, Cornwallis ordered hundreds of horses slaughtered and thrown into the York River. Then, with rations dwindling for his troops, he expelled thousands of black auxiliaries from the encampments. Hessian officer Johann Ewald found this shameful. "We had used them to good advantage and set them free, and now, with fear and trembling, they had to face the reward of their cruel masters." Ewald found "a great number of these unfortunates" half-starved and hiding in the woods. Joseph Plumb Martin, the private we have encountered before, also saw "herds of Negroes" in the woods, "scattered about in every direction, dead and dying with pieces of ears of burnt Indian corn in the hands and mouths, even of those that were dead." But Cornwallis was not so merciless as it appears. With surrender imminent, every black man and woman was a hairbreadth away from certain return to slavery. Forced out of the British fortifications, the black refugees at least had a chance of making an escape. General Charles O'Hara, a senior officer in Cornwallis's army, remembered leaving four hundred black refugees with provisions to get them through smallpox and placing them in "the most friendly quarter in our neighborhood," where he begged "local residents to be kind to the refugees he had once sheltered."[57]

When the Americans and French entered Yorktown on October 19, they found "an immense number of Negroes" lying dead "in the most miserable manner" from smallpox. Within days of the British surrender, planters descended on Yorktown and began hiring American soldiers to ferret surviving ex-slaves out of the woods. Private Joseph Martin was among those who accepted a guinea (twenty-one shillings) per head for those he rounded up. Writing of his wartime experiences much later, he remembered how some of the American soldiers would not hand over the former slaves of John Banister, a Virginia planter and legislator, "unless he would promise not to punish them."[58]

Thus ended the greatest tragedy of the American Revolution for African Americans. Those expelled from the British fortifications at Yorktown had little chance for escape, and even that chance had been severely minimized by the raging smallpox epidemic that stalked Cornwallis's march eastward from Richmond to Yorktown. Seven years later, Jefferson estimated that about 27,000 of some 30,000 Virginia slaves who fled to the British died of smallpox and camp fevers. Historians have argued recently that Jefferson greatly exaggerated the number of absconding Virginia slaves at 30,000. Current research suggests one-third that many. But the patriarch of Monticello was right about the horrendous effect of smallpox. The fate of his own absconding slaves was probably typical. Of the thirty-four who fled to the British, at least fifteen died from typhus and smallpox. He recovered nine others after the Yorktown surrender and sold or gave most of them away within a few years.[59] The others escaped and were lost to him—and to history. The British southern campaign, meant to bring the Americans to their knees, marked the greatest slave rebellion in American history. Though a remarkable testimony to the slaves' courage and their determination to be free, disease and the outcome of the Yorktown siege put most of the black refugees in shallow graves after only the briefest taste of partial freedom.

Defending Virginia

After the British moved the war south in late 1778, Virginia's middling and poor citizens faced some of the class inequities that had left Philadelphia's cobblestones stained with blood in 1779. Depreciation of paper money and the corresponding price increases were not so much the problem, because farmers fared better than urban workers in this kind of deranged economy.

Rather, tensions and violence within the patriot ranks sprang from the old problem of mobilizing citizen-soldiers. In the early years of war, the gentry-controlled legislature, leavened by some middle-class representatives, relied primarily on bounties in order to supply Virginia's quota for the Continental army. When insufficient numbers of the unmarried, the young, and especially the poor enlisted voluntarily, the legislature instituted a partial draft whereby magistrates in each county would "fix upon and draught" for three-year terms men who in their judgment could "be best spared and will be most serviceable"—the "lazy fellows who lurk about and are pests to society." [60] In actuality this was not a draft but an impressment system that shielded the gentry and middle classes entirely from Continental army service. Thus, by 1777, Virginia had abandoned the idea of citizen-soldiers and moved to the European view that a professional army built from the ranks of the poor was a necessity.

But the poor were not cooperative; they resisted the draft, deserted by droves once in the army, and in some western counties were as likely to join Loyalist bands as fall in for patriot militia duty. When a draft lottery was instituted in tidewater counties in 1781, a thousand men stormed Northumberland County Courthouse near the Potomac to break up the proceedings. Several thousand more broke up draft proceedings at Accomac County Courthouse in spring 1781. Similarly, in the interior, crowds of ordinary farmers and artisans, wielding clubs and poles, chased off military recruiters.[61] In many counties, sheriffs could collect no taxes to support mobilization.

By 1778–79, Virginia had to offer higher bounties and shorter terms of service. For gentlemen such as Edmund Pendleton, the lower class's insistence on larger enlistment bounties and eighteen-month rather than three-year terms of service showed how the "demon of avarice and spirit of extortion seem to have expelled the pure patriotism from the breasts of those who usually compose armies." The notion of the state's cellar dwellers practicing extortion against slave- and land-rich Virginians was novel, but there is a kernel of truth in it; the poor were unwilling to fight for the upper and middle classes, who rarely joined the Continental army, unless decently compensated for putting their lives on the line. Even larger bounties and shorter enlistment contracts brought meager results. By March 1778, in the heart of Patrick Henry's Hanover County, Robert Honyman noted that the recruiting plan "scarce advances at all" with "none at all offering for that service." Two

months later, Virginia had fulfilled only about one-third of the quota requested by Congress—a "horrible deficiency," in Washington's view. One
army chaplain believed that "Virginia makes the poorest figure of any state in
the recruiting way."[62]

With the British invasion imminent in late 1779, Virginians turned to their
county-based militia for home defense. But here, too, class antagonism complicated mobilization. In theory, all men between the ages of sixteen and sixty
were responsible for militia duty, and indeed the names of a large proportion
of them were inscribed on the militia rolls. But over the course of the war, the
willingness to respond to calls to arms ebbed away. If many of the lowest class
of Virginians had resisted service in the Continental army, would they and
middle-class Virginians in militia units ride to the sound of British guns? Virginia's legislators had reason to doubt this because, by 1780, they were beset
with remonstrances and petitions complaining of the burdens the war was
placing on common farmers. Virginia commoners complained especially of
the high taxes imposed to provide generous bounties that would entice the
lower class into the regular army. On top of this, militia call-outs caused
"great uneasiness and disquiet in the country," as Berkeley County militiamen complained in November 1780. "Harrassed" with call-outs that took
them away from their fields and their families, they hoped that the state could
turn to "that class of men" who "depend upon the [military] field for his
living."[63]

The debate over defending Virginia was thus conducted against a background of militia protests concerning the class injustice that had hampered
wartime mobilization all along. In early 1780, for example, the Charlotte
County militia petitioned the state legislature that "the poor among us who
scarce obtain a precarious subsistence by the sweat of their brow are called
upon as often and bound to perform equal military duty in defense of their
little as the great and opulent in defense of their abundance." But in fact the
opulent frequently did not do their part because they "often find means to
screen themselves altogether from those military services which the poor and
indigent are on all occasions taken from their homes to perform in person."[64]
Many other petitions charged Virginia's upper class with armchair patriotism, demonstrated by their reluctance to take the field.

With Cornwallis's armies pushing from the Chesapeake Bay deep into the
Virginia interior in 1780, the state's legislature looked desperately for a way to

dip deeper into the reservoir of manpower. How could Virginians be induced to defend their own state? The assembly had three choices: Compel all Virginians to share equally in the military burden; lure the lower and middling people into service while shielding the gentry; or free enslaved Virginians to fill the depleted ranks of white men.

With no time for further dallying, the legislature considered a radical plan advanced by representative Joseph Jones, wealthy delegate to the Continental Congress. Sensitive to the class-based complaints of Virginia's lower ranks that the land- and slave-rich planters were the state's most culpable war dodgers, Jones proposed that each enlistee receive, in addition to the land bounty of three hundred acres, a healthy slave between the ages of ten and forty years. These "bounty slaves" would come from slave owners with more than twenty slaves, each of whom would surrender every twentieth slave. Masters would be compensated by deducting from their taxes over the next eight years the appraised value of the slave. In effect, Jones was asking the legislature, which he believed had few slaveholders with as many as twenty slaves, to raise an army fighting for liberty through a modest redistribution of the state's slave property.

From gentrified Virginians came howls of protest. Jones wrote Madison that the "Negro holders in general already clamour against the project and will encounter it with all their force." Narrowly defeated, the bill was modified. Each enlistee would receive a land bounty at the end of the war, enough to enfranchise him, and either sixty pounds in specie (gold or silver) or a slave between the ages of ten and thirty. Some Virginia gentlemen, including James Madison, objected to the perversity of luring soldiers to fight for liberty with bounties of shackled dark-skinned men and women. "Would it not be as well," he wrote legislator Jones, "to liberate and make soldiers at once of the blacks themselves as to make them instruments for enlisting white soldiers?" This, thought Madison, would "certainly be more consonant to the principles of liberty which ought never to be lost sight of in a contest for liberty." But compromising the principles of liberty was not what worried most of the gentry; rather, it was a plan that would redistribute the state's slaves and might even "bring on a revolution in this state," as Theodorick Bland, a Virginia delegate to Congress, put it.

Nonetheless, the law took effect in October 1780 as Cornwallis's army approached. Giving up on the notion of the slave as soldier, Virginia's legislature turned to the plan for slaves as bounty. Even with a much enhanced bounty plan, the mobilization barely worked. Surveying the scene in May 1781, with Cornwallis penetrating Virginia's interior, Baron von Steuben judged that "The opposition to the law in some counties, the entire neglect of it in others, and an unhappy disposition to evade the fair execution of it in all [counties] afford a very melancholy prospect."[65]

That class rifts had compromised Virginians' attempts at mobilization to counter the British invasion became apparent as soon as Benedict Arnold's British contingent of 1,200 men landed at Hampton Roads on December 30, 1780. Using captured boats, Arnold's men pushed up the James and Chickahominy rivers. General Thomas Nelson's militiamen were no match for the Queen's Rangers led by Colonel John Simcoe. Simcoe's Rangers routed the Virginia militiamen at Richmond on January 5, 1781, put the torch to part of the town, and quickly scattered another militia unit at Charles County Courthouse three days later. Washington sent Baron von Steuben south with Lafayette in an effort to encircle Arnold's forces, but von Steuben first had to shape up the Virginians into a real fighting force. What he encountered must have made him wish he was back at Valley Forge in the bitter winter three years before. Von Steuben thought he could pull together five thousand militiamen, and this was not an unrealistic number given Virginia's white population of 280,000, the second largest of the thirteen states. At one county courthouse where a militia call-out was supposed to have produced five hundred men, he was shocked to find five men awaiting him, three of whom quickly deserted.[66]

Later in the spring of 1781, Virginia militiamen again disgraced themselves. They put up a mild struggle before relinquishing Petersburg to Simcoe's Queen's Rangers on April 25. Only the arrival of Lafayette with 1,200 Continentals, mostly from New England and New Jersey, kept Richmond from falling to the British again. Von Steuben minced no words: "I shall always regret that circumstances induced me to undertake the defense of a country where Caesar and Hannibal would have lost their reputation, and where every farmer is a general but where nobody wishes to be a soldier."[67]

The summer of 1781 brought a final chance for Virginia's militiamen to redeem themselves. The young, Oxford-trained Banastre Tarleton, feared throughout the South for his rapierlike light-cavalry strikes, made a lightning assault on Charlottesville on June 4, having moved 150 miles west from Cornwallis's main army near Jamestown. The Virginia militia had plenty of chances to resist as Tarleton's strike force moved thirty to forty miles a day through Petersburg, Amelia Court House, Prince Edward Court House, Charlotte, New London, and Bedford. As Tarleton's "army mounted on race-horses," as Lafayette described the British legion, moved to capture Governor Thomas Jefferson and the Virginia legislature, the state's government fled en masse to the hills, aided not in the least by Virginia militiamen. The Virginia militia had proved worthless. The most recent historian of the militia calls this "the almost complete breakdown of mobilization in Virginia."[68] Only Daniel Morgan's North Carolina riflemen and the arrival of General Anthony Wayne with the Pennsylvania Continentals crimped Tarleton and other British units.

One of the reasons for the abysmal militia turnouts was that too many officers, and some of the enlisted men, were fearful of leaving farms and plantations in the hands of slaves who were flocking to the British whenever the redcoated army appeared. Writing just after the war, Edmund Randolph, to become the state's governor in 1786, excused the militia's nonperformance because the "helpless wives and children were at the mercy not only of the males among the slaves but of the very women, who could handle deadly weapons, and these could not have been left in safety in the absence of all authority of the masters and of union among neighbors." Protecting slave property had trumped the common defense of Virginia. When the British raided Hampton, in Elizabeth City County, in the fall of 1780, militia officers didn't even try to keep the rank and file under arms. "Every man who had a family" could fall out and "do the best for them they could," county officials informed the legislature. James Innes told Jefferson that "no aid of militia could ever be drawn from the part of the country immediately invaded."[69] In one of the greatest ironies of the American Revolution, Virginians decided that controlling their slave property was more important than fighting the British for independence in the seventh year of the war. If necessary, they would make terms with the British, at least temporarily, rather than see themselves stripped of slaves.

As Tarleton's and Arnold's regiments approached, many planters packed their valuables, gathered their slaves, and moved "up the country" to escape the British. In late May, Robert Honyman noted in his diary that many Virginians were moving their "Negroes, cattle, horses etc. from the route which it is supposed they [the British] will take." Such famous patriots as Richard Henry Lee, George Mason, and Edmund Pendleton fled for the hills. Those who didn't suffered the fate of John Banister. During the first Tarleton raid on Petersburg, eleven of Banister's slaves fled to the British; when the red-coats returned in early May, all his other slaves took to their heels.[70]

The paramount desire of Virginia's slaveocracy in putting slave mainte-nance ahead of common defense was not lost on militiamen of modest means. Since the beginning of the war, militiamen had complained that those with slaves were advantaged because they had captive laborers to work the fields at home while they served on the military field. The "poorer sort," petitioned Chesterfield County militiamen, "have not a slave to labour for them" when they were called out. In June 1781, even as Jefferson and the Virginia legisla-tors were fleeing Charlottesville, the Rockbridge and Pittsylvania County militia petitioned that they were not in the position of slave owners and were unwilling to respond to the call to arms "in such a manner as would . . . totally ruin themselves, their wives and children." While principal slave owners ig-nored the recruiting laws or found ways to be invalided off the militia rolls so they could flee for the hills in the face of the British advance, "poor men with-out a single slave, with a wife and many small children to maintain" were being reduced "to the most indigent circumstances and hard grinding want." Once again, in the hour of greatest need, Virginia's deep entrenchment in slavery proved a "touchstone for class divisions among white Virginians."[71]

Native American Agonies

While the African American struggle for liberation reached a climax in the concluding years of war, Native Americans engaged in a desperate defense of their revolutionary goals. This was necessarily carried out in several frontier zones, because the expansionist campaigns of American frontiersmen were regional rather than national and were conducted variously by Continental army units, state militias, and even self-appointed local white marauders. In some of these encounters, Native Americans were split between conservative accommodationists trying to remain neutral or accede to American demands on their lands and radical militants determined to defend their ancient home-lands and sure that bowing to white demands only sharpened the appetites of land-hungry farmers. On the American side, men of moderation tried to keep Indians neutral and attempted to restrain trigger-happy frontiersmen. Opposing them were Indian haters bent on genocidal policies and possession of Indian land.

In the northern sector, the Iroquois remained divided. The Mohawk,

Seneca, Cayuga, and many Onondaga radicals had already cast the die to defend their lands and political autonomy by allying with the British. But the conservative Oneidas and Tuscaroras kept faith with the Americans. Launching a new wave of frontier raids in spring 1779, the militant Iroquois meant to deprive the Americans of one of their richest wheat belts. Putting farmhouses, barns, gristmills, and sawmills to the torch was more important than killing their enemies. In the valleys of the Mohawk, Monongahela, and Delaware rivers, militia units were ineffective in stopping the Indian marauders. "Our Country is on the eve of breaking up," wrote one militia officer to Pennsylvania's Supreme Executive Council. "There is nothing to be seen but desolation, fire, and smoke, as the inhabitants [are] collected at particular places. The enemy burns all the houses that [the frontier families] have evacuated."[72]

By the summer of 1779, General Washington made regaining an upper hand over the Iroquois rather than the British his priority. As late as September 1778, he had concluded that "to defend an extensive frontier against the incursions of Indians and the banditti under Butler and Brant is next to impossible," but now state leaders in New York and Pennsylvania changed his mind. Committing one-third of his army, Washington made the destruction of the Iroquois "the main American military effort of the year." Four times in the summer of 1779, American forces carried the battle to the heart of Iroquoia. Washington's orders were explicit: to "lay waste all the settlements around . . . that the country may not be merely overrun but destroyed." The first attack was inexplicably on the villages of the mostly neutralist Onondaga. The torching of three Onondaga villages and the taking of thirty-three prisoners, including one of Joseph Brant's children, drove three hundred Onondaga warriors to the British side. Within weeks, they reduced the white frontier village of Cobleskill to ashes.[73]

Brant's Volunteers were in the thick of the summer campaigns. The American expeditionary forces under General John Sullivan, General James Clinton, and Colonel Daniel Brodhead, some 4,600 strong with 1,200 horses and 700 cattle, outmanned, outgunned, and out-provisioned Brant's Volunteers, Butler's Rangers, and about five hundred Iroquois warriors. Washington knew that Sullivan's expedition was unlikely to face regular British units, which were fully occupied along the coast. Nonetheless, anticipating intense battles with the Iroquois, Washington advised Sullivan and Clinton "to rush on with the war whoop and fixed bayonet" and "make rather than receive attacks." But the expeditionary campaign saw only one pitched battle. At the Indian village at Newtown (near today's Elmira, New York) in late August the Iroquois-Tory contingent at first held its ground, only to be routed by the American forces. Heavily outnumbered and unable to defend their villages, Brant and his rangers avoided set battles, while the Iroquois villagers evacuated their homesites. Major Jeremiah Fogg recounted that "Not a single gun was fired for eighty miles on our march out or an Indian seen on our return." Brant's Volunteers contented themselves with pummeling the villages of the Oneida and Tuscarora allied with the Americans.[74]

In a largely uncontested scorched-earth campaign, matches and axes proved more important than guns. The American armies razed Indian villages, burned 160,000 bushels of corn, girdled thousands of fruit trees in ancient orchards, and took a limited number of prisoners. General Sullivan reported triumphantly to Congress that "the whole country [was] explored in search of Indian settlements, and I am well persuaded that, except one town situated near the Allegana [Allegheny] . . . there is not a single town left in the country of the Five Nations." Sullivan missed one other town in his account, but he was nearly right about destroying almost all Iroquois villages. Historian Page Smith calls it "the most ruthless application of a scorched-earth policy in American history," rivaled only by Sherman's Civil War march to the sea or the American search-and-destroy missions of the Vietnam War.[75] The ruthlessness reached an extreme when American soldiers plundered Indian graves to carry off the prized burial items customarily laid alongside deceased Iroquois. Other soldiers skinned bodies "from the hips down for bootlegs." An Onondaga chief testified that when Sullivan's troops attacked his town they "put to death all the women and children, excepting some of the young women, whom they carried away for the use of their soldiers and were afterwards put to death in a more shameful manner."[76]

The winter of 1779–80, which brought bitter cold and the deepest snow in recent years, was a time of dying, dysentery, and displacement for some three thousand Iroquois people, most of whom took refuge in the British fort at Niagara on the south shore of Lake Ontario. There the British fed and resupplied them. Sullivan had destroyed villages, granaries, and orchards, but not warriors; for all this devastation, he did not take the fight out of Brant and the other Iroquois. Americans had expected "overtures of peace" from the Iroquois, as New York's governor believed, but instead they got renewed warrior fury. "The nests are destroyed," recounted Major Fogg, "but the birds are still on the wing." Fogg could not have been more right. "We do not look upon ourselves as defeated," one Iroquois chief assured the British, "for we have never fought." A Cayuga chief at Fort Niagara echoed the thought, promising that come spring they would avenge their losses: "If it is the will of the Great Spirit [that we] leave our bones with those of the rest of our brethren, rather than evacuate our country or give our enemy room to say we fled from them," they would fight to the end.[77]

True to this word, some one thousand Iroquois, fighting with five hundred Tory rangers, sought revenge the next spring. Sweeping out of Fort Niagara even before the spring thaws of 1780, war parties devastated American farmlands and villages in New York's Schoharie Valley. Through the summer they matched the destructiveness of Sullivan's army a year before. Nothing stood in their way, for after Sullivan, Clinton, and Brodhead's men returned in "rags and [with] emaciated bodies," Washington sent them south to counter Cornwallis's southern campaign. Only local militiamen—a dispirited, weakly equipped lot—were left to protect the New York–Pennsylvania frontier. By autumn 1780, hardly an American settlement west of Schenectady existed. The Iroquois destroyed at least 150,000 bushels of wheat, while farming families streamed eastward for protection.[78] In Pennsylvania's Susquehanna River valley, south of Mohawk country, and on the state's western frontier all the way to the forks of the three rivers that joined at Pittsburgh, the situation was much the same. It was as if an immense army of locusts dressed in American uniforms had devastated Iroquoia in the summer of 1779, to be followed by an army of locusts dressed in Indian garb and British uniforms that laid waste to the American frontier farmlands the following summer.

In the spring and summer of 1781, with the New York and Pennsylvania militias near collapse and Washington's Continental army fully engaged in North Carolina and Virginia, the Tory and Iroquois men commanded by Joseph Brant and Sir John Johnson, William Johnson's son, struck again. This time, the American resistance was stiffer. Rallied by Colonel Marinus Willett, a New York City merchant and former leader of the Sons of Liberty, eight hundred militiamen slowed down the Tory-Iroquois marauders. The vicious cycle of depredation and counterdepredation repeated itself, as the men of two agricultural societies tried to maim each other through crop destruction, village razing, and battles of attrition. By the time Cornwallis surrendered at Yorktown on October 18, 1781, the frontier war in New York and Pennsylvania had reached a stalemate; but there was little left to destroy on either side.

From 1779 to 1781, while frontier wars in Iroquoia and western New York and Pennsylvania devastated both Indian and American farming life, another contest of long duration reached a climax east of the Mississippi River and north of the Ohio River all the way to the Great Lakes. Here the War of Independence turned into a war of conquest. The precarious grip of the British in this vast territory, weaker than in New York and Pennsylvania, provided a stage onto which the young George Rogers Clark could stride to claim his place as one of the heroes of American storybooks.

When the minutemen at Concord and Lexington were skirmishing with the British, Clark was twenty-three years old and living restlessly on a farm not far from Jefferson's Monticello. Farming was far too dull for this strongly built man with flaming red hair. What he loved was the wilderness west of Charlottesville, and what he hated was the Indians who lived there—the Shawnee, Ottawas, Hurons, Potawatomis, Kickapoos, Winnebagos, Chippewas, Sauk, and Foxes. In the early 1770s, Clark had explored and surveyed lands drained by the Ohio River in what was to become Kentucky. In 1774 he became a militia captain in Dunmore's War. Thereafter, with a contingent of admiring men, he took up huge tracts of land along the Kentucky River. Full of ambition and martial ardor, he began scheming at conquering what would become known in American history as the Old Northwest. His short-term goal was to prevent a collapse of Governor Dunmore's 1774 treaty with the Shawnee, by which they pledged neutrality. With the British promising supplies to the tribes, Clark argued, Virginia's back door to the prized lands beyond the Cumberland Gap was in great danger. But his long-term goal was possession of the entire Northwest.[79]

Clark's plan of conquest did not materialize for almost two years. But on January 3, 1778, he got what he wanted from Virginia's legislature and Governor Patrick Henry: logistical support and a colonel's commission to raise seven companies of militiamen. The intermediate targets of this incursion were the small British forts at Kaskaskia and Vincennes, in today's Illinois and Indiana. Both were surrounded with small gatherings of French-speaking farmers who had been incorporated into the British orbit after 1763. The ultimate target was the British stronghold at Detroit—the key to controlling the vast North American heartland. If the Americans could take these three garrisons, they could lay claim to a territory as large as the thirteen colonies.

Clark's official charge was to defend the small settlements of Virginians in Kentucky; his secret orders were to accomplish the mission he laid before his promoters—storm Kaskaskia, Vincennes, and Detroit, thereby wresting an empire from the native peoples and their British allies. Clark found recruiting tough going, almost as difficult as for the recruiting sergeants in Virginia's tidewater counties. How could he get volunteers, he pondered, "to be taken near a thousand [miles] from the body of their country to attack a people five times their number, and merciless tribes of Indians . . . , determined enemies to us?" Clark's zealousness produced not more than two hundred men, and some of them deserted as soon as they heard the details of what they believed to be a suicidal adventure. But on June 26, 1778, Clark and his contingent on the Ohio River headed downstream for hundreds of miles to the junction of the Tennessee River. From there they marched 120 miles northwest.

On July 5, Clark captured Kaskaskia without firing a shot. The word of the French alliance with the Americans made easier Clark's job of winning over the farming French *habitants* and their allied Illinois native peoples. Now, Vincennes, 150 miles to the east, was next. Sending Kaskaskia's French priest and doctor to Vincennes to announce that Kaskaskia had pledged allegiance to the "Republic of Virginia," Clark also took Vincennes without a fight.

Clark's ultimate objective, Detroit, was a harder matter. But he did not have to make the six-hundred-mile expedition to Detroit to reach his prized objective. Rather, Detroit came to him. The British garrison's commanding officer, Lieutenant Governor Henry Hamilton (also the governor of Canada), started south on October 7, 1778, to expel Clark from the trans-Appalachian country. Starting with 175 soldiers (many of them Frenchmen who had joined the British army) and 60 Shawnee warriors, Hamilton gathered other Indian warriors along the way. On December 17, after an incredible seventy-one-day march, Hamilton's force of five hundred retook Vincennes, where the French militiamen refused to fight and only a handful of Virginia militiamen remained since Clark had withdrawn most of them to Kaskaskia.

Nearly a thousand miles west of the main scene of the War for Independence, Clark gambled and won. The enlistment terms of many of his men had expired, and he was down to about one hundred wilderness-toughened soldiers. But Clark, bolstered by one hundred French recruits, decided to march on Vincennes in February 1779, through miles of heavy snow and boggy terrain saturated by an early spring thaw. Clark knew his attack was risky, but he was hardly a fainthearted man. To his good fortune, most of Hamilton's Shawnee auxiliaries had gone back to their villages and the French *habitants* in the town of Vincennes were ill-disposed to fight alongside the British since they had earlier pledged allegiance to the Americans. After marching for eighteen days over 150 miles through atrocious conditions, Clark invested the town and surrounded the fort at Vincennes. Clark then called for Hamilton's surrender on honorable terms. When Hamilton tarried, Clark and his men pushed five Indians they had just captured into clear view of the fort. There they tomahawked four of the five. One of them, a young Ottawa chief, wrenched the tomahawk from his skull and mockingly handed it back to his executioner before collapsing in a torrent of blood. Clark spared the fifth, the eighteen-year-old son of Chief Pontiac, when one of his captains pleaded that Pontiac, some years before, had saved his life. Hamilton capitulated with seventy-nine men on February 24; on the next day he surrendered the fort.

The execution of the four Indians, with the terms of surrender under negotiation, became two different stories told by Clark and Hamilton after the war. Victors' stories become enshrined in a nation's mythology and end up in history books; losers' stories are suppressed or forgotten. In his expedition journal, first published in 1791, Clark passed over the execution of the four captured Indian warriors with the briefest mention, though he had described the grisly incident fully in a letter to George Mason at the time. Hamilton's journal, which remained unpublished until 1951, featured the butchery. "One . . . was tomahawked either by Clark or one of his officers," Hamilton had noted ironically in his journal, "the other three, foreseeing their fate, began to sing their death song and were butchered in succession, though at the very time a flag of truce was hanging out at the fort and the firing had ceased on both sides. . . . The blood of the victims was still visible for days afterwards, a testimony of the courage and humanity of Colonel Clark." Hamilton further described how Clark met him directly after the executions with "his hands and face still reeking from the human sacrifice in which he had acted as chief priest" and "told me with great exultation how he had been employed." Clark then promised Hamilton that "for his part, he would never spare man, woman, or child of them on whom he could lay his hands." It was a genocidal promise kept many times in the last stages of the war.[80]

Clark dreamed of capping his heroics at Vincennes with the capture of

Detroit. Neither Virginia nor the Continental Congress would give him the men, supplies, and money for a new expedition. But he remained in the so-called Western Department, hoping to fight against a British regiment in Detroit reconstituted with Indian auxiliaries. After Hamilton's contingent made a daring assault on the American settlements in Kentucky in 1780 and took 350 prisoners, Clark made another of his famous marches through rough terrain—480 miles in thirty-one days—to descend on the Shawnee in August 1780. Rather than seeing the "Big Knives" raze their home village at Chillicothe, the Shawnees burned it themselves. They then fought hard at Piqua, another of their villages, located on the Mad River. Clark's artillery pieces provided the crucial advantage in the American victory. After the Shawnees fled, Clark's men burned cornfields and gathered whatever booty they could find, including unearthed burial objects. Even the scalps of disinterred Shawnees became part of the plunder. One of Clark's trophies was Joseph Rogers, his cousin. A prisoner of the Shawnee for two years, Rogers had adopted Indian customs and fought alongside the Shawnee against the Kentuckians at Piqua. Clark watched his cousin die of a battle wound after Rogers fell into the hands of his Kentucky contingent.

As much as he craved a fight with the British at Detroit in 1781, Clark was never able to raise enough money or men for the assault. Instead he tangled with Joseph Brant. Two charismatic leaders propelled to leadership roles by the incessant irregular warfare in the trans-Appalachian region, they met in the summer of 1781. Brant had reached Detroit by foot and sail that spring and for the next three months helped rally Huron, Ottawa, Chippewa, Potawatomi, and Miami warriors to head off the rumored Clark attack on Detroit. Moving south, Brant watched Clark and his men pass by to fortify forts that protected the Kentuckians from British-Indian attacks. Then Brant sprang his trap, ambushing one hundred Pennsylvania militiamen near the junction of the Little Miami and Ohio rivers as the Pennsylvanians moved to join Clark. The annihilation left forty-one Americans dead and all the others captured—the worst defeat in the *pays d'en haut* suffered by the Americans.[81] This ended Clark's dream of taking Detroit.

Brant spent the winter of 1781–82 in Detroit, and it was probably here where he heard the news of Cornwallis's surrender at Yorktown. But that did not end the war in the Illinois country. Brant's hammer blow deprived Clark of a crack unit that might have enabled him to march on Detroit, but given the condition of his Virginia and Kentucky volunteers, this may not have been possible anyway. One of Clark's captains described "the wretched situation of the few troops remaining westward. Many of them have been in service for two years past and never received a shoe, stocking, or hat and none of them any pay." They were probably no better off than the troops of the Western Department that General William Irvine described in spring 1782: "I never saw troops cut so truly a deplorable and at the same time despicable a figure. No man would believe from their appearance that they were soldiers; nay, it would be difficult to determine whether they were *white men*."[82] It was no wonder, then, that through 1780–82, the thin line of Americans in the border area, suffering desertions, grew thinner.

Hundreds of miles south of the Kentucky-Illinois country, another chapter of the conflict of expansion unfolded in the last years of the war. The ability of the Cherokee and other southern Indian nations to protect themselves depended on a continuing flow of weapons, ammunition, and trade goods from the British. That flow of goods hinged, in turn, on British control of ports of entry—on the Atlantic coast at Savannah, Georgia, and Charleston, South Carolina; and on the Gulf of Mexico coast at Pensacola, Florida, and Mobile, Alabama. The military strength of the warrior nations was formidable on paper: about 6,000 Creek, 7,000 Choctaw, 3,000 Cherokee, and 750 Chickasaw. But the warriors were only as good as the British supplies reaching them. Equally important, they were internally divided, particularly the Cherokee. In addition, they never fought as a united, intertribal Indian force.

For both the militant and accommodationist Cherokees, this became agonizingly evident. It will be remembered from chapter 5 that the Cherokees led by the older chiefs remained in their much devastated ancient towns in the hill country of the Carolinas, where they pledged to fight the Americans no more, while the Cherokee irreconcilables led by Dragging Canoe had built new villages on the Chickamauga River in today's Tennessee. From there, the militants cheered the British capture of Augusta and Savannah, Georgia, in 1778–79 because this opened up a new supply line along the Savannah River for the British to furnish them trade goods. Dragging Canoe's warriors operated with the British to seize control of parts of the Georgia and South Carolina interior. This was enough for Virginia to launch a punishing expedition against the irreconcilable Cherokees in April 1779. Though the Virginians destroyed eleven towns and most of their food supplies, the defiant Cherokee "are not yet conquered," Dragging Canoe told a Shawnee delegation in July 1779. As Cornwallis swept north out of South Carolina in 1780, the militant Chickamaugan Cherokee went on the warpath again. This led Governor Thomas Jefferson in June 1780 to call up 250 militiamen to prosecute another attack. Jefferson explicitly charged the officers of the Washington and Montgomery County militia units to take "great care that no injury be done to the friendly part of the [Cherokee] nation," and expressed his confidence that no Carolinians, who were to join the Virginians, "would propose to confound together the friendly and hostile parts of the Cherokee nations." The friendly Cherokees "have our faith pledged for their protection," he reminded the units taking the field.[83]

But Indian hating led to the destruction of the accommodationist Cherokees rather than the militants who had followed Dragging Canoe to the Chickamauga. Colonel Arthur Campbell led the Virginia militiamen, while the hotheaded John Sevier, one of the first North Carolinians to follow the path blazed by Daniel Boone into the Holston River valley on the eve of the Revolution, led a North Carolina contingent. The little army of about seven hundred marched toward the Chickamaugan towns in December 1780. But they stopped fifty miles short, with the men apparently queasy about taking on the fiercely irreconcilable young Cherokee warriors. Closer at hand was far easier quarry—the friendly, less combative Cherokees.

Charging that the neutralist Cherokee were foxes in sheeps' clothing, secretly plotting with the British, Sevier and Campbell fell on seventeen neutral Cherokee towns, where they burned a thousand houses, storehouses, and lodges and destroyed 50,000 bushels of corn. The work was easy because most of the Cherokee fled their homes, trying to avoid the Americans. In a detailed letter, Colonel Campbell told Jefferson about how his men saw the Cherokees "in force stretching along the hills" but how they "quietly let us pass on in order without firing a gun."[84] Immediately, the Virginians marched into Chota, the Cherokee's "beloved town," where they killed thirteen men who offered no resistance. Desperately trying to stop the killing, Cherokee ceremonial chief Nancy Ward reached Campbell to make an overture for peace. The niece of Attakullakulla, Ward was well known to the Virginians and Carolinians for warning frontiersmen on the Watauga River five years earlier of Dragging Canoe's imminent attack. But Campbell "evaded" the overture in order to complete the destruction of the Cherokee towns. "No place in the Overhill country remained unvisited," Sevier reported with satisfaction.[85] It was the southern equivalent of Sullivan's scorched-earth expedition of 1778 in Iroquois country, except that in this case the devastated region was that of

*Nancy Ward went down in the annals of American history as the "good In-
dian," because she counseled accommodation with the American frontiersmen
and saved many of them by warning of imminent Cherokee attacks. Here she
is shown with a plaque inscribed "Watauga 1776" to commemorate her aid to
the Tennessee frontiersmen. Nearby, in Benton, Tennessee, the Nancy Ward
chapter of the Daughters of the American Revolution maintains her burial
place. Visitors get an encapsulated mythology from a tablet that calls her
"Princess and Prophetess of the Cherokee Nation. The Pocahontas of Tennessee, the Constant Friend of the American Pioneer."**

the friendly Cherokee. For the militant Cherokees in the towns established
under Dragging Canoe's leadership, this was confirmation of the treachery of
the Americans.

While razing Chota, Campbell's militiamen found what historians have

---

*Carolyn Thomas Foreman, Indian Women Chiefs (Washington, D.C.: Zenger Publishing Co., 1976), 82.

called the archives of the Cherokee nation—treaties, letters, and commissions. Among them was the smoking gun proving the duplicity of the accommodationist Cherokee, or so say many historians. But the evidence is based on Colonel Arthur Campbell's statement to Jefferson that he found documents in Chota "expressive of their hostile designs on us." Yet Campbell gave no details about the "hostile designs," the documents have never been found, and there is no mention of them in the extensive papers of Thomas Jefferson. Against this shaky evidence are the facts that only one Indian village offered resistance of any kind, and only one man in the American strike force of seven hundred was injured or killed by the Cherokees. For their part, the militiamen killed twenty-nine men and took seventeen prisoners.

The entry of the Spanish into the war on the American side in mid-1779 began to turn the tide against the southernmost Indian nations. British-controlled Mobile fell to a Spanish fleet in February 1780. Only the presence of some two thousand Creek and Choctaw gunmen at Pensacola kept the Spanish from capturing that key British port in the same year. But the Spanish fleet, with seven thousand men, returned in April 1781 and took the port after a month-long siege. Augusta, Georgia, fell to the Americans a month later. These British losses of the pivotal port cities "marked the end of effective functioning of the [English] Southern Indian Department."[86] And with the departing British troops went British traders and supplies for their Indian allies.

The collapse of the British-Indian war effort in 1781 put the Americans in the position to secure a long-term peace with the still populous southern tribes. But complicating this desire—in fact nullifying it—was the hunger for national expansion that had burgeoned over the previous six years. When they were not fighting, southern frontiersmen had conducted what historian Colin Calloway calls "a squatters' invasion of the upper Tennessee country." William Fleming, a frontier leader, acknowledged as much to Jefferson in February 1781: "[T]he burning of their huts and destruction of their corn, will I fear make the whole [Cherokee] Nation our irreconcilable Enemies, and force them for sustenances to live altogether by depredation on our frontiers or make an open junction with our foes, as the loss they have sustained in men is little or nothing."[87] A month later, with the battered Cherokee accommodationists still suing for peace, North Carolina's John Sevier returned with 180 horsemen to destroy fifteen other Cherokee towns from which the Indians had fled in panic. This unprovoked assault brought a sharp rebuke from Colonel William Christian, who had commanded the expedition against the Cherokee in 1776: "People of all ranks appear to have a desire to encroach upon Indian lands; this will throw great obstacles in the way of a treaty. . . . The only inducements the Indians can have for treating are for us to do them justice respecting their land and to subsist their families this summer."[88] But the victors were in no way ready to be magnanimous.

Radical Mutineers

As George Rogers Clark was etching his place in history in the trans-Appalachian wilderness and Virginia and North Carolina militiamen were razing friendly Cherokee towns, Joseph Plumb Martin, a long-term enlistee in Washington's Continental army, was reaching the limit of his endurance. Looking back on the Revolution, Martin remembered how his unit of the Connecticut Line, after a cruel subzero winter and what he called "the monster hunger still attending us," nearly mutinied in May 1780. For five months they had received no pay and their meager meat rations had just been halved. "The men were exasperated beyond endurance," remembered Private Martin. "They could not stand it any longer; they saw no other alternative but to starve to death, or break up the army, give all up, and go home. . . . Here was the army starved and naked, and there their country sitting still and expecting the army to do notable things while fainting from sheer starvation."[89]

Martin recounted years after the war how his regiment joined with others of the Connecticut Line to rise up against their officers. One officer, Colonel Jonathan Meigs, was bayoneted in a scuffle with an enlisted man. But in the end, the men desisted. "We therefore still kept upon our parade in groups, venting our spleen at our country and government, then at our officers, and then at ourselves for our imbecility in staying there and starving in detail for an ungrateful people who did not care what became of us, so they could enjoy themselves while we were keeping a cruel enemy from them."[90]

Two months later, in July 1780, one of their officers, Lieutenant Ebenezer Huntington, almost invited the men to mutiny. Writing to his brother, the twenty-six-year-old Yale graduate described how "the insults and neglects which the army have met with beggars all description. . . . They can endure it no longer. I am in rags, have lain in the rain on the ground for 40 hours past, and only a junk of fresh beef and that without salt to dine on this day. . . . I despise my countrymen. I wish I could say I was not born in America. I once gloried in it but am now ashamed of it."[91]

Washington himself was near his wit's end in 1780. The provisioning system had nearly broken down, the desertion rate had skyrocketed, and morale was at an all-time low. "It would be well for the troops," he wrote Robert Morris in December 1780, "if like chameleons, they could live upon air, or, like the bear, suck their paws for sustenance during the rigor of the approaching season."[92] Officers had their hands full quelling repeated rumblings of mutiny, but were utterly incapable of dealing with the causes of it.

In January 1781, with the supply system crumbling and Continental paper dollars—which served as pay for the army—plummeting in value, a large-scale mutiny finally broke out. This time it was the Pennsylvania Line, quickly followed by the New Jersey Line. In this double mutiny we can see in capsule form all of the difficulties of managing a war that only about a quarter of the nation's peoples supported ideologically and an even smaller number supported materially. The way the mutineers conducted and expressed themselves also tells us how they exemplified the democratic values of revolutionary radicals. Insubordination and direct defiance of officers' authority is the most radical action any man under arms can take. In the army rule book, no mutiny is justifiable, and the penalty for it is immediate trial, sentencing, and execution. However, the Pennsylvania and New Jersey enlisted men revolted against their officers in the name of some of the most basic goals of the American Revolution—social justice, equality, and fair play. It says volumes that most of the mutineers' officers, even Washington himself, believed the men rose up with justification.

The mutiny of January 1781 came as no surprise. As early as November 1775, a company of Pennsylvania riflemen had mutinied in Cambridge, Massachusetts, and soon thereafter Washington lost a significant part of his army through massive desertions. Harsh new "Articles of War" passed by Congress the next year increased the number of capital offenses and specifically made desertion punishable by death, but even this did little to stop desertion and mutiny. For the entire course of the war, deserters in huge numbers dropped behind and disappeared during the interminable route marches. "By midwar," writes military historian Charles Patrick Neimeyer, "mutiny, actual or threatened . . . , became commonplace in the Continental army."[93]

Storm signals went up one after another. In the year before the major mutiny of January 1781, three smaller mutinies erupted. The first came at West Point on January 1, 1780, when the Massachusetts Line revolted in the middle of the most severe winter since 1740–41. In May, two regiments of the Connecticut Line, disgusted with no pay for five months and short rations for several weeks, turned out and prepared to march away in defiance of their officers. The officers restored order and pragmatically exercised lenity against the leaders. But this did little to improve the mood and morale of the soldiers. A month later, thirty-one men of New York's First Regiment deserted at Fort Schuyler, apparently to join the British. One of their officers pursued them with Oneida auxiliaries, who overtook the men and shot thirteen of them dead.

For the Pennsylvania Line, the causes of such mutinies—no pay and scarce food and clothing—were all too familiar. Just a month before the January 1781 mutiny, Brigadier General Anthony Wayne warned Pennsylvania's Supreme Executive Council of the desperate condition of his troops, who were quartered for the winter at Morristown in northern New Jersey. Dry bread, a bit of meat, worn-out coats, and tattered blankets, each shared by three soldiers, "is but wretched living and shelter against the winter's piercing cold, drifting snow, and chilling sleets." He might have added that with their pay in arrears by a year, many of the married men were staggering to cope with an especially cruel situation. "Our soldiery are not devoid of reasoning faculties," wrote Wayne. "They have now served their country for near five years, poorly clothed, badly fed, and worse paid. . . . They have not seen a paper dollar in the way of pay for near twelve months."[94] If his 2,473 men were not paid, fed, clothed, and assured that the enlistment bounty of one hundred acres of land would actually be given, they would desert, as they had been doing in massive numbers over the previous year. Beyond desertion beckoned mutiny.

This was a situation that the Continental Congress had wrestled with from the outset, beginning with the inability of the states to meet the supply quotas for uniforms, boots, food, tents and blankets, and arms and ammunition set to conduct the war. For men in the field, it was unfathomable that they starved in a country of agricultural plenty and were "bare footed, bare legged, bare breeched," as one Massachusetts officer expressed it.[95] When they could bear it no more, they took the desperate chance that mutiny might bring the Congress to its senses or bring the people in the states to understand that the war could not be continued with a starving, unpaid, unclothed army.

North Carolina's legislature, just a year before the Pennsylvania Line's mutiny, heard a pathetic tale from the widow of one soldier executed for leading a mutiny in the North Carolina Line. Ann Glover could not bring her husband back, but she reasoned that the state owed her support for her small children and should offer his pay, which was fifteen months in arrears. "The poor soldiers" were "possessed of the same attachment and affection to their families as those in command," she wrote. "[I] ask you what must the feeling of the man be who fought at Brandywine, at Germantown, and at Stony Point and did his duty, and when on another march in defense of his country, with poverty staring him full in the face, he was denied his pay?" The *Connecticut Courant* echoed the thought: "How is it that the poor soldier's wives in many of our towns go from door to door, begging a supply of the necessaries of life at the stipulated prices, and are turned away, notwithstanding the solemn agreements of the towns to supply such?"[96]

The largest mutiny of the war erupted on January 1, 1781, a day of special significance. This was the day on which the three-year enlistments of many men in the Pennsylvania Line expired, or at least that was their understanding of their contracts. Many wished to put three miserable years behind them, but most were willing to reenlist under the new bounties offered since the previous July—about twenty-seven dollars in hard money and certificates for two hundred acres of land after the war. But their officers told them that Congress meant their enlistment extended for the duration of the war, whether that be three, five, or seven years. This enraged the men, who insisted that they had enlisted for three years *or* the duration of the war, meaning whichever came first.

About ten o'clock P.M. on January 1, the men revolted. Returning from an officers' elegant regimental dinner, their leaders found men pouring from their huts brandishing their arms, cheering loudly, and gathering on the parade ground. One captain trying to control his unit was shot mortally. Seizing the artillery pieces, loading them with grapeshot, and breaking open the magazine filled with powder and balls, the men took control of the encampment. They rejected General Wayne's attempt to address them, telling him they intended to march to Philadelphia, where they would meet face-to-face with the congressmen "to see themselves righted" by those who had wronged them.

The ensuing melee left one officer dead, two others shot, and many others suffering wounds inflicted by musket butts, bayonets, and stones. At four-thirty in the morning, Wayne frantically scribbled a letter to Washington. "It is with inexpressible pain that I now inform your Excellency of the general mutiny and defection which suddenly took place in the Pennsylvania Line . . . last evening. Every possible exertion was made by the officers to suppress it in its rise, but the torrent was too potent to be stemmed."[97] By noon the next day, almost all enlisted men had joined the mutineers. Falling in order under their elected sergeants, they marched southward out of camp. Nearly one-fourth of Washington's Continental army was now in full revolt.

Wayne's main concern was that the men would join the British, who were only two days' march to the east in New Jersey. Receiving word of the mutiny, the British sent promises to give the mutineers their back pay in hard money and the choice of serving with the British or going their own way. The mutineers assured Wayne they had no intention of defecting to the enemy; they were stalwart patriots to the core but had been badly served and would bear ill treatment no longer. "If that is your sentiments," Wayne answered, "I'll not leave you, and if you won't allow me to march in your front, I'll follow in your rear."[98] And so the march began. According to one witness, the men marched "in the most perfect order and seemed as if under military discipline." After electing a "board of sergeants," almost the entire army trudged south, marching by their own rules and imposing their own discipline. Within two days the mutineers had reached Princeton. Controlling the town, they appropriated Nassau Hall, the College of New Jersey's single building, which the board of sergeants used as a meeting place.

What kind of men were these mutineers? To judge by the Eleventh Regiment, led by Lieutenant Colonel Adam Hubley, they were mostly young, poor, and foreign-born. The majority of the Eleventh's twenty-five sergeants and twenty-two corporals were immigrants—ten born in England, nine in Ireland, three in Scotland, sixteen in unspecified countries, and only nine in the colonies. Of those in the rank and file whose birthplaces were recorded in the muster lists, eighty-seven came from Ireland, thirty-seven from England, eight from Germany, six from Scotland, and fifty-six from the American colonies. The occupations of two companies recorded on the muster lists show a heavy proportion of ordinary workers (laborers, farmers, weavers, shoemakers, tailors, soap boilers, and coopers), and a sprinkling of higher tradesmen (saddlers, carpenters, blacksmiths, watchmakers, tobacconists, and silversmiths).[99]

The men had tasted fire under severe conditions. They had fought under Anthony Wayne at the Battle of Monmouth (New Jersey) in suffocating heat in June 1778, where they performed ably in the fiercest part of the fight, though they were "almost starving," as Alexander Hamilton, Washington's aide-de-camp, reported. Months later, they stormed the British stronghold at Stony Point at midnight on July 15, 1779. In September 1780, hundreds of them marched sixteen miles in an astounding four hours to secure West Point as Benedict Arnold, defecting to the British, tried to deliver the stronghold to the enemy. These grizzled, battle-hardened men, accustomed to rigorous discipline, seemed to Private Joseph Martin like an army of gypsies. Martin described the baggage train of Continental army units as they passed down the west side of the Hudson River six months before the mutiny. "When that of the middle states passed us," he remembered, "it was truly amusing to see the number and habiliments of those attending it; of all specimens of human beings, this group capped the whole. A caravan of wild beasts could bear no comparison with it. There was 'Tag, Rag and Bobtail'; 'some in rags and some in jags,' but none 'in velvet gowns.' Some with two eyes, some with one, and some I believe with none at all. They 'beggared all description'; their dialect too was as confused as their bodily appearance was odd and disgusting. There was the Irish and Scotch brogue, murdered English, flat insipid Dutch, and some lingoes which would puzzle a philosopher to tell whether they belong to this world or some 'undiscovered country.' "[100] Martin was right about the awful condition of their uniforms and the babel of tongues, but he was wrong in what he implied about the men's mettle.

Handed General Wayne's anguished notice of the mutiny, Washington pondered his options. He discarded the idea of calling up the New Jersey militia to stop the Pennsylvanians, because the New Jersey Line was itself unreliable and in any event the militia was too small to overawe the mutineers. Washington also rejected the idea that Congress flee Philadelphia before the mutineers arrived, because this sign of weakness might encourage the angry soldiers to vent their spleen "upon the persons and properties of the citizens" (by which Washington meant the many wealthy Philadelphians whom soldiers saw as wan supporters of the American cause). With no good options, Washington directed Wayne to listen to the mutineers' grievances and promise careful consideration of their complaints. The commander in chief could hardly have done otherwise because he in fact agreed with their grievances. Indeed, so often had Washington unsuccessfully implored Congress to support his troops that he took some grim satisfaction in the revolt. "The circumstances will now point out more forcibly what ought to be done," he wrote Congress, "than anything that can possibly be said by me on the subject."[101]

Meanwhile, the alarmed Continental Congress agreed to coordinate with Pennsylvania's Supreme Executive Council to dissuade the mutineers from pressing on to Philadelphia. A joint committee, escorted by light horsemen from Philadelphia, reached Trenton on January 6 to meet with the mutineers' board of sergeants. Joseph Reed, president of Pennsylvania's executive council, and General Wayne began the negotiations at Princeton the next day. For the first time in the American Revolution, noncommissioned officers of Washington's army parleyed the terms of the soldiers' enlistment directly with their commanding general and the head of the nation's most populous state.

Both sides put proposals on the table. Then Reed and Wayne listened to accounts of how the soldiers had been enlisted with dishonest promises and practices. After hurried discussions, Reed and Wayne agreed to the men's main demands: that they would be given total amnesty and not be considered traitors for their mutiny, and that no man would be held to service beyond what he had voluntarily agreed to. Disputed terms of enlistment would be put before a commission, and the soldier's oath on his understanding of the terms would be accepted in the absence of official enlistment papers. Those leaving the service would receive back pay, adjusted for inflation; the wretched condition of the soldiers' clothing would be remedied as soon as possible. General John Sullivan, part of the congressional negotiating committee, wrote to Chevalier Anne-César de La Luzerne, French minister to the United States, that "Perhaps history does not furnish an instance of so large a body of troops revolting from the command of their officers, marching in such exact order, without doing the least injury to individuals, and remaining in this situation for such a length of time, without division or confusion among themselves, and then returning to their duty as soon as their reasonable demands were complied with." Sullivan was almost ready to pin medals on the mutineers, who had "no officer to command them and no force to prevent their joining the enemy for which they had repeated invitations; yet, though they well knew they were liable to the severest punishment for their revolt, they disdained the British officers with a firmness that would have done honor to the ancient Romans."[102]

Finding enlistment papers proved cumbersome and often impossible; in the absence of the papers, the word of the individual enlisted man was accepted. By the end of January, about 1,250 of the 2,473 men took discharges. The other half were furloughed until March 15, when they were told to rendezvous at various locations after a reorganization of the troubled Pennsylvania Line.

Even as hundreds of Pennsylvania soldiers were heading home—with pockets empty of real wages but holding certificates that promised back pay and land bounties—the New Jersey Line mutinied. The five hundred men in winter quarters at Pompton, New Jersey, had the same grievances as the Pennsylvania Line, and they were spirited up by news of the January 1 mutiny. On January 20, about two hundred of them revolted. Washington and Congress took a hard line, fearful of losing the entire army and knowing they could quell a small rebellion. Dispatching units of New Englanders from West Point under the command of Major General Robert Howe, Washington demanded unconditional surrender and ordered the positioning of cannons to maim the mutineers in their huts if they persisted, and the instant execution of "[a] few of the most active and incendiary leaders." Howe picked one mutinous leader from each regiment and detailed six others to form a firing squad. Kneeling in the snow a short distance from the first mutineer to be executed, all six members of the firing squad deliberately missed their target. A second squad finished the job.[103] The Connecticut physician serving with the New Jersey Line recorded in his journal that "This was a most painful task; being themselves guilty, they were greatly distressed with the duty imposed upon them, and when ordered to load some of them shed tears."[104] Two of the three singled out for execution fell before the firing squad; Howe pardoned the third mutineer at the last moment.

Four months later, after being on furlough, eight hundred men of the Pennsylvania Line reported for duty to York, Pennsylvania, and readied themselves for a march south to join General Lafayette for a showdown with Cornwallis's army. But they would not march until General Wayne suppressed a small-scale mutiny. This time the grievance was over the value of state-issued paper money. Because it was worth about one-seventh of hard money and losing its value day by day, enlisted men regarded it as so much wallpaper. But this time, freshly uniformed and well-fed, most men did not join the disaffected. Wayne moved quickly to cure the "distemper" with "a liberal dose of nitre." He clapped six mutineers into irons, conducted an instant drumhead trial, and detailed a firing squad to execute four of them. The wife of one of the four, Macaroney Jack, ran to her husband to embrace him for the last time, only to be "felled . . . to the ground" by a tremendous sword blow from one of the attending officers. A volley of musket fire from a distance of ten feet blew the heads off the four mutineers in "a most painful scene." The next day the Pennsylvania Line marched south to demonstrate, as the flamboyant Wayne put it, that his men "shall produce a conviction that death has no terrors when put in competition with our duty and glory." At the siege of Yorktown, Wayne's men proved him right. Lieutenant Colonel Henry ("Light Horse Harry") Lee called Wayne's soldiers "bold and daring," men who "would always prefer an appeal to the bayonet to a toilsome march."[105]

But toilsome marching was not yet over, nor was the matter of back pay, as we will see in the next chapter. For now, the mistreated Pennsylvania Line, mostly composed of young immigrant men, had served their nation and made their point. They hadn't the slightest doubt about which side they were on or where they wanted to live out their lives. But they still had a vision of the country they wanted to hand down to their children. That vision would be challenged at the end of the war and in the following years by those who thought the Revolution had gone much too far in putting power in the hands of ordinary people.

8

TAMING THE
REVOLUTION

1780–1785

"THE PEOPLE FIRED WITH A JUST RESENTMENT [WILL] RISE LIKE A whirlwind and spurn them from the earth and take the power again into their own hands."[1] When Boston newspaper readers scanned this crackling, ominous sentence in the spring of 1780, they no doubt knew that it related to the upheaval of Massachusetts farmers who were struggling with the lack of specie to pay their taxes, the fear of losing their land at auction to satisfy their debts, and continued resentment at the constitution that stripped many of them of the right to vote. Also in everyone's mind was the dismal state of the war effort—British successes in their southern campaign, a Continental army suffering massive desertions and close to disbanding for lack of supplies, and virtually insolvent state and congressional governments. In Congress and in some state legislatures, this had brought conservatives to the fore—men who had disliked radical democratic reform since 1775 and were now moving energetically to curb the power of the people. Their "presiding genius," as one historian has called him, was Robert Morris of Philadelphia, the very man despised by ordinary people for his careful attention to amassing wealth and his faint concern for the lower orders.[2]

A weak central government was what radical revolutionaries wanted, because they prized popular and local control of taxation and the power of annually elected legislators to prevent the concentration of wealth and power in the hands of the elite. After all, the Revolution began in reaction to taxes imposed from afar by the English government, where power concentrated in king and Parliament had brought arbitrary rule and invasions of the rights of citizens. But now, for many war-weary Americans, stronger government and new measures to restore fiscal stability seemed unavoidable. Writing in September 1780, when the war against Great Britain for independence was still in doubt and the nation's public credit and fiscal policy were in a state of collapse, the precocious twenty-three-year-old Alexander Hamilton, Washington's aide-de-camp and a skillful writer, pinpointed how conservatives saw the Continental Congress hobbled in prosecuting the war: "The [Articles of] Confederation . . . gives the power of the purse too entirely to the state legislatures. It should provide perpetual funds, in the disposal of Congress, by a land tax, poll tax, or the like. All imposts upon commerce ought to be laid by Congress and appropriated to their use. For without certain revenues, a government can have no power. That power which holds the purse-strings absolutely must rule."[3]

From 1780 until the end of the war in 1783, conservative delegates, led by merchants and lawyers from mid-Atlantic states, gained the upper hand in Congress. Their cardinal idea was to yoke the self-interest of the wealthy, particularly merchants, money holders, and large landowners, to the nation's problems. According to Morris's unsentimental philosophy, it was reasonable to reward the wealthy, even lavishly, to save the nation. Only sound money, taxation to retire discredited paper currency, and a laissez-faire posture toward merchant activity could salvage the struggling republic. This reform also required "a clean sweep of such radical paraphernalia as tender laws, price regulation, embargoes, and anti-monopoly laws," all of which had been passed at the height of radical influence to ease the pain of the worst positioned people of the nation.[4] Taming the social and political radicalism of the Revolution was equally important to the Morris circle.

Along with obliterating populist restrictions, Congress, in Morris's view, must find a reliable source of revenue to restore financial stability and pay for continuing the war. This meant a federal tax of some kind. Of taxes available, one on imported goods became the tax of choice. Though the delegates of twelve states agreed to levy a federal import duty of 5 percent on imported goods, called the "impost," by summer 1782, Rhode Island's delegates scuttled it. Morris predicted disaster; but to the rescue came huge loans and gifts from Holland and France and sharp reductions in the numbers of state militia and Continental troops—from a height of 90,000 in 1776 to 45,000 in 1780 to 29,000 in 1781. In 1782 and 1783, when Washington conducted only small military operations, these numbers fell to 18,000 and 13,000, greatly reducing war expenditures. Morris's administrative efficiency, along with his ability to get the states to contribute more of their quotas of men and matériel than before, also helped get the nation through until peace came in 1783.

Conservatives were smitten with Morris's acumen, particularly in stabilizing the currency, restoring the credit of the nearly bankrupt nation, and laying the foundations for a strong central government with moneyed men playing key roles. Like trying to purge a sick patient with strong emetics, the physician-financier Morris would administer heroic doses of fiscal reform that might hurt the patient grievously in the short run but rebuild the sick man's constitution for a healthy future.

Morris's policies have been debated vigorously by historians and economists ever since the early 1780s. Doubtless, he satisfied conservatives at the time—most of them known as tepid revolutionaries and some as outright Tories—and rewarded them with policies that would presumably solve the fiscal problems besetting the emerging nation. But Morris's policies attracted sharp criticism from those certain that his grand schemes rewarded the few while wounding the many. By March 1784, when he resigned his post, Morris had aroused great fear that he had built an "Aristocratical Junto" that would "destroy the Liberties of this Country," as Samuel Osgood wrote John Adams, at that time abroad in England.[5]

Robert Morris had contempt for ordinary people, intensified by the Fort Wilson firefight in late 1779. His leathery insensitivity to their struggles and his horror of a government by, of, and for what New Englanders called "the body of the people" provided the adrenaline that sparked his energy. Nothing satisfied Morris more than blunting the radical impulses of the previous years and discrediting the Pennsylvania Constitution of 1776. As a man of massive wealth, hugely increased during the depths of the war, he was supremely insensitive to the poor. A former slave trader and present slave owner, he had little sympathy for African Americans. As for Native Americans, his interest was only in the profits he could accrue by speculating in their lands. He was the embodiment of "the acquisitive spirit of wartime Philadelphia," as Thomas Doerflinger, the main historian of the city's revolutionary-era merchants, has said. It was not "virtue and patriotism" that motivated him but "getting and spending." More than almost anyone else among the Quaker city's shrewd merchants, he "was somehow able to manipulate the fiscal reins of government with one hand while multiplying his fortune with the other."[6] Many believed he was the nation's wealthiest man. Nobody better represented the growing separation between wealth and want. And no leader seemed more intent than Morris to roll back the popular movements that had been essential to precipitating and prosecuting the Revolution.

While the "reign of the financier" played itself out from 1780 to 1784, the vast majority of the many peoples of America had neither the leverage nor the ability to concoct a scheme for rescuing the nation from the collapse of the fiscal system. Their day-to-day life was far more mundane than Morris's and often precarious. Many were still involved in the war with England, both directly and indirectly, with some still in the firing zone while others were disengaging from the war and trying to recoup their livelihoods, reknit their families, and think about how government rewarded or punished them at the state and local levels. It is the ideas, actions, and hopes of the mass of people below Robert Morris that concern us in this chapter. The challenges in the last years of the war differed from group to group, whether African Americans, Native Americans, fighting men, women, or ordinary people of the North and South. But all of them inhabited a world a vast distance from that of Robert Morris.

"Band of Brotherhood"

The glow from the Yorktown surrender that suffused both American civilians and men in uniform in late 1781 did not end the struggle of Washington's army of the poor to get the minimal treatment they had fumed over for six years: promised wages, food sufficient to sustain life, shoes, socks, shirts, and blankets to ward off frostbite, and decent medical treatment. All of these unmet rudimentary requirements of military service haunted the lives of the soldiers as much as they had in 1776 or 1778. The main part of Washington's Continental army marched north through Baltimore, Philadelphia, and New York to Newburgh, where they set up winter quarters in 1781–82 along the Hudson. Other parts of the army moved south, including the unit of the Pennsylvania Line commanded by Brigadier General Anthony Wayne, to fall under the command of Rhode Island's Major General Nathanael Greene. By April 1782, now in Georgia to free the interior from

British control, the men were back to a state of rags and short rations. Putting up placards, the men asked: "Can soldiers do their duty if clad in rags and fed on rice?"[7]

As had happened so many times before, such conditions led to mutiny. This time disaffection hatched a plan to abduct General Greene and hold him hostage until he met the mutineers' demands. But one day before the planned abduction, several soldiers betrayed the mutineers. Singling out Sergeant George Goznall of the Second Pennsylvania as the ringleader, Wayne promptly ordered his execution. Wayne and his motley crew of Pennsylvanians marched southward, where they joined Georgia militiamen. For months, Wayne's men kept the British pinned down in Savannah while skirmishing with Creek warriors supplied by the British. After the British evacuation of Savannah in July 1782, Wayne's contingent moved northward to join General Greene in an attempt to recapture Charleston. When the British withdrew from the South's largest seaport town in December 1782 with four thousand Tory refugees and thousands of slaves, everyone knew that the war was winding down. All Americans now awaited the outcome of peace negotiations in Paris.

Winding down meant that the effusions of blood were nearly over; yet the nation's army still seethed with righteous anger. In the three months before word finally arrived from Paris that the peace treaty had been signed, Washington, his generals, and the Continental Congress had to cope with two crises precipitated by the unmet promises made to the "band of brotherhood," as Private Joseph Plumb Martin called the men of the Continental army.

Just two days before the dispatches from Congress's peace commissioners arrived on March 12, 1783 (having taken fourteen weeks to cross the Atlantic in stormy seas), with the glad tidings that a preliminary treaty had been hammered out, officers in the main part of Washington's army, huddled in winter quarters at Newburgh, New York, addressed their commanding officer with bitter words born of exhausted patience. If Congress failed to rectify their grievances, they would refuse to disband and "retire to some unsettled country," presumably the western frontier. In this event, Congress would lose its army, the nation would be disgraced, and the mutineers would retire with their weapons as a disaffected thorn in the side of the shaky new nation.

Washington's sympathy for his men was real, for he knew intimately about their starvation, the rags that substituted for uniforms, the insufferable arrears in pay, the plunging value of the paper money they intermittently received, Congress's dallying on the promised lifetime half-pay pension for officers, and the uncertainty of the promised land bounties. He remembered well how he had warned Congress on at least seven occasions the previous autumn about the dark mood of the officers "about to be turned into the world soured by penury and what they call the ingratitude of the public, involved in debts, without one farthing of money to carry them home, after having spent the flower of their days and many of them their patrimonies in establishing the freedom and independence of their country, and suffered everything human nature is capable of enduring on this side of death."[8] He also knew that a delegation of officers, headed by New York's Major General Alexander McDougall, had presented the same grievances to Congress two months before to no avail. He probably did not know that Major John Armstrong, Jr., aide-de-camp to General Horatio Gates, had composed the address. But Washington had never wavered in the conviction that the military must always subordinate itself to civil authority. Yet this time, it was his officers who had promised mutiny and withdrawal from the nation, with the inference that the enlisted men under them would follow.

Although the so-called Newburgh Conspiracy seemed to unite the officers with their bedraggled enlisted men, the officers were mostly tending to their own interests. They knew that state and congressional support of the army, limited and insufficient from the beginning, had wavered even more as the fighting drew to a close and everyone awaited the peace treaty. They also knew about the public displeasure with the promised lifetime half-pay pensions for officers, first offered by Congress in 1778 for those who pledged to serve for the duration of the war. Most of the officers were from New England, and they knew that their delegates to Congress had heatedly opposed pensions, regarding them as the foundation of a military-caste anathema to a republic. Such sentiment opposing pensions of any kind for officers grew through 1782 and early 1783, especially among ordinary people struggling under heavy tax burdens.

For Private Martin's "family of brothers," the officers' issue of pensions was not theirs, because nobody at any time had promised them more than a land bounty and monthly wages. Martin never even mentioned the officers' threatened mutiny at Newburgh in his journal of six years' service in the Continental army. What the privates of the army wanted was to go home, but to go home with the promised pay and bounties. General Henry Knox advised Washington of this as the commander in chief composed his address to the officer mutineers: "Will the three years men who came out upon large bounties and their wages secured by a private contract at home tarry a moment after they are told by Congress they may go?" Washington's mind was made up by Knox's advice to ask the officers, "When the soldiery forsake you, what will be your situation? Despised and insulted, by an enraged populace, exposed to the revenging hand of justice, you will then flee to caves and dens to hide yourselves from the face of day and of man."[9]

In deciding to face the officers down, Washington may also have understood that those in Congress who were campaigning for a stronger central government with the power to impose taxes, led by Robert Morris, were collaborating with some of his officers to threaten civil authority. This would frighten members of Congress who had resisted—and killed—the plan to empower Congress to levy impost taxes in order to rescue the nation from its fiscal crisis. The officers' threat to revolt was just what Robert Morris and the so-called nationalists of his group wanted. Nothing could be more effective than a group of revolting Continental army officers seeking greater central powers. It was reminiscent, as historian E. James Ferguson, has said, of Oliver Cromwell's Roundheads, "who, in an analogous situation during the Puritan Revolution [of the mid-seventeenth century] had turned on Parliament and subdued it when an attempt was made to disband them without pay."[10]

Sizing up the situation with plenty of advice from Henry Knox, the old Massachusetts warrior who had been at Bunker Hill and rose to major general of artillery, Washington defused the powder keg masterfully. Rather than trying to ferret out the precipitators of the officers' revolt and execute them on the spot, he called their bluff and turned an ugly situation to his advantage. Gathering together officer representatives of each regiment on March 15, he read an address he had labored over for nearly five days. "Gentlemen, by an anonymous summons, an attempt has been made to convene you together," he began; "how inconsistent with the rules of propriety! How unmilitary! And how subversive of all order and discipline, let the good sense of the army decide." Here he drew on eight years of leadership and the fund of reverence he had built up for his unwavering service to the nation. In a stroke of genius, he then pulled a letter from his pocket from a member of Congress promising that the officers would not be left in the lurch. Taking his glasses from his uniform to read the letter, he told the men "that he had grown grey in their service and now found himself growing blind." One of the officers present remembered later that "there was something so natural, so unaffected, in this appeal as rendered it superior to the most studied oratory. It forces its way to the heart, and you might see sensibility moisten every eye."[11] Washington then made his plea—rather more of an order—that the men desist, trust him to promote the interests of his army with Congress, and condemn in their own way Major Armstrong's threatening address. The shamefaced officers withdrew, patriotism won the day, and Washington prevailed.

Three months after the Newburgh Conspiracy, with all of America still awaiting the final peace treaty, the second crisis arose. This time it was enlisted men, not officers, who mutinied—and not high on the Hudson River but in the shadow of the statehouse in Philadelphia where Congress met. Barracked on the edge of the city were hardened veterans of the Continental army supplemented by new short-term Pennsylvania recruits who had never seen a redcoat or fired a gun at the enemy. Their barrack mates also included several hundred men of the Maryland Line. By June 1783, most of the men were grumbling over having received no pay since the previous December. Now their officers told them that Congress had ordered Washington's army to disband and that the Pennsylvania Line would be furloughed and paid in "Morris notes"—certificates to be redeemed at a later point by Congress's superintendent of finance. If this promise-to-pay arrangement rankled, worse still was the order to issue pay notes only for February, March, and April, with January, May, and June payments held in abeyance.

Hearing this, the soldiers revolted. On June 13, 1783, sergeants from each unit joined to send a remonstrance to Congress demanding their full pay. Hearing of this, hundreds of other men of the Pennsylvania Line, barracked at Lancaster, marched to Philadelphia to join their comrades. Two elected captains of the combined units carried their case to the statehouse, where the Continental Congress and the state's executive council had conducted the war for nearly seven years. Years of broken promises and shabby treatment brought tempers to a boil. Surrounding the statehouse on June 21, the insurgent soldiers gave Pennsylvania's president, Joseph Reed, twenty minutes to answer their demands. Without immediate satisfaction "they would turn ... an enraged soldiery on the [state's Supreme Executive] Council ... and do themselves justice."[12]

Inside the statehouse, Pennsylvania's Supreme Executive Council fenced with Congress. Who would rescue the dignity of the American government? Some volunteered the Philadelphia militia. But the militia's sympathies lay with the soldiers, not Congress or the state executive council. The militia captains told the council that "it would be imprudent" to call on the radical militia—a polite way of saying that the militiamen would just as soon shoot congressional delegates as turn against their brothers. Held hostage, the nation's government searched for a way out of the impasse. Congress's delegates were hardly heartened by the "thousands of citizens" gathered to witness the standoff "crying 'stand for your rights!'" as a veteran of the Pennsylvania Line later recalled.[13]

In midafternoon, the soldiers permitted the nation's government to file out of the statehouse and repair to their lodgings. Unable to gain assurances that it could be protected, Continental Congress president Elias Boudinot glumly ordered Congress to leave the city and move forty-five miles north to Princeton, New Jersey. After receiving promises that they would get full pay, the mutineers melted away. The affronted Continental Congress did not return to Philadelphia thereafter until 1790.

For the mutinous militiamen in midsummer of 1783 and their compatriots furloughed two hundred miles to the north at Newburgh and West Point, the future was as uncertain as it had been when they joined the army of the dispossessed. Private Joseph Plumb Martin remembered it vividly in his old age. He recalled how his captain summoned the men on June 11, 1783, just a few days before the mutiny in Philadelphia, and announced that the men were free to go—not completely released from service but furloughed, which meant "permission to return home, but to return to the army again if required." The soldiery now began to say their goodbyes, as much "a band of brotherhood as Masons and, I believe, as faithful to each other," remembered Martin. Some left "the same day that their fetters were knocked off." Others remained a day or so "to get their final settlement certificates, which they sold to procure decent clothing and money sufficient to enable them to pass with decency through the country and to appear something like themselves when they arrived among their friends."[14] Many of the soldiers trekked down the Hudson River to New York City, just as those furloughed in Philadelphia walked ninety miles north, where "a very great number," with only Morris notes of dubious value in their hands, "offered themselves up for employment" on British ships preparing to evacuate the British army, American Loyalists, and several thousand former slaves who had fought under the banner of George III. It was much the same for the First Regiment of Rhode Island. Ragged and penniless, many of them lame and sick, they tramped northward from Yorktown for nearly four hundred miles to reach their homes.[15]

Martin recounted the bitterness in their mouths as their "warworn weary limbs" carried them home. "When the country had drained the last drop of service it could screw out of the poor soldiers, they were turned adrift like old worn-out horses, and nothing said about land to pasture them upon." They had been promised one hundred acres of bounty land, and Congress did indeed designate "soldiers' land" in the Northwest Territory. But Martin recalled that "no care was taken that the soldiers should get them. No agents were appointed to see that the poor fellows ever got possession of their lands; no one ever took the least care about it, except a pack of speculators who were driving about the country like so many evil spirits, endeavoring to pluck the last feather from the soldiers." Martin was right that "the soldiers were ignorant of the ways and means to obtain their bounty lands, and there was no one appointed to inform them." Looking back many years as he reflected on his discharge from the army and his "band of brotherhood," he summed up: "The truth was, none cared for them; the country was served, and faithfully served, and that was all that was deemed necessary. It was, soldiers, look to yourselves, we want no more of you."[16]

Apart from the bounty lands, the final cruelty to the soldiers was how the states and Congress handled the resolution of their wages, the problem that had figured so importantly in the recurrent mutinies. Private Martin remembered the terms exactly: six and two-thirds dollars a month in Continental currency, to be paid monthly. But payments stopped in August 1777, according to his recollection, and the payment wouldn't have mattered much after that when a month's salary by 1778 "was scarcely enough to procure a man a dinner." Congress, he believed, "was ashamed to tantalize the soldiers any longer with such trash [promissory notes], and wisely gave it up for its own credit." As for specie payment, he received one month's pay only once, on the march to Yorktown in the summer of 1781. "The country was rigorous in exacting my compliance to *my* engagements to a punctilio, but equally careless in performing her contracts with me; and why so?" Martin asked bitterly. His answer went to the heart of one of revolutionary radicalism's main formulations: "One reason was because she had all the power in her own hands, and I had none. Such things ought not to be."[17]

The men of Rhode Island's First Regiment must have agreed heartily with Martin's stinging comments. Black and white soldiers alike, once back in their home states, tried to get their unpaid wages. For some black soldiers, this struggle went on while former masters attempted to reenslave them. The pay came by dribs and drabs. Some soldiers were still trying to get the balance of their pay in 1789.[18] This would leave thousands of men, many with families, disgruntled, disillusioned, and resentful—a reservoir of men inclined to seek radical solutions to their problems.

Peace Without Peace

As the war in the South reached a spasmodic conclusion in Georgia and the Carolinas after the British surrender at Yorktown in October 1781, war in the West hardly stopped at all. Nor did the 1783 Treaty of Paris bring peace to the interior Indian nations. It might have been otherwise. A few important white leaders experienced in negotiating with Indian chiefs in the *pays d'en haut* thought that peace was achievable on the western frontier if state governments could restrain white land encroachers. Such a man was George Morgan, a former Indian trader who represented the Continental Congress at Pittsburgh from 1776 to 1779. Morgan had worked skillfully with village chiefs to keep Delawares, Munsees, Wyandots, Mingos, and many of the Shawnee neutral for the first three years of war. Contributing to this neutrality was the work of pacifist Moravian missionaries among the Delaware. But Morgan always worked against the grain of frontiersmen. As early as 1777, he reported the frontiersmen's "ardent desire for an Indian war on account of the fine lands those poor people possess." Pennsylvania frontiersmen were hell-bent "to massacre some who have come to visit us in a friendly manner and others who have been hunting on their own lands, the known friends of the Commonwealth."[19]

In 1778, Americans cudgeled the Delaware into an alliance. Promised an adequate supply of trade goods and seeing an opportunity to wrest independence from their Six Nation overlords, Quequedegatha (George White Eyes to white Americans) and other headmen agreed to the Treaty of Pittsburgh, which they believed only committed them to giving free passage to American troops who would build a fort to protect the Delaware villages in Ohio country. The chiefs took an interest in what proved to be a cynical American proposal that the Delaware might join the United States as a fourteenth state and even have representation in Congress. The treaty also included a first clause that spoke nobly "that all offences or acts of hostilities by one, or either of the contracting parties against the other, be mutually forgiven and buried in the depths of oblivion, never more to be had in remembrance."[20] This clause would soon assume a strange visage.

After the treaty signing, American negotiators insisted that the Delaware warriors join the fight against the British. The rebuilt fort at Pittsburgh became the base from which Brigadier General Lachlan McIntosh, commander of the Western Department, launched an offensive in November 1778. George White Eyes joined the expedition to guide them, though his warriors refused. He never returned. American officers claimed he died of smallpox, but the historical record shows that he was murdered by the militiamen and secretly buried. "Thus was lost," writes historian Randolph Downes, "one of the most trusting Indian friends the American people ever had."[21]

Most Delawares now went over to the British side. Some still hoped for supplies from the Americans and maintained their allegiance. But another treacherous blow by the Americans in 1780 washed away the remaining pro-American sentiment. Captain Daniel Brodhead, commander at Fort Pitt and veteran of Sullivan's scorched-earth campaign two years before, shattered the Treaty of Pittsburgh in April 1781 with an unprovoked attack on the central Delaware town of Coshocton. After razing the cluster of Delaware villages, Brodhead's men executed all but four male Delaware prisoners and tomahawked a Delaware peace emissary from behind as he was negotiating with Brodhead.[22]

By 1781, the bloodlust of the frontiersmen seemed unquenchable. It was true that renegade young Delaware warriors had killed whites, especially those encroaching on their lands. "The backcountry settlers, however," writes historian Richard White, "lumped all Indians together and the results proved disastrous for American Indian policy. Indian haters killed or alienated the very men who were willing to act as alliance chiefs or mediators for the Americans.... Indian hating did not concentrate on enemies. Indian haters killed Indians who warned them of raids. They killed Indians who scouted for their military expeditions. They killed Indian women and children.... Murder gradually and inexorably became the dominant American Indian policy, supplanting the policies of Morgan, of the Congress, and of the military."[23]

Indian hating and the genocidal policy that it embodied came to a gory

377

climax as winter descended in late 1782 at the Moravian mission village of Gnadenhutten ("Huts of Grace") on the banks of the Muskingum River in eastern Ohio. German immigrant missionaries had worked among the Delaware people since the 1740s and had seen them through the ravages of the Seven Years' War and Pontiac's Rebellion. As in these earlier conflicts, the Delaware fragments wished only to remain pacifists and devout Christians as the American Revolution ran its course. But when most of the nonpacifist Delawares reluctantly allied with the British near the end of the war, British agent Matthew Elliott insisted in the autumn of 1782 that the Christianized Delawares and their missionaries, John Heckewelder and David Zeisberger, withdraw to the west, where on the banks of the Sandusky River in Ohio country the British and their Indian allies could protect them.[24]

During a difficult winter, the nearly starved Moravian-led Delawares received permission to return through winter snow to their abandoned villages to gather unharvested corn for their people. Before reaching their villages, they ran into a militant Delaware war party that had murdered an American woman and child. Telling their pacifist brethren that they were expecting American militiamen to pursue them, the war party left the village. Hot behind them, Pennsylvania militiamen led by Captain David Williamson fell upon the group of Christianized Indians—twenty-eight men, twenty-nine women, and thirty-nine children—at Gnadenhutten and those brought in from the neighboring Christian village of Salem. Insisting that the pious Delawares had been part of the killing of the American woman and child, Williamson's men voted to execute them, with a minority protesting unsuccessfully that these were harmless Christians who had adopted the ways of whites. The Delawares clung together, sang hymns, and prayed through the night.

On the morning of March 7, 1782, in a grisly replay of the Paxton Massacre of nineteen years before, militiamen dragged the helpless Delawares by twos and threes to a cabin later described by the militiamen as "the slaughter house." One of the militiamen bludgeoned fourteen Indians with a cooper's mallet before turning the job over to another soldier. "My arm fails me," he said. "Go on with the work. I have done pretty well." Williamson's men scalped the corpses and divided the trophies. Burning the village to the ground, they confiscated scores of Indian horses. Only two of the ninety-six Delawares survived to spread the word about the massacre. Hearing a report of the massacre, the Pennsylvania legislature condemned the barbarous

John Vanderlyn, whose life-size portraits of George Washington and the Marquis de Lafayette hang in the U.S. House of Representatives to the wonderment of millions of visitors, probably had more impact on Americans with his 1804 painting of the murder of Jane McCrea near Saratoga in 1777. McCrea was the fiancée of a soldier in British general John Burgoyne's army. Vanderlyn shows the ferocious, muscular warriors mercilessly poised to scalp and kill the defenseless young woman (who was, in fact, felled by American bullets). Heralded as an important work of art as Jefferson was finishing his first term as president, The Murder of Jane McCrea *seared into the American mind the stereotype of the Indian as a remorseless savage and justified the dispossession of Indian land in the new republic. No Native Americans could paint their version of savagery, but the historical record is clear that the number of Indian women slaughtered by American warriors far exceeded the deaths of white women like Jane McCrea.*

behavior of the militiamen as "an act disgraceful to humanity." But as would happen so many times on the westward-moving frontier, no action was taken against the commanding officer or the men under him. Neither the Pennsylvania legislature nor the Continental Congress saw fit to investigate the matter. The motto "the only good Indian is a dead Indian" had moved from a generalized feeling among white frontiersmen to unofficial state and federal policy.

The Delawares aligned with the British always had uneasy relations with their Christianized brethren, but the massacre at Gnadenhutten intensified their hatred of the American frontiersmen. Their appetite for revenge was further whetted a few weeks after the Gnadenhutten bloodbath when frontier militiamen continued their rampage of ethnic cleansing on an island near Fort Pitt, where a small group of friendly Delawares were encamped. They had served the Americans at Fort Pitt as hunters and guides; two had been commissioned by the Americans as captains. Driving off a small regular army contingent guarding them, the militiamen killed all but two of the Delawares.

Ten weeks later the Indians got their revenge. Emboldened by the slaughter of pacifist and friendly Delawares, the militiamen under Captain David Williamson wanted to continue westward to wipe out what they regarded as the nests of Ohio country Indians who had repeatedly raided white settlements. This time they were joined by a few regulars from Fort Pitt and a surgeon's mate. Also with them was the personal aide of Fort Pitt's new commander, Brigadier General William Irvine—a Russian nobleman, Count Rosenberg, who had fled his country after a dual, disappeared into the American wilderness, and taken the American name of John Rose. Commanding the men was an intimate friend of George Washington's, Colonel William Crawford, who had fought in the Seven Years' War at Washington's side and was Washington's land agent in the transmontane Appalachians. Nearly five hundred short-term militiamen voted for the officer to lead the expedition, and Crawford nosed out David Williamson, who became second in command.

Heading west in late May 1782, most of them with horses, controlling the militiamen became a test of Crawford's leadership. Unruly, untrained, and opportunistic, the men were difficult to keep together in any kind of disciplined formation for the ten days it took to move west 150 miles from Fort Pitt to the Sandusky plains, where the main Indian towns were located. The slow progress proved fatal. Shadowing the Americans, Indian scouts knew exactly where the enemy was each day, and the Americans' dawdling pace allowed time for Butler's Rangers to move into the area to join the Delaware, Wyandot, and Mingo warriors of the Sandusky region. They encircled the Americans and engaged them on June 4, 1782. In a brisk skirmish, Indian warriors killed or wounded twenty-four militiamen. Retreating into the woods, the Americans spent the next day arguing about a strategy before deciding to attempt a nighttime retreat. Although they were supposed to withdraw in a column, the undisciplined frontiersmen disintegrated at the first burst of Indian fire. Fleeing eastward for the Ohio River, the panicked militiamen fell by scores to pursuing Delaware, Shawnee, Mingo, and Butler's Rangers. Among those captured was the expedition's commander, William Crawford. All of the built-up hatred, from the Delaware attempts to remain neutral to the assassination of George White Eyes to the Gnadenhutten massacre, fell upon Washington's lifelong friend. Tormented, scalped, and burned at the stake, he perished before the eyes of John Knight, the American surgeon, who escaped as he was being taken to a nearby Shawnee town for execution. It took only a year before Knight's story of Crawford's grisly death came off the press in Philadelphia, to become another key piece of literature feeding indiscriminate Indian hating. The story of the Gnadenhutten massacre of women and children, meanwhile, went untold.

Joseph Brant and the militant Iroquois had ended the war almost as it began: raids against Americans in the Mohawk River valley, along the Hudson River, and even west into Pennsylvania and the Ohio country. Recovering from Sullivan's village-razing expedition, they had once again gained the upper hand from the Mohawk to the Ohio, even obliging the Americans to abandon Fort Stanwix. Through the eyes of Brant, the Iroquois and their allied tribes had more than held their own, a judgment confirmed by historians since. When the Indians heard that the treaty of peace signed by British and American signatories made not the slightest mention of Iroquois interests and ceded all Indian land east of the Mississippi to the Appalachians to the United States, they were thunderstruck. The British fought hard in the peace negotiations to protect the property of the American Loyalists who had held constant to the king, but they made no attempts to bargain on behalf of their Indian allies. In one of the lamest rationalizations in the history of treaty making Lord Shelburne, head of George III's ministry, defended the preliminary articles of peace by explaining that "the Indian nations were not abandoned to their enemies; they were remitted to the care of neighbors, whose interest it was as much as ours to cultivate friendship with them, and who were certainly the best qualified for softening and humanizing their hearts." "Almost at the lowest tide of effectiveness of its Indian policy," writes Downes, "the vanquished [Americans] had become the victors."[25]

For British officers and Indian administrators in Iroquois country, the British abandonment of their dark-skinned allies was a horrendous embarrassment. Mohawk chief Kanonaron, known to the English as Captain Aaron Hill, upbraided the British commander at Fort Detroit that the Iroquois "were a free people subject to no power on earth." They "were the faithful allies of the King of England, but not his subjects," and therefore George III had "no right whatever to grant away to the States of America their rights or properties without a manifest breach of all justice and equity."[26]

Peace with England actually emboldened American frontiersmen to continue their war against Native Americans. George Rogers Clark launched his second expedition against the Shawnee on November 1, 1782, *after* word had arrived of agreement on the articles of peace. The interior tribes sought help from the British, still at Fort Detroit, and it was in the British interest to support them because they hoped to control the immensely profitable fur trade of the upper Great Lakes area after the war, by itself the main reason for retaining Canada. But in October 1783, Congress announced that it was master of all land east of the Great Miami and Maumee rivers from Lake Erie to the north and the Ohio River to the south—a great part of the unconquered lands of the Delaware, Wyandot, Miami, and Shawnee. One historian writes that "for imperial aggressiveness and outright effrontery this document takes a front rank in the annals of American expansion," and describes it as "nothing less than an open declaration of war."[27]

Fearing that such a policy would cement an uprising of a general Indian confederacy, Congress pursued what has been called a "policy of modified aggression." Yet frontiersmen were still swarming into Indian territory as a treaty with the Iroquois and their allied tribes was called for in September 1784. The Iroquois chiefs had little choice but to meet with the Americans in September and October of 1784 at Fort Stanwix to sign what they believed would be an honorable peace with both sides laying down their weapons. Yet the Fort Stanwix treaty was anything but honorable. The Iroquois, writes Anthony Wallace, "would lose over the council table the lands and the political sovereignty that white armies had been unable to seize by force." Congress operated as if the Iroquois were conquered people who had lost the war and therefore should be treated as subjects. From the American viewpoint, the British had lost and therefore their Indian allies surrendered their sovereignty, and the ownership of their soil, south of the Great Lakes and east of the Mississippi River. Thus, at Fort Stanwix, the United States would "give" peace to the Iroquois and allow them such pieces of land as they deemed fit. As subjects, they might be "civilized" as the salving water of Christianity gradually washed away their inferiority. Most whites, especially frontiersmen, doubted Indians could be improved or that they could coexist, though some, missionaries in particular, urged the effort. Washington gave blunt expression to the prevailing view: that one way or another Indians must withdraw from the settlers' path once England had surrendered its right to the vast trans-Appalachian west: "The gradual extension of our settlements will as certainly cause the savage as the wolf to retire; both being beasts of prey though they differ in shape."[28]

The Fort Stanwix treaty of 1784 was purportedly signed between Congress and the Iroquois Confederacy, including the Six Nations' western dependents and allies—the Shawnee, Wyandot, Chippewa, Delaware, and so forth. As Wallace describes it, "negotiations were held at gunpoint, hostages were unexpectedly demanded and taken by the United States for the deliberate purpose of coercion of the Indian delegates; the tone of the Continental commissioners was insulting, arbitrary, and demanding; and two Indians given up by the Seneca to be punished according to white law were lynched by a mob shortly after the treaty." Joseph Brant stormed out of the conference in disgust remarking, "we are sent in order to make peace and . . . we are not authorized to stipulate any particular cession of land."[29]

Some of the Iroquois war chiefs resisted the draconian terms dictated by the American commissioners, but the Iroquois were badly split and in a nearly impossible situation. Arthur Lee, one of the commissioners, lectured the chiefs that "You are a subdued people; you have been overcome in a war which you entered into with us, not only without provocation, but in violation of most sacred obligations."[30] All of this was fiction. But with their options severely limited, the chiefs yielded most of their land. Not unexpectedly, the chiefs found that the treaty was deemed unacceptable back in their villages. Yet uncertain of British military support, the Iroquois tacitly accepted it. In 1785, American commissioners forced similar treaties at Fort McIntosh on the western allies of the Iroquois whereby the Wyandot, Ottawa, Chippewa, and Delaware surrendered all but fragments of eastern and southern

Ohio—reservations in the wilderness—where they "were to remain on sufferance."[31] The War of Independence and the war to reform American society had reached climaxes simultaneously with the war of national expansion. Joseph Brant, who knew his Mohawk people could never return to the Mohawk River valley, began paving the way for his people to move to the Grand River region of southern Canada.

The story in Indian country to the south was much the same: murderous attacks carried out by small groups becoming genocidal state policy. Reeling from wartime losses and the collapse of their British allies by 1782, the Cherokee were nearly helpless in fending off the heavily armed frontiersmen pouring onto their lands. Even Dragging Canoe's Chickamauga secessionists wanted peace. But a negotiated peace was not what Virginian and Carolinian frontiersmen wanted. Some of their leaders, such as Virginia's governor, Benjamin Harrison, believed that "Indians have their rights and our justice is called on to support them. Whilst we are nobly contending for liberty, will it not be an eternal blot on our national character if we deprive others of it who ought to be as free as ourselves?"[32] But frontiersmen wanted a dictated peace. In the fall of 1782, John Sevier, as much an Indian hater as George Rogers Clark, led an expedition to raze the Chickamauga towns. In January 1783, the aged Cherokee chief Oconostota gave a talk before the Americans at the Cherokee holy town of Chota. Almost blind and about to die of tuberculosis, one of the Europeans' lethal microbial bullets, the chief spoke of how "All the old warriors are dead. There are now none left to take care of the Cherokees, but you and myself, and for my part I am become very old. And this beloved town of Chota belongs to you."[33]

Nonetheless, Chickamauga Cherokees held out hope that the British, with only Saint Augustine as a foothold in the Lower South, would continue the fight. Some Cherokee warriors trekked northward to live among and fight alongside the Shawnee as the war came to an end. But resistance to the land-hungry Americans was almost suicidal in the face of huge odds—some 150,000 Native Americans were outnumbered sixteen to one by the end of the war. In ceding huge portions of their homelands to the Americans in the Treaty of Hopewell in November 1785, the Cherokees hoped for fixed and durable boundaries beyond which the Americans would not cross. This was not to be.

South of the Cherokee, the Creek confederacy—a loose coalition of town-centered people whose local interests usually trumped loyalty to the Creek people at large—struggled too with the closing stages of the war. Most of them had refused to join the militant Cherokees during the war and maintained their neutrality until 1778, much sobered by the repeated devastation of Cherokee villages by American expeditions. But as was the case for so many other Indian nations, choices amidst the maelstrom of war hung on maintaining supply links—to either the British or the Americans—and the fear of the swelling white population always eyeing fertile Indian lands.[34] George Galphin, Georgia's most important Creek Indian trader and frontier leader, exerted himself prodigiously to keep the Creeks supplied; but keeping frontiersmen from tangling with Creeks in hopes of gaining their land required just as much of his time and talent.

The British capture of Savannah in December 1778 and their incursions into the up-country toward Augusta, gathering Loyalist support along the way, swung most of the Creeks to the British side. Accompanying the British was Alexander McGillivray, son of the Scottish immigrant Indian trader Lachlan McGillivray, who had married a Creek-French woman from the important Wind Clan. McGillivray was to become the Joseph Brant of the South—thoroughly bilingual and bicultural, and firmly aligned with the British because of his hatred of the voraciously land-hungry white settlers. Joining the British at Savannah with seventy Creek warriors, McGillivray was part of the plundering army that carried off slaves and captured Augusta in September 1780. This victory, however, was actually the beginning of the end. When the Spanish capture of Pensacola and Mobile in spring 1781 dried up the Creeks' source of British trade goods, the tables turned. The 1782 campaigns of Generals Nathanael Greene and Anthony Wayne mopped up British resistance, which ceased with their evacuation of Savannah and Charleston. The war had thus turned against the side the militant Creeks had chosen, leaving neutralists equally vulnerable, as had been the case with accommodationist Cherokee and Delaware.

At the Treaty of Augusta in western Georgia in November 1783, compliant pro-American and neutralist Creek chiefs tried to buy peace in the manner of Cherokee and other tribal chiefs facing land-avid frontiersmen. By ceding eight hundred square miles between the Ocmulgee and Oconee rivers, the Creeks hoped for harmony and security. Alexander McGillivray, their recently appointed chief, knew better. Like Dragging Canoe of the Cherokees, McGillivray refused to participate in peace talks, counting on the British to remember Creek support. Hearing rumors that the British would cede East Florida to the Spanish, Chief Fine Bones of the principal Creek town of Coweta asked the British commanders at Saint Augustine, "Why will they [the British] turn their backs on us and forsake us? We never expected that men and warriors, our friends, would throw us into the hands of our enemies. . . . If the English mean to abandon the land we will accompany them. We cannot take a Virginian [Creek term for Americans] or Spaniard by the hand. We cannot look them in the face." Gaining power as chief spokesman for the Creek confederacy, McGillivray echoed the thought, complaining bitterly that "this nation gave proofs of unshaken fidelity and at the close of it to find ourselves betrayed to our enemies and divided between Spaniards and Americans is cruel and ungenerous."[35] Thus, the Creeks ended the war like the Cherokees, as a bitterly divided people.

When the definitive Paris peace treaty arrived, McGillivray and other militant Creek chiefs denounced it and strengthened their hand by signing a treaty with the Spanish at Pensacola in June 1784. This put the Creeks under Spanish protection and assured them the crucial supply of trade goods that would protect them, as they put it cleverly, "from the bears and other fierce animals."[36]

Though the Spanish had supported the Americans in the latter stages of the war, they now looked to their own interests across the southernmost tier of North America. For McGillivray, the feeling was much the same as the Chickamaugan Cherokee: Short of support from some other power than the victorious Americans, "we may be forced to purchase a shameful peace and barter our country for a precarious security." Addressing the Continental Congress in 1785, McGillivray spoke for most of the Indian nations now facing the victorious Americans without British allies. "We chiefs and warriors of the Creek, Chickasaw, and Cherokee Nations . . . protest against any title, claim, or demand the American Congress may set up for or against our lands, settlements, and hunting grounds in consequence of the . . . treaty of peace between the King of Great Britain and the states of America." Pointing out that the Indian nations were not participants in the peace negotiations, they vowed "to pay no attention to the manner in which the British negotiators . . . [have] drawn out the lines of the lands in question ceded to the States of America." Georgians and Carolinians, McGillivray continued, "have divided our territories into counties and sat themselves down on our land as if it were their own. . . . While they are addressing us by the flattering appellations of Friends and Brothers, they are stripping us of our natural rights by depriving us of that inheritance which belonged to our ancestors and hath descended from them to us since the beginning of time."[37] It was through McGillivray's emergence as a power broker between the Creeks and the Spanish that he was able to bring greater political cohesion to the decentralized, often fractious Creek people. This would serve the Creeks well in the next decade.

For all of its power, the victorious new nation found the proud Creek and Chickamaugan warriors capable of holding their own. An English visitor at the end of the war wrote of how "nothing is more common than to hear" the Americans "talk of extirpating them from the face of the earth, men, women, and children." But in 1786–87, Cherokee and Creek war parties, aided by the Shawnee, drove Americans from disputed lands in Georgia and Tennessee, the first of a series of American setbacks that obliged the government to look toward negotiating with Indian leaders instead of "extirpating" them. It occurred to some American leaders, especially Henry Knox, who was appointed secretary of war in 1785, that Indians were the most patriotic of all the combatants involved in the American Revolution if patriotism was defined as the willingness to sacrifice everything for the good of the whole. "Instead of a language of superiority and command," he asked Congress, "may it not be politic and just to treat with the Indians more on a footing of equality?"[38]

Southern Fissures

Hundreds of miles north of the Creek nation, the Marquis de Chastellux, after three convivial days of spirited conversation with Jefferson at Monticello, settled down in Williamsburg to reflect on what he had seen during a month-long trip through Virginia in April 1782. Born to a military family, Chastellux had arrived with the French fleet under Rochambeau at Newport in July 1780, had sailed into the Chesapeake Bay as a major general of the French troops the next summer, took part in the siege of Yorktown in October 1781, and marched northward with the French all the way to New England the summer following Yorktown. A keen observer and accomplished writer, Chastellux puzzled over the European-like conditions he found in the Virginia countryside. Neither in Rhode Island, Pennsylvania, New York, nor New Jersey had he seen "the state of poverty in which a great number of white people live in Virginia." "It is in this state, for the first time since I crossed the sea, that I have seen poor people." Stitched between the wealthy plantations he had visited, "where the Negro alone is wretched," he found "miserable huts ... inhabited by whites, whose wane looks and ragged garments bespeak poverty." Chastellux knew all about the dismal peasantry of France, where he was born in 1754; but the grinding poor of American farmers in the rich soils of Virginia shocked him. How was it, he wondered, "in a country where there is still so much land to clear, [and] men who do not refuse to work," that such men "could remain in misery?" The answer, he learned, was that a small fraction of Virginia's white men owned almost all the good land of the state, concentrated in "immense estates" of many thousand acres, and that these land-rich grandees—men like Washington, Jefferson, Mason, and Madison—refused to "sell [even] the smallest portion of it" because the planters "always hope to increase eventually the number of their Negroes."[39]

Chastellux also witnessed another phenomenon he had never seen in his years of army service in France: The invading British army had plundered the countryside in the spring of 1781, taking "fruit, fowl, and cattle," only to have this "hurricane ... followed by a scourge yet more terrible." The scourge, he related, was "a numerous rabble, under the names of Refugees and Loyalists" who "followed the army, not to assist in the field, but to share the plunder." These were not wealthy Loyalists firmly attached to the king but the poor Virginians who had resisted the draft, resented the unequal burdens that the rich tried to place on the shoulders of the poor, and rioted to stop drafts and military recruitment after the British invasion in 1780. Descending on the plantations of wealthy patriot leaders, they "stripped the owners" of everything but "furniture and clothing." Even the latter became booty, as Chastellux heard from William Byrd III, who related his "distress that they had forcibly taken the very boots from off his feet." Chastellux called them "robbers," but what he was describing was the forced redistribution of property at the hands of Virginia's desperately poor—men for whom lofty principles about natural rights and freedom as trumpeted by wealthy Virginia patriots had little meaning.[40]

Chastellux's comments alert us to the fact that as the War of Independence was winding down after Yorktown, the war against poverty and the yawning gap between rich and poor was far from over. Even the most fervent revolutionary leaders of Virginia, men such as Patrick Henry and Richard Henry Lee, were focused mostly on the issue of independence from England. None except one advocated even partial leveling of their highly stratified society, where tenant farmers greatly outnumbered landowners. Jefferson made a truly radical stab by writing into his drafts of the 1776 Virginia constitution a clause giving fifty acres of land to each landless adult white man on the assumption that political democracy was unsustainable without economic democracy. This proved unacceptable to most legislators, and thereafter Jefferson became mostly an armchair radical, speaking of a "natural aristocracy" of virtuous and talented individuals open to all comers and waxing eloquent about a nation of self-sufficient yeoman farmers.

But how could poor Virginians acquire land to become the industrious, incorruptible citizens who would form the bedrock of the republic? Jefferson's first answer was that by abolishing entail and primogeniture wealthy landowners could distribute their property more equally to all their progeny and thus broaden the base of the narrow and powerful aristocracy. Jefferson always prided himself on this reform, telling John Adams that he had "laid the axe to the root of pseudoaristocracy."[41] Primogeniture and entail was the ancient rule of passing one's estate intact to the eldest son, which had been used effectively to perpetuate Virginia's aristocracy. Jefferson's bill to abolish entail in Virginia, which enforced primogeniture, passed by a single vote in 1776. This was indeed an important reform, frightening enough for the land- and slave-rich Landon Carter to call Jefferson a "midday drunkard" for the "cursed bill" that betrayed his class by taking the first step to loosen up the nearly feudal system of concentrated economic power. But it was a reform that redistributed property mostly within upper-level Virginia families, not in Virginian society at large.[42]

Jefferson's second solution for a class-torn society was cheap western land, and he looked to Kentucky as the land bank that would rescue impoverished white Virginians. To be sure, he did his part in cleansing Kentucky of Shawnee and other native peoples in order to open it for white settlement. But providing access to that land also depended on blocking the powerful companies of speculators who sought control of it, and whose prices usually put the land out of the reach of the desperate white farmers who had plundered plantations on the trail of Cornwallis's army. Jefferson was himself only a minor investor in these companies, but he did little to stop them.[43] The problem would eventually fall into the hands of the federal government after the seaboard states relinquished their western land claims to the Continental Congress.

In Maryland, the travails of the poor were usually worsened, not improved, by the war. Like other southern states, Maryland had great difficulty in filling its quota of soldiers for Washington's Continental army or even getting its county militia units to turn out. Those who were recruited or drafted were mostly poor. If they were married, service in the army further impoverished their families, because wives and children lost a key part of their family's productive capacity. The appeals of the destitute in Charles County, across the Potomac River separating northern Virginia from Maryland, are typical. One man whose five grown sons had joined him in enlisting in the Continental army appealed for aid to support five other young children. Another appealed that the loss of two sons who had enlisted at age sixteen stripped away most of the family's labor, leaving him desperate to "get me and my family the necessaries of life." A woman with two small children and pregnant with a third had only her own labor to support her family, leaving her in "a very distressed situation" where "they must unavoidably suffer exceedingly unless relieved."[44] For those widowed by a husband's death in the army, the situation was nearly irreparable. Yet Maryland's lower classes were better off than those in Virginia because the gentry—under the nation's most conservative state constitution—had enacted radical fiscal reform that reapportioned the tax burden more fairly and gave debtors some relief by making depreciated paper money legal tender.

However, Marylanders could not escape the scarcity of hard money and credit that swept the entire country in the latter stages of the war. This led to a torrent of foreclosures, forced property sales, and imprisonments for debt. Nearly everyone was affected, but the hardest hit were those with the smallest cushion of liquidity. For middling farmers, the war's end brought distress in the form of an economic recession and taxes heavier than they could possibly pay. What raised the tax burden in particular was the states' agreement in 1780, under Robert Morris's urging, to absorb the burden of back pay for Continental army troops. Like every other state, Maryland issued certificates for back pay, but these certificates held their value only through tax collections. This led to tax increases in 1780–83.

When the tax collector knocked on the door and the cupboard was bare, what was an ordinary farmer supposed to do? The answer in Maryland was a pragmatic one, derived from the accommodation that Maryland's elite had earlier been forced to reach with those beneath them. Tax collectors and sheriffs in the mid-1780s, now elected rather than appointed as in colonial days, cut straitened taxpayers some slack, making few attempts to haul delinquent farmers away from their fields and families to fill small county jails. Even magistrates adjourned court sessions in order to postpone judgments. If they did not, they faced what Charles County judges experienced in 1786 when they decided to move ahead with cases leading to imprisonment for debt. Before they could issue judgments, a crowd rushed into the courthouse to stop the proceedings. Supporting the mob from behind the scenes was none other than Walter Hanson, the state's chief justice.[45] When creditors took debtors to court, most magistrates delayed the proceedings or refused to apply the law strictly while waiting for a more robust economy to salvage the situation. Here the informal law of equity, trumping contract law, was one of the fruits of revolution on behalf of the least powerful.

The safety valve for poor Marylanders, and for those in every other state, was to tramp west. One Maryland tenant farmer, concluding that it was "most impossible for the poor man to live," joined the "incessant migrations to the farther regions," as Johann David Schoepf, a visiting observer, described it.[46] As we will see in the epilogue, this was not always the hoped-for remedy. A close friend of Jefferson's, Elizabeth House Trist, traveling through the western lands to which poor Americans were flocking at the end of the war, saw mostly desperate poverty. "Everyone thinks their troubles the greatest, but I have seen so many poor creatures . . . whose situation has been so wretched. . . . Here is a poor family encamped . . . A man and his wife, their father and mother, and 5 children . . . on their way to the Cumberland River and had not a morsel of bread for the last three months. They had buried one of the oldest of their sons a little while before. The poor children, when they saw us, cry'd for some bread."[47] We have no way of knowing whether this was the typical experience of those rushing like lemmings toward the western lands, though it is certain that the better off they were as they left their eastern homes, the better the chances they had of thriving in the lands being vacated by retreating Native Americans.

Farther south, in South Carolina's backcountry, the matter of tax collections and debt recovery was almost minor in view of the beastly experiences in the last years of the war. *Annus mirabilis,* the year of the Yorktown triumph for Americans, had been *annus horribilus.* The sharp division between poor farmers of the backcountry and the wealthy slaveocracy of the coastal low country that had erupted in 1775–76 simmered during the next five years. The patriot state government sitting in Charleston deployed such militia units as could be spared from slave-patrol duty to root out Loyalists between

1775 and 1779, succeeding partially by driving some of them out of the state and convincing others to switch sides. William Henry Drayton, president of the South Carolina Provincial Congress, played the role of a "political missionary" who preached "the gospel of liberty" to "a largely uninterested audience." Offering Cherokee land as bounty for joining patriot militia units, and even suggesting that enslaved Indians would be awarded as well, did not suppress backcountry Loyalism. But generally, South Carolinians, whatever their political allegiances, profited from their remoteness from the war until 1779. "The bulk of the people were scarcely sensible of any revolution or that the country was at war," wrote David Ramsay, a contemporary Charleston physician and historian of the war. Since South Carolina was one of the chief suppliers of provisions for the war-torn northern states, plantation owners, farmers, artisans, and wagoners busied themselves more with making money out of the war than with protecting their liberties.[48]

But as the British mounted their invasion in 1779, to judge by James Simpson, an important Tory leader, "there were still great numbers who continue firm in their opposition and were become most violent in their enmity to those by whom they had been oppressed." However, the British overestimated the number of Loyalists who would spring to action once the king's troops made a show of force. The British also greatly injured their cause by trying to force those preferring neutrality into British units, a policy that backfired and drove many neutrals into the patriot camp. The British occupation of South Carolina and Georgia in 1780 turned a simmering conflict into "a virtual civil war."[49]

This civil war, described by historian Clyde Ferguson as "a fratricidal conflict characterized by ruthlessness and undisguised brutality," was not neatly defined by class categories, but it unmistakably had a classist dimension. Though most up-country Loyalist leaders were men of some wealth, as measured by land and slaves, "in their effort to attract followers they played on widespread resentments against the wealthier planters and merchants of the coast."[50] From 1779 to 1783, the Lower South, as military historian Don Higginbotham describes it, "was ravaged by the war as no other section of the country. Its governmental processes had collapsed, and its society had disintegrated to the point that it approached John Locke's savage state of nature."[51]

That the Loyalist and patriot militia units were about evenly divided, as were the Continental and British army contingents, contributed to the partisan, bushwhacking warfare that kept South Carolina ablaze for several years.

The savagery of the fighting, the ferocity of plundering forays, and particularly the atrocity killings of surrendering men by both sides seemed to have begun with the British killing of captured patriots, though the historical record on this remains cloudy. By June 1781, General Nathanael Greene deplored how "The Whigs and Tories persecute each other with little less than savage fury. There is nothing but murders and devastations in every quarter." Greene's aide, William Pierce, was equally horrified: "Such scenes of desolation, bloodshed, and deliberate murder I never was a witness to before"; patriots and Tories were slitting "each other's throats, and scarce a day passes but some poor deluded tory is put to death at his door. For want of civil government the bands of society are totally disunited and the people by copying the manners of the British have become perfectly savage."[52]

The destruction of the landscape was as thorough as the scorched-earth expedition of General Sullivan into the Iroquois country two years before. In 1782 General William Moultrie, riding one hundred miles eastward from the backcountry after a prisoner exchange, described a countryside previously flush with "live-stock and wild fowl of every kind . . . now destitute of all. It had been so completely chequered by the different parties, that not one part of it had been left unexplored; consequently, not the vestiges of horses, cattle, hogs, or deer was to be found. The squirrels and birds of every kind were totally destroyed." Moultrie's scouts confirmed that "no living creature was to be seen except now and then a few [vultures] picking the bones of some unfortunate fellows, who had been shot or cut down and left in the woods above ground."[53]

Clearly, South Carolinians hated each other as was the case in no other state. Charles O'Hara, a British officer, believed that some hot-blooded temperamental differences among South Carolinians explained the yen for butchery and "no prisoners taken" mentality. "The violence of the passions of these people are beyond every curb of religion and humanity," he wrote; "every hour exhibits dreadful, wanton mischiefs, murders, and violence of every kind, unheard of before." At the end of the war, Aedanus Burke, a jurist and political leader, believed that South Carolina's patriots were so inured to killing indiscriminately that they had "reconciled their minds to killing each other."[54]

The orgy of killing left South Carolina devastated like no other state. After the British withdrew in 1782, state leaders acted quickly to reinstitute civil government and to stop "the daily scenes of the most horrid plundering and murder," where vengeance, as General Greene worried, "would dictate one universal slaughter." With a policy of pardon and reconciliation toward Tories, the state government largely succeeded. But this did not stop the confiscation of the estates of Tories, many of whom left South Carolina with the British. This was the obvious way to raise revenue for the devastated state, and the desire for it was concentrated in the plundered and replundered backcountry. The first postwar legislature made a gesture toward democratizing landholding by preventing the confiscated Loyalist estates from falling into the hands of land jobbers with ready money to win at auction. Legislators boasted that by limiting the size of tracts to five hundred acres, they had blocked the "voracious appetites" of eager "landjobbers." But the law said nothing about how many tracts an individual could buy. Thus one already land-rich South Carolinian acquired 5,723 acres; another 5,208. Of the eighty-two slaves from one Loyalist estate who went on the block in May 1783, half were purchased by one man. "The wealthy," wrote one observer are . . . invited to a dangerous accumulation of riches."55

In the immediate aftermath of war, South Carolina's aristocracy, which in prewar days had ruled with less opposition than in any other part of America, felt itself challenged. Additional seats in the lower house of the legislature for Charleston and backcountry voters did not exactly create a political revolution; but the electorate installed the first artisan lawmakers—a blacksmith, a house carpenter, and a wagon master, for example—and country novices who prided themselves on forming a "malcontented party . . . from the lower class." Men of wealth, accustomed to holding the reins of political power, fumed at accusations that "enormous wealth is seldom the associate of pure and disinterested virtue," or charges that the city was divided into two parties responding to "Democracy and the Revolution" and "Tories and Aristocrats." An expanded press in Charleston reported a disputatious, often bitter, political dialogue where distrust was more often evident than actual issues over which the two emerging parties fought. "There appears to be a swell of insolence and sinister design in many of the leading men," wrote one democracy stalwart in 1784, "which plainly indicates a settled plan of ruling by a few with a rod of iron."56

Among the most important points of contention were taxes and the conduct of lawyers. South Carolinians of middling means spilled a great deal of ink attacking lawyers' fees, lawyers' pettifogging, and lawyers' deliberately prolonging court cases. This had been one of the major complaints of backcountry men since before the Revolution. But only in the matter of taxes did any reform emerge. In 1784, the legislature changed the patently inequitable taxing of marginally productive backcountry land at the same rate as low-country rice and indigo plantation land. Thereafter, land was assessed according to "quality and yield"; "the rice planters agreed to pay to justify their political dominance," as historian Jerome Nadelhaft has said.[57] Seeds were in the ground for a democratization of South Carolina polity. But for now the planter slaveocracy, though rattled, had yielded little.

Northern Struggles for Equity

Like fellow patriots of ordinary means in southern states, northern commoners felt the sting of drastic fiscal reform beginning in 1780. With the war now centered in the South, fierce debates over ramped-up taxation procedures moved to the center of state politics. The stabilization of the currency was a boon for money and security holders, principally seaboard merchants, but a bane for farmers, especially in the western counties. Complaints of impossible tax burdens reeked of class hostility. "A Citizen of the States" in November 1780 railed that ordinary men had "no money in their hands" because it it had "got into the hands of a few fortunate individuals who have amassed great wealth." "That envy which is apt to attend fortunes suddenly acquired," "Citizen" warned, would break out and roil the commonwealth. Even President Joseph Reed, whom nobody accused of radicalism, called Robert Morris "a pecuniary dictator" and believed that "the rich" who hoarded the gold and silver were the main tax evaders because they regarded their hard money "as too sacred to be touched for taxes."[58]

Robert Morris enlisted Tom Paine to pen "The Crisis Extraordinary," in which he gamely tried to convince Americans that their tax burden was not heavy and that the war effort would collapse if Congress could not support the army. But this did not convince farmers standing on the brink of personal collapse. In 1780–82, they threatened tax collectors, refused to sell their land as the only way to pay taxes, and mobbed assessors. The possibility of a new revolution was all too apparent. One writer warned in February 1783 that Pennsylvanians submitting "to one fraction of an over or unjust tax . . . will . . . deserve that slavery which their valor has snatched from them. . . . When one part of the community is to be exacted on to please and serve another, then disorder follows: to this may be imputed many of the Revolutions that [have] laid the world in blood; our own is a recent instance; why then will the men of influence lay a foundation for another, or is war so desirable as to induce us to contrive a continuation of it among ourselves?"[59]

Though President Reed confided to Washington that "we have miscalculated the abilities of the country and entirely the disposition of the people to bear taxes," conservatives, who had gained a small legislative majority in Pennsylvania, pressed forward with tax collections. They followed Robert Morris's dictum that the nation's credit—and its future—depended on fiscal reliability. Sheriffs' sales at auction to satisfy debts and tax collections rose rapidly by 1782, and foreclosures, mostly on farmers' goods, more than doubled between 1782 and 1784. Public animosity grew as the already fragile tissue of trust that bound the people to the Continental Congress began to disintegrate. In York County in 1784, men of small means complained bitterly that they had sacrificed "blood and treasure to secure . . . independence," only to see their farm goods sold to pay the "grievous and insupportable load of taxes" that were conferring windfall profits for rich men speculating in wartime securities. From another county came angry charges that new fiscal policies allowed a "merciless, rapacious creditor . . . to sacrifice the property of his debtor by a public sale," thus reducing "great numbers of . . . good people . . . from a state of competency to beggary."[60] Those of slender means, at the moment when victory against the British seemed almost assured, believed that their plight overturned the entire idea of a revolution inspired by creating a *novus ordo seclorum* (a new order of the ages).

As in Maryland and Virginia, Pennsylvania farmers and rural artisans were not without defenses. Their elected tax collectors, understanding the plight of friends and neighbors, often refused to dun for taxes or provide the courts with the names of tax delinquents. Elected country justices often colluded by refusing to conduct court proceedings in debt cases. If cases were held, juries sometimes refused to convict. And at auctions to distrain farm goods local people either stayed away or refused to bid. The constitution of 1776, which provided for the public election of tax assessors, sheriffs, and court justices, was serving them well. As peace arrived and economic conditions failed to improve, rural Pennsylvanians did their best to thwart the agenda of Robert Morris and his friends because they saw that it allowed, as one petition to the state government put it, "a few private citizens to acquire an influence in . . . the government subversive to the dearest rights of the people."[61]

For the farmers of Massachusetts, as in Pennsylvania, the pinch of drastic fiscal reform after 1780 was inversely related to access to eastern markets. Western Massachusetts farmers did not enjoy the advantage of yeomen close to the eastern markets, where supplying the armies and navies—either British or American—had often brought good times, if not prosperity. By 1778 farmers of the hill counties of the Berkshires were suffering under heavy war taxes, a chronic shortage of hard money, and the debts they had incurred. By early 1779, farmers in towns such as Hancock, bristling with anger, rioted to keep land they occupied after its Tory owners had been evicted.[62] By May, they were massing to keep the superior court from meeting in Great Barrington since the lack of a state constitution, they reasoned, gave no basis for the courts to meet. In many towns they instructed their delegates to the new constitutional convention that all judges, from justice of the peace to superior court judge, should be elected by the people, that all free men should enjoy the vote, and that elections should be held annually.

Though disappointed with the rigged results of the ratification of the constitution of 1780, most of the western farmers were spent after watching the creaking judicial system function so fitfully during five years of war for lack of a proper constitutional foundation. Yet radical democracy in western Massachusetts was far from dead. Amid economic stress, it resurfaced with explosiveness shortly after the legislature declared the constitution of 1780 ratified. Wartime dislocations struck many parts of the state, but nowhere more than in the western farming communities. Under the superintendent of finance's plan endorsed by Congress, the state legislature in 1781 began retiring paper money issued during the war, repealed the law that made paper money legal tender, and levied heavier taxes to be paid in silver to effect these changes. This may have been sound fiscal policy, but the common farmer saw it only as the growing scarcity of a circulating medium, a manipulation of the unstable money market, and an increasingly onerous tax burden that primarily benefited the rich. The view of "A Citizen of Philadelphia," whose essays on free trade and finance caught the eye of Massachusetts readers when the *Independent Chronicle and Universal Advertizer* published them in the spring of 1780, expressed their anger accurately. The new Morris plan, the fourth essay read, "will raise the great money-holders into nabobs so rich there will be no living with them. They have already, it is generally thought, much more than their share." By long experience, "Citizen" continued, "overgrown riches ... are dangerous to any community" and "will bring the inevitable ruin of many poor people."[63]

Confirming this prediction, falling farm prices, scarcity of hard money (which courts ruled the only medium for discharging debts), and sharply rising taxes drove many farmers to the wall by 1781. These were not the poorest people, who paid little taxes since they owned scarcely any property, but rather the middling farmers looking for a better future. For them, what was especially grievous was a tax system based primarily on land, which shielded from taxation the main source of merchants' income: personal property in ships, money at interest, stock-in-trade, and even unimproved land held for speculative gain. "In no other New England state was the demand for tax reform and relief greater," writes the historian of revolutionary taxation politics, "and in none did it receive a less sympathetic response from government."[64]

Farmers had only two avenues of relief: get their representatives to convince the state legislature to change the tax system and make paper money legal tender for discharging debts and paying taxes, or get a suspension of civil suits in court until economic conditions improved. Beyond that lay only forcible closing of the courts. Western farmers, writes Robert Taylor, their main historian, "worked hard for both solutions."[65] Throughout the western counties of Worcester, Berkshire, and Hampshire, ordinary men flouted the property requirement for suffrage in attending town meetings where petitions to the legislature were drafted. But the legislature, dominated by eastern mercantile interests, blocked legislative remedies. Petitioning the county courts for relief was equally unsuccessful. Now farmers faced bankruptcy and the sale of their farms at auction to satisfy their creditors. Staring them in the face were laws compelling county court judges to issue warrants allowing sheriffs to seize from a debtor whatever goods would satisfy the debt. This did not include a man's clothes, furniture, or tools of trade; but it included cattle, horses, grain, orchard fruit, or anything else that might bring in money at auction. "With money scarce and buyers few," writes Taylor, "a man might see his goods knocked down for a trifle of their real worth to satisfy a small debt. When the sum owed was larger or when sufficient goods were lacking, real estate could be appropriated to satisfy executions. . . . In default of personal or real estate, a debtor went to jail." One petition from a western town in 1782 cried that the tiny jail, twenty-eight by thirty-six feet in size, was bursting with nearly ninety men unable to pay their debts.[66]

Not surprisingly, western farmers, most of whom had fought in the Revolution, reverted to the actions that had pushed the revolutionary movement forward less than a decade before. Calling extralegal town and county conventions, as at Hadley on February 11, 1782, they demanded a suspension of civil actions. Two weeks later in Pittsfield, three hundred townsmen gathered, took a straw vote on whether or not to prevent the court of common pleas from functioning, determined that two-thirds favored such a radical step, and told the judges to adjourn until the next term. A justice of the peace from the tiny town of Lanesborough, serving as the aggrieved farmers' leader, told the judges that "the courts had to be ripped up before the General Court [the state legislature] would listen to petitions from the people."[67]

Western Massachusetts now tottered on the brink of repudiating courts established under the newly installed constitution. Propping them up were creditors in the old commercial towns along the Connecticut River. Gathering a month after the Pittsfield court closing, many Berkshire-region citizens agreed that closing courts and suspending the law augured a "fatal tendency" to the commonwealth. But beleaguered farmers knew that the clerk of this convention was a well-known former Tory and conservative opponent of the democratic reforms urged by most western towns when the state constitution was being written.

Appearing on the scene to lead the protests was an agrarian radical preacher who had never figured before in public affairs. Forty-two years old, Samuel Ely had graduated two decades before from Yale College and then served briefly as an evangelical minister in the small Connecticut town of Somers. Conservative parishioners there disliked his message championing the poor and pronouncing them closer to God than the wealthy. In 1771, he described himself in a published sermon as "much despised by the great and by the fashionable world" and likened himself to Job, who appealed "to God's tribunal for a trial," when the rich denied justice to the poor. Ousted from Somers in 1773, Ely wandered west to the Massachusetts hill country, where he served the unchurched as an itinerant preacher. Already he was known as "the friend of the suffering and oppressed and the champion of violated rights," a man—according to Reverend Timothy Dwight, the conservative Congregational preacher who detested Ely—who "industriously awakened the jealousy of the humble and ignorant against all men of superior reputation as haughty, insolent and oppressive." "This insistence that the righteous poor could defy corrupt earthly authority and ground their actions in a direct appeal to God," writes historian Alan Taylor, "lay at the heart of rural New England's post-Revolutionary insurgencies."[68]

During the war, Ely drifted northward, where he fought against General

John Burgoyne's army as they moved to crush the New Englanders in August 1777. A veteran of the Battle of Bennington, in what would become Vermont, where the Americans achieved a stunning victory, Ely took up residence in Hampshire County at the end of the war. There he became one of the fiercely ascetic itinerant evangelists who were sweeping subsistence farmers into their folds in the hilly frontier towns of northern and western New England. With his volatile mixture of incendiary religion and politics—almost a replica of the North Carolina Regulator phenomenon explored in chapter 2—Ely crystallized the mounting anger at new, merchant-friendly economic policies.[69]

Calling on those gathered in fear of the decisions of the county court of common pleas and the supreme court sitting in 1782, Ely allegedly shouted: "Come on my brave boys, we will go to the wood pile and get clubs enough and knock their grey wigs off and send them out of the world in an instant." The supreme court now faced the same decision that General Gage had confronted eight years before: Retreat in the face of a worked-up crowd or step in quickly to quell a revolt in progress. The supreme court took the latter course. Ordering Ely's arrest, the judges convicted him, fined him fifty pounds, and ordered him jailed in Springfield. But this boomeranged. Joseph Hawley, the old radical from Northampton, warned that war veterans of the river valley towns were coming to the defense of debtors. Having an additional grievance of their own—the state had refused to accept the certificates for back wages they had received in lieu of hard money as payment of taxes—they were "on the point of turning to the mob and . . . will become outrageous and the numbers who will side with them will be irresistible." In mid-June Hawley's warning materialized. Men gathering from various towns marched to Springfield under the leadership of Reuben Dickinson, a Revolutionary War captain, sprang Ely and several debtors from jail, and headed northward. Hot in pursuit came the sheriff with fifty soldiers. Ely escaped amid a bone-bruising fracas. When the sheriff insisted on three hostages, all Revolutionary War officers, for the return of Ely, the insurgent farmers complied. But a day later, six hundred men marched on Northampton to spring the hostages too. Bloodshed was averted only when it was agreed that, if freed, the three army officers would bring Ely in. Three months later, authorities arrested Ely, and he remained in jail until March 1783, when he was released by the general court in a gesture of reconciliation.[70]

Conservatives preferred to think of Ely's Rebellion, as it came to be called, as a local, short-lived flare-up. In fact, it was a prelude to Shays's Rebellion, which erupted three years later in western Massachusetts and was accompanied by rural insurgency in many parts of the new nation. Joseph Hawley, old and infirm, but more moderate than in his radical days, knew that the men of the Berkshire towns who had sprung to arms to fight the British were livid at the betrayal of what they believed they had fought for. What they saw around them were growing divisions between ordinary citizens who worked by the sweat of their brow and wealthy, money-hungry men who seemed to control the apparatus of government. For the benefit of these men, debtors had to pay high court and lawyers' fees, relinquish their personal property, and in many cases go to jail for no other offense than their inability to pay taxes or debts. Meanwhile, the furloughed Massachusetts soldiers of the Continental Line waited vainly for their wages, "vastly in arrear," as one captain told Hawley. "Many of the insurgents say that our soldiers get none of it [state tax revenues] . . . , that it cost them much to maintain the Great Men under George the 3rd, but vastly more under the Commonwealth and Congress," Hawley wrote a friend a few days after the Springfield jailbreak in mid-June 1782. "We have had it huzza[h]ed for George the third within 8 rods of our Court House" and "particular houseburnings have been repeatedly threatened with amazing bitterness." Hawley urged the legislature to send a fact-finding committee to western Massachusetts to study the problems and find remedies for the deep-seated animosity that was growing with "amazing rapidity." "I was told . . . by as calm and sedate a man as any I have seen of their number," he advised a well-placed friend, "that two thirds of these western people" believed that the revolutionary leaders of Boston and eastern Massachusetts "were the men who have brought all their burdens upon them, which they are told they should have been forever free from" by resisting the Hutchinson circle aligned with the British. Hawley learned in no uncertain terms that the insurgents vowed "they would take care how they were catched again."[71]

An aging Sam Adams and two other legislators made their way west as a grievance committee of the legislature, and they sensibly began their fact-finding in the little town of Conway, where Samuel Ely lived. The committee convened a town meeting to air the issues. But true to the spirit of insurgency that had spread throughout the region, the Conway citizens insisted on a convention of all the towns. Thus, delegates from forty-four Massachusetts towns assembled at Hatfield in early August to present their grievances about heavy taxes; lack of specie to pay debts; high court fees and salaries for government officials; and the suspension of habeas corpus, which the legislature had ordered for six months beginning in June—in sum a system of privilege and inequity that was beggaring the western Massachusetts countryside. The general court met these grievances partway by reducing some court fees and making personal property such as cattle, flour, and pine boards legal tender.

Such partial remedies quieted the western countryside for several years, at least to the extent that no uprisings of ordinary men stopped the courts from functioning. But repeated incidents made sheriffs' work unenviable. In September 1782, a crowd of farmers, led by a Revolutionary War major, rescued a pair of oxen destrained by a sheriff to satisfy a creditor's suit at law. In May 1783, a crowd of sixty marched with bludgeons to keep county judges from holding court. Three months later, in Northampton, one of Samuel Ely's friends tried to spring from jail another Ely supporter. In all these cases, authorities were able to muster enough men to thwart the insurgents. But "tumults and disorders," as several towns petitioning the general court for relief called them, continued because a great many citizens agreed with Justus Wright, an Ely supporter, who asked from jail in a letter published in the *Hampshire Herald*: "Are we not governed by aristocracy, only allowing one word to be transmitted, noble to ignoble; and are not officers in the state, even those who partake of the smallest share of the spoils . . . as great tyrants as Louis the fourteenth—judge ye."[72] Western Massachusetts benefited from a good crop in 1784 and from a reduction of the tax burden that year by the legislature. But radical agrarianism was still smoldering, as would soon become apparent in the farmers' insurgency known as Shays's Rebellion.

Leaving America

For African Americans, the closing years of the long war marked new opportunities, sharp disappointments, and great uncertainties. Much depended on how they had spent the war, where they were located as peace arrived, and what alternatives lay before them. For the thousands who were enfolded in the British armies, the decisions were almost entirely out of their hands. For those who had fought with the Americans or stayed out of the war altogether, the future was anything but certain, though signs appeared that the American victory over England might be capped by the patriots' attempt to redeem their virtue through resolving the massive contradiction of fighting for freedom while enslaving one-fifth of the population.

In the southern states, a new chapter of the African diaspora began months before the peace treaty of 1783 arrived in the triumphant new nation. Thousands of slaves still in the grasp of their Loyalist masters huddled within British encampments in Savannah, Georgia, and Charleston, South Carolina, mingling with former slaves who had gained their freedom by fleeing their patriot masters and fighting with the British. How would the British deal with this strange combination of the free and the enslaved after American forces reversed early defeats in the British southern campaign of 1779–81, pinning the British regiments thereafter in the coastal seaports?

The British faced the issue first in Savannah. Nobody contested the right of Loyalists with slaves in tow to leave with the British. Already the state government had seized the estates of many of them, selling the land and buildings at auction to patriot bidders. But what about the slaves who had fled their patriot masters and found refuge with the British? When the British fleet came into sight in the spring of 1782 to evacuate the British army and Loyalist supporters, Georgia's legislature urgently petitioned the English commander to allow planters to cross British lines and claim their former slaves. The British commander refused, leaving the Americans to deplore how the Crown officials "hurried away with our Negroes."[73] About four thousand African Americans sailed away from Savannah in July 1782, most of them as slaves. With British shipping inadequate to carry them all, some slaves went with their masters on small private ships, while others in small craft and even canoes traveled southward along the coast to British Florida.

As the British completed the Savannah evacuation, other Crown officials prepared to repeat the process in Charleston. In the summer of 1782, they awaited the decision of the American and British commissioners, who had argued for months over the question of fugitive slaves. The Americans' best card in this diplomacy was the threat to repudiate debts owed to British merchants before the Revolution. On the other hand, the British could return the refugees if the Americans promised not to confiscate the property of South Carolina Loyalists. Finally, officials in London decided not to surrender any refugee slave explicitly promised freedom, or any whose military service for the British might lead to ugly reprisals if the black rebel was forcibly returned to a former master. For the latter, the British promised full compensation to former owners.

Rarely in the history of concluding a war has such a scene as now occurred come to happen. The only way to decide whether a man or woman had been promised freedom or legitimately feared reprisal if returned to his or her master was by hearing the African American's own testimony. Thus, by agreement, a committee of Loyalist civilians and British officers met at the statehouse in early November 1782 to listen to the refugees' stories. Waiting in line by the hundreds to give their accounts, many freed people were cajoled by former patriot masters to return to their plantations. But inducing those who had tasted freedom to refasten their chains was, by definition, an absurdity. One planter "used every argument I was master of to get them to return, but to no effect. . . . Several of them . . . told me with an air of insolence they were not going back."[74] South Carolina planters were sure that sympathetic British members of the board coached the refugees so their stories would be convincing. But what slave needed to know what to say? Major General Alexander Leslie was staggered by the number of slaves who came forward to plead for freedom. "From the numbers that may expect to be brought off," he wrote Sir Guy Carleton, British officer in charge of evacuation, "including their wives and children, if to be paid for will amount to a monstrous expense." As the British officers accepted the black refugee stories, the Loyalist Americans resigned from the committee in disgust. John Rutledge, former South Carolina governor, believed that the commissioners ruled in favor of "almost every Negro, man, woman, and child, that was worth the carrying away."[75]

For the slaves still in the grasp of Loyalists poised to leave South Carolina, the problem was different. To stay off the departing ships, not on them, was their only hope for freedom, because almost the entire British flotilla was sailing for the West Indian slave colonies where sugar planters practiced the cruel institution at its worst. "Secreted away by her friends," wrote one Loyalist master, his enslaved woman "got out of the way of the evacuation and remains" in the state. Another Loyalist reported that his male slave "ran away overnight when they were to embark the next morning."[76] How many slipped away is not known, and only fragments of evidence remain to tell us how many of those who escaped found their way to freedom.

As the British fleet at Charleston prepared the final stages of evacuation in December 1782, an uneasy collection of white Loyalists, their slaves, and free black men and women to whom the British promised freedom filed onto the ships. One debarkation report numbered 5,327 black evacuees out of a total of 9,127 passengers. Other reports suggest that the total number was at least 10,000 and perhaps even 12,000. Far more of them were slaves than freemen. In one debarkation list, only 160 African Americans were on ships headed for New York, Nova Scotia, and England, and these are the most likely to have been free. About 2,960 others sailed for Jamaica and Saint Lucia in the West Indies, almost all scheduled for a continued life in slavery. Those who went to East Florida, about 2,210, were also bound for the old life of bondage in a new location.[77] Many others, perhaps several thousand, had been trafficked out of Charleston in the months leading up to evacuation, often sold by British officers bent on leaving America with something to show for their trouble.

East Florida was still a wilderness when the British ships began unloading their human cargo in December 1782. Spanish colonization for two hundred years had reduced the Indian population drastically, but Spanish settlers were still scattered thinly, with a small number of slaves. The old fortress and mission town of Saint Augustine was little more than a dusty collection of crude houses. Scattered in the hinterland were small assemblages of refugee slaves living off the land. Now East Florida became a major asylum for Loyalists. East Florida had joined Nova Scotia as a new frontier, pinning the British at the two extremities of the North American Atlantic seaboard. By early 1783, the evacuations of Savannah and Charleston, along with Cornwallis's surrender at Yorktown, added about 11,000 people to the sparsely populated colony. Sixty percent of them were slaves.

Set to work cultivating rice, indigo, and corn, and producing tar and turpentine from pine forests, some nine thousand slaves found themselves pawns again when England ceded East Florida to Spain in January 1783 as part of the peace negotiations ending the American war. South Carolina and Georgia legislatures tried to prevent their removal in the hope that their planters could recover them. But the Spanish governor resisted, leaving the Loyalist slave refugees in Florida to move to Jamaica, the Bahamas, and other British West Indian islands. Seven years of hoping and fighting for liberty had yielded these evacuees nothing. Thousands of them perished in hurricanes and a deadly yellow-fever epidemic in the late 1780s.

In the North, the other half of the British army prepared to evacuate New York City after word of the final peace treaty arrived in June 1783. Here lived the other large contingent of African Americans who had reached the British lines. But in contrast to those in Savannah and Charleston, these were almost all free men, women, and children. That did not assure them continued freedom, however. The coming of peace, remembered Boston King, the South Carolina slave escapee, "diffused universal joy among all parties, except us who had escaped from slavery and taken refuge in the English army." For four years he and his wife had been part of roving British forces and had arrived in New York by ship. But now, in 1783, "a report prevailed at New-York, that all the slaves, in the number 2000, were to be delivered up to their masters, altho' some of them had been three or four years among the English. This dreadful rumor," King related in his autobiographical account, "filled us all with inexpressible anguish and terror, especially when we saw our old masters coming from Virginia, North-Carolina, and other parts, and seizing upon their slaves in the streets of New-York. . . . For some days we lost our appetite for food, and sleep departed from our eyes."[78]

Then the British officers assured King and his brethren that they would not be surrendered to their former owners. "Each of us received a certificate [of freedom] from the commanding officer at New-York, which dispelled our fears and filled us with joy and gratitude," King remembered. They were to be transported to Nova Scotia—a decision reached painfully by the British. Clearly, the black Loyalists now guaranteed freedom for life could not be taken to any of England's Caribbean sugar islands. Jamaica, Bermuda, Antigua, Barbados, Saint Kitts, Saint Lucia, and all the others were built on slave labor and had no place for a large number of free blacks. England itself wanted no influx of ex-slaves, for London and other major cities already felt themselves burdened by growing numbers of impoverished former slaves seeking public support. Nor was East Florida much of an option since that, too, was a slave colony and in any event was being pawned to Spain. Only Nova Scotia remained, suitable because slavery had not taken root in this easternmost part of the Canadian wilderness, which England had acquired from France at the end of the Seven Years' War. Here, amidst the sparsely scattered old French settlers, the remnants of Indian tribes, and the more recent British settlers, including hundreds of Loyalists from the American colonies, Boston King and all the others clambered off British ships in the winter of 1783 to start life anew. But new lives would have to be created alongside several thousand British soldiers discharged in America after the war, men who chose to move to Canada rather than return to England. To British dischargees and black refugees the British government offered land, tools, and rations for three years.

In the "Book of Negroes," kept exactly by the British in New York, are inscribed 2,775 black Loyalists' names and ages, as well as the places where they had toiled as slaves. Probably another two thousand had earlier left New York City and other northern port towns on merchant and troop ships.[79] If smallpox and camp fevers hadn't wiped out thousands of African Americans who joined the British, the evacuation would have been much larger, probably at least twice as large. Nearly 40 percent of the evacuees were females, and children made up about one-quarter of the whole. They came from every region of the former American colonies, with the largest number from Virginia and the Carolinas. Many had toiled for the "founding fathers" of the new American nation, and it is certainly conceivable that on the voyage to Nova Scotia the slaves of Thomas Jefferson, George Washington, James Madison, Patrick Henry, Charles Carroll, and John Laurens recounted stories of their enslavement and their escape.

Among them were Thomas Peters, the slave from Wilmington, North Carolina, we met in chapter 4, along with his wife and two children. The ship on which the Peters family debarked was blown off course by the late-fall gales in 1783, and had to seek refuge in Bermuda for the winter. They set forth the following spring, reaching Nova Scotia in May, months after the rest of the black settlers had arrived. Peters led his family ashore at Annapolis Royal, a small port on the east side of the Bay of Fundy that looked across the water to the coast of Maine. There he became a leader of the African Canadians for nearly a decade.

Finding Freedom

Of black Americans who survived the war, the vast majority did not leave American shores but remained to toil and carry on the struggle to end slavery where most of them had been born. In the northern states, African Americans and white abolitionist allies tried to capitalize on the promise of revolutionary radicalism. Though a loosely organized national effort had produced American independence, slavery had to be combated state by state, locale by locale, and even person by person. About one in ten African Americans lived in the northern states and perhaps half were still enslaved when the British and Americans signed the Treaty of Paris in 1783. One of them, a slave named Mum Bett, showed how the humblest African descendants could be agents of change.

Mum Bett grew up enslaved in the small town of Sheffield in western Massachusetts and heard her share of the white townsmen's rhetoric in their struggle for freedom from British oppression. Colonel John Ashley, her master, was a wealthy landowner and merchant who had fought for freedom early in the war. Mum Bett's own husband had fallen on a Massachusetts battlefield. But this blood sacrifice for the emerging nation did not bring her freedom, though Massachusetts had opportunities to abolish slavery in its six years of wrestling with a state constitution.[80]

Widowed and the mother of a small daughter, Mum Bett brooded about the words in the Declaration of Independence that she had heard recited. While waiting on Colonel Ashley's table, she told her master that "in all they said she never heard but that all people were born free and equal, and she thought long about it, and resolved she would try whether she did not come in among them." In 1781, an incident occurred, of the sort common to the tension that was built into the relationship between enslavers and the enslaved, that brought the matter to a head. When an argument arose between Mum Bett's sister and their mistress, Mum Bett threw herself between her sister and the angry woman, who swung a heated kitchen fire shovel during the dispute. Mum Bett received the blow on her arm, "the scar of which she bore to the day of her death." Outraged, she stalked from the house and refused to return. When her master appealed to the local court in Sheffield for the recovery of his slave, Mum Bett called upon Theodore Sedgwick, a rising lawyer from nearby Stockbridge, to ask if Massachusetts' new state constitution, with its preamble stating that "all men are born free and equal," did not apply to her.

Sedgwick took the case. He argued before the county court in Great Barrington that Mum Bett and Brom, a fellow slave in the Ashley household, were "not dumb beasts" and therefore entitled to the same privileges as other human beings whose skin was pigmented differently. When the all-white jury agreed that the preamble to the state constitution made no exception to the principle that all men are both free and equal, the case set a precedent. Thereafter, Mum Bett called herself Elizabeth Freeman. Two years later, in the Quok Walker case, where a runaway slave appealed that he should be free, the state supreme court upheld the jury decision in Elizabeth Freeman's case. A century and a half of slavery in Massachusetts ended with the striking words: "Is not a law of nature that all men are equal and free? . . . [Are] not the laws of nature the laws of God? Is not the law of God then against slavery?"

After gaining her freedom, Elizabeth Freeman worked as a housekeeper for the Sedgwicks for many years. She later set up her own household with her daughter. In the hill towns of western Massachusetts, she became a noted midwife and nurse, revered for her skills in curing and calming her patients. Years later, after her death in 1829, Sedgwick's son commemorated Freeman's strength: "If there could be a practical refutation of the imagined superiority of our race to hers, the life and character of this woman would afford that refutation. . . . She uniformly . . . obtained an ascendency over all those with whom she was associated in service. . . . Even in her humble station, she had, when occasion required it, an air of command which conferred a degree of dignity. . . . She claimed no distinction but it was yielded to her from her superior experience, energy, skill, and sagacity." Catherine Sedgwick, her friend, remembered Freeman saying emphatically that "Any time while I was a slave, if one minute's freedom had been offered to me, and I had been told I must die at the end of that minute, I would have taken it—just to stand one minute on God's *airth* a free woman—I would."[81]

Another Massachusetts slave found freedom but not security. Enslaved in the 1720s in what is Ghana today, Belinda served Isaac Royall, one of Boston's wealthiest slave traders and slave owners for many years before he fled to England as a Loyalist in 1775. The revolutionary Massachusetts government confiscated his estate, including his many slaves. Belinda's new owner, whose name is lost to history, freed her, perhaps because at her advanced age she was more a burden than a useful worker. In 1782, at about age seventy, Belinda applied for a small pension. "Fifty years her faithful hands have been compelled to ignoble servitude for the benefit of an Isaac Royall, until, as if nations must be agitated and the world convulsed, for the preservation of that freedom which the Almighty Father intended for all the human race, the present war commenced," read her petition. "The face of your petitioner is now marked with the furrows of time, and her frame feebly bending under the oppression of years, while she, by the laws of the land, is denied the enjoyment of one morsel of that immense wealth, a part whereof hath been accumulated by her own industry and the whole augmented by her servitude." Belinda's argument that she could be paid from the sale of her slave master's large estate convinced the state government to pay her fifteen pounds—but only for one year.[82]

Just as Elizabeth Freeman was unwilling to wait for white conscience to respond to the natural-rights rhetoric of the revolutionary era, a large group

Susan Sedgwick, later an accomplished novelist, painted Elizabeth Freeman in 1811 as a woman nearing seventy. Eighteen years later, Freeman left a will bequeathing to her daughter a black silk gown belonging to Freeman's African-born father and a short gown that her African-born mother had worn. Freeman was buried in the Sedgwick family plot in the Stockbridge, Massachusetts, burial ground.

of slaves in Maryland moved aggressively at the end of the war to get what they believed God gave them. The case began with Mary Butler of Prince Georges County, but the outcome also affected hundreds of other slaves in neighboring counties. All of them were descended from Eleanor Butler (called Nell), an Irish indentured servant who had come to Maryland more than a century before. When Butler agreed to marry an African slave, Lord Baltimore, the colony's proprietor, opposed the marriage, asking Nell "how she would like to go to bed" with Charles, the African slave. Nell, according to the story passed down from generation to generation, replied that "she rather go to bed with Charles than his Lordship." One of Irish Nell's grand-sons and one of her great-granddaughters had sued for freedom before the American Revolution, arguing that they descended from a woman who was white and not herself enslaved. But the court ruled against them. Now, in 1783, the Prince Georges County court passed the tangled matter on to the General Court of Maryland's Western Shore. The matter was resolved only when the Maryland Court of Appeals, after several years of litigation, ruled that Mary Butler was "entitled to liberty" because they could find no proof that her great-great-grandmother, known as Irish Nell, had been sentenced to slavery for marrying an African slave.[83]

Though Mary Butler walked free, all the other slaves descended from Irish Nell had only a precedent to work with and resistant masters to contend with. But scores of them pressed suits. Year by year, well into the 1790s, Irish Nell's descendants gained their freedom, to the dismay of their owners.

African Americans in other states hoped that the end of slavery might come with the end of the war. Pushing their cause were members of the Society of Friends in Pennsylvania and New Jersey. Ceaseless prodding by Anthony Benezet and a handful of other Quaker reformers began to build on the crusade they had launched on the eve of the war. The war itself had gone hard with Quakers, some of them exiled from Pennsylvania as Loyalists and others hated for their refusal to bear arms on behalf of the emerging nation. But the war had fulfilled their darkest prophecies of suffering, and many Friends emerged from it convinced that they must return to their former ways of plain living and dedicate themselves to righting the wrongs swirling around them. Nothing was more wrong, they believed, than the continuation of slavery. At the Philadelphia Yearly Meeting in 1783, more than five hundred Friends from Pennsylvania, Delaware, and New Jersey signed a petition to the Continental Congress to prohibit a reopening of the slave trade by those "prompted from avaricious motives" in contradiction of "the solemn declarations often repeated in favour of universal liberty."[84] Congress did not comply and South Carolina and Georgia resumed importation.

Although they failed at the national level, the Quakers were more success-ful in Pennsylvania, where they took up the enforcement of the gradual abo-lition act of 1780. Benezet described how black Philadelphians came to him "almost daily and sometimes more" seeking help. Some slave owners were creating loopholes in the abolition act by selling their slaves out of the state, sending pregnant women across the border to Maryland or Virginia where their children would be born into perpetual slavery, and in other ways circumventing the law. Two dramatic cases of suicide galvanized reform-minded Philadelphians to revive the abolition society they had founded in 1775. One "sensible" free black Philadelphian, Benezet related, was denied a writ of habeas corpus to prevent his forced departure from the city. Desperate to avoid reenslavement, he "hung himself to the great regret of all who knew him." Another African American, "having pressingly, on his knees, solicited a friend, without success, to prevent his being sent away to the southward" from his family, threw himself from the deck of a ship as it sailed down the Delaware River.[85]

After these heart-wrenching suicides, a small group of Philadelphians revived the Pennsylvania Abolition Society, just a few months before Benezet's death. Reaching out to every neighborhood and church in the city, the core group built a mostly middle-class organization of artisans, shopkeepers, and lesser merchants. Shoemaker Samuel Richards became its first president; shoemaker James Starr and schoolteacher John Todd served as treasurer and secretary. But the workhorse was an unassuming forty-three-year-old Quaker tailor, Thomas Harrison. His shop became the listening post, information center, and place of temporary refuge for African Americans fleeing their masters. Harrison and his wife, a Quaker minister, knew pain enough of their own. Sarah Harrison gave birth nine times between 1765 and 1778, and seven times the Harrisons buried children. But the irrepressible Thomas Harrison, described by a contemporary as "a lively, bustling man with a roguish twinkle in his eye," became the abolition society's most important representative, listening to the stories of African Americans, assigning their cases to members of the Acting Committee, posting security with the courts in particular cases, and negotiating with individual masters and mistresses to avoid court action.

As slaves came forward hoping to secure their freedom or that of their children, the PAS litigated at least twenty-two cases in 1784 and many more thereafter as word spread of its work. The aggressive litigation strategy troubled some Philadelphians and more outsiders, who protested that it strained interstate harmony in a nation struggling to establish itself. Arguing on behalf of a fellow Virginian, George Washington put the case strongly. When his acquaintance had entered the state with a slave, the PAS sued on behalf of the bondman's freedom. Two years later when the case came to trial, the Virginian was obliged to return to defend himself. "When slaves who are happy and contented with their present masters are tampered with and seduced to leave them," wrote Washington to Philadelphia's Robert Morris, and when practices of this kind "fall on a man, whose purse will not measure with that of the Society, and he loses his property for want of means to defend it, it is oppression . . . and not humanity because it introduces more evils than it can cure."[86] The argument that any slaves were content to be living in a perpetual bondage that was passed to all their children must have seemed laughable to PAS members, not to mention the slaves. In any case, Washington's argument did not prevail.

One of the PAS's most important services was to copy out by hand the freedom papers of slaves emerging from bondage. This was invaluable to any freedperson who had the misfortune of losing his or her freedom papers and being seized by bounty hunters whom southern slave masters commissioned to recapture fleeing or presumed runaway slaves. Many free men and women found themselves snatched from the streets and put on ships headed southward. Sometimes it was a case of mistaken identity; other times it was case of kidnapping for a price. The very first freedom paper copied into the large PAS Manumission Books was that of "Richard," with no surname indicated. This was Richard Allen, not much known at the time but soon one of the young men who stepped out of the shadows to become part of the rootstock of postwar black society.

Born in 1760, Allen grew up as a slave to the family of Benjamin Chew, a wealthy conservative lawyer in Philadelphia who maintained a plantation in southern Delaware, where the labor force was mostly enslaved. Chew sold Allen's family to a neighboring Delaware farmer just before the Revolution, and it was here that Richard experienced a religious conversion at the hands of itinerant Methodists. Richard's master also fell to the power of the Methodist message. Nudged along by economic necessity in the war-torn economy, he let Richard and his brother purchase their freedom. In 1780, with the war still raging, the twenty-year-old Richard gave himself the surname of Allen and began a six-year religious sojourn. Interspersing work as woodcutter, salt wagon driver for the revolutionary army, and shoemaker with stints of itinerant preaching, he trudged over hundreds of miles to preach before black and white audiences. In the mid-1780s, he attracted the attention of Francis Asbury, about to become the first American Methodist bishop. Asbury sent Allen to Philadelphia to preach to the free African Americans who worshiped at Saint George Methodist Church—a rude, dirt-floored building in the German part of the city. Allen soon became the city's foremost black leader. He went on to create the first independent black church in the city, organize the first black school, and found the Free African Society, which ministered to the needs of people coming out of slavery.[87]

Elsewhere, other black men stood forward in the early years of the new republic. Prince Hall became a resolute organizer of free black Bostonians. The slave of merchant William Hall, Prince Hall had worshiped at the church of Andrew Crosswell, a radical evangelist who had preached against slavery since the 1740s. Hall received his freedom in 1770 and established the first black Masonic lodge in America with the aid of British soldiers occupying the town in 1775–76. An associate of Phillis Wheatley, he waged a campaign against slavery during the war. After slavery was abolished by judicial decree, Hall continued his efforts to combat the low pay and deep prejudice that most black Bostonians faced.

Farther north, in Massachusetts, Lemuel Haynes (whom we met in chapter 5) became an inspiration for aspiring African Americans. After the war, he supported himself doing farm labor while preparing for a lifetime in the ministry. "One-time minute man," says John Saillant, his recent biographer, he "never wavered in his patriotism," and "he articulated more clearly than anyone of his generation, black or white, the abolitionist implications of republican thought." Haynes understood what half a million fellow African Americans were up against: Early in the revolutionary struggle, political leaders up and down the seaboard agreed that slavery was an affront to the natural rights on which republicanism was built, but as the war wound down, the dominant theoreticians of republican ideology—men such as Thomas Jefferson and James Madison—were seeing black people *themselves,* rather than the institution of slavery, as corrosive to "the great republican experiment." "The eradication of slavery," writes Saillant, "and the extension to blacks of the liberty and security of an antislavery republican state were, in Haynes' mind, essential to republican governance and republican life."[88] Haynes knew that many men who were revered for their leadership roles in the struggle for independence were themselves complicit in the monstrous contradiction of black Americans perpetually trapped in slavery in the midst of a so-called republican experiment.

Licensed to preach in 1780—the first ordained black clergyman in the United States—Haynes led a white congregation in Middle Granville, Massachusetts. There he met Elizabeth Babbitt, a white woman who bucked the tide of prejudice against interracial marriage. Nine children were born of this marriage that lasted for more than fifty years. One white minister, later to become president of Amherst College, remembered that Haynes sermonized with "no notes but spoke with freedom and correctness. . . . There was so much of truth and nature in [his sermons] that hundreds were melted into tears." In 1788, Haynes became the pastor in Rutland, Vermont, where he served for thirty years. It was here, in a state that had abolished slavery in 1777, that his thoughts ripened on how black Americans would fit into a republican scheme of government. After a long tenure in Rutland, Haynes moved on to his final pastorate in South Granville, New York, where he served through his seventies. After Haynes died, his biographer called him "a sanctified genius," a man whose life story could "hardly fail to mitigate the unreasonable prejudices against the Africans in our land."[89]

Defenders of slavery in the northern states were clearly on the defensive by 1784; it was already clear, to be confirmed by the first federal census in 1790, that free African Americans were to be the rule rather than the exception. In 1785, Jefferson believed that opponents of abolition in the North were no more numerous than the occasional murderers and robbers who roamed the countryside and predicted that "in a few years there will be no slaves northward of Maryland."[90] But in the southern states, where nearly nine of every ten African Americans still lived as peace became official, only guarded optimism about abolishing slavery could be found, and that was only in Maryland and Virginia. Yet the majority of southern slaves lived in the Upper South. If Maryland and Virginia had crossed the Rubicon, could the Carolinas and Georgia have resisted?

As the war drew to a close, many leaders in Maryland, such as Luther Martin and Gustavus Scott, or Virginians such as George Mason, Patrick Henry, George Wythe, Thomas Jefferson, Arthur Lee, and Edmund Pendleton, publicly advocated the gradual abolition of slavery. The Marquis de Chastellux believed that Virginians "in general . . . seem grieved at having slaves, and are constantly talking of abolishing slavery and of seeking other means of exploiting their lands." Chastellux was doubtless too optimistic in saying that "this opinion . . . is almost universally accepted." But he had inquired carefully into the matter and found that younger men, especially the educated, were moved by "justice and the rights of humanity." As for their fathers, the concern was more practical—that slave "labor is neither so productive nor so cheap as that of day laborers or white servants" and that "epidemical disorders, which are very common [among slaves] render both their property and their income extremely precarious."[91]

Boosting the chance of expunging slavery from southern republican soil was the rise of radical evangelical Christianity in the South. For populist Methodist evangelists such as Freeborn Garretson and David Rice, slaveholding was interlocked with other sins such as gambling, horse racing, and sabbath breaking—all afflictions of the self-indulgent gentry class. Among the Methodists, the fastest-growing denomination in the South, leaders such as Francis Asbury and Thomas Coke spread the antislavery gospel and circulated resolutions condemning slavery in the early 1780s. At the famous Christmas meeting of 1784, Methodist leaders banned all those who held slaves and called upon all slaveholders to provide for the manumission of their chattel property at specified times. "We view," they wrote, "the practice of holding our fellow creatures in slavery . . . as contrary to the golden law of God on which hang all the law and the prophets, and the unalienable Rights of Mankind, as well as every principle of the Revolution."[92] The Methodists had now joined the Quakers in making allegiance to their faith and allegiance to slaveholding incompatible and unallowable.

The decreasing profitability of slave labor in the Upper South influenced some planters shifting from tobacco to wheat cultivation to liberate their slaves. Still, there was in every emancipating slave owner some sentiment that slavery was immoral, unnatural, and inimical to revolutionary republicanism. Otherwise, slave owners would merely have sold bondmen and bondwomen who could no longer be profitably employed to planters in areas where slavery was still profitable. In some cases, especially in manumitting aged slaves who were no longer able to work, little altruism was involved. But the manumitting documents themselves include language infused with the doctrine of natural rights, often interwoven with expressions of Christian conscience. "The constant reiteration of antislavery ideals," writes historian Ira Berlin, "suggests that most manumitters took them to heart." When one man freed slaves because, to quote one Virginian, "it is contrary to the command of Christ to keep fellow creatures in bondage," his neighbors were often affected.[93]

The rapid growth of the free black population in the Upper South gives a final, if rough, indication of antislavery sentiment. Maryland's free black population was 1,818 in 1755, rose slowly before the Revolution, and reached 8,000 by 1790 and nearly 20,000 by the turn of the century. In Virginia, where a census in 1782 showed 1,800 free blacks, the number more than doubled in the two years after the liberal manumission law took effect and swelled to nearly 13,000 by 1800. Delaware's free population of African Americans, only 3,899 in 1790, grew to 8,268 in 1800. To be sure, free blacks made up only one of eight Upper South blacks by 1800. Yet in the absence of a compensated gradual emancipation law, thousands of slaveholders were nonetheless disentangling themselves from coerced labor. The idea had indeed spread that a republic based on natural-rights theory could not survive without emancipating the enslaved fifth of the population. A "general consensus" had emerged in the revolutionary era, as David Brion Davis has concluded, "that black slavery was a historical anomaly that could survive for a time only in the plantation societies where it had become the dominant mode of production."[94] A transformative moment seemed at hand.

Women of the Republic

When galloping inflation led to the price-control crisis in seaboard cities in 1779 and Washington's tattered army suffered greatly, two high-visibility women in Philadelphia swung into action. Esther de Berdt Reed was the wife of the president of Pennsylvania's Supreme Executive Council and Sally Franklin Bache was the daughter of Benjamin and Deborah Franklin. Nailing up a broadside around the city titled "The Sentiments of an American Woman," they announced that American women were "born for liberty" and refused to "bear the irons of a tyrannic Government." In earlier societies, they reminded Philadelphians, politically active women had strode into the public arena to save their people. Ancient Rome was "saved from the fury of a victorious enemy by the efforts of Volumnia," and at other times when cities were under siege "the Women have been seen ... building new walls, digging trenches with their feeble hands, furnishing arms to their defenders, they themselves darting the missile weapons on the enemy." Was it not "the Maid of Orleans who drove from the kingdom of France the ancestors of those same British, whose odious yoke we have just shaken off and whom it is necessary that we drive from this Continent"?[95]

Having prepared the public, Reed and Bache organized a battalion of

In painting this scene of Philadelphia women binding the wounds of casualties of the Battle of Germantown, Peter Frederick Rothermel may have been inspired by the Philadelphia women of the Civil War who launched the U.S. Sanitary Commission in 1861 to provide medical relief to wounded soldiers and sailors.

women to go door to door to raise money for Washington's ragged, demoralized army. Loyalist Anna Rawle sputtered, "Of all absurdities the ladies going about for money exceeded everything." But the women's battalion collected about 300,000 paper dollars and proposed to convert it to specie that would provide each soldier about $2 cold cash. Washington rejected this proposal, afraid it would increase his soldiers' discontent at getting only depreciated paper money for their regular pay. Instead, the women used the money to buy linen and made it into 2,200 shirts for the threadbare soldiers. Historian Linda Kerber has called the Reed-Bache broadside "an ideological justification for women's intrusion into politics that would become the standard model throughout the years of the early Republic."[96]

Jefferson believed that American women would be "too wise to wrinkle their foreheads with politics," but in the latter stages of the war increasing numbers of women believed they could not do otherwise. Some were in a position to think and act forcefully because they were married to leaders such as John Adams. Abigail knew very well that John listened to her and that she was as much a councillor as were Indian women to male tribal chiefs. Moreover, she saw that the emerging republic could be no better than the wisdom and virtue of its young women. "America will not wear chains while her daughters are virtuous," she told a male friend.[97] Even if women were barred from formal politics, the country would still have to rely on them because mothers would have the crucial role of molding the sons and daughters in whom the nation's future resided.

Abigail still grated that John and all his male colleagues would not revise the laws that made women's property "subject to the control and disposal of our partners, to whom the law have given a sovereign authority." This reform awaited the nineteenth century. Yet she and many other women like her remained dedicated to the public welfare though "deprived of a voice in legislation [and] obliged to submit to those laws which are imposed upon us." She reminded her friend that American women's patriotism and sacrifice during the war "equals the most heroic of yours" in spite of the unfair laws they lived under that were "sufficient to make us indifferent to the public welfare."

Abigail was correct as usual in her assertion about "women's patriotism and sacrifice during the war," but she may not have known the full extent of this. Mostly she thought about the women who tended the farms and the shops while their husbands were serving in the army; often she wrote about the economic and psychological burdens that the war placed on nearly everyone. But she had only limited experience with the hazards and hardships of the masses of ordinary women who, during the agonizingly long war, left their homes to follow their husbands, brothers, and sons into the fray or flocked to the army simply to find work. The number who followed the British army—in a case of counterpatriotism—was also very large.

The number of women who nursed the sick and wounded soldiers, washed and mended their clothes, hauled water and cooked their food, satisfied their sexual urges, and served as messengers and ammunition passers cannot be determined, because the women signed no articles of enlistment and had no official status. Modern studies estimate that several thousand women served with the Continental army, and it is possible that as many served with the British. A British intelligence report in 1778 described "the rebel army" at White Plains, New York, where "friends to government [Loyalists]" estimated the army at 14,000 and "that the women and wagoners make up near the half of their army."[98]

Most of the women were poor, as were the men they served. Many were runaway indentured servants. Washington wrestled with the problem of legions of camp followers for the entire war. On the one hand they slowed down troop movements and intensified the issue of finding food for the army. On the other hand, he knew the army would "lose by desertion, perhaps to the enemy, some of the oldest and best soldiers" if he cast off their wives, relatives, and lovers.[99] Often women had to do with half rations, but that was also true for most of the men during much of the war.

Always trying to limit the number of women following his army, Washington could do no more than issue orders—with scant results. Near the end of the war, he issued a general order establishing a ratio of one woman for each fifteen men. There was no way to enforce this, and it cut against the needs of the men who were already prone to desertion because of the awful conditions they had to endure. Nor could officers always control the women, who almost by definition were a tough lot. Early in the war General Anthony Wayne had to cope with striking laundresses seeking an adequate wage. In another case, when Washington led his army through Philadelphia in 1777, just before the British occupation of the city, he was unsuccessful in his attempt to make the camp followers disappear. "Not a woman belonging to the army is to be seen with the troops on their march through the city," he ordered. But no sooner had his regiments passed by than women sprang from courtyards and alleys and fell in behind the men, "demanding by their very presence, their share of respect."[100]

The army, in fact, could not do without women. In one of countless examples, Mary Frazier, a Pennsylvania farmer's wife, made daily rounds to collect from neighbors what they could spare for the soldiers—blankets, worn-out socks, bits of yarn. As her granddaughter later recounted, she took these castoffs home "where they would be patched and darned and made wearable and comfortable.... She often sat up half the night, sometimes all, to get clothing ready. Then with it, and whatever could be obtained for food, she would have packed on her horse and set out on the cold lonely journey to the camp—which she went to repeatedly during the winter." At Yorktown in

1781, Sarah Osborn, wife of a New York blacksmith, was one of many who cooked and washed for the American troops and brought them food under fire because, as she remarked to Washington, "it would not do for the men to fight and starve too."[101]

Away from the fields of battle, the nation's women found themselves in a conflict without bullets—the refashioning of a new civic role for women. As Linda Kerber explains, it had two connected goals. The first was bursting the old stereotype of women as irrational, unsteady, and incompetent in public affairs; in its place came the model woman who was rational, competent, and steadfast. The second goal was using this competence to stand forth as "monitors of the political behavior of their lovers, husbands, and children."[102] This campaign on the home front gradually took shape as the war trailed off and would be burnished to a gloss in the years after the war.

Women also maintained the standards for civic virtue. Not all women were as punctilious as Abigail Adams in insisting that women should "judge how well her husband and sons met their responsibilities," but this was the ideal created during the course of the long war.[103] What made this urgent was the widespread feeling by the end of the war that the Americans had fashioned a great and dangerous paradox: Victorious against the world's mightiest military power, they had lost the virtue required to maintain an independent republic. "Our morals are more depreciated than our currency," judged David Ramsay halfway through the war, and a few years later he lamented that the "declension of our public virtue" had produced "pride, luxury, dissipation and a long train of unsuitable vices [that] have overwhelmed our country." "Selfishness has so far prevailed over that patriotic spirit which at first wrought wonder through the Continent," echoed William Gordon to Washington, "that I have little dependence on the virtue of the people."[104] The correspondence of wartime leaders, both military officers and politicians, is dotted with similar expressions of anguish over selflessness replaced by selfishness.

Thus "virtue," before the war a masculine quality that citizen-warriors demonstrated by sacrificing self-interest for the common good and sacrificing individual lives for the good of the whole society, had to be retooled and feminized in peacetime if the noble new democratic experiment was to succeed. In this rescue operation, the salvaging of the human traits upon which a republic could be built and sustained lay much in the hands of women. With virtue inculcated by women, the nation might overcome the decay of masculine virtue that the war brought on. Women would be the moral bookkeepers and instructors in the new, raw, boisterous American society. It would take another decade after peace arrived in 1783 to complete the refashioning of women of the republic, but the process was under way.

Epilogue

SPARKS FROM THE ALTAR OF '76

IN 1802, ARRIVING IN BALTIMORE AFTER AN ABSENCE FROM AMERICA of fifteen years, Thomas Paine began a series of letters "To the Citizens of the United States." In what he called "sparks from the altar of Seventy-six," he tried to explain to a new generation what the American Revolution was all about. In the eighth letter, published in June 1805, he reminded Americans that "The independence of America . . . was the opportunity of *beginning the world anew,* as it were; and of bringing forward a *new system* of government in which the rights of *all* men should be preserved that gave *value* to independence." For Paine, matters had gone amiss. The rights of all men had never been fully acknowledged, and in the years he had been away the accomplishments of the radical revolutionists to begin the world anew had been sullied. Pennsylvania's revised constitution of 1790 stood as a prime example of betraying the Revolution. After years of inveighing against it, conservatives had finally scuttled the radical constitution of 1776. Gaining power in the state legislature, they had called a new constitutional convention and then ripped out some of the most democratic features of the original constitution. They gave power to veto laws passed by the elected legislature to a governor as well as handing him "a great quantity of patronage . . . copied from England." They replaced the unicameral lawmaking assembly with a

Thomas Paine had left America in 1787, just before the Constitutional Convention convened in Philadelphia, had visited Paris briefly, and then gone to see his aged parents in England. His sojourn there ended in 1792, when the English government hounded him out of the country for what they regarded as seditious libel in the second half of The Rights of Man. *Thereafter, in France, he had been elected to the assembly in the French Revolution and had set the world ablaze with* The Age of Reason, *a no-holds-barred attack on aristocracy and established religion.*

two-house legislature where the upper house was reserved for those with wealth. Worst of all, they scaled back white adult male suffrage, making "artificial distinctions among men in the right of suffrage." It was a constitution unworthy of America, Paine believed, and it was put into place without its ratification by the people.[1]

Four months after Paine's letter on the betrayed Revolution appeared in a Philadelphia newspaper, John Adams was still at work on the autobiography he had started in 1802. Writing from his study in Braintree, Massachusetts, he, too, was reflecting on the meaning of the American Revolution because he was working on the years of 1776–78 at this very moment. Paine leaped to Adams's mind as he wrote his old friend Benjamin Waterhouse, leader of Harvard's medical school, who had tutored the young John Quincy Adams in Leyden when Abigail and John were there in 1781. Whether Adams had been following Paine's letters to "the Citizens of the United States" is uncertain, but it probably didn't matter. His views of Paine had been fully formed years before. Taking up his pen on October 29, 1805, Adams wrote that Paine was "a mongrel between pig and puppy, begotten by a wild boar on a bitch wolf." Working up a lather at the thought of Paine, he continued that "never before in any age of the world" was such a "poltroon" allowed "to run through such a career of mischief." Yet Adams was an astute observer as well as a maker of history; so thinking further, he conceded that "I know not whether any man in the world has had more influence on its inhabitants or affairs for the last thirty years than Tom Paine." Responding to a letter from Waterhouse in which the eminent doctor had called the revolutionary era the "Age of Frivolity," Adams allowed that he "would not object if you had named it the Age of Folly, Vice, Frenzy, Fury, Brutality, Daemons, Buonaparte, Tom Paine, or the Age of the Burning Brand from the Bottomless Pit, or anything but the Age of Reason." The last reference, of course, was to Paine's scathing attack on aristocracy and organized Christian religion, read the world over since its publication in Paris in 1794. We can imagine Adams sighing as he tried to sum up the response to Waterhouse: "Call it then the Age of Paine."[2]

Did Adams mean the age of *pain* as well as the "Age of Paine"? Probably so, to judge by everything Adams wrote about his revolutionary experiences. For him, self-interest and avarice had repeatedly trumped public virtue, threatening to sunder the republic. And it gnawed at him that his own contributions received so little credit. For the inegalitarian Adams, who had become a Federalist after the states ratified the Constitution of 1787, pain was almost an everyday affair during his presidency from 1797 to 1801. Steering the nation through a near war with France and coping with the French and Haitian revolutions earned him many enemies, and his unpopularity increased for signing the Alien and Sedition Acts under which his administration jailed the most important newspaper editors of the Democratic-Republican Party that opposed him. The scurrilous election campaign against Jefferson in 1800 deprived him of a second term and sent him back to Braintree full of bitterness and remorse.

Many people of the new republic agreed with Adams that it was an age of pain, and some seconded his view that ultrademocratic ideas had gone too far and should be resisted and neutralized in order to secure order and stability. But for many of the nation's peoples, including the Native Americans struggling within the nation's borders, the pain consisted mostly of the unfulfilled promises of revolutionary radicalism. For them, the most radical dreams had been diluted, deferred, or dashed. Yet, as we will see, the leaders of radical reform, and those who followed their lead, were not in the habit of supinely kneeling before those who wanted to return American society to its elitist moorings. For them, sparks from the "altar of '76" still furnished the inspiration to fight on.

The Dream Deferred

African Americans had reached a crossroads during the Revolution, with one large contingent casting their lot with the British and the others hoping against hope that white Americans would honor their founding principles by making all people free and equal. Estimates vary, but historians agree that tens of thousands of adult slaves, along with many of their children, made their declarations of independence by fleeing to England's protective flag. In this gamble, disease turned out to be their worst enemy. It is likely that not more than one-third of those who fled to the British lines survived the Revolution. Of those who were free, most were on their way to the easternmost province of Canada as Americans celebrated peace.

Nova Scotia would not be the land of dreams that Boston King, Thomas Peters, David George, and the others of the latest African diaspora hoped for. Peters settled at Digby, "a sad, grog drinking place," as one visitor called it. About five hundred white and a hundred black families were like so much flotsam thrown up on the shores of Nova Scotia. But once there, the British promises of land, tools, and provisions fell far short of their expectations. Black families found themselves segregated in impoverished villages, given scraps of often untillable land, deprived of the rights normally extended to British subjects, and forced to work on road construction in return for the promised necessities. Gradually they were reduced to peonage.

By 1790, after six years of hand-to-mouth existence in a land of dubious freedom, Peters concluded that his people must find their freedom elsewhere. Deputized by two hundred black families, Peters composed a petition to English authorities and agreed to carry it personally across the Atlantic. Sailing from Halifax that summer, he reached London with little more in his pocket than the plea for fair treatment in Nova Scotia or resettlement "wherever the wisdom of Government may think proper to provide for [my people] as free subjects of the British Empire."[3]

Peters arrived in London at a momentous time. English abolitionists were bringing to a climax four years of lobbying for a bill in Parliament to abolish the slave trade. Though merchant slave trade interests defeated the bill, the abolitionists won approval for chartering the Sierra Leone Company with trading and settlement rights on the African coast. The recruits for the new colony would be the ex-slaves from America then living in Nova Scotia and free blacks from England ready to return to the African homeland.

After almost a year in London, Peters returned to Halifax, and from there he eagerly spread the word that the English government would provide free transport for any black Nova Scotians who wished to go to Sierra Leone. On the African coast, they would receive at least twenty acres per man, ten for each woman, and five for each child. John Clarkson, the younger brother of one of England's best-known abolitionists, traveled with Peters to coordinate and oversee the resettlement plan. Fifty-four years old, Peters now began a journey on foot to spread word of the chance to return to Africa. Working through black preachers, the principal leaders in the Canadian black communities, the two men spread the word. The return to Africa soon took on overtones of the Old Testament delivery of the Israelites from bondage in Egypt. Clarkson described the scene at Birchtown, a black settlement near Annapolis, where in October 1791, 350 black people trekked through the rain to the church of their blind and lame preacher Moses Wilkinson to hear about the Sierra Leone Company's resettlement terms. Pressed into the pulpit, the English reformer "rose up and explained . . . the object, progress, and result of the embassy of Thomas Peters to England."[4] Applause burst forth frequently as Clarkson spoke, and in the end the entire congregation vowed its intent to make the exodus out of Canada in search of the promised land. In the next three days, 514 men, women, and children inscribed their names on the rolls of prospective emigrants. They were soon joined by seven hundred more from other black communities.

As black Canadians streamed into Halifax at the end of 1791, Peters and Clarkson inspected each of the fifteen ships sent to convoy the emigrants back to Africa. They ordered some decks removed, ventilation holes fitted, and berths constructed so this trip across the Atlantic would not mimic the horrors of the passage that every African remembered. On January 15, 1792, under sunny skies and a fair wind, the fleet weighed anchor and stood out from Halifax harbor. Crowded aboard the ships were men, women, and children whose collective experiences in North America described the entire gamut of slave travail. Included was the African-born Charles Wilkinson, who had fought with the British Black Pioneer unit, accompanied by two small daughters and his mother. Also aboard was David George, founder of the first black Baptist church to be formed among slaves in Silver Bluff, South Carolina. There, too, was Moses Wilkinson, who had escaped his Virginian master in 1776 and had become a revered preacher in Nova Scotia. Preacher Boston King, the South Carolina slave who had escaped his master, joined the British, and debarked from New York City in 1783, was also included, as was Harry Washington, who had fled his master at Mount Vernon in 1776. Eighty-year-old Richard Herbert, a laborer, was among the throng, but he was not the oldest. That claim fell to a woman whom Clarkson described in his shipboard journal as "an old woman of 104 years of age, who had requested me to take her that she might lay her bones in her native country."[5]

The winter gales, the worst in the memory of seasoned crew members, created a wretched ocean crossing of nearly eight weeks. Two of the fifteen ship captains and sixty-five black émigrés died en route. Legend tells that Thomas Peters, sick from shipboard fever, led his shipmates ashore in Sierra Leone singing, "The day of jubilee is come; return ye ransomed sinners home." For those who made it, the American Revolution was now complete. Peters lived only four months longer and was buried at Freetown, where his descendants live today. He had crossed the Atlantic four times, lived in French Louisiana, North Carolina, New York, Nova Scotia, New Brunswick, Bermuda, London, and Sierra Leone. He had worked as a field hand, millwright, ship hand, casual laborer, and soldier. He had waged a three-decade struggle for the most basic political rights, for equality, and for human dignity. His struggle was individual at first, as he tried to burst the shackles of slavery, but he merged his individual efforts with those of thousands of other slaves who made the American Revolution the first large-scale rebellion of Africans in North America. Out of thousands of acts of such defiance and militancy grew a legend of black strength, struggle, and vision for the future.

For the much larger number of African Americans who remained in America, the 1783 treaty recognizing the independence of the United States was only a diplomatic nicety. In fact, it narrowed their options. With no British military establishment offering freedom to black refugees, African Americans had to carry on the struggle for freedom and equality within a victorious white American society still rankling at the British escape hatch that had offered slaves freedom. Regarding American soil as their own, since it was the place where their toil and tears had made the land flourish, and in most cases their place of birth, they would have to pursue their agenda of freedom and equality within the bosom of the new white republic.

"We are determined to seek out for ourselves, the Lord being our helper," wrote Richard Allen a few years after the Revolution.[6] By this time, free black Americans were congregating in inland towns and seaboard cities where they saw the best opportunities to find jobs, marriage partners, and black churches. Their numbers grew to about 3,500 in New York City, 6,400 in Philadelphia, and 1,350 in Baltimore by 1800. In cities and small towns, most northern African Americans made the transit from slavery to freedom. This often had to be accomplished in the face of white hostility, because many white Americans saw free black people as more threatening than slaves. But in spite of such animosity, they created the foundations of black urban life—churches, schools, self-improvement societies, and mutual-aid associations—while cultivating an ethic of self-reliance that became a key attribute in making the long walk to freedom and equality.[7]

The Last Best Chance

Though the tenth of African Americans who lived in the postwar North began fashioning new lives for themselves beyond the expectations of white Americans, most of whom doubted their ability to function as free people, the greatest radical reform of the revolutionary era pertinent to black Americans, the abolition of slavery, slipped away. This was the great hope of those who believed the Revolution would mark the dawn of a new day for the sons and daughters of Africa. Though the prospect of liberty for slaves was real enough at war's end, it vanished in a few sorrowful years. Of all the missed opportunities in American history, it was the most tragic.

Viewing the political landscape and worrying about how the newly independent American republic could survive while one-fifth of its people were still in chains, Mathew Ridley, a Baltimore merchant, wrote in 1786 that slavery was "one of those evils that will be very difficult to correct [because] of all

Richard Allen founded the breakaway African Methodist Episcopal Church, which would become the largest black Christian denomination in the world. In raising money to build an independent black church in 1791, Allen's democratic sensibility shone through in his rationale that "men are more influenced by their moral equals than by their superiors . . . and . . . are more easily governed by persons chosen by themselves . . . than by persons who are placed over them by accidental circumstances."*

reformations those are the most difficult to ripen where the roots grow as it were in the pockets of men."[8] Ridley was right, but he was addressing only half of the problem. Reform-minded white Americans confronted two main issues in abolishing slavery: First, how slave owners would be compensated for their immense investment in human labor—the economic problem; second, how freed people would fit into the social fabric of the new nation—the social problem. Solutions to these two thorny matters, freighted with two

---

*Gary B. Nash, *Forging Freedom: The Formation of Philadelphia's Black Community* (Cambridge, MA: Harvard University Press, 1988), 113.

centuries of history, hinged on a willingness to make pocketbook sacrifices and to envision a biracial republic. The Revolution's natural-rights under-pinnings demanded a resolution of this glaring inconsistency. For many Americans, the question was not about *whether* slavery should be abolished but *when* and *how*. Yet to the crushing disappointment of hundreds of thou-sands of African Americans, elected white representatives provided little leadership in solving these problems.

It became evident at the Constitutional Convention of 1787 that the revolu-tionary generation, while providing a constitutional capstone to their achieve-ment, would not do what was essential to create "a more perfect union." Northern as well as southern delegates tried to bury the issue of abolition and leave slavery in place, all the while drawing a thin veil over the problem that even the most talented political theorists could not make disappear. By the time the revolutionary generation was in its grave, the best opportunity for abolishing slavery had been lost.

That this happened was not inevitable. Yes, the obstacles were huge, in-cluding the fragility of the newly independent nation, the threat of South Carolina and Georgia to secede if slavery was tampered with, and the reluc-tance of northern states to be part of a national remedy for a national prob-lem. At the same time, five interlocking factors after the war made this the opportune time for abolishing slavery. First, it was the era when the senti-ment for ridding American society of a blood-drenched labor system widely agreed to be abominable was the strongest. Second, it was the moment when the part of the new nation most strenuously resisting abolition, the Lower South, was most precariously situated and thus ill-suited to break away from the rest of the nation.[9] Third, it was a period when the school of thought called environmentalism was in full sway, positing that the degraded condi-tion of slaves was a matter of social conditioning, not innate inferiority, and that therefore no inborn disability stood in the way of emancipation. Fourth, it was a time when the opening of the vast trans-Appalachian West provided the wherewithal for a compensated emancipation, and when the use of this western domain as an instrument for binding the nation together had seized the public mind. Lastly, the outbreak of black rebellion in Saint Domingue in 1791, and the thunderclap 1794 decision of the French revolutionary govern-ment to emancipate half a million slaves, fed the belief that the entire Western world was trembling with the prospect of reversing the sordid, three-century history of European-sponsored Atlantic slavery.

What might have removed the formidable obstacles that stood in the way of capitalizing on conditions favorable for ending slavery was inspired leadership from those who emerged at the end of the Revolution as national heroes. But when they were most needed, these leaders failed to lead. North of Virginia and Maryland, John Adams and Benjamin Franklin used little of their political influence and gigantic respect to ally themselves with clergymen and reformers pushing the abolitionist agenda. As northerners, they might not have moved political leaders in the South, where most slaves lived, but they could have worked to convince the North that its contributions toward a compensated emancipation were essential to solving what was not just a regional but a national problem.

Southern leaders, especially Virginia's Jefferson and Washington, were strategically positioned to help the nation pay off the promissory notes contained in the language of the Declaration of Independence and almost every state constitution. Both had huge funds of moral and political capital to draw upon. Both knew of their unusual leverage. And both professed a hatred of slavery and a desire to see it ended in their own time.

Washington, as Henry Wiencek has recently shown, had been troubled for a decade by slavery, calling it the "foul stain of manhood" and contemplating, as the war drew to an end, whether he might be the key figure in securing the unalienable rights of man.[10] Pushing him hard was the dashing young Marquis de Lafayette, who had virtually become Washington's surrogate son.

From abroad, the French nobleman acted on what apparently were earlier talks with Washington about rooting slavery out of America. In early 1783, Lafayette proposed that the nation's conquering hero join him in a grand experiment to free the American slaves. Lafayette promised to purchase an estate on the coast of French Guiana, and there their slaves would be settled in preparation for freedom. "Such an example as yours might render it a general practice," wrote Lafayette, and he even imagined that "if we succeed in America," he would devote himself to spreading the experiment to the West Indies. "If it be a wild scheme," Lafayette concluded, "I had rather be mad this way than to be thought wise in the other tack."[11]

Washington did not dismiss the idea. He knew he might be the exemplar whom others would follow. "I shall be happy to join you in so laudable a work," he wrote Lafayette, and would welcome seeing his adoptive son to discuss the details "of the business." At Mount Vernon the next summer, the two men discussed the experiment. William Gordon, the Boston minister who would write one of the first histories of the American Revolution, recalled that Washington "wished to get rid of his Negroes, and the Marquis wished that an end might be put to the slavery of all of them." Gordon also played on Washington's enormous clout, urging that, teamed with Lafayette, "your joint counsels and influence" might accomplish emancipation, "and thereby give the finishing stroke and the last polish to your political characters."[12]

Nine months later, in May 1785, the Methodist leaders Francis Asbury and Thomas Coke visited Mount Vernon to solicit Washington's support for a petition they intended to deliver to Virginia's House of Delegates urging a gradual emancipation of slaves. Like everyone else, they knew that Washington's fortitude and integrity had taken root in America's heart and nowhere more so than in Virginia. Washington reiterated his wish to end slavery and told the Methodists that he "had signified his thoughts on the subject to most of the great men of the state." He declined to sign the petition but promised he would "signify his sentiments to the Assembly by letter" if they "took it into consideration."[13]

Virginia's legislature took the petition under consideration in November 1785 and summarily rejected it, though not, according to James Madison, "without an avowed patronage of its principle by sundry respectable members." Among the supporters was the immensely respected George Wythe, law professor at the College of William and Mary and Jefferson's ally in overhauling Virginia's code of laws during the Revolution. Contrary to his promise to Asbury and Coke, Washington did not write the letter supporting a gradual abolition of slavery.[14]

Later that year, Robert Pleasants, from an old-stock slave-owning family of Virginia Quakers, again appealed to Washington's "fame in being the successful champion of American liberty." "It seems highly probable to me," Pleasants wrote Washington, "that thy example and influence at this time towards a general emancipation would be as productive of real happiness to mankind as thy sword may have been." How would history remember him, Pleasants asked, if "impartial thinking men" read "that many who were warm advocates for that noble cause"—the cause of liberty and the rights of mankind—should now withhold that inestimable blessing from any who are absolutely in thy power and after the right of freedom is acknowledged to be the natural and unalienable right of all mankind.[15]

By this time, Lafayette had purchased an estate in French Guiana and was settling his slaves there with promises of freedom. But Washington was now waffling, much to the dismay of Lafayette, who wrote, "I would never have drawn my sword in the cause of America if I could have conceived thereby that I was founding a land of slavery." Rather than confessing his own change of heart on freeing his slaves, Washington blamed "the minds of the people of this country," who would not tolerate Lafayette's "benevolence" and "humanity." Contrary to James Madison's report that "sundry respectable persons" had argued on behalf of the Methodist petition for a gradual abolition act, Washington claimed it "could scarcely obtain a reading."[16]

The Virginian who, next to Washington, had the greatest moral capital and political influence to trade upon also declined the opportunity to help end the system of coerced labor that he professed to hate and knew compromised the American attempt to create a republic for all nations to emulate. Both for economic and ideological reasons, Thomas Jefferson squandered the respect he enjoyed as a national leader and internationally famous son of the Enlightenment. Dragged into a life of debt by his attachment to never-ending renovations and expensive furnishings at Monticello, he buried the thought of giving freedom to the several hundred slaves surrounding him there. At his death, he left so many debts that almost all of his slaves were sold at auction to satisfy his creditors.

Even if Jefferson's self-indulgence had not hobbled his professed desire to free his slaves, his view of people of African descent as indelibly inferior tainted all his thoughts about repairing the Achilles' heel of the new republic. Jefferson could not imagine white and black people living together in freedom—or so he said, though for most of his life he lived at Monticello surrounded by black people. Africans were "inferior to the whites in . . . mind and body," he contended, because they were "originally a distinct race, or made distinct by time and circumstances." Some historians today doubt that Jefferson actually believed in this doctrine of the inherent inferiority of black people but instead used it to shield himself from charges of gross duplicity. David Grimsted, for example, wastes no words in calling Jefferson's racist theorizing "obvious self-serving hypocrisy"—a pseudotheory advanced "to palliate the brutal exclusions from all civil and most human rights of those blacks that so contributed to his and his society's convenience."[17]

Nothing could better express the dismay of black Americans over Jefferson's moral retreat than the words of Benjamin Banneker, a free black mathematician and almanac writer. In his fifties, Banneker implored Jefferson in

1791 to rethink his views about African inferiority and tasked him for continuing to hold slaves at Monticello. "I apprehend you will embrace every opportunity to eradicate that train of absurd and false ideas and opinions which so generally prevail with respect to us, and that your sentiments are concurrent with mine, which are that one universal father hath given being to us all and that he hath not only made us all of one flesh but that he hath also without partiality afforded us all the same sensations, and endowed us all with the same faculties." Reminding Jefferson of his oft-quoted words in the preamble of the Declaration of Independence that "all men are created equal and that they are endowed by their creator with certain unalienable rights," Banneker chided the Squire of Monticello for "detaining by fraud and violence so numerous a part of my brethren under groaning captivity and cruel oppression." Should not Jefferson "be found guilty of that most criminal act, which you professedly detested in others"?[18]

If Washington had carried through with his pledge in 1783 to join Lafayette in "the grand experiment," if Jefferson, Madison, and a few other luminous Virginians who professed to hate slavery had stepped forward to support the Methodists' appeal to the Virginia legislature in 1785 for a gradual emancipation plan, and if northern leaders such as John Adams and Benjamin Franklin had drawn on their vast respect to support such a plan, the course of history might have changed at that moment. Eighty years later, more than 600,000 American lives were lost accomplishing the goal of emancipation, roughly one for each of the slaves in the new United States as of 1785.

The Indispensable Enemy

As we have already seen, Native Americans suffered disastrous losses in the war of the American Revolution. Facing a white society that was heavily armed and determined to seize the western lands that the Proclamation Act of 1763 denied white settlers, nations such as the Iroquois, Delaware, Shawnee, Wyandot, Cherokee, and Creek were forced by American commissioners to cede most of their land at gunpoint. White population buildup that had caused straitened economic conditions in seaboard settlements found a safety valve in western lands. Pouring across the Appalachians even before Benjamin Franklin, John Adams, and John Jay affixed their signatures to the peace treaty with England, thousands of settlers ignored treaty boundary lines and thumbed their noses at their elected state governments and the Continental Congress. Looking east, Native Americans had to make hard choices while confronting this human torrent.

Joseph Brant, the Mohawk leader we have followed through most of this book, appeared on the scene once more to play a crucial role in attempts to forge a pan-Indian alliance that could stem the white tide in the Old Northwest. Having cowed the tribes closest to the settlers' frontier—the Iroquois, Delaware, Wyandot, Chippewa, and Ottawa—congressional commissioners in 1786 planned to humble the westernmost tribes, the Shawnee, Miami, Potawatomi, Kickapoo, and others. But meanwhile, Brant worked his own woodland diplomacy, trying to gather many tribal leaders together for a grand parley at Detroit late in 1786. He had just returned from his second voyage to England, where he did not receive what he most hoped for— promises of military support. But England promised Brant a generous compensation for Iroquois losses in the war and gave him enough encouragement to return home determined to rally England's wartime Indian allies for further resistance to the overweening Americans. Brant knew that for his own people, the Mohawks and other Iroquois, the future lay in moving north of Lake Erie and Lake Ontario where the British had granted them land in the Grand River region of Lower Canada. Yet he felt compelled to play out his years on a larger stage, working to rally the Ohio River valley tribes in defense of their homelands.

Trekking into Ohio country in September 1786 with fifty-seven Iroquois delegates to parley with the Shawnee at their main town of Wapakoneta (in today's west central Ohio), Brant narrowly escaped a punitive expedition of two thousand militiamen led by George Rogers Clark and Benjamin Logan that burned seven Shawnee towns, killed many warriors, and captured women and children. In another incident of violating the rules of civilized warfare, the Americans slaughtered Old Melanthy, a friendly Shawnee headman, under a flag of truce. "Melanthy would not fly, but displayed the thirteen stripes and held out the articles of the Miami treaty," Colonel Josiah Harmar wrote, "but all in vain; he was shot down, . . . although he was their prisoner." Yet Clark withdrew, still not strong enough to attack the towns farther west of the Wabash River.[19]

Moving on to Detroit, Brant awaited the gathering of headmen from all the western tribes. In December, a moving speech was made, probably by Brant, reviewing the entire course of history since Europeans had invaded

North America. "It is certain that before Christian Nations visited this continent we were the sole lords of the soil. . . . The Great Spirit placed us there! And what is the reason why we are not still in possession of our forefathers' birth rights?" The answer was all too obvious: that intertribal rivalry and ancient animosities had allowed the Europeans to pursue the age-old policy of divide and conquer. "The interests of any one nation should be the interests of us all," the orator counseled; "the welfare of the one should be the welfare of all the others."[20]

The speech carried the day. Ten nations of the Ohio country spoke as one in an address to Congress calling for a reconsideration of the shotgun treaties of Fort Stanwix and Fort McIntosh. They had not been conquered, they insisted, and they had not lost their land except by intimidation and fraud. Until new negotiations took place, the surveyors laying off lands in the ceded parts of Indian country should lay down their instruments. If the United States rejected these requests, the Indian confederacy would fight.

Congress paid little heed to the address. By mid-1787, with the Constitutional Convention drawing up a new plan of government, Congress was near the end of its life. Nor were the western tribes able to maintain a united front, beset as in the past by intratribal and intertribal disputes. Once reorganized after ratification of the Constitution, the United States would do exactly what Pennsylvania's president John Dickinson promised in addressing the western tribes: Unless they quit resistance to the American treaties forced on them "we will instantly turn upon them our armies that have conquered the king of Great Britain . . . and extirpate them from the land where they were born and now live."[21]

The western Indian nations did not bow to such bluster. Preferring death to supine retreat, they resisted. Supplied by the British from Detroit and other posts in Lower Canada, the western Indian confederacy repulsed American invading armies under the command of General Josiah Harmar in 1790 and General Arthur St. Clair in 1791, only to lose to the army of General Anthony Wayne in 1794 at the Battle of Fallen Timbers.

To the south, the Creek leader Alexander McGillivray waged a similar resistance to white settlers coveting the rich lands possessed for centuries by his people. "Our lands are our life and breath," wrote McGillivray. "If we part with them, we part with our blood. We must fight for them." In 1786–87, Creek warriors drove encroaching settlers out of Tennessee's Cumberland River valley and sent them fleeing eastward from the Georgia frontier.

Knowing that Georgians had put a price on his head, McGillivray assured a friend in 1787, a month before the Constitutional Convention began its deliberations, that "if I fall by the hand of such [assassins], I shall fall a victim in the noblest of causes . . . maintaining the just rights of my country. I aspire to . . . meriting the appellation of preserver of my country, equally with those chiefs among you, whom from acting on such principles, you have exalted to the highest pitch of glory." McGillivray was confident that "if after every peaceable mode of obtaining redress of grievances having proved fruitless, having recourse to arms to obtain it be marks of the savage and not the soldier, [then] what savages must the Americans be."²²

Like the Ohio country Indian nations, the Creeks held their own against the land-hungry Georgians and South Carolinians for a time, and even obtained a treaty with the new American government in 1790 that guaranteed the Creek nation "all their lands within the limits of the United States." The Treaty of New York, writes historian Michael Green, "was an end run around Georgia which reversed the position of the Creek Nation and that state in their relations with the United States" by making illegal Georgia's militant Indian policy and prohibiting Georgia from treating separately with the Creeks.²³ This conciliatory treaty reflected a hard, cold fact—that the revenue-starved federal government preferred peace to a militant expansion of frontiersmen that the government could not back up with regular army units.

Known now by the Creeks as "The Great Beloved Man," McGillivray conducted what in the long run was a losing fight that cost both Creeks and Americans dearly. By the time he died in 1793 at age thirty-four, state militias, newly funded federal armies, and frontier irregulars were finally overwhelming the Indian nations in both the northern and southern regions, culminating in enormous new land cessions. In the course of these wars, the humanitarian language of the "utmost good faith" clause of the Northwest Ordinance of 1787 was all but forgotten. In its last significant act, the Continental Congress had pledged to native peoples that "their lands and property shall never be taken from them without their consent; and in their property, rights and liberty, they never shall be invaded or disturbed, unless in just and lawful wars authorized by Congress." It was a promise honored in the breach. In continuing the war of national expansion, the new nation turned its back on the revolutionary ideal of just and equitable relations with the "first people" of the continent. No political leader, at the state or federal level, voiced strenuous objection. Only such a man as George Morgan, former Indian trader and Indian agent for the Continental Congress, raised a lonely voice. "At what time do a people violate the law of nations, as the United States have done with regard to the northwestern Indians?" asked Morgan in 1793. "Only when they think they can do it with impunity. Justice between nations is founded on reciprocal fear. Rome whilst weak was equitable; become more strong than her neighbors, she ceased to be just. The ambitious and powerful are always unjust. To them the laws of nations are mere chimeras."[24]

The Chickamaugan Cherokee also knew this. Like McGillivray, Dragging Canoe hoped for a Spanish alliance. The Spanish governor of Florida had assured him that "you, our brothers the red men, are not without friends," and pointed out that "If it had not been for the Spanish and French, the British would have subdued them [the Americans] long ago." Supplied by the Spanish, the Chickamaugan Cherokee continued to attack Carolinian invaders of their lands in 1784–85, while hoping that the Treaty of Hopewell, which included a new cession of land from Chief Old Tassel and other accommodationist Cherokee chiefs in 1785, would stem the American squatter invasion. This was not to happen. "Your people settle much faster on our lands after a treaty than before," Old Tassel complained bitterly in 1786.[25] State governments failed to restrain further white land incursions and countenanced the murder of Old Tassel, who in 1788 had come peacefully to confer with white authorities about boundary disputes and frontier bloodletting. At this, most of the peace-seeking Cherokee moved south to northern Georgia, with most of their warriors joining Dragging Canoe's Chickamaugans.

By the time Dragging Canoe died in 1792, the determined resistance of the Chickamaugan Cherokee had brought some respect from white southerners. In the Treaty of Tellico Blockhouse in 1794, the Cherokee relinquished more land to white Carolinians, but this at least gave them breathing room and fostered a flowering of Cherokee culture in the early nineteenth century. Almost all of the leaders of this era—John Ross, Major Ridge, and John Walker—came from Dragging Canoe's militant Cherokee offshoot.[26]

Can the pro-British stance of most Native Americans and their resistance after the war to onrushing white settlers be counted as a failure of judgment on their part? No. Had they sided with the Americans they would have fared no better, as the dismal postwar experience of the Tuscaroras, Oneidas, and Catawbas demonstrates. The Oneidas and Tuscaroras, though guaranteed by

the Treaty of Fort Stanwix in 1784 that they "shall be secured in the possession of the lands on which they are now settled," quickly lost most of their
land to white settler depredations and New York's relentless pressure on
tribal chiefs to give up their remaining land. They "dwindled to nothingness
in the State of New York," according to Barbara Graymont, the main historian of the Iroquois revolutionary experience. Repeated petitions to Congress
for loss of their land and for aid in relieving the sordid poverty they had sunk
to by the time Washington became the nation's first president brought them
little in return. Thinking itself merciful, Congress awarded the Stockbridge
people $200 and the Oneida $148 per year.[27]

Even Indians who had abandoned their own people to support the American cause got little succor after the Treaty of Paris in 1783. Nonhelema, the
Shawnee sister of Cornstalk, who was murdered with his son in 1777, is a
good case in point. Even after the shameful slaughter of her brother and
nephew, Nonhelema served the Americans as a messenger and translator.
Congress denied the old and impoverished woman the two thousand acres
she requested, but after receiving many pleas awarded her a suit of clothes
and a blanket each year, along with rations if she could reach one of the forts
in the Ohio country.[28]

Joseph Brant, Alexander McGillivray, and Dragging Canoe were the ex-
emplars of pan-Indian resistance after the peace without peace. The spiritual
heirs of such war-tempered Indian chiefs were a new generation of resistance
leaders in America's heartland—Tecumseh, Black Hawk, Red Jacket, Handsome Lake, Sequoyah, and many others. In their three-decade struggle to
defend their homelands, ending with the War of 1812, they lost in the proxi-
mate sense. What they won, however, was a piece of history, for they kept
lit the lamp of resistance and passed on their revolutionary struggle to their
children and their children's children. Memory of the long and bloody post-
revolutionary era lives on yet today. What we proudly call the Spirit of '76 in
our white-oriented history books had its counterpart in the red Spirit of
'76, which has been at the ideological core of the Indian rights movement
of the 1970s and its successors. Today, the descendants of the militant Chickamaugan Cherokees "in Oklahoma and in the mountains of North Carolina,"
says Dragging Canoe's biographer, "can still repeat with pride Dragging
Canoe's statement to the Shawnee delegation: 'We are not yet conquered.' "[29]

The Veterans' Cheat

In fighting the War of Independence, the Continental Congress struggled mightily with a paradox familiar to American lawmakers today: The people want a lot from government but seem almost innately allergic to taxes. Supplying the American army and paying its soldiers plagued Congress from the beginning because Congress had no revenue of its own—not one penny. Rather, it relied entirely on requisitioning appropriations from the thirteen states and depended on their compliance. Not until the Constitution of 1787 was ratified the next year would the federal government have the power to tax. In this improbable situation, Congress faced incessant grumbling, persistent desertion, and repeated mutinies from within Washington's Continental army.

One way to stanch the hemorrhaging of the army was to promise pensions for those who would reenlist. Congress did so only for officers. In desperate straits in 1778, it promised officers half pay for life if they agreed to serve for the remainder of the war and seven years thereafter. In 1780, Congress authorized pensions for the widows and orphans of those who had died. In 1783 Congress reduced the pensions to five years of full pay—not actually paid in cash but in certificates redeemable for cash at some point in the future. None of these provisions affected very many officers for it was uncommon for men to step forward for such indeterminate and lengthy stints of service. In the meantime, enlisted men were promised nothing.

It was hardly in the spirit of yearning for a more egalitarian society that the widows and orphans of enlisted men received no pensions. But even worse, affecting tens of thousands of men, was one of the first decisions made by Congress after Washington became president in 1790—to fund at face value the certificates issued during the war to pay enlisted men's salaries (and the officers' five-year pensions). Most soldiers had sold their certificates to money speculators at war's end for between two and two and a half shillings on the pound (twenty shillings). This was all the pieces of paper could command because it was doubtful they could ever be turned in for full-value payment in specie with interest added. Mostly poor and desperate to rebuild their lives, the soldiers took what they could get. Something was better than nothing.

But in 1790 Washington's secretary of the treasury, Alexander Hamilton,

The 1832 pension act passed by Congress gave full-pay benefits to both enlisted men and officers if they had served at least two full years. Two years later, their widows received pensions. The debates over these pensions may have inspired William Ranney, who had fought in the Texas army in 1836 to secure the Lone Star Republic, to paint this romanticized version of ordinary soldiers returning home. Most returned in rags, many shoeless, and very few had a horse and cart to make the trek back to their villages and farms.

proposed to use federal revenue, much of it derived from sale of western lands, to pay off the certificates at their full face value in hard money plus interest for seven years. As icily self-confident as Robert Morris, Hamilton had little concern that this would be seen as inequitable, for, after all, this windfall for speculators would be the solder that welded them to the national interest. However, a friend of Hamilton, Morris, and the other advocates for a powerful central government run by the nation's financial elite stepped forward on behalf of Joseph Plumb Martin and his band of brotherhood.

Pelatiah Webster, a laissez-faire free-trade and anti–price control advocate during the war, the most skillful political economist of the day, and a part of Robert Morris's conservative nationalist group, strongly opposed a measure that would heap wealth on those who had snapped up the pay certificates when soldiers were selling them at a fraction of their value. The veterans now learned that everyone would be taxed to pay off the certificates at full value plus interest—a bonanza 800 percent profit for those who held them. By itself, the plan would increase the gap between the rich and poor. In "A Plea for Poor Soldiers," Webster called the plan a "perversion," an "absurdity," and a "shameful injustice." At the end of the war, he argued, fighting men "submitted with patience to accept their discharge" with no real pay but only certificates with numbers written on them, and "returned home as they could with empty hands and dry lips." But now they would get none of the difference between the face value of the certificates and the price they sold them at in their desperation. The subtitle of "A Plea for Poor Soldiers" gave Webster's argument in capsule form: "To demonstrate that the soldiers and other public creditors, who really and actually supported the burden of the war, HAVE NOT BEEN PAID, OUGHT TO BE PAID, CAN BE PAID, and MUST BE PAID."[30] It was a battle lost in the First Congress, which adopted Hamilton's plan for assuming and funding the Revolutionary War debt. But the bitterness of all the losers, most notably those who fought and won the war, lingered for many years.

Not until 1818, thirty-five years after the war ended, did Congress move to reward the soldiers and sailors who survived, and by this time only a small fraction of some 300,000 who served were still alive and able to prove they were impoverished. Fourteen years later, in 1832, Congress passed a comprehensive pension act for any survivor, officer or enlisted man, rich or poor, still alive and able to provide satisfactory proof of at least six months' service. Only a few thousand septuagenarians and octogenarians had the nation's bounty bestowed on them.[31]

Small-Producer Persistence

Just as the war of national expansion did not end in 1783, the revolutionary radicalism of small producers continued after the war and at times even intensified. This would not happen absent the reassertion of power by conservative revolutionaries in the latter years of the war—men bent on constraining the power centered in the popularly elected state legislatures. "During this last phase of the Revolution," writes Alan Taylor, "gentlemen and yeomen who had cooperated against the British fell out over the nature of property, whether power would be diffused locally or consolidated

DEBORAH SAMPSON.

Published by H. Mann 1797

Deborah Sampson Garnett was among the successful invalided pensioners of the Continental Line. Six years after receiving a pension in 1803, she petitioned Congress that the pension be given retroactively from 1783, the year of her discharge, to 1803. Congress denied the petition.

centrally, and whether extralegal crowds retained any legitimacy in the new republic."[32]

Backcountry unrest grew out of some of the same tensions that had marked the tenant uprisings in New Jersey and New York from the 1740s to 1760s and in the Regulator insurgencies in the Carolinas in the 1760s and 1770s. Access to reasonably priced land, security of homesteaded property, an adequate circulating medium, and equitable taxes were the main concerns of ordinary farmers seeking escape from the marginal existence that had prevailed in the old areas of settlement. Confiscation of Loyalist property held the promise of distributing land widely, but most of the land in fact fell into the hands of well-to-do men, not poor yeoman farmers. Even opening the frontier lands from which Native Americans were being driven brought struggling men of the soil face-to-face with affluent men seeking even greater landed wealth. For most farmers seeking economic security, the end of the Revolution brought greater freedom from British mercantilist policies, but it did not bring equality or enhanced economic opportunities. The result was renewed popular upheaval—a succession of bloody confrontations between entrepreneurs preaching the doctrine of unrestrained capitalism and small farmers clinging to traditional ideas of fair prices, debt relief, greater economic opportunity, and mutuality of economic exchanges preserved in the name of the community's benefit.

In the aftermath of revolution, the scramble for advantage reignited the earlier Vermont radicalism personified by Ethan Allen. In fact, Allen himself, now old and grizzled, lent his experience to the frontier disputes between rival speculators from Pennsylvania and Connecticut. Spreading sparks from the altar of '76, he told poor Susquehanna settlers in 1785, four years before his death, to "crowd your settlements, add to your numbers and strength; procure fire-arms, and ammunition, be united among yourselves.... Liberty and Property; or slavery and poverty are now before us."[33] Susquehanna territory radicals spoke of "the Vermont Plan" as their stratagem. Though unsuccessful, they provided inspiration for similar breakaway frontier states—Franklin and Transylvania in the Kentucky country, for example—where the hope of cheap land, escape from wealthy land speculators, and light taxes beckoned ordinary men and their families.

Postrevolutionary agrarian radicals spoke the same language of the Green Mountain Boys and Carolina Regulators—"that laboring men had a God-given right to claim and improve wilderness land"—but they were fortified with the righteousness of men who had fought and shed blood on the battlefields where independence had been won.[34] It was virtually impossible to breathe more fire than Ethan Allen, but those who tried had the additional argument that their cause was now against those who were traducing the revolutionary principles of natural rights and social justice.

The key natural right thrown in the faces of great proprietors and companies that controlled the price of land after the war was the old argument

445

advanced by the Green Mountain Boys and Regulators: The farmer's labor that improved wilderness land gave him a legitimate title to it. The American Revolution for them meant more than independence from England; it offered the possibility of a land where small producers did not live under the rule, as Alan Taylor puts it, of "moneyed parasites who did not live by their own labor but, instead, preyed on the many who did."[35] If the Revolution meant only a continuation of the great landed proprietors' hold on the Hudson River region or the Carolina backcountry or the trans-Appalachian frontier lands opening up, then the Revolution had been lost for its surviving veterans, who would lapse back into economic dependency as tenant farmers or wage workers. Expensive land, excessive rents, heavy taxes, and exorbitant legal fees, all the work of land companies owned by wealthy speculators, paved the way to slavery.

Correlatively, a republic of freedom-loving, slavery-hating men would emerge from widely and fairly distributed land. This was not a radical idea of the revolutionary era but the insistence of America's radical revolutionaries that the wisdom of England's seventeenth-century Levellers and eighteenth-century "commonwealthmen" still provided the best way forward. The seventeenth-century English radical belief that "where there is inequality of estates there must be inequality of power" still pertained: Inequality would spawn dependency, and dependency would destroy political liberty. Now, as in eighteenth-century "commonwealthman" thought, "a free people are kept so by no other means but an equal distribution of property." It followed, then, after the war, that "when men's riches are become immeasurably or surprisingly great, a people who regard their own security ought to make a strict enquiry how they came by them and oblige them to take down their own size, for fear of terrifying the community or mastering it."[36]

This ideology of yeoman farmers and small producers animated not only frontier farmers along the arc of settlement from Maine to Georgia. In New Jersey, the small state pinched between larger, more populous, and richer New York and Pennsylvania, Abraham Clark was a herald of the same message. Clark had signed the Declaration of Independence and served as a New Jersey delegate to the Continental Congress for most of the war. Distressed at how soured postwar conditions had deluged the courts with suits for debt, set creditors upon debtor farmers demanding payment in specie, and jammed jails with ordinary people unable to satisfy their creditors, Clark took up his pen in 1785 to spell out how men of "wealth and renown" were corrupting the democratic promise of the Revolution. Moneyed men, who were "not ... under the necessity of getting their bread by industry" were feeding on "the labor of the honest farmer and mechanic." How, after all, had New Jersey been transformed from "a howling wilderness to pleasant fields, gardens, towns, and cities," except by the sweat off the brows of productive laborers?[37]

In *The True Policy of New Jersey Defined* (1786), Clark returned to the labor theory of value that sustained insurgent pre-revolutionary New Jersey farmers. The job of lawmakers, he lectured, was to "help the feeble against the mighty and deliver the oppressed out of the hands of the oppressor." Attacking men of wealth who hoarded hard money and then withheld it from circulation while taking debtors to court for their inability to pay them in specie, Clark deplored this "avaricious thirst for gain" that was causing farms to be "sold far below ... value, to the breaking of families and increase of poverty." "That inequality of property which is detrimental to a republican government," he predicted, would soon turn a republican state of husbandmen into a European-like aristocratic state of "lords and tenants." "Our boasted liberty may prove but a delusive dream."[38]

In this yearning for a more equitable society, agrarian radicals and laboring men in the cities took satisfaction when some of the new nation's trumpeters of untrammeled capitalism fell from their height; sometimes their love of freedom from price controls, debt-relief legislation, and other curbs on free-market activity proved excessive. Every city knew of such self-inflicted wounds. Philadelphia's Robert Morris was the most spectacular case of riches-to-rags. After stepping down as Congress's superintendent of finance in 1784, he went on a spree of wild speculation in western lands, overextended himself, declared bankruptcy in 1798, and languished in debtor's prison for the last three years of his life. Perhaps thinking of the old saying, "Grasp all, lose all," on his way to debtor's prison, Morris wrote to John Nicholson, his land scheme partner: "My money is gone, my furniture is to be sold, I am to go to prison and my family to starve. Good night." To relieve desperate overcrowding at Philadelphia's prison, the city's board of inspectors sent female prisoners to Morris's huge uncompleted marble mansion a block away.[39]

Curbing the piling up of great wealth or even worrying about the growing disparity between wealth and want was not the main concern of farmers remote from seaboard sites of capital accumulation. The price control failure of the late 1770s had taught them that managing an economy in times of stress

447

was akin to redirecting a river's course. Rather, maintaining their economic independence, providing for their families, and warding off a descent into poverty were their main concerns. But in the mid-1780s, and many times thereafter, they saw themselves again slipping to the brink of penury and dependency. When this happened, they took the law into their own hands—one of the main lessons of the Revolutionary experience. This occurred most dramatically in central and western Massachusetts in 1786 when Daniel Shays, a Revolutionary War officer, led farmers in militant court closings and sheriff mobbings of the kind that had led Massachusetts into revolution twelve years before. Facing farm foreclosures, unable to pay taxes and small debts in the specie required by the legislature, and knowing that seaboard merchants controlled the limited supply of gold and silver, the farmers rocked the state to its core. In a revolt involving about one-quarter of all adult men, Shays's followers arrayed themselves against their elected government. Governor James Bowdoin's privately financed army eventually suppressed the rebellion (which occurred on a smaller scale in other states). But we can see that ordinary farmers had their limits. With sprigs of pine needles in their farmer's hats, signifying the liberty tree prized in New England, they marched to the tune of England's late-seventeenth-century radical thinker, Algernon Sidney, who maintained that "That which is not just is not law and that which is not law ought not to be obeyed."[40]

The leather-apron men of the inland towns and seaboard cities also wrestled with the less than rosy prospects they faced in the wake of America's world-shaking victory over Great Britain. Many of them were expectant capitalists, hoping for a surge in American-manufactured goods and optimistic about the release of American producers from English mercantilist policies. This often allied them with merchants and lawyers. But for many others, particularly in the lower trades such as shoemaking, coopering, and tailoring, the postwar economic slump and the closure of the huge British West Indian market to American products caused great pain.

What galled craftsmen particularly after the war was the willingness of seaport merchants to import a flood of British-manufactured goods. Merchants forbidden to send locally crafted goods to the West Indian market were glad enough to accept British-crafted goods. This set artisan against merchant, a fracture repaired only when the economy revived later in the 1780s. Out of this conflict, artisans began to understand the need to band together as an interest group. Thus, tradesmen and small manufacturers formed cross-craft societies in all the cities—predecessors of central trade unions. In Boston, the "tradesmen and manufacturers" appealed to merchants "like a band of brothers whose interests are connected." Similar organizations took form in New York, Philadelphia, Baltimore, and Charleston. Although they had some success in getting duties placed on imported English goods, giving local craftsmen a bit of an advantage, attempts at uniting the trade policies of the various states—an attempt "to cement a general union"—largely failed.[41]

Many of the artisans and most of the mariners came out of the Revolution with a radical heritage and more sharply defined democratic, antideferential sensibilities. Nowhere was this more evident than in Boston. Merchants and lawyers, supported by some of the wealthier artisans, proposed a reorganization of the town meeting so that the venerable open-air gatherings of the populace, led by a moderator, would be replaced by an elected mayor and aldermen. In theory they would bring order, efficiency, and financial stability to New England's capital seaport. This was the old dream of conservatives for two generations, voted down and seen as an elitist power grab. Proposed again in 1784, it aroused ordinary Bostonians to call it a "detestable Hutchinsonian plan" (aptly associating it with Lieutenant Governor Thomas Hutchinson's similar attempt at municipal reorganization in the 1740s) that would "engross the whole power of the town" in the hands of the rich. At a raucous town meeting in 1784, efforts to present the plan were met with shouts of "No incorporation. No mayor and aldermen. No innovations." Faced with "an unabated roaring," the "gentlemen of character" left Faneuil Hall to await another day. Further attempts in 1785 and 1786 met with the same determined defense of the town meeting by the "low people," as one Bostonian called them.[42]

In other cities, craftsmen built on the gains they had made in the course of fomenting the American Revolution by electing men of their own class to local and state governing bodies. In New York, in the first election after the departure of the British along with some 20,000 Loyalists, voters sent artisans and small merchants to the legislature. There they made confiscation of Loyalists' property a legislative priority. Meanwhile, radical politicians, such as Albany's Abraham Yates, championed the rights of productive men while resisting the determination of political centralizers to remove power from the hands of ordinary people. In Charleston, artisans and maritime workers formed the Marine Anti-Britannic Society in late 1783 to oppose "aristocratical principles endeavoured to subvert and destroy every genuine idea of real republicanism." Crowd demonstrations in 1784–85, threatening British merchants, lawyers, and opulent Charleston families who were believed to be betraying the promise of the Revolution, convinced Edward Rutledge that the previously obscure men who had risen to positions of authority during the war "found it very difficult to fall back in the ranks."[43]

Those embracing unrestrained capitalism were winning the day by the time the Constitutional Convention met in 1787, but the tenacity of commitments to a rough equality of citizens lived on deep into the nineteenth century, not only among working people but in influential writers and intellectuals as well.

Passing the Torch

In 1810, thirty-five years after she first told her husband to "remember the ladies," Abigail Adams was still nudging her aging mate about the need to "destroy the foundation of all pretensions of the gentlemen to superiority over the ladies." Her goal? "[To] restore liberty, equality, and fraternity between the sexes."[44] With all the power he had acquired as an internationally acclaimed diplomat and second president of the United States, John Adams had done little to advance women's rights. But Abigail and many of the women of her generation, though failing to get recognition for women's full rights as citizens, were conceding nothing. She had been a prime voice for change in gender relations as the Revolution got under way; she had achieved little of what she wanted; she had made her peace with her brilliant, irascible husband; but she held true to her vision of a changed society, where a woman's sphere was broadened and a female could fully develop and utilize her talents.

If Abigail Adams could not convince her husband, she could shape the values and commitments of her children. Abigail did not live long enough—she died in 1818, eight years before her husband's death—to see John Quincy Adams address Congress in 1838, where he insisted that women, though they lacked the vote, should have the right to petition the nation's legislative body. We can imagine that Abigail's son, as he spoke on behalf of stopping a gag rule to take women's petitions off Congress's table, had in mind his comment to his brother at the time of their mother's death: that "her life gave the lie to every libel on her sex that was ever written."[45]

Long before American women became fully involved in the radical abolition movement of the 1830s, where they strode onto public ground that their revolutionary fathers would not yield, their revolutionary-era mothers had become privately involved in benevolent and educational institutions serving the nation's interest. In every city after the war, women founded charitable societies to relieve the miseries of widows, orphans, prostitutes, and the illiterate. Usually connected to churches, these organizations provided opportunities for "female collective behavior." The organizing, writing, publicizing, and speaking skills that women honed within these organizations primed them and their daughters for the abolitionist, suffragist, temperance, penal, public-education, and other reform movements of the 1820s and beyond. This was the work of middle- and upper-class women, for those below them followed lives of labor that afforded little time for public and philanthropic affairs.[46]

If the middle-class revolutionary woman could not be an enfranchised woman, she could become an educated woman with a sharpened political consciousness and a changed sense of herself. The postrevolutionary era bristled with new female academies, bringing education to a much broader swath of American society. The rationale for the educated woman was simple: Republican government would stand or fall on the intelligence, wisdom, morality, and public-mindedness of its citizens. Inasmuch as child-rearing was the mother's main business, the young could hardly be raised properly as citizens without educated mothers. In Philadelphia, Benjamin Rush's "Thoughts on Female Education" (1787) pushed forward a rationale meant to undermine generations of conventional thinking about women's inherently frail minds. Rather than educating women to be dependent upon men, he urged training women to be the molders of young men's character. "Let the ladies of a country be educated properly," he wrote, "and they will not only make and administer its laws but form its manners and character." The proposed curriculum for the Young Ladies' Academy that Rush helped establish departed sharply from English models, which favored subjects that made the woman an ornament of her husband—a "sensible, virtuous, sweet-tempered woman" who knew how to draw, dance, and play drawing room instrumental music. By contrast, the American woman of the new republic needed far more utilitarian knowledge so that she could monitor the morals of her society and train the children of the republic. Thus, bookkeeping, writing, history, geography, science, and religion must have a place in female education.[47]

Beginning in the 1780s, the sharp literacy gap between men and women began to close. This would narrow over many decades; but "no social change in the early Republic affected women more emphatically," writes historian Linda Kerber, "than the improvement of schooling, which opened the way into the modern world." It was a sign of how much work lay ahead that a Philadelphia male in 1792 sneered at a woman and called her "deluded" for having proposed a "University Established for Women."[48] But this was also a sign that women were seeking what they had never sought before in America—equality of education and a claim to equal intellectual capabilities. It may not be coincidence that this call for a woman's university came shortly after a Philadelphia printer published Mary Wollstonecraft's *Vindication of the Rights of Women,* the era's most muscular statement of women's capabilities and the rights they deserved.

By the 1790s, the renegotiation of gender roles and talk of women's rights began to put potent, if half-formed, ideas on the blank slate where Abigail Adams attempted to write them in 1776. The role of republican motherhood, argues Linda Kerber, was a "conservative, stabilizing one" because it created a new and important yet limiting role for women, in which they could not fully capitalize on "the radical potential of the revolutionary experience."[49] Ironically, men would not allow women to become full-fledged citizens, but cast them in the role of training men for full-fledged citizenship. Yet the arrival of Mary Wollstonecraft's *Vindication of the Rights of Women* in 1792— quickly republished and widely circulated—began to change all that. Like a sputtering teapot, the Revolution had raised the issue of women's rights intermittently; but now, in the 1790s, the dynamic English radical woman brought water to a boil. "The rights of humanity," she wrote, "have been . . . confined to the male line from Adam downwards," but now she called for extending universal rights to the excluded half of humanity. Within a year, Wollstonecraft's *Vindication* ricocheted up and down eastern North America. "The Rights of women are no longer strange sounds to an American ear," wrote Elias Boudinot, a New Jersey leader, in 1793. "They are now heard as familiar terms in every part of the United States." In effect, the women's rights talk spurred by Wollstonecraft's broadside challenge to male superordination, as historian Rosemarie Zagarri has put it, forced both men and women to struggle with "two conflicting principles: the equality of the sexes and the subordination of women to men."[50]

The idea of rational, competent, politically sensate, even independent women was brought forth and given potential by the women of the Revolution, not to be realized in their own lifetimes but handed down to their daughters and granddaughters. For several decades, women occupied an ambiguous terrain created by intermediate steps toward citizenship and self-conscious political identity. Once planted, however, the seeds of women's suffrage and equal female rights could not be torn from the soil. But another generation would be born before women could forthrightly play public roles as reformers, public speakers, and religious leaders. As Kerber aptly puts it, "the price of stabilizing the Revolution was an adamant refusal to pursue its implications for race relations and the relations of gender, leaving to subsequent generations to accomplish what the Revolutionary generation had not."[51]

In *The Wealth of Nations*, published in 1776 as the Declaration of Independence reached England, Adam Smith had written that "civil authority, so far as it is instituted for the security of property, is in reality instituted for the defense of the rich against the poor, or of those who have some property against those who have none at all."[52] This was precisely what conservative revolutionaries had in mind as they tried to squash the popular movements of the early war years. For these reluctant revolutionaries, "freedom," "security," and "order" were the watchwords of *their* revolution. Challenging them from below were those who honored "equality" and "equity" as the watchwords of *their* revolution. For the people whom this book has featured, the Revolution was visionary and experimental. They did not expect it to have an end point, final victory, or triumphant success. Rather it was a revolution of beginnings, of partial achievements, of deferred dreams—in short, an ongoing process where the transformative work must be passed like a torch to the next generation. Philadelphia's Benjamin Rush, no radical himself, shrewdly expressed this in 1787: "The American war is over, but this is far from the case with the American Revolution. On the contrary, nothing but the first act of the great drama is closed."[53] In this vein, to think of the American Revolution as incomplete is very different from arguing that it was a failure, even for those with the most expansive ideas about a truly free, just, and equal society.

Revolutions are always incomplete. Almost every social and political convulsion that has gone beyond first disruptions of the *ancien régime* depended on mass involvement; and that in itself, in every recorded case of revolutionary insurgency, raised expectations that could not be completely satisfied. In this sense, there has never been such a thing as a completed revolution. So it was with the American Revolution.

Yet promoting and prosecuting the Revolution instilled in ordinary and subjected people a new sense of themselves, a certitude that they had been instrumental in one of the most mold-shattering, mass action movements of recorded history, and in a comradeship born of fighting against formidable odds. Such awareness of their political importance and their certainty about the justness of their causes insured that the ideas of ardent radicals would not be driven underground. Very seldom in history do a people imagine a new world, see it within their grasp, and then give it up. Every unfulfilled element of the Revolution—abolition of slavery; full citizenship for all free people; greater women's rights; the integrity of Native American land and political sovereignty; the entitlements of laboring people on farms and in cities; more equitable taxes; public education; religious toleration—reemerged in the late eighteenth and early nineteenth centuries. Some of these planks in the radical platform, such as strict limits for legislators or gender equality, are still agenda items today.

Another measure of the Revolution's partial success for the unacknowledged radicals was the grudging concessions made to them by those who wanted their labor but not their political and social involvement. Reasserting power from the top of society, convinced that ordinary Americans had not learned to exercise freedom responsibly and had threatened order and security in the new nation, conservative revolutionaries moved energetically to hobble popularly elected state legislatures as well as county and city governments. Yet if conservatives tried to create a new American ruling class by the late 1780s, this ruling class would have to hold power gingerly, always making accommodations, always negotiating, always returning to the people. Patrician politicians could still refer to the people "out of doors" as a rabble, a mob, or the *canaille;* but they knew, like New York's Robert R. Livingston, that uttering such taunts did not obviate the need to "swim a stream which is impossible to stem, to yield to the torrent if they hoped to direct its course."[54] Having elbowed their way into the political system; having pried open legislative-assembly debates to public view; having institutionalized the rotation of offices, term limits, and annual elections; having elected their militia officers; and having known through intimate experience that they had been instrumental to the genesis and conduct of the Revolution, the common people did not easily give up what they had achieved. This is why elected leaders knew they were obliged to return to a broadened electorate perennially for permission to continue holding power; they knew that ordinary Americans were done with deference. Radical reformers might be contained but not ignored. "We must consult the rooted prejudices [of the people at large]," admitted Boston's Nathaniel Gorham, a merchant accustomed to giving orders, "if we expect their concurrence in our propositions."[55]

By eliminating the boundaries between the rulers and the ruled, always the constructs of entrenched elites, the people examined in this book—all of them animated by a sense of freedom, justice, or dignity denied—could no more step away from the revolutionary agendas they had created than a mountain stream fed by melting snow can halt its rush to the valleys below. What they learned from insurgent experiences—about themselves as well as about strategies for contesting power holders—would be passed down to the next generation, where weighty questions would be asked over and over again: How far should liberty be extended? What kind of men should rule the republic? How much equality would be necessary to keep concentrated economic power from turning into concentrated political power?

Never again would the mass of American people believe that the right to rule public affairs should be pinned to wealth and status achieved in the private realm. But never, not even to this day, could common ground be found on an egalitarian democracy. Radical democrats of the revolutionary era were not able "to begin the world over again," as Tom Paine had thought might happen in midwar. But they had begun to remake America, leaving to their descendants and political heirs the hard work of structuring society more equally in ways appropriate to a democratic polity.

ACKNOWLEDGMENTS

My fascination with the American Revolution first came from schoolboy absorption with the historical novels of Kenneth Roberts. *Rabble in Arms*, *Lydia Bailey*, *Oliver Wiswell*, and others stirred my blood and brought to life the revolutionary era with the kind of emotion and descriptive power that few historians achieve. Later I discovered Roberts's biases and contemporary political convictions; but by that time, in the 1960s, I was embarked on graduate studies in early American history and turned from historical novels to historical archives. Since then, the American Revolution has been my constant companion—in the lecture hall, the seminar room, and dozens of libraries and historical societies. This book culminates four decades of reading, resaerching, and writing about the American Revolution.

My own work on the American Revolution has centered on African Americans, Native Americans, and ordinary people, especially the artisans, laborers, and mariners of the late-eighteenth-century cities. Much of that work is woven into this book. More broadly, I have tried to synthesize the work of an ever-growing number of historians whose scholarship, collectively, has opened up new understandings of the American Revolution. A number of them are of special importance for pioneering studies in the 1960s and 1970s that refocused the attention of those who cared to listen about forgotten Americans and buried dimensions of the Revolution. For many years, Alfred F. Young has been an intellectual shepherd to a flock of young scholars interested in the radical impulses leading to and unleashed by the American Revolution. He has contributed fascinating studies of the Boston shoemaker George Robert Twelves Hewes and Deborah Sampson Gannett, the woman who fought in the war as a man. Staughton Lynd and Jesse Lemisch blazed the way with studies of farmers, artisans, and blue water mariners, thus opening up the neglected world of plebeian people. John Shy laid foundations for a revised social history of military affairs in the Revolution. Benjamin Quarles, Peter Wood, and Ira Berlin showed the importance of African Americans in how the revolution unfolded; and David Brion Davis and Winthrop Jordan created monumental studies of Anglo-American racial attitudes and the construction of antislavery arguments. Mary Beth Norton and Linda Kerber administered potent doses of memory-recovering medicine as it pertained to the half of American society that was female in the revolutionary era. Native Americans began to receive their due as Anthony F. C. Wallace, Francis Jennings, and Barbara Graymont began lighting the lanterns by which we now see. All of these scholars produced pioneering studies in the 1960s and 1970s, creating a new dynamic upon which others have built.

Those who have followed the pathbreaking histories of the Revolution mentioned above are numerous and prolific. Keeping up with the mountainous literature on the American Revolution requires strong eyes and a rigorous work schedule. Much of this more recent work is acknowledged in the footnotes. After more than four decades of rich scholarship, we have before us an American Revolution that our parents and grandparents never knew. Little could he know, his vision clouded by pessimism about how Americans seemed to care little about remembering the Revolution, when John Adams wrote a friend in 1817, that he regarded "the true history of the American Revolution and of the establishment of our present constitution as lost forever." (Michael Kammen, *Season of Youth: The American Revolution and the Historical Imagination* [1978], 19)

Alfred Young, Marcus Rediker, John Howe, Doug Greenberg, Bob Gross, and Ron Hoffman have pored over my manuscript, offered shrewd and supportive criticisms, and saved me from errors. Master historians themselves, they exemplify the good-heartedness and intellectual camaraderie that has made academic life so rewarding. Wendy Wolf, my editor at Viking/Penguin, has cheered me on and improved the book through deft editorial interventions.

The staff at the Library Company of Philadelphia has made that great repository of early American materials the most satisfying venue that a scholar can imagine. At UCLA, the staff of the Young Research Library has faithfully assisted this scholar who has been inhabiting their haunts for thirty-eight years. Research assistants Grace Lu and Rosa Segura have been of good cheer as they ably assisted me in preparing this book. Marian Olivas has nudged me into the world of electronic data retrieval and cyberediting.

Pacific Palisades
December 2004

NOTES

In quoted material from eighteenth-century sources, I have modernized spelling, capitalization, and punctuation.

Introduction

1. Lester J. Cappon, ed., *The Adams-Jefferson Letters: The Complete Correspondence between Thomas Jefferson and Abigail and John Adams*, 2 vols. (Chapel Hill: University of North Carolina Press, 1959), 2:451–52.
2. Michel-Rolph Trouillot, *Silencing the Past: Power and the Production of History* (Boston: Beacon Press, 1995), 47.
3. John Adams to Elbridge Gerry, 2 May 1785, *Microfilms of the Adams Papers* (Boston: Massachusetts Historical Society, 1954), reel 364, quoted in Marcus Cunliffe, *George Washington, Man and Monument* (Boston: Little, Brown, 1958), 159; Charles F. Adams, ed., *Works of John Adams: Second President of the United States: With a Life of the Author, Notes and Illustrations*, 10 vols. (Boston: Little, Brown, 1850–56), 10:133.
4. Thomas Jefferson to James Madison, 14 February 1783, *Papers of Thomas Jefferson*, 31 vols., ed. Julian Boyd (Princeton, NJ: Princeton University Press, 1950–), 6:241, quoted in Jay Fliegelman, *Declaring Independence: Jefferson, Natural Language, and the Culture of Performance* (Stanford, CA: Stanford University Press, 1993), 93; Page Smith, *John Adams*, 2 vols. (Garden City, NY: Doubleday, 1962), 2:940; Nathanael Emmons, *A Discourse, Delivered on the Annual Fast in Massachusetts, April 9, 1801* (Wrentham, MA: Nathaniel Heaton, Jr., 1801), 22.
5. Letter to George Washington (1796), *The Complete Writings of Thomas Paine*, 2 vols., ed. Philip S. Foner (New York: Citadel Press, 1969), 2:723; Charles Lee is quoted in Samuel W. Patterson, *Knight Errant of Liberty: The Triumph and Tragedy of General Charles Lee* (New York: Lantern Press, 1958), 254.
6. Benjamin Rush to John Adams, 12 February 1812, *The Spur of Fame: Dialogues of John Adams and Benjamin Rush*, eds. John A. Schutz and Douglass Adair (San Marino, CA: Huntington Library, 1966), 210; Boyd Stanley Schlenther, *Charles Thomson: A Patriot's Pursuit* (Newark: University of Delaware Press: 1990), 204.
7. David Ramsay, *The History of the American Revolution*, 2 vols. (Philadelphia: R. Aitken & Son, 1789), 1:12, 356.

8. Quoted in Lester Cohen, "Creating a Usable Future: The Revolutionary Historians and the National Past," in *The American Revolution: Its Character and Limits*, ed. Jack P. Greene (New York: New York University Press, 1987), 325.

9. Mercy Otis Warren, *History of the Rise, Progress, and Termination of the American Revolution: Interspersed with Biographical, Political, and Moral Observations*, 2 vols., ed. Lester H. Cohen (Indianapolis, IN: Liberty Classics, 1988), 1:145–46.

10. Quoted in Gary B. Nash, *First City: Philadelphia and the Forging of Historical Memory* (Philadelphia: University of Pennsylvania Press, 2002), 83.

11. Benson John Lossing, *Pictorial Field-Book of the Revolution: Illustrations, by Pen and Pencil, of the History, Biography, Scenery, Relics, and Traditions of the War for Independence*, 2 vols. (New York: Harper and Brothers, 1851–52; reprint, Cottonport: Polyanthos, 1972), 1:ix; 2:292 n, 411, 744.

12. Elizabeth F. Ellet, *The Domestic History of the American Revolution* (1850), 234, quoted in Linda K. Kerber, *Toward an Intellectual History of Women* (Chapel Hill: University of North Carolina Press, 1997), 65–67.

13. David S. Reynolds, ed., *George Lippard, Prophet of Protest: Writings of an American Radical, 1822–1854* (New York: P. Lang, 1986), 4; Nash, *First City*, 165–66.

14. George Lippard, *Thomas Paine: Author-Soldier of the American Revolution* (Philadelphia, 1852), 1–2.

15. Ibid. 2.

16. Quoted in Nash, *First City*, 217–18.

17. *National Era*, 10 July 1847, quoted in Sidney Kaplan and Emma Nogrady Kaplan, *The Black Presence in the Era of the American Revolution* (Amherst: University of Massachusetts Press, 1989), 44.

18. Frederick Law Olmsted, *A Journey in the Seaboard Slave States with Remarks on Their Economy* (New York: Mason Brothers, 1859), 214–15.

19. Christopher Hill, *The World Turned Upside Down: Radical Ideas during the English Revolution* (New York: Viking Press, 1972), 13–14.

20. Roger Wilkins, *Jefferson's Pillow: The Founding Fathers and the Dilemma of Black Patriotism* (Boston: Beacon Press, 2001), 6, 7.

Chapter 1: Roots of Radicalism

1. *Pennsylvania Journal*, 24 April 1776, in Philip S. Foner, ed., *The Complete Writings of Thomas Paine*, 2 vols. (New York: Citadel Press, 1969), 2:82.

2. John Adams to Mercy Otis Warren, 7 July 1807, *Correspondence between John Adams and Mercy Warren* (New York: Arno Press, 1972), 338; Merrill Jensen, *American Revolution within America* (New York: New York University Press, 1974), 1.

3. Edward Countryman, " 'Out of the Bounds of the Law': Northern Land Rioters in the Eighteenth Century," in *The American Revolution: Explorations in the History of American Radicalism*, ed. Alfred F. Young (DeKalb: Northern Illinois University Press, 1976), 46.

4. Brendan McConville, *These Daring Disturbers of the Public Peace: The Struggle for Property and Power in Early New Jersey* (Ithaca, NY: Cornell University Press, 1999), 157; Board of Proprietors (1748), quoted in ibid, 156; Countryman, " 'Out of the Bounds of the Law,' " 43.

5. McConville, *Daring Disturbers*, 157.

6. Quoted in Francis Jennings, *The Invasion of America: Indians, Colonialism, and the Cant of Conquest* (Chapel Hill: University of North Carolina Press, 1975), 181.

7. McConville, *Daring Disturbers*, 32; Countryman, " 'Out of the Bounds of the Law,' " 48; "Answer of the Rioters to the Publication of the Proprietors and Speech of

Samuel Nevill" (August 1747), in *Archives of the State of New Jersey*, 1st series, eds. William A. Whitehead et al. (Newark, NJ, 1880–1949), 7:39–42.

8. Countryman, " 'Out of the Bounds of the Law,' " 44.

9. McConville, *Daring Disturbers*, 165, 172.

10. Ibid., 83, quoted in Gary B. Nash, *Urban Crucible: Social Change, Political Consciousness, and the Origins of the American Revolution* (Cambridge, MA: Harvard University Press, 1979), 207; McConville, *Daring Disturbers*, 88.

11. Quoted in Countryman, " 'Out of the Bounds of the Law,' " 48.

12. William G. McLoughlin, *New England Dissent, 1630–1833* (Cambridge, MA: Harvard University Press, 1971), 335; quoted in Alan Heimart, *Religion and the American Mind from the Great Awakening to the Revolution* (Cambridge, MA: Harvard University Press, 1966), 208.

13. Quoted in Peter Linebaugh and Marcus Rediker, *The Many-Headed Hydra: Sailors, Slaves, Commoners, and the Hidden History of the Revolutionary Atlantic* (Boston: Beacon Press, 2000), 88.

14. Quoted in Henry Mayer, *A Son of Thunder: Patrick Henry and the American Revolution* (New York: Franklin Watts, 1986), 34.

15. Frank Lambert, *Inventing the "Great Awakening"* (Princeton, NJ: Princeton University Press, 1999), 139; Mayer, *Son of Thunder*, 35–36.

16. Mayer, *Son of Thunder*, 36.

17. Quoted in Patricia U. Bonomi, *Under the Cope of Heaven: Religion, Society, and Politics in Colonial America* (New York: Oxford University Press, 2003), 125–26.

18. Rhys Isaac, "Religion and Authority: Problems of the Anglican Establishment in Virginia in the Era of the Great Awakening and the Parsons Cause," *William and Mary Quarterly*, 3rd ser., 30 (1973): 23.

19. Bonomi, *Under the Cope of Heaven*, 152–57.

20. Mayer, *Son of Thunder*, 39–40.

21. Quoted in Gary B. Nash, *Red, White, and Black: The Peoples of Early America*, 4th ed. (Upper Saddle River, NJ: Prentice Hall, 2000), 232–33.

22. Quoted in David H. Corkran, *The Cherokee Frontier: Conflict and Survival* (Norman: University of Oklahoma Press, 1962), 15.

23. Peter Wraxall and Charles H. McIwain, *An Abridgment of the Indian Affairs . . . Transacted in the Colony of New York, from the Year 1678 to the Year 1751* (Cambridge, MA: Harvard University Press, 1915), 219.

24. Marion Eugene Sirmans, *Colonial South Carolina: A Political History, 1663–1763* (Chapel Hill: University of North Carolina Press, 1966), 335.

25. William Shirley to Lords of Trade, 1 December 1747, *Correspondence of William Shirley, Governor of Massachusetts and Military Commander in America, 1731–1760*, 2 vols., ed. Charles H. Lincoln (New York: Macmillan, 1912), 1:418.

26. Quoted in Linebaugh and Rediker, *Many-Headed Hydra*, 110, 145–57.

27. [John Wise,] "Lover of his Country," in *An Address to the Inhabitants of the Province of the Massachusetts-Bay in New England* (Boston, 1747).

28. [Boston] *Independent Advertiser*, 8 February 1748 and 11 January 1748, quoted in Linebaugh and Rediker, *Many-Headed Hydra*, 217.

29. *Boston Gazette*, 5 May 1760. The following account is a condensed version of Nash, *Urban Crucible*, 274–81.

30. *Boston Gazette*, 12 May 1760.

31. William V. Wells, *The Life and Public Services of Samuel Adams*, 3 vols. (Boston: Little, Brown, 1865), 1:44.

32. L. H. Butterfield, ed., *Diary and Autobiography of John Adams*, 4 vols. (New York: Atheneum, 1964), 3: 355, 357.

33. William Tudor, *The Life of James Otis: Containing Also, Notices of Some Contemporary Characters and Events from the Year 1760 to 1775* (Boston: Wells and Lilly, 1823), 172 n.

34. *Boston Evening Post*, 21 March 1763.

35. "The Conversation of Two Persons under a Window on Monday Evening the 23rd of March" (Boston, 1765); *Boston Evening Post*, 7 March 1763; *Boston Gazette*, 28 February 1763.

36. *Boston Evening Post*, 7 March 1763.

37. James Hart Merrell, *Into the American Woods: Negotiators on the Pennsylvania Frontier* (New York: Norton, 1999), 288.

38. James H. Hutson, *Pennsylvania Politics, 1746–1770: The Movement for Royal Government and Its Consequences* (Princeton, NJ: Princeton University Press, 1972), 97.

39. The following account is a revised version of Nash, *Urban Crucible*, 150–56; the quotations are documented on pp. 60–61 n. 85, 87, 91, and 99.

40. "The Plain Dealer, No. III" (Philadelphia, 1764), in *The Paxton Papers*, ed. John R. Dunbar (The Hague: M. Nijhoff, 1957), 369.

41. John Dickinson, *A Speech, Delivered in the House of Assembly of the Province of Pennsylvania, May 24th, 1774* (Philadelphia: William Bradford, 1764), iv.

42. This account here and in the following five paragraphs is a condensation of Nash, *Urban Crucible*, 286–90; the sources used there are identified on pp. 504–5 n. 63–82.

43. *The Election Medley* (Philadelphia, 1864).

44. Jared Sparks, ed., *The Works of Benjamin Franklin*, 10 vols. (Boston, 1844), 7: 268; J. Philip Gleason, "A Scurrilous Colonial Election and Franklin's Reputation," *William and Mary Quarterly*, 3rd series, 18 (1961): 70.

45. Robert R. Desrochers, " 'Not Fade Away': The Narrative of Venture Smith, an African in the Early Republic," *Journal of American History* 84 (1997): 40–66, provides background and context for Smith's life account.

46. Vincent Carretta, ed., *Unchained Voices: An Anthology of Black Authors in the English-Speaking World of the Eighteenth Century* (Lexington: University Press of Kentucky, 1996), 369–85 for all quoted excerpts.

47. Quoted in Peter Wood, " 'Liberty Is Sweet': African-American Freedom Struggles in the Years before White Independence," in *Beyond the American Revolution: Explorations in the History of American Radicalism*, ed. Alfred F. Young (DeKalb: University of Northern Illinois Press, 1993), 152.

48. Quoted in Nash, *Red, White, and Black*, 183.

49. Fred Anderson, *Crucible of War: The Seven Years' War and the Fate of Empire in British North America 1754–1756* (New York: Knopf, 2000), 160.

50. Wood, " 'Liberty Is Sweet,' " in Young, *Beyond the American Revolution*, 156.

51. Ibid. 152.

52. Benjamin Lay, *All Slave-keepers, That Keep the Innocent in Bondage, Apostates* (Philadelphia, 1737), 106.

53. Quoted in Gary B. Nash and Jean R. Soderlund, *Freedom by Degrees: Emancipation in Philadelphia and Its Aftermath* (New York: Oxford University Press, 1991), 51; Winthrop D. Jordan, *White over Black: American Attitudes toward the Negro* (Chapel Hill: University of North Carolina Press, 1968), 273.

54. Quoted in Gary B. Nash, *Forging Freedom: The Formation of Philadelphia's Black Community* (Cambridge, MA: Harvard University Press, 1988), 31; Nash and Soderlund, *Freedom by Degrees*, 52.

55. Ibid., 52–53.

56. William McKee Evans, "The American Paradox: The Evolution and Crisis of a Racial System," unpublished ms., 165.

Chapter 2: Years of Insurgence, 1761–1766

1. Dirk Hoerder, *Crowd Action in Revolutionary Massachusetts* (New York: Academic Press, 1977), 97.

2. Ibid., 101; for a detailed account of the Stamp Act Crisis, see Edmund S. and Helen M. Morgan, *The Stamp Act Crisis: Prologue to Revolution* (Chapel Hill: University of North Carolina Press, 1953; 1995).

3. William Gordon, *The History of the Rise, Progress, and Establishment of the Independence of the United States: Including an Account of the Late War; and of the Thirteen Colonies, from Their Origin, to That Period*, 4 vols. (London, 1788), 1:178; the account below follows my analysis in *Urban Crucible: Social Change, Political Consciousness, and the Origins of the American Revolution* (Cambridge, MA: Harvard University Press, 1979), 292–300.

4. Samuel Waterhouse, *Proposals for Printing by Subscription the History of Adjutant Trowel* [Thomas Dawes] *and Bluster* [James Otis] (Boston, 1766); *Boston Gazette*, 11 January 1762, and 6 April 1763; *Boston Evening Post*, 14 December 1771.

5. William Henry Whitmore, *Annual Reports of the Record Commissioner of Boston, 1876–1909*, 39 vols. (Boston: Rockwell and Churchill, 1876–1909), 17:152.

6. Thomas Hutchinson, "A Summary of the Disorders . . . ," Massachusetts Archives, Boston, 26:182–84.

7. David S. Lovejoy, *Rhode Island Politics and the American Revolution, 1760–1776* (Providence, RI: Brown University Press, 1958), 99–113, for full account of this incident.

8. Quoted in Morgan and Morgan, *Stamp Act Crisis*, 199.

9. Ibid., 154, 200; Lovejoy, *Rhode Island Politics*, 108.

10. Lovejoy, *Rhode Island Politics*, 103; quoted in Carl Bridenbaugh, *Cities in Revolt: Urban Life in America, 1743–1776* (New York: Knopf, 1955), 309; 403–4.

11. Peter Oliver, *Origin and Progress of the American Revolution: A Tory View*, eds. Douglass Adair and John A. Schutz (San Marino, CA: Huntington Library, 1961), 54–55.

12. Quoted in Morgan and Morgan, *Stamp Act Crisis*, 181.

13. Quoted in F. L. Engelman, "Cadwallader Colden and the New York Stamp Act Riots," *William and Mary Quarterly*, 3rd series, 10 (1953): 560–69. This account follows Nash, *Urban Crucible*, 300–305.

14. Jesse Lemisch, *Jack Tar vs. John Bull: The Role of New York's Seamen in Precipitating the Revolution* (New York: Garland, 1997), 79; another valuable account is Roger J. Champagne, *Alexander McDougall and the American Revolution in New York* (Schenectady, NY: Union College Press, 1975).

15. Edward Countryman, *A People in Revolution: The American Revolution and Political Society in New York, 1760–1790* (Baltimore: Johns Hopkins University Press, 1981), 39.

16. Jerome J. Nadelhaft, *Disorders of War: The Revolution in South Carolina* (Orono: University of Maine Press, 1981), 10.

17. Samuel Wharton to Benjamin Franklin, 13 October 1765, *The Papers of Franklin*, 36 vols., ed. Leonard W. Labaree et al. (New Haven, CT: Yale University Press, 1959–), 12:315–16; William Bradford to New York Sons of Liberty, 15 February 1766, quoted in Francis Von A. Cabeen, "The Society of the Sons of Saint Tammany of Philadelphia," *Pennsylvania Magazine of History and Biography* 25 (1901): 439.

18. Oliver, *Origin and Progress of the American Revolution*, 65.

19. Thomas Gage to Henry Conway, 23 September 1765 and 8 November 1765, in *The Correspondence of General Thomas Gage*, ed. Clarence E. Carter, 2 vols. (New Haven, CT: Yale University Press, 1931), 1:67, 72–73.

20. Ibid., 67.

21. Robert A. Rutland, ed., *The Papers of George Mason, 1725–1792*, 3 vols. (Chapel Hill: University of North Carolina Press, 1970), 1:61–62; Woody Holton, *Forced Founders: Indians, Debtors, Slaves, and the Making of the American Revolution in Virginia* (Chapel Hill: University of North Carolina Press, 1999), 138–39.

22. Holton, *Forced Founders*, 139.

23. Jeffrey J. Crow, *The Black Experience in Revolutionary North Carolina* (Raleigh: North Carolina Department of Cultural Resources, Division of Archives and History, 1977), 28, 42.

24. Peter Wood, " 'Liberty Is Sweet': African-American Freedom Struggles in the Years before White Independence," in *Beyond the American Revolution: Explorations in the History of American Radicalism*, ed. Alfred F. Young (DeKalb: Northern Illinois University Press, 1993), 157–58.

25. Ibid., 157, 159.

26. Peter Wood, " 'Taking Care of Business' in Revolutionary South Carolina: Republicanism and the Slave Society," in *The Southern Experience in the American Revolution*, eds. Jeffrey J. Crow and Larry E. Tise (Chapel Hill: University of North Carolina Press, 1978), 277–78.

27. Darold D. Wax, "Negro Resistance to the Early American Slave Trade," *Journal of Negro History* 51 (1966): 11.

28. David Brion Davis, *The Problem of Slavery in the Age of Revolution, 1770–1823* (Ithaca, NY: Cornell University Press, 1975), 45; James Otis, *The Rights of British Colonies Asserted and Proved* (Boston, 1764), quoted in Davis, *The Problem of Slavery*, 441–42.

29. Otis, *The Rights of British Colonies*, in Davis, *The Problem of Slavery*, 408.

30. Quoted in Patricia Bradley, *Slavery, Propaganda and the American Revolution* (Jackson: University of Mississippi Press, 1998), 99.

31. *Newport Mercury*, 11 January 1768, in Lovejoy, *Rhode Island Politics*, 134–35; Bernard Bailyn, *The Ideological Origins of the American Revolution* (Cambridge, MA: Harvard University Press, 1967), 235.

32. Richard Bland, *The Colonel Dismounted: Or the Rector Vindicated, in a Letter Addressed to His Reverence: Containing a Dissertation upon the Constitution of the Colony* (1764); John Camm, *Critical Remarks on a Letter Ascribed to Common Sense* (Williamsburg, VA: Joseph Royle, 1765), quoted in Bailyn, *Ideological Origins*, 235–36.

33. L. H. Butterfield, ed., *Diary and Autobiography of John Adams*, 4 vols. (New York: Atheneum, 1964), 2:182–83.

34. Daniel K. Richter, *Facing East from Indian Country: A Native History of Early America* (Cambridge, MA: Harvard University Press, 2001), 10.

35. Quoted in Charles Patrick Neimeyer, *America Goes to War: A Social History of the Continental Army* (New York: New York University Press, 1996), 93.

36. Richard White, *The Middle Ground: Indians, Empires, and Republics in the Great Lakes Region, 1650–1815* (Cambridge, England: Cambridge University Press, 1991), 257.

37. Gregory Evans Dowd, *A Spirited Resistance: The North American Indian Struggle for Unity, 1745–1815* (Baltimore: Johns Hopkins University Press, 1992), 33–40 for this account of Neolin.

38. Richter, *Facing East*, 196.

39. Quoted in Howard Peckham, *Pontiac and the Indian Uprising* (Chicago: University of Chicago Press, 1961), 119; Gregory Evans Dowd, *War Under Heaven: Pontiac, the Indian Nations, and the British Empire* (Baltimore: Johns Hopkins University Press, 2002), 91.

40. Johnson is quoted in Richter, *Facing East*, 193; for Amherst, see Fred Anderson, *The Crucible of War: The Seven Years' War and the Fate of Empire in British North America 1754–1756* (New York: Knopf, 2000), 538.

41. Richter, *Facing East*, 199.
42. Ibid., 200.
43. Ibid., 208.
44. Johnson is quoted in Francis Paul Prucha, *American Indian Policy in the Formative Years* (Lincoln: University of Nebraska Press, 1970), 19; and, White, *Middle Ground*, 310.
45. George Sims, "An Address to the People of Granville County" (1765), in Marvin L. Michael Kay, "The North Carolina Regulation, 1766–1776: A Class Conflict," in *The American Revolution: Explorations in the History of American Radicalism*, ed. Alfred F. Young (DeKalb: Northern Illinois University Press, 1976), 84.
46. Mark Jones, "Herman Husband: Millenarian, Carolina Regulator, and Whiskey Rebel," Ph.D. diss., Northern Illinois University, 1983, 72.
47. Marjoleine Kars, *Breaking Loose Together: The Regulator Rebellion in Pre-Revolutionary North Carolina* (Chapel Hill: University of North Carolina Press, 2002), 53, 138.
48. Richard J. Hooker, ed., *The Carolina Backcountry on the Eve of the Revolution: The Journal and Other Writings of Charles Woodmason, Anglican Itinerant* (Chapel Hill: University of North Carolina Press, 1969), 104; Kars, *Breaking Loose*, 105.
49. Hooker, *Woodmason*, 240–41.
50. Kay, "North Carolina Regulation," 87.
51. Kars, *Breaking Loose Together*, 142.
52. Quoted from William K. Boyd, ed., *Some Eighteenth Century Tracts Concerning North Carolina* (Raleigh, NC: Edwards & Broughton, 1927), 268–71, 368–70; Kay, "North Carolina Regulation," 88; Kars, *Breaking Loose*, 157.
53. Kars, *Breaking Loose*, 147.
54. Staughton Lynd, *Antifederalism in Dutchess County, New York: A Study of Democracy and Class Conflict in the Revolutionary Era* (Chicago: Loyola University Press, 1962), 38–39; Sung Bok Kim, *Landlord and Tenant in Colonial New York: Manorial Society, 1664–1775* (Chapel Hill: University of North Carolina Press, 1978), 377–78.
55. Irving Mark, *Agrarian Conflicts in Colonial New York, 1711–1775* (Port Washington, NY: I. J. Friedman, 1965), 142–43; Edward Countryman, " 'Out of the Bounds of Law': Northern Land Rioters in the Eighteenth Century," in Young, *The American Revolution*, 45.
56. Kim, *Landlord and Tenant*, 377–78.
57. Ibid., 379.
58. Ibid., 381.
59. Lynd, *Dutchess County*, 98 n. 48; Thomas J. Humphrey, "Poor Men Were Always Oppressed By the Rich: William Prendergast and the Revolution in the Hudson River Valley, 1727–1811," in *The Human Tradition in U.S. History: The American Revolution*, eds. Ian K. Steele and Nancy Rhoden (New York: Scholarly Resources, 2000), 86.
60. Kim, *Landlord and Tenant*, 387; Countryman, " 'Out of the Bounds of the Law,' " in Young, *American Revolution*, 47.
61. Kim, *Landlord and Tenant*, 388.
62. Ibid., 388–89.
63. Mark, *Agrarian Conflicts*, 140 n. 45, 144.
64. Countryman, " 'Out of the Bounds of the Law,' " in Young, *American Revolution*, 49.
65. Mark, *Agrarian Conflicts*, 146.
66. Merrill Jensen, *The Founding of a Nation: A History of the American Revolution, 1763–1776* (New York: Oxford University Press, 1968), 32.
67. Mark, *Agrarian Conflicts*, 149.
68. Anderson, *Crucible of War*, 722.

Chapter 3: Building Momentum, 1766–1774

1. Quoted in Gary B. Nash, Julie Roy Jeffrey, John R. Howe, Peter J. Frederick, Allan F. Davis, and Allan M. Winkler, *The American People: Creating a Nation and a Society*, 5th ed. (New York: Longman, 2001), 174; L. H. Butterfield, ed., *Diary and Autobiography of John Adams*, 4 vols. (New York: Atheneum, 1964), 1:263.
2. Edmund Burke, *On the American Revolution: Selected Speeches and Letters*, ed. Elliot R. Barkan (New York: Harper & Row, 1966), 5.
3. Henry Mayer, *A Son of Thunder: Patrick Henry and the American Republic* (New York: Franklin Watts, 1986), 212–13.
4. Gary B. Nash, *Urban Crucible: Social Change, Political Consciousness, and the Origins of the American Revolution* (Cambridge, MA: Harvard University Press, 1979), 320; Woody Holton, *Forced Founders: Indians, Debtors, Slaves, and the Making of the American Revolution in Virginia* (Chapel Hill: University of North Carolina Press, 1999), 97.
5. *New-York Gazette*, 11 July 1765, "The Commercial Conduct of the Province of New-York Considered . . ." (New York, 1767), 11–12.
6. John Adams, "Dissertation on Canon and Feudal Law," quoted in Richard D. Brown, *The Strength of a People: The Idea of Informed Citizenry in America, 1650–1870* (Chapel Hill: University of North Carolina Press, 1996), 54.
7. *New York Post-Boy*, 8 November 1756, quoted in Brown, *Strength of a People*, 51.
8. Jacob Duché, quoted in Lawrence Arthur Cremin, *American Education: The Colonial Experience, 1607–1783* (New York: Harper & Row, 1970), 517.
9. Adams, "Canon and Feudal Law," in Brown, *Strength of a People*, 56–57.
10. *Boston Gazette*, 14 March 1768, quoted in Dirk Hoerder, *Crowd Action in Revolutionary Massachusetts, 1765–1780* (New York: Academic Press, 1977), 156.
11. Quoted in John C. Miller, *Sam Adams: Pioneer in Propaganda* (Stanford, CA: Stanford University Press, 1936), 302.
12. Quoted in ibid., 207.
13. Joshua Coffin and Joseph Bartlett, *A Sketch of the History of Newbury, Newburyport, and West Newbury, from 1635 to 1845* (Boston: S. G. Drake, 1845), 235.
14. A. B. [Augustine Birrell], *Proposals for Erecting and Encouraging a New Manufactory* (New York, 1770).
15. Morris to John Penn, 20 May 1774, in Merrill Jensen, ed., *American Colonial Documents to 1776*, in *English Historical Documents* (London: Eyre & Spottiswoode, 1955), 10:861–63.
16. *Pennsylvania Chronicle*, 27 March 1767; *To the Free and Patriotic Inhabitants of the City of Philadelphia* (Philadelphia, 1770); *Pennsylvania Chronicle*, 5 July 1770.
17. Quoted in Charles S. Olton, *Artisans for Independence: Philadelphia Mechanics and the American Revolution* (Syracuse, NY: Syracuse University Press, 1975), 53.
18. *A Tradesman's Address to His Countrymen* (Philadelphia, 1772); *Pennsylvania Gazette*, 22 September 1773; Joseph Reed, quoted in Merrill Jensen, *The American Revolution within America* (New York: New York University Press, 1974), 36.
19. Quoted in Jerome J. Nadelhaft, *The Disorders of War: The Revolution in South Carolina* (Orono: University of Maine, 1981), 11; Jensen, *Revolution within America*, 37.
20. Marjoleine Kars, *Breaking Loose Together: The Regulator Rebellion in Pre-Revolutionary North Carolina* (Chapel Hill: University of North Carolina Press, 2002), 169.
21. Quoted in ibid., 171–72; Kars's assessment is on p. 271.
22. Quoted in ibid., 183–85.
23. Ibid., 186, 188.
24. Ibid., 195; William Stevens Powell, *The Regulators in North Carolina: A Documen-*

tary History, 1759–1776 (Raleigh, NC: State Department of Archives and History, 1971), 302, for the pamphlet.

25. Kars, *Breaking Loose*, 197.
26. William Lawrence Saunders, *The Colonial Records of North Carolina*, 10 vols. (Raleigh, NC: P. M. Hale, 1886–1890), 9:1167.
27. Kars, *Breaking Loose*, 198–203.
28. Ibid., 203–5.
29. Ibid., 207–8.
30. *Boston Gazette*, quoted in Pauline Maier, *From Resistance to Revolution: Colonial Radicals and the Development of American Opposition to Britain, 1765–1776* (New York: Knopf, 1972), 197 n. 57; for Stiles, Kars, *Breaking Loose*, 208.
31. Edward Countryman, " 'Out of the Bounds of Law': Northern Land Rioters in the Eighteenth Century," in *The American Revolution: Explorations in the History of American Radicalism*, ed. Alfred F. Young (DeKalb: Northern Illinois University Press, 1976), 39.
32. Charles A. Jellison, *Ethan Allen: Frontier Rebel* (Syracuse, NY: Syracuse University Press, 1969), 34.
33. Quoted in Michael A. Bellisles, *Revolutionary Outlaws: Ethan Allen and the Struggle for Independence on the Early American Frontier* (Charlottesville: University Press of Virginia, 1993), 82; Jellison, *Ethan Allen*, 38.
34. Jellison, *Ethan Allen*, 62, 59; John Pell, *Ethan Allen* (Boston: Houghton Mifflin, 1929), 41.
35. Alan Taylor, *Liberty Men and Great Proprietors: The Revolutionary Settlement on the Maine Frontier* (Chapel Hill: University of North Carolina Press, 1990), 193.
36. Jellison, *Ethan Allen*, 93.
37. Taylor, *Liberty Men and Great Proprietors*, 7–8.
38. Darline Shapiro, "Ethan Allen: Philosopher-Theologian to a Generation of American Revolutionaries," *William and Mary Quarterly*, 3rd series, 21 (1964): 242–43; John Locke, *Two Treatises of Government*, ed. Peter Laslett (Cambridge, England: Cambridge University Press, 1960), 306–7.
39. Shapiro, "Ethan Allen," 244–46.
40. Countryman, " 'Out of the Bounds of the Law,' " 47; Bellisles, *Revolutionary Outlaws*, 105; Chester Town Meeting Records, 10 October 1774, quoted in Bellisles, *Revolutionary Outlaws*, 107.
41. Arthur Lee, *An Essay in Vindication of the Continental Colonies of America from the Censure of Mr. Adam Smith, in His Theory on Moral Sentiments: With Some Reflections on Slavery in General* (London, 1764), quoted in David Grimsted, "Anglo-American Racism and Phillis Wheatley's 'Sable Veil,' 'Length'ned Chain,' and 'Knitted Heart,' " in *Women in the Age of the American Revolution*, eds. Ronald Hoffman and Peter J. Albert (Charlottesville: University Press of Virginia, 1989), 399.
42. Arthur Lee, "Address on Slavery," *Virgina Gazette*, 19 March 1767, reprinted in Gary B. Nash, *Race and Revolution* (Madison, WI: Madison House, 1990), 92–96.
43. Edmund S. Morgan, "The Puritan Ethic and the American Revolution," *William and Mary Quarterly*, 3rd series, 23 (1967): 3; see Holton, *Forced Founders*, 70 n. 49 for identification of "Philanthropos."
44. Henry Wiencek, *An Imperfect God: George Washington, His Slaves, and the Creation of America* (New York: Farrar, Straus, and Giroux, 2003), 161; Paul Finkelman, *Slavery and the Founders: Race and Liberty in the Age of Jefferson* (Armonk, NY: M.E. Sharpe, 2001), 113–14.
45. Quoted in Finkelman, *Slavery and the Founders*, 113.
46. *Virginia Gazette* (Rind), 25 January 1770, in Mayer, *Son of Thunder*, 167.

47. Stephen B. Weeks, *Southern Quakers and Slavery: A Study in Institutional History* (Baltimore: Johns Hopkins University Press, 1896), 214; Paul Finkelman, *The Law of Freedom and Bondage: A Casebook* (New York: Oceana Publications, 1986), 116–23; David Brion Davis, *The Problem of Slavery in Western Culture* (Ithaca, NY: Cornell University Press, 1966), 196.

48. Mayer, *Son of Thunder*, 168.

49. Ibid., 169–70.

50. Thomas E. Drake, *Quakers and Slavery in America* (New Haven, CT: Yale University Press, 1950), 88.

51. Charles W. Akers, *The Divine Politician: Samuel Cooper and the American Revolution in Boston* (Boston: Northeastern University Press, 1982), 107; for Cooke's *A Sermon Preached at Cambridge . . . : Being the Anniversary for the Election of His Majesty's Council for the Said Province* (Boston, 1770), see Bernard Bailyn, *The Ideological Origins of the American Revolution* (Cambridge, MA: Harvard University Press, 1967), 239.

52. A. Leon Higginbotham, *In the Matter of Color: The Colonial Period* (New York: Oxford University Press, 1978), 347.

53. Ray Raphael, *A People's History of the American Revolution: How Common People Shaped the Fight for Independence* (New York: New Press, 2001), 237.

54. Patricia Bradley, *Slavery, Propaganda and the American Revolution* (Jackson: University Press of Mississippi, 1998), 64, 80.

55. Davis, *Problem of Slavery in Western Culture*, 274; L. H. Butterfield, ed., *Letters of Benjamin Rush*, 2 vols. (Philadelphia: American Philosophical Society, 1951), 1:81.

56. Bailyn, *Ideological Origins*, 239.

57. David Waldstreicher, *Runaway America: Benjamin Franklin, Slavery, and the American Revolution* (New York: Hill and Wang, 2004) may sweep the shadows away.

58. Quoted in Gary B. Nash and Jean R. Soderlund, *Freedom by Degrees: Emancipation in Philadelphia and Its Aftermath* (New York: Oxford University Press, 1991), x.

59. Quoted in Gary B. Nash, *Forging Freedom: The Formation of Philadelphia's Black Community, 1720–1840* (Cambridge, MA: Harvard University Press, 1988), xii.

60. Benjamin Quarles, *The Negro in the American Revolution* (Chapel Hill: University of North Carolina Press, 1961), 38.

61. Alexander Starbuck, *The History of Nantucket, County, Island, and Town* (Boston: C. E. Goodspeed, 1924), 621–23, quoted in Drake, *Quakers and Slavery*, 88; "Lover of Constitutional Liberty," in *Appendix: Or, Some Observations on the Expediency of the Petition of the Africans Living in Boston* (Boston, 1773); Coffin and Bartlett, *History of Newbury*, 241.

62. John Adams to Jeremy Belknap, 21 March 1795, in *Massachusetts Historical Society Collection*, 5th ser., 3 (1877): 402, in Quarles, *The Negro in the American Revolution*, 39 n.

63. Linda K. Kerber, *Women of the Republic: Intellect and Ideology in Revolutionary America* (Chapel Hill: University of North Carolina Press, 1980), 85; "Lover of Constitutional Liberty."

64. Herbert Aptheker, *A Documentary History of the Negro People in the United States*, 3 vols. (New York: Citadel Press, 1969), 1:7.

65. Sidney Kaplan and Emma Nogrady Kaplan, *The Black Presence in the Era of the American Revolution* (Amherst: University of Massachusetts Press, 1989), 13, 15.

66. W. Robert Higgins, "The Ambivalence of Freedom," in *The Revolutionary War in the South—Power, Conflict, and Leadership: Essays in Honor of John Richard Alden*, eds. John Richard Alden and Robert Higgins (Durham, NC: Duke University Press, 1979), 45.

67. Quoted in Holton, *Forced Founders*, 7.
68. For background see Tom Hatley, *The Dividing Paths: Cherokees and South Carolinians through the Era of Revolution* (New York: Oxford University Press, 1993).
69. Richard White, *The Middle Ground: Indians, Empires, and Republics in the Great Lakes Region, 1650–1815* (Cambridge, MA: Cambridge University Press, 1991), 351.
70. Quoted in John Mack Faragher, *Daniel Boone: The Life and Legend of an American Pioneer* (New York: Holt, 1992), 81.
71. Ibid., 88–89.
72. William Johnson to Earl of Dartmouth, 4 November 1772, quoted in White, *Middle Ground*, 315.
73. White, *Middle Ground*, 315.
74. Ibid., 316–17.
75. Ibid.
76. John Bohstedt, "The Myth of the Feminine Food Riot: Women as Proto-Citizens in English Community Politics, 1790–1810," in *Women and Politics in the Age of the Democratic Revolution*, eds. Harriet Branson Applewhite and Darline Gay Levy (Ann Arbor: University of Michigan Press, 1990), 21.
77. Quoted in Nash et al., *The American People*, 130. For background see Nancy Woloch, *Women and the American Experience*, 2nd ed. (New York: McGraw-Hill, 1994).
78. Quoted in Carl Bridenbaugh, *Cities in the Wilderness: The First Century of Urban Life in America, 1625–1742* (New York: Knopf, 1955), 341.
79. Brendan McConville, *These Daring Disturbers of the Public Peace: The Struggle for Property and Power in Early New Jersey* (Ithaca, NY: Cornell University Press, 1999), 124–29.
80. Grimsted, "Anglo-American Racism and Phillis Wheatley's 'Sable Veil,' " 374.
81. Mary Beth Norton, " 'My Resting Reaping Times': Sarah Osborn's Defense of Her Unfeminine Activities," *Signs* 2 (1976): 515–29; Grimsted, "Anglo-American Racism and Phillis Wheatley's 'Sable Veil,' " 382.
82. Grimsted, "Anglo-American Racism and Phillis Wheatley's 'Sable Veil,' " 378; Ezra Stiles, quoted in Mary Beth Norton, *Liberty's Daughters: The Revolutionary Experience of American Women, 1750–1800* (Boston: Little, Brown, 1980), 132.
83. David Brion Davis, *The Problem of Slavery in the Age of Revolution, 1770–1823* (Ithaca, NY: Cornell University Press, 1975), 24.
84. Grimsted, "Anglo-American Racism and Phillis Wheatley's 'Sable Veil,' " 341; for more on Wheatley, see Henry Louis Gates, *The Trials of Phillis Wheatley: America's First Black Poet and Her Encounter with the Founding Fathers* (New York: Basic Books, 2003).
85. This verse and those following are taken from Vincent Carretta, ed., *Phillis Wheatley: Complete Writings* (New York: Penguin Books, 2001).
86. Grimsted, "Anglo-American Racism and Phillis Wheatley's 'Sable Veil,' " 349 n. 24.
87. Linda K. Kerber, *Toward an Intellectual History of Women* (Chapel Hill: University of North Carolina Press, 1997), 76.
88. Peter Oliver, *Origin and Progress of the American Revolution: A Tory View*, eds. Douglass Adair and John A. Schutz (San Marino, CA: Huntington Library, 1961), 61.
89. Alfred F. Young, "The Women of Boston: 'Persons of Consequence' in the Making of the American Revolution, 1765–76," in Applewhite and Levy, *Women and Politics*, 196; Norton, *Liberty's Daughters*, 159.
90. Quoted in Barbara Clark Smith, "Was the American Revolution a Bourgeois Revolution?" in *The Transforming Hand of Revolution: Reconsidering the American Revolution as a Social Movement*, eds. Ronald Hoffman and Peter J. Albert (Charlottesville: University Press of Virginia, 1996), 47.

91. Nash, *Urban Crucible*, 335; Oliver, *Origin and Progress*, 63–64.
92. Quoted in Kerber, *Women of the Republic*, 42.
93. Quoted in Holton, *Forced Founders*, 89.
94. Nash, *Urban Crucible*, 344; *Newport Mercury*, 13 December 1773, in Edmund Sears Morgan, *The Puritan Ethic and the American Revolution* (Indianapolis, IN: Bobbs-Merrill, 1970), 9.
95. Smith, "Was the American Revolution . . . ?" 49; Morgan, *The Puritan Ethic*, 12.
96. Smith, "Was the American Revolution . . . ?" 51–52.
97. Kerber, *Toward an Intellectual History*, 80–81; Hoerder, *Crowd Action*, 241; Oliver, *Origin and Progress*, 97–98; Lee Newcomer, *The Embattled Farmers: A Massachusetts Countryside in the American Revolution* (New York: King's Crown Press, 1953), 55.
98. Quoted in Mayer, *Son of Thunder*, 158–59.
99. Ibid., 158–59.
100. L. P. Little, *Imprisoned Preachers and Religious Liberty in Virginia* (Lynchburg, VA.: J. P. Bell, 1938), quoted in Mayer, *Son of Thunder*, 159.
101. Mayer, *Son of Thunder*, 160; for extensive coverage, see Rhys Isaac, *The Transformation of Virginia, 1740–1790* (Chapel Hill: Unversity of North Carolina Press, 1982), part 2.
102. Mayer, *Son of Thunder*, 162–63.
103. Ibid., 164–65.
104. Isaac, *Transformation of Virginia*, 201–2.

Chapter 4: Reaching the Climax, 1774–1776

1. Nathaniel Niles, "Two Discourses in Liberty" (July, 1774), in Roger Bruns, *Am I Not a Man and a Brother: The Antislavery Crusade of Revolutionary America, 1688–1788* (New York: Chelsea House, 1977), 321; Joshua Coffin and Joseph Bartlett, *A Sketch of the History of Newbury, Newburyport, and West Newbury, from 1635 to 1845* (Boston: S. G. Drake, 1845), 340.
2. Philip S. Foner, ed., *The Complete Writings of Thomas Paine*, 2 vols. (New York: Citadel Press, 1969), 2:18.
3. This account of the Society for the Relief of Free Negroes and early abolitionism in Pennsylvania follows Gary B. Nash and Jean R. Soderlund, *Freedom by Degrees: Emancipation in Philadelphia and Its Aftermath* (New York: Oxford University Press, 1991), chapter 3.
4. Gary B. Nash, *Forging Freedom: The Formation of Philadelphia's Black Community, 1720–1840* (Cambridge: Harvard University Press, 1988), 44.
5. Nash and Soderlund, *Freedom by Degrees*, 80.
6. Julian Boyd et al., eds., *Papers of Thomas Jefferson*, 31 vols. (Princeton, NJ: Princeton University Press, 1950–), 1:130, 253, 263.
7. Abigail Adams to John Adams, 22 September 1774, *Adams Family Correspondence*, 6 vols, eds. L. H. Butterfield et al. (Cambridge, MA: Harvard University Press, 1963–1993), 1:161–62; Leonard Woods Labaree et al., eds., *The Papers of Benjamin Franklin*, 36 vols. (New Haven, CT: Yale University Press, 1959–), 11:397–99.
8. Sidney Kaplan and Emma Nogrady Kaplan, *The Black Presence in the Era of the American Revolution* (Amherst: University of Massachusetts Press, 1989), 15–16; the Worcester County petition was published in *Massachusetts Spy*, 21 June 1775.
9. Robert Allen Rutland, ed., *The Papers of James Madison: Presidential Series*, 4 vols. (Charlottesville: University Press of Virginia, 1984–), 1:129–30; *Georgia Gazette*, 7 December 1774; Herbert Aptheker, *American Negro Slave Revolts* (New York: International Publishers, 1963), 201.

10. Sylvia R. Frey, *Water from the Rock: Black Resistance in a Revolutionary Age* (Princeton, NJ: Princeton University Press, 1991), 55; Thomas Gage to John Stuart, February or March, 1775, quoted in Frey, *Water from the Rock*, 55.

11. Woody Holton, *Forced Founders: Indians, Debtors, Slaves, and the Making of the American Revolution in Virginia* (Chapel Hill: University of North Carolina Press, 1999), 144–45; *Virginia Gazette*, 4 May 1775, quoted in Frey, *Water from the Rock*, 55.

12. Holton, *Forced Founders*, 141; Frey, *Water from the Rock*, 56.

13. Merrill Jensen, *The Founding of a Nation: A History of the American Revolution, 1763–1776* (New York: Oxford University Press, 1968), 602.

14. Ibid., 609; Henry Laurens to John Laurens, *Papers of Henry Laurens*, 16 vols., eds. Philip M. Hamer, George C. Rogers, and David R. Chesnutt (Columbia: University of South Carolina Press, 1968–2003), 10:160 n. 14; Frey, *Water from the Rock*, 57.

15. Peter H. Wood, " 'Taking Care of Business' in Revolutionary South Carolina: Republicanism and the Slave Society," in *The Southern Experience in the American Revolution*, eds. Jeffrey J. Crow and Larry E. Tise (Chapel Hill: University of North Carolina Press, 1978), 285.

16. Benjamin Quarles, *The Negro in the American Revolution* (Chapel Hill: University of North Carolina Press, 1961), 19.

17. Holton, *Forced Founders*, 155.

18. Lund Washington to George Washington, 3 December 1775, *Papers of George Washington, Revolutionary War Series*, 12 vols., eds. Philander D. Chase et al. (Charlottesville: University Press of Virginia, 1988), 2:480.

19. Holton, *Forced Founders*, 156; John E. Selby, *The Revolution in Virginia: 1775–1783* (Charlottesville: University Press of Virginia, 1988), 67.

20. Ibid., 69–74; Holton, *Forced Founders*, 156.

21. Quarles, *The Negro in the American Revolution*, 30; Elizabeth Fenn, *Pox Americana: The Great Smallpox Epidemic of 1775–82* (New York: Hill and Wang, 2001), 58–61.

22. Frey, *Water from Rock*, 59–61.

23. Peters's story is adapted from Gary B. Nash, "Thomas Peters: Millwright and Deliverer," in *Struggle and Survival in Colonial America*, eds. David G. Sweet and Gary B. Nash (Berkeley: University of California Press, 1981), 69–85.

24. Jeffrey J. Crow, *The Black Experience in Revolutionary North Carolina* (Raleigh: North Carolina Department of Cultural Resources, 1977), 56–57.

25. Quarles, *The Negro in the American Revolution*, 20 n. 3.

26. Ibid., 32; Nash, *Forging Freedom*, 45; "Extract of a Letter from Philadelphia," 6 December 1775, published in *Morning Chronicle and London Advertiser*, 20 January 1776, in *Letters on the American Revolution, 1774–1776*, ed. Margaret Willard (Port Washington, NY: Kennikat Press, 1968), 233.

27. The account of Logan follows Anthony Wallace, *Jefferson and the Indians: The Tragic Fate of the First Americans* (Cambridge, MA: Harvard University Press, 1999), 1–13; Logan's lament is on p. xvi.

28. Holton, *Forced Founders*, 30, 33.

29. Ibid., 34; Richard White, *The Middle Ground: Indians, Empires, and Republics in the Great Lakes Region, 1650–1815* (Cambridge, England: Cambridge University Press, 1991), 356–62, provides a detailed account.

30. White, *Middle Ground*, 364.

31. Edward J. Cashin, " 'But Brothers, It Is Our Land We Are Talking About': Winners and Losers in the Georgia Backcountry," in *Uncivil War: The Southern Backcountry During the American Revolution*, eds. Ronald Hoffman, Thad W. Tate, and Peter J. Albert (Charlottesville: University Press of Virginia, 1985), 245.

32. Holton, *Forced Founders*, 36.
33. Barbara Graymont, *The Iroquois in the American Revolution* (Syracuse, NY: Syracuse University Press, 1972), 50.
34. Charles A. Jellison, *Ethan Allen: Frontier Rebel* (Syracuse, NY: Syracuse University Press, 1969), 118.
35. Quoted in Gary B. Nash, *Landmarks of the American Revolution* (New York: Oxford University Press, 2003), 23.
36. Joseph Brant, quoted in Page Smith, *A New Age Now Begins: A People's History of the American Revolution*, 2 vols. (New York: McGraw-Hill, 1976), 1:596; Isabel Thompson Kelsay, *Joseph Brant, 1743–1807: Man of Two Worlds* (Syracuse, NY: Syracuse University Press, 1984), 155.
37. Jellison, *Ethan Allen*, 160.
38. Kelsay, *Joseph Brant*, 161, 166.
39. Ibid., 172.
40. David Ammerman, *In the Common Cause: American Response to the Coercive Acts of 1774* (Charlottesville: University Press of Virginia, 1974), 106–9.
41. Peter Oliver, *Origin and Progress of the American Revolution: A Tory View*, eds. Douglass Adair and John A. Schutz (San Marino, CA: Huntington Library, 1961), 56; for extensive coverage of Boston, see Richard D. Brown, *Revolutionary Politics in Massachusetts: The Boston Committee of Correspondence, 1772–1774* (New York: Norton, 1976).
42. Ray Raphael, *The First American Revolution: Before Lexington and Concord* (New York: New Press, 2002), 66; the following paragraphs are derived from Raphael's account, part 2.
43. L. Kinvin Wroth, *Province in Rebellion: A Documentary History of the Founding of the Commonwealth of Massachusetts, 1774–1775* (Cambridge, MA: Harvard University Press, 1975), 51.
44. Oliver, *Origin and Progress*, 153; Thomas Gage to Barrington, 26 June 1775, quoted in John S. Pancake, *This Destructive War: The British Campaign in the Carolinas, 1780–1782* (Tuscaloosa: University of Alabama Press, 1985), following "Table of Contents."
45. Thomas Young to John Lamb, 19 November 1774, quoted in Roger Champagne, *Alexander McDougall and the American Revolution in New York* (Syracuse, NY: Syracuse University Press, 1975), 74; for Seabury, Merrill Jensen, *The American Revolution within America* (New York: New York University Press, 1974), 43.
46. Jensen, *American Revolution within America*, 239.
47. Edward Countryman, *A People in Revolution: The American Revolution and Political Society in New York, 1760–1790* (Baltimore: Johns Hopkins University Press, 1981), 102, 129, 134.
48. Paul A. Gilje, *The Road to Mobocracy: Popular Disorder in New York City, 1763–1834* (Chapel Hill: University of North Carolina Press, 1987), 61.
49. Jensen, *American Revolution within America*, 39–40.
50. *Pennsylvania Packet*, 30 April 1775.
51. Quoted in Stephen Lucas, *Portents of Rebellion: Rhetoric and Revolution in Philadelphia, 1765–1776* (Philadelphia: Temple University Press, 1976), 185.
52. David Freeman Hawke, *In the Midst of a Revolution* (Philadelphia: University of Pennsylvania Press, 1961), 102–5; Pauline Maier, "Dr. Thomas Young and the Radicalism of Science and Reason," in *Old Revolutionaries: Political Lives in the Age of Samuel Adams* (New York: Knopf, 1980), 101, 107, 109.
53. Maier, *Old Revolutionaries*, 120–21.

54. Eric Foner, *Tom Paine and Revolutionary America* (New York: Oxford University Press, 1976), 64.
55. This paragraph draws heavily on Steven Rosswurm, *Arms, Country, and Class: The Philadelphia Militia and "Lower Sort" During the American Revolution, 1775–1783* (New Brunswick, NJ: Rutgers University Press, 1987), chapter 2.
56. "Diary of James Allen," *The Pennsylvania Magazine of History and Biography* 9 (1885): 184–86.
57. David Freeman Hawke, *Paine* (New York: Harper & Row, 1974), 35.
58. "Forester's Letter II," in Foner, *Writings of Thomas Paine*, 2:67.
59. Hawke, *Paine*, 44.
60. Ibid., 49.
61. Quoted in John C. Miller, *The Origins of the American Revolution* (Boston: Little, Brown, 1948), 460.
62. Worthington Chauncey Ford et al., eds. *Journals of the Continental Congress, 1774–1789*, 34 vols. (Washington, DC: U.S. Government Printing Office, 1904–1937), 4:358; Hawke, *Midst of Revolution*, 134.
63. Hawke, *Midst of Revolution*, 136.
64. Thomson, quoted in Rosswurm, *Arms, Country, and Class*, 85.
65. Ibid., 89–97, for the quotes in this and the next paragraph.
66. Holton, *Forced Founders*, 165.
67. Michael A. McDonnell, "Popular Mobilization and Political Culture in Revolutionary Virginia: The Failure of the Minutemen and the Revolution from Below," *Journal of American History* 85 (1999): 952, 953, 955.
68. Ibid., 959. This account is derived from McDonnell's essay; quotes are from pp. 946, 960, 962, and 964.
69. Holton, *Forced Founders*, 179, 180, 182–83.
70. McDonnell, "Popular Mobilization," 965.
71. Landon Carter Diary, 1 May 1776, in Holton, *Forced Founders*, 202; Holton quotes Lee in *Forced Founders*, 185, 187.
72. Braxton to Landon Carter, 14 April 1776, in *Letters of Delegates to Congress, 1774–1789*, 26 vols., eds. Paul Hubert Smith and Ronald M Gephart (Washington, DC: U.S. Government Printing Office, 1976–2000), 3:522; Landon Carter to George Washington, 9 May 1776, in *American Archives*, 4th ser., 9 vols., ed. Peter Force (Washington, 1837–1853), 6:389–92, quoted in Jensen, *Revolution within America*, 45.
73. Francis Lightfoot Lee to Landon Carter, 21 May 1776, quoted in Holton, *Forced Founders*, 186; the second quote is from 193.
74. Jensen, *Revolution within America*, 40–41.
75. Ibid., 42, 48.
76. Ibid., 43.
77. "Diary of James Allen," *Pennsylvania Magazine of History and Biography*, 9 (1885): 184–86; Jensen, *Revolution within America*, 47.
78. John Adams, 3 June 1776, in *Papers of John Adams*, 11 vols., ed. Robert Joseph Taylor (Cambridge, MA: Harvard University Press, 1979), 4:235; John Adams to Abigail Adams, 14 April 1776, *Adams Family Correspondence*, 1:381.
79. Ibid., 382.
80. Abigail Adams to John Adams, 31 March 1776, *Adams Family Correspondence*, 1:369–71.
81. Ibid., 382–83.
82. Bernard Bailyn, ed., *Pamphlets of the American Revolution, 1750–1765* (Cambridge, MA: Harvard University Press, 1965), 420–22, for Otis pamphlet; John Adams to

Abigail Adams, 14 April 1776, *Adams Family Correspondence*, 1:382–83; Lynne Withey, *Dearest Friend: A Life of Abigail Adams* (New York: Free Press, 1981), 81.

83. Abigail Adams to Mercy Otis Warren, 27 April 1776, *Adams Family Correspondence*, 1:397–98.

84. Abigail Adams to John Adams, 10 May 1776, *Adams Family Correspondence*, 1:402; John Adams to James Sullivan, *Papers of John Adams*, 4:212–13 n. 2.

85. Abigail Adams to Elizabeth Shaw, 19 July 1799, Shaw Family Papers, Library of Congress; quoted on www.umkc.edu/adamsa.htm.

Chapter 5: The Dual Revolution, 1776–1778

1. Elizabeth A. Fenn, *Pox Americana: The Great Smallpox Epidemic of 1775–1782* (New York: Hill and Wang, 2001), 53–54.

2. L. H. Butterfield et al., eds., *Adams Family Correspondence*, 6 vols. (Cambridge, MA: Harvard University Press, 1963–1993), 2:30; Richard M. Ketchum, "The Day New York Declared Its Independence," *New York Times*, 4 July 2003, A21, for "melted majesty."

3. *Adams Family Correspondence*, 2:46; Jefferson's original draft with Congress's changes is published in Garry Wills, *Inventing America: Jefferson's Declaration of Independence* (New York: Vintage Books, 1979), 374–79.

4. Pauline Maier, *American Scripture: Making the Declaration of Independence* (New York: Knopf, 1997), 122.

5. Roger Wilkins, *Jefferson's Pillow: The Founding Fathers and the Dilemma of Black Patriotism* (Boston: Beacon Press, 2001), 5, 50.

6. Michael Foot and Isaac Kramnick, *Thomas Paine Reader* (New York: Penguin Books, 1987), 109.

7. James Forten, *Letters from a Gentleman of Colour* (1813), reprinted in Herbert Aptheker, *A Documentary History of the Negro People in the United States*, 3 vols. (New York: Citadel Press, 1969), 1:60.

8. Jack P. Greene, "All Men Are Created Equal: Some Reflections on the Character of the American Revolution," in *Imperatives, Behaviors, and Identities: Essays in Early American Cultural History*, ed. Jack P. Greene (Charlottesville: University Press of Virginia, 1992), 236–67, especially 264–67; Gordon S. Wood, "Equality and Social Conflict in the American Revolution," *William and Mary Quarterly*, 3rd series, 51 (1994): 707; William Freehling, "The Founding Fathers and Slavery," *American Historical Review*, 77 (1972): 80ff.

9. Abigail Adams to John Adams, 22 September 1774, *Adams Family Correspondence*, 1:162; "African Slavery in America," in *The Complete Writings of Thomas Paine*, 2 vols., ed. Philip S. Foner (New York: Citadel Press, 1969), 2:17.

10. Samuel Hopkins, *A Dialogue Concerning the Slavery of the Africans* (1776; reprint, New York: Arno Press, 1970), 570–71; Thomas G. West, *Vindicating the Founders: Race, Sex, Class, and Justice in the Origins of America* (Lanham, MD: Rowman & Littlefield, 1997), 7.

11. Lee, "Extract from an Address [on Slavery] in *Virginia Gazette*, 19 March 1767," in Gary B. Nash, *Race and Revolution* (Madison, WI: Madison House, 1990), 92; Henry Wiencek, *An Imperfect God: George Washington, His Slaves, and the Creation of America* (New York: Farrar, Straus, and Giroux, 2003), 161 for Jefferson.

12. Robert Allen Rutland, ed., *The Papers of George Mason, 1725–1792*, 3 vols. (Chapel Hill: University of North Carolina Press, 1970), 1:277; William James Van Schreeven and Robert L. Scribner, *Revolutionary Virginia, The Road to Independence*, 7 vols. (Charlottesville: University Press of Virginia, 1973–1983), 7:454 n. 16; and discussion

in Rutland, *Papers of George Mason*, 1:289; Henry Mayer, *A Son of Thunder: Patrick Henry and the American Revolution* (New York: Franklin Watts, 1986), 300.

13. Benjamin Quarles, *The Negro in the American Revolution* (Chapel Hill: University of North Carolina Press, 1961), 63.

14. Simon Winchester, *The Professor and the Madman: A Tale of Murder, Insanity, and the Making of the Oxford English Dictionary* (New York: HarperCollins, 1998), 89–90; Samuel Johnson, *Political Writings*, ed. Donald J. Greene (New Haven, CT: Yale University Press, 1977), 454; last quote from David Waldstreicher, *Runaway America: Benjamin Franklin, Slavery, and the American Revolution* (New York: Hill and Wang, 2004), 212.

15. John Lind, *An Answer to the Declaration of the American Congress* (London, 1776), 107, quoted in Wills, *Inventing America*, 73.

16. Thomas Jefferson, "Preamble," in *Papers of Thomas Jefferson*, 31 vols., ed. Julian Boyd et al. (Princeton, NJ: Princeton University Press, 1950–), 1:377–79; the phrase is on p. 378.

17. Anthony F. C. Wallace, *Jefferson and the Indians: The Tragic Fate of the First Americans* (Cambridge, MA: Harvard University Press 1999), 51–52.

18. Thomas Jefferson, *Notes on the State of Virginia*, ed. William Harwood Peden (New York: Norton, 1972), 62.

19. Georgiana Nammack, *Fraud, Politics, and the Dispossession of the Indians: The Iroquois Land Frontier in the Colonial Period* (Norman: University of Oklahoma Press, 1969), 31; Edmond Atkin, *Indians of the Southern Colonial Frontier: The Edmond Atkin Report and Plan of 1755*, ed. Wilbur Jacobs (Columbia: University of South Carolina Press, 1954), 38.

20. Brickell quoted in James Axtell, "The White Indians of Colonial America," *William and Mary Quarterly*, 3rd series, 32 (1975): 86.

21. Colin G. Calloway, *American Revolution in Indian Country: Crisis and Diversity in Native American Communities* (Cambridge, England: Cambridge University Press, 1995), 92.

22. Robert Joseph Taylor, ed., *Papers of John Adams*, 11 vols. (Cambridge, MA: Harvard University Press, 1979), 4:221; for Charles Lee, Charles Patrick Neimeyer, *America Goes to War: A Social History of the Continental Army* (New York: New York University Press, 1996), xiii.

23. James Kirby Martin and Mark Edward Lender, *A Respectable Army: The Military Origins of the Republic, 1763–1789* (Arlington Heights, IL: H. Davidson, 1982), 89; John W. Shy, *A People Numerous and Armed: Reflections on the Military Struggle for American Independence* (New York: Oxford University Press, 1976), 15.

24. Shy, *People Numerous and Armed*, 13.

25. Robert A. Gross, *The Minutemen and Their World* (New York: Hill and Wang, 1976), 148–53.

26. Neimeyer, *America Goes to War*, 17, quoting Jonathan Smith, *Peterborough, New Hampshire in the American Revolution* (Peterborough, NH: Peterborough Historical Society, 1913).

27. Shy, *People Numerous and Armed*, 168.

28. Bernard Bailyn and Barbara DeWolfe, *Voyagers to the West: A Passage in the Peopling of America on the Eve of the Revolution* (New York: Knopf, 1986), 25–26; Neimeyer, *America Goes to War*, 9 for "Line of Ireland"; Aaron Spencer Fogleman, *Hopeful Journeys: German Immigration, Settlement, and Political Culture in Colonial America, 1717–1775* (Philadelphia: University of Pennsylvania Press, 1996), 2, table 1.1.

29. A. Roger Ekirch, *Bound for America: The Transportation of British Convicts to the Colonies, 1718–1775* (Oxford, England: Clarendon Press, 1987), 115.

30. Neimeyer, *America Goes to War*, 24, 34.
31. Ibid., 9; Bailyn and Wolfe, *Voyagers to the West*, 326, 346.
32. Washington quoted in Edmund S. Morgan, *Inventing the People: The Rise of Popular Sovereignty in England and America* (New York: Norton, 1988), 163; see also George Washington, *Writings of George Washington from the Original Manuscript Sources, 1745–1799*, 39 vols., eds. John Clement Fitzpatrick and David Maydole Matteson (Washington, DC: U.S. Government Printing Office, 1931–1944), 4:124; 6:5.
33. James Kirby Martin, ed., *Ordinary Courage: The Revolutionary War Adventures of Joseph Plumb Martin* (1830; reprint, St. James, NY: Brandywine Press, 1993), 61–63.
34. Ibid., 62–63.
35. Benjamin Rush to John Adams, 12 February 1812, *The Spur of Fame: Dialogues of John Adams and Benjamin Rush*, eds. John A. Schutz and Douglass Adair (San Marino, CA: Huntington Library, 1966), 207–9.
36. Neimeyer, *America Goes to War*, 133, 137–38.
37. Sidney Kaplan and Emma Nogrady Kaplan, *The Black Presence in the Era of the American Revolution* (Amherst: University of Massachusetts Press, 1989), 120.
38. John Saillant, *Black Puritan, Black Republican: The Life and Thought of Lemuel Haynes, 1753–1833* (Oxford, England: Oxford University Press, 2003), 15.
39. Ruth Bogin, " 'Liberty Further Extended': An Antislavery Manuscript by Lemuel Haynes," *William and Mary Quarterly*, 3rd series, 40 (1983): 85–105.
40. Kaplan and Kaplan, *Black Presence*, 120.
41. Ibid., 10–11.
42. Gary B. Nash, introduction to Quarles, *The Negro in the American Revolution*, xiii–xiv.
43. Ibid., xiv.
44. Neimeyer, *America Goes to War*, 73; new research has revealed many more Indians and African Americans in the first stage of the war. See George Quintal, Jr., *Patriots of Color, " 'A Peculiar Beauty and Merit': African Americans and Native Americans at Battle Road and Bunker Hill,"* unpublished report for Boston National Historical Park, February 2002.
45. Wiencek, *An Imperfect God*, 218; Lorenzo Greene, "Black Regiment of Rhode Island," *Journal of Negro History* 37 (1952): 144.
46. Louis Wilson, "Rhode Island's First Rhode Island Regiment—The Black Regiment, 1777–1780," unpublished paper, 8.
47. Ibid., 1.
48. William C. Nell, *The Colored Patriots of the American Revolution* (Boston: R. F. Wallcut, 1855), 127, quoted in Kaplan and Kaplan, *Black Presence*, 65.
49. Neimeyer, *America Goes to War*, 83, quoting François Jean Marquis de Chastellux, *Travels in North America*, 2 vols. (Chapel Hill: University of North Carolina Press, 1963), 2:229.
50. Wiencek, *An Imperfect God*, 245; Wilson, "Rhode Island's Black Regiment," 20.
51. Rhys Isaac, *Landon Carter's Uneasy Kingdom: Revolution and Rebellion on a Virginia Plantation* (New York: Oxford University Press, 2004), 3–4, 7–11.
52. Gary B. Nash, *Forging Freedom: The Formation of Philadelphia's Black Community* (Cambridge, MA: Harvard University Press, 1988), 57.
53. Graham Russell Hodges, *Slavery and Freedom in the Rural North: African Americans in Monmouth County, New Jersey, 1665–1865* (Madison, WI: Madison House, 1997), 96–104 for full account of Tye.
54. Abigail Adams to John Adams, 31 July 1777, *Adams Family Correspondence*, 2:295.
55. John Adams to Abigail Adams, 11 August 1777, ibid., 2:305.
56. Barbara Clark Smith, *After the Revolution: The Smithsonian History of Everyday Life in the Eighteenth Century* (New York: Pantheon Books, 1985), 35–36.

57. Ibid., 37, 39.

58. Ibid., 39.

59. Barbara Clark Smith, "Food Rioters and the American Revolution," *William and Mary Quarterly*, 3rd series, 51 (1994): 11.

60. Smith, "Food Rioters," 3–38; for French, Smith, *After the Revolution*, 9.

61. Abigail Adams to John Adams, 20 April 1777, *Adams Family Correspondence*, 2:217–18.

62. Smith, "Food Rioters," 24, 29.

63. Ronald Hoffman, *A Spirit of Dissension: Economics, Politics, and the Revolution in Maryland* (Baltimore: Johns Hopkins University Press, 1973), 197–98.

64. Ibid., 195.

65. Ibid., 195, 198.

66. Ibid., 187–88; 201.

67. Ibid., 205.

68. Ibid., 198.

69. William Eddis, *Letters from America*, ed. Aubrey C. Land (Cambridge, MA: Harvard University Press, 1969), 65.

70. Council of Safety to Continental Congress's president, John Hancock, in Hoffman, *Spirit of Dissension*, 197–98.

71. Hoffman, *Spirit of Dissension*, 200.

72. Ibid., 186, 189–90.

73. Ibid., 227.

74. Keith Mason, "Localism, Evangelicalism, and Loyalism: The Sources of Discontent in the Revolutionary Chesapeake," *Journal of Southern History* 56 (1990): 40.

75. Ibid., 23.

76. Charles Carroll of Carrollton and Charles Carroll of Annapolis in *Dear Papa, Dear Charley: The Peregrinations of a Revolutionary Aristocrat*, 4 vols., ed. Ronald Hoffman (Chapel Hill: University of North Carolina Press, 2001), 2:858.

77. Hoffman, *Spirit of Dissension*, 210.

78. Ronald Hoffman and Sally D. Mason, *Princes of Ireland, Planters of Maryland: A Carroll Saga, 1500–1782* (Chapel Hill: University of North Carolina Press, 2000), 323–24.

79. Hoffman, *Spirit of Dissension*, 220; Hoffman, *Dear Papa*, 2:859.

80. Edward Countryman, *A People in Revolution: The American Revolution and Political Society in New York, 1760–1790* (Baltimore: Johns Hopkins University Press, 1981), 116.

81. Staughton Lynd, *Class Conflict, Slavery, and the United States Constitution, Ten Essays* (Indianapolis, IN: Bobbs-Merrill, 1968), 69.

82. Ibid., 72–73.

83. William Smith, *Historical Memoirs of William Smith, 1778–1783*, 2 vols., ed. William Henry Waldo Sabine (New York: New York Times, 1969–1971), 2:128, 131–34, 136, quoted in Staughton Lynd, *Who Should Rule at Home?: Dutchess County, New York in the American Revolution* (Indianapolis, IN: Bobbs-Merrill, 1961), 74.

84. Lynd, *Dutchess County*, 77.

85. Neimeyer, *America Goes to War*, 92; for congressional Indian policy, see Jack M. Sosin, "The Use of Indians in the War of the American Revolution: A Re-Assessment of Responsibility," *Canadian Historical Review* 46 (1965): 101–21.

86. Francis Jennings, "The Indians' Revolution," in *The American Revolution*, ed. Alfred F. Young (DeKalb: Northern Illinois University Press, 1976), 322.

87. Isabel Thompson Kelsay, *Joseph Brant, 1743–1807: Man of Two Worlds* (Syracuse, NY: Syracuse University Press, 1984), 173; the following account of Brant draws

heavily on Kelsay's biography and on Barbara Graymont, *The Iroquois in the American Revolution* (Syracuse, NY: Syracuse University Press, 1972).

88. James E. Seaver, *A Narrative of the Life of Mrs. Mary Jemison*, ed. June Namias (1884; reprint, Norman: University of Oklahoma Press, 1992), 98.

89. For Butler, see Howard Swiggett, *War Out of Niagara: Walter Butler and the Tory Rangers* (Port Washington, NY: Ira J. Friedman, 1963).

90. W. Max Reid, *Mohawk Valley: Its Legends and Its History* (New York: G. P. Putnam's Sons, 1901), in Swiggett, *War Out of Niagara*, 28.

91. Page Smith, *A New Age Now Begins: A People's History of the American Revolution*, 2 vols. (New York: McGraw-Hill, 1976), 2:911; Graymont, *Iroquois in the American Revolution*, 135.

92. Graymont, *Iroquois in the American Revolution*, 143.

93. Ibid., 159.

94. Ibid., 181.

95. Calloway, *American Revolution in Indian Country*, 124–25.

96. Anthony F. C. Wallace, *The Death and Rebirth of the Seneca* (New York: Knopf, 1970), 140.

97. E. Raymond Evans, "Notable Persons in Cherokee History: Dragging Canoe," *Journal of Cherokee Studies* 2 (1977), 176.

98. "Henry Stuart's Account of His Proceedings with the Cherokee Indians About Going Against the Whites," *Colonial Records of North Carolina*, 10: 764, quoted in Hatley, The *Dividing Paths: Cherokees and South Carolinians Through the Era of Revolution* (New York: Oxford University Press, 1993), 218; Calloway, *American Revolution in Indian Country*, 189–91.

99. Nathaniel Sheidley, "Hunting and the Politics of Masculinity in Cherokee Treaty-Making, 1763–1775," in *Empires and Others: British Encounters with Indigenous Peoples, 1600–1850*, eds. M. J. Daunton and Rick Halpern (Philadelphia: University of Pennsylvania Press, 1999), 167–186.

100. Edward J. Cashin, " 'But Brothers, It Is Our Land We Are Talking About': Winners and Losers in the Georgia Backcountry," in *An Uncivil War: The Southern Backcountry during the American Revolution*, eds. Ronald Hoffman, Thad W. Tate, and Peter J. Albert (Charlottesville: University Press of Virginia, 1985), 251–52; Evans, "Dragging Canoe," 182.

101. Hatley, *Dividing Paths*, 199–200; 194.

102. Calloway, *American Revolution in Indian Country*, 164.

103. Ibid., 166.

104. Richard White, *The Middle Ground: Indians, Empires, and Republics in the Great Lakes Region, 1650–1815* (Cambridge, England: Cambridge University Press, 1991), 384.

105. James Hart Merrell, *The Indians' New World: Catawbas and Their Neighbors from European Contact through the Era of Removal* (Chapel Hill: University of North Carolina Press, 1989), 215.

106. Ibid., 215; James H. O'Donnell, *Southern Indians in the American Revolution* (Knoxville: University of Tennessee Press, 1973), 44.

107. Edward Manning Ruttenber, *History of the Indian Tribes of Hudson's River* (1872; reprint, Port Washington, NY: Kennikat Press, 1971), 286–87.

108. Quoted in Calloway, *American Revolution in Indian Country*, 103; also Jeanne Ronda and James P. Ronda, " 'As They Were Faithful': Chief Hendrick Aupaumut and the Struggle for Stockbridge Survival, 1757–1830," *American Indian Culture and Research Journal* 3 (1979): 43–55.

Chapter 6: Writing on the Clean Slate, 1776–1780

1. L. H. Butterfield, ed., *Diary and Autobiography of John Adams*, 4 vols. (New York: Atheneum, 1964), 3:355–58 for Adams's ruminations on making government.
2. Samuel Miller, *A Brief Retrospect of the Eighteenth Century*, 2 vols. (New York: T. and J. Swords, 1803), 2:251–52.
3. Quoted in Willi Paul Adams, *The First American Constitutions: Republican Ideology and the Making of the State Constitutions in the Revolutionary Era* (Chapel Hill: University of North Carolina Press, 1980), 23–24.
4. Philip S. Foner, ed., *The Complete Writings of Thomas Paine*, 2 vols. (New York: Citadel Press, 1969), 1:6–7, 45; Marc W. Kruman, *Between Authority and Liberty: State Constitution Making in Revolutionary America* (Chapel Hill: University of North Carolina Press, 1997), 32.
5. Kruman, *Between Authority and Liberty*, 17–18.
6. J. Paul Selsam, *The Pennsylvania Constitution of 1776: A Study in Revolutionary Democracy* (New York: Octagon Books, 1971), 139.
7. "To the Privates of Several Battalions of Military Associators in the Province of Pennsylvania," broadside (Philadelphia, 1776), Historical Society of Pennsylvania.
8. Clinton Lawrence Rossiter, *The Political Thought of the American Revolution* (New York: Harcourt, Brace & World, 1963), 120–21.
9. Kruman, *Between Authority and Liberty*, 88; Adams, *First American Constitutions*, 179.
10. Ronald Hoffman, *A Spirit of Dissension: Economics, Politics, and Revolution in Maryland* (Baltimore: Johns Hopkins University Press, 1973), 170–72; The Committee of Mechanics of New York City, quoted in Adams, *First American Constitutions*, 179.
11. Selsam, *Pennsylvania Constitution of 1776*, 148–49.
12. "Thoughts on Government," in *Papers of John Adams*, 11 vols., ed. Robert Joseph Taylor (Cambridge, MA: Harvard University Press, 1979), 4:86–93.
13. William Hooper, quoted in Kruman, *Between Authority and Liberty*, 150; "K," "Remarks on the Constitution of Pennsylvania," *Pennsylvania Packet*, 15 October 1776.
14. Selsam, *Pennsylvania Constitution of 1776*, 199.
15. This account follows Steven Rosswurm, *Arms, Country, and Class: The Philadelphia Militia and "Lower Sort" during the American Revolution, 1775–1783* (New Brunswick, NJ: Rutgers University Press, 1987), 93–108.
16. Benjamin Rush to Anthony Wayne, *Pennsylvania Magazine of History and Biography* 70 (1946): 91; Benjamin Rush to Anthony Wayne, 24 September 1776, *Letters of Benjamin Rush*, ed. L. H. Butterfield (Philadelphia: American Philosophical Society, 1951), 1:114–15, 137, 148; John Adams quoted by Benjamin Rush in Rush to Adams, 12 October 1779, *Letters of Benjamin Rush*, 1:240.
17. Kruman, *Between Authority and Liberty*, 88–89; James Sullivan to [Elbridge] Gerry, 6 May 1776, in *Papers of John Adams*, 4:212 n. 2.
18. John Adams to James Sullivan, 26 May 1776, *Papers of John Adams*, 4:210; Adams, *First American Constitutions*, 31; "people's war" quoted in John E. Ferling, " 'Oh That I Was a Soldier': John Adams and the Anguish of War," *American Quarterly* 36 (1984): 264.
19. Timothy Dwight, *Travels in New England and New York*, 4 vols., ed. Barbara Miller Solomon (Cambridge, MA: Harvard University Press, 1969), 2:405; William Hooper, quoted in Gordon S. Wood, *The Creation of the American Republic, 1776–1787* (Chapel Hill: University of North Carolina Press, 1969), 233; Robert J. Taylor, ed., *Papers of John Adams*, 4:81, 88.

20. Michael A. Bellisles, *Revolutionary Outlaws: Ethan Allen and the Struggle for Independence on the Early American Frontier* (Charlottesville: University Press of Virginia, 1993), 135.

21. Ibid., 131, 136.

22. Allen Soule and John A. Williams, eds., *Laws of Vermont* (Montpelier, VT: H. E. Armstrong, Secretary of State, 1964), 5–8; Bellisles, *Revolutionary Outlaws*, 172, 235.

23. Bellisles, *Revolutionary Outlaws*, 159, 160.

24. Ibid., 341 n. 12.

25. Ibid., 178.

26. Hoffman, *A Spirit of Dissension*, 169–70; Edward C. Papenfuse and Gregory A. Stiverson, eds., *The Decisive Blow Is Struck: A Facsimile Edition of the Proceedings of the Constitutional Convention of 1776 and the First Maryland Constitution* (1787; reprint, Annapolis: Hall of Records Commission, 1977), np; Kruman, *Between Authority and Liberty*, 99.

27. Hoffman, *A Spirit of Dissension*, 171.

28. Ibid.

29. Charles Carroll of Carrollton and Charles Carroll of Annapolis, *Dear Papa, Dear Charley: The Peregrinations of a Revolutionary Aristocrat*, 4 vols., ed. Ronald Hoffman (Chapel Hill: University of North Carolina Press, 2001), 2:940 n. 5.

30. Carroll and Carroll, *Dear Papa*, 2:941.

31. *Maryland Gazette*, 15 August 1776, quoted in Kruman, *Between Authority and Liberty*, 95.

32. Paperfuse and Stiverson, *The Decisive Blow Is Struck*, np.

33. Hoffman, *Spirit of Dissension*, 181.

34. Kruman, *Between Authority and Liberty*, 40.

35. Judith Apter Klinghoffer and Lois Elkis, " 'The Petticoat Electors': Women's Suffrage in New Jersey, 1776–1807," *Journal of the Early Republic* 12 (1992): 166; "Essex," *New York Journal*, 6 March 1776, quoted in Kruman, *Between Authority and Liberty*, 105; Larry R. Gerlach guesses that "Essex" was William DeHart in *Prologue to Independence: New Jersey in the Coming of the American Revolution* (New Brunswick, NJ: Rutgers University Press, 1976), 473 n. 63; Klinghoffer and Elkis, "Petticoat Electors," 160; Mary Beth Norton, *Liberty's Daughters: The Revolutionary Experience of American Women, 1750–1800* (Boston: Little, Brown, 1980), 191–93.

36. Kruman, *Between Authority and Liberty*, 103, 104–5.

37. Abigail Adams, quoted in Charles W. Akers, *Abigail Adams: An American Woman* (Boston: Little, Brown, 1980), 52.

38. Oscar Handlin and Mary Flug Handlin, eds., *The Popular Sources of Political Authority: Documents on the Massachusetts Constitution of 1780* (Cambridge, MA: Harvard University Press, 1966), 231.

39. John Chester Miller, *Sam Adams: Pioneer in Propaganda* (Boston: Little, Brown, 1936), 355.

40. John Winthrop to John Adams, 1 June 1776, *Papers of John Adams*, 4:223–24.

41. John Winthrop to John Adams, 23 June 1776, ibid., 4:332–33.

42. Kruman, *Between Authority and Liberty*, 30.

43. For constitution making in Massachusetts, I have followed Stephen E. Patterson, *Political Parties in Revolutionary Massachusetts* (Madison: University of Wisconsin Press, 1973), and the documents in Robert J. Taylor, ed., *Massachusetts: Colony to Commonwealth: Documents on the Formation of Its Constitution, 1775–1780* (Chapel Hill: University of North Carolina Press, 1961).

44. James Warren to John Adams, 22 June 1777, in *Warren-Adams Letters*, 2 vols.

(Boston: Massachusetts Historical Society, 1917–1925), 1:334–35; 22 June 1777, in *Papers of John Adams*, 5:230 and 10 July 1777, 5:244–45.

45. *Independent Chronicle and the Universal Advertiser*, 10 July 1777, quoted in Elisha P. Douglass, *Rebels and Democrats: The Struggle for Equal Political Rights and Majority Rule During the American Revolution* (Chapel Hill: University of North Carolina Press, 1955), 172–73.

46. Douglass, *Rebels and Democrats*, 175.

47. Many of the town votes and criticisms are printed in Handlin and Handlin, *Popular Sources of Political Authority*.

48. Robert Joseph Taylor, *Western Massachusetts in the Revolution* (Providence: Brown University Press, 1954), 59; *Continental Journal and Weekly Advertiser*, 9 April 1778, in Douglass, *Rebels and Democrats*, 179 n. 52.

49. Douglass, *Rebels and Democrats*, 177; Taylor, *Massachusetts: Colony to Commonwealth*, 69.

50. Theophilus Parsons, quoted in Kruman, *Between Authority and Liberty*, 104; and Douglass, *Rebels and Democrats*, 182.

51. Quoted in John R. Howe, *The Changing Political Thought of John Adams* (Princeton, NJ: Princeton University Press, 1966), 82.

52. Mercy Otis Warren, 29 July 1779, in *Papers of John Adams*, 7:102.

53. Patterson, *Political Parties*, 234–37.

54. E. Francis Brown, *Joseph Hawley: Colonial Radical* (New York: Columbia University Press, 1931), 176–84; Hawley, quoted in Adams, *First Constitutions*, 211.

55. Patterson, *Political Parties*, 245.

56. Kruman, *Between Authority and Liberty*, 94; Patterson, *Political Parties*, 240–41.

57. Quoted in Gregory H. Nobles, " 'Yet the Old Republicans Still Persevere': Samuel Adams, John Hancock, and the Crisis of Popular Leadership in Revolutionary Massachusetts, 1775–1790," in *The Transforming Hand of Revolution: Reconsidering the American Revolution as a Social Movement*, eds. Ronald Hoffman and Peter J. Albert (Charlottesville: University Press of Virginia, 1995), 276.

58. Quoted in Richard D. Brown, *The Strength of a People: The Idea of an Informed Citizenry in America, 1650–1870* (Chapel Hill: University of North Carolina Press, 1996), 52; Brown examines "the recognition of the informed citizen" as the "bulwark of revolutionary liberty" in chapter 3.

Chapter 7: Radicalism at Floodtide, 1778–1781

1. Warren is quoted in Lester Cohen, "Creating a Usable Future: The Revolutionary Historians and the National Past," in *The American Revolution: Its Character and Limits*, ed. Jack P. Greene (New York: New York University Press, 1987), 316. The fiscal crisis is fully explored in E. James Ferguson, *The Power of the Purse: A History of American Public Finance* (Chapel Hill: University of North Carolina Press, 1961).

2. John K. Alexander, "The Fort Wilson Incident of 1779," *William and Mary Quarterly*, 3rd series, 31 (1974): 593; the following account draws upon Alexander's article and Steven Rosswurm, *Arms, Country, and Class: The Philadelphia Militia and "Lower Sort" During the American Revolution, 1775–1783* (New Brunswick, NJ: Rutgers University Press, 1987), chapter 7.

3. Ronald Schultz, *Republic of Labor: Philadelphia Artisans and the Politics of Labor, 1720–1830* (New York: Oxford University Press, 1993), 47.

4. *Pennsylvania Packet*, 10 December 1778; Jared Sparks, ed., *The Writings of George Washington*, 12 vols. (Boston: American Stationers' Company, 1847), 6:91.

5. William B. Reed, *Life and Correspondence of Joseph Reed*, 2 vols. (Philadelphia: Lindsay and Blakiston, 1847), 2:142.
6. Rosswurm, *Arms, Country, and Class*, 178.
7. Ibid., 180–86.
8. Ibid., 180.
9. Eric Foner, *Tom Paine and Revolutionary America* (New York: Oxford University Press, 1976), 169.
10. Ibid., 170, 187–88.
11. The Meschianza is described in Gary B. Nash, *First City: Philadelphia and the Forging of Historical Memory* (Philadelphia: University of Pennsylvania Press, 2002), 98–100.
12. *Pennsylvania Packet*, 21 January 1779.
13. Rosswurm, *Arms, Country, and Class*, 197, 242.
14. "The Address of the Committee . . . to the Fellow-Citizens throughout the United States," quoted in Douglas M. Arnold, "Political Ideology and the Internal Revolution in Pennsylvania, 1776–1790," Ph.D. diss., Princeton University, 1976, 131; Rosswurm, *Arms, Country, and Class*, 194–99.
15. Schultz, *Republic of Labor*, 56.
16. Rosswurm, *Arms, Country, and Class*, 205–6.
17. Alexander, "Fort Wilson Incident," 601; Schultz, *Republic of Labor*, 59.
18. Rosswurm, *Arms, Country, and Class*, 214.
19. . L. H. Butterfield, ed., *Letters of Benjamin Rush*, 2 vols. (Philadelphia: American Philosophical Society, 1951), 1:243–44.
20. Rosswurm, *Arms, Country, and Class*, 220; Nash, *First City*, 104; Alexander, "Fort Wilson Incident," 589.
21. Foner, *Paine*, 178, quoting "To the Merchants and Traders of Philadelphia."
22. Rosswurm, *Arms, Country, and Class*, 232–33.
23. Nash, *First City*, 99–100.
24. Petition of Connecticut Negroes from County of Fairfield, 11 May 1779, in Herbert Aptheker, *A Documentary History of the Negro People in the United States*, 3 vols. (New York: Citadel Press, 1969), 1:10–11.
25. Page Smith, *A New Age Now Begins: A People's History of the American Revolution*, 2 vols. (New York: McGraw-Hill, 1976), 2:1343; Aptheker, *A Documentary History*, 1:12–13.
26. Gary B. Nash and Jean R. Soderlund, *Freedom by Degrees: Emancipation in Philadelphia and Its Aftermath* (New York: Oxford University Press, 1991), 101–2, for quotations in this and the next two paragraphs. This analysis of the Pennsylvania gradual emancipation law is drawn from ibid., 100–105.
27. Robert W. Fogel and Stanley L. Engerman, "Philanthropy at Bargain Prices: Notes on the Economics of Gradual Emancipation," *Journal of Legal Studies* 3 (1974): 377–401.
28. Nash and Soderlund, *Freedom by Degrees*, 111.
29. Ibid., 111.
30. Ibid., 112.
31. Ibid.
32. Sylvia Frey, *Water from the Rock: Black Resistance in a Revolutionary Age* (Princeton, NJ: Princeton University Press, 1991), 85.
33. Benjamin Quarles, *The Negro in the American Revolution* (Chapel Hill: University of North Carolina Press, 1961), 60.
34. Quoted in Gregory D. Massey, *John Laurens and the American Revolution* (Columbia: University of South Carolina Press, 2000), 120, 132–33.

35. Henry Wiencek, *An Imperfect God: George Washington, His Slaves, and the Creation of America* (New York: Farrar, Straus, and Giroux, 2003), 227.
36. Ray Raphael, *Founding Myths: Stories That Hide Our Patriotic Past* (New York: New Press, 2004), 177; Mercy Otis Warren is quoted in Massey, *Laurens*, 139.
37. Frey, *Water from the Rock*, chapter 3.
38. Wiencek, *An Imperfect God*, 233–34.
39. Frey, *Water from the Rock*, 113; Clinton is quoted in Robert Olwell, *Masters, Slaves, and Subjects: The Culture of Power in South Carolina Low Country, 1740–1790* (Ithaca, NY: Cornell University Press, 1998), 249.
40. Frey, *Water from the Rock*, chapter 4.
41. Ibid., 118–19.
42. The accounts of both David George and Boston King appear in Vincent Carretta, *Unchained Voices: An Anthology of Black Authors in the English-Speaking World of the Eighteenth Century* (Lexington: University Press of Kentucky, 1996).
43. Johann von Ewald, *Diary of the American War: A Hessian Journal*, trans. and ed. Joseph P. Tustin (New Haven, CT: Yale University Press, 1979), 305.
44. Phillip D. Morgan, "Black Society in the Lowcountry, 1760–1810," in *Slavery and Freedom in the Age of the American Revolution*, eds. Ira Berlin and Ronald Hoffman (Charlottesville: University Press of Virginia, 1983), 109.
45. Quarles, *Negro and the American Revolution*, 108–9
46. Ibid., 109.
47. David Ramsay, *History of South Carolina: From Its First Settlement in 1670 to the Year 1808*, 2 vols. (Trenton, NJ, 1785), 1:312–14, cited in Olwell, *Masters, Slaves, and Subjects*, 251.
48. David Ramsay to Benjamin Rush, 18 May 1779, in Robert Brunhouse, ed., *David Ramsay, 1749–1815: Selections from His Writings*, Transactions of the American Philosophical Society, vol. 55, pt. 4 (Philadelphia: American Philosophical Society, 1965), 60.
49. Frey, *Water from the Rock*, 119; Elizabeth A. Fenn, *Pox Americana: The Great Smallpox Epidemic of 1775–82* (New York: Hill and Wang, 2001), 116–28, for the lethal smallpox epidemic.
50. Frey, *Water from the Rock*, 172–75.
51. Ibid., 150–59.
52. Lucia Stanton, *Free Some Day: The African-American Families of Monticello* (Charlottesville, VA: Thomas Jefferson Foundation, 2000), 56; Fenn, *Pox Americana*, 129; Frey, *Water from the Rock*, 167; Ewald, *Diary*, 305.
53. Frey, *Water from the Rock*, 168.
54. Ibid., 169.
55. Ewald, *Diary*, 305–6.
56. Fenn, *Pox Americana*, 129.
57. Ewald, *Diary*, 335–36; James Kirby Martin, ed., *Ordinary Courage: The Revolutionary War Adventures of Joseph Plumb Martin* (1830; reprint, St. James, NY: Brandywine Press, 1993), 141–42; Fenn, *Pox Americana*, 130.
58. Martin, *Ordinary Courage*, 141–42.
59. Stanton, *Free Some Day*, 52–57.
60. For Virginia's draft difficulties, see Michael A. McDonnell, "Popular Mobilization and Political Culture in Revolutionary Virginia: The Failure of the Minutemen and the Revolution from Below," *Journal of American History* 85 (1999): 6.
61. H. J. Eckenrode, *The Revolution in Virginia* (1916; reprint, Hamden, CT: Archon Books, 1964), 237–49; Henry Mayer, *A Son of Thunder: Patrick Henry and the American Republic* (New York: Franklin Watts, 1986), 344.

62. Michael McDonnell, "Class and Class Struggles During the American Revolution," unpublished paper, 2003, 7, 24 n. 30.
63. Ibid., 9.
64. Ibid., 15; McDonnell discusses the slave bounty scheme addressed in next three paragraphs on pp. 15–18. The quotations are on pp. 1, 16, 17.
65. McDonnell, "Popular Mobilization," 976.
66. Smith, *A New Age Begins*, 2:1627.
67. Ibid.
68. McDonnell, "Class and Class Struggles," 12.
69. Ibid., 14.
70. Ibid., 13; John E. Selby, *The Revolution in Virginia: 1775–1783* (Charlottesville: University Press of Virginia, 1988), 275.
71. McDonnell, "Class and Class Struggles," 14.
72. Anthony F. C. Wallace, *The Death and Rebirth of the Seneca* (New York: Knopf, 1970), 141.
73. Ibid., 141; Isabel Thompson Kelsay, *Joseph Brant, 1743–1807: Man of Two Worlds* (Syracuse, NY: Syracuse University Press, 1984), 155.
74. Smith, *A New Age Begins*, 2:1164, 1175; a detailed analysis of the Sullivan expedition is Joseph R. Fischer, *A Well-Executed Failure: The Sullivan Campaign Against the Iroquois* (Columbia: University of South Carolina Pres, 1997).
75. Smith, *A New Age Begins*, 2:1172.
76. Colin G. Calloway, *American Revolution in Indian Country: Crisis and Diversity in Native American Communities* (Cambridge, England: Cambridge University Press, 1995), 51, 53.
77. Smith, *A New Age Begins*, 2:1175; Fischer, *A Well-Executed Failure*, 192.
78. Kelsay, *Joseph Brant*, 298.
79. This account of Clark follows Smith, *A New Age Begins*, 2:chapters 8–9; and Richard White, *The Middle Ground: Indians, Empires, and Republics in the Great Lakes Region, 1650–1815* (Cambridge, England: Cambridge University Press, 1991), chapter 9.
80. White, *Middle Ground*, 368, 376–77.
81. Kelsay, *Joseph Brant*, 312–13.
82. Smith, *A New Age Begins*, 2:1218.
83. E. Raymond Evans, "Notable Persons in Cherokee History: Dragging Canoe," *Journal of Cherokee Studies*, 2 (1977), 184; Julian Boyd, ed., *Papers of Thomas Jefferson*, 31 vols. (Princeton, NJ: Princeton University Press, 1950–), 3:447–49.
84. Arthur Campbell to Thomas Jefferson, 15 January 1781, *Papers of Jefferson*, 4:359–61.
85. Calloway, *American Revolution in Indian Country*, 204–5.
86. James H. O'Donnell, *Southern Indians in the American Revolution* (Knoxville: University of Tennessee Press, 1973), 114.
87. O'Donnell, *Southern Indians*, 109, 205.
88. William Christian to Thomas Jefferson, 10 April 1781, *Papers of Jefferson*, 5:395–96.
89. Martin, *Ordinary Courage*, 109.
90. Charles Patrick Neimeyer, *America Goes to War: A Social History of the Continental Army* (New York: New York University Press, 1996), 7.
91. Ebenezer Huntington, *Letters Written by Ebenezer Huntington during the American Revolution* (New York: C. F. Heartman, 1915), 86–89.
92. Wayne E. Carp, *To Starve the Army at Pleasure: Continental Army Administration and American Political Culture, 1775–1783* (Chapel Hill: University of North Carolina Press, 1984), 181.
93. Neimeyer, *America Goes to War*, 146; the fullest account of the mutiny is in Carl Van

Doren, *Mutiny in January: The Story of a Crisis in the Continental Army* (New York: Viking Press, 1943).

94. Van Doren, *Mutiny in January*, 33.
95. Wayne Bodle, *The Valley Forge Winter: Civilians and Soldiers in War* (University Park: Pennsylvania State University, 2002), 128.
96. Charles Royster, *A Revolutionary People at War: The Continental Army and American Character* (Chapel Hill: University of North Carolina Press, 1979), 296–97.
97. Smith, *A New Age Begins*, 2:1607; for Wayne see Paul David Nelson, *Anthony Wayne: Soldier of the Early Republic* (Bloomington: Indiana University Press, 1985).
98. Smith, *A New Age Begins*, 2:1608.
99. Van Doren, *Mutiny in January*, 43.
100. Martin, *Ordinary Courage*, 117–18.
101. Smith, *A New Age Begins*, 2:1616.
102. Ibid., 2:1619.
103. Neimeyer, *America Goes to War*, 152–53.
104. Smith, *A New Age Begins*, 2:1622.
105. Neimeyer, *America Goes to War*, 154; Van Doren, *Mutiny in January*, 236.

Chapter 8: Taming the Revolution, 1781–1785

1. *Boston Independent Chronicle*, 4 May 1781, quoted in Oscar Handlin and Mary Flug Handlin, *Commonwealth: A Study of the Role of Government in the American Economy: Massachusetts, 1774–1961*, rev. ed. (Cambridge, MA: Harvard University Press, 1969), 32.
2. E. James Ferguson, *The Power of the Purse: A History of American Public Finance* (Chapel Hill: University of North Carolina Press, 1961), 109.
3. Ibid., 107.
4. Ibid., 115; for Morris's fiscal policies see Clarence Lester Ver Steeg, *Robert Morris, Revolutionary Financier: With an Analysis of His Early Career* (Philadelphia: University of Pennsylvania Press, 1954).
5. Quoted in Ferguson, *Power of the Purse*, 176.
6. Thomas Doerflinger, *Vigorous Spirit of Enterprise: Merchants and Economic Development in Revolutionary Philadelphia* (Chapel Hill: University of North Carolina Press, 1986), 212–13.
7. Carl Van Doren, *Mutiny in January: The Story of a Crisis in the Continental Army* (New York: Viking Press, 1943), 236; for Wayne see Paul David Nelson, *Anthony Wayne: Soldier of the Early Republic* (Bloomington: Indiana University Press, 1985).
8. Quoted in Charles Royster, *A Revolutionary People at War: The Continental Army and American Character* (Chapel Hill: University of North Carolina Press, 1979), 334; the Newburgh Conspiracy is dissected by Richard H. Kohn, "The Inside History of the Newburgh Conspiracy: America and the Coup d'Etat," *William and Mary Quarterly*, 3rd series, 27 (1970): 187–220.
9. Quoted in Royster, *Revolutionary People at War*, 336.
10. Ferguson, *Power of the Purse*, 157–58; Richard H. Kohn, *Eagle and Sword: The Federalists and the Creation of the Military Establishment in America, 1783–1802* (New York: Free Press, 1975), chapter 2; and Kohn, "Inside History of the Newburgh Conspiracy."
11. Page Smith, *A New Age Now Begins: A People's History of the American Revolution*, 2 vols. (New York: McGraw-Hill, 1976), 2:1770.
12. Charles Patrick Neimeyer, *America Goes to War: A Social History of the Continental Army* (New York: New York University Press, 1996), 156.

13. Steven Rosswurm, *Arms, Country, and Class: The Philadelphia Militia and "Lower Sort" During the American Revolution, 1775–1783* (New Brunswick, NJ: Rutgers University Press, 1987), 247.

14. James Kirby Martin, ed., *Ordinary Courage: The Revolutionary War Adventures of Joseph Plumb Martin* (1830; reprint, St. James, NY: Brandywine Press, 1993), 160–61.

15. Lorenzo Greene, "The Black Regiment of Rhode Island," *Journal of Negro History* 37 (1952): 173.

16. Martin, *Ordinary Courage*, 162.

17. Ibid., 164.

18. Greene, "Black Regiment of Rhode Island," 172 n. 11.

19. Gregory Evans Dowd, *A Spirited Resistance: The North American Indian Struggle for Unity, 1745–1815* (Baltimore: Johns Hopkins University Press, 1992), 75; Richard White, *The Middle Ground: Indians, Empires, and Republics in the Great Lakes Region, 1650–1815* (Cambridge, England: Cambridge University Press, 1991), 384.

20. Colin G. Calloway, ed., *The World Turned Upside Down: Indian Voices From Early America* (New York: St. Martin's Press, 1994), 190–93 for treaty.

21. Randolph C. Downes, *Council Fires on the Upper Ohio: A Narrative of Indian Affairs in the Upper Ohio Valley Until 1795* (Pittsburgh: University of Pittsburgh Press, 1940), 217; Calloway, *Revolution in Indian Country*, 37.

22. White, *Middle Ground*, 388–89; Dowd, *Spirited Resistance*, 82–83.

23. White, *Middle Ground*, 384.

24. This account of the Gnadenhutten massacre follows Daniel K. Richter, *Facing East from Indian Country: A Native History of Early America* (Cambridge, MA: Harvard University Press, 2001), 222–23; Dowd, *Spirited Resistance*, chapter 4; and Dale Van Every, *A Company of Heroes: The American Frontier, 1775–1783* (New York: William Morrow, 1962), 302–5.

25. Barbara Graymont, *The Iroquois in the American Revolution* (Syracuse, NY: Syracuse University Press, 1972), 262; Downes, *Council Fires*, 276.

26. Graymont, *Iroquois in the American Revolution*, 260.

27. Downes, *Council Fires*, 284.

28. Anthony F. C. Wallace, *The Death and Rebirth of the Seneca* (New York: Knopf, 1970), 149; Reginald Horsman, *Expansion and American Indian Policy, 1783–1812* (East Lansing: Michigan State University, 1967), 9.

29. Wallace, *Death and Rebirth*, 152.

30. Graymont, *Iroquois in the American Revolution*, 280–82.

31. Wallace, *Death and Rebirth*, 152–53.

32. James H. O'Donnell, *Southern Indians in the American Revolution* (Knoxville: University of Tennessee Press, 1973), 128.

33. Calloway, *Revolution in Indian Country*, 207.

34. David H. Corkran, *The Creek Frontier, 1540–1783* (Norman: University of Oklahoma Press, 1967), chapter 17.

35. Ibid., 323–24.

36. This and the following quoted passage are from James H. Merrell, "Declarations of Independence: Indian-White Relations in a New Nation," in *The American Revolution: Its Character and Limits*, ed. Jack P. Greene (New York: New York University Press, 1987), 202.

37. John Walton Caughey, *McGillivray of the Creeks* (Norman: University of Oklahoma Press, 1938), 91–92.

38. Quoted in Merrell, "Declarations of Independence," 199; Horsman, *Expansion and American Indian Policy*, 41–42.

39. François Jean Marquis de Chastellux, *Travels in North America*, 2 vols., ed. Howard C. Rice, Jr. (Chapel Hill: University of North Carolina Press, 1963), 2:438.

40. Ibid., 2:378.

41. Quoted in John E. Ferling, *Setting the World Ablaze: Washington, Adams, Jefferson, and the American Revolution* (New York: Oxford University Press, 2000), 157; for Jefferson's vacillating views on reforms benefiting his ideal yeoman farmer, see Roger G. Kennedy, *Mr. Jefferson's Lost Cause: Land, Farmers, Slavery, and the Louisiana Purchase* (New York: Oxford University Press, 2003).

42. Holly Brewer, "Entailing Aristocracy in Colonial Virginia: 'Ancient Feudal Restraints' and Revolutionary Reform," *William and Mary Quarterly*, 3rd series, 54 (1997): 307–46.

43. Anthony Wallace, *Jefferson and the Indians: The Tragic Fate of the First Americans* (Cambridge, MA: Harvard University Press, 1999), chapter 1.

44. Jean Butenhoff Lee, *The Price of Nationhood: The American Revolution in Charles County* (New York: Norton, 1994), 168–69.

45. Jean Lee, "Lessons in Humility: The Revolutionary Transformation of the Governing Elite of Charles County, Maryland," in *The Transforming Hand of Revolutions: Reconsidering the American Revolution as a Social Movement*, eds. Ronald Hoffman and Peter J. Albert (Charlottesville: University Press of Virginia, 1996), 103–5.

46. Gregory A. Stiverson, *Poverty in a Land of Plenty: Tenancy in Eighteenth-Century Maryland* (Baltimore: Johns Hopkins University Press, 1977), 141–42.

47. Annette Kolodny, "Travel Diary of Elizabeth House Trist: Philadelphia to Natchez," in *Journeys in New Worlds: Early American Women's Narratives*, ed. William L. Andrews (Madison: University of Wisconsin Press, 1990), 185–88.

48. Edward Countryman, *The American Revolution*, rev. ed. (New York: Hill and Wang, 2003), 153; Keith Krawczynski, *William Henry Drayton: South Carolina Revolutionary Patriot* (Baton Rouge: Louisiana State University Press, 2001), 248–49.

49. Clyde Ferguson, "Carolina and Georgia Patriot and Loyalist Militia in Action, 1778–1783," in *The Southern Experience in the American Revolution*, eds. Jeffrey J. Crow and Larry E. Tise (Chapel Hill: University of North Carolina Press, 1978), 175–76; Rachel Klein, "Frontier Planters and the American Revolution: The South Carolina Backcountry, 1775–1782," in *An Uncivil War: The Southern Backcountry during the American Revolution*, eds. Ronald Hoffman, Thad W. Tate, and Peter J. Albert (Charlottesville: University Press of Virginia, 1985), 38.

50. Ferguson, "Patriot and Loyalist Militia," 180; Klein, "Frontier Planters," 49.

51. Don Higginbotham, *The War of American Independence: Military Attitudes, Policies, and Practice, 1763–1789*, (New York: Macmillan, 1971), 361, 375; Robert M. Weir, " 'The Violent Spirit,' The Reestablishment of Order, and the Continuity of Leadership in Post-Revolutionary South Carolina," in Hoffman et al., *Uncivil War*, 70–98.

52. Royster, *A Revolutionary People at War*, 277–78; Jerome J. Nadelhaft, *The Disorders of War: The Revolution in South Carolina* (Orono: University of Maine Press, 1981), 60.

53. Weir, "The Violent Spirit," 76.

54. Royster, *A Revolutionary People at War*, 279; Weir, "The Violent Spirit," 76.

55. Nadelhaft, *Disorders of War*, 71, 77–78, 241 n. 30.

56. Ibid., 105, 107–9.

57. Ibid., 126–27.

58. *Pennsylvania Gazette*, 8 November 1780, quoted in Robert A. Becker, *Revolution, Reform, and the Politics of American Taxation, 1763–1783* (Baton Rouge: Louisiana State University Press, 1980), 185; Robert Levere Brunhouse, *The Counter-Revolution in Pennsylvania, 1776–1790* (New York: Octagon Books, 1971), 99 for "dictator."

59. *Pennsylvania Packet*, 13 February 1783, quoted in Becker, *Revolution, Reform*, 187.
60. Terry Bouton, "Rural Insurgency in Post-Independence Pennsylvania," *Journal of American History* 87 (2000): 861–63, 865.
61. Ibid., 865.
62. Robert J. Taylor, *Western Massachusetts in the Revolution* (Providence, RI: Brown University Press, 1954), 94.
63. *Independent Chronicle and Universal Advertizer*, 27 April 1780.
64. Becker, *Revolution, Reform*, 118.
65. Taylor, *Western Massachusetts*, 110–12.
66. Handlin and Handlin, *Commonwealth*, 33, 110–11.
67. The Lanesborough complaint and that in the next paragraph are from ibid., 111–12.
68. Timothy Dwight, *Travels in New England and New York* (London, 1821), quoted in Robert E. Moody, "Samuel Ely: Forerunner of Shays," *New England Quarterly* 5 (1932): 106; Alan Taylor, *Liberty Men and Great Proprietors: The Revolutionary Settlement on the Maine Frontier* (Chapel Hill: University of North Carolina Press, 1990), 106.
69. Stephen A. Marini, *Radical Sects of Revolutionary New England* (Cambridge, MA: Harvard University Press, 1982), chapter 5.
70. Taylor, *Western Massachusetts*, 112, 116.
71. Moody, "Samuel Ely," 112–13, 114.
72. Taylor, *Western Massachusetts*, 121.
73. Sylvia Frey, *Water from the Rock: Black Resistance in a Revolutionary Age* (Princeton, NJ: Princeton University Press, 1991), 174.
74. Quoted in Robert Olwell, *Masters, Slaves, and Subjects: The Culture of Power in South Carolina Low Country, 1740–1790* (Ithaca, NY: Cornell University Press, 1998), 269.
75. Frey, *Water from the Rock*, 178.
76. Olwell, *Masters, Slaves, and Subjects*, 269.
77. Frey, *Water from the Rock*, 177–83; George Smith McCowen, *The British Occupation of Charleston, 1780–82* (Columbia: University of South Carolina Press, 1972), 149 n.
78. Boston King's *Memoir of the Life of Boston King*, first published in 1798, is reprinted in Vincent Carretta, *Unchained Voices: An Anthology of Black Authors in the English-Speaking World of the Eighteenth Century* (Lexington: University Press of Kentucky, 1996), 351–68; the quoted passage is on p. 356.
79. Cassandra Tybus, *Jubilee Is Come: Black Freedom and the American Revolution*, (Boston: Beacon Press, forthcoming), chapter 4.
80. This account of Mum Bett follows Sidney Kaplan and Emma Nogrady Kaplan, *The Black Presence in the Era of the American Revolution* (Amherst: University of Massachusetts Press, 1989), 244–48.
81. Catharine Maria Sedgwick, "Slavery in New England," *Bentley's Miscellany*, 64 vols. (London, 1853), 34:421.
82. Ibid., 243–44.
83. Lee, *The Price of Nationhood*, 211–16.
84. Gary B. Nash and Jean R. Soderlund, *Freedom by Degrees: Emancipation in Philadelphia and Its Aftermath* (New York: Oxford University Press, 1991), 114.
85. Ibid., 114; the description of Harrison in next paragraph is documented on p. 124.
86. Quoted in ibid., 123.
87. I have treated Allen at length in *Forging Freedom: The Formation of Philadelphia's Black Community, 1720–1840* (Cambridge, MA: Harvard University Press, 1988) and "New Light on Richard Allen: The Early Years," *William and Mary Quarterly*, 3rd series, 46 (1989): 332–40.
88. John Saillant, *Black Puritan, Black Republican: The Life and Thought of Lemuel*

Haynes, 1753–1833 (New York: Oxford University Press, 2003), 47; the quote below is from ibid., 49.

89. Kaplan and Kaplan, *Black Presence*, 120.
90. Quoted in Gary B. Nash, *Race and Revolution* (Madison, WI: Madison House, 1990), 14.
91. Chastellux, *Travels in North America*, 2:439.
92. Nash, *Race and Revolution*, 15.
93. Ira Berlin, *Slaves Without Masters: The Free Negro in the Antebellum South* (New York: Pantheon Books, 1975), 18.
94. David Brion Davis, *Slavery and Human Progress* (New York: Oxford University Press, 1984), 82.
95. Quoted in Gary B. Nash, *First City: Philadelphia and the Forging of Historical Memory* (Philadelphia: University of Pennsylvania Press, 2002), 97–98.
96. Linda K. Kerber, *Women of the Republic: Intellect and Ideology in Revolutionary America* (Chapel Hill: University of North Carolina Press, 1980), 278.
97. The words of Abigail Adams in this and the next paragraph are taken from Charles W. Akers, *Abigail Adams: An American Woman*, 2nd ed. (New York: Longman, 2000), 84.
98. Linda Grant DePauw, "Women in Combat: The Revolutionary War Experience," *Armed Forces and Society* 7 (1981), 210; Holly A. Mayer, *Belonging to the Army: Camp Followers and Community during the American Revolution* (Columbia: University of South Carolina Press, 1996), 1.
99. Ray Raphael, *A People's History of the American Revolution: A Common People Shaped the Fight for Independence* (New York: New Press, 2001), 110.
100. Mary Beth Norton, *Liberty's Daughters: The Revolutionary Experience of American Women, 1750–1800* (Boston: Little, Brown, 1980), 213; Raphael, *People's History*, 112.
101. Quoted in Gary B. Nash, *Landmarks of the American Revolution* (New York: Oxford University Press, 2003), 80, 82.
102. Linda K. Kerber, " 'History Can Do It No Justice,': Women and the Reinterpretation of the American Revolution" in *Women in the Age of the American Revolution*, eds. Ronald A. Hoffman and Peter J. Albert (Charlottesville: University Press of Virginia, 1989), 36.
103. Akers, *Abigail Adams*, 216.
104. Quoted in Lester Cohen, "Creating a Usable Future: The Revolutionary Historians and the National Past," in Greene, *The American Revolution: Its Character and Limits*, 314.

Epilogue: Sparks from the Altar of '76

1. Philip S. Foner, ed., *The Complete Writings of Thomas Paine*, 2 vols. (New York: Citadel Press, 1969), 2:956, 992–1007. For Paine's return to America, see David Freeman Hawke, *Paine* (New York: Norton, 1974), part 4.
2. Adams to Waterhouse, in *Statesman and Friend: Correspondence of John Adams with Benjamin Waterhouse, 1784–1822*, ed. Worthington Chauncey Ford (Boston, 1927), 31.
3. Quoted in James W. St. G. Walker, *The Black Loyalists: The Search for a Promised Land in Nova Scotia and Sierra Leone, 1783–1870* (New York: Africana, 1976), 95.
4. Quoted in Ellen Wilson, *The Loyal Blacks* (New York: Capricorn Books, 1976), 205.
5. Gary B. Nash, "Thomas Peters, Millwright and Deliverer," in *Struggle and Survival in Colonial America*, eds. David B. Sweet and Gary B. Nash (Berkeley: University of California Press, 1981), 83.

6. Richard Allen, *The Life Experience and Gospel Labors of the Rt. Rev. Richard Allen* (Nashville, TN: Abingdon Press, 1983), 21.

7. Gary B. Nash, "Forging Freedom: The Emancipation Experience in the Northern Seaport Cities, 1775–1820," in *Slavery and Freedom in the Age of the American Revolution*, eds. Ira Berlin and Ronald Hoffman (Charlottesville: University Press of Virginia, 1983), 3–48.

8. Quoted in Duncan J. MacLeod, *Slavery, Race, and the American Revolution* (London: Cambridge University Press, 1974), 75.

9. I have argued the case concerning South Carolina and Georgia's precarious position in *Race and Revolution* (Madison, WI: Madison House, 1990), 25–29.

10. Henry Wiencek, *An Imperfect God: George Washington, His Slaves, and the Creation of America* (New York: Farrar, Straus, and Giroux, 2003), 251.

11. Lafayette to George Washington, 5 February 1783, *Lafayette in the Age of the American Revolution: Selected Letters and Papers, 1776–1790*, 5 vols., ed. Stanley Idzerda (Ithaca, NY: Cornell University Press, 1977), 5:90–93.

12. Wiencek, *Imperfect God*, 262; William Gordon to George Washington, 30 August 1784, *The Papers of George Washington: Confederation Series*, 6 vols., eds. W. W. Abbot and Dorothy Twohig (Charlottesville: University Press of Virginia, 1992), 2:64.

13. Albert Matthews, "Notes on the Proposed Abolition of Slavery in Virginia in 1785," Colonial Society of Massachusetts *Publications* 6 (1904): 376–77.

14. Nash, *Race and Revolution*, 14–15.

15. Paul Finkelman, *The Law of Freedom and Bondage: A Casebook* (New York: Oceana Publications, 1986), 116; Robert Pleasants to George Washington, 11 December 1785, in *Am I Not a Man and a Brother: The Antislavery Crusade of Revolutionary America, 1688–1788*, ed. Roger Bruns (New York: Chelsea House, 1977), 508–9.

16. Wiencek, *An Imperfect God*, 261, 263.

17. David Grimsted, "Anglo-American Racism and Phillis Wheatley's 'Sable Veil,' 'Length'ned Chain,' and 'Knitted Heart,' " in *Women in the Age of the American Revolution*, eds. Ronald Hoffman and Peter J. Albert (Charlottesville: University Press of Virginia, 1989), 415.

18. Banneker's letter is reprinted in Sidney Kaplan and Emma Nogrady Kaplan, *The Black Presence in the Era of the American Revolution* (Amherst: University of Massachusetts Press, 1989), 139–44.

19. Isabel Thompson Kelsay, *Joseph Brant, 1743–1807: Man of Two Worlds* (Syracuse, NY: Syracuse University Press, 1984), 401–2; Randolph C. Downes, *Council Fires on the Upper Ohio: A Narrative of Indian Affairs in the Upper Ohio Valley Until 1795* (Pittsburgh, PA: University of Pittsburgh Press, 1940), 298.

20. Downes, *Council Fires*, 300.

21. Daniel K. Richter, *Facing East from Indian Country: A Native History of Early America* (Cambridge, MA: Harvard University Press, 2001), 224.

22. Alexander McGillivray to James White, 8 April 1787, quoted in John Walton Caughey, *McGillivray of the Creeks* (Norman: University of Oklahoma Press, 1938), 33; *American State Papers: Documents, Legislative and Executive of the Congress of the United States . . . Class II. Indian Affairs* (Wilmington, DE: Scholarly Resources, 1972), 7:18.

23. Michael Green, "Alexander McGillivray," in *American Indian Leaders: Studies in Diversity*, ed. R. David Edmunds (Lincoln: University of Nebraska Press, 1980), 54–56.

24. Quoted in Downes, *Council Fires*, 249.

25. E. Raymond Evans, "Notable Persons in Cherokee History: Dragging Canoe," *Journal of Cherokee Studies* 2 (1977): 185; Colin G. Calloway, *American Revolution in*

Indian Country: Crisis and Diversity in Native American Communities (Cambridge, England: Cambridge University Press, 1995), 209.

26. For a full account, see William G. McLoughlin, *Cherokee Renascence in the New Republic* (Princeton, NJ: Princeton University Press, 1986).

27. Barabara Graymont, *The Iroquois in the American Revolution* (Syracuse, NY: Syracuse University Press, 1972), 286–91; Calloway, *American Revolution in Indian Country*, 105.

28. Calloway, *American Revolution in Indian Country*, 169.

29. Evans, "Dragging Canoe," 187.

30. Webster's "A Plea for Poor Soldiers," was published in his *Political Essays on the Nature and Operation of Money, Public Finances, and Other Subjects* (Philadelphia, 1791; New York: Burt Franklin, 1969), 306–75.

31. John Phillips Resch, *Suffering Soldiers: Revolutionary War Veterans, Moral Sentiment, and Political Culture in the Early Republic* (Amherst: University of Massachusetts Press, 1999), chapter 4.

32. Alan Taylor, "Agrarian Independence: Northern Land Rioters after the Revolution," in *Beyond the American Revolution: Explorations in the History of American Radicalism*, ed. Alfred F. Young (DeKalb: Northern Illinois University Press, 1993), 223.

33. Alan Taylor, " 'To Man Their Rights': The Frontier Revolution," in *The Transforming Hand of Revolution: Reconsidering the American Revolution as a Social Movement*, eds. Ronald Hoffman and Peter J. Albert (Charlottesville: University Press of Virginia, 1996), 249.

34. Taylor, "Agrarian Independence," in Young, *Beyond the Revolution*, 224.

35. Ibid., 225.

36. Charles Blizter, ed., *The Political Writings of James Harrington: Representative Selections* (New York: Liberal Arts Press, 1955), 98; John Trenchard and Thomas Gordon, *Cato's Letters*, 6th ed., 4 vols. (London, 1755), 3:207–8.

37. Ruth Bogin, "New Jersey's True Policy: The Radical Republican Vision of Abraham Clark," *William and Mary Quarterly*, 3rd series, 35 (1978): 105.

38. Abraham Clark, *The True Policy of New Jersey Defined*, quoted in Bogin, "New Jersey's True Policy," 106, 109.

39. Quoted in Thomas M. Doerflinger, *Vigorous Spirit of Enterprise: Merchants and Economic Development in Revolutionary Philadelphia* (Chapel Hill: University of North Carolina Press, 1986), 326; Bruce H. Mann, *Republic of Debtors: Bankruptcy in the Age of American Independence* (Cambridge, MA: Harvard University Press, 2002), 98.

40. Algernon Sidney, *Discourses Concerning Government* (London, 1698), quoted in Staughton Lynd, *Intellectual Origins of American Radicalism* (New York: Pantheon Books, 1968), 101.

41. Alfred F. Young, "Artisans and the Constitution: Boston" unpublished ms., 21–23.

42. Van Beck Hall, *Politics Without Parties: Massachusetts, 1780–1791* (Pittsburgh, PA: University of Pittsburgh Press, 1972) 171–73.

43. James Haw, *John and Edward Rutledge of South Carolina* (Athens: University of Georgia Press, 1997), 184–86.

44. John Schutz and Douglas Adair, eds., *Spur of Fame: Dialogues of John Adams and Benjamin Rush, 1805–1813* (San Marino, CA: The Huntington Library, 1966), 170.

45. Linda K. Kerber, *Women of the Republic: Intellect and Ideology in Revolutionary America* (Chapel Hill: University of North Carolina Press, 1980), 112; last quote is from Charles Akers, *Abigail Adams: An American Woman* (New York: Longman, 2000), 219.

46. Kerber, *Women of the Republic*, 111.

47. Rush is quoted in Linda K. Kerber, *Toward an Intellectual History of Women* (Chapel Hill: University of North Carolina Press, 1997), 40; the second quote is from Mary Beth Norton, *Liberty's Daughters: The Revolutionary Experience of American Women, 1750–1800* (Boston: Little, Brown, 1980), 268–69.

48. Kerber, *Women of the Republic*, 196; *American Museum* 9 (1792, Pt. 1), quoted in Kerber, *Toward an Intellectual History of Women*, 196.

49. Kerber, *Toward an Intellectual History of Women*, 58–62.

50. Wollstonecraft is quoted in Rosemarie Zagarri, "The Rights of Man and Woman in Post-Revolutionary America," *William and Mary Quarterly*, 3rd series, 55 (1998): 207, 210. Zagarri's statement is on p. 204.

51. Kerber, *Toward an Intellectual History of Women*, 98.

52. Adam Smith, *Wealth of Nations*, ed. Edward Cannan (New York: Random House, 1937), 674.

53. Benjamin Rush, "An Address to the People of the United States" (1787).

54. Robert R. Livingston, quoted in Alfred F. Young, "Afterword," in *Beyond the American Revolution: Explorations in the History of American Radicalism* (DeKalb: Northern Illinois University Press, 1993), 335.

55. Quoted in ibid., 336.

ILLUSTRATION CREDITS

page xix. Morristown National Historical Park

page xxv. Library of Congress

page 17. © Trustees of the British Museum

page 27. The Library Company of Philadelphia

page 40. The Quaker Collection, Haverford College, Pennsylvania

page 54. All rights reserved, The Metropolitan Museum of Art. Bequest of Charles Allen Munn, 1924 (24.90.1566a).

page 69. Haverford College Library, Haverford, PA, Quaker Collection, no. 850

page 74. Courtesy of The North Carolina State Archives

page 95. Courtesy of The Bostonian Society/Old State House

page 102. The Library Company of Philadelphia

page 131. Courtesy of The Anschutz Collection

page 140. Courtesy of the Massachusetts Historical Society

page 142. © 2004 Museum of Fine Arts, Boston. Gift of Joseph W. R. Rogers and Mary C. Rogers.

page 153. The Library Company of Philadelphia

page 154. Private collection: photo, Gavin Ashworth

page 177. © National Gallery of Canada, Transfer from the Canadian War Memorials, 1921

page 184. Museum of the City of New York, J. Clarence Davies Collection 29.100.2337

page 217. Munson-Williams-Proctor Arts Institute, Museum of Art, Utica, New York, 58.284

page 226. Stockbridge Library Association Historical Collection

page 227. Courtesy Alexander A. McBurney

Illustration Credits

page 254. Collection of The New-York Historical Society

page 255. Chicago Historical Society

page 273. Courtesy of The Historical Society of Pennsylvania Collection, Atwater Kent Museum of Philadelphia

pages 308–9. Collection of The New-York Historical Society

page 321. Historical Society of Pennsylvania

page 355. Photograph by David Ray Smith; for more information on Nancy Ward see http://SmithDRay.tripod.com/nancyward-index-5.html

page 379. Wadsworth Atheneum, Hartford. Purchased by the Wadsworth Atheneum.

page 410. Massachusetts Historical Society, Boston, MA, USA/Bridgeman Art Library

page 418. Courtesy of the Pennsylvania Academy of Fine Arts, Philadelphia. Bequest of Henry C. Gibson.

page 424. Collection of The New-York Historical Society

page 430. Moorland-Spingarn Research Center, Howard University

page 442. Dallas Museum of Art, The Art Museum League Fund, Special Contributors and General Acquisitions Fund

page 444. American Antiquarian Society

INDEX

Index